ISSUES IN AGRICULTURAL COMPETITIVENESS

IAAE OCCASIONAL PAPER SERIES

No. 1–*Papers on Current Agricultural Economic Issues*

No. 2–*Rural Challenge*

No. 3–*Rural Development: Growth and Inequity*

No. 4–*Agriculture and Economic Instability*

No. 5–*Government Intervention in Agriculture: Cause and Effect*

No. 6–*Issues in Agricultural Development: Sustainability and Cooperation*

No. 7–*Issues in Agricultural Competitiveness: Markets and Policies*

IAAE Occasional Paper No. 7

Issues in Agricultural Competitiveness

Markets and Policies

Edited by
Roger Rose, Carolyn Tanner
and Margot A. Bellamy

International Association of Agricultural Economists

Published by
Dartmouth Publishing Company Limited
Ashgate Publishing Company
Gower House
Croft Road
Aldershot
Hants GU11 3LR
England

Ashgate Publishing Company
Old Post Road
Brookfield
Vermont 05036
USA

British Library Cataloguing in Publication Data
Issues in agricultural competitiveness : markets and
policies : proceedings of the twenty-second International
Conference of Agricultural Economists, held at Harare,
Zimbabwe, 22-29 August 1994. - (IAAE occasional paper ; no.
7)
1.Agriculture - Economic aspects - Congresses 2.Competition
- Congresses
I.Rose, Roger II.Tanner, Carolyn III.Bellamy, Margot A.
IV.International Association of Agricultural Economists
V.International Conference of Agricultural Economists (22nd
: 1994 : Harare, Zimbabwe)
338.1

Library of Congress Cataloging-in-Publication Data
International Conference of Agricultural Economists (22nd : 1994 :
Harare, Zimbabwe)
Issues in agricultural competitiveness markets and policies :
proceedings of the Twenty-first International Conference of
Agricultural Economists, held at Harare, Zimbabwe, 23-29 August 1994
/ edited by Roger Rose, Carolyn, Tanner, Margot A. Bellamy.
p. cm. – (Occasional paper (International Association of
Agricultural Economists) ; no. 7)
ISBN 1-85521-634-5 (pb)
1. Agriculture–conomic aspects–Congresses. 2. Agriculture and state–
Congresses. 3. Competition, International–Congresses. I. International
Association of Agricultural Economists. II. Title. III. Series: I.A.A.E.
occasional paper ; no. 7.
HD1405.I58 1994
338.1–dc21 97-15982
CIP

ISBN 1 85521 634 5

Printed and bound by Athenaeum Press, Ltd.,
Gateshead, Tyne & Wear.

CONTENTS

FOREWORD

This book is the seventh in the IAAE *Occasional Paper* series. It contains the 45 contributed papers — together with the discussion opening and summary of general discussion presented at the Twenty-Second International Conference of Agricultural Economists, Harare, Zimbabwe, 22–29 August 1994. A companion publication, *Agricultural Competitiveness: Market Forces and Policy Choice* (edited by G.H. Peters and Douglas D. Hedley), published in 1995, contains the plenary and invited papers presented at the conference and also appears under the imprint of the Dartmouth Publishing Company.

The contributed papers were refereed using a double blind refereeing process. The 45 papers presented in contributed paper sessions and published in full were selected from a total of 257. A further 119 papers were selected for presentation in the poster programme. The 44 referees representing 24 countries and 6 continents, were Giovanni Anania (Universita degli studi della Calabria), Malcolm D. Bale (World Bank), Vishwa Ballabh (Institute of Rural Management, India), Herbert I. Behrmann (University of Natal), Olof Bolin (Swedish University of Agricultural Sciences), John R. Brake (Cornell University), Elisabetta Croci-Angelini (University of Siena), Elmar R. da Cruz (Empresa Brasileria de Pesquisa Agropecuária), Dana G. Dalrymple (US Agency for International Development), Cristina C. David (International Rice Research Institute), Paulo F.C. de Araujo (University of Sao Paulo), Eugenia M. de Rubinstein (Universidad Catolica de Chile), Fumio Egaitsu (The University of Tokyo), Robert Evenson (Yale University), John Graham (IDRC), Harold Guither (University of Illinois), Larry Harrington (Centro International de Mejoramiento de Maiz y Trigo), D.R. Harvey (University of Newcastle Upon Tyne), Marvin L. Hayenga (Iowa State University), M.A. Jabbar (International Livestock Centre for Africa), Habibullah Khan (National University of Singapore), Yoav Kislev (Hebrew University of Jerusalem), Donald Larson (The Ohio State University), Gordon MacAulay (The University of Sydney), Paavo Makinen (Ministry of Agriculture and Forestry, Finland), Laurent Martens (University of Gent), Joseph G. Nagy (Hunting Technical Services, Pakistan), James Obben (University of Brunei Darussalam), Tongroj Onchan (Kasetsart University), Sushil Pandey (International Rice Research Institute), Epictetus Patalinghug (University of the Philippines), Ewa Rabinowicz (Swedish University of Agricultural Sciences), Thomas Reardon (Michigan State University), Günther Schmitt (Georg-August-Universität Göttingen), David B. Schweikhardt (Michigan State University), Chamhuri Siwar (University of Kebangsaan), Reza Soltani (Shiraz University), Stefan Tangermann (Georg-August-Universität Göttingen), Luther G. Tweeten (The Ohio State University), Cornelis L.J. van der Meer (National Council for Agricultural Research, The Netherlands), Michele Veeman (University of Alberta), Vijay S. Vyas (Institute of Development Studies, Jaipur), Timothy O. Williams (International Livestock Centre for Africa) and Hiroshi Yamauchi (University of Hawaii).

The International Association of Agricultural Economists is grateful to the referees for their efforts in reviewing the papers. A particular debt is also owed to the Australian Bureau of Agricultural and Resource Economics (ABARE) where Marian Hinds, Vicki Bell and Julie Murley undertook the onerous task of preparing the papers in camera ready format prior to their printing. The editing work was led by Roger Rose (ABARE), with major input from Carolyn Tanner (University of Sydney) and Margot Bellamy (CAB

International, Wallingford, UK). Roger Rose also undertook the task of organising the contributed paper sessions at Harare Conference. The poster paper sessions were in the capable hands of Kenneth Thomson (University of Zimbabwe). At the conference Emma Matimati (University of Zimbabwe) provided important secretarial assistant to the organisers. The staff of Dartmouth Publishing Company, in particular John Irwin and Sonia Hubbard, were constantly supportive and tolerant of delays in preparation of the test. We cannot disguise the fact that delays did occur though the authors who have waited for their papers to appear, and those who wished to read them, are assured that the late publication could not possibly have been foreseen when the work of editing and preparation was put in hand.

The views expressed in the papers are the responsibility of the authors, and are not necessarily those of the IAAE or of the institutions with which authors and editors are associated.

G.H. Peters
IAAE Proceedings Editor
Queen Elizabeth House
University of Oxford

REKHA MEHRA*

Women's Land Rights and Sustainable Development

Abstract: Unequal and insecure access to land undermine women's farm productivity, limit employment options, depress their earnings, and degrade the environment. Factors limiting women's access to land include legal discrimination, land scarcity, inappropriate government policies, and lack of political power and social status. Policies to promote sustainable development rather than focusing on family planning, as is commonly done, should directly support women's economic activities. Especially needed to enhance women's investment incentives and to encourage them to take a longer-term view on the environment are policies to strengthen their land rights. To enhance women's capacity to act upon these incentives and build their human capital, policies are needed to improve their access to resources and services such as credit, agricultural extension, new technologies, and better education and health care.

INTRODUCTION

When policy-makers take account of women in development planning they focus principally on their reproductive roles. Where women are concerned, policy-makers have come to regard family planning as the key to promoting sustainable development because of the popular view that rapid population growth is the main factor slowing economic growth and accelerating resource depletion and environmental degradation. This emphasis on women's reproductive roles is reflected in the skewed distribution of donor financial resources between population programmes and programmes targeted at women's economic development. For instance, US bilateral assistance to population programmes has ranged between $240–350 million per year over the past decade while funding for women-in-development programmes averaged $5.6 million a year in the same period.

This paper argues that such a predominant focus on women's reproductive roles is misplaced for at least two reasons. First, it ignores women's productive roles which are the basis of their interaction with the environment and of economic and social change (Lycette, 1993). Second, it deflects attention from the more fundamental causes of poverty and environmental degradation — factors such as the unequal distribution of resources and power between women and men and between classes. By documenting women's unequal access to one critical resource — land — the paper shows how this inequality constrains women's productivity and undermines the environment. It then examines the causes of the inequality and suggests ways to enhance women's access to land.

WOMEN'S LIMITED AND INSECURE ACCESS TO LAND

Few women in developing countries have secure and independent access to land. In most places, women cannot legally or customarily inherit wealth or property, including land. Nor are they generally permitted to own land in their own right, and when they are, few women actually do (Seager and Olson, 1986). From the Food and Agriculture Organization's (FAO) estimates of 167 million landless or near-landless households, one can infer that at

* International Centre for Research on Women, USA.

least that many women are landless or near-landless (Sinha, 1984)[1]. Patrilineal inheritance predominates in both traditional and modern land tenure systems and when women need to meet traditional responsibilities of providing food for their households, they are granted use and not ownership rights.

Women's Restricted Rights: Traditional Tenure Systems

Studies have shown that traditional land tenure arrangements emphasizing communal use rights, because they are clear on use, exclusion, and transfer of land, are effective in enabling communities both to meet their basic economic needs and to use available resources in a sustainable manner (Brink and Bromley, 1992; and Cleaver and Schreiber, 1992). Such systems are regarded as relatively favourable to women, in that, unlike modern tenure systems, they guarantee both economic access and incentives for conservation (Collins, 1991). Closer examination reveals, however, that tenure under traditional systems can be quite secure for men but not for women (Cleaver and Schreiber, 1992; Rocheleau, 1988; and Wynter, 1990). Where women have use rights to land, they are rarely free to act as independent agents; their rights tend to be restricted and use-specific. They cannot, for example, use their land for commercial purposes. This is because women's rights derive from their status as wives or wards — that is, mothers, daughters, sisters, or widows — and their degree of access to land varies with, and reflects, the social status of the male members of the household (ILO, 1989). When women's status changes through divorce or widowhood, they are vulnerable to losing their land rights and hence their access to a livelihood.

Women's Deteriorating Rights Under Modern Tenure Systems

Women tend to face even greater difficulties in obtaining access to land under modern tenure systems. In fact, their land rights tend to deteriorate when governments institute land reform, land registration or resettlement schemes. Land registration programmes throughout Africa (for example, in Ethiopia, Guinea-Bissau, Kenya and Zimbabwe) have failed to give women title to land even where they had customary access to land prior to registration (Davison, 1988; Palmer, 1985; and Jacobs 1991). In Latin America, women were similarly left out of the agrarian reform process of the 1960s and 1970s. In four of thirteen countries for which gender disaggregated data were available, Deere (1987) found that women comprised 4–25 percent of beneficiaries because land titles were not given to women but to household heads, who were assumed to be men. Even in households recognized as female-headed, few women were given land. Recent reforms in China have also overlooked women. With the collapse of rural communes in the early 1980s, land was redistributed primarily among men, in effect reversing the 1947 agrarian reform which had given women separate land deeds (*New York Times,* 28 July 1992). The reality that the vast majority of women — whether in traditional or modern tenure systems — are either landless or have limited and insecure access to land has important consequences for sustainable development.

THE CONSEQUENCES OF WOMEN'S LIMITED AND INSECURE ACCESS TO LAND

Economic theory suggests that security of tenure is linked to higher productivity and better land management (Panayotou, 1993). By reducing farmer risk and raising expected profitability, secure tenure provides the proper incentive for farmers to make investments in the long-term productivity of their land. Where tenure is secure, farmers are more inclined, for example, to invest in slower growing tree crops, or productivity-enhancing inputs, or more labour-intensive land conservation practices, thereby raising both productivity and the quality of their land. Where tenure is insecure (because land is untitled or disputed, or there is multiple and overlapping ownership) the resulting uncertainty discourages the investments needed to improve land productivity. This in turn has a negative impact on the environment.

There is no reason to think that women farmers behave any differently from (or respond less rationally to negative incentives than) their male counterparts. The evidence suggests that, by undermining incentives for long-term investments, insecure tenure among women likewise has a negative effect on both farm productivity and environmental sustainability. The effects may even be more pronounced for female than male farmers because women lack access to credit and other productivity-enhancing resources and services.

Impact on Productivity and Employment

Where women do have access to land and cultivate their own fields but are less productive than men, household food security is reduced, women's own earnings are depressed, and total household income is lower. In many African countries, where women are the main food producers, low and sometimes declining productivity among women can significantly jeopardize national food security. Evidence from northern Sudan shows that social and cultural factors strongly discourage women from even cultivating land they do not regard as their own. When Sudanese men migrated in search of employment in the 1970s, women farmers did not cultivate their husbands' lands because they regarded such investment as risky, given the ease of divorce and the widespread practice of polygamy. They were willing to incur the short-term risk of both land deterioration and food shortages resulting from not working their husbands' land (Schuler, 1986).

Women farmers are less productive than men farmers not because they are less efficient but because they generally farm smaller amounts of lower quality land, and have more restricted access to complementary resources, new technologies and adult labour. An extensive literature documents the skewness of service delivery and access to inputs in the developing world in favour of male producers on better land (Ahmed, 1985; Berger *et al.*, 1984; ILO, 1989; and Staudt, 1982). A review of settlement schemes in Indonesia, Malaysia, Sri Lanka and Papua New Guinea shows that services were provided only to men (ILO, 1989). Households headed by women tend to be most disadvantaged. Studies in Zimbabwe and Botswana show that households headed by women produced less and were poorer than households headed by men because women had less or poorer quality land and more limited access to farm technologies, services, and markets (ILO, 1989).

A key constraint for women is the lack of access to institutional credit. Paradoxically, a major reason why women are unable to obtain bank credit is that land is often required as collateral, and women generally do not have title to land. Women are also unable to obtain loans from agricultural cooperatives because cooperative membership is dominated by male farmers, and available credit funds are often targeted to improve the cash crops grown by men rather than the food crops more commonly grown by women. Women farmers are estimated to receive just 10–15 percent of institutional credit available in developing countries (Staudt, 1982). This pressures them to seek credit in informal credit markets where the cost of borrowing is higher, driving down the profitability of their investment and their incentive to invest.

Finally, landless women's employment and earnings options are severely restricted. Because they have little or no education and training to seek other employment opportunities, landless women can at best find work for low pay as wage labourers or tenants on the land of others. Wage labour is generally intermittent and poorly paid work: unemployment and underemployment due to seasonality are high, and wages for female agricultural labour tend to be low both absolutely and relative to male wages. In Sri Lanka, for example, average daily wages for women farm workers in the unorganized sector are one-quarter to one-third less than men's wages (United Nations, 1989). Because women have less education than men and lack vocational skills and training, their occupational mobility is restricted. Women are also less likely than men to migrate to seek work because of their household and childcare responsibilities as well as cultural constraints. Altogether, employment and earnings options for landless women are severely restricted.

Environmental Effects

Extensive documentation is available on the damaging environmental effects of land shortages, insecure tenure, and uncertain land rights (Colchester and Lohmann, 1993; Cruz *et al.,* 1992; Myers, 1991; and Panayotou, 1993). Problems include over-use and abuse of fragile lands, shortening of fallow periods, deforestation, and related ecological problems that are the secondary effects of the initial degradation. Although there is a great shortage of data on the environmental effects of insecure tenure among women, the material that is available confirms that tenure insecurity contributes to environmental degradation by undermining incentives for long-term investment. These negative effects are magnified by women's time constraints and lack of access to resources and supporting services.

A study in Ruhengiri prefecture of Rwanda shows growing land scarcity, shrinking fallow periods, and increasing use of marginal lands for farming (Randolph and Sanders, 1988). Farmer investment in land is low, land quality is declining rapidly, and soil erosion is a severe problem. Weaknesses in women's land rights are a key contributing factor. Although women are the primary farmers they do not own or inherit land but, provided they have young children to support, they are granted use rights on male owned lands. Their holdings are generally small and scattered, with individuals farming up to six different parcels of land. Also, women have virtually no access to institutional credit or extension services designed to improve farmer productivity and ability to manage land.

The decline of common property rights, including limitations on community access to common lands and the separation of use and management of common areas, has contributed significantly to deforestation. In the 1970s, 90 000 square kilometres of forests worldwide were lost annually, more than one-quarter of them for fuelwood which is the primary energy source for the poor in those developing countries where biomass fuels are available (Myers, 1991). In many places, because women are the ones mainly responsible for collecting fuelwood from common lands, growing scarcity is reflected in increases in the amount of time that women spend collecting fuelwood (Agarwal, 1986; ILO, 1987; and FAO, 1987). In Bara, Sudan, over a single decade, the time that women spent walking to obtain fuelwood increased from 15 to 30 minutes to one or two hours (Agarwal, 1986). By exacerbating women's time burdens, the growing scarcity of fuelwood contributes to further degradation by reducing the time available for other activities, including environmental protection and maintenance. Time constraints are often cited as reasons why women either discontinue conservation practices or fail to adopt them. In the Caribbean, for instance, these factors have caused the deterioration of irrigation systems, the disappearance of cultivation terraces, and increased soil erosion (van Herpen and Ashby, 1991).

While more research on the effects of insecure tenure among women on the environment and development is needed, the available evidence strongly suggests the importance of strengthening women's land rights to enhance productivity and mitigate environmental degradation. This requires understanding the factors that currently limit women's land rights.

BARRIERS TO WOMEN'S ACCESS TO LAND

Barriers to women's access to land include two sets of influences; on the supply side, factors that affect land availability, and on the demand side, factors that affect the ability of women themselves to obtain and retain land.

Supply Side Factors

The supply of land is limited — most importantly by discriminatory laws — as well as by land scarcity and regulatory policies that concentrate land ownership.

Legal discrimination Legal discrimination against women's ownership and inheritance of land is widespread. Laws or customs prohibiting women from holding land, although not unknown, are relatively uncommon. More commonly, problems arise because laws governing women's rights to property, land, and inheritance are complex, overlapping, and sometimes contradictory. In matters that most affect property ownership — marriage, family and inheritance — modern laws frequently defer to customary and personal laws, often to the detriment of women.

Personal laws in some countries (e.g., Botswana, Kenya, Lesotho and Sri Lanka) actually discriminate against women (Schuler, 1986). In Lesotho, a woman who marries becomes a minor; her husband becomes her legal guardian and he is entitled to administer their joint estate. In practice, a woman cannot control the disposition of property because rights devolve upon male relatives in case of divorce or the death of a husband (Schuler, 1986). In Venezuela and Costa Rica, the wife inherits farmland if her husband dies or abandons her, but inheritance laws specifically designate sons, not daughters, as next in line of succession (Deere, 1987).

Laws are especially discriminatory regarding women's access to agricultural land. In India, for example, women have practically no right to inherit agricultural land (Agarwal, 1988). Despite the passage of the Hindu Succession Act (1956), which was intended to improve women's rights, the law has been interpreted so as to deny women access to agricultural land. In some Indian states, laws explicitly exclude widows and daughters from inheriting agricultural land (Schuler, 1986). Kenya's Succession Act (1972), intended to provide gender equality in inheritance, fails to do so because agricultural land was left under customary law, which denies women the right to inherit farmland (FAO, 1979).

Even where laws are equitable, women may not know their legal rights. In addition, implementation may be biased, and law enforcement may be inadequate or prejudiced against women. In Bolivia and Honduras, agrarian reform laws explicitly providing for the inclusion of female heads of household as beneficiaries were implemented in such a way as to exclude women. Women simply were not regarded as agriculturalists (Deere, 1987).

Increasing land scarcity Between 1965 and 1988, per capita land availability declined in all developing regions except Latin America and the Caribbean (Table 1). This reflected diminishing land availability in most countries (Jazairy *et al.,* 1992). Government policies that promote concentration of land in the hands of wealthy, often urban-based, large landowners are a major factor in the growing scarcity of land. Governments often expropriate vast tracts of land, sometimes retaining them as state lands and sometimes making them available to large, commercial producers and commercial logging enterprises (Colchester and Lohmann, 1993). Policies pursued by post-independence governments have exacerbated land scarcity. Governments offer incentives for commercialization or export-crop production that raise the demand for land among large commercial landholders, often at the expense of smallholders (Jazairy *et al.*, 1992; and Colchester and Lohmann, 1993). As fertile lands are converted, land distribution becomes increasingly skewed. Less land is available for smallholders. In eight of the 23 countries for which data are available, land distribution became more skewed by the 1980s (Jazairy *et al.*, 1992).

Table 1 *Changes in Arable Land Per Head of Agricultural Population, by Developing Region, 1965–1988 (hectares)*

Region	1965	1988
Asia	0.29	0.23
Sub-Saharan Africa	0.59	0.43
Near East and North Africa	0.82	0.77
Latin America and the Carribean	1.01	1.27

Source: Jazairy *et al.* (1992).

Environmental degradation is another important factor that restricts the supply of land. For the past 45 years, agriculture, deforestation and overgrazing have caused moderate to extreme soil degradation on 1.2 billion hectares (or almost 11 percent) of the world's vegetated surface (WRI, 1992). Worldwide losses of arable land continue, with 70 000 square kilometres of farmland — a large proportion in the developing regions — abandoned each year (Fornos, 1991). The inadequacies of the government policies described above contribute to the degradation. In Central and South America, for instance, government incentives for cattle exports made it possible for large landholders to take over great amounts of fertile lands for extensive cattle grazing. Smallholders, meanwhile, were pushed onto less fertile lands, on which intensive crop farming causes environmental damage (Thiesenhusen, 1991).

As the supply of arable land diminishes and competition for land intensifies, women are particularly disadvantaged in acquiring land. There is some evidence that this is already happening. Palmer (1991) found that in African countries affected by land scarcity, the quantity and quality of land assigned to women tended to decline first.

Demand Side Factors

Even where land is available and laws are not unfavourable, women may be unable to acquire land because they are too poor or because social and cultural factors deter them from asserting their limited rights.

Poverty Worldwide, more women than men are poor, and the numbers of poor women are growing even faster than those for men, especially in the rural areas of developing nations (Jazairy *et al.*, 1992). In 1988, an estimated 564 million rural women lived below the poverty line, representing an increase of 47 percent since 1965–70. In comparison, the number of men living below the poverty line (375 million) increased 30 percent over the same period.

A significant factor explaining rural poverty in many countries is the increasing number of households headed by women (14–45 percent) (Buvinic, and 1993; Jazairy *et al.*, 1992). In Bangladesh, for instance, the proportion of households headed by women as a percentage of all rural households has risen from 5–7 percent to 16 percent over a 20-year period. Such households tend to be overrepresented among the poor. In a review of 60 empirical analyses, Buvinic and Rao Gupta (1993) found that 44 of these studies established that households headed by women were poorer than those headed by men.

As a consequence of their poverty, women are unable to acquire land even when laws permit. In Kenya, for example, recent laws do not prevent women from owning property, but most women cannot afford to acquire it (Schuler, 1986). Moreover, poverty prevents women from benefiting from some reforms; for example, women may be unable to take advantage of privatization that entails titling and registration because they cannot afford the costs of registration (Dickerman, 1989).

Social and cultural constraints Women may also be prevented from asserting land rights by generally accepted social and cultural values. In Wadi Kutum, Sudan, where a titling scheme registered most of the land owned by women in men's names, the women did not protest because, customarily, they were not permitted to conduct relations with the state (Rahama and Hoogenboom, 1988).

Lack of status and power Because they lack status and power within the community, women are often unable to exercise the limited land rights they do have. In India, for example, women are conditioned by custom to accept the idea that sisters should not 'deprive' brothers of property (FAO, 1979). Even though modern bilateral inheritance laws grant women rights to land, women's claims to land under these laws are strongly resisted or circumvented by male relatives. Women are often encouraged to relinquish their claims to land in favour of their brothers. When women baulk, they are subjected to litigation, threats, harassment, beatings and, in extreme cases, murder by male relatives (Agarwal, 1988). Because women lack political power, they generally are unable to seek and obtain support for their rights in court. In India, for example, local panchayats (village governments) support families in pressuring daughters to sign away their shares of land in favour of their brothers (Agarwal, 1988).

It is important to note, however, that women have not always passively accepted their lack of land rights. Nor have they let their inferior economic, political, and social status deter them from expressing their discontent and demanding their rights. At various times, they have taken collective action to demand land rights: efforts include resistance to a fundamentalist challenge to women's land rights during the 1950s in the Malaysian State of Negeri Sembilan and the Bodhgaya movement in India, in the 1970s, in which landless women demanded ownership of the plots they cultivated, independent of men (Stivens, 1985; and Agarwal, 1988).

STRENGTHENING WOMEN'S LAND RIGHTS: CONCLUSIONS AND RECOMMENDATIONS

This paper shows that the disincentives to investment due to women's lack of access to land and insecure tenure undermine productivity and the environment. Given the growing urgency of environmental problems and the sluggishness of economic development, efforts to promote sustainable development require a broadened focus and a shift in the allocation of resources to take into account women's productive roles, an important element of which is strengthening women's land rights.

Measures needed to enhance women's access to land include legal reforms to give women direct and independent control of land unmediated by male relatives; procedures to include women in on-going land titling and registration programmes; and stricter enforcement of women's land rights where they are relatively secure. Needed also are changes in government policies to reduce land concentration and to improve women's access to common property resources. Community management or comanagement of government owned common property areas would improve women's access, assuming their full and equal participation in community management processes.

Needed to address the demand side constraints to women's access to land are measures to reduce women's poverty, enhance their productivity, and build their human capital including better access to credit, agricultural extension, new technologies, more education, and quality health care. Policies to strengthen women's land rights, complemented by policies to improve their access to productive resources and services, can enhance women's investment incentives and capacity, improve their productivity, and enable them to take a longer term view on the use and management of the environment and natural resources thereby strengthening sustainable development.

NOTE

1 The landless or near-landless are defined as people with little or no land 'even to meet the barest minimum needs of the individual' (Sinha, 1984).

REFERENCES

Agarwal, B., 1986, *Cold Hearths and Barren Slopes – The Woodfuel Crisis in the Third World*, The Riverdale Company, Inc., Riverdale, Maryland.

Agarwal, B., 1988, 'Who Sows? Who Reaps? Women and Land Rights in India', *Journal of Peasant Studies,* Vol. 15, No. 4, pp.531–581.

Ahmed, I. (ed.), 1985, *Technology and Rural Women: Conceptual and Empirical Issues,* George Allen & Unwin, London.

Berger, M., DeLancey, V. and Mellencamp, A., 1984, *Bridging the Gender Gap in Agricultural Extension,* International Center for Research on Women, Washington, D.C.

Buvinic, M., 1993, 'Population Policy and Family Planning Programmes: Contributions From A Focus

On Women', Paper presented at the Population Summit of the World's Scientific Academics, New Delhi, India, 24–27 October.

Buvinic, M. and Rao Gupta, G., 1993, 'Targeting Poor Women-Headed Households and Women-Maintained Families in Developing Countries: Views on a Policy Dilemma', paper prepared for the Population Council/ICRW Joint Programme on 'Female Headship and Poverty in Developing Countries', International Centre for Research on Women, Mimeo, Washington, D.C.

Cleaver, K. and Schreiber, G., 1992, *The Population, Agriculture and Environment Nexus in Sub-Saharan Africa*, Africa Region, World Bank, Washington, D.C.

Colchester, M. and Lohmann, L. (eds.), 1993, *The Struggle for Land and the Fate of the Forest*, Zed Books Ltd, London.

Collins, J.L., 1991, 'Women and the Environment: Social Reproduction and Sustainable Development', in Gallin, R.S. and Ferguson, A. (eds.), *The Women and International Development Annual, Volume 2*, Westview Press, Boulder, Colorado.

Cruz, M.C., Meyer, C.A., Repetto, R. and Woodward, R., 1992, *Population Growth, Poverty, and Environmental Stress: Frontier Migration in the Philippines and Costa Rica*, World Resources Institute, Washington, D.C.

Davison, J. (ed.), 1988, *Agriculture, Women, and Land: The African Experience*, Westview Press, Boulder, Colorado.

Deere, C.D., 1987, 'The Latin American Agrarian Reform Experience', in Deere, C.D. and Leon, M. (eds.), *Rural Women and State Policy: Feminist Perspectives on Latin American Agricultural Development*, Westview Press, Boulder, Colorado.

Dickerman, C.W., 1989, *Security of Tenure and Land Registration in Africa: Literature Review and Synthesis*, Land Tenure Center, University of Wisconsin, Madison, Wisconsin.

FAO (Food and Agriculture Organization of the United Nations), 1979, *The Legal Status of Rural Women*, Economic and Social Development Paper No. 9, Rome.

FAO (Food and Agriculture Organization of the United Nations), 1987, *Restoring the Balance*, Rome, Italy.

Fornos, W., 1991, 'Strategies for Survival: The Population/Environment Connection', *Toward the 21st Century*, No. 8, Washington DC; Population Institute.

ILO (International Labour Office), 1987, *Linking Energy with Survival: A Guide to Energy, Environment and Rural Women's Word*, ILO, Geneva.

ILO (International Labour Office), 1989, *Women and Land*, Report on the Regional African Workshop on Women's Access to Land as a Strategy for Employment Promotion, Poverty Alleviation and Household Food Security held in Harare, Zimbabwe, October 17–21, 1988, Programme on Rural Women, Rural Employment Policies Branch, ILO, Geneva.

Jacobs, S., 1991, 'Land Resettlement and Gender in Zimbabwe: Some Findings', *The Journal of Modern African Studies*, Vol. 29, No. 3, pp.521–528.

Jazairy, I., Alamgir, M. and Panuccio, T., 1992, *The State of World Rural Poverty: An Inquiry Into Its Causes and Consequences*, New York University Press for the International Fund for Agricultural Development (IFAD), New York.

Lycette, M., 1993, *Women, Population and the Environment: A Misplaced Focus*, Environment Series No. 1, International Centre for Research on Women, Washington, D.C.

Myers, N., 1991, 'The World's Forests and Human Populations: The Environmental Interconnections', in Davis, K. and Bernstam, M.S. (eds.), *Resources, Environment, and Population: Present Knowledge, Future Options*, Oxford Press for *Population and Development Review*, London.

Palmer, I., 1985, *The Impact of Agrarian Reform on Women*, Kumarian Press, West Hartford, Connecticut.

Palmer, I., 1991, *Gender and Population in the Adjustment of African Economies: Planning for Change*, Women, Work, and Development Number 19, ILO, Geneva.

Panayotou, T., 1993, *Green Markets: The Economics of Sustainable Development*, International Center for Economic Growth, San Francisco.

Rahama, A. and Hoogenboom, A., 1988, 'Women Farmers, Technological Innovation and Access to Development Projects', *Development*, Vol. 4, pp.71–77.

Randolph, S. and Sanders, R., 1988, 'Constraints to Agricultural Production in Africa: A Survey of Female Farmers in the Ruhehgeri Prefecture of Rwanda', *Studies in Comparative International Development*, Vol. 13, No. 3, pp.78–98.

Rocheleau, D.E., 1988, 'Women, Trees, and Tenure: Implications for Agroforestry', in Formann. L. and Bruce, J.W. (eds.), *Whose Trees? Proprietary Dimensions of Forestry*, Westview Press, Boulder, Colorado.

Schuler, M. (ed.), 1986, *Empowerment and the Law: Strategies of Third World Women*, OEF International, Washington, D.C.

Seager, J. and Olson, A., 1986, *Women in the World: An International Atlas*, Simon and Schuster, New York.

Sinha, R., 1984, *Landlessness: A Growing Problem*, FAO, Rome, p.15.

Staudt, K.A., 1982, 'Women Farmers and Inequities in Agricultural Services', in Bay, E. (ed.), *Women and Work in Africa*, Westview Press, Boulder, Colorado.

Stivens, M., 1985, 'The Fate of Women's Land Rights: Gender, Matriliny, and Capitalism in Rembau, Negeri Sembilan, Malaysia', in Afshra, H. (ed.), *Women, Work, and Ideology in the Third World*, Tavistock Publications, New York, USA.

Thiesenhusen, W., 1991, 'Implication of the Rural Land Tenure System for the Environmental Debate: Three Scenarios', *The Journal of Developing Areas*, Vol. 26, pp.1–24.

United Nations, 1989, *World Survey on the Role of Women in Development*, United Nations, New York.

van den Brink, R. and Bromley, D.W., 1992, *The Enclosure Revisited: Privitization, Titling, and the Quest for Advantage in Africa*, Cornell Food and Nutrition Program, Ithaca, New York.

van Herpen, D. and Ashby, J.A. (eds.), 1991, *Gender Analysis in Agricultural Research: Proceedings of an Internal Workshop*, Centro Internactional de Agricultura Tropical, Cali, Colombia.

WRI (World Resources Institute), 1992, *World Resources 1992–1993*, Oxford University Press for WRI, New York.

Wynter, P., 1990, 'Property, Women Fishers and Struggles for Women's Rights in Mozambique', *Sage*, Vol. 7, pp.33–37.

DISCUSSION OPENING — Korotoumou Oattara *(The Ohio State University, USA)*

The objective in the paper was to demonstrate that unequal access to land by women undermines the environment. The author gives numerous examples throughout the developing world to illustrate several barriers that prevent women's access to land. However, it is not very clear from the paper how unequal land rights for women have affected the environment. The author admits that not enough data are available to show the negative effect of insecure land tenure among women on the environment. Further research and more rigorous works needs to be done to prove this point.

The author refers to the lack of institutional credit as a major constraint to women's access to land. It has to be recognized that in most sub-Saharan African countries, land ownership rights are not very well defined. Therefore, women are not the only ones who do not utilize institutional credit due to the lack of collateral such as land; men have to rely on informal finance as well.

That women receive only 10–15 percent of institutional credit, as reported by the author, may not be directly linked to their lack of land ownership. There is really no need for targeted credit programmes where women would be the principal beneficiaries as a solution to the problem. In fact, programmes that cater to both genders have been successful in their attempt to overcome gender biases. The village savings and credit associations (VISACAs) in The Gambia (West Africa) are a vivid example that perpetuation of any existing discrimination can be alleviated or even eliminated by careful planning (Ouattara *et al.* 1994). The single most important feature behind the VISACAs' success is a sound institutional design that lets all villagers participate in the decision-making process, irrespective of gender. Collateral substitutes are used to grant loans to both women and men. Women are given leadership roles, with their inclusion in the management committees, and granted full voting rights. The end result is a remarkable female presence (52 percent of membership). The VISACAs have created an environment that welcomes women as equal partners in spite of the fact that in Gambian villages, men and women are used to doing business separately. No targeting of any group based on gender, or activity, has been necessary to achieve a remarkable result. Clearly, programmes like VISACAs that are based on the right institutional design need to be encouraged.

The solutions stated in the conclusion to address the demand-side constraints to women's access to land such as poverty reduction, human capital building, and better access to financial services remain valid, although great care is required in their implementation.

Reference

Ouattara, K. *et al.* (1994), '*Financial Innovation and Women in Rural Africa: The Village Savings and Credit Associations in The Gambia*', Paper presented at the AAEA meeting, San Diego, California, August.

HUGO DE GROOTE*

Women's Income Versus Family Income as a Determinant for Food Security, an Example from Southern Mali

Abstract: The simple neo-classical household model presents a major problem — the cooperative unique household utility function might not always be appropriate. More specifically, women's and men's utility functions might be different. To accomodate the problem, this paper explores the possibility of an enlarged household model. This model also includes two other elements that have recently received major attention, credit and seasonality. The analysis of data from southern Mali indicates that, in contrast to the family's total income, the family's assets and women's income have a positive effect on the nutritional status of pre-school children in the pre-harvest season. The relationship does not hold in the period after the harvest. This indicates that the women's utility function differs from that of the family as a whole, and that the seasonality of the income is very important.

INTRODUCTION

In recent years the simple neo-classical household model (Singh, Squire and Strauss, 1986) has come under increased scrutiny. The cooperative unique household utility function might not always be appropriate to study development problems. More specifically, women's and men's utility functions might be different, which would require a new approach in development work and research (Haddad, 1993). In recent literature, evidence that a household does not constitute a unified economy has been presented and new research approaches have suggested for (Guyer and Peters, 1987; Wilk 1989; Feldstein, Poats, Cloud and Norem, 1989).

Due to a perception that traditional development projects were biased towards men, projects and policies targeted specifically at women and a new academic field 'Women in Development' have emerged. The assumption underlying this new approach is that resources entering the household are not distributed independently of the person who acquires or manages them. In other words, different individuals have different utility functions that are not necessarily in harmony with the abstract overall household utility function. A common example of this policy change is the targeting of women in order to increase food security. In many countries women are perceived to be responsible for providing food for the household. Assuming that women derive a higher utility than men from providing food to children, an increase in women's income or production would have a higher effect on food security than would a similar increase for men.

In this framework, the Freedom From Hunger Foundation (FFH) provides credit services to poor rural women in southern Mali. In a group-lending, poverty bank, system the women are provided with small loans to be paid back in weekly instalments. The repayments are organized in a group meeting in which loan management is discussed, but which also serves as a vehicle for health and nutrition education. The first loans were provided in 1989 and the program now reaches several hundred households (Lassen and

* Equipe de Systèmes de Production et de Gestion des Resources Naturelles, Mali/Royal Tropical Institute, The Netherlands.

Mknelly, 1992). The program is funded by USAID, who invited the International Food Policy Research Institute (IFPRI) to study its impact on income, production and food security. A field study was executed in 1993, and the first results are presented here.

CONCEPTUAL FRAMEWORK

In the basic agricultural household model, the household is assumed to have a unique utility function, based on the consumption of market goods, home consumption and leisure for any production cycle (Singh, Squire and Strauss, 1986). The household allocates time and assets for home production and wage labour to maximize its welfare. These relations are depicted in Figure 1. Although the allocation of time, assets, production and consumption of different individuals can play different roles and can therefore be modelled explicitly within the framework, the utility function is necessarily unique.

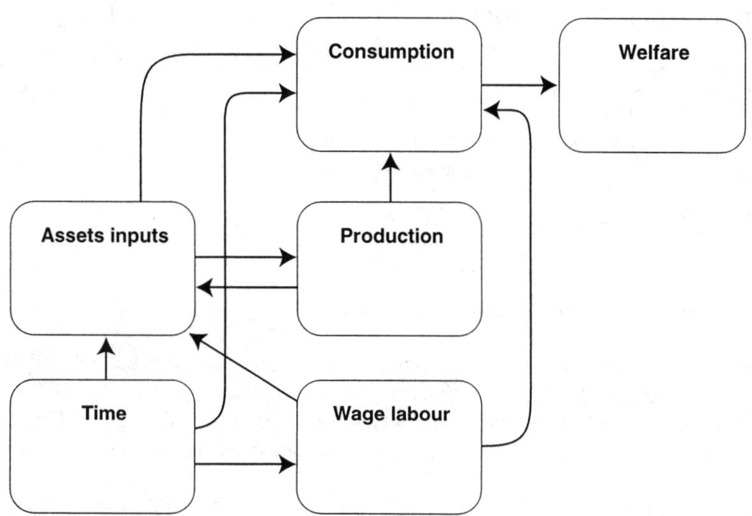

Figure 1 *The Household Model — General Conceptual Framework*

To respond to the reality in southern Mali and to reflect the problems under discussion the model needs three extensions; seasonality, credit and intra-household resource allocation. Mali has a distinct rainy season and one main harvest. This has obvious effects on agricultural production and therefore on home consumption, but also on time allocation and health (Sahn 1989). Food and income are generated in a short period after the harvest, while food, labour and other inputs are needed before the harvest especially. The direct effect of seasonality is illustrated in the bottom right corner of Figure 2, while its rippling effect is presented by undulating arrows.

Credit can alleviate the effects of this one main harvest by smoothing consumption and allowing for timely investments over different seasons, as well as over different years. It allows for an increase in inputs if so needed, but also for consumption smoothing between seasons, while leaving assets where they are needed in the long run (Iqbal, 1986). The effects are illustrated on the top left corner of Figure 2.

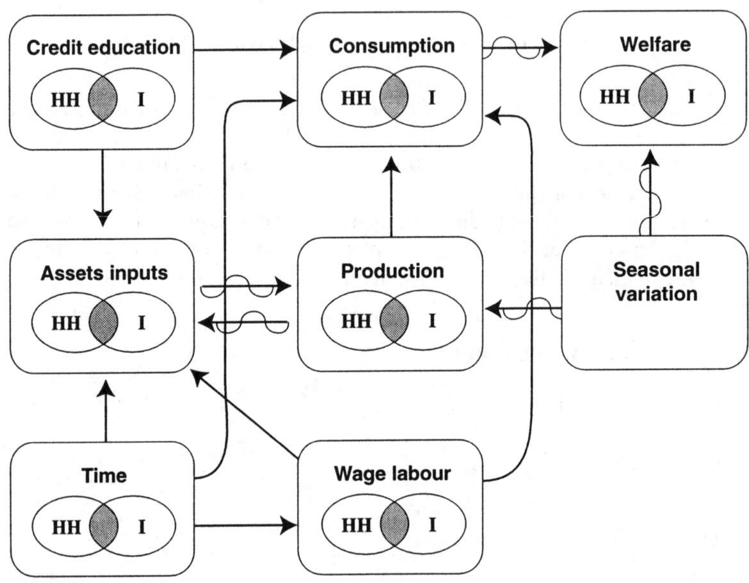

Figure 2 *The Household Model — Seasonal Variability*

Intra-household resource allocation and individual welfare effects need to be included to allow for different individual utility functions, the basic assumption in projects focused on women. Moreover, the effects of those projects have to be traced through; different allocations of resources by individuals, assets, production, consumption and time use (Haddad, 1993).

Explicitly, the household or individual household members derive utility from, among other things, health and nutritional status:

(1) $U(B, X, H, L)$ where

$U =$ utility
$B =$ nutritional status
$X =$ consumption goods
$H =$ health
$L =$ leisure

To maximize utility, the household allocates resources according to first order conditions for demand functions as well as for production functions. Nutritional status can be seen as a health production function whose inputs are decided through those first order conditions (Behrman and Deolalikar, 1988). The basic assumption for such a function is that nutritional status is positively related to assets and income (both monetary and in-kind), through increased food consumption and better health care:

(2) $B(A, I)$ where $A =$ assets
$I =$ income

Thus, if women derive a higher utility from a better nutritional status of the children, and they have freedom to spend their own income, the effect of their income on nutritional status will be higher than that of family income, all other things being equal. A further assumption is that most of the income is agriculture related and earned in the post-harvest season. Due to the discounting over time in the utility function, consumption will decrease over time until the new harvest. Extra income in the pre-harvest season would then be spent on the items which deliver high utility in a period of low consumption, such as food. If indeed women's utility function differs from men's, the effect should be more noticeable in this season. The health nutrition function has to reflect time and individual differences. Income I of the health production function is therefore represented by a matrix:

$$I_{11} \cdot\cdot$$
$$I = \cdot I_{it} \cdot \text{ where } i = \text{individuals or group of individuals}$$
$$\cdots \qquad t = \text{time during year}$$

Now that the theoretical groundwork is laid out in the previous section, the hypotheses to be tested can be stated formally as follows. The family and the women's income have a positive effect on children's nutritional status. The latter has à higher effect than the former, and its effect is more pronounced in the pre-harvest season.

SOUTHERN MALI, A COMPLEX REALITY

Freedom From Hunger started its program in the district ('arrondissement') of Dogo, subregion ('cercle') of Bougouni, in southern Mali. Although recently other districts in the same subregion have been included, the IFPRI research was limited to this first district. Dogo has a population of 31 500 for an area of more than 3000 km^2 (10.5 people per km^2), dispersed over 85 villages (CMDT, 1992).

The district of Dogo is accessible from the town of Bougouni in the dry season over an unpaved road of 55 km. It is also linked all year round with an unpaved road to the excellent paved road from Bamako to Bougouni (Figure 3).

Southern Mali is situated in the wooded savannah of West Africa. Bougouni has an average yearly rainfall of 1089mm (1941–1980) spread over about seven months (Sivakumar, Konate and Virmani, 1984). The rain falls from April to October (see Figure 4), and the harvest of the principal crops follows shortly thereafter. This rainfall pattern dominates the agricultural year.

The household in Dogo, defined as a group of related people who eat and work together, is an extended family, consisting of the descendants of one male individual, and their wives. The structure is patrilocal, patrilinear and polygamous. A typical household is composed of a male head, his wives and their children. Daughters leave the household when they marry, but sons and younger brothers of the household head stay with their wives and children.

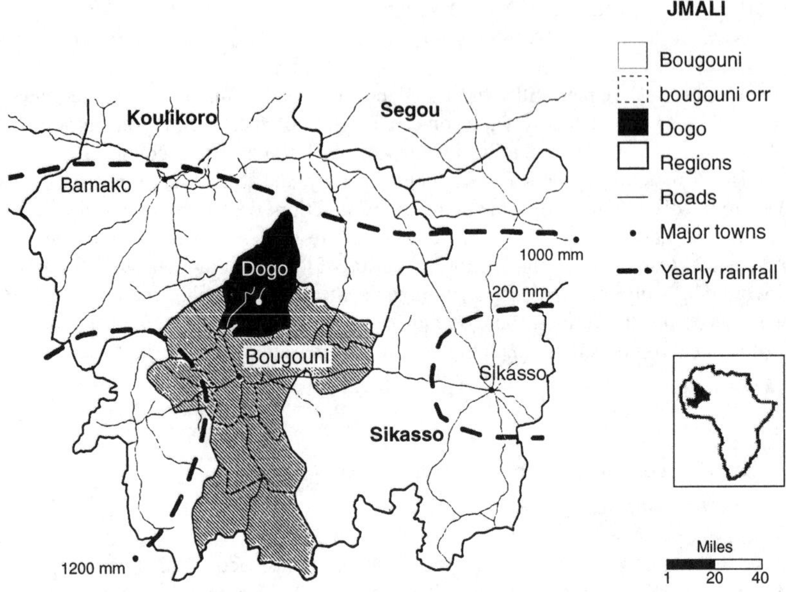

Figure 3 *Mali — IFPRI Credit and Education Survey*

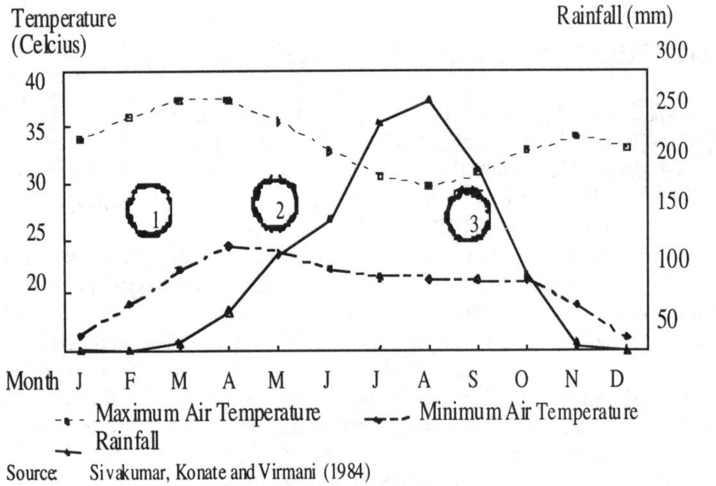

Figure 4 *Climate in Southern Mali — Average Monthly Temperature and Rainfall in Bougouni (1941–1980)*

The household has common lands, that are cultivated together, but individuals can have small personal plots and can own animals. The head of the household is in charge of common grain production and the stocks for the year. Generally, the younger women take turns cooking for the whole household. Once women have daughters-in-law, they leave the cooking to the latter.

Thus, for the analysis of income effects on nutritional status we have to distinguish four groups of adults: head of the household, non-head men, younger women (defined here as those who prepare meals) and elder women (who no longer cook).

DATA COLLECTION

Based on a Rapid Rural Appraisal (De Groote *et al.,* 1993) and a survey optimization program (De Groote, 1993) a stratified two-stage PPS sampling design was chosen, resulting in 100 households for each of the two strata, villages with the FFH project and villages without. There were three rounds of the survey. In the first round, late February to early April 1993, the head of the household, an additional adult man, and the women who cooked the previous day were interviewed on their income, expenditure, food consumption and credit, and all women and children under 15 were measured for weight and height. Based on the experience from the first round, an older woman who no longer cooks was added to the sample for the subsequent rounds, in April-May and in August-September.

RESULTS

Family Composition, Income and Assets

Table 1 *Family Composition*

	Group	Mean	St. dev.
	Head of Household*	0.97	0.18
Male	Adults, not head of hh	3.73	4.34
	5–19 years	2.64	2.7
	0–4 years	1.55	1.89
Female	Elder (not cooking)	1.24	1.66
	Young (married, cooking)	3.11	2.81
	Unmarried, ≥ 5 years	3.71	3.8
	0–4 years	1.34	1.58
Total	Total number of hh members	18.29	
	Household members present	17.02	15.03
	Adult equivalent	11.17	9.86

Note: * 18 percent female; 91per cent illiterate, 90 per cent muslim.

The households have an average of 17 members present at the time of the interview with a maximum of 99. Besides the head, 82 per cent of whom are male, there are four other adult males on average. The average family has three younger cooking women, one older woman, six school-age and three pre-school children. The total household income (including home consumed agricultural production) is estimated at almost 500 000 FCFA (at US$1 = 260 FCFA this is roughly $2000, before the 50 percent devaluation of 1994) for a family of 17. Agriculture provides 95 percent of that income, and half of that comes from cotton, all of which is sold. The other half comes mostly from cereals such as millet, sorghum and corn, which are primarily used for home consumption.

Table 2 *Family Income and Assets*

		Number		Value	
		Mean	St. dev.	FCFA	St. dev.
Assets	Land available	15.21	23.7		
	Land cultivated	7.7	5.99		
	Cattle	10.83	14.61	324 900	438 300
	Small ruminants	4.95		34 650	
	Animal traction	0.675		192 377	
Income	Cotton			236 248	295 204
	Other agric. income			234 386	
	Non-agric. income			26 217	53 078

Table 3 *Women's Income (1 year)*

		Production			Sales		
		Mean	St. dev.	N	Mean	St. dev.	N
Young women (who cook)							
	Crops	16 688	21 999	156	731	2198	40
	Animals	835	3720	19	649	3171	18
	Non-agr.[1]	2032	4346	135			
	Total	19 556		156	1380	3914	50
Older women (exempt)							
	Crops	14 254	16 441	156	1340	4831	40
	Animals	2238	13 960	19	920	4405	18
	Total	16 492	24 815	156	2260	6788	50

Note: [1] January-March only.

The majority of women have some private agricultural activity, valued at 17 000 FCFA per woman year, but the production goes almost completely to home consumption. Women's non-agricultural monetary income is small in comparison, 2000 FCFA for the first quarter of the year. It comes about equally from three sources; trading of agricultural products, petty trading, and the production of shea nut butter. It is for the first two activities, which take place in the local weekly markets, that the FFH credit is well suited and used.

Nutritional Status (Dependent Variables)

A common indicator for nutritional status of pre-school children (under 6 years) is the weight for height Z-score (WHZ), which is a comparison of the weight for height ratio of each child with that of a standard (US) population, expressed in standard deviations. The results show that in March the mean WHZ is –0.56, or more than half a standard deviation lower than the standard population. In September, the pre-harvest season, the mean WHZ drops to –0.74.

Table 4 *Anthropometric Measurements*

Time	Weight for Height Z			Body Mass Index		
	Mean	St. dev.	N	Mean	St. dev.	N
March	–0.56	1.34	519	20.40	2.37	607
May	–0.58	1.11	462	20.43	2.46	568
September	–0.74	0.91	254	19.45	2.62	188

The standard indicator for adults is the body mass index (BMI) which is calculated as the weight divided by the height squared. A BMI under 18.5 is generally considered a sign of malnutrition. The BMI for adult women in March is 20.4 and drops seriously in September.

Analysis

The dependent variable used in the regression is the Weight for Height Z-score for all children under the age of five years. The analysis was repeated with the same independent variables for the Z-scores of the three rounds. The following indicators of family income and assets were retained:

- household size, expressed as adult equivalent (ADEQUIV)
- household agricultural production of the previous year, in 1000 FCFA/adult equivalent (AG_FAM)
- household's number of cattle per adult equivalent (BOV_FAM).

All indicators of women's income were adjusted for family size and composition by multiplying first by the number of women in the household in the specific group (since only one woman per group was interviewed), and divided by the adult equivalent of the household. Thus, the variables used were:

- last year's agricultural production by women of the household, 1000 FCFA/adult equivalent (AG_WOM)
- young women's non-agricultural income for the household, in 1000 FCFA/adult equivalent: from January 1 to the first interview in March (NA_YW1), from March to May (NA_W2), from May to September (NA_YW3)
- older women's non-agricultural income for the household, in 1000 FCFA/adult equivalent: from January 1 to their first interview in May (NA_OW2), from May to September (NA_OW3).

The results of the regressions are presented in Table 5. In the first round only the coefficient of family size is significantly different from zero. This negative relationship shows up in every round, indicating that children suffer more malnutrition in larger families. Women's non-agricultural income has no significant effect, while women's agricultural income and family assets as measured by cattle have a positive effect, but only at the 88 per cent level.

In the second round young women's income has a clear and positive effect. The exact interpretation is as follows: if the young women's non-agricultural income of this period increases by 1000 FCFA ($4) per adult equivalent (11/family on average), the WHZ increases by 0.042. The women's agricultural production has a surprising negative effect, while older women's income has no effect. Family's assets as measured by cattle have a strong positive effect. In the third round only the young women's non-agricultural income of the second period has a significant effect, while family size keeps its negative effect. No effect of agricultural production is positive in this shortage period.

Table 5 *Regression of Weight-for-Height Z-scores of Pre-schoolers on Income Variables*

	First round		Second round		Third round	
	b	*t*	*b*	*t*	*b*	*t*
NA_YW1	0.068	0.956	–0.015	–0.272	–0.065	1.141
NA_YW2		0.042	1.949	0.033	1.878	
NA_YW3	0.290	0.235				
NA_OW2		0.215	1.017	0.092	0.443	
NA_OW3	0.001	0.353				
AG_WOM	0.012	1.579	–0.016	–1.969	–0.010	–0.995
AG_FAM	0.001	0.630	0.001	0.582	0.003	1.465
BO_FAM	0.087	1.585	0.090	1.817	–0.091	–1.349
ADEQUIV	–0.010	–1.830	–0.006	–1.054	–0.011	–1.646
Constant	–0.649	–3.689	–0.611	–3.675	–0.582	–2.732
N	0.423		0.340		0.201	
R^2	0.031		0.028		0.068	
S	1.330		1.120		0.892	

CONCLUSIONS AND IMPLICATIONS

Younger women's non-agricultural income does have a significant effect on children's nutrition in the pre-harvest season, while no such effect is obtained for older women or for younger women in the post-harvest period. Women's agricultural income, on the other hand, has at most an effect in the post-harvest season. Family agricultural production does not seem to have any effect, but family's size has a clear negative effect.

The major result of the study is that the season in which income is generated and the gender of the provider are important. The significant variable, women's non-agricultural income in the pre-harvest season, has both a gender and a seasonal component, which can not yet be distinguished here. Projects are, however, justified in promoting this kind of income generation, since it does have a positive impact on the nutritional status of pre-school children. Further analysis of the data should show how an increase in women's income influences expenditure on food and other items.

REFERENCES

Behrman, J. and Deolalikar A., 1988, 'Health and Nutrition', in Chenery, H. and Srinivasan, T.N. (eds.), *Handbook of Development Economics*, Vol. I, Elsevier Science Publishers B.V.

CMDT, 1992, *Monographie de Bougouni*, Compagnie Malienne pour le Développment du Textile, Bamako.

De Groote, H., 1993, 'Optimizing Survey Design for Developing Countries', Paper presented at the American Agricultural Economics Association meetings, Orlando, August.

De Groote H., Dembele I., Sidibe, M. and Sidibe, N., 1993, 'Pre-Etude sur l'Impacte du Programme Credit avec Education', International Food Policy Research Institute, Mimeo, Bamako.

Feldstein, H.S., Poats, S.V., Cloud, K. and Norem, R., 1989, 'Intra-household Dynamics and Farming Systems Research and Extension Conceptual Framework and Worksheets', in Feldstein, H.S. and Poats, S.V. (eds.), *Gender and Agriculture: Case Studies in Intra-Household Analysis*, Kumarian Press, West Hartford, Connecticut.

Guyer, J. and Peters, P. (eds.), 1987, 'Conceptualizing the Household: Issues of Theory and Policy in Africa', *Development and Change*, Vol. 18, No. 2, pp.197–328.

Haddad, L., 1993, 'Intra-Household Allocation, a Multi-Country Research Proposal', International Food Research Institute, Mimeo,Washington, D.C.

Iqbal, F., 1986, 'The Demand and Supply of Funds among Agricultural Households in India', in Singh, I., Squire, L. and Strauss, J. (eds.), *Agricultural Household Models*, Johns Hopkins University Press, Baltimore, Maryland.

Lassen, C.A. and Mknelly, B., 1992, 'Freedom from Hunger's New Credit-Led Approach to Alleviate Hunger: Is It Working?', Freedom From Hunger, Mimeo, University of California, Davis.

Sahn, D. (ed.), 1989, *Seasonal Variability in Third World Agriculture, The Consequences for Food Security*, Johns Hopkins University Press, Baltimore, Maryland.

Singh, I., Squire, L. and Strauss, J., 1986, *Agricultural Household Models*, Johns Hopkins University Press, Baltimore, Maryland.

Wilk, R. (ed.), 1989, *The Household Economy, Reconsidering the Domestic Mode of Production*, Westview Press, Boulder, Colorado.

DISCUSSION OPENING — Benon Gazinski *(Agricultural University, Poland)*

In the past, economists neglected the importance of factors other than pure economics, particularly items that were, by nature, difficult to measure and include in the cost equation. They ignored the fact that the human being not always acts as a Homo economicus. Non-economic motivations of the human behaviour, the heritage of culture, in which people grow up, the structure of values they follow; all these have a significant impact on the framework of economic relations.

A strong call for change arose from the natural environment, facing the prospect of disaster. Modern, high-input, intensive agriculture has more and more resembled a sportsman doped by drugs. In sharp contrast, the idea of organic farming has been developing, emerging not only from the environmental concern but from philosophical reflection on the cultural message related to agricultural activities and representing a shift in lifestyle.

A failure of a concept of direct technology transfer from developed countries to the third world and a realization that development is not a commercial commodity contributed to the change from the typical style of thinking of the economists. It has become evident that the cultural factors and structures of human populations have to be considered for effective solutions to the issues of economic and social development to be worked out.

Let's turn from such a broad perspective to the paper of Hugo De Groote, considering the issue of womens' incomes in relation to the nutritional status of the family. As evidenced by the experiment in Southern Mali, some economic questions can not be solved without insight into the mechanisms and links which regulate the functioning of communities.

The author argues that it is not enough to treat the family as a coherent and uniform unit in the fulfilment of development projects. Differences in individuals' utility functions have to be considered. It is argued in the paper that an increase in womens' income would have a more pronounced effect on the food security of families than would a similar increase for men — because women have the role of assuring the daily food for the families. The econometric results support that argument.

I suggest that findings in the paper suggest three broad areas of further investigations and discussions. The first concerns the relationship between the model and reality. A coherent and well-designed model may still misrepresent the performance of the real system. The question is not only how to improve the model's performance but how to improve the interpretations of the outcome. Second, what lessons can be drawn from the paper for the practice of international and aid programmes? Is a strategy to increase womens' incomes sufficient or too simplified and mechanistic. Is there a danger of external action damaging the coherence of the family? How can harm be avoided while assisting the development? Third, how can De Groote's experiences and approach be applied to other areas and issues of development of local communities. Finally, does contemporary economics constitute an enemy or an ally in preserving the great heritage of cultures of nations all over the world?

JAAKKO KANGASNIEMI AND THOMAS REARDON *

Demographic Pressure and the Sustainability of Land Use in Rwanda[1]

Abstract: Increasing land scarcity forces Rwandan farmers to expand the area under food crops at the expense of pasture, fallow, and forest. Since the non-cropping uses of land provide more vegetative cover against erosion than most food crops, land scarcity appears to be associated with unsustainable land uses. However, demographic pressure also pushes farmers to grow crops in dense associations, which increases vegetative cover on cultivated fields. The estimated relationship between farm size and protective crop cover depends crucially on how the measure of vegetative cover is adjusted to account for high cropping densities. Without any adjustment, the association between land scarcity and erosive land use is strong; with the adjustment used here, it disappears, except for high altitude areas, where bananas, the only major food crop that protects land well against erosion, do not grow well.

INTRODUCTION

Does demographic pressure make agriculture less sustainable in developing countries? Literature presents two conflicting hypotheses (National Research Council, 1993). The pessimistic, 'Ricardian,' hypothesis is that when population grows, farmers tend to mine their soils and expand cultivation to marginal, easily erodible land. The higher the rate of population growth and the more fragile the environment, the greater is the rate of erosion.

The optimistic hypothesis is that because land-scarce farmers depend on land productivity for food security, they attempt to prevent degradation. Above all, they use their relatively abundant labour to adopt more sustainable labour-intensive land use practices and to invest in soil conservation. In Rwanda, the pessimistic hypothesis has much credibility. The most densely populated country on the African continent, Rwanda has an average farm size below one hectare (DSA, 1992). Farming has already expanded to cover the easily erodible hillsides. Almost one-third of cultivable fields are now located on slopes of 20 degrees or more. In a 1991 survey by the Ministry of Agriculture, 40 percent of field blocks were reported by their cultivators as degraded.

Yet economic theory could support either hypothesis. On the one hand, it suggests that land-scarce poor farmers may have a high rate of time preference and may sacrifice long-term sustainability for immediate food security. On the other hand, theory suggests that as population growth changes the relative endowments of land and labour, it also may change relative prices so that using labour to maintain the productivity of land becomes more attractive. In the end, the question is empirical and depends significantly on the characteristics of the land uses (crops) farmers can choose in a specific environment.

To understand fully what determines how sustainable are the land uses farmers choose, ideally one would first model the determinants of land use, and then model their impacts on the farming environment. The space here is too brief for both, so we focus on the second, and ask directly whether increasing land scarcity, reflected in miniaturization of farms, is associated with Rwandan farmers having unsustainable land uses. This

* Visiting Specialist, Michigan State University, USA, Outposted in the Division of Agricultural Statistics (DSA), Ministry of Agriculture (MINAGRI), Kigali, Rwanda, Michigan State University, USA, respectively.

addresses an important unresolved debate in a context that should tell much about the future sustainability of agriculture in Africa.

We examine this longitudinal question with cross-sectional data by comparing how well the land uses chosen by more and less land-scarce farmers protect the land against erosion. Land use is here defined to include the allocation of land to different uses (crops, pasture, fallow, and woodlot) and cultural practices such as intercropping and crop planting density. This definition excludes treatment of soil conservation investments, which are studied with the same data base by Clay and Reardon (1994).

DATA AND METHODS

This study uses data for 821 sample households that derive from the detailed rural household survey conducted in 1991 by the Division of Agricultural Statistics (DSA), Ministry of Agriculture and Livestock of Rwanda.

Our approach has four steps. First, we categorize farm households into landholding quartiles according to their land scarcity using the criterion of cultivable land per adult equivalent.[2] All pastures, fallows, and woodlots are considered cultivable. Second, we compare over quartiles the average index of the protective crop cover on farm fields, without controlling for other factors. Third, we repeat the comparison with stratifications for agroclimatic zone and for altitude.

Fourth, to control better for agroclimatic factors we use regression analysis with observations aggregated over fields to farm-household observations. The control variables include rainfall and altitude. In addition, a multiplicative dummy variable is introduced to allow the coefficient for farm size to differ for high altitudes where bananas do not grow well (MINAGRI, 1978). The hypothesis is that since bananas are highly caloric and also protect the land well against erosion, the areas where few bananas are grown would show a stronger link between erosive land uses and demographic pressure.

The dependent variable in the analysis is an index of the protective vegetative cover provided by crops or other land use such as pasture, known as the C-value (erosion index measuring crop protective cover). Soil scientists use C-values together with data on slope, rainfall, and soil type to predict erosion (Wischmeier and Smith, 1978). The C-value itself is not a measure of erosion but, other things being equal, a lower C-value indicates less erosion. Depending on the varieties and cultural practices, the protective cover provided by a given crop varies widely and its C-value needs to be estimated empirically for different environments. The crop-specific C-values used in this paper are estimated in Lewis (1986) and Lewis, Clay and Dejaegher (1988) based on Rwandan field data.

Although C-values are specific to cultural practices such as weeding and mulching, the C-value estimates used here are the same for all farm-size quartiles. However, it is known that all major crops show 50–100 percent higher yields on the fields of the most land-scarce quartile compared to those of the least land-scarce quartile (Uwamariya, Kangasniemi, and Reardon, 1993). This suggests that small farmers (in terms of cultivable land per adult equivalent) use much more labour per unit of land than large farmers. The impact of this on the protective crop cover is unclear, since while some ways of using additional labour (weeding) are likely to expose land to erosion, others (mulching) clearly increase soil protection and crop cover.

Since more than one-half of cultivated fields in Rwanda are intercropped, a key question is how to estimate C-values for crop associations. Because few empirically-based estimates were available for crop associations, we used C-values estimated for purely cropped fields to compute C-values for the associations. Our unadjusted C-value is an average of crop-specific C-values weighted by the estimated land shares of each crop in a given association. However, DSA's data show that planting densities on intercropped fields are higher than on purely cropped fields, which suggests that there is more vegetation, and thus more crop cover against erosion. Also DSA's field experiments indicate that the average C-value of the crops grown in the association overstates the C-value (exposure to erosion) of the association (Lewis 1986). In the literature, reduced erosion is mentioned as one of the reasons farmers continue to rely on intercropping (Fussel and Serafini, 1985).

To adjust C-values for high densities we divide the unadjusted C-value by the sum of the densities of the crops grown in the association (for technical details, see Kangasniemi, 1993). On average, the adjustment reduces C-values (increases soil protection, ceteris paribus) of the intercropped fields from 0.20 to 0.13.

Rwanda's main export crop, coffee, is usually mulched and has a very low C-value (0.02). Also forest (C = 0.06), fallow (C = 0.10), and pasture (C = 0.10) cover the land well. Of the main food crops, only bananas have a low C-value (0.04), whereas beans (0.19), tubers (sweet potato: 0.23, potato: 0.22, and cassava: 0.26), and cereals in particular (maize: 0.35 and sorghum: 0.40) provide much less protective cover against erosion.

Table 1 shows the differences in land use by farm-size quartiles. The smallest farms, compared to the other quartiles, dedicate more of their cultivable land to bananas, tubers, cereals, and coffee. They cultivate a larger share of their land at the expense of pasture, fallow and forest.

Table 1 *Land Allocation by Farm Size Quartile*

	Farm Size Quartile (Ares/AE)				C-value
	0–9 ares	9–15 ares	15–26 ares	26– ares	
Cereals	12%	12%	10%	9%	0.35–0.40
Tubers	26%	24%	22%	13%	0.22–0.26
Beans	16%	15%	12%	10%	0.19
Fallow/Pasture	9%	13%	19%	30%	0.10
Forest	5%	5%	8%	13%	0.06
Banana	18%	19%	18%	15%	0.04
Coffee	6%	5%	5%	4%	0.02
Other	7%	7%	7%	6%	0.02–0.35

Source: DSA/MINAGRI Survey Data, Agricultural Year 1991.
Note: Means shares for seasons A and B, weighted by farm size.

RESULTS

Results of the C-value calculations for the cultivated, cultivable, and intercropped fields of each farm size quartile at the national level are shown in Table 2. All differences between the quartiles that show up in the table are significant at the 0.1 percent level.

Table 2 *Crop Cover Indices by Farm Size Quartile*

	Cultivable Fields		Cultivated Fields		Intercropped Fields		
	Density-adjusted C-value	Un-adjusted C-value	Density-adjusted C-value	Un-adjusted C-value	Density-adjusted C-value	Un-adjusted C-value	Total Density
Farm Size per Adult Equiv.							
0– 9 ares	0.13	0.17	0.14	0.19	0.11	0.19	1.889
9– 15 ares	0.13	0.17	0.14	0.18	0.13	0.20	1.758
15–26 ares	0.13	0.16	0.14	0.18	0.13	0.20	1.698
26– ares	0.12	0.14	0.14	0.17	0.14	0.20	1.585

Source: DSA/MINAGRI Survey Data, Agricultural Year 1991.
Notes: Means weighted by field size. All visible differences significant at 1 percent level.

When land use on *all fields* is examined, the unadjusted C-values show that land-scarce households allocate their land to uses that provide less protective cover against erosion than the uses chosen by those with more land. However, the density-adjusted C-values show no clear relationship, suggesting that small farmers (in terms of cultivable land per adult equivalent) make up much of the difference by growing crops in higher densities.

This key result is compatible with the finding that there are no significant differences between farm size quartiles in the share of fields reported as degraded (Clay, 1993).

Table 3 *Erosivity (C-value, or Crop Cover) Indices by Farm Size, Zone and Altitude*

	Agroclimatic zone					Altitude (m)	
	North West	South West	North Central	South Central	East	–1900	1900–
Farm Size per Adult Equiv.							
0–9 ares	0.17	0.11	0.12	0.11	0.11	0.12	0.17
9–5 ares	0.18	0.12	0.13	0.11	0.11	0.12	0.16
15–26 ares	0.17	0.12	0.12	0.11	0.11	0.12	0.14
26– ares	0.15	0.10	0.11	0.11	0.10	0.12	0.12

Source: DSA /MINAGRI Survey Data, Agricultural Year 1991.
Notes: Mean Adjusted C-values of cultivable fields weighted by field size. All visible differences between quartiles significant at 1 percent level.

When only *cultivated fields* are compared, neither measure suggests that demographic pressure pushes farmers to grow more erosive crops. Due to the higher densities on their intercropped fields, land-scarce farmers may actually generate less exposure to erosion on their cultivated fields. Thus, the reason they do worse or at least not better than larger farmers when all fields are compared is that they need to cultivate a larger share of their land at the expense of pasture, fallow, and forest.

The examination of the subset of *intercropped fields* shows that land-scarce farmers have substantially higher cropping densities on their intercropped fields. This covers their intercropped fields better against erosion than do their less land-scarce neighbours.

The result that the degree of protective crop cover is almost the same on small and on large farms holds well in three of the five agroclimatic zones (Table 3). In the North West, agricultural land uses are more erosive than elsewhere, particularly on small farms. The reason presumably is that much of the North West is of too high an altitude for bananas, which are the only major food crop that covers the land well against erosion. Differences in banana production may also explain the results for the North Central zone. To explore this further, comparisons were also made separately for altitudes below and above 1900 metres. At the high altitudes, which cover roughly one-quarter of Rwanda's cultivable land, land scarcity was strongly associated with erosive land use practices.

Table 4 shows that using regression analysis to control for rainfall and altitude with does not change the basic results presented above. The first equation confirms the finding that when the estimates of crop cover are adjusted downward for densely intercropped fields, farm size is not significantly associated with erosive land use, except for the high altitude areas. The most important determinant of crop cover is altitude, largely because few bananas are grown at high altitudes.

Table 4 *Regression Results for Crop Cover Index (Cultivable Fields)*

Independent Variable	Dependent Variable	
	Adjusted C-value	Unadjusted C-value
Intercept	0.00641	0.09889
(*t*)	(0.70)	(2.28)
Rainfall (cm)	–0.00025	–0.00085
(*t*)	(-5.88)*	(-4.25)*
Altitude (100m)	0.00871	0.00592
(*t*)	(14.52)*	(2.08)
Land (ares/ad.eq.)	–0.00003	0.00340
(*t*)	(0.54)	(12.88)*
Land*dummy for alt.> 1900 metres	–0.00048	0.00008
(*t*)	(-4.09)*	(-0.15)
Adj. R Square	0.24	0.21

Source: DSA/MINAGRI Survey Data, 1991.
Note: * significant at the 1 percent level.

The second equation (Table 4, right column) illustrates that without the adjustment for density, the result is entirely different. If small farmers are not 'given credit' for their higher cropping densities in the calculation of the C-values, land scarcity appears to make land use much more erosive. In contrast, the association of crop cover with altitude becomes insignificant if the higher densities at low altitudes are not accounted for.

CONCLUSIONS

Although increasing land-scarcity forces Rwandan farmers to cultivate a larger share of their land at the expense of forest, pasture, and fallow, it also encourages them to grow more perennials and to grow crops in dense associations. While the expansion of cultivation contributes to erosion, especially when it occurs on easily erodible steep slopes, perennials and dense associations are a form of intensification that makes land use more sustainable. The estimated net impact of these changes depends crucially on how one adjusts the estimates of vegetative crop cover for high cropping densities. With the adjustment used here, small farmers do not appear to have substantially more erosive land uses than large farmers, except in the high-altitude areas.

Our adjustment for high cropping densities reduces the estimated C-values on the intercropped fields of the smallest farm-size quartile almost by one-half, which may be too generous. On the other hand, no adjustment was made for purely cropped fields, which probably also have higher cropping densities on small farms than on large farms. Without field experiments, it is impossible to say whether our adjustment is too optimistic.

With or without adjustment for high cropping densities, land uses appear erosive at high altitudes, where few bananas are grown. Crop cover on these areas is poor and is becoming less protective with increasing land scarcity. Moreover, fields in high altitude areas are much steeper than elsewhere, which makes them even more vulnerable to erosion. At high altitudes, finding ways to channel the additional labour provided by population growth to soil conservation through investments such as anti-erosion ditches and terraces and land use practices such as mulching and agroforestry is a major challenge. Since much of the environmentally sustainable labour-based intensification at lower altitudes involves banana production, agricultural research on banana varieties that grow well on high altitudes might have a high payoff in terms of environmental sustainability and long-term food security.

In sum, our cross-sectional comparisons give only limited support for the hypothesis that demographic pressure makes land use less sustainable. Although this gives some optimism regarding the environmental impacts of population growth in the nearby future, it does not change the fact that during the recent past population growth has already forced Rwandan farmers to cultivate marginal lands. On the steep slopes, the current levels of crop cover are insufficient to control erosion. The current rate of land degradation is alarming, and measures to reduce it are badly needed. To design policies that promote soil conservation investments and land use practices that protect the soil against erosion, especially on easily erodible areas, decision makers need information on the determinants of investments and land use. Research that provides such information deserves priority in Rwanda and other countries facing similar problems.

NOTES

[1] We are grateful to Dan Clay for his suggestions. We are also grateful for USAID/Kigali's Rwanda Add-on and to USAID/ARTS/FARA/FSP's Productivity Add-on for support for this research as part of the Food Security II Cooperative Agreement at Michigan State University, and to the Division des Statistiques Agricoles (DSA), Ministère d'Agriculture et de l'Elevage, Rwanda for use of data. We are also grateful for comments on an earlier version by Akin Adesina. The ideas and interpretations expressed herein are those of the authors and are not necessarily shared by the sponsoring agencies.

[2] Conversion into adult equivalents is based on Miniplan (1988).

REFERENCES

Clay, D. C., 1993, 'Fighting an Uphill Battle: Demographic Pressure, the Structure of Landholding, and Land Degradation in Rwanda', unpublished draft manuscript, Michigan State University, Department of Sociology, East Lansing.

Clay, D. and Reardon, T., 1994, 'Determinants of Farm-Level Conservation Investments by Rwandan Farm Households', Contributed Paper to the International Association of Agricultural Economists Twenty-Second Conference, Harare, Zimbabwe, pp. 210– 221 of this volume.

DSA, 1992, *Enquête Nationale Agricole 1990: Production, Superficie, Rendement, Elevage et Leur Evolution 1984-1990*, Publication DSA No. 26, Division Des Statistiques Agricoles, Ministère de l'Agriculture et de l'Elevage, Republique Rwandaise, Kigali, Rwanda.

Fussel, L.K. and Serafini, P.G., 1985, ''Crop Associations in the Semi-Arid Tropics of West Africa: Research Strategies Past and Future', in Ohm, H.W. and Nagy, J.G. (eds.), *Appropriate Technologies for Farmers in Semi-Arid West Africa*, Purdue University.

Kangasniemi, J., 1993, 'Estimating Vegetative Cover (C-values) for Crop Association', Division of Agricultural Statistics, unpublished research note, Ministry of Agriculture and Livestock, Republic of Rwanda.

MINAGRI, 1978, *Guide Pratique de l'Agronome: Première Partie: Les Principales Cultures du Rwanda: Les Conditions de Production*, Ministère de l'Agriculture et de l'Elevage, Kigali, Rwanda.

MINIPLAN, 1988, *Enquête Nationale sur le Budget er la Consommation des Ménages (Milieu Rural), Volume 4: Consommation Alimentaire en Milieu Rural*, Ministère du Plan, République Rwandaise, Kigali, Rwanda.

National Research Council (US), 1993, Committee on Sustainable Agriculture and the Environment in the Humid Tropics, *Sustainable Agriculture and the Environment in the Humid Tropics*, National Academy Press, Washington, D.C.

Lewis, L.A., 1986, 'Predicting Soil Loss in Rwanda', unpublished research note, Graduate School of Geography, Clark University, Worcester, Maryland, and Division of Agricultural Statistics, Ministry of Agriculture and Livestock, Republic of Rwanda, Kigali, Rwanda.

Lewis, L.A., Clay, D.C. and Dejaegher, Y.M.J., 1988, 'Soil Loss, Agriculture, and Conservation in Rwanda: Toward Sound Strategies for Soil Management', *Journal of Soil and Water Conservation*, Vol. 43, No. 5, pp.418–421.

Uwamariya, L., Kangasniemi, J. and Reardon, T., 1993, 'La Productivité Agricole au Rwanda, 1989-1990: La Productivité Moyenne de la Terre, du Travail, et la Rentabilité de la Terre, et les Fonctions de Production', draft Working Paper, Division Des Statistiques Agricoles, Ministère de l'Agriculture et de l'Elevage, Republique Rwandaise, Kigali, Rwanda.

Wischmeier, W.H. and Smith, D.D., 1978, *Predicting Rainfall Erosion Losses, a Guide to Conservation Planning*, Agricultural Handbook No. 537, US Department of Agriculture, Washington, D.C.

DISCUSSION OPENING — K.J. Thomson *(University Of Aberdeen, UK)*

The paper addressed directly a major issue in a country currently suffering a human disaster depicted nightly on our TV screens.

In the introduction, two potentially interesting theoretical issues are raised, though not (understandably) resolved. First, it is suggested that rate of time preference depends on poverty and the land resources of farm families. Second, it is suggested that the land/labour ratio affects the sustainability of land management practices (in passing, it may be noted that in developed countries, non-sustainable land management occurs, often in labour scarce regions. Either of these issues might reward further more general analysis.

The empirical analysis in the paper is of course crucially dependent on the nature and reliability of the C-values and the adjustment process undertaken by the authors for intercropping. Since the C-value itself, and the adjustment arithmetic, are technical measures directly related to actual erosion, the result may be sensitive to the nature of the dependent variable rather than the erosion damage ultimately in focus. Since land management apparently makes a great difference to yields (+50 to 100 per cent), and presumably to erosion too, more sophistication may be justified here. Turning to he results, the differences in the tables are rather small (one or two points) although asserted to be statistically significant at the 1 per cent level, and some information on variability in the data would be welcome.

The paper thus, represents an interesting but partial attack on a crucial problem in African agriculture, as elsewhere. Its narrow data base and analytic focus inevitably suggest the need for further information on such matters as the land management practices of the farming communities involved, including their responses to increased erosion itself. Meanwhile, one can only hope that such analyses are not overwhelmed by events such as the current emergency in Rwanda.

GENERAL DISCUSSION — Michelle Veeman, Rapporteur *(University of Alberta, Canada)*

Discussion of the paper by Rekha Mehra included comments on elements of the social structure that limit women's access to land and a query about the impact of matrilineal, as versus patrilineal descent on women's land rights. Dr Mehra argued that the impact of matrilineal descent in providing women with access to land is reduced due to the prevalence of patriarchal societies and the tendency for women's location to change after marriage. Other points of discussion included possibilities and limitations of women's access to employment and the question of whether increased access to land, as versus other employment opportunities, would better increase family food security. The need for targeting of programs, such as credit, specifically toward women was advocated by one discussion participant and disputed by another. A challenge to this author, repeated by several speakers, queried the demonstration of a clear linkage between women's access to land and adverse environmental effects.

Hugo De Groote's paper on women's income versus family income as a determinant of food security for Mali was, in the absence of the presenter, briefly summarized by the discussant, Benon Gazinski, who noted that it is based on a survey of male household heads. (Dr De Groote was not able to present his paper until a later session). This issue was raised by a participant who noted that surveys of male household heads tend to elicit different responses and policy prescriptions than when women are interviewed.

Numbers of comments on the paper by Jaako Kangasniemi and Thomas Reardon were directed to the focus on cropping patterns, specifically inter-cropping, relative to a broader range of resource management practices to combat land degradation, and a lack of information on the erodibility index and their adjustments to this index. The apparent small difference between size classes shown in the tables were the subject of several comments. The suggestion, in the verbal presentation, that commodity tax and price policy might be useful to encourage less erosive cropping practices was also challenged by several speakers. The authors responded that although differences between size classes appeared to be small, on average, there are sizeable differences in erodibility at high altitudes. While acknowledging that the scope of the paper is narrower than the broad problems of erosion and population pressure, Kangasniemi and Reardon noted that farmer's investment and labour-intensive practices to control erosion, such as ditching, by small farmers are expressly excluded from this paper but are considered in another paper; presented at this conference, based on the same data set (Clay and Reardon, pp.210–219 of this volume).

Participants in the discussion included D.G.R. Belshaw, Steven Franzel, Theodora S. Hyuha, Rosebud Kurwijib, Bongiwe Njobe, Mark Odhiambo, P.C. Sarkar, Nana M. Tanko and Joachim von Braun.

STEPHAN VON CRAMON-TAUBADEL*

Policy Preference Functions: The Implications of Recent Developments

Abstract: The policy preference function (PPF) approach continues to be the subject of considerable interest in agricultural economics. Recent work has added sophistication and strengthened the approach's theoretical underpinnings. In this paper, several implications of this recent work are considered. First, the distinction between the PPF and the surplus transformation curve (STC) is stressed. Estimated PPF weights are derived from what we know about the STC. We actually know very little about the PPF itself. Second, the relationship between the number of interest groups and the number of policy tools in PPF models is discussed. The relationship that is mathematically necessary may not correspond to that which is suggested by our intuition about reality. Hence, it may be that PPF modelling is often inappropriate. Finally, the stochastic nature of PPF estimates is discussed, and a simple method for quantifying the variability of these estimates is illustrated.

INTRODUCTION

The last two decades have seen a sustained interest in the policy preference function approach[1]. Recent work has added sophistication and strengthened the approach's theoretical underpinnings. For example, Bullock (1993) investigates the basic assumptions and methodology of the PPF approach; Love, Rausser and Burton (1990) develop more sophisticated methods of estimating and validating PPFs; von Cramon-Taubadel (1992) considers the interpretability of empirical PPF results.

In this paper I explore some implications of this recent work. As Bullock (p.1) points out, 'Though PPF studies have appeared frequently over the past two decades, explanation of their methodology is sparse'. His formal analysis of the basic assumptions of revealed PPF studies leads to several important insights. I begin by discussing two of these insights; the importance of the distinction between the STC and the PPF, and the relationship between the number of policy tools available to the policy maker and the number of interest groups that are influenced by these tools. Second, inspired by Love, Rausser and Burton, I discuss the stochastic nature of PPF estimates.

WHAT DO WE REALLY KNOW ABOUT THE PPF?

It is important to recognize that revealed PPF weights measure the marginal rate of transformation at a point on the STC and that this STC is conditional on the welfare measures that are assumed to motivate the pertinent interest groups. The local characteristics of the PPF itself are only deduced *indirectly* based on the *assumption* that the PPF has been maximized and, therefore, must be concave and tangent to the STC at this point[2].

Hence, empirical PPF results simply tell us that the policy maker's preferences could be represented by any function that is tangent to the STC at a certain point while restricting

* Institut für Agrarökonomie, Christian-Albrechts-Universität zu Kiel.

the degree of convexity of this function's contours[3]. This isn't very much; indeed, a cynic might argue that economists have, once again, mathematically belaboured a simple fact — that governments in industrialized nations generally choose to transfer income to farmers, despite the inevitable dead-weight losses.

Suppose we are interested in more. For example, suppose that we wish to identify which changes in PPF weights reflect shifts in political preferences and which changes result from shifts in the STC (von Cramon-Taubadel, p.376ff) or to predict how a policy such as the EU's intervention price for milk will respond to a change in the world market price. To address such questions, we need more information about the PPF than just its slope at a number of points in time. Broadly speaking, there are two approaches to gathering such information depending on whether or not we are willing and able to estimate an explicit functional form for the PPF (Oskam, 1988).

If we do not wish to specify a functional form, revealed preference theory provides tests that can be used to determine whether an observed series of prices and consumption bundles is consistent with stable preferences. Hence, as a first step, it is possible to use empirical PPF results to test whether a policy-maker's preferences have changed over time. However, it is well known that these tests are not strong[4]. In von Cramon-Taubadel's application to the EU's wheat and barley policies, tests of WARP and SARP indicate that the policy-maker's preferences did not change between 1973 and 1989, even though, *a priori*, we might expect that they did[5]. Applications to countries that have witnessed major changes in farm policies — New Zealand in 1984, the EU in 1992 — could help determine whether these tests can help add to what we know about the PPF.

A potentially more fruitful approach is to try to estimate a specific functional form for the PPF. If we could estimate such a function, we would, for example, be able to make conditional forecasts of policy behaviour. Oskam (1988) argues in favour of this approach and discusses several functional forms that are both simple to employ and flexible. Love, Rausser and Burton discuss the relationship between the game structure that is assumed to underlie the policy making process and the form of the PPF.

Unfortunately, most agricultural applications are likely to be hampered by a lack of degrees of freedom. In practice, we only observe one policy-maker's reaction to different sets of conditions on the political market. Because observations are usually annual, the resulting time series are short. In the case of the EU we are limited to perhaps 25 observations, which is few in comparison to the number of parameters implied by even a simple model[6]. Oskam (1988) and Oskam and von Witzke (1990) suggest increasing the number of available observations by using information contained in so-called 'non-decisions' — alternative tools and/or levels of tools that the policy-maker has considered but decided not to implement. Such information can result in a more accurate specification of the STC and, hence, add to what we know about the PPF. However, as Oskam (p.36) acknowledges, it is difficult to define a non-decision[7].

In the procedure outlined by Love, Rausser and Burton the question of degrees of freedom is addressed first by considering at least $g-1$ policy tools simultaneously, where g is the number of PPF parameters, and second by using time series data. As will be discussed below, the first suggestion may not be feasible. As regards the use of time series, it was pointed out above that these are generally short. Moreover, Love, Rausser and Burton (p.11) note themselves that empirical PPF analysis typically deals with reduced form specifications that do not explicitly define an underlying political structure. This abstraction is necessary because the variables that describe the political structure —

lobbying costs and strategies, for example — are generally unobservable. However, the functional form of the PPF and the PPF weights themselves depend on these variables. Hence, if the political structure is not constant over time, it is not reasonable to treat time series data as a series of observations on one function.

Finally, it is important to recognize that all increases in our knowledge of the PPF that result from assumptions regarding its form are entirely conditional on these assumptions. There is no sense in which the data have been made to reveal more; we have more information *ex post* because we have added it *ex ante*. No matter how we twist and turn, empirical PPF weights only describe the slope of a many dimensional and possibly shifting function at a relatively small number of discrete points.

INTEREST GROUPS AND POLICY TOOLS: THE STRUCTURE OF PPF MODELS

Bullock (1993, p.10ff) analyses the relationship between the number of distinct interest groups whose welfare the policy maker is manipulating (n), and the number of policy tools at the policy-maker's disposal (m). The structure of the PPF model is such that a unique solution — in other words, a unique set of PPF weights — is only guaranteed if the number of available tools equals the number of interest groups less one, $m = n - 1$. If $m < n - 1$, an infinite number of solutions exist, and if $m > n - 1$, there will be either one solution or none at all. In the latter case, a solution will only exist if government policies are efficient, in other words, if the relative PPF weights implied by the chosen levels of each policy tool are equal[8]. Bullock (p. 18) suggests that in the case where the number of policy tools is 'too large' relative to the number of interest groups $(m > n - 1)$, the PPF method will 'generally' fail to find a solution.

This result has important implications for many aspects of PPF work. Consider first Love, Rausser and Burton's result that in order to estimate the PPF, the number of policy tools considered must greater than or equal to the number of PPF parameters less one, $m \geq g - 1$. g will depend on both the functional form that is chosen and n, the number of interest groups considered. Generally, g will be considerably larger than n; in the example discussed above (Footnote 4), $g = 9$ and $n = 3$. However, if $m \geq g - 1$ and $g > n$, then $m > n - 1$ and we are unlikely to find a unique solution to the PPF problem. Hence there appears to be a contradiction between the constraints that must be imposed to estimate PPFs and the conditions that ensure that the PPF can be solved for a unique set of weights.

This result also has implications for the construction of PPF models. In constructing a PPF model, it is generally necessary — if only for reasons of simplicity — to make aggregation assumptions regarding m and n. However, as Bullock (p.12) states, 'If after objective preliminary study the $m = n - 1$ assumption does not seem reasonable, it may be that the political power of interest groups cannot be reasonably measured using PPF methodology'. Intuition on the relative sizes of m and n can run in two directions. Arguments such as Lee's (1989, p.188) — that nearly 20 interest groups lobbied in connection with sugar policy in the 1985 US Farm Bill — suggest that n may be larger than m and is certainly larger than PPF studies usually assume. On the other hand, it may be that many of these groups had largely overlapping interests, thus reducing n.

Furthermore, the size of m depends on how we define feasible policies, or what is included in Oskam's definition of a non-decision. An example is the EU's wheat policy. If we consider only the intervention price — which has determined producer and consumer prices for most of the CAP's history — then $m = 1$ and it is only possible to derive relative PPF weights for two interest groups. If we wish to derive weights for three groups, m must be increased. One option is to assume that the intervention price is really two tools, a producer price and a consumer price, that have been explicitly pegged the same level year after year. Another option might be to add a policy tool in the form of a non-decision. For example, we could assume that the policy maker has considered the use of deficiency payments each year, but decided not to implement them, that is, set them equal to 0. If this is a valid approach, then m can be made quite large indeed and we may find ourselves permanently faced with the difficult $m > n - 1$ situation.

THE STOCHASTIC NATURE OF ESTIMATED PPF WEIGHTS

To quote Love, Rausser and Burton (p.20), 'A major criticism of previous work on PPFs is that the stochastic nature of estimated parameters has been swept aside'. The authors proceed to identify two sources of uncertainly in the PPF. One source might be labelled economic. Uncertainty arises — even if we assume that we have identified the correct measure for interest group welfare — because we are not sure exactly how policy changes are translated into changes in interest group welfare. The other source is political. The policy-maker cannot be sure that the welfare changes he generates will have the desired political results because he does not know exactly how welfare changes are translated into interest group activity by the political process — in essence, the policy-maker does not know exactly what the PPF weights are.

The latter, or political, source of uncertainty may not be important for attempts to estimate reduced form PPFs. The policy-maker may not be sure exactly which set of PPF weights prevails and, hence, which set of transfers maximizes his utility. Nevertheless, we can reasonably assume that he will base his decision on a set of expected weights. Hence, it may be possible to ignore political uncertainty as long as we are not interested in estimating the parameters that relate PPF weights to underlying political variables. In a sense, we can acknowledge this source of uncertainty and proceed to analyse the 'expected' PPF.

It is more difficult to dismiss economic uncertainty. PPF weights are derived by measuring the slope of the STC at the point that corresponds to the chosen levels of policy tools. Our estimates of this slope are conditional on the estimates of market parameters such as elasticities that we employ. Again, we might assume that the policy-maker bases his decision on a set of expected values for these parameters; nevertheless, we do not know what these expected values are. If the policy-maker's expected parameters differ from those that we employ, then the PPF weights that we calculate will differ from those that are actually implicit in his decisions.

The following analysis takes a very simple and purely illustrative approach to investigating the impact of this problem on the confidence that we can have in estimated PPF weights. A simple two-group (producer and consumer/taxpayer) PPF model of the EU's wheat market was constructed as outlined in Sarris and Freebairn (1983) using linear supply and demand functions and supply and demand elasticities of 0.2 and –1.3, respectively. Assume that these elasticities have been estimated econometrically and are significantly different from 0 at exactly the 5 percent level. Hence, they have *t*-values of roughly 2 and standard errors of 0.1 and 0.65, respectively[9]. Next, although we do not know exactly what elasticities the policy-maker uses, assume that different values are used according to these distributions. In other words, assume that the policy-maker is most likely to use elasticity values that are close to our econometric estimates and, following a *t*-distribution, less likely to use values that differ.

For each marketing year between 1973 and 1991, the PPF model was solved 5000 times, each time using actual EU data on wheat prices and quantities, and a pair of elasticity values drawn randomly from the above distributions[10]. The result was a set of 5000 consumer and producer PPF weights — p and c respectively — for each year. Using these results, the range that contains 95 percent of the p/c ratios was calculated for each year. This analysis was repeated under the assumption that the supply and demand elasticities are significant at the 1 percent {0.1 percent} level (*t*-values of roughly 2.6 {3.3} and standard errors of 0.077 and 0.5 {0.061 and 0.4}, respectively) and the results are presented in Figure 1.

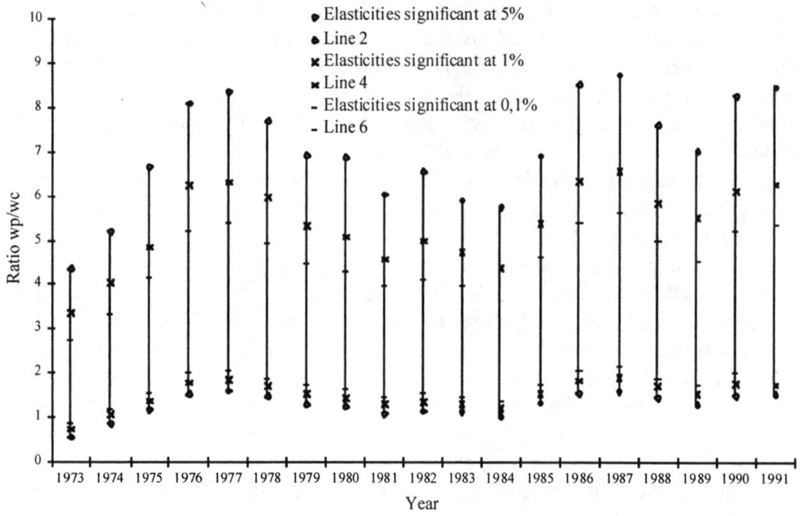

Figure 1 *The Ratio of Producer to Consumer PPF Weights: Simulated 95 Percent Confidence Intervals for EU Wheat Policy 1973–1991*

The ranges displayed in Figure 1 are large, even under the assumption that we have relatively precise knowledge of the supply and demand elasticities that the policy-maker uses. This suggests that we cannot be very certain of estimated PPF weights and that ignoring the stochastic nature of these estimates might be misleading. For example, Bullock (1993, p.16ff) estimates a simple PPF model of the US wheat market that includes 2 groups (producers and consumer/taxpayers) and 2 policies (acreage control and an export subsidy). Since $m > n - 1$, this model will only yield a solution if policy is efficient as discussed above. Bullock's results indicate that policy is not efficient since the ratios p/c corresponding to the two policy tools are not equal; one ratio is 1.09 and the other is 2.04[11]. However, this difference is well within the ranges displayed in Figure 1 and may not be large enough to enable us to conclude with reasonable certainty that policies are inefficient.

Of course, these results depend critically on the underlying assumptions — in particular the distributions associated with the elasticities of supply and demand, and the assumption that the unknown elasticities used by the policy maker are drawn from these distributions. Bullock draws his conclusions from a completely different PPF model which might be less susceptible to the uncertainly discussed here. Refining this analysis would be an interesting area for further research.

CONCLUSIONS

The main conclusions that must be drawn from the discussion above seem quite discouraging. We do not know very much about the PPF itself beyond a few revealed points and some basic assumptions about its shape. The prospects for finding out more about the PPF from observations alone are not very encouraging. Hence, our ability to make predictions and detect changes in policy preferences on the basis of empirical PPF work remains limited.

At the same time, the construction of PPF models seems to be caught between often contradictory mathematical and practical considerations. The relationship between the numbers of interest groups and policy tools has important implications for the tractability of PPF models and more careful consideration must be given to reasonable criteria for determining both. In particular, if we define the number of policy tools broadly to include any tool that might reasonably have been used, we may find ourselves consistently concluding that observed policy is not efficient and, hence, that the PPF approach is not valid.

Finally, preliminary results suggest that the confidence intervals associated with estimated PPF weights might be fairly large. These results are based on several very contestable assumptions, but the simulation method used could be refined and generalized. More information on issues such as these is needed if PPF analysis is to become a useful practical tool.

NOTES

1 See Swinnen and van der Zee (1993) for a brief summary of the literature.

2 Bullock (1993, pp.7–10) is the first to make this point clearly and demonstrate that a number of researchers have failed to appreciate it. For example, von Cramon-Taubadel (1992, p.389) claims that a PPF he estimates is not concave in the policy tools he considers. However, his tests actually indicate that the STC is not concave. Hence, his results cannot be interpreted as a failure of the PPF method. Love *et al.* (p.17) also claim erroneously that second order conditions on the PPF must be checked to ascertain that the PPF has been maximized.

3 Specifically, the PPF contours must be at least more convex than the STC in the case of a (locally) convex STC. Beghin and Foster (1992, p.789) recognize that any second order tests which are carried out will pertain to the STC and not the PPF, but do not explicitly acknowledge the possibility of an optimum at a point where the STC is convex.

4 I thank David Bullock for pointing out that this is especially true if the STC is not linear, in other

words if the marginal rate of substitution is not constant as it is in the case of linear constraints in Varian's tests.

[5] For example, in the mid-1980s when the EU adopted a more conservative price policy and enlarged to include Spain and Portugal.

[6] With only three groups, the simple second order quadratic form discussed by Love *et al.* (1990, p.13), for example, involves 9 parameters.

[7] For example, we might consider the EU's direct income transfers to grain producers as feasible but rejected prior to 1992 — in other words, a non-decision. However, perhaps these transfers were never seriously considered prior to 1992 and, hence, cannot be considered a non-decision.

[8] See Bullock (1993, p.16ff) and Beghin and Foster (pp.788–789).

[9] For simplicity these estimates are assumed to have a covariance of 0.

[10] Simulations were performed using the random number generator in GAUSS.

[11] Bullock (1993, p.17), transformed to make them comparable with the results in Figure 1.

REFERENCES

Beghin, J. and Foster, W., 1992, 'Political Criterion Functions and the Analysis of Wealth Transfers', *American Journal of Agricultural Economics*, Vol. 74, No. 3, pp.787–794.

Bullock, D., 1993, *In Search of Rational Government: What Political Preference Function Studies Measure and Assume*, Manuscript, University of Illinois, Department of Agricultural Economics.

von Cramon-Taubadel, S., 1992, 'A Critical Assessment of the Political Preference Function Approach in Agricultural Economics', *Agricultural Economics*, Vol. 7, No. 3/4, pp.371–394.

Lee, D., 1989, Discussion opening for Lopez, R. and Sachtler, K., 'Politico-economic Analysis of the US Sugar Programme', in Greenshields, B. and Bellamy, M. (eds.), *Government Intervention in Agriculture: Cause and Effect*, International Association of Agricultural Economists Occasional Paper No. 5, Aldershot, Hants, UK, pp.181–188.

Love, H., Rausser, G. and Burton, D., 1990, 'Policy Preference Functions: Grand Themes and New Directions', Paper presented at the meetings of the Western Agricultural Economics Association, Vancouver, British Colombia, May.

Oskam, A., 1988, *Decision Based Economic Theory*, Staff Paper P88–38, Department of Agricultural and Applied Economics, University of Minnesota.

Oskam, A. and von Witzke, H., 1990, *Agricultural Policy Preference: Wheat in the United States 1981–1990*, Staff Paper P90–68, Department of Agricultural and Applied Economics, University of Minnesota.

Sarris, A. and Freebairn, J., 1983, 'Endogenous Price Policies and International Wheat Prices', *American Journal of Agricultural Economics*, Vol. 65, No. 1, pp.214–224.

Swinnen, J. and van der Zee, F., 1993, 'The Political Economy of Agricultural Policies: A Survey', *European Review of Agricultural Economics*, Vol. 20, No. 3, pp.261–290.

JEAN-CHRISTOPHE BUREAU, V. ELDON BALL, JEAN PIERRE BUTAULT AND AHMED BARKAOU*

Productivity Gaps Between European and United States Agriculture

Abstract: A set of purchasing power parities was constructed for the inputs and the outputs of the agricultural sector in 10 European countries and the United States. This made it possible to deflate both spatially and in time the nominal agricultural accounts. Real values of inputs and outputs made it possible to construct spatial indexes of productivity. These indexes measure the productivity gaps between countries for a given year. Extrapolation between 1973 and 1989 measures how these gaps have changed over time. The results show that the productivity of the United States has been 20 percent higher than the average productivity of European agriculture. This gap has persisted over time. However, large discrepancies exist in Europe and a few countries such as The Netherlands obtain a higher productivity than the United States.

INTERNATIONAL PRICE AND QUANTITY INDEXES

A purchasing power parity is an exchange rates that equalizes the price of a basket of goods in two countries. Although most of the applications have focused on the final consumption of Gross Domestic Product, PPPs can be constructed for other baskets of goods[1]. PPPs are constructed for the inputs and outputs of the agricultural sector in the European Community and the United States. Using PPPs as spatial deflators, real values are then constructed, which are more meaningful indicators of production and consumption levels than simple conversions into dollars using nominal exchange rates. Real values of inputs and outputs are used to compute multilateral indexes of productivity between countries, that is, measures of the gaps in productivity for a given year (as opposed to different growth rates over time). In this paper, spatial comparisons in the agricultural sector are extrapolated over time in order to investigate the changes in productivity gaps between US and EC agriculture between 1973–90.

METHODOLOGY AND DATA

The EKS index number is used to construct PPPs and real values. The EKS index relies on the idea that the best way to compare a pair of countries is to use a bilateral Fisher index (that is, a geometric average of a Laspeyres and Paasche index, Diewert, 1992). When the comparison involves more than two countries, a matrix of bilateral Fisher indexes can lead to inconsistent results. The EKS index ensures transitivity of the comparisons between $I(I > 2)$ countries (Eurostat, 1983). The EKS price index between country A and country B is expressed as:

$$(1)\quad P_{EKS_{A-B}} = \left[\prod_{k=1}^{I} P_F\left(p^B, p^k, y^B, y^k\right) / P_F\left(p^A, p^k, y^A, y^k\right)\right]^{\frac{1}{I}}$$

* INRA-Economie, Grignon, ERS-USDA, Washington, D.C., INRA-Economie Forestiére, ENGREF, Nancy, respectively.

where P_F is the bilateral Fisher price index between A and B, and a country k. A direct EKS quantity index can be obtained in the same way using Fisher quantity indexes.

Prices, real values and productivity are compared for 10 members of the EC-10 and the USA. Real values and price indexes (PPPs) are constructed for agricultural production as well as for the inputs used in the sector. For the year 1985, a bilateral PPP for each basic heading level commodity (for example, wheat) is constructed as the ratio of prices in national currency between countries. The real value is implicit. Prices and real values are then computed for a more aggregated list of commodities (for example, grains) using EKS index numbers. At this level, the spatial indexes for 1985 are matched to the time series indexes (base 1 in 1985) for each country. Time series indexes are Fisher indexes between 1973 and 1985. This double deflation (space and time) leads to the construction of a complete set of PPPs and real values for every year of the period (Ball *et al.,* 1994). The annual productivity indexes (such as in Table 1) are expressed relative to the aggregate EC-10 in 1985.

The construction of the set of PPPs for the agricultural sector requires a huge amount of data since it is necessary to get a price per kg in 1985 for every input and output at the basic heading level (that is, 63 outputs and 24 inputs) (Ball *et al.,* 1994). A PPP was also constructed for the livestock capital, machinery and buildings. PPPs on land and labour were computed using a user cost. Numerous sources were used to obtain price data. Most of the data for the USA were collected from the National Agricultural Statistical Service (NASS) and the Economic Research Service (ERS) of the US Department of Agriculture. Data were obtained for the EC from Eurostats' Farm Accountancy Data Network, as well as numerous national sources. Unpublished data were provided by many statistical agencies, the OECD, Eurostat and some farm business associations. In the US, deficiency payments were included in the output prices. The European accounts (source Eurostat) were matched to the US accounts (source ERS) on the basis of the European accounting rules. A stock of capital was constructed (Ball *et al.*, 1993) for all countries from series of Gross Formation of Fixed Capital (GFCF). The Permanent Inventory Method was used to generate series of stock of productive capital and series of economic depreciation. A truncated normal vintage distribution and hyperbolic decay were assumed. The PPPs for capital were constructed (Conrad and Jorgenson, 1985). Values and quantities for livestock were calculated for 1985 using 15 types of farm animals. The volume of labour is an estimation of the number of hours worked, expressed in Annual Worker Units (AWU).

PRODUCTIVITY GAPS AND PRICE DIFFERENCES BETWEEN US AND EC AGRICULTURE

Over the 1973–89 period, the growth rate of the volume of agricultural production is comparable in the EC and in the USA at, respectively, 1.8 and 1.7 percent. Although the growth rate of EC production was high in the beginning of the period, supply limitation measures in the EC have lowered this rate at the end of the period. Export programs and a weaker dollar helped US exports stimulate production in the 1980s. A gap of 10 percent between the volume of production in the USA and in the EC-10 in the beginning of the period can also be observed in 1989.

Table 1 *Spatial Indexes of Productivity and Annual Growth Rates of Productivity*

Annual indexes, base 100 for aggregate EC-10 in 1985

	GER	FRA	ITA	NET	B-L	UK	IRL	DEN	GRE	USA	EC10
1973	73.2	87.8	62.6	110.3	108.2	86.3	70.4	85.8	67.5	104.0	79.0
1974	76.7	87.4	63.7	115.2	111.7	89.9	73.7	98.1	68.2	93.0	80.7
1975	75.7	85.9	67.0	113.4	104.2	84.8	77.0	87.3	71.4	99.1	80.1
1976	74.5	83.5	64.2	114.4	103.2	82.4	73.6	84.6	71.0	96.8	78.1
1977	78.5	86.3	65.4	118.5	106.7	89.1	78.4	91.8	67.0	105.2	81.0
1978	80.6	91.6	66.3	122.5	111.4	91.7	78.1	91.5	73.1	98.2	83.9
1979	79.8	97.3	69.9	124.3	110.8	92.3	72.9	91.5	70.2	102.2	86.0
1980	81.1	96.9	73.5	123.3	112.8	97.6	75.7	94.4	76.5	98.0	88.3
1981	82.0	97.7	75.0	130.4	115.9	99.4	74.3	99.4	77.0	112.1	89.9
1982	89.5	108.2	77.2	135.6	119.4	103.7	79.7	106.5	77.7	115.1	96.0
1983	87.2	105.7	81.2	131.6	118.1	101.3	81.0	103.5	74.0	100.2	95.1
1984	91.7	111.9	78.7	139.7	122.9	111.9	88.4	118.8	76.7	119.0	99.4
1985	88.8	113.6	82.0	137.2	123.5	109.6	87.4	120.9	78.5	129.9	100.0
1986	94.3	115.8	83.9	143.3	126.7	108.7	84.9	123.6	82.7	130.0	102.8
1987	91.7	119.4	87.7	139.0	123.9	110.2	89.2	119.9	81.4	132.4	103.9
1988	95.9	121.0	88.1	142.8	128.4	110.6	90.3	128.3	91.3	127.5	106.6
1989	98.0	124.5	91.0	147.5	129.7	114.2	90.1	134.1	95.9	137.5	109.9

Spatial index 73–74–75, base 100 for aggregate EC-10 in '74'.

	GER	FRA	ITA	NET	B-L	UK	IRL	DEN	GRE	USA	EC10
'74'	94	109	81	141	135	110	92	113	86	124	100

Spatial index 1987–88–89, base 100 for aggregate EC-10 in '88'.

	GER	FRA	ITA	NET	B-L	UK	IRL	DEN	GRE	USA	EC10
'88'	89	114	83	134	119	105	84	119	84	124	100

Annual growth rate, percent ('88'/ '74').

	GER	FRA	ITA	NET	B-L	UK	IRL	DEN	GRE	USA	EC10
'88'/ '74'	1.7	2.4	2.3	1.7	1.2	1.7	1.4	2.5	1.9	2.1	2.1

Note: '74' = average 1973–74–75. '88' = average 1987–88–89.

In the EC-10, the growth rate of agricultural production is very different between countries — 3.2 percent a year in The Netherlands, compared to 1.2 percent a year in the Belgium-Luxembourg Economic Union (BLEU). The highest growth rate is achieved in The Netherlands, due to a dramatic increase in production of pigs, poultry, flowers and vegetables which has persisted over the period. In Denmark, an increase in pig and wheat production contributed to a high growth, although it has declined during the last years of the period. The growth rate in the Republic of Ireland and the UK was very high at the beginning of the period, concurrent with EC membership which resulted in a sudden increase in prices. Although the growth rate of BLEU production is the lowest in the EC, it has increased in recent years.

Despite these different rates of growth, the share of each country in the volume of production has not changed very much. It is worth noting the progression of The Netherlands, which had a volume share of 7.5 percent of EC production in 1973 and 9 percent in 1989.

Real values of outputs and inputs were used to calculate spatial indexes of productivity. Table 1 presents total factor productivity figures for the beginning and end of the period. Table 1 also shows how the productivity gaps have changed over time. In Table 1 the base is 100 for the EC in 1985. The table of annual indexes makes possible both spatial comparisons (for instance, rows give the relative level of productivity of the USA compared to the EC in a given year) as well as time series comparisons (columns give the growth in productivity for a given country). In the three-year average at the end and the beginning of the period (Table 1) the base is 100 for the EC during the three-year period.

The total productivity of US agriculture is 23 percent higher than the total productivity of the aggregated EC-10. This gap remains constant between '74' (that is, average of 1973–74–75) and '88', since the growth rate of productivity in the EC is similar to the US growth rate, about 2.2 percent a year. However, two periods can be distinguished. After a lower growth rate between 1973 and 1981, the gains in the USA are superior to the gains in the average EC after 1981.

If the EC countries are considered independently, the productivity of US agriculture remains lower than the productivity of The Netherlands over the period. The gap, however, tends to decrease: Dutch productivity was 14 percent higher than that of the USA in '74', and only 8 percent higher in '88'. US agriculture is more productive than that of any European country, even if the gap between the US and Denmark, as well as between the USA and France, has decreased over time (from 10 percent in '74' to 4 percent in '88' for the USA compared to Denmark and from 14 percent to 9 percent for the USA compared to France).

Denmark, France and Italy show a growth rate of global productivity higher than the European average, as the Belgium-Luxemburg Economic Union and Republic of Ireland achieve lower rates. However, Italy and Greece remain among the low productivity countries at the end of the period.

DIFFERENT INPUT COMBINATIONS

The input combinations are very different between countries, so are the partial productivities (Table 2). The high productivity levels of US agriculture can be explained partially by the availability of land, which allows the USA to substitute intermediate inputs for land. Intermediate inputs per hectare are 15 times lower than in The Netherlands. The quantity of land per unit of aggregate output is higher in the USA than in any European country (Table 2). The high productivity of labour and intermediate inputs compensate the poor partial productivity of land. In Europe, the productivity of land reflects not only high yields of major crops, but also the structure of the output mix and substitutions with other inputs. For instance, in '88' the yields for wheat were 2.5 t/ha in Greece, compared to 5.7 t/ha in France, 6.4 t/ha in UK and 7.3 t/ha in The Netherlands. However, if the whole quantity of aggregate production is considered, Greece appears to use a relatively small quantity of land to produce one unit of output, due to high production of fruit and vegetables. The opposite is true for UK and French agriculture, where the quantity of land per unit of output is high, since these countries use extensive grazing areas for animal production. High yields with specialization in land saving production (horticulture, pigs, intensive milk production), generate very high land productivity in The Netherlands.

Table 2 *Spatial Indexes of Partial Productivity Average 73–89 (E10=100); Annual Growth Rate of Productivity ('88'/ '74')*

Partial productivity: average 1973–89

	GER	FRA	ITA	NET	B-L	UK	IRL	DEN	GRE	EC10	USA
Intermediate inputs	79	107	151	87	79	80	114	80	161	100	104
Land	126	85	113	363	206	63	44	115	115	100	29
Capital	62	122	95	139	154	112	106	88	167	100	91
Labour	135	125	57	255	224	177	66	217	40	100	286
Total	94	111	78	146	131	112	87	119	80	100	121

Annual growth rate of partial productivity : ('88'/'74')

	GER	FRA	ITA	NET	B-L	UK	IRL	DEN	GRE	EC10	USA
Intermediate inputs	0.0	–0.1	–1.0	0.6	–0.2	1.2	–1.1	0.6	–0.9	0.1	0.4
Land	1.7	2.5	2.2	3.4	1.8	1.5	2.6	2.8	0.7	2.1	1.6
Capital	1.1	1.4	0.5	–0.8	–0.8	0.9	1.3	2.0	–1.2	0.9	3.6
Labour	4.2	4.8	4.2	4.4	4.0	3.1	4.2	6.5	4.0	4.3	4.1
Total	1.7	2.4	2.4	1.7	1.2	1.7	1.4	2.5	1.9	2.1	2.1

These differences in land productivity are explained by very different uses of intermediate inputs. Clearly, The Netherlands have substituted intermediate inputs for land to cope with a shortage of arable land. Given the very high rates of fertilization and the very intensive use of feedstuffs, the productivity of the intermediate inputs is high and demonstrates how efficient the Dutch farmers are in the use of these intermediate inputs. This productivity of the variable inputs is only 13 percent below the EC average. The productivity of labour and capital is very high too. Dutch agriculture succeeds in saving land, capital and labour, using a large amount of intermediate inputs in a very efficient way. This explains the impressive performance of The Netherlands in terms of total productivity.

Despite the extensive land use of US agriculture, partial productivities of intermediate inputs and fixed capital are not very high. Productivity of intermediate inputs is only 4 percent higher than in the EC, because of the low yields in the grain sector. Productivity of intermediate inputs is 9 percent lower than the EC average, even though it has improved more over the period (growth rate of 4.1 percent a year compared to 1.3 percent in the EC). The low investment in the USA after 1985 has not influenced the production. The source of high total factor productivity in US agriculture is mainly the high productivity of labour, about three times as high as the EC average, due to the large size of farms as well as the high level of mechanization.

The total productivity of French agriculture is about 10 percent above the EC average, due to the good productivity of intermediate inputs and fixed capital. Productivity of labour is low in France, compared to the other North-European countries. Large less-favoured areas and highlands contribute to a low average land productivity, despite high yields in the crop sector.

The total productivity of UK agriculture is lower than that of France, Denmark or The Netherlands. German agriculture is among the least productive in the EC. This confirms the finding of other studies about productivity as well as costs of production in Germany. It has been suggested that the main explanation for this is small farm size and over-mechanization, which both generate a low productivity of capital and labour, compared to other North-European countries. Of course, when looking at these figures, one should remember that since reunification, German agriculture is no longer dominated by small farmers. Large Eastern farms have to be taken in consideration.

Good productivity of intermediate inputs can be found in Southern agriculture (Italy and Greece), partly due to the large share of fruit and vegetables in the total production. Another reason is the low use of variable inputs in some disadvantaged areas. Italian and Greek agriculture has remained very labour-intensive. However, the low productivity of labour reflects not only substitutions between labour and capital, but also reveals an excess of labour on the farms, and a certain form of 'hired unemployment'. Because of this poor productivity of labour, total factor productivity is low compared to the EC average. The growth rate of total productivity in Italy is higher than the EC average. However, Greek agriculture does not seem to catch up and a gap of –20 percent between the average total productivity in Europe and in Greece persists at the end of the period.

In general, there is little change in the ranking of the different countries in terms of total productivity over the period. The situation of Germany, Belgium and Republic of Ireland, compared to the EC average, has worsened during the period. The situation of Denmark, France and Italy has improved.

CONCLUSION

Productivity is the main determinant of real prices in the long term. Compelling evidence of this can be seen by comparing changes in prices of computers, a sector where high rates of productivity have been achieved, with changes in the prices of some services where almost no productivity gains have been achieved. In most of industrialized countries, real agricultural prices have decreased more than prices in the aggregate economy. Lower costs of food have freed resources, and have fostered economic growth. This was achieved thanks to a high rate of productivity growth in agriculture, compared to other sectors (Jorgenson and Gollop, 1992).

Productivity indexes are one of the most relevant indicators of long term trends in real prices and competitiveness. Sectoral studies show that the comparatively more rapid efficiency gain in a country is the major reason why long-run average costs decrease relatively to other countries (Fuss and Waverman, 1985). Productivity enhances the competitive and financial position of a nation within the international community. In the agricultural sector, productivity differences are a much more important determinant of costs of production than are low input prices (Bureau and Butault, 1992).

This paper shows that productivity gaps between the most productive country (The Netherlands) and the least productive (Greece) in the sample are considerable. Although the USA is not as productive as The Netherlands, US total factor productivity is much higher than that in the EC as a whole. US productivity growth has kept in pace with the EC since 1973 and remains the best guarantee for the competitiveness of US agriculture in the future, whatever the issue of international negotiations.

NOTE

[1] These global PPPs based on the GDP are published by several international organization (OECD, 1987, Eurostat, 1983). These PPPs are used in comparative studies of price levels. They form the basis from which the over-valuation or under-valuation of a currency is determined, since the rate of PPP can be compared to the Nominal Exchange Rate (NER). They are usually used to compute real GDP per capita, which is a major issue for international organizations, since it is an important element in the determination of loans and international payments.

REFERENCES

Ball, V.E., Bureau, J.C., Butault, J.P. and Witzke, H.P., 1993, 'The stock of capital in the European Community Agriculture', *European Review of Agricultural Economics*, Vol. 20, No.4, pp.437–450.

Ball, V.E., Barkaoui, A., Bureau, J.C. and Butault, J.P., 1994, *Productivity Differences and Relative Levels of Prices in the Agricultural Sector: European Community and the United States, 1973–90*, Economic Research Service, US Department of Agriculture, Washington, D.C.

Bureau, J.C. and Butault, J.P.,1992, 'Productivity Gaps, Price Advantages and Competitiveness in E.C. Agriculture', *European Review of Agricultural Economics*, Vol. 19, No. 1, pp.25–48.

Conrad, K. and Jorgenson, D.W., 1985, 'Sectoral Productivity Gaps Between the United States, Japan and Germany', in Berlin, Duncker and Humbolt, '*Probleme und Perspektiven der weltwirschaflichen entwincklung*', pp.335–347.

Diewert, W.E., 1992, 'Fisher Ideal Output, Input and Productivity Indexes Revisited, *Journal of Productivity Analysis*, No. 3, pp.211–248.

Eurostat, 1983, *Comparison in Real Values of the Aggregates of SEA 1980*, Statistical Office of the European Communities, Luxembourg.

Fuss, M. and Waverman, L., 1985, *Productivity Growth in the Automobile Industry, 1979–1980: A Comparison of Canada, Japan and the United States*, National Bureau of Economic Research, Working Paper No. 1735, Cambridge, Massachusetts.

Jorgenson, D.W. and Gollop, F., 1992, 'Productivity Growth in U.S. Agriculture: A Postwar Perspective', *American Journal of Agricultural Economics*, Vol. 3, No. 74, pp.745–751.

OECD, 1987, *Purchasing Power Parities and Real Expenditures 1985*, Department of Economics and Statistics, OECD, Paris (Updated 1992).

MARY A. MARCHANT, STEVEN A. NEFF AND MEI XIAO*

Political Economy of United States and European Union Dairy Policy Choice

Abstract: Policy interventions in dairy markets are pervasive in industrialized countries. Resistance to domestic agricultural policy reform in the USA and the EU is partially responsible for delays in reaching a GATT Uruguay Round agreement. We explain US and EU dairy policy choices by analyzing the influence of key domestic variables. Empirical results for the US price support and the EU intervention price show a dominant influence of the support (intervention) price in the previous year. US farm income, stocks, and government costs also influenced US policy-makers' choice of the price support level. In the EU, where multiple policy instruments are used, government costs influence both production and surplus disposal policies. The EU chooses dairy policies sequentially — first the farm support policies and then surplus disposal policies. The results imply that trade policy reforms will be most acceptable if farm incomes can be maintained without increasing government support expenditures.

INTRODUCTION

Through 7 years of negotiation in the Uruguay Round of the General Agreement on Tariffs and Trade (GATT), the USA and the EU[1] locked horns over agricultural policy differences, including methods of domestic support and export competition. Resistance to reform in such countries as the USA and the EU was partially responsible for delaying a GATT Uruguay Round agreement. By understanding why regions choose the policies they do, the relative importance of key variables affecting policy choice are identified and can be used to anticipate policy responses to major developments, such as the GATT.

US and EU dairy policies make an excellent case study for agricultural policy choice. The USA is second only to the EU in world milk production. Dairy policy is important in the agricultural support budgets of both the USA and the EU. As an example of the large and variable government expenditures, US dairy program costs ranged from $700 million to $2.6 billion in the 1980s. Dairy averaged 7 percent of US farm support costs in the late 1980s, with an average annual expenditure of $1.6 billion. The budget problem is even more severe in the EU, where dairy has historically received the greatest amount of government support, averaging 18 percent of EU agricultural spending at $6 billion annually, with the largest portion used for export subsidies.

Government domestic and trade policies play a significant role in US and EU dairy markets, unlike other important commodities (for example, pork) with much less policy direction. Also, significant dairy policy changes took place in both the USA and EU during the 1980s, fueling dramatic price changes on international markets and realized in both domestic markets (Marchant, Neff, and McCalla, 1992). By contrast, the sugar markets in the USA and the EU also have heavy policy involvement, but there have been no significant policy changes in sugar since 1982.

Dairy product markets are among the most distorted agricultural markets in the world, as evidenced by high ratios of domestic prices to international prices in many countries. In

* University of Kentucky, Economic Research Service, US Department of Agriculture and University of Kentucky, respectively.

the decade 1982–1991, US support prices averaged 1.85 times the international milk price equivalent, as composed from international prices for butter and skim milk powder (which we refer to as powder). For the EU during the same time, the intervention milk price equivalent was more than twice the international milk price equivalent.

The support price is the primary US dairy policy instrument. The authorizing legislation specified that the manufacturing milk price would be supported through purchases of manufactured dairy products (MDP) by the Commodity Credit Corporation (CCC). The CCC offers to purchase MDP from handlers at the support purchase price, equalling the price support level plus a make allowance (processing margin).

European Union dairy policy was created in 1962, upon adoption of the Common Agricultural Policy (CAP). EU domestic dairy policies are targeted at two different levels, production and surplus disposal. The EU supports minimum producer prices through support purchases (called intervention in the EU) of butter and powder, similar to the support purchase prices used in the USA. The other key production policy variable is the marketing quota, a supply control measure instituted in 1984 by the EU Council of Ministers in an effort to decrease costly surpluses generated by the intervention price policy. The EU disposes of surpluses through subsidized domestic consumption and export subsidies. We estimate the policy choice function for subsidized EU domestic consumption of powder as the subsidy rate for use in calf feed, the largest use of EU powder. Similarly for butter, we estimate the policy choice function for the subsidy rate for butter use by food manufacturers, the largest category of subsidized domestic consumption.

US AND EU DAIRY POLICY CHOICE MODELING

There is a growing literature that incorporates political decisions into commodity models, making the models more realistic, particularly for highly regulated markets. In order to endogenize government behaviour, one must be familiar with a wide body of literature on political economy. Publications which survey this literature include Young, Marchant, and McCalla (1991); Carter, McCalla and Sharples (1990); Rausser, Lichtenberg, and Lattimore (1982); and Buchanan *et al.* (1978). In general, Buchanan *et al.* surveyed political economic theory, while the other publications surveyed empirical modeling of this theory as it relates to agricultural policy.

Economists differ on the approach used to endogenize government behaviour. Rausser, Lichtenberg and Lattimore categorized empirical analyses of government behaviour into 2 groups: (1) analytical derivation followed by estimation of policy instruments from policy preference or criterion functions (criterion function models) and (2) direct estimation of policy instrument behavioural equations (behavioural models). Proponents of criterion function models, which analytically derive and then estimate policy instruments, include Rausser and Freebairn (1974), Zusman (1976), Zusman and Amiad (1977), Sarris and Freebairn (1983), Paarlberg (1983), Paarlberg and Abbott (1986), Riethmuller and Roe (1986) and Lopez (1989). Behavioural models, which directly specify and then estimate policy equations, include Abbott (1979a and 1979b), Lattimore and Schuh (1979), and Dixit and Martin (1986). Models which use both criterion function and behavioural approaches include De Gorter (1983), Gardner (1987), and Marchant

(1993). Beghin and Foster (1992), Rausser and Foster (1990), Beghin (1990), and Love, Rausser and Burton (1990) have recently added to the political economy literature.

Unfortunately for researchers of policy choice, many policies do not continue for extended periods of time. The result is a limited time series with few observations for estimation purposes, as in the case of the EU marketing quota. In the case of dairy policies, only a few of the main policy instruments have existed over a long time period compared to other short-lived policies, e.g., the US Dairy Termination Program. Not only are the policies changeable and sometimes brief, but social priorities change. An example is budget expenditure for dairy programs, which is far more important in the USA in 1993 than it was in the 1970s and the early 1980s. Econometrically, these changes in social priorities mean that variables used to explain policy choices can have changing coefficients.

General Theoretical Model of Dairy Policy Choice and US Model Specification

Since this paper is limited to an analysis of factors that influence dairy policy choice, only dairy policy choice equations are estimated, as opposed to a structural model of the dairy industry. A general form for policy-makers' choice of the US support price for MDP follows. (Note, the functional form for this model also describes the EU intervention prices, as shown below.)

(1) $\hat{P}_t^{Spt} = f\left[P_{t-1}^{Spt}; Stocks; GC; Y^{Farm}; Z\right]$

where:

P^{Spt}	=	US support price
$Stocks$	=	government stockpiles
GC	=	government costs
Y^{Farm}	=	domestic farm income
Z	=	a vector of other exogenous variables

Equation (1) describes the support price as function of five general groups of variables based on economic and political economic theory. (1) Institutional inertia — following the hypothesis that, once a policy is in place, it does not change dramatically, we expect a positive relationship between the support price in the current year and the support price in the previous year (Allison, 1971; Lavergne, 1983; Von Witzke, 1990; and Young, 1987). (2) Stocks — we expect stocks to be negatively related to the price support level; that is, as stocks rise, policy-makers should lower the guaranteed minimum support price level in an effort to reduce over production and the build up of costly stockpiles of MDP. (3) Government costs — as the budgetary costs rise, the price support level should fall (Infanger, Bailey, and Dyer, 1983; De Gorter, 1983; and Von Witzke, 1990). (4) Domestic farm income — as farm income level falls, policy-makers may attempt to improve farm incomes by raising the price support level, so a negative relationship is expected (Dixit and Martin, 1986; and Gardner, 1987). (5) A vector of other applicable exogenous variables; for example, international variables following the hypothesis that policy-makers consider the international market when choosing domestic policy instruments (Lattimore and Schuh, 1979; Sarris and Freebairn, 1983; Paarlberg, 1983; Paarlberg and Abbott, 1986; and Von Witzke, 1990); or a variable representing special interest groups, following the hypothesis that political influence, as measured by campaign contributions or economic rent can influence policy-makers' decisions (Sarris and Freebairn, 1983; Caves, 1976; and Krueger, 1974).

Empirical Estimation of the US Policy Choice Model

Data were obtained from the US Department of Agriculture, the Bureau of Labor Statistics (BLS), and the Federal Election Commission (FEC). A dummy variable was included for years in which Congress enacted farm legislation. Ordinary least squares (OLS) estimations used annual time series data, beginning in 1951, depending on data availability for specific variables. Presented below are empirical estimation results for US dairy policy choice of the price support level for MDP ('*t*' statistics are listed below estimated coefficients).

$$(2)\quad \hat{P}^{Spt}_{t} = \underset{(2.3)}{0.391} + \underset{(42.8)}{1.13}\, P^{Spt}_{t-1} - \underset{(-5.3)}{0.043}\, Exp(Stk)_t - \underset{(-2.2)}{0.022}\, Y^{Farm}_{t-1} + \underset{(3.7)}{0.008}(GR-GC)^{US}_{t-1}$$

$R^2 = 0.99$ F = 1152 h = 0.45 n = 31

$$(3)\quad \hat{P}^{Spt}_{t} = \underset{(0.03)}{0.005} + \underset{(32.6)}{1.31}\, P^{Spt}_{t-1} + \underset{(2.87)}{0.005}(GR-GC)^{US}_{t-1} - \underset{(-6.0)}{0.053}\left[\frac{GC^{MDP}}{GC^{Ag}}\right]_{t-1} - \underset{(-5.8)}{0.62}\,(P^{Spt} - P^{Wld})_{t-1}$$

$R^2 = 0.99$ F = 815 h = –0.3 n = 15

where previous definitions hold and

$Exp(Stk)$	=	expected additions to government stockpiles
$(GR-GC)^{US}$	=	US Federal Government deficit, i.e., government revenues minus government costs
GC^{MDP} / GC^{Ag}	=	government costs for the dairy program as a share of government costs for all agricultural programs
P^{Wld}	=	world price for manufactured dairy products

Equation (2) was estimated at an aggregate level using nominal prices, where expected stocks were measured as actual additions to government stocks, assuming perfect foresight, and farm income was measured as the change in net farm income. The difference between Equations (2) and (3) was that Equation (3) has fewer observations but includes two more independent variables, both of which were significant: (1) the costs to government of the dairy program relative total agricultural program costs, and (2) the difference between the support price and the world price for MDP.

Empirical results indicated a common set of explanatory variables which appeared to affect policy-makers' choice of the support price: (1) the support price in the previous year, supporting the hypothesis that institutional inertia is important; (2) the dairy program's share of total agricultural program costs to government, where, as the cost share increased in the previous period, the support price fell; (3) the difference between the support price and the world price, where a positive price distortion resulted in a lowering of the support price; (4) expected additions to CCC stocks, that is, as stocks increased, the support price fell; (5) change in net farm income, that is, as farm income fell, support prices rose, and (6) US Federal Government deficit, where as the deficit increased, the support price fell. (Estimations using real prices indicated that the first three variables were significant.) Empirical results were good in terms of statistical significance and properties, and reinforced empirical results of prior research, described above.

Theoretical Model and Empirical Results for EU Dairy Policy Choice

The theoretical policy equations and empirical estimation results are described below for four key EU dairy policies: (1) intervention price, (2) marketing quota, (3) EU domestic subsidized consumption rate, and (4) subsidized export rate. Annual time series data ranging from 1978 through 1992 (depending on the variable) were used for estimation.

Intervention price

$$(4)\quad P_t^{Intv} = f(P_{t-1}^{Intv};\ Y_{t-1}^{Farm};\ Stock_{t-1};\ GC_t^{CAP};\ Z)$$

where previous definitions hold and

P^{Intv} = EU intervention price

GC^{CAP} = EU government costs spent on the Common Agricultural Policy

The 'Z' vector for the EU represents, in addition to the considerations mentioned for the USA, the presence of the milk marketing quota and the particular interests of member states, where individual members may have more or less than equal influence on EU policy choice based on their political power (comparable to political influence by special interest groups). The only 'Z' variable that proved quantifiable was the marketing quota, which is included as a dummy independent variable set equal to 1 for the years since it was implemented in 1984 and equal to 0 before 1984. Empirical results are presented in Equations (5) and (6) for powder and (7) and (8) for butter.

$$(5)\quad \hat{P}_t^{Intv} = \underset{(1.8)}{168} + \underset{(4.6)}{0.6}\, P_{t-1}^{Intv} + \underset{(2.8)}{0.02}\, Y_{t-1}^{Farm} + \underset{(2.1)}{0.08}\, Stock_{t-1} - \underset{(-1.8)}{0.006}\, GC_t^{CAP}$$

$R^2 = 0.98$ Adj $R^2 = 0.97$ $F = 104$ $n = 15$

$$(6)\quad \hat{P}_t^{Intv} = \underset{(1.6)}{223} + \underset{(4.0)}{0.6}\, P_{t-1}^{Intv} + \underset{(2.2)}{0.02}\, Y_{t-1}^{Farm} + \underset{(1.5)}{0.07}\, Stock_{t-1} - \underset{(-1.7)}{0.006}\, GC_{t-1}^{CAP} + \underset{(0.4)}{27}\, M_t^{Q}$$

$R^2 = 0.98$ Adj $R^2 = 0.96$ $F = 76$ $n = 15$

$$(7)\quad \hat{P}_t^{Invt} = 1456 + 0.6P_{t-1}^{Invt} + 0.002\,Y_{t-1}^{Farm} - 0.03\ Stock_{t-1} - 0.01\ GC_t^{CAP}$$

(3.0) (3.0) (0.1) (–0.8) (–0.07)

$R^2 = 0.65$ Adj. $R^2 = 0.51$ $F = 5$ $n = 15$

$$(8)\quad \hat{P}_t^{Invt} = 1089 + 0.4\ P_{t-1}^{Invt} + 0.04\,Y_{t-1}^{Farm} + 0.1\ Stock_{t-1} - 0.01\ GC_t^{CAP} - 495\ M_t^{Q}$$

(2.6) (2.6) (1.7) (1.2) (–0.81) (–2.5)

$R^2 = 0.79$ Adj. $R^2 = 0.68$ $F = 7$ $n = 15$

where previous definitions hold and

$M^Q =$ marketing quota dummy variable

The overall model is significant at the 1 percent level for both powder models and for the butter model that included the marketing quota dummy variable, while Equation (7) was significant at the 2 percent level. The previous intervention price is significant at the 1 percent level in all cases except in Equation (8), where it was significant at the 3 percent level. For the stock variable, we expected a negative sign. Although most of the estimated results had a positive sign, the stock variable was insignificant in most cases. The government cost variable had the correct sign and is most significant in Equation (5). The marketing quota appeared to affect the butter intervention price but not the nonfat powder intervention price. The farm income variable had a positive sign in all of the estimated equations and its level of significance varied, but was most significant for the powder models. Our original hypothesis was that if farm incomes fell in the previous year, the EU would raise the intervention price in an effort to achieve the domestic goal of raising farm incomes. EU farm incomes rose in 11 of 15 observations, while in the USA the changes in farm incomes were equally split between rising and falling observations.

One possible explanation is asymmetric decision making where policy-makers strive to improve farm incomes by increasing the support price if the change in farm incomes is negative (a negative relationship), but may wish to continue this trend by further increasing the intervention price if the change in farm income is positive (a positive relationship). Support price increases are always politically popular with farmers, especially so in the EU because there was an explicit policy to bring farm incomes up to nonfarm incomes. The political counterweights to farmers are consumers and the budget. Unless consumers are mobilized (not the case) or there is a binding budget constraint (only occasionally the case), higher support prices are popular.

Milk marketing quota

$$(9)\quad M_t^Q = f(Stock_t; GC_t^{CAP}; SX_{t-1})$$

where previous definitions hold and

$SX =$ subsidized export rates

The goal of the marketing quota is to decrease both government stocks acquisition and government expenditures by restricting milk production without having to reduce intervention prices. We expect that the marketing quota will be negatively related to EU government expenditures, stock levels, and subsidized export rates. If CAP costs or stocks are high, quotas are reduced as a correction. Similarly, high export subsidy rates indicate both an oversupplied international market and surplus disposal problems, that may be avoided by reducing the quota. Although the marketing quota is for milk, rather than for butter and skim milk powder, variables for stocks and export subsidies are in terms of products. We accordingly specified the marketing equation twice, using the milk marketing quota as the dependent variable in both and the cost of the CAP as an independent variable in both, but with butter stocks and the butter export subsidy in Equation (10) and powder stocks and the powder export subsidy in Equation (11). This was practical and also served as a test to determine if one product dominated the choice of the marketing quota level.

$$(10)\quad M_t^Q = \underset{(24)}{121\,093} - \underset{(-4.4)}{0.8}\ GC_t^{CAP} + \underset{(0.2)}{0.8}\ Stock_t^{Butter} - \underset{(-1.1)}{4.6}\ SX_{t-1}^{Butter}$$

$R^2 = 0.86$ Adj $R^2 = 0.75$ F = 8 n = 8

$$(11)\quad M_t^Q = \underset{26}{117\,799} - \underset{(-4)}{0.65}\,GC_t^{CAP} - \underset{(-1.4)}{2.9}\ Stock_t^{Powder} - \underset{(-0.8)}{2.0}\ SX_{t-1}^{Powder}$$

$R^2 = 0.91$ Adj $R^2 = 0.85$ F = 14 n = 8

Both marketing quota equations were significant at the 5 percent level and virtually all variables exhibited the correct sign, although limited to a short series by the fact that quotas were only instituted in 1984. The government cost variable was significant at the 1 percent level for powder and at the 5 percent level for butter. Although the result was slightly stronger for the equation using butter variables, neither formulation showed stocks or export subsidies to be significant.

Subsidized EU consumption rates

$$(12)\quad SEC_t = f(Stock_{t-1}; GC_t^{CAP}; P_{t-1}^{Intv})$$

where previous definitions hold and

SEC = subsidized domestic consumption

Subsidized domestic consumption is a surplus disposal strategy (as is subsidized exports), in contrast to the above production policy instruments. We expect that the rate of subsidized consumption is negatively related to government expenditures. If government costs are high, then policy-makers may seek to reduce government costs by decreasing the subsidy rate. Domestic consumption subsidy rates should be positively related to stocks as policy-makers strive to reduce stockpiles and avoid further intervention buying by more intensive use of subsidies. Internal EU subsidies are primarily in the form of animal feed for powder and discount prices to bakeries for butter. Insufficient butter data were available for proper estimation. Empirical results for subsidized powder are presented in Equation (13).

$$(13)\quad SEC_t = -19.7 \;\; -0.01\, GC_t^{CAP} + \; 0.1 \;\, Stock_{t-1} + 0.5\, P_{t-1}^{Invt}$$
$$(-0.3) \;\; (-3.6) \qquad\qquad (3.9) \qquad\qquad (7)$$
$$R^2 = 0.88 \quad \text{Adj. } R^2 = 0.85 \qquad F = 27 \quad n = 15$$

For EU domestic subsidies of powder, of which a large proportion is used for animal feed, the estimated equation is significant at the 1 percent level. The government cost variable, the lagged stock variable and the lagged intervention price were all significant at the 1 percent level and had the correct signs. If CAP costs are relatively high, the Commission may opt for a low subsidy to defer some expense until budgetary slack returns. If stocks are already high, a higher subsidy will help to reduce the stocks. If the intervention price in the previous year was high, a high export refund may be desirable to prevent additional surpluses from depressing the EU market.

Subsidized EU export rates

$$(14)\quad SX_{t-1} = f(Stock_{t-1}; GC_{t-1}^{CAP}; ER_t; P_{t-1}^{Intv})$$

where previous definitions hold and

ER = exchange rates

Export subsidies are another surplus disposal strategy which dispose of large EU surpluses on the world market at the world price using export restitution payments. The estimated equation includes independent variables similar to the EU domestic subsidy equation and we expect the same sign for explanatory variables. In addition, exchange rates (US$/ECU) are now included, where we expect a positive relationship between the exchange rate and the export subsidy rate because a weakening US dollar results in lower international prices as reflected in European currencies, thus requiring higher EU export subsidies. Empirical results are presented in Equations (15) for powder and (16) for butter.

$$(15)\quad SX_t = -1139 + \; 0.6 \;\, Stock_{t-1} + 0.1\, GC_t^{Dairy} \; - \; 0.03 \;\, GC_t^{CAP} + 1138\, ER_t + \; 0.3 \;\, P_{t-1}^{Invt}$$
$$(-4.8) \quad (5.3) \qquad\qquad (2) \qquad\qquad (-4.2) \qquad\qquad (2.9) \qquad (0.9)$$
$$R^2 = 0.94 \;\; \text{Adj. } R^2 = 0.88 \quad F = 15 \qquad n = 11$$

$$(16)\quad SX_t = 5937 + \; 0.6 \;\, Stock_{t-1} + 0.16\, GC_t^{Dairy} \; - \; 0.02 \;\, GC_t^{CAP} + \; 190 \;\, ER_t - \; 1.6 \;\, P_{t-1}^{Invt}$$
$$(2) \quad (3.4) \qquad\qquad (1.5) \qquad\qquad (-1.5) \qquad\qquad (0.2) \qquad (-2.2)$$
$$R^2 = 0.88 \qquad \text{Adj. } R^2 = 0.76 \qquad F = 7 \quad n = 11$$

where previous definitions hold and

GC^{Dairy} = EU Dairy Program Government Costs

Overall, the estimation results for the export subsidy rate for powder were significant at the 1 percent level, and at the 2 percent level for butter. In terms of signs, the stock variable was positively correlated with export subsidy rates, as expected; thus, as stocks increased, export subsidies were used for surplus disposal. The stock variable was highly significant in both equations, at the 1 percent level for powder and at the 2 percent level for butter. Government costs had different signs depending on their origin — dairy program costs were positively correlated with subsidized exports, as expected, since subsidized exports are a large component of program costs. Altenatively, government costs for CAP were negatively correlated with dairy export subsidies. This makes sense from the viewpoint that if CAP costs are high and the Ministers do not want them to increase, they may choose a less expensive form of surplus disposal than subsidized exports; thus, they are negatively correlated. Government cost variables were significant in the powder equation but insignificant in the butter equation. As expected, the US$/ECU exchange rate was positively correlated with subsidized exports. It was significant in the powder equation at the 3 percent level but insignificant for butter. The lagged intervention price was significant at the 8 percent level for butter, but insignificant for powder. The intervention price was expected to carry a positive sign because a high intervention price in the previous year would tend to produce a greater need for surplus disposal through a higher export refund rate. The mixed signs and mixed significance of the intervention price lead us to discount the importance of the prior year's intervention price.

ASSESSMENT AND IMPLICATIONS OF RESULTS

Results for both the USA and EU show a dominant influence of the support (intervention) price in the previous year, which supports the institutional inertia hypothesis discussed above. US farm income, stocks, and government costs also appeared to influence US policy-makers' choice of the price support level.

In the EU, additional policy instruments are used. Government costs appear to influence both production and surplus disposal policies. Public stocks significantly influence EU surplus disposal policies. From a dairy policy perspective, which may be applicable to other commodities, the EU appears to choose policies sequentially — first choosing farm level support policies and then choosing surplus disposal policies. If the farm policies produce a large surplus, the surplus disposal policy instruments are then changed accordingly to minimize the consequent budget costs and stocks. While the limited number of observations may hinder statistical analysis, we were able to establish a connection between budget costs and the marketing quota decisions.

The statistical results, in combination with the Uruguay Round agreement, point toward likely policy approaches to current and future challenges. For the United States and the European Union in the Uruguay Round, an understanding of each other's agricultural policies was not sufficient to assure that an agreement could be reached. But such an understanding was necessary, however, for each to propose solutions acceptable to both parties, which were then offered for general consideration by all contracting parties of the GATT. This analysis may not extend to other subsectors of the agricultural economy, or to political forces that affect policy decisions. This research does contribute to gaining an understanding of the factors which influence US and EU dairy policy choice, which can be used in the broader context of trade negotiations.

NOTE

1 As of 1 November, 1993, the European Community was renamed the European Union.

REFERENCES

Abbott, P.C., 1979a, 'Modeling International Grain Trade With Government-controlled Markets', *American Journal of Agricultural Economics*, Vol. 61, No. 1, pp.22–31.

Abbott, P.C., 1979b, 'The Role of Government Interference in International Commodity Trade Models', *American Journal of Agricultural Economics*, Vol. 61, No. 1, pp.135–140.

Allison, G., 1971, *The Essence of Decision: Explaining the Cuban Missile Crisis*, Little, Brown and Co., Boston.

Beghin, J.C., 1990, 'A Game-Theoretic Model of Endogenous Public Policies', *American Journal of Agricultural Economics*, Vol. 72, No. 1, pp.138–148.

Beghin, J.C. and Foster, W.E., 1992, 'Political Criterion Functions and the Analysis of Wealth Transfers', *American Journal of Agricultural Economics*, Vol. 74, No. 3, pp.787-794.

Buchanan, J. M. and others, 1978, 'The Economics of Politics', *The Institute of Economic Affairs*, Vol. 18, pp.1–194.

Carter, C. A., McCalla, A. F. and Sharples, J., 1990 (eds.), *Imperfect Competition and Political Economy: The New Trade Theory in Agricultural Trade Research*, Westview Press, Boulder and London.

Caves, R.E., 1976, 'Economic Models of Political Choice: Canada's Tariff Structure', *Canadian Journal of Economics*, Vol. 9, pp.278–300.

De Gorter, H., 1983, 'Agricultural Policies: A Study in Political Economy', Ph.D. dissertation, University of California at Berkeley.

Dixit, P.M. and Martin, M.A., 1986, *Policymaking for US Commodity Programs: A Case Study of the Coarse Grains Sector*, Foreign Agricultural Economic Report No. 219, Economic Research Service, US Department of Agriculture, Washington, D.C., USA.

Gardner, B.L., 1987, 'Causes of US Farm Commodity Programs', *Journal of Political Economy*, Vol. 95, No. 2, pp.290–310.

Infanger, C.L., Bailey, W.C. and Dyer, D.R., 1983, 'Agricultural Policy in Austerity: The Making of the 1981 Farm Bill', *American Journal of Agricultural Economics*, Vol. 65, No. 1, pp.1–9.

Krueger, A., 1974, 'The Political Economy of the Rent Seeking Economy', *American Economic Review*, Vol. 64, No. 3, pp.291–303.

Lattimore, R.G. and Schuh, G.E., 1979, 'Endogenous Policy Determination: The Case of the Brazilian Beef Sector', *Canadian Journal of Agricultural Economics*, Vol. 27, No. 1, pp.1–16.

Lavergne, R.P., 1983, *The Political Economy of U.S. Tariffs: An Empirical Analysis*, Harcourt-Brace-Jovanovich Academic Press, New York.

Lopez, R.A., 1989, 'Political Economy of US Sugar Policies', *American Journal of Agricultural Economics*, Vol. 71, No. 1, pp.20–31.

Love, H.A., Rausser, G.C. and Burton, D.M., 1990, 'Policy Preference Functions: Grand Themes and New Direction', invited paper at the annual meeting of the Western Agricultural Economics Association, Vancouver, Canada.

Marchant, M.A., 1993, *Political Economic Analysis of US Dairy Policies and European Community Dairy Policy Comparisons*, Garland Publishing, New York.

Marchant, M.A., Neff, S. and McCalla, A., 1992, 'Domestic Policy Interdependence: Analysis of Dairy Policies in the US and the EC', in Bellamy, M. and Greenshields, B. (eds.), *Issues in Agricultural Development: Sustainability and Cooperation*, International Association of Agricultural Economists Occasional Paper No. 6, Brookfield, Vermont, pp.339–343.

Paarlberg, P.L., 1983, 'Endogenous Policy Formation in the Imperfect World Wheat Market', Ph.D. dissertation, Purdue University.

Paarlberg, P.L. and Abbott, P.C., 1986, 'Oligopolistic Behavior by Public Agencies in International Trade: The World Wheat Market', *American Journal of Agricultural Economics*, Vol. 68, No. 3, pp.528–542.

Rausser, G.C. and Freebairn, J.W., 1974, 'Estimation of Policy Preference Functions: An Application to US Beef Import Quotas', *Review of Economics and Statistics*, Vol. 56, pp.437–449.

Rausser, G.C. and Foster, W.E., 1990, 'Political Preference Functions and Public Policy Reform', *American Journal of Agricultural Economics*, Vol. 72, No. 3, pp.641–52.

Rausser, G.C., Lichtenberg, E. and Lattimore, R., 1982, 'Developments in Theory and Empirical Applications of Endogenous Government Behavior', in Rausser, G.C. (ed.), *New Directions in Econometric Modeling and Forecasting in US Agriculture*, Elsevier/North-Holland Publishing Co., New York, Chapter 18.

Riethmuller, P. and Roe, T., 1986, 'Government Intervention in Commodity Markets: The Case of Japanese Rice and Wheat Policy,' *Journal of Policy Modeling*, Vol. 8, No. 3, pp.327–349.

Sarris, A. and Freebairn, J., 1983, 'Endogenous Price Policies and Wheat Prices', *American Journal of Agricultural Economics*, Vol. 65, No.2, pp.214–24.

Von Witzke, H., 1990, 'Determinants of the U.S. Wheat Producer Support Price: Do Presidential Elections Matter?', *Public Choice*, Vol. 64, pp.155–65.

Young, L., 1987, 'The Formation of Wheat Policies in the U.S., Canada and Japan: Case Studies of Endogenizing Policy Behavior', Ph. D. dissertation, University of California at Davis.

Young, L., Marchant, M. and McCalla, A., 1991, *The Political Economy of Agricultural Trade: A Review of the Literature on Domestic Policy Behavior and International Price Formation,* Agriculture and Trade Analysis Division, No. AGES 9103, Economics Research Service, US Department of Agriculture, Washington, D.C.

Zusman, P., 1976, 'The Incorporation and Measurement of Social Power in Economic Models', *International Economic Review*, Vol. 17, No.2, pp.447–462.

Zusman, P. and Amiad, A., 1977, 'A Quantitative Investigation of a Political Economy: The Israeli Dairy Program', *American Journal of Agricultural Economics*, Vol. 59, No. 1, pp.88–98.

GENERAL DISCUSSION — P.J. Lund, Rapporteur *(Ministry of Agriculture, Fisheries and Food, UK)*

Both of the (only two) discussants present had been asked to discuss the same paper (that by Eldon Ball *et al.*). In presenting this paper J-C Bureau said that the objective was to make multinational comparisons, across both space and time, output and productivity, thus identifying both differential growth rates and gaps in productivity. In order to do this it was necessary to obtain price indices, for both outputs and inputs, which could be applied across both space (comparisons between countries) and time. Hence the use of Purchasing Power Parities (PPPs). The presentation (and the paper) did not elaborate on the complex details of the methodology but focussed on the results which, was claimed, would provide a basis for econometric modelling of supply responses.

David Lee (Cornell, USA) opened the discussion of this paper by asking how sensitive the results were (e.g. to choice of deflations) and whether there were common determining factors.

Similar points were made by the other opening discussant, Ellen Hanak Freud, (IRAD, France). She asked how sensitive the results were to methodological choices (such as 1985 as the base year for the PPPs) and how wide is the margin of error in the results (the non-stochastic nature of the procedure not having generated confidence intervals etc.). She went on to ask about the causal factors which might explain the obscured differences, in particular the role of policy intervention. However, one might question whether the effects of policy are not better examined at commodity rather than industry level. Ulrich (Germany) raised an important methodological point; that opportunity costs (e.g of non labour inputs) differ considerably between countries reduces the usefulness of comparisons of productivity in which some common proxy is used. Other speakers raised the problems of measuring labour and capital inputs, the latter being dependent on estimates of asset lives. This led into a discussion of the role of the production of some commodities (notably pigs) within farmers' mix of outputs, which was lively rather than conclusive.

Jean-Marc Boussard (France) offered to open the discussion on the von Cramon-Taubadel paper. He questioned why it is necessary to know a government PPF and why it should be linear (is this a necessary assumption?). More fundamentally be questioned whether it is reasonable to assume rationality on the part of politician. He provided examples to the contrary and concluded that political decisions are a matter of chance. In similar vein, Rausser (USA) questioned whether preference functions exist. It was also suggested that there is lots of evidence to indicate that politicians are not systematically attempting to maximize something. However, although fundamental these comments did not address the more technical aspects of von Cramon-Taubadel's paper, on which there was relatively little discussion.

There was relatively little discussion of the Marchant *et al.* paper, though one person questioned whether the apparent influence of previous policy level may not simply reflect auto-correlation in the dependent variable and Revell (UK) pointed out that EU quota changes are not (in the main) reversible.

MICHAEL LYNE, MICHAEL ROTH AND BETSY TROUTT*

Land Rental Markets in Sub-Saharan Africa: Institutional Change in Customary Tenure

Abstract: Data show that rental markets for agricultural land held under customary forms of tenure in sub-Saharan Africa are often constrained, despite potential benefits for many households. The notion that conditions necessary for land rental will emerge in response to increasing population pressure and better prospects in farming is questioned. Attention is focused on the 'supply' of institutional change and on interest groups opposed to changes in customary tenure. The implication is that farmer support programs are unlikely to realize their full potential unless they are accompanied by strategies designed to make endogenous changes in customary tenure more predictable.

INTRODUCTION

This paper investigates rental markets for agricultural land in regions of sub-Saharan Africa (SSA) where land is scarce and customary institutions influence security of tenure and transaction costs. Despite the advantages of renting and the wide range of contractual arrangements (including cash rentals, sharecropping and 'lending' land in return for regular tributes) that has emerged in response to imperfections in other markets, rental markets appear to be constrained in SSA. Research conducted by Thomson and Lyne (1993) in the homelands of South Africa suggests that land is under-utilized because it is uncertain whether rented land will be returned to lessors. Such tenure insecurity deprives the lessor of rental income, and the lessee of access to productive lands. It is therefore important (a) to corroborate the evidence and (b) to ask why these markets are constrained if renting has positive welfare implications for a significant number of rural households. The question does not challenge claims that customary tenures have responded to demands generated by population growth and better prospects in farming, but it does recognize that there is a 'supply' side to institutional change. This process involves collective action and is influenced by power and ideology. Concerted opposition to rental markets could come from several quarters within a community, and will influence both the direction and extent of institutional change. Clearly, policy questions relating to intervention cannot be answered without knowledge of the forces that shape local institutions.

EVIDENCE OF CONSTRAINED RENTAL MARKETS

In the homelands of South Africa land is not abundant and households face very different economic opportunities owing to the existence of a highly differentiated wage labour market, although farm sizes tend to be uniformally small. While the vast majority of rural households derive only a small fraction of their total earnings from farming, a significant number of households are very dependent upon agriculture. In a recent (1991) survey conducted in parts of rural KwaZulu, 43 percent of the households wanted to rent land left

* University of Natal, South Africa, University of Wisconsin, USA and University of Wisconsin, USA, respectively.

Financial assistance from the Human Science Research Council is gratefully acknowledged. Views expressed in this paper are those of the authors and not necessarily those of the HSRC.

idle by neighbours yet only 5 percent did so. Of those that did not rent, 70 per cent claimed that transactions were 'too risky' — a finding consistent with Thomson and Lyne's argument. Risk and high transaction costs raise the reservation price of potential lessors and tend to confine the population of tenants to farmers who can cover the risk premiums charged by lessors. Empirical studies conducted in KwaZulu have shown that renting is virtually synonymous with more intensive cropping and surplus production even though lessors attempt to reduce their chances of losing land by renting to close friends and relatives (Nieuwoudt and Vink, 1989). There is little information regarding the extent of private rental transactions in the other homelands, but a survey of commercial farmers conducted in the Transkei during 1992 revealed that 21 per cent of the respondents rented land in. However, within the subset that operated land under customary tenure only, the proportion was lower (13 per cent) and the majority claimed that renting was not allowed. Even amongst these emerging farmers, land was farmed more intensively by those renting in (Table 1).

Bruce (1989) noted that wealthier farmers with draft animals could no longer rent in land from other households that lacked oxen following the draconian enforcement of reform legislation that prohibited tenancy arrangements in the communal areas of Ethopia. In Senegal, he observed that landholders were unwilling to observe the custom of 'loaning' land after laws enacted in 1964 recognized the right to continued occupancy of those individuals cultivating land. Similarly Roth (1993) reports that respondents surveyed in Somalia's lower Shebelle region were wary of renting land out owing to legal provisions banning transactions and frequent disputes involving tenants who refused to return land at end of the agreed term.

The *de facto* situation is that land is often under-utilized even though it is not abundant and is sought by farmers. In the Barolong and Eastern Bangwaketse regions of Botswana where competition for farmland is strong, large areas remain uncultivated. Gulbrandsen's (1985) report on these regions also mentions sharecroppers and borrowers claiming land, and tenants losing their investments on rented land. In Nigeria (Parsons, 1971), Ghana, Cameroon and Zanzibar (Feder and Noronha, 1987), tenants wishing to plant perennial crops have been denied access to land in case they claim title by virtue of their length of possession.

RENTAL MARKET ACTIVITY, EFFICIENCY OF LAND USE AND EQUITY

Where small farm-households value their land rights as a form of social security, rental transactions are a more reliable indicator of allocative efficiency in agriculture than land sales. Renting will not only bring idle land into use but, where leasing out is risky, it will also tend to transfer land to farmers confident of their ability to cover the risk premiums charged by lessors. Hence, an inverse relationship is expected between rental market activity and the productivity gap (income per hectare operated) between farmers who rent land in and households that do not. Table 1 presents statistics computed for households sampled in four regions of Uganda, and in the Transkei and KwaZulu. In Uganda and KwaZulu, the samples were drawn from populations of rural households but the Transkei survey was confined to emerging farmers (surplus producers). Land is not considered abundant in any of the regions with the possible exception of Bukuya and Kabulasoke subcounties in Uganda, and evidence of off-farm employment in each region suggests that households face different opportunity costs in farming. Consequently, if potential lessors perceive renting to be risky, the productivity gap between farmers who *rent* land in and *other* households should be highest in the samples where the incidence of renting is lowest.

The data show that renting transfers land to farmers who gross more income per hectare operated, and that the income difference does widen in favour of renters as the incidence of renting diminishes. A comparison of net incomes would provide a more accurate test of the market's efficiency advantages but cost data were recorded only in KwaZulu. Deducting expenditure on improved seed, fertilizer and chemicals yields a per hectare gross margin significantly higher on land operated by renters in this region where the rental market is particularly weak.

From an equity perspective, a land rental market resulting from secure tenure and contracts avoids the problem of landlessness associated with land sale. Potential lessors need only rent out land that they do not require in the short-term, and do not have to relocate. Provided that rental arrangements are voluntary, removing constraints to renting will create positive opportunities for many households — particularly the poorest (Table 1). Landholders who are either unwilling or unable to use all of their land would gain opportunities to earn rental income, and households short of land for subsistence or commercial farming would gain opportunities to extend their farming operation. However, fixed transaction costs and imperfections in related markets (e.g. discriminatory access to cheap credit) will influence the distribution of benefits generated by these opportunities, and the emergence of conditions necessary for a rental market could harm many households (discussed later). Under customary tenures where farm size patterns tend to be egalitarian, the distorting effects of fixed transaction costs and other market imperfections may be unimportant. The data in Table 1 show that renters (smaller and possibly younger families) are generally land poor relative to other households, and that renting tends to equalize areas operated. In short, the evidence does not contradict the view that tenancy, as a voluntary market response, is neither inherently nor inevitably damaging to the interests of the poor. Support for this view comes from a survey of sharecroppers in Lesotho. Lawry (1993) found that households sharing land out had more land but less liquidity, fewer resident workers and more widows and elderly people as heads than households sharing land in. Due to their severe liquidity problems, households sharing land out seldom provided any inputs other than labour. Conversely, Riddell (undated) reports that sharecropping arrangements were the only access to land by the poor in a highland Madagascar study. Clearly, rental transactions sustain many households that would otherwise be destitute.

CAUSES OF INEFFICIENT LAND RENTAL MARKETS

For the purpose of this paper, an 'efficient' land rental market will be defined as one which accomplishes the productivity and equity gains referred to in the previous section. Viewed from this perspective, an efficient rental market would require the usual neoclassical conditions needed for an efficient sale market, viz. security of tenure and low transaction costs. Whilst it is often claimed that tenure is secure under the indigenous systems operating in Africa, Feder and Noronha add the qualification that customary tenure is secure only when it refers to the ability to use land for a certain period and for a defined purpose without disturbance. The situation may change when the holder attempts a land transaction. In Place and Roth's (undated) terminology, security of tenure has breadth, duration and assurance components. Following this approach, transaction costs are expected to vary inversely with security of tenure. For example, a potential tenant seeking exclusive rights to a parcel may find transaction costs prohibitive if there are many legitimate claimants, each possessing inclusive rights to the same parcel owing to the high cost of discovering the owner and establishing his or her rights. Here, high transaction costs faced by the tenant are matched by tenure insecurity (inadequate breadth of rights) on the part of the users. Risks that reduce tenure security could also be viewed as raising transaction costs. Uncertainty about institutions and laws that would be applied to disputes, unpredictable judgements, and fuzzy procedures to establish or defend contracts would undermine the assurance component of tenure security. Alternatively, the risk premiums attracted by these circumstances could be interpreted as transaction costs.

Other things being equal, exclusive use rights to land enhance tenure security or reduce transaction costs and are therefore central to an efficient land rental market. Table 2 lists six 'institutional' variables that convey information about tenure security and transaction costs in each of the regions included in Table 1. Data relating to small irrigation farmers in the Shebelle region of Somalia (1987–88) and the Green Zones of Maputo in Mozambique (1991) are also presented. Statistics describing the continuous variables were estimated from observations recorded in household samples, but scores assigned to the dichotomous variables (one indicates the presence of an attribute, and zero otherwise) summarize the results of case studies and personal observations made by the authors.

As expected, there is a strong inverse relationship ($r = -0.94^{**}$ across regions) between the incidence of renting and the proportion of respondents who perceived transactions to be risky or subject to customary restrictions. Whilst it might be anticipated that tenure would be most secure in regions where the incidence of land purchase or land titles is highest, neither of these variables was significantly correlated with rental market activity. There is some evidence of a positive correlation between renting and the incidence of purchased land ($r = -0.75$) despite legal prohibitions on land markets in Somalia and Mozambique. The reverse holds for land titles ($r = -0.46$). This result most likely reflects legal restrictions on transfers that accompanied land registration in the Transkei, Somalia and Mozambique but it is also consistent with the view that titling is neither a sufficient nor a necessary condition for a rental market, and that it may aggravate tenure insecurity by creating conflicting claims to land. The remaining variables suggest that rental markets are more active where (a) procedures for establishing contracts are transparent, (b) local precedents set in land disputes confirm security of tenure, and (c) national law sanctions local precedents. However, it is not obvious why some regions are characterized by local institutions that constrain renting. The following section attempts to identify factors that influence endogenous shifts in customary land tenure.

Table 1 *Rental Market Activity and Farm Characteristics in Regions of Uganda, Transkei and KwaZulu*

Region	Busaana		Kabulasoke		Bukuya		Kibinge		Transkei (emerging farmers)		KwaZulu	
	Rent	Other	Rent	Other	Rent	Other	Rent	Other	Rent	Other	Rent	Other
Households observed	51	72	35	72	33	91	28	98	11	42	7	125
% Hhlds renting in	41		33		27		22		21		5	
Farm size (ha)	0.43	1.86	0.80	2.42	2.48	11.33	0.52	2.56	8.54	9.02	0.83	1.36
Area operated	0.84	1.80	1.34	2.30	3.38	11.25	0.77	2.50	11.81	9.02	1.39	1.36
Income/Ha operated ($)	41	42	19	18	7	4	46	26	601	400	167	73
Gross margin/ha operated											95	30
Farm income	34	75	26	41	23	47	35	65	7102	3606	232	100
Non-farm income	28	17	24	26	29	20	33	30	4212	3623	2769	1838
Household income	62	92	50	67	52	67	68	95	11 314	7229	3001	1038
Family size	5.12	6.24	4.37	5.29	3.85	4.81	4.68	6.49	11.18	7.86	7.29	7.38

Note: 1000 USh = 1 US$ (1992); R2.78 = 1 US$ (1992, Transkei) and R2.63 = 1 US$ (1991, KwaZulu).

Table 2 *Rental Market Activity and Institutions in Regions of Uganda, Transkei, Somalia, KwaZulu and Mozambique*

Region	Uganda				Transkei (emerging farmers)	Somalia	KwaZulu	Mozambique
	Busaana	Kabulasoke	Bukuya	Kibinge		Shebelle		Maputo
Households observed	123	107	124	126	53	113	132	121
Households renting in	41	33	27	22	21	7	5	0
% households that:								
– perceive customary restraints or undue risk in land rental	2	33	25	34	43	81	69	68
– purchased land	31	29	19	28		25	0	9
– have title to some land	11	20	21	14	51	32	0	58
Rental procedures transparent	1	1	1	1		0	0	0
Precedents affirm tenure security	1	1	1	1		0	0	0
Land sale upheld by national laws	1	1	1	1	0	0	0	0

INSTITUTIONAL CHANGE

Several African studies have reported correlations between changes in customary tenure and changes in socio-economic conditions. Feder and Noronha (1987) summarize the popular view that secure tenure and low transaction costs emerge in response to population growth, the adoption of high value crops and improvements in communications and extension services. The generic explanation starts with land becoming relatively scarce owing to population pressure and better prospects for commercial farming. According to Ault and Rutman (1979), this should induce a system that assigns exclusive rights to land because farmers have an incentive to invest but are unable to internalize the benefits of their effort unless they can exclude other users (free-riders). Rigorous application of this Coasian 'transaction cost' approach helps to identify groups whose members share a common interest in a collective good (e.g. exclusive land rights), but there is no guarantee that steps will be taken to acquire the collective good just because people experience similar shifts in potential net benefits when relative prices change. Curiously, the 'transaction cost' approach ignores problems of collective action, like high transaction costs in large groups (Olson, 1971). Historical evidence quoted in support of the model rarely refutes claims that commercial farming may have been the result, rather than the cause, of a shift towards exclusive land rights. Whilst the causal relationship between population growth and individual tenure appears to be more predictable, some authors suggest that population pressure may constrain, not hasten, the evolution of exclusive land rights (Parsons, 1971; Lawry, 1993). Rural communities are not homogenous, and population growth could favour groups opposed to local precedents that reinforce security of tenure. Such groups influence the 'supply' of institutional change.

One example of 'supply-side' interest groups identified in the land tenure debate distinguishes between smallholders who rely mainly on wage employment and those who rely primarily on farming. Lawry contends that increasing population pressure on land in Lesotho has strengthened the former group, overwhelming farmer demands for more marketable land rights. Like Parsons, he attributes opposition from non-farmers to fears that a land market will jeopardize their social security. However this argument ignores the mutual benefits afforded by land rental. Of course, when households rely on secondary use rights to land a shift towards exclusive rights could threaten security. Opposition to exclusive land rights has also been attributed to livestock owners and tribal authorities. Lyne and Nieuwoudt (1990) noted that stockowners in KwaZulu resisted attempts by farmers to rent idle land because their supply of communal grazing diminished when fallow land was cultivated. In the same region, Thomson and Lyne found that some chiefs disallowed rental contracts between prospective lessors and sugar-cane farmers. They reason that tribal authorities oppose land markets where they rely on their control over land allocation to prevent political rivals from settling in their domain. Alternatively, tribal authorities may empathize with households who rely on secondary use rights to land, or they may be predisposed to special interest groups, like influential stockowners who keep cattle as store of wealth.

The Marxist view that institutions are transformed by class struggle has obvious appeal but there are equally obvious questions about how the classes should be defined. Further, Marxists, like their 'transaction cost' counterparts, tend to ignore the problems of collective action that may preclude a struggle or resistance. Nevertheless, by stressing the relevance of political organize, ideology and the distribution of wealth as elements of institutional change, they do focus attention on the need for compensation. Unless acceptable substitutes can be offered to losers (e.g. options to exchange secondary use rights for serviced residential sites, shares in ranching corporations, etc.) attempts by local authorities to sanction or allocate exclusive land rights will continue to meet with opposition, and government recommendations for enclosure and rental transactions would be contentious if they were imposed. To alter the evolution of land tenure from an unpredictable, organic process to a more pragmatic one, government would also have to support research, document transactions, disputes and precedents, disseminate information, and ensure that national laws sanctioned local precedents.

CONCLUSIONS

The data presented in this paper show that renting closes productivity gaps by transferring land to farmers who can use it more effectively, and that, far from damaging the interests of the poor, it sustains many households that would otherwise be destitute. Unfortunately, land rental markets are often constrained in SSA because customary tenure is not secure and transaction costs are high. These problems stem largely from two sources; either the user does not have exclusive land rights (i.e. the breadth of rights is inadequate) or the risk of losing land as a result of a transaction is too high. In theory, titling could resolve these problems but, even if its consequences were acceptable, it poses formidable logistical problems that may aggravate tenure insecurity by creating conflicting claims to land. Instead, attention has turned to ways of facilitating an endogenous shift toward exclusive land rights.

On the one hand, policies based on the Coasian 'transaction cost' model stress the importance of support programs that will encourage farmers to press for exclusive land rights. This approach ignores the problems of collective action and disregards groups opposed to precedents that reinforce tenure security. Resistance is likely where households are dependent upon secondary use rights to land that primary users wish to enclose. As a result, the outcome of such induced innovation is unpredictable, and could be highly undesirable. If the policy succeeds, it could produce distress sales and land grabbing. Conversely, failure implies a constrained land rental market (i.e. losses in efficiency, equity, experience and information), meagre incentives to conserve and improve land, and limited response to the support programs.

On the other hand, adaptive policies emphasize strategies intended to make changes in customary tenure more predictable. In particular, they recognize the need to compensate people whose welfare is threatened by tenure security, including tribal authorities who often control the information and functions that set precedents and revise customary tenure. Apart from identifying and providing suitable forms of compensation, adaptive policies aim to transform privileges into rights and to reduce transaction costs.

Clearly, adaptive programs would be appropriate and more effective when there are worthwhile opportunities in farming. Likewise, farmer support programs are unlikely to realize expected changes in customary tenure or production if they are not accompanied by adaptive programs. In practice it may be useful to include the latter as components of any farmer support program.

REFERENCES

Ault, D.E. and Rutman, G.L., 1979, 'The Development of Individual Rights to Property in Tribal Africa', *Journal of Law and Economics*, Vol. 22, No. 1, pp.163–182.

Bruce, J.W., 1989, 'The Variety of Reform: A Review of Recent Experience with Land Reform and the Reform of Land Tenure, with Particular Reference to the African Experience', Land Tenure Center, University of Wisconsin, Madison.

Feder, G. and Noronha, R., 1987, 'Land Rights Systems and Agricultural Development in Sub-Saharan Africa', *World Bank Research Observer*, Vol. 2, pp.143–165.

Gulbrandsen, O., 1985, 'Access to Agricultural Land and Communal Land Management in Eastern Botswana', Land Tenure Research Paper No. 81, University of Wisconsin, Madison.

Lawry, S.W., 1993, 'Transactions in Cropland Held Under Customary Tenure in Lesotho', in Bassett, T.J., and Crummey, D.E. (eds.), *Land in African Agrarian Systems*, University of Wisconsin Press, Madison, pp.57–74.

Lyne, M.C. and Nieuwoudt, W.L., 1990, 'The Real Tragedy of the Commons: Livestock Production in KwaZulu', *South African Journal of Economics*, Vol. 58, No. 1, pp.88–96.

Nieuwoudt, W.L. and Vink, N., 1989, 'Farm Household-Economics and Increased Earnings from Agriculture: Implications to Southern Africa', *South African Journal of Economics*, Vol. 57, pp.257–268.

Olson, M., 1971, *The Logic of Collective Action*, Harvard University Press, Cambridge, Massachusetts.

Parsons, K.H., 1971, 'Customary Land Tenure and the Development of African Agriculture', Land Tenure Center Paper No. 77, University of Wisconsin, Madison.

Place, F. and Roth, M. (undated), 'Land Tenure Security and Agricultural Performance in Africa: Overview of Research Methodology', Land Tenure Center, University of Wisconsin, Madison.

Riddell, J.C., undated, 'Dynamics of Land Tenure and Spontaneous Changes in African Agrarian Systems', Institutions and Agrarian Reform Division, FAO, Rome.

Roth, M., 1993, 'Somalia Land Policies and Tenure Impacts: The Case of the Lower Shebelle', in Bassett, T.J. and Crummey, D.E. (eds.), *Land in African Agrarian Systems*, University of Wisconsin Press, Madison, pp.298–326.

Thomson, D.N. and Lyne, M.C., 1993, 'Constraints to Land Rental in KwaZulu: Analysing the Transaction Costs', *Oxford Agrarian Studies*, Vol. 21, No. 2, pp.143–150.

DISCUSSION OPENING — Timothy O. Williams *(International Livestock Centre For Africa, Niger)*

This paper addresses a topical issue of particular relevance to agricultural development in sub-Saharan Africa. Agricultural land rental markets are poorly developed in Africa due to economic, social, legal and institutional contraints. These constraints impede the realization of efficiency and equity gains that could be expected from properly functioning land rental markets, particularly where farm land is scarce and rural population is growing fast.

Based on data from east and southern Africa, the paper shows that insecurity of customary tenure and high transaction costs are the main impediments to land rental markets. As a panacea, the authors reject policies based on the 'transaction cost' model arguing that these policies could produce unpredictable and undesirable outcomes. Instead, they advocate adaptive policies that aim to transform privileges enjoyed under customary tenure into property rights and compensate individuals whose welfare may be threatened by tenure security. However, contrary to the authors' claim, the policies they recommend do not invalidate the transaction cost model. Rather these policies represent additional measures that could be used to support the emergence of exclusive and assured land rights — the main proposition of the transaction cost approach.

Analytically, the usefulness of the paper is slightly diminished by the limited quantitative analysis reported and the inadequate coverage given to regions outside east and southern Africa. Except for tangential reference to findings of studies conducted elsewhere in Africa, no analysis is provided of the constraints and opportunities for emerging land rental markets in west and central Africa where the socio-economic conditions are different from those operating in east and southern Africa. Despite these shortcomings, the paper represents a valuable contribution to the growing literature on agricultural land rental markets in sub-Saharan Africa.

MARCOS GALLAGHER, STEPHAN J. GOETZ AND DAVID L. DEBERTIN*

Efficiency Effects of Institutional Factors: Limited-Resource Farms in Northeast Argentina

Abstract: This paper analyzes technical efficiency of limited-resource farms operating in a sub-tropical environment (Province of Misiones, Argentina). Property rights over land, the degree of market exposure and food support programmes are three institutional variables that are hypothesized to lead to departures from the production frontier. Econometric analysis indicates that market exposure and receipt of food transfers increase efficiency. No effect of land ownership is detected. We argue that slash-and-burn agricultural systems allow non-owners of land to operate as or more efficiently than landowners.

INTRODUCTION

This paper focuses on agricultural households which meet consumption requirements not only through market exchange but also directly through their own production. It examines: (a) property rights; (b) access to markets; and (c) in-kind income support programmes as determinants of technical efficiency of production. The purpose of the paper is to highlight the linkages between these 'non-traditional' factors and efficiency in farming situations where an important proportion of the household's consumption requirement is met through own production.

Research on these issues is not abundant. Property rights have been analyzed by scholars interested in sharecropping (e.g., Cheung, 1969). However, most of this research addresses agriculture in densely populated areas (in particular, Asia) or in areas of modern commercial farming (e.g., the USA). In contrast, this paper addresses a production situation characterized by the abundance of land and scarcity of capital. Similarly, little research has addressed the linkages between factors such as market-orientation and food-subsidy programmes on technical efficiency. These topics are explicitly analyzed here.

ECONOMICS OF LIMITED-RESOURCE FARMERS

Limited-resource farmer decision-making has received considerable attention in the literature (e.g., Wharton, 1965; and Valdés, Scobie and Dillon, 1979). T.W. Schultz's (1964) 'poor but efficient' hypothesis implies that farmers in traditional settings are efficient in their allocation process. However, in a context of rapid technical change, inefficiencies may exist as information gathering and analysis constitute a constraint for farmers who often have less-than-adequate schooling.

Small farms have been analyzed using different conceptual frameworks. Economists have modelled the farming unit as a simplified production process, in which a set of inputs is transformed into a set of outputs (see, for example, Hopper, 1965; and Massell, 1967). These studies generally neglect institutional aspects related to the internal working of

* University of Buenos Aires, University of Kentucky, University of Kentucky, respectively.

firms. Alternatively, systems scientists have emphasized the complex interactions typically found in small, tropical or sub-tropical farms. A holistic approach is advantageous, as problems faced by limited–resource farmers are rarely amenable to highly abstract models. Indeed, it has been argued that research into the economics of small-farmer agriculture should take into account:

> (a) The social milieu in which farm decisions are made, including customs of sharing and bequest; (b) the institutional setting and policy environment, including land tenure, credit and taxation; (c) the economic environment of farms, including long-term market prospects for inputs and outputs and, most importantly, understanding of the opportunity costs and transaction costs faced by farmers; and (d) the attitudes and personal constraints of farmers, including their desire or otherwise for change, for leisure, for education, for safety and for different foods, and their human and other capital (Hardaker, Anderson and Dillon, 1984, p.95).

Property rights over land, access to markets and access to safety nets provided by government agencies constitute three aspects of the 'social milieu' considered here.

Property Rights

Land tenancy studies have documented the efficiency of share-type arrangements (see Cheung, 1969; and Otsuka and Hayami, 1988). Share tenancy arrangements are generally accompanied by a well-defined set of rights both for the landowner as well as the tenant. Thus, resource allocation efficiency is not impaired. A different situation exists when property rights are ill-defined, or though defined cannot be enforced. Bottomley (1963) focuses on the inefficiency of common property in North Africa, while De Alessi (1980) provides a comprehensive review of the economic implications of different arrangements of property rights. In general, alternative property rights change the nature of incentives faced by economic agents, and therefore affect behaviour. In 'slash-and-burn' agriculture, where squatters occupy land on a *de facto* basis, uncertainty with respect to future control may give rise to inefficiencies in resource allocation. In particular, non-existent rights may affect incentives for land improvements, and hence productivity.

Access to Markets

Differential access to markets may result in differences in firm performance. Markets allow not only exchange of *products* but exchange of *information* as well. Access to markets, moreover, permits specialized production and therefore may result in a closer matching between resource availabilities and input requirements of production activities. This may also contribute to increased efficiency. Access to markets may be restricted by factors such as fixed costs for marketing output, fixed costs for information gathering necessary for decision-making (e.g., Goetz, 1992) or minimum output or quality requirements by purchasing agents in the case of formal or informal vertical integration (contracts).

Income Support

Income-support programmes vary widely in their objectives, scope and design. In Africa and Asia, food crises have frequently resulted in massive food-aid programmes. In other cases, transfers have been more modest. In countries attempting to increase agricultural output, food-support programmes targeted at poor families are an important policy tool. In particular, they dampen effects of increased agricultural prices that result when export taxes are reduced. One possible policy measure is to allow for relatively high food prices (thus providing incentives for production) while at the same time implementing targeted food transfer programmes for low-income households.

Relatively little research, however, has analyzed the production efficiency aspects of income-support measures such as food stamps and direct food aid. In general, these programmes benefit urban households more than rural households, as the former are net demanders and the latter are generally net suppliers of food. If a lump-sum food subsidy is given to an agricultural household, several outcomes are possible:

- If calorie supply is a binding constraint, labour effort can increase.
- A shift may occur from food to cash crops, with possible efficiency gains due to greater specialization. Availability of a 'safety net' may induce less conservative decision-making, and hence greater use of 'risk-increasing' inputs.
- Alternatively, food transfers may only substitute for market or self-consumption production. For this to happen, however, farmer behaviour must correspond to a lexicographic utility function in which leisure dominates over income once subsistence is assured.[1]

THE CASE STUDY

Most studies dealing with subsistence farming focus on low-income countries, where 50–70 percent of the labour force is typically engaged in agriculture. In contrast, this study deals with a middle-income country: Argentina. Here agriculture employs less than 12–14 percent of the labour force. Income levels, although well below those of OECD countries, are much higher than those of most African and Asian countries. Subsistence farms in Argentina are an exception rather than the rule, and are confined to the northern part of the country.

The farms studied here are located in the province of Misiones. This area constitutes a three million hectare region bordered to the east and north by Brazil, and to the west by Paraguay. Approximately 50 percent of the 35 000 farms in this region can be classified as subsistence or semi-subsistence farms (INTA Misiones, 1988). The farms are characterized by a slash-and-burn type of agriculture, with low usage of modern production inputs (herbicides, fertilizers and insecticides). Sixty percent of the farmers intercrop corn with soybeans; other intercropping systems such as corn with cotton, beans or manioc are found on approximately 30 percent of all farms. Land preparation, planting and weeding are carried out manually with the help of animal power. Crop technology varies among farms: distance between corn rows, for example, ranges from 60 to 160 cm (Scattini, 1987). Table 1 shows basic indicators of resource use and output. Even for a sample of similar farms, considerable heterogeneity exists. Total farm output (including both home-consumed and marketed output) is nine times larger for farms of stratum V compared to farms of stratum I.

The data set permits analysis of issues related to tenancy, market access and income support. Twenty-seven percent of the farmers sampled own the land they farm; the remainder are squatters who illegally occupy land owned either privately or publicly. Most of this land must be cleared of forest cover prior to cultivation. The importance of market integration (as measured by the proportion of output sold) varies considerably among farms: from 50 percent in the smaller farms to nearly 100 percent in the larger ones.

Though not reported in Table 1, farms in the sample received different amounts of food transfers. These were part of a food-support programme instituted in the mid-1980s, which periodically provided needy families with boxes of assorted foodstuffs (the 'PAN' programme).[2] Half of the households received transfers that are greater than zero but less than 20 percent of their total income. Very few households received more than 20 percent of their income from transfers.

Table 1 *Organization of Seventy-Five Small Farms*

		Strata				
	Units	I	II	III	IV	V
Net income:						
Range	'000A[a]	≤2	2 – 4	4 – 6	6 – 8	≥8
Average value	A	1217	2898	4676	6857	10 902
Output sold	%	47	70	84	87	94
Tobacco income	%	33	32	40	50	71
Percentage of farms	%	52	29	11	5	3
Crop area[b]	ha	3.9	4.7	4.4	4.4	8.0
Total capital[c]	A	1089	1652	1338	1877	5240

Source: The data set used for this study was obtained by the Extension Agency of INTA Misiones at Oberá. It was made available to us by Carlos Acuña.

Notes: [a] 'A' refers to 'australes', the Argentine currency. [b] 'Crop area' refers only to annual crops. [c] 'Capital' includes tools and production livestock. It excludes buildings, fences or production animals.

THE IMPACT OF NON-TRADITIONAL FACTORS

This paper analyzes the impact of non-traditional factors (property rights, access to markets and impact of food transfers) on production efficiency. The following model is used to represent the farm production environment (farm specific subscripts omitted):

(1) $Y = f(W, L, K, D, E) + v - u$

(2) $u = g(T, MA, I) + w$

In Equation (1), traditional factors of production (labour , land, capital, draught animals and other production expenses) are represented by inputs W, L, K, D and E, respectively. Y represents total output (both sold and consumed). Equation (2) represents the relationship between institutional variables and production efficiency. Variable T represents land-ownership. It is hypothesized that lack of property rights over land leads to a reduction in efficiency (measured by the average product of inputs $W - E$). This occurs because incentives for investments tied to land are severely reduced when uncertainty exists over future control of land. Variable MA represents access to markets and technology sources, and it especially represents factors that lead to differences in efficiency between farms where most output is consumed as opposed to those where it is sold. Lastly, variable I captures the effect of in-kind income transfers on resource allocation and production efficiency. Symbols v, u and w are error terms, where $E(v) = 0$, $E(u) \geq 0$ and $E(w) = 0$. Error term u is associated with farm-specific inefficiency.

A Cobb–Douglas type of production function is used to estimate the relationship implied by Equation (1):

$$(3) \quad y = \exp^{a0} W^{b1} L^{b2} K^{b3} S^{b4} W^{b5}$$

The inputs considered are labour (measured in adult-equivalent months), land (hectares), capital stock (australes invested in tools and production animals), draught animals and production expenses (outlays in australes for crop inputs). Tenancy status and the farm's production system variables act as shifters of the production surface. It is assumed that these variables have no impact on the individual elasticities of production (represented by the b_is) of the 'traditional' inputs of the production process. Equation (1) was estimated with the stochastic frontier estimation method in *LIMDEP* (Greene, 1992). Estimation of Equation (2) is accomplished with a linear model:

$$(4) \quad u = c_0 + c_1 T + c_2 MA + c_3 I$$

T is a dummy variable with value zero for non-owners of land and 1 otherwise. Variable MA is calculated as *Output Sold/(Output Sold + Output for Self-Consumption).* It is inversely related to self-sufficiency, and presumably self-sufficiency increases as access to markets and to technologies for cash food production is restricted.[3] Lastly, variable I is calculated as *Value of Food Transfer/Value of Total Output.*[4]

ESTIMATION RESULTS

Estimation results for Equations (3) and (4) are shown in Tables 2 and 3. The main emphasis of this paper is on the determinants of technical efficiency, and therefore only selected aspects of Table 2 are discussed. Production theory suggests that small firms should generally experience increasing returns to additional resources. However, the sum of the elasticities of Table 2 reveals decreasing returns to scale for these units: $\eta(t) = \partial Y(xt)/\partial t = 0.52$ (letting $b_2 = 0$). This suggests that in the case of labour-intensive production such as analyzed here, factors associated with technology, choice of activity and production specialization can have more impact than duplication of resources. The insignificant coefficient for land is probably characteristic of slash-and-burn, small-farmer agriculture, where constraints may be more related to capital, labour and managerial resources than to land. These farms, moreover, operate in a sub-tropical environment, with high transportation costs and output spoilage due to humidity and temperature. Increasing marketable surplus poses considerable problems for limited-resource farmers.

Table 3 shows that landownership is not significant in determining efficiency. This is surprising given the generally positive relation between property rights and efficiency found in other studies. However, slash-and-burn agriculture in situations characterized by an elastic supply of land presents some distinct characteristics. In particular, it allows squatters to 'move on' once productivity of a given land parcel has been reduced through cultivation. In sub-tropical agriculture, this may occur after a relatively few years. In fact, landownership may increase the cost of abandoning land that has deteriorated and may therefore contribute to *lower* and not higher productivity.

Table 2 *Production Function*

	Coefficient	*t*-value
a_0	6.875	10.12
b_1 (labour)	0.237	1.36*
b_2 (land)	–0.116	–0.72
b_3 (capital)	0.112	1.31*
b_4 (animals)	0.118	2.24**
b_5 (expenses)	0.079	4.30**

Notes: LogL = –64.75; n = 75 * = 0.10. ** = 0.01 for one-sided tests.

Table 3 *Determinants of Inefficiency*

	Coefficient	*t*-value
c_0	0.381	6.28
c_1 (ownership)	–0.003	0.19
c_2 (market)	0.153	7.57**
c_3 (PAN)	0.036	1.29*

Note: $R^2 = 0.46$.

Access to markets has a significant impact on efficiency. As mentioned previously, markets facilitate flows of information that are not available to self-sufficient individuals. Moreover, production for markets may give rise to increasing returns through specialization, and this may increase resource productivity even without a change in technology. On these farms, increasing returns may thus be related more to *market orientation* than to *overall input quantity* as measured by the elasticity of scale, η.

Food transfers have a positive impact on efficiency. This result is tentative. However, one can probably reject the hypothesis that receipt of food *decreases* farmer effort. The linkages between transfers and resource allocation at the farm level are probably subtle and involve changing patterns in the use of time of both spouses, changing proportions between cash and subsistence crops, and changing intensity of resource-use due to risk considerations.

CONCLUSION

This paper has explored the impact of non-traditional factors on the production efficiency of small farms. Three findings emerge. First, in slash-and-burn agriculture, property rights over land do not appear to influence technical efficiency at the individual farm level. Obviously, over time, shifting cultivation that is characteristic of slash-and-burn systems will cause degradation of production resources. In many areas of the world (including tropical and sub-tropical Latin America), land is relatively abundant and limited-resource farmers are free to move on as the productivity of their current parcel of land decreases.

Second, increased market-orientation is associated with increased efficiency. These results are tentative: although the stochastic frontier model separates random factors from managerial inefficiency, it is possible that this separation is not complete. For example, marketable surplus may increase with favourable random weather shocks, thus confounding the effects of variables v and u in Equation (1). Lastly, food transfers appear to increase efficiency of production. Whether this is due to better nutrition or more possibilities for specialization is an important topic for future research.

NOTES

[1] This could also occur when demand for output at the individual farm level is highly inelastic. High transactions costs could lead to this situation.

[2] PAN ('bread' in Spanish) is the acronym for the 'Programa Alimentario Nacional (National Nutritional Programme). This programme was implemented in the mid-1980s as a direct support to low-income families.

[3] Ideally, *MA* should be measured by variables such as costs of transportation (a function of distance to markets, type of roads, etc.), farmer education and extension contacts. This information, however, is not available.

[4] The value of food transfers is obtained by pricing all 'PAN' food boxes received by the household.

REFERENCES

Bottomley, A., 1963, 'The Effect of Common Ownership of Land upon Resource Allocation in Tripolitania', *Land Economics*, Vol. 39, pp.91–95.

Cheung, S.N.S., 1969, *The Theory of Share Tenancy*, University of Chicago Press, Chicago.

De Alessi, L., 1980, 'The Economics of Property Rights: A Review of the Evidence', *Research in Law and Economics*, Vol. 2, No. 1, pp.1–47.

Goetz, S.J., 1992, 'A Selectivity Model of Household Food Marketing Behavior in Sub-Saharan Africa', *American Journal of Agricultural Economics*, Vol. 74, No. 2, pp. 444–452.

Greene, W.H., 1992, *LIMDEP Version 6.0–User's Manual and Reference Guide*, Econometric Software, Inc.

Hardaker, H.B., Anderson, J.B. and Dillon, J.L., 1984, 'Perspectives in Assessing the Impacts of Improved Agricultural Technologies', *Australian Journal of Agricultural Economics*, Vol. 28, Nos. 2 and 3, pp.87–108.

Hopper, W.D., 1965, 'Allocation Efficiency in a Traditional Indian Agriculture', *Journal of Farm Economics*, Vol. 47, pp.611–624.

INTA Misiones, 1988, Investigación en Chacras de Pequeños Productores de la Provincia de Misiones (Research in Farms of Small Producers of the Province of Misiones), Mimeo.

Massell, B.F., 1967, 'Farm Management in Peasant Agriculture: An Empirical Study', *Food Research Institute Studies*, Vol. 7, No. 2, pp.205–215.

Otsuka, K. and Hayami, Y., 1988, 'Theories of Share Tenancy—A Critical Review', *Economic Development and Culture Change*, Vol. 57, pp.31–88.

Scattini, L., 1987, Estudio de los Sistemas Productivos del Pequeño Productor en el Area de Influencia de la Agencia de Extensión Rural de L.N. Alem (A Study of Small-Farmer Production Systems in the Area of the L.N. Alem Extension Agency), Mimeo.

Schultz, T.W., 1964, *Transforming Traditional Agriculture*, Yale University Press, New Haven.

Valdés, A., Scobie, G.M. and Dillon, J.L. (eds.), 1979, *Economic Analysis and the Design of Small Farmer Technology*, Iowa State University Press, Ames, Iowa.

Wharton, C.R. (ed.), 1965, *Subsistence Agriculture and Economic Development*, Aldine.

DISCUSSION OPENING — Csaba Forgacs *(Budapest University of Economics)*

The efficiency issue is one of the most exciting topics among agricultural economists all over the world. The competitiveness of farmers basically depends on economic efficiency and we would like to know more about the influence of separate factors on it. Substantial research work has been devoted to limited-resource farmer decision-making. But what models are appropriate to measure the results? The simplified input–output models, models based on systems theory and the holistic approach reflect different levels of complexity of agricultural performance. In the literature less attention is paid to the effects of the non-traditional factors on efficiency. An advantage of this paper is that it focuses on three institutional factors and investigates them as determinants of technical efficiency of production: property rights; access to markets, and in-kind income support programmes. It argues that slash-and burn down agricultural systems allow non-owners of land to operate as efficiently as landowners, or more efficiently.

Studies dealing with subsistence farming mainly focus on low-income countries. This case is an exception by selecting a middle-income country, Argentina, for a case study. The data series collected permits analysis of issues dealing with tenancy, market access and income support in the case of 75 farms. Twenty-seven percent of the farmers owned the land while the rest are squatters, occupying illegally either privately or publically owned land.

As the paper says, production theory suggests that small firms should generally experience increasing returns to additional resources, However, in this case decreasing returns to scales are observed. The explanation is '..in the case of labour-intensive production such as analyzed here, factors associated with technology, choice of activity and production specialization can have more impact than duplication of resources. The insignificant coefficient for land is probably characteristic of slash-and burn, small-farmer agriculture'.

Surprisingly, the results show that land ownership is not significant in determining efficiency. This contradicts the results of other studies which found a positive relationship between property rights and efficiency. Elastic supply of land is used as the explanation. There is a significant positive relationship between market access and efficiency. The increasing level of productin for markets may lead to increasing retuns through specialization, which may have a positive effect on productivity.

The authors points out that '...in slash-and-burn agriculture property rights over land do not appear to influence technical efficiency at individual farm level' but admit that shifting cultivation is a characteristic of this system which will cause degradation of productive resources. Theoretically, there may be a contradiction between the two statements. The first is true if we use a static approach. But using a dynamic model, this statement would mean that in regions with abundant land, farmers are not interested in becoming landowners. With degradation of the land resource due to the slash-and-burn production, returns to land will decrease over time.

Although it was shown that market access has a positive effect on technical efficiency, the paper mentions that this result is a tentative one. Does it mean that market access can increase efficiency under given circumstances only? If the answer is yes, then what is the explanation?

Finally food transfers are shown to have a positive influence on production efficiency. But can we state that the bigger the food transfers, the higher the positive influence on technical efficiency of production? At this point, the authors underline the necessity for future research.

Y. KHATRI, T.S. JAYNE AND C. THIRTLE*

A Profit Function Approach to the Efficiency Aspects of Land Reform in Zimbabwe[1]

Abstract: The purchase of commercial farm land in Zimbabwe for resettlement has been a factor in government policy since independence in 1980, but from 1980 to 1989 only 52 000 families were relocated. The Land Acquisition Bill of 1992 made compulsory purchase easier and at present the government has announced its intention to considerably increase the rate of resettlement. But Zimbabwe has a serious food security problem and the output effects of land redistribution are a matter of dispute. The World Bank estimate that 3 million hectares of commercial farmland are under-utilized is contested by the Commercial Farmer's Union. Fitting a normalized restricted profit function to the data for the commercial sector allows estimation of the shadow price of commercial farm land. We find that the model suggests that the World Bank is correct, in that the marginal value product of land is negative, meaning that there is under-utilization. However, negative values of capital assets are common when real interest rates are negative, so the result should be treated with some caution. Also, the problem of identifying the un-utilized land is not trivial and redistributing intra-marginal land would have output effects.

INTRODUCTION

'Zimbabwe's one million communal farm households are restricted to half of the total area suited for agricultural production. The other half is occupied by 4500 large-scale commercial farmers, most of whom are white. To compound this inequality, the communal lands have a much lower agricultural potential; 74 percent of communal land is in natural regions IV and V, and 51 percent of the commercial farming area is in natural regions I-III (CSO, 1989). This grossly unequal land distribution is the most fundamental and least tractable of all Zimbabwe's problems. It is also a significant cause of food insecurity in the rural areas.' (Christensen and Stack, 1992).

There is also, in theory, an efficiency argument for land redistribution, since in any dual economy output can be increased by redistributing resources until their marginal products are equal in the two sectors. But it is widely accepted that the communal farmers cannot produce at the same level as the commercial farmers, without considerable support, and the government is already under extreme pressure to cut expenditures. Without considerable investment, the expectation is that food production would decrease, exacerbating the food security problem. The cost of resettling 52 000 families in 1980–89 has been about $112 million (Bratton, 1991). Christensen and Stack (1992) estimate that 420 000 rural and 125 000 urban households are suffering from chronic food insecurity. In this respect the land reform issue in Zimbabwe is quite different from the situation in South Africa, where output exceeds consumption by a wide margin and food grains are exported at below cost. Self-sufficiency indexes for South Africa (100 = sufficiency), show grain production at 150, horticultural products at 132 and livestock production at 98 (van Zyl *et al.*, 1993). Thus, South Africa can afford to redistribute land, even if the result is a substantial decline in output, but Zimbabwe cannot ignore the possibility that land reform could result in even greater food security problems.

* Birkbeck College, University of London, Michigan State University and University of Reading, respectively.

The food output effect of reducing the commercial acreage is currently being disputed. The World Bank (1991) estimates that there are about 3 million hectares of unused, or under-utilized, commercial farmland, suitable for crop production, that would be suitable for resettlement. This contention is contested by the Commercial Farmers' Union.

Whereas many of the arguments over land reform are complex, the value of marginal land in the commercial sector can be estimated quite simply. One legacy of the colonial past is that Zimbabwe has a statistical system not much different from that of the UK, which has collected agricultural statistics for the national income accounts that can be used for the estimation of production relationships. The data for the commercial sector are qualitatively not much different from the information available in European countries (indeed, better than some). These data were used for the Total Factor Productivity estimates in Thirtle *et al.*, (1993), but direct comparison of the two sectors was deliberately avoided, on the grounds that they are too dissimilar. However, by fitting production, cost, or profit functions to the two sectors separately, estimates of variables such as marginal products and shadow prices of inputs can be derived. These indicate relative factor scarcities, allowing quantification of the costs and benefits of reallocating resources between the two sectors.

THE DUAL PROFIT FUNCTION APPROACH

The profit function provides estimates of a full range of economic variables, whereas the production function and the TFP index concentrate only on the physical relationships between inputs and outputs. The commercial and communal sectors (Jayne, *et al.*, 1993) are treated as single production units to which the restricted or variable profit function (Lau 1972, 1976) is applied. Consider a multiple output technology producing $Y(y_1,...,y_m)$, with the respective expected output prices $P(p_1,...,p_m)$, using n variable inputs $X(x_1,...,x_m)$, with prices $W(w_1,...,w_m)$. Define variable expected profits as:

$$(1)\quad \pi = m\sum_{i=1}^{m} p_i y_i - \sum_{j=1}^{n} w_j x_j = P'Y - W'X$$

Normalising the profit function with respect to an output or input price has the practical advantages of ensuring that the homogeneity requirement is met and reducing the number of parameters to be estimated. The normalized expected profit function can be represented as:

$$(2)\quad \prod{}^* = \prod{}^*\left(\frac{P}{w_0},\frac{W}{w_0};Z,\Theta\right) = \frac{\pi^*(P,W;Z,\Theta)}{w_0}$$

where w_0 is the price used for normalization, P is the output price vector, W is input prices, Z is a vector of fixed inputs, Θ is the vector of 'shift' variables (such as R&D) that increase productivity over time, and '*' indicates optimized levels. The numeraire input demand can be obtained residually from Equation 2 as:

$$(3)\quad x_0^* = -\prod{}^* + P'Y^* - W'X^*$$

The functional form employed is the generalized quadratic, which is defined as:

$$(4)\quad \prod = \alpha_0 + \alpha'\hat{P} + \delta'\Theta + \frac{1}{2}\hat{P}'\beta\hat{P} + \frac{1}{2}\Theta'\Phi\Theta + \hat{P}'\gamma\Theta$$

where $\hat{P}$ is the stacked vector of normalized output and input prices, $(P,R)'$ and Θ is the stacked vector of quasi-fixed, fixed and conditioning factors $(Z,\theta)'$. The vector $\alpha\,(\alpha_1,..,\alpha_{m+n-1})$ and matrices $\beta(\beta_{ij};\ i,j=1,...,m+n-1)$, $\varnothing(\varnothing_{gh};\ g,h=1,...,K+L)$ and $\gamma(\gamma_{ig};\ i=1,...,m+n-1,\ g=1,...,k+1)$ contain the parameter coefficients to be estimated. Applying Hotelling's lemma, we derive the optimal levels of output supply and input demand:

$$(5)\quad y_i^* = \alpha_i + \sum_{j=1}^{m} \beta_{ij}p_j + \sum_{j=m+1}^{m+n-1} \beta_{ij}w_j + \sum_{g=1}^{k+1} \gamma_{ig}\Theta_g,\quad i=1,...,m$$

$$(6)\quad -x_i^* = \alpha_i + \sum_{j=1}^{m} \beta_{ij}p_j + \sum_{j=m+1}^{m+n-1} \beta_{ij}w_j + \sum_{g=1}^{k+1} \gamma_{ig}\Theta_g,\quad i=m+1,..,m+n-1$$

and the level of the numeraire input can be derived residually from Equation 2.

Denoting non-normalized or actual expected prices with a superscript 'A', the elasticities of outputs and inputs to prices for the non-numeraire cases are:

$$(7)\quad \eta_{ij} = \frac{1}{w_0}\beta_{ij}\frac{p_j^A}{y_i},\quad i,j=1,...,m$$

$$\eta_{ij} = -\frac{1}{w_0}\beta_{ij}\frac{w_j^A}{x_i},\quad i,j=m+1,...,m+n-1$$

and the price elasticities relating to the numeraire are derived from Equation (3).

Convexity of the profit function with respect to prices requires that the own-price elasticities should be positive for an output and negative for an input. The cross-price elasticities for pairs of inputs are negative for complementary inputs and positive for substitutes. For pairs of outputs, positive cross-price elasticities imply complementarity in supply and output substitutes are indicated by negative cross-products.

If the elements of Θ are treated as short-run constraints on production, we can derive the effects of relaxing the Θ variable constraints on the output and variable input levels. We can derive these effects in elasticity form by logarithmic differentiation of Equations 5 and 6 (and Equation 3 for the numeraire input) with respect to the elements of Θ:

$$\varepsilon_{ih} = -\frac{\Theta_h}{y_i}\gamma_{ih},\quad i=1,...,m;\ h=1,...,k+1$$

$$(8)\quad \varepsilon_{jh} = -\frac{\Theta_h}{x_j}\gamma_{jh},\quad j=m+1,...,m+n-1; h=1,...,k+1$$

$$\varepsilon_{og} = -(\delta_g + \sum_{j=1}^{k+1} \Phi_{gj}\Theta_j)\frac{\Theta_g}{x_0}, \quad g = 1,..,k+1$$

Shadow prices for the variables in the Θ vector can be derived as partial derivatives of the profit function (Diewert, 1974; Huffman, 1987). The derived shadow values can be interpreted equivalently as (a) the marginal change in profits for an increment in a particular element of Θ (b) as the imputed rental value for an additional unit of that factor or (c) the effects on expected profit of relaxing the particular constraint represented by each Θ variable. The shadow value equations are:

$$(9) \quad \lambda_g = \frac{\partial \pi}{\partial \Theta_g} = w_0 \frac{\partial \prod}{\partial \Theta_g} = w_0(\delta_g + \sum_{h=1}^{k+1} \Phi_{gh}\Theta_g + \sum_{i=1}^{m} \gamma_{ig}p_i + \sum_{j=m+1}^{m+n-1} \gamma_{jg}w_j$$

The shadow value of land (treated as fixed) provides the implicit value in production as opposed to the market price. The difference between the market price and shadow value indicates whether land is over, under or optimally utilized. The shadow prices of the other conditioning factors (such as R&D) can be used to assess their effectiveness.

RESULTS AND INTERPRETATION

The data are described in some detail in Thirtle *et al.* (1992). For the commercial sector the outputs are; food crops (Y1), industrial crops (Y2) and livestock and livestock products (Y3). The variable inputs are hired labour (XL), livestock inputs (XV), chemical/crop inputs (XC), and running costs (XO). The two capital inputs, farm vehicles (CAP) and Buildings (BLD) are treated as quasi-fixed. The total area of land (LAND) in the commercial sector is included as a fixed input. Other fixed, exogenous or conditioning factors included are, research and extension (RES), rainfall (RAIN), world agricultural patents (PAT) (included to catch the effects of technological spillovers).

Table 1 summarizes the short-run elasticities of supply and variable input demand with respect to prices, quasi-fixed inputs and conditioning factors at the variable means. The significant own-price supply and demand elasticities (on the diagonal) have the expected sign and are of plausible magnitudes[2]. The own-price elasticity of the industrial crop aggregate has the wrong sign, but the *t*-statistic indicates that the elasticity is not significantly different from zero. Apart from livestock-related inputs (not significant), the variable input own-price elasticities have the expected signs. All the own-price output supply and input demands are inelastic.

For the outputs, complementarity (substitutability) is indicated by a positive (negative) cross-price elasticity. Thus, industrial crops and livestock are complements and food crops are not related to industrial crops or livestock, due to the *t* values. Input complementarity (substitutability) is indicated by a negative (positive) cross-price elasticity. Thus, livestock inputs and running costs are complementary and crop inputs and running costs are substitutes. Labour, livestock inputs and crop inputs are all substitutes for one another.

If we consider the quasi-fixed, fixed and conditioning factors as constraints in production, the long-run output and variable input elasticities with respect to these factors can be regarded as the responses to relaxing these constraints. The quasi-fixed inputs are stock variables that are endogenous in the long-run, but changing their levels requires investment. Thus, in the short-run, the costs of adjusting these stock levels may be considered in terms of foregone production. The levels of the conditioning variables are assumed to be beyond the control of farmers and the costs of adjustment are not considered to be incurred by farmers. Thus, since the reported elasticities are short-run, we might predict net negative output elasticities with respect to fixed and quasi-fixed factors and positive output elasticities with respect to the conditioning factors representing technology. However, the effect on individual outputs cannot easily be predicted, as changing capital stock levels or technology levels may favour certain outputs and also affect the variable input levels, which in turn affects output.

Table 1 *Estimated Elasticities*[a]

Exp	Dependant Variable						
Var	Y1	Y2	Y3	XL	XV	XC	XO[b]
P1	**0.8**	**−0.08**	**−0.10**	−0.15	−0.44	0.36	0.33
	(4.4)	(−0.99)	(−1.2)	(−3.8)	(−4.4)	(2.92)	(1.6)
P2	**−0.19**	**−0.31**	**0.47**	0.33	0.68	−0.29	0.37
	(−0.98)	(−1.6)	(2.8)	(4.1)	(3.6)	(−1.8)	(0.73)
P3	**−0.14**	**0.28**	**0.83**	−0.44	−0.21	−0.53	0.49
	(−1.2)	(2.8)	(3.4)	(−3.9)	(−0.74)	(−3.9)	(1.5)
WL	−0.24	0.22	−0.5	**−0.11**	**0.33**	**0.27**	**0.06**
	(−3.8)	(4.1)	(−3.9)	(−1.4)	(1.95)	(2.97)	(0.34)
WV	−0.34	0.22	0.11	**0.16**	**0.33**	**0.3**	**−0.84**
	(−4.4)	(3.6)	(0.74)	(1.95)	(0.97)	(2.76)	(−3.2)
WC	0.34	−0.11	−0.35	**0.16**	**0.36**	**−0.4**	**0.32**
	(2.9)	(−1.8)	(−3.9)	(2.97)	(2.76)	(−3.8)	(1.9)
WO	−0.32	−0.15	−0.34	**0.04**	**−1.1**	**0.33**	**−0.84**
	(−1.6)	(−0.73)	(−1.5)	(0.34)	(−3.2)	(1.9)	(−1.2)
CAP	**−1.29**	**0.33**	**1.4**	**0.34**	**2.1**	**−0.46**	**11.9**
	(−1.8)	(0.78)	(3.6)	(1.8)	(4.5)	(−0.9)	(3.4)
BLD	**−0.14**	**−0.69**	**−1.88**	**0.07**	**−0.74**	**0.99**	**−6.2**
	(−0.2)	(−1.8)	(−4.4)	(0.37)	(−1.54)	(2.0)	(−3.4)
LAND	**−0.24**	**−0.54**	**1.0**	**1.1**	**0.6**	**0.14**	**4.7**
	(−0.49)	(−2.0)	(3.4)	(7.8)	(1.7)	(0.4)	(3.1)
RES	**0.9**	**−0.12**	**−0.16**	**−0.04**	**0.5**	**0.96**	**−1.6**
	(2.1)	(−0.5)	(−0.64)	(−0.39)	(1.8)	(3.2)	(−1.2)
PAT	**0.58**	**−0.07**	**−0.24**	**−0.27**	**0.06**	**0.48**	**−2.7**
	(1.7)	(−0.4)	(−1.4)	(−3.4)	(0.3)	(2.1)	(−2.2)

Notes: [a] *t*-values are in parentheses; the critical value is taken to be 2.26.
[b] *t*-values are not computed for numeraire input elasticities as the numeraire input and the derived elasticities are gained residually from Equation (6).

The food crop output elasticities follow the predicted pattern; with respect to machinery, building stock and land the elasticities are negative (but insignificant), and positive with respect to research and international technology spillovers. All the elasticities for the industrial crops are insignificant and for livestock, machinery and land appear to increase output, even in the short-run.

The effects of changes in the fixed inputs and technology variables on the variable inputs are mostly insignificant, but increasing machinery increases livestock inputs and running costs. Increasing buildings reduces running costs and increasing land raises both labour inputs and running costs. For the technology variables, R&D increases crop inputs (which is reasonable, since improved varieties use more fertilizer and pesticide), but technology spillovers reduce both labour inputs and running costs. This is entirely sensible, since the majority of patents are for machinery.

SHADOW PRICES

The shadow prices for the quasi-fixed, fixed and conditioning factors provide measures of the implicit value in production of additional units of the factors. In equilibrium, the shadow price of a quasi-fixed factor should equal its opportunity cost, or rental value. Excess capacity or under-utilization of a quasi-fixed input would be indicated by an estimated shadow price less than the opportunity cost. Similarly, under investment is indicated by a shadow value greater than the opportunity cost, indicating that revenue can potentially be increased by increasing the stock of the quasi-fixed factor until the shadow price equals the opportunity cost (Berndt and Fuss, 1986; Morrison, 1986).

The economic reasoning behind these propositions is sound enough, but does not take good account of economies with persistent high inflation and negative interest rates. In such circumstances, the opportunity cost of capital investment is negative, but rental rates are not. For Zimbabwe, the opportunity cost is taken to be the real return on bank deposits: the rate has been negative since 1976. For long-term investments, such as 25–year government stock, the average real rate of interest has been negative since the mid-1980s.

This implies that a rational farmer should invest in capital up to the point where the return is negative. The Zimbabwe case is further complicated by rationing and allocation of farm machinery, which would suggest that the supply is inadequate (at these prices). These factors should be taken into account in interpreting Table 2, which reports the mean values of the estimated shadow prices of capital, buildings, land and the technology variables. As the capital stocks are derived as aggregate values divided by capital price *indexes*, there are no appropriate and observable corresponding market rental prices. The appropriate opportunity cost of machinery capital is assumed to be proportionate to and the same sign as the real rate of return on bank deposits (Bouchet, 1987) and similarly, we expect the opportunity cost of buildings to be proportionate to and the same sign as the real rate of interest on 25–year stock.

There is no simple way to interpret the results. The estimated shadow price of capital was negative throughout the period, but was increasingly negative post-independence. This is wholey consistent with the increasingly negative real interest rate, post-1976. With no further information this should be taken to mean over-investment in machinery in the early part of the period. The annual series cannot be reported here, but the opportunity cost criterion shows over-capitalization up to 1976. This is not surprising, since sanctions were in force until independence and since then the shortage of foreign exchange has limited imports. From the employment viewpoint, the 'shortage' of machinery is a positive factor, as an increasingly negative opportunity cost of capital implies that machinery should have been further substituted for labour. The employment consequences of getting prices wrong to this extent are shown in Thirtle *et al.*, (1993b), for South African agriculture.

For buildings, the results are not significant, but if they were, the shadow price is positive up to 1981 and negative thereafter and is thus consistent with the real returns on long term financial investments. The shadow price of land is negative and highly significant. A negative shadow price for land implies that land area is not an effective constraint to production in the commercial sector. The shadow values become even more negative over the period, even after the policy of land redistribution from the commercial sector to the communal areas. Possible reasons for this include the adoption of new chemical and biological technologies that effectively substitute for land. This is supported with respect to the food crop and industrial crop outputs by the negative elasticities of these outputs with respect to land area. It is also possible that the land redistribution has only removed under-utilized or low quality land from the commercial sector. Even after about 15 percent of the commercial land has been purchased for resettlement, land still does not represent an effective constraint to production.

Table 2 *Shadow Prices of Fixed Inputs and Conditioning Factors*

SP of CAP	OC of CAP	SP of BLD	OC of BLD	SP of LAND	SP of R&D	SP of PAT
–0.82	–2.27	0.0105	1.02	–72.4	1.5	108.8
(–8.44)		(0.13)		(–8.2)	(0.74)	(4.2)

Note: *t*-values in parentheses.

Lastly, the shadow price of patents is positive and significant, indicating that international spillovers are important. This cannot be easily quantified because the series is the number of patents registered, which has no obvious connotations, in terms of financial magnitudes. However, R&D, which has an insignificant shadow price, was significant for food crops (Table 1), and for this a rate of return can be estimated (Stranaham and Stonkwiler, 1986). Assuming a lag of five years we derive an estimated internal rate of return to public sector research of 36 percent.

Thirtle *et al.*, (1993) derived an IRR of 43 percent using the same approach, in a primal translog production function model. However, no account was taken of international spillovers in that model, implying that some upward bias existed in the estimated IRR due to the omission of international spillovers.

CONCLUSIONS

The model suggests that the World Bank is correct, in that the marginal value product of land is negative, meaning that there is under-utilization. However, negative values of capital assets are common when real interest rates are negative, so the result should be treated with some caution. The extent of the distortions of macroeconomic variables, such as the interest rate, must have a considerable effect on the efficiency of resource allocation in the agricultural sector. The combination of the over-valued exchange rate and negative real interest rates would lead to undue substitution of capital for labour. With unemployment estimated at about one million, minimising employment in agriculture makes no sense at all, and has only been restricted by the shortage of foreign exchange.

NOTES

[1] The authors would like to thank USAID for generous financial support for part of this work.
[2] The elasticities that are meaningful are in bold print; the others are not discussed.

REFERENCES

Berndt, E. R. and M. A. Fuss, 1986, 'Productivity Measurement with Adjustments for Variations in Capacity Utilization and Other Forms of Temporary Equilibrium', *Journal of Econometrics,* Vol. 33, pp.7–29.

Bouchet, F. C., 1987, 'An Analysis of the Sources of Productivity Growth in French Agriculture', *1960-1984*, Unpublished Ph.D. Thesis, Virginia Polytechnic Institute and State University, Blacksburg, Virginia.

Bratton, M., 1991, 'Ten Years After: Land Redistribution in Zimbabwe, 1980-90', in Prosterman, Temple and Hanstad (eds.), *Agrarian Reform and Grassroots Development: Ten Case Studies*, Curry Foundation.

Christensen, G. and Stack, J., 1992, *The Dimensions of Household Food Insecurity in Zimbabwe, 1980-91*, Working Paper No.5, Food Studies Group, Oxford, England.

Diewert, W. E., 1974, 'Applications of Duality Theory', in Intriligator, M.D. (ed.) *Frontiers of Quantitative Economics*, Volume 2, and Kendrick D.A., North-Holland Publishing Company, Amsterdam.

Jayne, T., Khatri, Y. and Thirtle, C., 1993, *Determinants of Productivity Change in Zimbabwean Agriculture: Implications for Research and Policy*, University of Reading.

Lau, L. J., 1972, 'Profit Functions of Technologies with Multiple Inputs and Outputs', *Review of Economics and Statistics*, Vol. 54, No. 1, pp.281–289.

Lau, L.J., 1976, 'A Characterisation of the Normalised Restricted Profit Function', *Journal of Economic Theory*, Vol. 12, No. 1, pp.131–163.

Morrison, C. J., 1985, 'On the Economic Interpretation and Measurement of Optimal Capacity Utilisation with Anticipatory Expectations', *Review of Economic Studies*, Vol. 52, No. 2, pp. 295–310.

Stranaham, H.A. and Stonkwiler, J.S., 1986, 'Evaluating the Returns to Post Harvest Research in the Florida Citrus-Processing Subsector', *American Journal of Agricultural Economics*, Vol. 68, No.1, pp.88–94.

Thirtle, C., Atkins, J., Bottomley, P., Gonese, N. and Govereh, J., 1993, 'The Efficiency of the Commercial Agricultural Sector in Zimbabwe, 1970–89', *Hull Papers in Developing Area Studies*, No.6.

Thirtle, C., Atkins, J., Bottomley, P., Gonese, N., Govereh, J. and Khatri,Y., 1993, 'Agricultural Productivity in Zimbabwe', 1970-89, *Economic Journal*, Vol. 103, No. 417, pp.474–480.

Thirtle, C., Sartorius von Bach, H. and van Zyl, J., 1993, 'Total Factor Productivity in South African Agriculture, 1947-91', *Development Southern Africa*, Vol. 10, No. 3, pp.301–18.

van Zyl, J., van Rooyen, C.J., Kirsten, J. and van Schalkwyk, H., 1993, 'Land Reform in South Africa: Options to Consider for the Future', Paper presented at the ESRC Development Economics Study Group, London.

World Bank, 1991, *Country Report, Zimbabwe*, Washington, D.C.

DISCUSSION OPENING — Mamou K. Ehui *(United Nations Econonomic Commission For Africa)*

The paper written by Dr Khatri *et al.*, is an important and interesting piece of work, both conceptually and empirically. It is interesting conceptually because the application of duality theory to the agriculture sector has become very popular recently. This is due to many of its advantages in terms of flexibility in the specification of factor demand and output equations use for policy analysis, and mainly because duality permits a very close relationship between economic theory and practice. Empirically the paper is an important piece of work because it raises the very important concern of Zimbabwean policymakers; that of land redistribution and its eventual consequences on the food security situation. The paper thus provides both a theoretical and an empirical contribution to the understanding of implications of land reforms. I read the paper with respect and I must congratulate the authors on their success in obtaining fairly satisfactory results that are consistent with a priori expectations and findings of the World Bank. However, since the paper treats an important policy issue and involves many explanatory variables, its results also lead to several conflicting and unanswered questions.

To open the discussion, I want to raise a series of questions which hopefully will help us to reconsider their conclusions or reanalyse the study. Starting with the data, I would like to know more about the type of data, the quality and how it has been analyzed. I can understand that space limitations did not allow presentation of some details. But, for this type of analysis, aggregation problems must be expected. How are variables like capital and buildings measured? Improper measurements can lead to inconsistency of the coefficients. I consider these issues to be an important because elasticity estimates are usually very sensitive to data construction.

The second point that is worth raising is linked to the model specification and the regression technique used. There are some dynamic issues that should have been modelled explicitly. For example, the effects of R&D or the generation of new technologies on hired labour and prices must be questioned, especially the long run effects. Changes in fixed variables such as vehicles and buildings are likely to be driven by both productivity and price indices. My suggestion is that the profit function and the demand and supply fuctions could have been estimated simultaneously.

The third point that I would like to raise is related to the interpretation of the results. It seems to me that the authors have derived theory and the empirical evidence from the model. It should have been the other way around. For example, it is said that industrial crops and livestock are complements and food crops are not related to industrial crops or livestock due to *t*-values. The authors went even further by indicating that input complementarity is indicated by the negative cross price elasticity. Thus livestock inputs and running costs are complementary and crop inputs and running costs are substitutes. And all these are based on the significance of t values. These conclusions could be true, but I would like the author to consider the following questions. What if the model is mispecified? What if the data are not reliable? What if we have opposite signs, would the conclusion be the same? I think it could have been better to compare the results with real life situations. I leave this to people who know Zimbabwe very well to testify. The authors could have gone further by asking what would have happened to the shadow price of land if all government subsidies were removed? Would communal land owners be able to exploit unutilized land at its optimal capacity?

The question of food security does not seem to be addressed. Does the expected ouptut increase from land reform contribute to acheiving greater food security? As you know, food security is not only a matter of increasing production, but also of improving support services such as credit, infrastructure and policies so that less fortunate people can have access to minimun requirements. The issue is of capital importance because food security problem is likely to be more acute for communal land users to whom unutilized land is being redistributed. Perhaps in this case, and given that implications for food security issue have been raised, the duality problem should account for both price as well as non price factors.

In my opinion, the questions that I have raised have important implications both for the model and the conclusion. I leave these open for discussion.

GENERAL DISCUSSION — Terrence S. Veeman, Rapporteur *(University of Alberta, Canada)*

All the papers in this session, as the Chair, H. Behrmann (South Africa) noted, dealt with land issues: land rental markets in sub-Saharan Africa where land was scarce but underutilized; impacts of property rights, market access and food transfers on the technical efficiency of small scale farms in north-east Argentina where land is plentiful; and efficiency aspects of land reform in Zimbabwe where land is currently very inequitably distributed and large-scale commercial farming by a tiny racial minority occurs on the nation's best land.

It was suggested that the initial presentation on land rental market in sub-Saharan Africa used the tools of the transactions cost approach to arrive at its conclusions, rather than denying that approach to the analysis of land tenure and institutional change. It was also queried whether the policy recommendations, while sensible, arose tightly out of the analytical framework. Debate also ensued on whether widows on customary land could retain use rights and utilize land rental as a vehicle for cash flow on whether use rights and rental income would revert back to the headman. In any event, it was concluded that an evolutionary shift to more exclusive and assured property rights in land would foster a more active land rental market in the region.

The paper on Argentina, ably presented by H. Pagoulotos in the absence of the authors, focussed on small scale farming, largely by squatters, in a slash-and-burn type of cultivation. The main concern of the audience, echoed by the discussant, was that such shifting cultivation was unlikely to be sustainable in the long run. The short-run static conclusion that property rights were not a significant institutional influence on technical efficiency of these small scale farms was very unlikely to hold in a dynamic and long-run setting. It was noted, however, that the paper involved interesting econometric techiques for isolating the influence of institutional factors such as ownership and food transfers on technical inefficiency.

The most lively audience reaction was to the paper on land reform in Zimbabwe, the host country. There can be no denying the equity rationale for land reform in Zimbabwe. What is less clear is the efficiency impact of land reform and whether (and to what extent) land held by the commercial farming elite is under-utilized, as alleged by the World Bank. There were varying critiques of the profit function (duality) approach used by the authors, including the lack of attention to institutional detail (such as the inability to sub-divide land) historic input market distortions, concerns about unreliable data, the lack of consideration of risk and dynamic features, and the general applicability of such sophisticated models to the conditions of less developed countries. The author, in trying to use the duality approach to estimate the shadow prices of factors including land, cautioned that the finding of a negative shadow price for land did not necessarily imply the underutilization of land but might have resulted from the very adverse macro-economic conditions which had often prevailed during the time period in southern Africa.

Taking part in the discussion were M. Hubbard (UK), G. Rozell (Malawi), F. Mucavele (Mozambique), R. Johnson (New Zealand), S. Dittoh (Ghana), O. Mbatia (Kenya), K. Muir-Leresche (Zimbabwe), H. Walker (Zimbabwe), S. Ehui (Côte d'Ivoire), C. Mataya (Malawi) and M. Lyne (South Africa).

GODFREY J. TYLER*

Macro-Economic Policy, Export Competitiveness and Poverty in Kenya: A General Equilibrium Analysis

Abstract: A Computable General Equilibrium model based on a Social Accounting Matrix for Kenya is used to simulate the effects of a 10 percent devaluation combined with a more progressive tax regime and elimination of indirect industrial taxes. For each policy simulation two specifications for the labour markets are adopted, the first assuming abundant supplies of labour at given nominal wages and the second assuming fixed supplies so that wages are determined endogenously. These crucially affect the results. The poor are better off under both scenarios; but only under the first (preferred) assumption does the policy also result in a large boost to GDP, to exports, particularly agricultural exports and to a dramatic improvement in the balance of payments, while maintaining real investment and essential government expenditure.

INTRODUCTION

Compared to most other sub-Saharan African countries, Kenya has been a success story. However, it has suffered from a number of problems, many of which have become accentuated in recent years. Chief among these is the deterioration of its balance of payments situation, with rising external debt. Moreover, its relatively fast real economic growth has only been able to keep 1–1.5 percentage points above the rate of growth of population. Hence, combined with the unequal distribution of wealth and income, there has been continuing poverty. There has been considerable debate about the extent to which some of the problems have been self-inflicted, see for example Killick (1981). However, there is little doubt that the decline in Kenya's terms of trade since the mid-1970s has been almost entirely outside its control. The extent to which the slower growth of the volume of exports compared to that of imports is an entirely external problem is more debatable.

The view taken here of Kenya's problems is one very much in line with that expressed by Killick (1985). He sees one of the main questions as being how to solve the balance of payments problem without accentuating poverty and without reducing Government basic needs provision to the poorest. He believes that improved agricultural performance should help both the balance of payments and poverty alleviation. Structural changes, brought about partly by maintaining a competitive real exchange rate, should be backed up by fiscal and monetary restraint, while protecting real investment. This implies reduction in overall consumption but he argues for progressive taxation (see also World Bank 1983) to ensure that reduction in expenditure, especially government expenditure on social services, does not hurt the poor. Whether or not there has to be an actual reduction in consumption (private and/or government) is, in our view, a moot point. There is no doubt that to solve a balance of payments problem there has to be a reduction in domestic absorption for a given level of national income, but it may be possible to increase both the level of output and the excess of exports over imports, so that domestic absorption is maintained or even enhanced.

* Oxford University, UK.

We are not in a position to comment on the degree of fiscal and/or monetary restraint needed. It is, of course, the usual IMF message for most LDC governments facing deficits on external and internal accounts, inflation or debt problems. The message was echoed recently for Kenya by Julin and Levin (1992) who believe that excessive increases in government expenditure have fuelled inflation, such that the 1990 depreciation in the nominal exchange rate has not resulted in the required real devaluation. In connection with the latter, Bigsten (1990) believes there is a need for a further lowering of the exchange rate, with top priority being given to export promotion, the foreign exchange situation still being a constraint on growth.

In a previous paper (Tyler and Akinboade, 1992), simulation of a 10 percent devaluation on the Kenyan economy was shown to be, in general, a very successful policy, particularly in a situation of unemployed or underemployed labour resources. However, the policy resulted in a small reduction in real investment. In this paper, we explore through simulation the implications of combining a devaluation with other policy measures. The first measure considered is the elimination of indirect taxes on industrial commodities. This is expected to lower the price of industrial commodities needed for capital investment and hence allow the maintenance of the same level of real investment with a smaller monetary outlay, and also through the reduction of price distortions is expected to have a beneficial effect throughout the economy. However, the resulting reduction in government tax revenue needs to be redressed and this is done by introducing a more progressive direct tax structure. No serious study of Kenya's tax structure has been carried out recently but, in view of the known inequitable distribution of primary incomes, it is difficult not to conclude that further progressive moves would be feasible. They may, of course, not be politically acceptable at the present time.

THE MODEL AND DATA

The model used is a computable general equilibrium (CGE) model based on a social accounting matrix (SAM) for the Kenyan economy. Such models are now widely accepted as being particularly appropriate for the analysis of the impact of macro-policy changes on the whole economy and on the distribution of income at the household level (Demery and Addison, 1987; Helleiner, 1987). It is, like most models applied to the problems of developing countries, concerned purely with the 'real' side of the economy. It is not designed to take account of the monetary side, such as the money supply, domestic credit, interest rates, foreign currency reserves, etc. A description of the model and the results of some previous policy simulations appear in Tyler and Akinboade (1992). The approach is based on that of Drud, Grais and Pyatt (1985).

In essence the CGE model consists of a large set of structural equations (linear and non-linear) linking productive activities, factor markets, households, government and the rest of the world — with production, employment, consumption, savings, trade and market prices being, in general, endogenously determined. As it is based on a SAM the accounting framework ensures internal consistency. Thus the usual national accounting identities hold. There are three production activities, agriculture, manufacturing industry and services. The primary inputs of labour of various categories, capital stock and 'operating surplus' combine in a constant-returns-to-scale Cobb–Douglas production function to produce value added. The latter is combined with purchased intermediate inputs in fixed Leontief fashion to produce gross output, at producer prices. Imports are assumed to be available in perfectly elastic supply at fixed world prices. However, the demand for Kenya's exports is assumed to depend on the price of these relative to the world market price of comparable goods, with elasticities of demand of 3.0, 1.5 and 1.0 for agriculture, industry and services, respectively. Income accruing to the various household groups from ownership of factors (labour, capital, etc.) is assumed to be allocated to consumption, savings, remittance transfers and direct taxes in fixed value shares. Total consumption expenditure is then allocated to commodities in fixed proportions in quantity terms. Similarly, government income, mainly from direct and indirect taxation, is allocated to transfers to households, to consumption expenditure and to savings in fixed value shares, the shares taken from the original SAM. The government is assumed in the present model not to have any control over this allocation and therefore not able to run a current budget deficit. However, it can change rates of direct and indirect taxation. It is important to note that, as there is no separate item for government investment in this model, government savings represent the budget surplus over current expenditure only. Total savings in the economy, by government, households, companies and from foreign capital inflow, are distributed to investment in the three sectors in fixed value shares. Capital inflow or foreign savings is specified as a residual. It meets the gap between total savings and total investment. By definition it is identically equal to the current account deficit.

The SAM refers to the year 1976, which is still the most recent data set. Study of more recent partial data suggest that the general pattern of the results and the magnitude and direction of change indicated from the simulations using the 1976 data still have relevance for policy choice in present-day Kenya.

For example, comparing the most recent figures, for 1988 to 1990, (World Bank, 1991) with 1976, and expressed as a percentage of GDP at market prices, private consumption has only decreased from 62 percent to 61 percent, government consumption has increased from 17 percent to 19 percent and domestic savings have decreased marginally from 21 percent to 20 percent. Net indirect taxes have increased from 12 percent to 14 percent. In 1976 the government had a small current budget surplus; in 1988 there was a small current deficit, after a number of years of large deficits. Taking into account government capital expenditure there were overall deficits in all years, being 5.8 percent in 1976 and 4.2 percent in 1988.

Population has, of course, grown dramatically, being estimated at 14.3 million in 1976 and 23.3 million in 1989. There have also been structural changes, with agriculture's share of GDP decreasing from approximately 40 percent to 30 percent and a concomitant increase in services' share from 40 percent to 50 percent. Industry's share has remained roughly constant at 20 percent. Employment in manufacturing industry has increased by about 60 percent, roughly in line with the increase in the overall labour force. At the same time real earnings have decreased by about 25 percent. The major difference has been in the external balance. The current account deficit (before official transfers) was about 4.6 percent of GDP in 1976. Since then it has fluctuated widely; disappearing in 1977, reaching nearly 14 percent in 1978 and 1980, dipping to 2.6 percent in 1986 and reaching 10.5 percent in 1989. External debt has grown, from being about one-and-a-half times export earnings in 1976 to about five times in 1989.

RESULTS OF POLICY SIMULATIONS

As previously stated the three policy simulations reported here are: (a) elimination of domestic indirect taxes in the industrial sector, (b) the elimination of these taxes combined with increased rates of direct taxation on middle-income and rich households and (c) the foregoing policy changes combined with a 10 per cent devaluation.

The results are presented in Table 1. A selection only of the important indicators are reported. The first column contains the actual levels of the variables in millions of Kenyan pounds in the base year. All prices (including wages) are taken as unity in the base year solution, hence the physical quantity of production, consumption, employment, etc. are represented in money terms. The remaining columns of the Table present the results of the policy experiments, as percentage changes from the base solution, in two blocks. Block A assumes an unlimited supply of labour in all categories at constant wages. Employment of each category of labour is thus determined endogenously by the demand for such labour. Block B assumes fixed total supplies of each category, so that wages are determined endogenously by demand in a situation of full employment.

As previously intimated a major concern is the impact of macro-policy changes on the real incomes of the poor. Hence the table includes employment and wages of urban unskilled and skilled labour and of rural self-employed labour, these being major sources of income for the urban and rural poor. To give an indication of the changes in income distribution, the real consumption of the middle-income households is also given. To save space, that of upper-income households is excluded; changes in their consumption are however very similar.

Elimination of Industrial Taxes

The elimination of domestic indirect taxes in the industrial sector has a number of far-reaching consequences. As would be expected, industrial market prices decrease, by 13–15 percent. As industrial commodities are intermediate inputs in all sectors, particularly agriculture and industry itself, costs of production are greatly reduced, providing a boost throughout the economy. Under assumption A, production in industry increases by 12 percent and in agriculture by 8 percent. Overall GDP in real terms increases by 6 percent. Under assumption B production is to a large extent constrained by the fixed supplies of labour. Hence, though industrial production increases by as much as 8 percent, production increase in agriculture is only 2 percent. GDP in money terms increases by the same amount as before (6.5 percent) but this is translated into an increase in real GDP of only 1.8 percent.

Under assumption A there is a 4 percent increase in exports, mainly of industrial origin, because of the increased competitiveness of Kenyan supplies, both producer and export prices falling by up to 5 percent. Export revenue, however, decreases somewhat, so that there is a slight deterioration in the current account balance. Under assumption B the trade situation hardly changes; the competitiveness of Kenyan exports is eroded by increases in the cost of primary inputs, especially wages.

The elimination of industrial taxes reduces government revenue from indirect taxes by 50 percent. This is only partly recompensed by an increase of 6 percent in direct taxes, from the general rise in incomes. Hence government expenditure is drastically reduced in monetary and real terms, by 17–20 percent. Government savings likewise suffer, so that

Table 1 *Policy Simulations*

		Percentage change from base solution					
		A[a]			B[a]		
	Base solution (K£m)	Eliminate industrial taxes (1)	(1) plus increased direct taxes (2)	(2) plus 10% devaluation (3)	Eliminate industrial taxes (1)	(1) plus increased direct taxes (2)	(2) plus 10% devaluation (3)
GDP at constant factor cost	1296.1	6.1	5.1	16.1	1.8	1.5	4.1
GDP deflator price index	-	0.5	0.4	1.1	4.7	4.4	12.3
Exports at constant prices[b]	478.1	4.4	4.6	20.9	-2.2	–0.8	2.8
Imports at constant prices[b]	461.6	1.4	0.4	3.3	0.4	–0.7	–0.1
Current account deficit	51.9	17.3	–1.6	–39.7	36.8	11.7	11.6
Direct taxes, etc.	196.7	5.9	32.6	47.4	5.8	33.0	46.6
Net indirect taxes	181.9	–50.3	–49.6	–42.6	–50.7	–51.1	–45.6
Government real expenditure[c]	215.2	–17.1	–3.7	5.9	–20.5	–7.5	–5.7
Domestic savings	242.3	–5.6	–1.7	9.9	–6.0	–1.7	8.5
Total real investment	294.2	2.1	1.7	–0.2	3.0	2.1	1.6
Urban unskilled							
employment	65.0	5.4	6.0	14.9	-	-	-
wages	-	-	-	-	6.4	7.7	18.0
Urban skilled							
employment	162.2	5.2	5.7	14.8	-	-	-
wages	-	-	-	-	6.2	7.4	17.8
Rural self-employment	334.3	7.2	4.9	18.9	-	-	-
wages (implicit)	-	-	-	-	6.2	4.2	15.6
Household real consumption							
Urban poor	89.2	9.9	11.8	19.3	7.0	9.3	11.1

Table 1 (continued) *Policy Simulations*

		Percentage change from base solution					
		A[a]			B[a]		
	Base solution (K£m)	Eliminate industrial taxes (1)	(1) plus increased direct taxes (2)	(2) plus 10% devaluation (3)	Eliminate industrial taxes (1)	(1) plus increased direct taxes (2)	(2) plus 10% devaluation (3)
Urban middle income	139.1	12.1	8.8	15.3	9.4	6.8	8.3
Rural very poor	42.2	12.6	11.1	21.3	8.5	8.1	10.2
Rural poor	62.3	12.2	10.4	21.0	8.0	7.2	9.6
Rural middle income	285.3	12.4	–0.2	9.4	8.2	–3.0	–0.8
Agricultural production	513.9	8.3	4.6	20.3	2.2	0.2	3.6
Agricultural producer prices	-	–0.1	–0.3	0.7	3.8	2.2	10.2
Industrial production	599.8	12.4	10.9	21.4	8.0	7.0	9.8
Industrial producer prices	-	–5.6	–5.7	–3.0	–2.7	–2.9	4.4
Service production	1114.5	2.7	3.9	11.4	–0.4	0.8	2.4
Service producer prices	-	–3.7	–3.7	–2.0	0	0.4	8.7
Agricultural market prices	-	–0.1	–0.3	1.0	3.6	2.1	10.2
Industrial market prices	-	–14.8	–14.9	–10.3	–13.1	–13.2	–6.0
Service market prices	-	–3.5	–3.4	–1.3	0	0.4	8.8

Notes: [a] Simulations A assume unlimited supplies of labour; Simulations B assume fixed supplies of labour.
[b] Excludes net factor payments and transfers.
[c] Excludes transfers to other institution.

though household savings increase in line with increased incomes, overall domestic savings decline by about 6 percent. This is not translated into decreased real investment, however, because capital goods, to a significant extent of domestic industrial origin, are now much cheaper. There is, in fact, a small rise in real investment of 2–3 percent.

Turning now to the impact on the poor, the effect of this policy change is favourable. Either employment or wages of workers in the relevant categories increase by between 5 and 7 percent. Combined with the overall decrease in consumer prices, the poor enjoy increases in real consumption of 10–12 percent under assumption A and 7–8 percent under assumption B. However, they suffer to an unknown extent from reduced overall government expenditure, some of which will inevitably entail cuts in health, education and other social expenditure.

Elimination of Industrial Taxes Plus Increased Direct Taxes

This policy experiment is designed to restore the state of government finances, while still benefitting from the removal of the distortionary effects of high indirect taxation. This is brought about by an increase in the direct tax incidence (including social security payments) for middle and upper-income households in both urban and rural areas. Specifically, the rates are increased as follows:

	Middle	Upper
Urban	From 9.7 to 14.6%	From 15.2 to 22.8%
Rural	1.2 to 12%	From 1.8 to 18%

Direct tax revenue now rises by a third compared to the base solution. With indirect taxes largely unaffected total government revenue rises dramatically, so that real government expenditure now only falls short of its original levels by between 4 and 7 percent. There is a slight dampening effect on real GDP and production increases are somewhat less. This is almost entirely due to lower domestic demand (exports remaining largely unaffected) from middle and upper income households. The impact of increased direct taxes is reduced real consumption of both these groups; however only in the case of rural households does their real consumption fall below that in the base solution (0.2 percent under assumption A and 3 percent under B).

With enhanced government income, government savings also rise, effectively making up for the drop in private savings from middle income and rich households, so that domestic savings are virtually restored to their original level. Total real investment remains unaffected. The balance of payments position is also hardly affected.

As regards the poor, their real income position remains largely unaffected by the change in taxation. Employment or wage increases are very similar to those in the first experiment. As retail price reductions are virtually identical, real consumption is also very similar.

Indirect and Direct Tax Changes Plus Devaluation

As previously intimated, the objective of this policy experiment was to combine the benefits of the cost-reducing effects of the previous experiments with the export-enhancing effects of a devaluation, so that the current account deficit could be reduced or eliminated, whilst maintaining real investment and government expenditure. Under assumption A this objective is successfully realized. With the 10 percent devaluation, virtually unchanged domestic currency prices translate into lower foreign exchange prices so that demand for Kenyan exports rises. Overall, exports at constant prices increase by 21 percent, with agricultural exports rising by 30 percent. With only a small increase in imports, the balance of payments dramatically improves, with a 40 percent reduction in the current account deficit. Overall GDP at constant prices increases by 16 percent, with hardly any inflationary effect. Because of the boost to incomes there is a large increase in revenue from direct taxes, so that government revenue now surpasses its level in the base solution. Real government expenditure therefore, helped by lower service sector prices, is now 6 percent above its original level.

A problem experienced in our earlier work with devaluation as the sole policy instrument was that of lower foreign savings consequent on an improved current account and hence, in spite of increased domestic savings, increased capital good prices led to a reduction in total real investment. Combined with the other policy instruments, however, domestic savings rise by 10 percent, total savings by 1 percent and real investment remains virtually constant.

Allied to the massive increase in production, employment rises by 15–19 percent over the base solution. This feeds through to increases of 19–21 percent in the real consumption of the poor. Even the middle and upper income households now enjoy greatly increased standards of living, with real consumption of those in urban areas up by 15 percent and those in rural areas up by 9 percent on the base solution.

Under assumption B, the effects of devaluation are much less satisfactory. It has a largely inflationary impact on the economy and real GDP is only 4 percent above the base solution. Producer and export prices now are higher than in the base solution, so that the competitive edge gained by Kenyan exports by the previous policy changes is lost. Exports and imports at constant prices hardly change, so that with increased costs of imports in domestic currency the current account deficit is slightly worse than the base solution. Government taxation revenue is about the same as under assumption A but with increased service sector costs real government expenditure is now down by 6 percent.

Wages, instead of employment, rise in scenario B, by as much as 18 percent for the urban unskilled. However, retail prices of agricultural and service sector goods are now 9–10 percent higher than in the base solution, with only industrial goods prices still benefitting to some extent from the earlier elimination of indirect taxes. Thus real consumption of the poor rises by much less than their money incomes, but it is still 10–11 percent higher than in the base solution. The only losers even in this scenario are the rural middle (and upper) income households, who suffer a minuscule 0.8 percent reduction in real consumption.

CONCLUSIONS

It is probably true to say that for countries relying very much on agricultural exports for their foreign exchange earnings and their industry dependent to a large degree on imported capital and intermediate goods, there are many external factors outside their control. Nevertheless, there are clearly a number of policy actions which governments of such countries can still take, depending on the particular situations facing them.

The results of the policy simulations indicate that elimination of indirect industrial taxes and a shift to a more progressive direct tax structure, combined with a 10 percent devaluation could be beneficial for the Kenyan economy and for poverty alleviation. Under the preferred assumption of abundant supplies of labour (Godfrey 1987), real GDP increases by 16 percent, overall exports by 21 percent (agricultural exports by 30 percent), the current account deficit shrinks by 40 percent, real government expenditure increases by 6 percent, real investment remains constant, employment grows by between 15 and 19 percent and, most importantly, the real consumption of poorer households is raised by between 19 and 21 percent.

The simplifying assumptions (for example those about competitive product and factor markets) necessary in a model of this type and its aggregative nature must be borne in mind. Nevertheless, the findings from the policy simulations, particularly on devaluation, are generally in line with the conclusions of several other studies eg. Balassa (1990), Bird (1983), Gulhati *et al.* (1986), Heller *et al.* (1988) and Killick (1984). It is therefore believed that the general pattern of the results has important implications for policy choice in Kenya. It suggests that with appropriate macro-economic policy actions there may be no conflict between improvements in the balance of payments position and the alleviation of poverty.

REFERENCES

Balassa, B., 1990, 'Incentive Policies and Export Performance in Sub-Saharan Africa', *World Development*, Vol. 18, No. 3, pp.383–91.

Bigsten, A., 1990, *Kenya*, Macroeconomic Studies, No.10, Swedish International Development Authority, Stockholm.

Bird, G., 1983, 'Should Developing Countries Use Currency Depreciation as a Tool of Balance of Payments Adjustment? A Review of the Theory and Evidence, and a Guide for the Policy Maker', *Journal of Development Studies*, Vol. 19, No. 4, pp.461–84.

Demery, L. and Addison, T., 1987, 'Stabilization Policy and Income Distribution in Developing Countries', *World Development*, Vol. 15, No. 12, pp.1483–98.

Drud, A., Grais, W. and Pyatt, G., 1985, *An Approach to Macroeconomic Model Building Based on Social Accounting Principles*, Discussion Paper Report No. DRD 150, Development Research Department, World Bank, Washington, D.C.

Godfrey, M., 1987, 'Stabilization and Structural Adjustment of the Kenyan Economy, 1975-85: An Assessment of Performance', *Development and Change*, Vol. 18, No.4, pp.595–624.

Gulhati, R. *et al.*, 1986, 'Exchange Rate Policies in Africa: How Valid is the Scepticism?', *Development and Change*, Vol. 12, No. 3, pp. 399-424.

Helleiner, G.K., 1987, 'Stabilization, Adjustment and the Poor', *World Development*, Vol. 15, No. 12, pp.1499-1513.

Heller, P.S., *et al.*, 1988, *The Implications of Fund-Supported Adjustment Programmes for Poverty: Experiences in Selected Countries*, Occasional Paper No. 58, International Monetary Fund, Washington, D.C.

Julin, E. and Levin, J., 1992, *Kenya: Macroeconomic Performance 1990*, Macroeconomic Studies No.30/92, Swedish International Development Authority, Stockholm.

Killick, T., 1981, 'The IMF and Economic Management in Kenya', Working Paper No. 4, Overseas Development Institute, London.

Killick, T., 1985, 'The Influence of Balance of Payments Management on Employment and Basic Needs in Kenya', *Eastern Africa Economic Review* (New Series),Vol. 1, No. 1, pp.57–69.

Tyler, G.J. and Akinboade, O., 1992, 'Structural Adjustment and Poverty: a Computable General Equilibrium Model of the Kenyan Economy', *Oxford Agrarian Studies*, Vol. 20, No. 1, pp.51–61.

World Bank, 1983, *Kenya: Growth and Structural Change*, World Bank, Washington, D.C.

World Bank, 1991, *World Tables 1991*, World Bank, Washington, D.C.

DISCUSSION OPENING — P. Lynn Kennedy *(Louisiana State University, USA)*

This discussion will proceed by reviewing the paper's methodology and empirical results. It will then offer criticisms and suggestions for improvements.

The underlying problem addressed by this paper is Kenya's deteriorating balance of payments situation, coupled with rising external debt. Using a computable general equilibrium model, based on a 1976 social accounting matrix of the Kenyan economy, policy simulations are conducted which seek to solve the balance of payments dilemma without worsening poverty or reducing the ability of the government to provide for the basic needs of the poor.

Three basic scenarios are used in this policy analysis: (a) the elimination of industrial taxes, (b) the previous scenario plus increased direct taxes and (c) the previous scenario plus a 10 percent currency devaluation. The above policy scenarios are simulated, first, assuming an unlimited supply of labour in all categories at a constant wage and, second, assuming fixed total supplies of labour in each category.

Under the assumption of unlimited labour the policy change simulating indirect and direct tax changes plus devaluation successfully meets the previously stated objectives. This scenario results in a nearly 40 percent decline in the current account deficit, an increase in real government expenditure and a relatively constant level of total real investment. In addition, employment and consumption are increased in all sectors.

The results of the simulation using the fixed total labour supply assumption are, as noted by the author, much less satisfactory in achieving the policy objectives. An increase in Gross Domestic Product is attained at the expense of high levels of inflation. The current account deficit increases while real government expenditures decrease. This scenario results in an increase in wages, ranging from 15.6 percent for rural self-employed labour to 18.0 percent for urban unskilled labour. However, due to the increase in retail prices, the increase in real household consumption is not nearly as large as the increase in wages. In fact, the rural middle income sector suffers a decline in real consumption.

One criticism would be that while abundant total labour may be a reasonable assumption, the idea that skilled and unskilled labour are both abundant seems to have its drawbacks. Where labour is not homogeneous, the assumption of an unlimited supply of skilled labour may be unrealistic. The actual supply and interchangeability of labour will undoubtedly fall in a range between assumptions A and B. A third assumption could, therefore, be incorporated in this model to better simulate the actual characteristics of the available labour force.

Another suggestion relates to a statement that moving towards a more progressive direct tax structure may prove to be politically unacceptable. By utilizing a CGE framework the effects of policy options on various segments of the economy are simulated. However, without a specific objective function, the analyst must use some degree of judgement as to the importance of solving the balance of payments problem, welfare assistance to the poor and other relevant political-economic factors. Incorporating some type of policy preference function into the current model would allow policy alternatives to be analyzed in a manner which seeks to solve the balance of payments problem without worsening the poverty situation and at the same time prove to be politically acceptable.

In conclusion, the methodology employed in this study can be used to find policy alternatives which improve the Kenyan current balance of payments problem without exacerbating the poverty situation under alternative labour force assumptions. Showing policy alternatives to be politically feasible will greatly enhance the usefulness of this analysis.

W. NEIL ADGER AND FLORIAN GROHS*

Aggregate Estimate of Environmental Degradation for Zimbabwe: Does Sustainable National Income Ensure Sustainability?

Abstract: Standard measures of economic growth do not adequately reflect changes in aggregate welfare over time. Sustainable national income is therefore defined as Net National Product with adjustments for the degradation of renewable and non-renewable capital. Productivity loss rather than replacement cost is the most theoretically correct way to value resource depletion. Modified net product is estimated for the agriculture and forestry sectors of Zimbabwe by valuing the loss of forest stock and soil erosion. The results show that traditional measures overstate the value of the agricultural sector's product by approximately 10 percent in 1989. It is argued that indicators of sustainable national income do not ensure sustainable development; as with all macroeconomic indicators, they do not account for distributional and equity issues which are at the crux of sustainable development, nor do they point to mechanisms which would ensure sustainable resource management. Indicators are therefore a necessary but not sufficient condition for the achievement of sustainable development.

INTRODUCTION

It has now been widely recognized that the standard measures of economic growth do not reflect changes in environmental quality or the changing stock of natural capital. The search for better measures at the national level has concentrated on recognizing social goals as part of sustainable development, and incorporating social indicators into measures such as the UNDP's Human Development Index (HDI) (UNDP, 1992). The HDI retains real GNP per capita as the central economic indicator in the index. It is equally necessary, in the search for indicators of sustainability, to correct national income measures in order to avoid the most obvious pitfalls. National income is the economic performance indicator with the central role in macroeconomic policy. A wide body of research has suggested how best to revise this critical indicator.

Even the least radical suggested revisions of adjusting national income for annually observable changes in stocks of renewable and non-renewable resources (Mäler, 1991), pose many obstacles to the estimation of a 'sustainable' national income measure, in that estimates of renewable and non-renewable resource use are imprecise and unreliable, and may be virtually impossible to replicate year on year. In this paper we first review the concept of sustainable income. It is important to highlight that if an economy experiences growth in what is defined as sustainable income, this may mean that the excesses of *unsustainable* resource use may be being minimized, but it does not ensure that a country

* University of East Anglia and University of Hohenheim, respectively. Neil Adger received research funding from the British Council under the University of Newcastle/University of Zimbabwe agricultural economics research link, which is gratefully acknowledged. Florian Grohs received financial support from DAAD (German Academic Exchange Service) and the University of Hohenheim, Centre for Tropical Agriculture which is also gratefully acknowledged. The authors would like to thank members of the Department of Agricultural Economics and Extension at the University of Zimbabwe and Dr Henry Elwell of the Institute for Agricultural Engineering, Borrowdale, Harare for assistance and advice.

is in a state of sustainable development as sustainable development, in its most widely accepted definition, is a wider concept incorporating ecological security and equity. Estimates of changes in natural capital stock for a single sector in Zimbabwe are presented. These are recognized as partial estimates, dealing only with forestry and soil renewable resources. The results show that the account significantly overestimates the net product of the sector, when the adjustments for capital loss are made. However, although the residual 'sustainable income' is positive, this does not necessarily indicate that Zimbabwe's land using sector is on a sustainable development path, as other necessary sustainable development criteria (such as social equity), may not be fulfilled. Distributional issues and potential land reform policies, as well as the impacts of structural economic reform on the resource base are not encompassed by macroeconomic indicators.

THE CONCEPT OF SUSTAINABLE NATIONAL INCOME

The most quoted principle of sustainable development is that offered by the Brundtland Commission: '...development that meets the needs of the present without compromising the ability of future generations to meet their own needs' (WCED, 1987). Two necessary conditions for sustainable development can be identified within the definition of sustainable development. These are intergenerational equity — as implied in the Brundtland definition — and equity in opportunity and human development, which is not only a desirable goal in itself, but is also necessary to safeguard intergenerational equity in resource use.

The implementation of these principles fundamentally leads to environmental and equity constraints on economic optimization. Thus in the context of the case study presented in this paper, a more accurate and sustainable measure of income generated from the agricultural sector does not determine whether the development path is sustainable or not. Sustainable development requires actual compensation for future welfare loss through resource degradation and actual redistribution of resources so that those with least resources are able to sustain their livelihoods. The main processes of land degradation in Zimbabwe are deforestation, overgrazing and soil erosion. There are various interpretations of the driving forces behind this — simple mismanagement of resources or non-allocation of private property rights in communal areas. As distribution of land and resources are crucial political questions in Zimbabwe, as elsewhere, political stances on the fundamental land reform question are often dressed in environmental clothes. Sustainable development demands both social equity and environmental conservation, so the expansion of the argument from sustainable indicators to policies for sustainable development is critical.

The premise underlying resource accounting is, as outlined above, that natural resources are essential to production and consumption for the maintenance of life supporting systems, as well as having intrinsic value in existence for intergenerational and other reasons. This leads to the conclusion that natural capital should be treated in a similar manner to reproducible capital in accounting terms, so that the ability to generate income in the future is reduced, if the stock falls. If a correct value can be placed on natural capital under an accounting system, the implication is that if stocks of natural capital are depleted to increase stocks of reproducible capital and it is assumed that there are no constraints on natural capital use (under a strong sustainability rule for example), then the ability to generate income in the future will be maintained (see Pearce and Atkinson, 1994).

All aspects of renewable and non-renewable resources should be incorporated into adjustments of the national accounting measure (see Adger, 1993). The empirical estimation in this paper is restricted to the agricultural sector accounts so the modifications are of the form:

$$(1)\quad \text{Modified } NNP = C + \dot{K}_M + (P_R - MC_R)\cdot(\delta Q)$$

where NNP = Net National Product, C = aggregate consumption, K_M = reproducible capital stock; MC_R = marginal cost of renewable; P_R = price of renewables; δQ = change in stock of renewable resource. The renewable resource degradation investigated is as a result of soil erosion and from deforestation.

RESOURCE DEPLETION IN ZIMBABWE

The relevance of the expansion of national accounts to include environmental capital is more critical in those economies with a high reliance on primary production, and development strategies based on these sectors. Zimbabwe is a natural resource dependant economy. Mining and quarrying accounted for 5.5 percent of GDP and agriculture 10.9 percent of GDP in 1987. The mining sector had decreased relative to the size of the economy in the previous 15 years, from 7.6 percent in 1974, and agriculture had also declined, although it now makes a greater contribution to overall exports. The share of agriculture products and raw materials ranged between 53 and 61 percent in the decade up to 1987. More crucially, up to 80 percent of the total population rely on agriculture as their major economic activity. At independence, in 1980, Zimbabwe inherited a highly skewed dual agricultural sector, characterized as an affluent, mainly white-dominated, large-scale commercial farming sector, with smallholder farming areas farmed by black families. The unequal land distribution aggravates environmental problems in the more densely populated smallholder farming areas. Erosion of the physical agricultural base through soil erosion and deforestation are important considerations in any assessment of the sustainability of income generation in the Zimbabwean economy. Given the importance of the agricultural sector in the Zimbabwean economy, the distribution of income and land leads to soil erosion, in particular, being a sensitive political issue. This sensitivity is further heightened in an era when post-colonial reform of the land-ownership and tenure systems is underway. Macroeconomic indicators do not reflect these distributional issues but rely on data formulated to give policy prescriptions at the sectoral level, must therefore be used with caution. Annual changes in environmental indicators, such as soil erosion and deforestation, are also difficult to assess.

Zimbabwe Forestry Sector

Although much attention is given to conserving present forest stocks in the humid tropics for their global environmental benefits, forests throughout the tropics and the developing world are the major source of primary energy through woodfuel and charcoal. So although deforestation of climax forest and major forested areas is a cumulatively global problem, the problems of obtaining fuelwood at relatively low prices in terms of money or labour is a much more immediate question at a local level. This role of woodfuel is often neglected in energy planning, especially where countries have been trying to develop non-traditional industrial sectors which require large and constant energy sources.

An energy accounting project in Zimbabwe in the 1980s (Hosier, 1986) concluded that a shortfall is likely to occur between the supply and demand for fuelwood, given the then present population and relative price levels in Zimbabwe, by 2000. The reduction of the total stocks of forests each year is the difference between the mean annual increment (*MAI*), which is the increase due to the growth of the existing stock, and the harvest. The estimated aggregate for 1987, shows a reduction in stock of 2.66 million tonnes of dry weight matter equivalent in the time period. This reduction in the stock of natural capital would not appear in the Net Product of Zimbabwe as traditionally measured, though the consequences of the use of other purchased fuels would be registered. If this reduction were to be reflected in a modified Net Product figure, by subtracting the depreciation of the physical stock valued at the rental value (following Hartwick, 1990) then for the forestry sector the following calculation is relevant:

$$(2)\quad NNP = C + \dot{K}_M (P_R - MC_R) \cdot (MAI - Q_R)$$

where P_R = market price for fuelwood; and MC_R = marginal cost of extraction.

The market price of fuelwood per tonne in 1987 (P_R) was estimated to be ZM\$68, taking a weighted average of urban and rural fuelwood prices based on various reported surveys. The imputed cost of extraction of fuelwood per tonne is derived from the estimated time to collect fuelwood in different regions, the shadow price being the minimum agricultural wage. The results are that net product should be reduced by the value of the physical depreciation of ZM\$93.77 million in 1987. If this is borne by the agricultural sector of the Zimbabwean economy, this represents a 9 percent reduction in the net product of the combined commercial and communal areas' agricultural net product as traditionally measured.

Soil Erosion

The value of soil erosion is often quantified in natural resource account studies as it is perceived as a threat to sustaining income and production in the long term, especially in agriculturally based economies. Soil erosion is amenable to estimation through physical models which can be extrapolated across land use data and is generally converted to economic accounts either through productivity loss or through replacement costs of the soil nutrients. The economic cost is generally calculated through two alternative measures.

The *change of productivity* technique uses the value of an erosion-induced yield decline as the damage cost of unabated erosion. It can be used to evaluate on-farm costs (decline of crop yield) and also for the off-farm costs of erosion (decline in irrigation area because of reduced dam capacity). Considering the on-farm costs of erosion, the soil is the relevant stock of natural capital. Its value can be defined as the capitalized net annual income stream generated by producing crops on the soil. The value of the lost production, that is, the change of productivity, reflects the erosion induced damages. The change of productivity technique allows for substitutions at the consumption level, that is, crops that could not be produced can be substituted for by imports of substitute crops. Depreciation of the soil is only considered up to the value of the crops produced on the soil. Previous investments, for instance to ameliorate the soil, are treated as sunk costs. The same applies to the off-farm impacts where only the change in dam yield is considered but not the investment costs of building the dam or a replacement at another location. The change of productivity technique is based on what can be called a weak sustainability constraint. It implies that the sum of natural and man-made capital stocks are non-declining and that substitutions between the two capital stocks are possible. It further allows substitutions at the consumption level. Food produced at a given site can be substituted with food produced at other sites which can lead to a situation where it is economically rational to deplete soil productivity at a given location. Empirical case studies for Mali (Bishop and Allen, 1989), Java (Magrath and Arens, 1989), Lesotho (Bojo, 1991) and Zimbabwe (Grohs, 1994) assessing the on-farm costs of erosion with the change of productivity technique revealed that the net annual costs of erosion are generally less than 1 percent of the agricultural GDP.

The *replacement cost* technique uses the costs that have to be incurred in order to replace a damaged asset. It is based on maintaining a certain stock of natural capital and does not measure the benefits of avoiding the damage. Considering the on-farm costs of erosion, the value of the soil equals the costs of replacing it completely, or at least parts of it, by replacing soil nutrients lost with mineral fertilizer. The replacement cost technique is based on what can be called a strong sustainability constraint. Stocking (1986) estimated the national costs of soil erosion for Zimbabwe with a similar approach based on replacement costs of nitrogen and phosphorus. The costs of erosion with his approach amount up to ZM$1.5 billion per annum (1985 prices), which is more than twice the value of the net agricultural product of the same year.

The purpose of the case study presented here is to determine the sustainable national income from a weak sustainability perspective, hence the productivity loss approach is used. Strong sustainability requires many rigid constraints on the use of renewable and non-renewable resources and substitution between them, and would require an ambitious redefinition of the role of economic growth (see Turner, 1993). In a study on cropland erosion in the smallholder areas in Zimbabwe, Grohs (1993) estimates the productivity loss due to erosion. Soil erosion lowers the productivity of the soil and the change in soil productivity induces an income loss for the farmer because the yields of his crops decline. The aggregate decline in crop yields is used to estimate the annual farm income losses through erosion. In particular, this approach combines three steps. First, average annual erosion rates of cropland erosion for smallholder areas are estimated using an the Soil Loss Estimator for Southern Africa (SLEMSA). The average rate of erosion for Zimbabwe's cropland in the communal areas is estimated to be around 40 t/ha annually, a comparably high soil loss. Second, the impact of erosion on yields is estimated with two soil–plant models. Assumptions on the erosion-productivity relationship (1 percent, 2 percent, or 3 percent yield loss per cm of soil lost) are then based on the model results. The erosion-induced farm income losses are in a third step, calculated with an economic model.

Assuming that erosion induces a 3 percent yield decline per cm of soil lost, smallholder farm income losses for 1988–89 average ZM$4.4 million (Grohs, 1993). The same approach is then applied to cropped land in the large-scale commercial farming sector. Erosion rates are considerably lower (on average 15 t/ha) because the land is less steeply sloped and better conserved. The net annual farm income loss calculated for the large-scale sector is lower and averages ZM$1.7 million. For both sectors, the costs of erosion sum up to about 0.6 percent of the agricultural GDP in 1989.

Agricultural Sector Accounts

The degradation of the resource base of soil and forest stock should then affect the net product as traditionally measured. The agricultural sector accounts are adjusted here in the first instance to reflect the role of that sector as the major location for primary natural resources. The agricultural sector accounts illustrate difficulties which also occur in national accounts. The communal area account, for example, because of lack of data, imputes value to production based on estimates of yields and areas which are not updated each year. The role of subsistence and informal economic activity tends to be ignored in market-based indicators because of this paucity of data. The communal area net product in Table 1 is not disaggregated into returns to the factors.

Table 1 *Modified Net Product for Commercial and Communal Agriculture Sector of Zimbabwe, 1987*

		ZM$ million (1987)
Output		2024
Input		987
Gross Product		1037
Less Depreciation K_M		62
Net Product		975
Less Depreciation K_N		99
Modified Net Product		876
of which	Labour (commercial sector)	333
	Farming Income	372
	Communal Sector	332
	Depreciation K_M	-62
	Depreciation K_N	-99

Sources: Zimbabwe Central Statistical Office (1989) and own calculations.
Note: Part of K_R forms part of Farming Income but is not reported separately. Communal sector accounts are not broken down into disbursement of net product.

Table 1 shows that with soil erosion (ZM$5.65 million (1987)) and forestry depletion (ZM$93.77 million (1987)), the traditional measure of net product for the sector overstates the sustainable contribution of this sector to growth by approximately 10 percent. So although both the communal and commercial farming sectors in Zimbabwe have increased productive sales and the returns to all productive factors impressively in the decade since independence (Thirtle *et al.*, 1993), this traditional accounting overstates the benefit to society in the long run.

DISCUSSION AND CONCLUSION

The need for sustainability modifications to national accounting systems has been recognized as an important contribution to better resource management as well as to the realization that economic growth (as measured by growth in traditional economic indicators) will not necessarily reduce poverty or protect the environment. However, data and estimates of environmental degradation are more unreliable than traditional macroeconomic indicators because of additional classification and estimation difficulties. Many types of environmental damages are only weakly documented and the linkages between environmental degradation and welfare impacts are often unclear. Even if the damages and linkages were known, it is still difficult to assign monetary values to these modifications. Finally, even if economic values can be assigned to the damages, it remains difficult to interpret them. The valuation of the existing stock of resources is still controversial.

Only *potentially* sustainable income is defined in making these adjustments. As an objective of economic policy, increasing the flow of sustainable income is desirable, and would serve to internalize the value of environmental assets into macroeconomic calculus. It will not, however, necessarily bring about *sustainable development*, because it does not address intragenerational equity issues or deal with exported environmental pollution. In short, sustainable development is a complex process which requires the recognition of the subjective positions of the decision-makers:

> ...economists need explicitly to recognise that sustainability is an equity question being debated in various moral discourses utilizing ecological reasoning and that sustainability will be chosen through politics (Norgaard, 1992, p.95).
>
> The degradation of the physical agricultural base through soil erosion and deforestation are important considerations in any assessment of the sustainability of income generation in the Zimbabwean economy. However, the questions of sustaining the level of natural resources is inextricably linked to the ownership and control of those resources (especially land), and hence to the distribution of the income, in the post-colonial period in Zimbabwe. As with all macroeconomic analyses, these issues are not addressed in the estimation sustainable income indicators. Thus the formulation and estimation of such indicators are a necessary but not sufficient condition for the achievement of sustainable development.

REFERENCES

Adger, W.N., 1993, 'Sustainable National Income And Natural Resource Degradation In Zimbabwe', in Turner, R.K. (ed.), *Sustainable Environmental Economics and Management: Principles and Practice*, Belhaven Press, London, pp.338–359.

Bishop, J. and Allen, J., 1989, 'The On-Site Costs of Soil Erosion in Mali', Environment Department Working Paper No. 53, World Bank, Washington, D.C.

Bojo, J., 1991, 'The Economics of Land Degradation: Theory and Applications to Lesotho', Stockholm School of Economics, Stockholm.

Grohs, F., 1993, 'Economics of Soil Degradation, Erosion and Conservation: A Case Study of Zimbabwe', PhD. dissertation, University of Hohenheim, Stuttgart, Germany.

Grohs, F., 1994, *Economics of Soil Degradation, Erosion and Conservation: A Case Study of Zimbabwe*, Vauk, Kiel.

Hartwick, J.M., 1990, 'Natural Resources, National Accounting And Economic Depreciation', *Journal of Public Economics*, Vol. 43, pp.291–304.

Hosier, R.H. (ed.), 1986, *Zimbabwe: Energy Planning for National Development*, Beijer Institute and Scandinavian Institute of African Studies, Stockholm.

Magrath, W. and Arens, P., 1989, 'The Costs of Soil Erosion on Java: A Natural Resource Accounting Approach', Environment Department Working Paper No. 18, World Bank, Washington, D.C.

Mäler, K.G., 1991, 'National Accounts and Environmental Resources', *Environmental and Resource Economics*, Vol. 1, pp.1–15.

Norgaard, R.B., 1992, 'Sustainability: The Paradigmatic Challenge To Agricultural Economists' in Peters, G.H. and Stanton, B.F. (eds.), *Sustainable Agricultural Development: the Role of International Cooperation. Proceedings of the Twenty-First International Conference of Agricultural Economists*, Aldershot, Dartmouth, pp.92–100.

Pearce, D.W. and Atkinson, G., 1994, 'Measuring Sustainable Development' in Bromley, D.W. (ed.), *Handbook of Environmental Economics*, Blackwell, Oxford.

Stocking, M., 1986, *The Cost of Soil Erosion in Zimbabwe in Terms of the Loss of Three Major Nutrients*, Consultants Working Paper No.3, FAO, Rome.

Thirtle, C., Atkins, J., Bottomly, P., Gonese, N., Govereh, J. and Khatri, Y., 1993, 'Agricultural Productivity in Zimbabwe, 1970–1990', *Economic Journal*, Vol. 103, pp.474–480.

Turner, R.K., 1993, 'Sustainability: Principles and Practice' in Turner, R.K. (ed.), *Sustainable Environmental Economics and Management: Principles and Practice*, Belhaven Press, London, pp.3–36.

UNDP (United Nations Development Programme), 1992, *Human Development Report 1992*, Oxford University Press, Oxford, UK.

WCED (World Commission on Environment and Development), 1987, *Our Common Future*, Oxford University Press, Oxford, UK.

Zimbabwe Central Statistical Office 1989, *Production Account of Agriculture, Forestry and Fisheries, 1980–1988*, Central Statistical Office, Harare.

DISCUSSION OPENING — Angelos Pagoulatos *(University of Kentucky, USA)*

The attempt to estimate the Modified Net Product for the agriculture and forestry sectors of Zimbabwe is consistent with the effort to refine the concept of Net National Product by accounting for the economic depreciation of exhaustible but renewable resources. In this paper, on-site soil erosion and fuelwood costs are addressed. It is not surprising to see the conclusion that a traditional macroeconomic indicator for welfare accounting is not able to reflect sustainable resource management. The underlying factors for achieving sustainable resource management and sustainable development must be found in the causes of environmental deterioration. Several factors may cause environmental deterioration, such as social and cultural factors, population growth, and economic conditions and policies. These factors create the incentives for current patterns of resource use and therefore a change in some of these factors, through policy actions designed to redirect incentives or eliminate price distortions, could be sufficient to achieve reductions in environmental deterioration. Examples of some economic factors are the international prices for important exports and imports, domestic agricultural and forest product prices, subsidies and taxes and alternative energy source national policies etc. Appropriate indicators for sustainability could then, and should be, identified to monitor the redirection of these factors as they provide necessary incentives for sustainable resource use.

It is understandable that limited data did not allow for more precise calculations and inclusion of secondary and off-site costs. The change-in-productivity approach to value environmental cost is appropriate. It is the concept of opportunity cost, which refers to the best alternative use, that is not followed in the determination of environmental costs. Rather, a concept of comparing present use to an assumed sustainable yield level which would produce no environmental deterioration is used in quantifying costs. Thus, all agricultural income foregone from declining soil productivity, through lower crop yields, is measured regardless of whether this sustainable alternative associated with zero environmental deterioration is viable and realistic. If it is not viable and realistic, the estimates of on-site soil erosion costs are overstated. Should sustainable resource use disregard the concept of opportunity cost?

Finally, the estimates presented in the analysis represent average values used, with no caveats. The use of average, rather than marginal, values can produce over or under estimation. Using average figures for soil productivity would over estimate the opportunity of cost soil productivity if land (soil productivity) is not scarce (the opposite if land is scarce). If scarcity of land (soil productivity) is to become relevant at some future date, then the current cost should include a user cost. The user cost would be smaller the further that date is into the future and the larger the discount rate used.

MANFRED WIEBELT AND RAINER THIELE*

A CGE Analysis of Policies to Combat Deforestation in Cameroon

Abstract: This paper provides a numerical general equilibrium assessment of forestry policies aimed at the reduction of tropical deforestation in Cameroon. Four different policy measures are distinguished, namely the provision of more secure timber concessions, a rise in the minimum size of trees that can be harvested, the establishment of national parks, and a tax on forest land. In the model simulations, all instruments are calibrated so as to achieve a prespecified increase in the volume of standing timber. The achievement of the ecological target is mainly due to the fact that the policies prevent the agricultural conversion of some forest land. From an ecological perspective, more secure property rights for concessionaires are the preferred option, because they most effectively deal with the main problem in Cameroon, that is the extremely short rotation period which does not allow the forest to regenerate. All policies lead to a moderate decline in real GDP.

INTRODUCTION

There is a consensus among resource economists that the tropical forests are excessively exploited (e.g. Pearce, 1990; Repetto, 1988). The overutilization results from two main factors driving a wedge between private and social costs of forest use: *market failure* and *policy failure*. Market failure is a consequence of the fact that tropical forests not only supply timber and land for agricultural conversion but also provide ecological benefits, which, because of their public good properties or the lack of property rights do not enter the individual decision making process. Some of these ecological benefits, such as the stabilization of the water cycle and the protection of soils against erosion and nutrient losses, affect only populations in tropical countries, while others, notably the fixing of carbon and the provision of habitat for a large share of the world's biological diversity, accrue to the whole world. Hence, local as well as global externalities have to be considered. Moreover, the pressure on tropical forests is frequently exacerbated by ecologically harmful government activities (Repetto and Gillis, 1988). These policy failures range from subsidized regional development programmes to general biases in the trade regime in favour of resource intensive production.

The present paper focuses on the local externalities of deforestation by investigating quantitatively the effects of forestry policy measures on the structure, growth and the utilization of forest resources of the Cameroonian economy. For this purpose, a computable general equilibrium (CGE) model was developed, which, unlike a partial equilibrium approach, captures the economy-wide repercussions of sectoral policies and hence allows for conclusions about structural responses and the change in land use patterns. The paper starts with a short description of the available policy options. It then

* Kiel Institute of World Economics, Germany. This study is part of the Kiel Institute of World Economics' research project. 'International and National Economic Policy Measures to Reduce the Emission of Greenhouse Gases by Protection of Tropical Forests' financed under grant II/67 310 by Volkswagen-Stiftung.

explains main features of the CGE model and presents the policy simulations for Cameroon. Finally, the results are briefly summarized.

POLICY OPTIONS

The local externalities of deforestation can be split up into a 'user cost' and an 'environmental externality' component (Barbier *et al.*, 1992). User costs denote the foregone future returns of using a resource today. The creation of adequate property rights ensures that the producers internalize these user costs. The external environmental costs of forest exploitation, such as watershed degradation and soil erosion, can be internalized by means of price and quantity policies.

The definition and enforcement of property or user rights is the basic precondition for individuals to include sustainability considerations into their decisions. Missing or ill-defined property rights encourage short-run profit maximization and thus lead to the over-exploitation of resources. In order to avoid this, the contractual arrangements for timber concessionaires have to be improved. One possibility is to base the duration of logging concessions for Cameroonian forests, most of which are state-owned, on a regeneration period of about 30 years, whereas licences are currently given for a maximum of five years (World Bank, 1989). Other arrangements, such as conditioning the continuation of short-term contracts on 'sustainable' harvesting practices or even the outright sale of the land, could also be applied (Barbier *et al.,* 1992). Moreover, the licences should be tradeable to provide an incentive for the concessionaires to maintain the value of their timber stands (Repetto, 1988).

Once the long-run privately efficient use of forest resources has been attained through the provision of property rights, the remaining external environmental costs can be internalized by imposing a tax. One possible solution is a tax on the use of tropical forest land. Since logging is ecologically less harmful then agricultural conversion, and since the cultivation of tree crops like coffee and cocoa causes less damage than the cultivation of food crops like rice and cassava, there is a rationale for varying tax rates.

Another possibility to narrow the gap between private and social costs of deforestation is to fix upper limits for the use of forest resources. The government could proscribe concessionaires from cutting trees until they have reached a certain age. The objective of such a selective logging regime is to account for the renewability of the tropical rain forest, thereby making a sustainable forest management possible.[1] A further option for the government is to set aside certain areas directly, for example, by establishing new national parks.

Theoretically, the local external environmental costs of deforestation should be internalized by employing a tax or a quantity measure in order to achieve an economic optimum. However, since the ecological costs of deforestation can only be estimated with high uncertainty and since damages may be irreversible, a safe minimum standard may, in practice, be a more adequate reference point for policy measures (Pearce and Turner, 1990, pp.317 ff.).

THE MODEL

The model used in the empirical analysis is a standard CGE model (Dervis *et al.*, 1982), extended by a forestry submodel (Dee, 1991).[2] A major advantage of the multisectoral approach is that it captures the implications of environmental and economic policy instruments for land use patterns. This is important, because the question of whether forests should be logged, or left as protected areas, or cleared entirely for agricultural use, is primarily one of land use patterns. The forestry submodel enables us to examine conventional forestry policy measures like resource taxes, secure property rights, selective logging regimes, and the setting up of national parks.

The treatment of the forestry sector can be examined through forest economics literature. The traditional economic problem is to find the rotation period[3] that maximizes the present value of net returns from the current and all future harvests, at given timber prices, harvesting costs, interest rates, and physical growth characteristics of trees (Bowes and Krutilla, 1985). While the traditional model does not take into account the environmental services provided by the forest, this model does by constraining harvests via the introduction of a minimum harvest age T^* (Nguyen, 1979). By means of such a selective logging regime the government can ensure that a certain minimum timber stock remains after each harvest. In the modified model, foresters choose the optimal harvest age T so as to maximize:

$$(1)\quad PV(T) = \frac{RR \cdot e^{-r(T-T^*)}}{1-e^{-r(T-T^*)}}$$

where PV is the present value of net returns per hectare, RR is the net return per hectare per rotation, $T-T^*$ is the rotation period, and r is the discount rate applied by the concessionaire. The first-order condition of the maximization problem is given by:

$$(2)\quad RR' = \frac{r \cdot RR}{1-e^{-r(T-T^*)}}$$

$$(2a)\ \text{with}\ RR = \left(P_x \cdot HV - RC\right)\cdot\left(1-t_F\right)$$

$$(2b)\ RR' = \partial RR / \partial T = P_x \cdot \partial HV / \partial T \cdot \left(1-t_F\right)$$

where HV denotes the volume of timber harvested per hectare per rotation, P_x the output price of timber, RC the harvest costs per hectare per rotation, and t_F a factor tax on forest land.

The interpretation of the first-order condition is that foresters should harvest at age T or, equivalently, choose the rotation period $T-T^*$, at which the marginal increase in net revenues from further growth of the forest RR' just equals the opportunity cost of delaying the harvest. The opportunity cost is the potential interest income foregone on the delayed receipt of harvesting revenues. The correction term in the denominator accounts for the fact that not only the current harvest but also future harvests are postponed, if the rotation period is extended.

Equation (2) reveals that an increase in the discount rate, which may be attributed to more insecure property rights for concessionaires, raises the opportunity costs of letting trees grow and hence leads to a shorter rotation period. A rise in the timber output price raises both the marginal revenues from further growth and the opportunity costs. Using the definitions in Equations (2a) and (2b), one can see that, with positive harvesting costs, the increase in RR is stronger than that in RR' so that the rotation period shortens. Finally, higher harvesting costs reduce opportunity costs, leading to an extension of the rotation period.

The physical growth of trees is described by a logistic functional form. Initially, trees grow very rapidly. Slower growth sets in as the stand matures, until growth stops when the climax state is reached. At any chosen rotation period, the physical growth characteristics of trees determine the volume of timber than can be harvested per hectare per rotation.

Logging technology is described by a Leontief function which combines land and a non-land input bundle consisting of capital, labour and intermediate inputs at the top of a multi-level production function. It is assumed that the bundle of non-land inputs is fixed per rotation, which gives rise to a form of increasing returns to scale (Dee, 1991). Within the input bundle, substitution possibilities between labour and capital and between imported and domestically produced intermediates are allowed.

Since the harvest volume HV above is defined per hectare per rotation, it has to be translated into annual output for the entire forest in order to make the forestry submodel compatible with the rest of the model. Assuming that the harvest per rotation is equally distributed over the years of the rotation period, annual timber output X from the whole harvested area B is

$$(3)\quad X = HV \cdot B/(T - T^{*})$$

The rest of the model follows conventional lines. Domestic supply of all sectors except forestry is given by a constant-returns Cobb–Douglas production function. In foreign trade, domestically produced goods and imports of the same product category are regarded as imperfect substitutes. In a similar way, differences in quality between domestically consumed and exported commodities are accounted for. In the household sector, it is assumed that there is only one representative consumer who buys consumer goods according to fixed expenditure shares. Government demand for final goods is defined using fixed shares of aggregate real spending on goods and services. The sectoral allocation of investable funds is determined by exogenously given share parameters.

In order to solve the CGE model, market clearing equations for the product and factor markets as well as macroeconomic equilibrium conditions for the balance of payments and the savings-investment balance must be specified. Supply and demand in product and factor markets is equilibrated by the adjustment of sectoral prices. For the factor markets it is assumed that the supply of each factor is exogenously fixed.[4] While sectoral capital stocks are assumed to be fixed within each period, labour and land are intersectorally mobile. Forest land moves towards the use in which the discounted returns to land are greater. Returns to forest land therefore adjust until their discounted values are equalized across sectors. With foreign savings set exogenously, equilibrium in the balance of payments is achieved via adjustments in the real exchange rate. As the nominal exchange rate is fixed in Cameroon, changes in the real exchange rate are the result of movements in the absolute price level. Finally, aggregate investment is the endogenous sum of private, government and foreign savings, i.e. the model is 'savings-driven'.

EMPIRICAL RESULTS

It is assumed that the target of the Cameroonian government is to achieve a specified increase in the volume of standing timber. For concreteness, the target for each policy measure is set at 5 million m^3, equivalent to about 20 percent of the biomass losses caused by one year's deforestation and degradation. The four policy instruments discussed above are distinguished.

The first is an increase in the length of forest leases. This has been modeled as a reduction of the discount rate which concessionaires apply to calculate their returns from forestry by 30 percent. The second option is an increase in the stipulated minimum harvest age of trees by eight years. The third option is a direct set-aside in the form of a national park. The increase in national parks has been modelled as a reduction in the total area of forest land available for forestry and agriculture by 220 000 ha. The final option is a tax on income from forest land. As the ecological damage varies according to land use patterns, the tax rates are varied accordingly, that is, 10 percent for forestry, 20 percent for export crops and 25 percent for food crops.

Table 1 shows the economic and ecological impact of each resource policy. It is striking that all policies induce a considerable reduction in forestry's production and exports, leading to increasing domestic producer prices. Wood processing is heavily penalized by increasing input costs because of its strong backward linkages to the forestry sector.

The change in the annual forestry activity level is determined by three variables (see Equation 3):

- the rotation period;
- the volume of timber harvested per hectare per rotation, and
- the area of land devoted to forestry.

The forestry sector adjusts these variables in different ways depending on the specific policy measure.

When the discount rate is lowered (Simulation 1), this reduces the opportunity cost of letting trees grow so that there is an incentive for concessionaires to extend the rotation period. Since the subsequent increase in the harvested volume per rotation does not fully compensate for the more infrequent harvests, the net result is a reduction in annual output and a rise in the timber price. As gross harvest revenues increase, because the rise in the timber price is stronger than the decline in harvests, and annual harvesting costs decrease, because the rotation period is extended, forestry net revenues and the stock value of land increase. This provides the price signal to attract additional land into forestry and thereby eases off the initial output reduction.[5] The reallocation of forest land contributes significantly to the achievement of the ecological target as it implies that the planned conversion of some forest areas does not take place. Furthermore, it has only minor effects on agricultural output and prices because forest land is only a small fraction of total agricultural land.

Table 1 *Consequences of Forestry Policies in Cameroon (percentage change)*

Policies / Indicators	30 percent reduction of discount rate in forestry	8 year increase in minimum harvest age	220 000 ha converted to national parks	Sector-specific factor tax on income from forest-land
	Simulation 1	Simulation 2	Simulation 3	Simulation 4
Real GDP	–0.2	–0.3	–0.3	–0.4
GDP deflator	0.0	0.3	0.3	–0.7
Total exports	–0.5	–1.4	–1.1	–0.8
Sectoral production				
Forestry	–4.4	–14.0	–10.0	–15.2
Wood processing	–3.8	–9.8	–6.8	–8.6
Food crops	–0.1	–0.1	–0.2	–0.7
Cash crops	–0.3	–0.2	–0.2	1.3
Sectoral prices				
Forestry	11.2	23.5	15.9	11.0
Wood processing	2.3	10.8	7.2	5.8
Food crops	0.1	0.2	0.2	0.3
Cash crops	0.0	0.2	0.2	–0.6
Sectoral exports				
Forestry	–10.0	–15.6	–11.2	–19.0
Wood processing	–6.5	–13.5	–9.5	–11.8
Cash crops	– 0.1	–0.2	–0.3	1.4
Use of forest land in agriculture:				
Food crops	–19.3	–19.2	–18.8	–20.9
Cash crops	–18.6	–18.1	–17.8	–15.7
in forestry:	1.2	1.4	–9.9	–15.2
Rotation period	10.3	5.8	–7.3	1.1
Harvest per rotation	4.7	–9.6	–7.4	1.1

Source: Own calculations based on the CGE model.

Note: All policies are calibrated to produce an increase in standing timber of about 5 million m^3 compared to the reference situation.

The primary impact of an increase in the minimum harvest age (Simulation 2) is that foresters have to wait for trees to grow larger before they harvest them, that is, the rotation period is shortened exogenously. This change in the logging regime reduces the opportunity costs of forest growth by making earlier harvests possible in the future. As a consequence, concessionaires increase the age at which they actually harvest the trees. On balance, the rotation period is extended. The change in the volume of timber harvested per rotation is the result of two offsetting factors. First, at any given minimum harvest age, the increase in the actual harvest age leads to a higher harvest volume. Secondly, the increase in the minimum harvest age reduces the harvestable timber volume by stipulating a higher amount of timber that has to be left after each harvest. In Cameroon, the second effect dominates the first and hence the harvest per hectare per rotation falls. An explanation of this result relies on the Cameroonian peculiarity that, because of very small and selective harvests, the timber volume in logged forests is very close to the maximum timber volume in virgin forests.[6] This implies an extremely low growth rate of trees so that delaying harvest does not yield much additional timber. Both the lower and less frequent harvests are translated into a decline in annual output and a rise of the timber price. The negative output effect is partly offset by an increase in the area of land devoted to forestry via the same mechanism as described for Simulation 1.

The establishment of a national park (Simulation 3) initially reduces the area available for forestry activities. As a consequence, annual output declines, pushing up the price of domestically produced timber. The higher output price provides an incentive for concessionaires to undertake more frequent harvests, because it raises the opportunity costs by more than the marginal revenues of forest growth (see above). The shorter rotation period, in turn, leads to smaller harvests per rotation. On balance, annual production falls and the output price increases. With gross revenues increasing more than annual harvesting cost, a rising stock value of forest land attracts land from agriculture thereby cushioning the output reduction in forestry.

A general taxation of forest land (Simulation 4) forces up the price of forest land in forestry as well as in agriculture and thus leads to a reduced demand for this factor in both sectors. As the frequency and the intensity of harvests adjust only marginally and compensate each other, the decline in annual output of the forestry sector is solely due to the reduction of forest land use.

The output losses in forestry and wood processing lead to moderate reductions of real GDP in the range of 0.2 to 0.4 percent, depending on the policy choice. Because of the weak linkages to other sectors there are only minor real adjustments in the rest of the economy. On the demand side, exports have to carry the major burden of adjustment. This is because forestry and wood processing are highly export oriented and because the export demand for forest products is very elastic. The sharp decline in exports of the timber industry would impose a significant constraint on the Cameroonian economy, especially in a situation in which export prospects for coffee, cocoa and oil are discouraging and the country has to look for alternative foreign exchange sources. Moreover, the wood industry is a relatively labour-intensive industry in which Cameroon may have a comparative advantage (World Bank, 1989).

CONCLUSIONS

This paper has provided a numerical general equilibrium assessment of policies to reduce tropical deforestation in Cameroon. It assumes that the Cameroonian government wants to achieve a specified increase in the volume of standing timber. This ecological target can be realized by each of the resource policies analysed: prolongation of forest leases; raising the minimum size of trees that can be harvested, establishment of a national park or a Pigou-tax on forest land. In all cases, the ecological gain is accompanied by a moderate economic loss. In order to obtain the overall welfare impact of the different measures, a valuation of the ecological effects would be necessary.

Since the main problem in Cameroon is the extremely short rotation period of around five years and the logging damage caused at each harvest, the best solution from an ecological point of view is to extend logging concessions. This measure would encourage concessionaires to take into account the regenerative capacity of the forests. It also has the lowest negative side effects on timber production and exports as well as real GDP.

NOTES

1 Foresters point out that it is possible to manage tropical forests sustainably, but that current management practices for the most part are unsustainable (Bruenig, 1990).

2 A detailed formal description of the model can be found in Thiele and Wiebelt (1993).

3 The rotation period is the length of time between two harvests on a specific area (here on one ha).

4 With respect to forest land, the assumption of a fixed aggregate supply seems appropriate for Cameroon, where the access of the forestry sector is restricted by the provision of concessions and where agricultural use is dominated by smallholders who are not able to open up new primary forests.

5 The 4.4 percent decline in annual output is the net result of a 10.3 percent increase in the length of the rotation period and two offsetting factors, namely a 4.7 percent increase in the harvest volume per rotation and a 1.2 percent increase in the land devoted to forestry: $-10.3 + 4.7 + 1.2 = -4.4$.

6 The average timber volume in logged forest is 266 m^3/ha as compared to 280 m^3/ha in virgin forests.

REFERENCES

Barbier, E., Burgess, J., Aylward, B. and Bishop, J., 1992, *Timber Trade, Trade Policies and Environmental Degradation*, LEEC Discussion Paper No. 92-01, London Environmental Economics Centre, London.

Bowes, M.D. and Krutilla, J.V., 1985, 'Multiple Use Management of Public Forestlands', in Kneese, A.V. and Sweeney, J. L. (eds.), *Handbook of Natural Resource and Energy Economics*, Vol. I. North-Holland, Amsterdam, pp.531–569.

Bruenig, E.F., 1990, 'Möglichkeiten nachhaltiger Forstwirtschaft in Regenwaldgebieten', *Nord-Süd aktuell*, Vol. 4, pp. 93–97.

Dee, P.S., 1991, *Modelling Steady State Forestry in a Computable General Equilibrium Context*, Working Paper Series, No. 91/8, National Centre for Development Studies, Canberra.

Dervis, K., de Melo, J. and Robinson, S., 1982, *General Equilibrium Models for Development Policy*, Cambridge University Press, Cambridge, England.

Nguyen, D., 1979, 'Environmental Services and the Optimal Rotation Problem in Forest Management', *Journal of Environmental Management*, Vol. 8, pp.127–136.

Pearce, D.W., 1990, *An Economic Approach to Saving the Tropical Forest*, LEEC Discussion Paper No. 90-06, London Environmental Economics Centre, London.

Pearce, D.W. and Turner, R.K., 1990, *Economics of Natural Resources and the Environment*, Johns Hopkins University Press, Baltimore.

Repetto, R., 1988, *The Forest for the Trees? Government Policies and the Misuse of Forest Resources*, World Resource Institute, Washington, D.C.

Repetto, R. and Gillis, M., 1988, *Public Policies and the Misuse of Forest Resources*, Cambridge University Press, Cambridge, England.

Thiele, R. and Wiebelt, M., 1993, *Modelling Deforestation in a Computable General Equilibrium Model*, Kiel Working Papers, No. 555, Kiel Institute of World Economics, Kiel.

World Bank, 1989, *Cameroon Agricultural Sector Report*, Washington, D.C.

DISCUSSION OPENING — Jean-Christopher Bureau *(INRA-ESR, France)*

I must say that my overall opinion of this paper is very good. I apologize to the authors for saying almost nothing on the many excellent aspects of their work, but my job is to focus on the few questionable points. Due to space limitations, little is said about the model, and it is quite difficult to make comments on the validity of the approach. I am supportive of the idea of using a CGE model in such an analysis which has proved to be very interesting (Jorgenson and Wilcoxen, 1990, for example). This paper also leads to some instructive results on the comparative effects of the four policies on Cameroon's economy. However, when a CGE model is used to investigate some very focused policy reforms, the conclusions are more sensitive to assumptions about the behaviour of the agents in the particular sector. Regarding the microeconomic effects, I would appreciate the authors clarifying a few points. I have five remarks that make me wonder if the authors have not overstated the positive aspects of policy no. 1 compared to the three alternatives.

I agree that a decrease in the discount rate should have desirable effects described by the authors. But I am not sure that one can draw conclusions on the effects of lease length from changes in the discount rate only. Longer leases may be a necessary but not sufficient condition for more sustainable management. As an illustration, consider the case of the Haitian peasant who cuts the few remaining trees down. Clearly there is a huge problem of lease length and the authors are perfectly right in emphasising this aspect. The main reason for erosion in Haiti is that you don't manage your trees for the long term when you know that any soldier with a machine gun can steal your land tomorrow. But even those who have reasonable land security are so desperate for short term cash that their preference for the present is almost infinite. Facing starvation, they cut down everything for immediate sale of charcoal. This is an extreme situation, but it is illustrative of many aspects. My friend Eldon Ball took me to his home country in Kentucky. I have the impression that the barren hills of Kentucky are due to a high preference for the present of the people up there, not because they fear that their property certificates will be cancelled in the near future.

The results of simulation no. 1 are attributed to changes in lease length, but there are cases where longer leases will not lead to letting trees grow. If loggers are small firms, they may be constrained in liquidity and have difficulty accessing credit. Large firms may also choose to cut trees in the first years of their lease if they fear political trouble, or anticipate falling timber prices in the future. Multinational firms with opportunities for logging all over the world but a limited amount of capial may prefer to make quick money and shift to other quick money in another country, even with long leases. So I think that attributing the results in no. 1 to longer leases is a bit optimistic.

A large share of the economic gains involved in policy no. 1 comes from the rise in timber price and the decrease in harvest costs that increase profitability of timber and attract land into forestry. One should not neglect two effects. First, lower harvest costs may generate other environmental damage (a resource is more quickly exhausted if collection costs are low). Second, it is likely that higher timber prices will lead to further depletion on marginal lands before attracting new land into forestry. The result of higher timber prices on the environment seems more ambiguous than the authors claim. Therefore, I agree with the authors about the importance of a long term horizon for the loggers, but I think that their conclusion about the benefits of policy no. 1 is excessive.

In simulation no. 2, as well as in simulation no. 1, there is a reduction in annual ouput, since the increase in the harvested volume per rotation does not fully compensate for the more infrequent harvests (no. 1) or does not compensate for the higher amount of timber that has to be left because of minimum harvest age (no. 2). This result is quite counter-intuitive. On a longer period, I have the feeling that more sustainable practices should lead to a higher annual output than cutting new born trees. The authors give a detailed explanation only for policy no. 2, that is that trees grow slowly, and delaying harvest does not bring much additional timber. This explanation is not very convincing. Timber output in Cameroon is close to the maximum possible. This may indicate that present logging is unsustainable. I would welcome some clarification.

The results of simulation no. 3 suggest that the conversion of some forests into national parks is not a satisfactory option. This is an interesting result, and is certainly useful to remind us that conservation of little oases of nature is a poor substitute for an ambitious policy for more sustainable practices, since it only creates more problems on non protected areas. However, one should not forget that national parks provide other benefits, and that it may be necessary to forbid timber harvesting in some areas, for instance, for protecting endangered species. When irreversibility occurs, the classical economics that the authors use in this paper is not sufficient (Madariage, McConnell 1987, Henry 1974, Fisher 1988, Fisher and Hanemann 1986).

I do not think the authors give enough credit to simulation no. 4 in the conclusion. The economic loss is moderate for a quite large ecological benefit caused by a large reduction in logging. In addition, revenue raised can be used for supporting reforestation and management of the forest. The literature on the welfare effect of Pigovian taxes is large and leads to complex developments. However, empirical evidence suggests that problems of deforestation often occur when loggers do not pay much for the access to a public resource. This may be a difficult political problem (see the difference between candidate Clinton's proposal and President Clinton's actions about North West forests in the USA). But keep Papua New Guinea in mind. Therefore, I appreciate the desire of the authors to be conclusive. But I would be more careful in emphasizing the benefit of policy no. 1 relative to the others.

Also note that the increase in lease length would not fundamentally change the logger's behaviour if the licence is not made tradeable. The optimal age for cutting trees is not necessarily equal to the regeneration period. Assume that this optimal age is 25 years, and that the lease length is set at the regeneration period of 30 years. That is, the concessionaire will cut the tree once at 25 years and then at 5 years and leave barren land, unless he can sell the discounted value of the 5 years growth to the next concessionaire.

If licences are tradeable, in a competitive market with perfect information, there is little interest in expanding lease length. This can only bring rigidity to the system and lead to inefficiencies. At any point in time, licences can be sold at a price that accounts for the age of each tree on the land. Theoretically, a perfect market for licences is a safer bet on sustainable management than longer leases which are not transferable. Privatization of land also has the same theoretical advantages. However, it raises other problems, such as the division into smaller plots at each generation (another cause of deforestation in many third world countries: better cut a tree than leave it to my brother), the very high cost of monitoring transfer that leads to non-written agreements (a tree on a plot claimed by several 'owners' has a very small chance of getting old: a creole proverb says that a goat with several owners always dies of starvation).

The relevance of the CGE model depends crucially on the reliability of the modelling of the logger's behaviour under the four policy simulations. Typically, this is often the weak point in using CGEs for modelling effects of sectoral reforms. One cannot avoid questionable assumptions about biological aspects and the microeconomic aspects (growth rates of the trees, rate of exhaustion of the resource, discount rates, fixed costs, substitution with other crops, etc.), the cumulated effect of these assumptions leads to a large standard error on the GDP change. This is not a criticism of the work presented here, but my general opinion is that more effort on the modelling of the forest management, and less effort on a sophisticated general equilibrium framework is often worth it. It is noteworthy that the adjustments in the rest of the economy are quite small in the results presented here. Most of the interest of a CGE framework comes from the endogenization of the price of timber, and the conclusions could have been roughly inferred from a partial equilibrium framework.

GENERAL DISCUSSION — Earl D. Kellogg, Rapporteur *(Winrock International)*

Deryke Belshaw (University of East Anglia) asked about the CGE model for Dr Tyler's paper assumptions.

- Will there not be a leakage of high income-earners' liquid funds out of Kenya (neighbours Uganda and Tanzania have freely convertible currencies) as a result of higher marginal tax rates, i.e. negative revenue elasticity from progressive direct taxation?
- Why is a price-maker position assumed for Kenya in world agricultural markets, rather than a price-taker position? In the latter case, devaluation enhances the producer price expressed in domestic currency (assuming a reasonable pass-through rate); elasticities of market supply and total supply response are then relevant in assessing effects on the national economy.
- The Kenya shilling has been appreciating through 1994, despite the domestic inflation rate well exceeding the trade weighted index of inflation in partner states. Can Dr Tyler throw any light on reasons for this?

There was some concern that Tyler's model did not include a welfare function that would be maximized.

Dr Tyler agreed with the discussion opener that if data were available, a different assumption could be made about the behaviour of the skilled compared to the unskilled labour market. He disagreed, however, about incorporating a social welfare function into a CGE model, even if this were possible. He said that he saw great merit in the economist presenting the results of the impact of various policy instruments on measurable variables such as GDP, the balance of payments, the incidence of poverty, etc, leaving the policy makers to choose.

The export demand elasticities were based on available studies and the formulation of export demand was similar to that used in may CGE models. With the high level of aggregation, product differentation is a necessary assumption within each sector. Hence Dr Tyler did not consider it appropriate to assume that Kenya is a price-taker for the heterogeneous product 'agriculture', which would imply a demand elasticity of infinity on world markets. He noted that the proposed increase in direct taxation, eg. for urban upper income households from 15–22 percent, is unlikely to lead to capital flight; it is an income tax and not a wealth tax and the preferred simulation results showed that the rich would still be better off, because of income growth.

Maurizio Merlo (University of Padova, Italy) asked the first two speakers — Neil Adger and Manfred Wiebelt — to what extent they considered the differences between forests that were natural stock versus forests that were cultivated plantations regarding offtake rates and degradation consequences in their model. Both presenters said they did not differentiate between degradation parameters for natural versus cultivated forests.

Richard Tiffin (University of Newcastle Upon Tyne) asked if Adger and Grohs thought the current price of a non-renewable resource adequately reflected the value of the resource to future generations. The response was that this was a difficult question. There were no present obvious, surperior and practical methods for valuing non-renewable resources in the model. New methods for pricing these non-renewable resources for future generations are being developed.

Professor Tiffin also asked if there was a case to be made for an upward adjustment of national income to account for current consumption which is foregone for the benefit of future generations eg. research and development expenditures. This question was not addressed.

T.S. Veeman (University of Alberta) asked if we should not focus on maintaining key or critical elements of the natural capital stock like those which lack substitutes) by employing the safe minimum standard of conservation rather than completely maintaining the natural capital stock. Adger replied that it was not sensible to follow the strong constraint of the model ie. no depreciation of natural non-renewable resources. He agreed a safe minimum standard of conservation approach would be better.

Dr. Wiebelt responded to discussion about the high discount rates used in his model, whether loss of biodiversity was included in the costs of degradation and if it would help to lengthen the time interval given in logging concessions so that fewer trees would be cut while they were relatively young. He indicated that he had to use high discount rates and that did bias the outcomes to more heavily count earlier rather than later costs and benefits. Because Cameroon logging companies harvest trees at near climax growth, extending the concession time would not help. Lastly, loss of biodiversity was not included in the model. If it is to be included, it would have to be exogenous to the system so inclusion way not add much to the model.

ROMEO M. BAUTISTA AND CLEMEN G. GEHLHAR*

Export Price Variability, Government Interventions and Producer Welfare: The Case of Egyptian Cotton

Abstract: This paper examines the effects of government interventions during 1965–91 on short-run price stability and long-run price incentives, as well as the further repercussions on producer income and welfare, for the main agricultural export crop (cotton) in Egypt. In contrast to most existing studies on agricultural pricing policies in developing countries that focus on either price stability or producer incentives as the central policy goal, the analysis considers the simultaneous effects of alternative policy regimes on those two objectives. In fact, what matters to risk-averse producers is not price variability *per se* but the variability of their income. The analysis finds that the pure stabilization benefit from government interventions is heavily dominated by the transfer benefit so that producer welfare is significantly improved in moving to either of the two counterfactual regimes of sectoral and economywide free trade.

INTRODUCTION

Government market interventions that create a wedge between domestic and foreign (or border) prices are often rationalized in terms of the need to reduce product-price variability for domestic producers in the face of uncertain and volatile world commodity prices.[1] For export crop producers in developing countries (LDCs), where capital markets are typically underdeveloped, domestic price stability can reduce the riskiness of income and promote consumption smoothing over time. Dampening world price fluctuations, however, is seldom unbiased; LDC governments have tended to reduce the peaks without raising prices in the troughs. This would explain, in part, the general empirical finding that government price interventions in developing countries have had the effect of reducing the average relative price of major agricultural products, especially of export crops (Krueger, Schiff and Valdés, 1988; and Bautista and Valdés, 1993).

It is useful to distinguish between government interventions that influence relative agricultural prices directly, that is, policies specifically aimed at the agricultural sector and indirectly, that is, those aimed at other production sectors (particularly, manufacturing) and macroeconomic policies that affect agricultural prices through the real exchange rate. They can be referred to simply as *direct* and *indirect* interventions. The actual (or historical) policy regime can then be compared with two counterfactual policy regimes: (a) sectoral free trade, in which there is an absence of direct interventions; and (b) economywide free trade, in which there is an absence of total (direct and indirect) interventions.

In this paper we examine the effects of government interventions in Egypt on the average level of producer prices of cotton, the country's most important export crop, and on their variability. Our approach is based on comparisons of historical (or actual) price data with the equilibrium values associated with the two hypothetical policy regimes of sectoral free trade and economywide free trade. In contrast to most existing studies that

* International Food Policy Research Institute, Washington, D.C.

assume either short-run price stability or long-run price incentives as the central policy goal, our analysis considers the simultaneous effects of government interventions on these two policy objectives. We also make an assessment of the income effects, in terms of average income and income variability, and of the repercussions on producer welfare based on the methodology developed by Newbery and Stiglitz (1981). The paper ends with some concluding comments on the implications of our findings for agricultural pricing policy in Egypt.

PRICE EFFECTS OF GOVERNMENT INTERVENTIONS

Since the early 1960s when the cotton sector was nationalized in Egypt, direct intervention has consisted of government controls on area planted to various cotton varieties, determination of the amount and varieties for export and domestic use, and crop procurement at fixed producer prices. There were insignificant increases in cotton procurement prices during the 1960s. Procurement prices have increased measurably since 1974, the year when 'Infitah' or open-door policy was declared. However, the average farmgate price of cotton continued to be much lower than the border price at the official exchange rate (Dethier, 1989).

Even with the comprehensive policy liberalization programme initiated in 1986, in which many aspects of government control on agricultural production, marketing and prices were dismantled, cotton continued to be subject to fixed producer prices and crop procurement. While decontrol and liberalization of the cotton sector have been delayed, large increases in the procurement price began in 1989. More recently, the government has developed a Cotton Liberalization Implementation Plan that will establish a 'free-market system for cotton production and marketing'.

The terms of trade for cotton corresponding to the historical and sectoral free-trade regimes can be represented, respectively, by:

(1) $P_1 = P_h / P_{na}$ and $P_2 = P_{bo} / P_{na}$

where P_h is the historical average procurement price of cotton, P_{bo} is the border price equivalent at the official exchange rate (E_o) and P_{na} is the non-agricultural price index. Since the entire cotton output is sold to the government during the period of analysis (1965–91), the farmgate (producer) price is equal to the procurement price. The weighted average of procurement prices for major cotton varieties is used here,[2] the weights based on the production of lint and waste (following Dethier, 1989, pp.50–52).

Domestic relative prices of tradable agricultural products are influenced not only by sector-specific policies but also — and more importantly and generally adversely (see Krueger *et al.*, 1988) — by economywide trade, fiscal, monetary, and nominal exchange rate policies. In Egypt, import restrictions to protect domestic industry and expansionary macroeconomic management have caused significant real exchange rate overvaluation, especially from 1979 until recently. The relative price of cotton under the policy regime of economywide free trade is given by:

(2) $P_3 = P_b^* / P_{na}^*$

where P_b^* is the border price of cotton evaluated at the 'equilibrium' exchange rate (E^*), and P_{na}^* is the non-agricultural price index with the tradable goods component calculated at border prices using the equilibrium exchange rate. The equilibrium exchange rate is defined as the exchange rate that would have prevailed under conditions of unrestricted foreign trade and balance-of-payments equilibrium (that is, no unsustainable imbalance in the current account).

Table 1 *Relative Producer Price of Cotton under Alternative Policy Regimes, 1965–91 (Egyptian pounds/tonne)*

	Historical (P_1)	Sectoral free trade (P_2)	Economy wide free trade (P_3)
1965	196	292	422
1966	187	260	394
1967	199	374	394
1968	174	230	323
1969	173	255	372
1970	174	255	391
1971	174	256	418
1972	188	258	381
1973	182	477	450
1974	215	572	626
1975	221	493	589
1976	269	419	680
1977	265	519	829
1978	244	314	584
1979	298	618	744
1980	273	559	614
1981	329	546	726
1982	292	372	524
1983	320	388	576
1984	273	396	734
1985	301	367	845
1986	299	395	804
1987	305	340	736
1988	340	555	1301
1989	416	1212	2922
1990	465	1438	2063
1991	474	1269	1797

Source: Authors' calculations.

Notes: P_1 = Producer price of cotton deflated by P_{na}.

P_2 = Border price of cotton evaluated at official exchange rate deflated by P_{na}.

P_3 = Border price of cotton evaluated at equilibrium exchange rate deflated by P_{na}^*.

Base year for P_{na} and P_{na}^* is 1979.

The annual values of P_1, P_2 and P_3 are shown in Table 1, based on the annual estimates of Dethier (1989) for 1965–84 and of the authors for 1985–1991 using the Krueger *et al.* (1988) methodology. The upper part of Table 2 contains the average price levels and instability values. Our measure of price instability is the detrended standard deviation, representing the dispersion of observed annual values around the trend line. In terms of average price incentives, it is evident that domestic cotton producers would have been better off without the direct or total interventions of the government during 1965–91. Table 2 also indicates that the adverse incentive effects of both sector-specific and economywide policies had been quite significant.

Did government interventions result in a less unstable domestic price for cotton producers? It would appear from Table 2 that sectoral policies were highly price stabilizing; by contrast, indirect interventions served to reduce only slightly the variability of domestic cotton prices. Overall, government interventions did lead to a much lower price instability for Egyptian cotton, the relative product price under each of the two counterfactual free-trade regimes being about three and a half times more unstable than the historical price.

Clearly, there has been a trade-off between long-run (average) price incentives and short-run (inter-year) price variability. The Egyptian government has managed to reduce substantially the volatility of annual world cotton prices but at a cost of significantly lowering the price incentives for domestic cotton producers.

EFFECTS ON PRODUCER INCOME AND WELFARE

What matters to risk-averse producers is not the price variability *per se* but the variability of their income. The supply response to the price changes associated with each policy regime is therefore an important consideration. In view of interdependencies in the production of cotton, rice, wheat, and maize in Egypt (Dethier, 1989), it is necessary to make the comparisons of producer income and welfare under the three alternative policy regimes based on the simultaneous presence or absence of government interventions affecting all four crops. Thus, in the sectoral free-trade regime, the interpretation would be that direct interventions in all four crops are absent.

Supply parameter estimates derived in Dethier (1989, Appendix I) are used in calculating annual values of producer income (value added) during 1965–91 under each of the two free-trade regimes. The calculated average level and instability index for each policy scenario are given in the lower part of Table 2. It is notable that cotton producer income during 1965–91 would have been significantly higher without direct interventions. Also, the removal of total interventions would have more than doubled the historical average income. In terms of income instability, Table 2 shows that sectoral policies had been effective in dampening income fluctuations markedly, and that economywide policies had a significant income-destabilizing effect for cotton producers.

Turning now to the evaluation of the effect on producer welfare associated with a shift from the historical policy regime to either of the two counterfactual regimes, we assume a von Neumann–Morgenstern utility function of income $U(Y)$ for the representative cotton producer.[3] Let Y_i and Y_j denote the income variables corresponding to the prices P_i and P_j associated with any two alternative policy regimes. The means of Y_i and Y_j are $\overline{Y}_i$ and $\overline{Y}_j$, respectively, the standard deviations are σ_{yi} and σ_{yj}, respectively.

Table 2 *Average Levels and Instability Indexes of Relative Cotton Prices and Producer Incomes, 1965 –1991*

	Average level	Instability (percent)
Relative prices		
P_1	268	14.2
P_2	497	49.1
P_3	787	53.7
Producer incomes		
Y_1	2614	17.8
Y_2	4329	42.5
Y_3	6663	23.3

Source: Authors' calculations.
Notes: P_1, P_2 and P_3 as defined in the notes to Table 1.
Y_1 = Value added measured at actual domestic prices.
Y_2 = Value added measured at border prices at official exchange rate deflated by P_{na}.
Y_3 = Value added measured at border prices at equilibrium exchange rate deflated by P^*_{na}.
Prices are in Egyptian pounds/tonne. Income is in Egyptian pounds.

The monetary benefit to the producers of a change from Y_i to Y_j is given by B in the following equation:

$$(3)\quad EU(Y_i) = EU(Y_j - B)$$

where E is the expectation operator. As shown by Newbery and Stiglitz (1981, p.93), using a Taylor series approximation for Equation (3) leads to:

$$(4)\quad \frac{B}{Y} = \frac{\overline{Y}_j - \overline{Y}_i}{Y_i} - \frac{1}{2} r(\sigma^2_{yj} - \sigma^2_{yi})$$

where r is the Arrow–Pratt measure of relative risk aversion.

The first term in the right-hand side of Equation (4) represents the 'transfer benefit', indicating the increase (or decrease) in average income associated with the shift from one policy regime to another. Table 2 shows, for example, that policy reform toward freer trade during 1965–91 would have produced a positive transfer benefit for cotton producers. The second term represents the pure stabilization benefit, or 'risk premium', indicating the monetary gain (loss) from a reduction (increase) in income instability. The higher the degree of risk aversion the greater is the relative importance of the risk premium to the total producer benefit from a policy change.

Table 3 presents estimates of the transfer benefit, risk premium, and net benefit for cotton producers resulting from a hypothetical change from the historical policy regime during 1965–91 to each of the two counterfactual regimes of sectoral and economywide free trade. The three alternative values assumed for the coefficient of relative risk aversion, 1.0, 1.5, and 2.0, are deemed reasonable (Binswanger, 1980; and Newbery and Stiglitz, 1981). A striking observation from Table 3 is that the risk premium is consistently dominated by the transfer benefit, so that producer welfare is improved in the policy shift toward either of the two free-trade regimes. The net benefit to cotton producers is quite substantial: removal of *direct* and *total* interventions will lead to increases in average income of more than 50 percent and 150 percent, respectively. Among the three alternative policy regimes, therefore, cotton producers would have gained the most from economywide free trade.

Table 3 *Calculated Producer Benefits, 1965–91 (percent)*[a]

	Transfer benefit	Risk premium	Net benefit
Sectoral free trade			
r=1.0	65.6	–7.5	58.1
r=1.5	65.6	–11.2	54.4
r=2.0	65.6	–14.9	50.7
Economy wide free trade			
r=1.0	154.9	–1.11	53.7
r=1.5	154.9	–1.71	53.1
r=2.0	154.9	–2.31	52.6

Source: Authors' calculations.
Notes: [a] Percentage of actual average income in 1965–91. r = coefficient of relative risk aversion.

CONCLUDING REMARKS

The results of our analysis indicate that cotton producers in Egypt have been penalized heavily by the distortionary price effects of sectoral policies, in particular the low procurement prices of cotton. Moreover, the economy wide policies adopted, including import protection to promote domestic industry and macroeconomic policies that overvalued the real exchange rate, exacerbated the incentive bias against cotton production.

On the other hand, government policies toward the cotton sector have been successful in reducing significantly the price variability for cotton producers. However, the amount of the risk premium (pure stabilization benefit) associated with the reduced income variability due to government interventions compared unfavourably with the negative transfer benefit resulting from the reduced average income for cotton producers. Our assessment, therefore, is that the removal of policy-induced biases against cotton production would have had a significantly positive effect on producer welfare.

These findings suggest to us that delays in implementing government plans to liberalize cotton production and marketing in Egypt will likely continue the welfare bias of sectoral policies against cotton producers. With respect to economywide policies, it is important that the recently initiated trade reforms toward lower tariff and non-tariff barriers (especially on highly protected manufactured products) be intensified and that prudent fiscal and monetary policies to strengthen the country's external account continue to be adopted. Among other things, this will reduce the degree of real exchange rate overvaluation, benefiting not only producers of cotton and other export goods but also those of import-competing products in agriculture and the rest of the economy.

NOTES

[1] According to Dethier (1989, p.41), 'stabilizing producer prices to insulate producers from instability in world prices has been a predominant objective of Egyptian agricultural policy'.

[2] That the aggregation bias is not a significant problem in the use of a weighted average farmgate price in the present study is suggested by the more or less parallel movement of the procurement prices for the major cotton varieties during 1983–91.

[3] In view of this, the distribution of producers' income and their differential aversion to risk are not taken into account in our analysis.

REFERENCES

Bautista, R.M. and Valdés, A. (eds.), 1993, *The Bias Against Agriculture: Trade And Macroeconomic Policies In Developing Countries*, ICS Press for IFPRI and ICEG, San Francisco, California.

Binswanger, H.P., 1980, 'Attitudes Towards Risks: Experimental Measurement Evidence in Rural India', *American Journal of Agricultural Economics*, Vol. 62, No. 3, pp.395–407.

Dethier, J-J., 1989, *Trade, Exchange Rate and Agricultural Pricing Policies in Egypt*, Vols. 1 and 2, World Bank Comparative Studies on the Political Economy of Agricultural Pricing Policies, World Bank, Washington, D.C.

Krueger, A.O., Schiff, M. and Valdés, A., 1988, 'Agricultural Incentives in Developing Countries: Measuring the Effect of Sectoral and Economywide Policies', *World Bank Economic Review*, Vol. 2, pp.255–271.

Newbery, D.M.G. and Stiglitz, J.E., 1981, *The Theory of Commodity Price Stabilization: A Study in the Economics of Risk*, Clarendon Press, Oxford, UK.

DISCUSSION OPENING — Paul W. Heisey *(International Maize and Wheat Improvement Center, Mexico)*

This interesting and well-written paper measures the effects of both direct and indirect policy measures on the level and stability of both producer prices and producer incomes. My remarks are directed less to criticism of the paper than to possible future research avenues that might lead both to more precise definition of the problem and to greater policy relevance.

In one sense the choice of country and crop (Egyptian cotton) makes it almost inevitable that one would find evidence suggesting very high levels of discrimination against export-crop producers. In situations in which discrimination is less obvious, would there be need for even more precise measurement of the price and other policy variables used in the analysis? Are there situations in which stabilization and incentive objectives are less obviously in conflict, and could in fact be pursued simultaneously?

There are several methodological questions whose answers might be useful to researchers attempting to duplicate or extend such a study. First, are there commodities for which world prices themselves are so distorted that they might be less relevant as a basis for welfare analysis? Second, the historical policy regime was marked by three separate phases. Although data may not allow it, it would be interesting to see if policy effects on levels and stability of price and income variables changed significantly from one historical regime to the next. Third, when regimes do change, how fast do producers adjust their expectations? The implicit assumption in the paper appears to be that they adjust immediately.

The paper adds to a very large body of literature demonstrating that governments in developing countries appear to discriminate systematically against agricultural producers. Presumed stability goals have only been partially met, and both prices and incomes are far below what they would have been in the absence of intervention. Given the analysis in the paper, the conclusions are not surprising. The authors suggest the Egyptian government should not delay, as it appears to be doing, further liberalization of the cotton market.

To give such conclusions greater policy relevance, further analysis might take a political economy perspective. Why did the government behave the way it did? Did it have objectives other than stabilization or producer incomes? Why has it started to change its policies? Are policy makers becoming more intelligent about how policies contribute to or detract from development goals? Do farmers now have a greater weight in the social welfare function? Or are policy makers' incentives now different from what they used to be? Finally, why has the government delayed its stated changes in policy?

CHRISTOPHER D. GERRARD AND JOHN SPRIGGS*

Optimal Price Stabilization Policies for Staple Grains: The Case of Maize in Eastern and Southern Africa

Abstract: In the context of (a) stability in domestic maize production, (b) a significant divergence between import and export parity prices for maize, and (c) random variability in world maize prices, Eastern and Southern African governments have for many years attempted to reduce the instability in domestic maize prices. However, governments face a trade-off between the fiscal costs of price stabilization and the degree of price variability allowed. This paper presents a dynamic stochastic simulation model that not only explores the nature of this trade-off, but also determines optimal government policies for domestic target prices and domestic target levels of stock in order to minimize the expected fiscal costs of maintaining given degrees of price stability.

INTRODUCTION

Governments of Eastern and Southern African countries such as Kenya, Malawi, Tanzania, Zambia and Zimbabwe have for many years operated price stabilization programs for their staple food grain, maize.

Generally speaking, prior to each marketing year, governments have announced the official producer and consumer prices for maize that are to prevail in the coming year. Then, as the year has unfolded, governments have attempted to enforce these official prices by means of an internal government monopoly and by quantity adjustments — either in government held stocks, in international trade, or in some combination of the two.

However, in the current economic climate of macroeconomic and sectoral structural adjustment, governments are realizing that their attempts to enforce such perfect price stability within years have been very costly.

On the one hand, they are starting to liberalize their domestic maize markets and to allow some intra-year price variability. On the other hand, in their particular situation, they may rationally choose not to deregulate domestic maize markets completely. They seek some optimal trade-off between the fiscal cost of price-stabilization and the degree of price variability allowed.

BACKGROUND

In a closed economy, in the absence of intertemporal exchange, the domestic consumption of maize will equal the domestic production of maize in any given year. Random variability in production, resulting (primarily) from changes in the weather, will require year to year variability in domestic prices in order to clear domestic markets. Given an intertemporal elasticity of substitution close to unity[1] this is unlikely to be Pareto optimal.

* University of Saskatchewan, Canada. This research has been supported in part by the Economic Development Institute of the World Bank.

If institutional constraints prevent private markets from bringing about a better intertemporal distribution of consumption[2], then the government could, as a first option, establish a domestic buffer stock to reduce intertemporal variability in consumption. However, the annual storage losses associated with a buffer stock operation reduce the potential Pareto improvement[3]

As an alternative, the government could establish a buffer fund — exporting surpluses in good years and importing in bad years — while earning interest on the capital invested in the fund rather than incurring storage losses on the capital invested in a buffer stock. However, the price spread between import and export parity prices increases the cost of a buffer fund. Additions to the buffer fund occur at the (lower) export parity price, while withdrawals occur at the (higher) import parity price[4]

Given random variability in world maize prices in addition to random variability in production, the optimal policy will probably involve some combination of a buffer stock and a buffer fund. Without knowledge of the government's intertemporal preferences, it is not possible to determine the optimal degree of price stability enforced[5] However, it is possible to map the trade-off between fiscal costs and price stability. For each degree of price variability allowed, it is also possible to determine the optimal domestic target price in relation to world prices and domestic self-sufficiency prices, and the optimal balance between a domestic buffer stock and a buffer fund.

THE MODEL

The complete model is presented in Table 1. Both domestic demand and supply curves are constant elasticity functions[6] while the supply curve incorporates both a Nerlovian partial adjustment process and a random component. Both demand and expected supply are known to the government. The expected self-sufficiency price (the intersection of the domestic demand and expected supply curves) is above the export parity price but below import parity — the typical situation in Eastern and Southern Africa (see also Figure 1).

The world price is modeled as a log-normally distributed random walk. The government's target price, P_t^*, is modeled as a weighted average of the expected self-sufficiency price for the current period and the world price of the previous period:

(1) $P_t^* = (1-\omega)SSP_t + \omega MP_{t-1}, \qquad 0 \le \omega \le 1$

The government's target level of stocks is a percentage of the expected domestic demand:

(2) $SK_t^* = \gamma QD(P_t^*) \qquad \gamma \ge 1\%.$[7]

For a given price band around the target price,

(3) $P_t^* - \delta \le P_t \le P_t^* + \delta \qquad \delta \ge 0\%$

The government can choose the parameters, ω and γ, in order to minimize the expected fiscal costs of enforcing this degree of price stability.

As illustrated in Figure 2, when production is high, the government will purchase supplies from the domestic market in order to prevent the price falling below the price floor. As it purchases supplies, then the government will either increase its stocks, export its purchases, or perform some combination of the two. Conversely, when production is low, the government will reduce its stocks and/or import in order to prevent the domestic price rising through the price ceiling. Stocks cannot, however, fall below zero. We assume (1) that the government's stocks will approach zero asymptotically; (2) that for

Table 1 *Dynamic Stochastic Model of Price Stabilization*

Domestic demand:	$QD_t = A \cdot P_t^{-\alpha}$	$\alpha = 0.3,\ A = SSQ_0 / SSP_0^{-\alpha}$
Domestic supply:	$QS'_t = B.P_t^{*\beta}$	$\beta = 0.5,\ B = SSQ_0 / SSP_0^{\beta}$
	$QS^e{}_t = (QS'{}_t)^{\lambda}.(QS^e{}_{t-1})^{(1-\lambda)}$	$\lambda = 0.2$
	$QS_t = QS^e{}_t.\exp(u_t)$	$u_t = N(0,10\%)$
Self-sufficiency quantity:	$SSQ_0 = 1750\ 000$ tonnes	
Self-sufficiency price:	$SSP_0 = \$120$/tonne	
	$SSP_t = \left(A / \left(B^{\lambda} \cdot QS^e_{t-1}{}^{(1-\lambda)} \right) \right)^{(1/(\alpha+\lambda\beta))}$	$t \geq 1$
World price:	$WP_0 = \$110$/tonne	
	$WP_t = WP_{t-1} \cdot \exp(v_t)$	$t \geq 1;\ v_t = N(0,\ 14.5\%)$
Import parity price:	$MP_t = Wp_t + \text{MCOST}$	MCOST = \$40/tonne
Export parity price:	$XP_t = WP_t +$ White maize Premium – XCOST	Premium = \$20 /tonne XCOST = \$70/tonne
Government target price:	$P^*{}_t = (1-\omega)\ SSP_t + wMP_{t-1}$	$0 \leq \omega \leq 1$
Government target stock level:	$SK^*{}_t = \gamma .\ QD(P^*{}_t)$	$\gamma \geq 1\%$
Domestic price:	$P^*{}_t - d \leq P_t \leq P^*{}_t + d$	$\delta \geq 0$
Net government purchases:	$NP_t = 0$	If $\mid P_t - P^*{}_t \mid < \delta$; or
	$NP_t = QS_t - QD_t$	If $\mid P_t - P^*{}_t \mid = \delta$
Government stocks:	$SK_t = (2\ SK^*{}_t)e^{\theta}/(1+e^{\theta})$	$\theta = (2/SK^*{}_t)(NP_t + SK_{t-1} - SK^*_t)$
Net exports:	$X_t - M_t = NP_t - (SK_t - SK_{t-1})$	
One-period cost:	$COST_t = (MP_t \cdot M_t) + (P_t \cdot NP_t) + (SKCOST \cdot SK_{t-1}) - (XP_t \cdot X_t)$	SKCOST = \$25/tonne
Net present value of cost:	$\sum_{t=1}^{T} \frac{COST_t}{(1+r)^t} - \frac{SSP_0\ (SK_T - SK_0)}{(1+r)^T}$	T= 10 years; $r = 7\%$

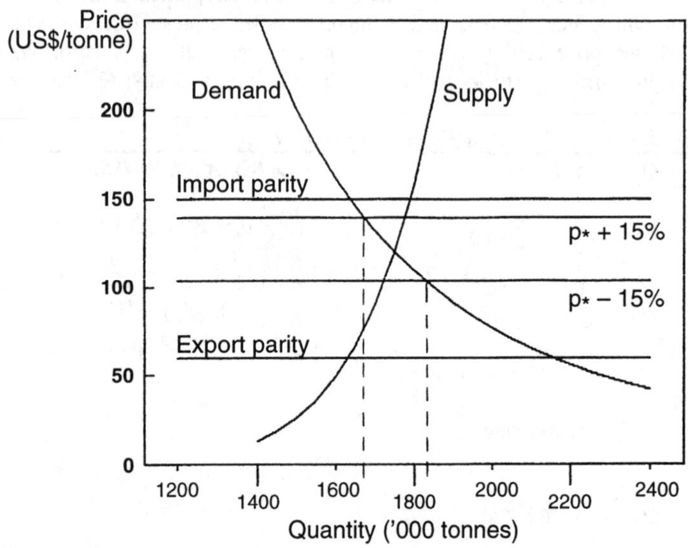

Figure 1

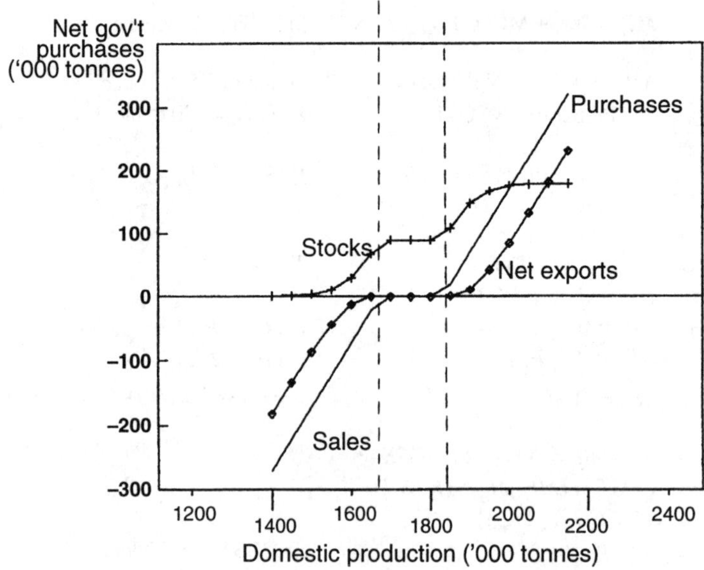

Figure 2

small departures from the target level of stocks, the government neither imports nor exports; and (3) that the government's stock depletion and stock acquisition responses are symmetric around the target level of stocks. As presented in Table 1, the government's stock equation that meets these three criteria is the following:

(4) $SK_t = (2SK_t^*)e^{\theta}/(1+e^{\theta})$, where $\theta = (2/SK_t^*)(NP_t + SK_{t-1} - SK_t^*)$

Net exports are a residual — the difference between net government purchases from the domestic market and the change in government-held stocks.

Less any revenues from exports, the one-period cost of enforcing price stability includes (1) the cost of imports, if necessary; (2) the cost of net purchases from the domestic market if any[8]; and (3) the annual costs of storing government stocks. The net present value of costs is the sum of the discounted one-period costs (over a 10 year simulation period) plus a discounted inventory valuation adjustment between the beginning and ending stocks.

The world price and domestic production are random variables with standard deviations of 14.5 percent and 10 percent respectively[9] For a given set of environmental parameters, in order to determine the optimal target price and target level of stocks that minimizes the expected fiscal costs of enforcing each degree of price stability, we calculated the average cost of 100 replicates for each of 120 different combinations of δ, ω and γ, as follows:

δ = 0, 5%, 10%, 15% and 20%;

ω = 0.00, 0.05, 0.10, 0.15, 0.20 and 0.25; and

γ = 1%, 3%, 5% and 7%.

Then, in order to determine the impact of two environmental parameters — the random variability in domestic production and the export parity price — on the expected fiscal costs, we duplicated the above for each environmental state[10].

THE RESULTS

The overall results are summarized in Figure 3. Each curve corresponds to one combination of the environmental parameters: the standard deviation of domestic production equalling 10 percent or 20 percent, and the white maize premium equaling $10 or $20 a tonne. The numbers in parentheses beside the 20 points on the four curves are the optimal values of ω and γ that minimize the expected fiscal costs of enforcing each degree of price stability.

As expected, for a given set of environmental parameters, there is an inverse relationship between the minimum expected fiscal costs and the degree of price variability allowed. The government must pay a higher cost to achieve a greater degree of price stability. Also, minimum expected costs increase as the random variability in domestic production increases and as the export parity price decreases (because the white maize premium decreases).

As illustrated in Figures 4 to 7, for each set of environmental parameters, the minimum expected cost function is saucer-shaped in ω and γ. For the five degrees of price stability and four environmental states represented in Figure 3, seven are interior solutions, five are corner solutions in which $\omega = 0$, and eight are corner solutions in which $\gamma = 1$ percent[11].

For a given environmental state, as the degree of price variability allowed decreases from 20 percent to 0, the government should generally reduce its target price P_t^* and increase its target level of stocks SK_t^*, in order to minimizes its costs. Also, as the standard deviation of domestic production increases and as the export parity price decreases, the government should reduce its target price and increase its target level of stocks[12].

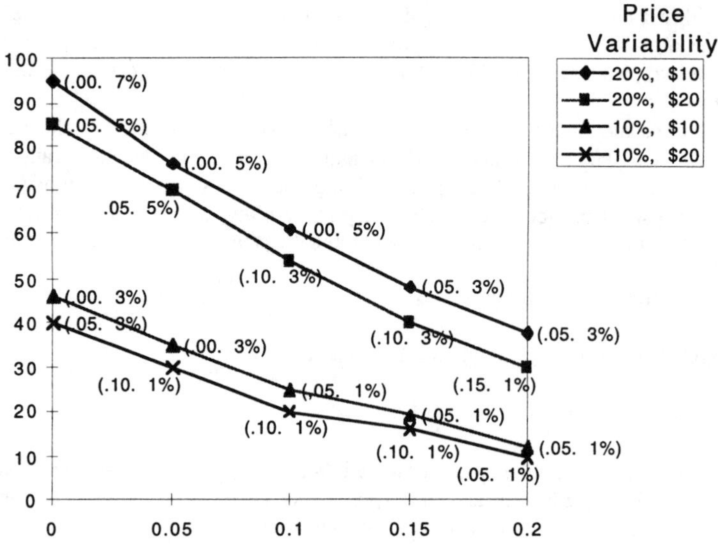

Figure 3 *Minimum Expected Costs*

The government must trade-off two factors that influence the minimum cost of enforcing a given degree of price stability. On the one hand, the target price determines the probability of imports and exports. The higher is the target price, the lower becomes the probability of imports, but the higher probability of exports. On the other hand, the import and export parity prices determine the fiscal cost of importing (at a price above the domestic market price) or exporting (at a price below the domestic market price). The lower is the export parity price the greater becomes the cost of exporting surplus production at a loss, and the more economic becomes a domestic buffer stock.

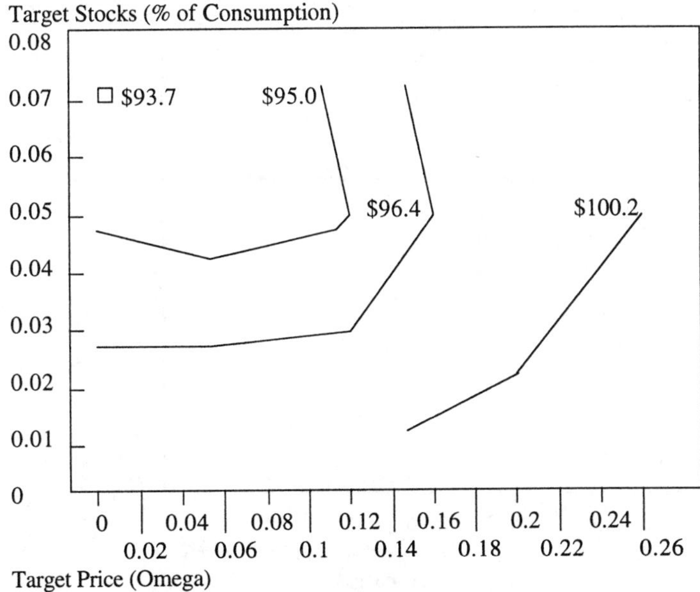

Figure 4 *Price Variability = 0% — St. Dev. = 20%, White Maize Prem. - $10*

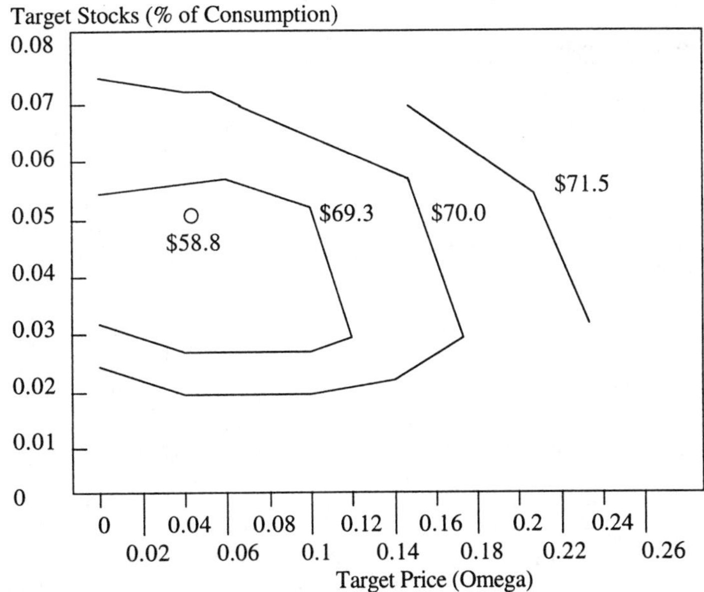

Figure 5 *Price Variability = 5% — St. Dev. = 20%, White Maize Prem. - $20*

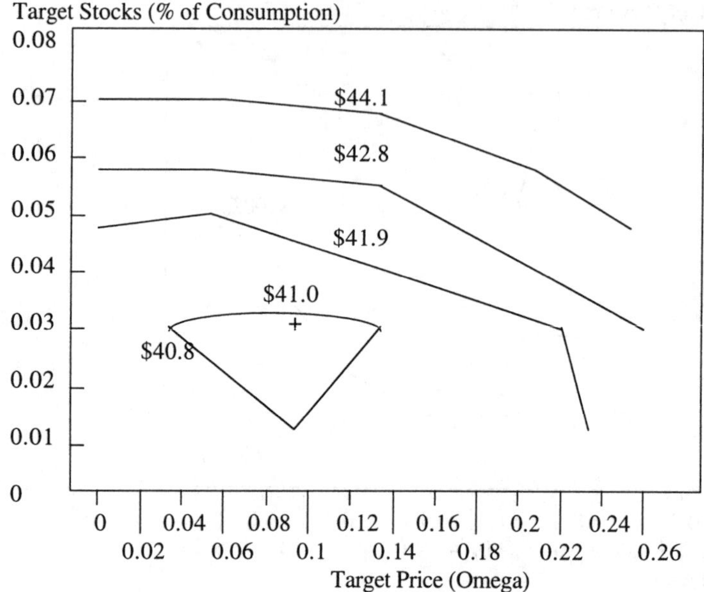

Figure 6 *Price Variability = 15% — St. Dev. = 20%, White Maize Prem. - $20*

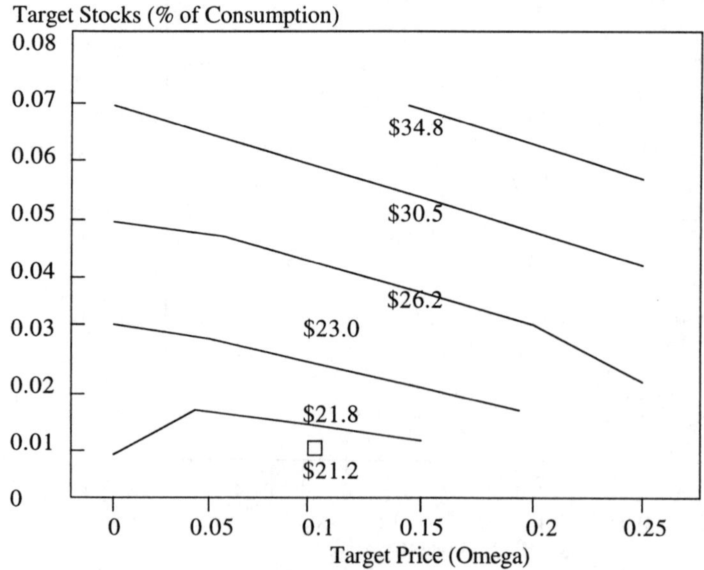

Figure 7 *Price Variability = 10% — St. Dev. = 10%, White Maize Prem. - $20*

CONCLUSION

This paper has presented a dynamic stochastic model of government price stabilization for maize in a typical Eastern of Southern African country. While the environmental constraints and parameters are representative of countries in the region, these could, with relative ease, be more closely calibrated to individual countries. Nonetheless, the basic results will likely continue to hold.

In the future, governments could decrease the cost of their price stabilization programs by allowing somewhat more intra-year price variability than in the past. In the context of random variability in domestic production, a significant divergence between import and export parity prices for maize, and random variability in world maize prices, optimal cost-minimizing policy will generally involve some combination of domestic buffer stocks and international trade. The greater the degree of price stability that the government desires, the closer should be the domestic target price to the expected self-sufficiency price, and the higher should be domestic buffer stocks.

Governments may have other elements in their objective function such as a desire to subsidize domestic consumers (since maize is a wage-good), or a political desire to minimize imports (since imported maize is generally yellow maize rather than white maize). The model could be adapted quite readily to incorporate the cost of these objectives as well.

NOTES

[1] According to Blanchard and Fischer (1989, p.44), empirical estimates of the intertemporal elasticity of substitution usually lie around or below unity.

[2] As a practical matter, since the establishment of government marketing boards for maize in Eastern Africa started in the 1930s, the establishment of private market alternatives, such as private inter-year stockholding and futures markets, have been hindered. Other institutional constraints include exchange controls and a relatively thin international market for white maize.

[3] In Kenya, Pinckney and Gotsch (1987), p.275, estimate annual storage losses to $25 a tonne per year, which equals about 30 percent per year.

[4] In the case of Kenya, Pinckney and Gotsch estimate that the cost of preparing maize for export is $70 a tonne, while the cost of importing maize (international plus domestic transportation costs) is $40 a tonne, for a price spread of $110 tonne. While the country may be able to realize a premium of, say, $20 a tonne when exporting white maize, this still leaves a price spread of $90 a tonne, which compares to the average world price of $110 a tonne over the last 20 years.

[5] As discussed by Knudsen and Nash (1993), pp.266–268, governments may desire price stability for political and macro economic reasons as well as for the micro economic reasons discussed here.

[6] The assumed demand elasticity of –0.3 and long-run supply elasticity of 0.5 are consistent with empirical estimates. See Pinckney and Gotsch (1987), and Gerrard (1983). Like previous authors in this literature, in order to focus on the issue of price instability around a trend, we assume stationarity in production and consumption.

[7] The minimum target level of stocks is greater than zero because of the time lag — typically 3 or 4 months — between placing orders for maize and receiving the imports at the border.

[8] Net government sales in order to prevent the domestic price from rising through the price ceiling represent, of course, a negative cost.

[9] These are the same values assumed by Pinckney and Gotsch (1987).

[10] For 48 000 replicates, at approximately 4 seconds a replicate, the computations took approximately 54 hours using EXCEL 4.0.

[11] Some of the apparent corner solutions may in fact be interior solutions with a value of ω between 0

and 0.05, or a value of γ between 1 and 3 percent.

[12] The minimum cost combination of ω and γ when price variability equals 20 percent, the standard deviation of domestic production equals 10 percent, and the white maize premium equals $20, is an outlier that does not conform completely to the above relationships.

REFERENCES

Blanchard, O.J. and Fischer, S., 1989, *Lectures on Macroeconomics*, MIT Press, Cambridge, Massachusetts.

Gerrard, C.B., 1983, 'Government-Controlled Food Grain Markets, External Trade in Food Grains and Agricultural Development: the Case of Four Countries in East Africa', in Greenshields, B.L. and Bellamy, M.A. (eds.), *Rural Development: Growth and Inequity*, Proceedings of the 18th International Conference of Agricultural Economists, Jakarta, Indonesia, 24 August–2 September, International Association of Agricultural Economists, Gower Press, Aldershot, pp.560–70.

Knudsen, O. and Nash, J., 1993, 'Agricultural Price Stabilization and Risk Reduction in Developing Countries', in Bautista, R.M. and Valdés, A., *The Bias Against Agriculture*, ICS Press, San Francisco, pp.266–68.

Pinckney, T.C. and Gotsch, C.H., 1987, 'Simulation and Optimization of Price Stabilization Policies: Maize in Kenya', *Food Research Institute Studies*, Vol. 20, No. 3.

DISCUSSION OPENING — Guillermo Flichman *(Institut De Montpellier, France)*

This paper proposes a method to optimize price stabilization policies with a particular application to maize production in Eastern and Southern Africa. In this particular application, domestic production can assure self-sufficiency in an average year, A model is proposed to set the target price (always between the internal self-sufficiency price and the previous period world price), given the preferences of the policy-makers in terms of the target level of stocks (defined as a proportion of domestic demand) and tolerated level of deviations around the target price. The model is simple, rigorous, and may help the decision-making process in a situation in which old rigid price policies, based on a fixed internal price, are going to be abandoned.

The principal critical comment I have concerns the way internal supply is represented in the model. As it is expressed in note 7, the focus is on the issue of price instability about a trend, assuming stationarity in production. The question that arises immediately is; can we reasonably expect that a change from a fixed, guaranteed, price to an uncertain one will not affect the level of supply? If farmers have a production mix integrating different crops, more or less risky, both in terms of natural conditions of production (weather) and expected price variability, a policy change that modifies the security status of maize, may completely change the relative position of this crop in the farmers' strategy.

I believe that the scenarios in which the value of g is bigger, should be associated with a lower level of maize production. The cost of policies allowing higher levels of g is probably higher than is calculated by the model. Complementary research at a micro-economic level, using farm production models, could provide the parameters to improve the model substantially.

M.K. EHUI AND S.K. EHUI*

Optimal Pricing of Primary Commodities in Developing Countries: A Model From Sub-Saharan Africa

Abstract: In most developing countries, especially in sub-Saharan Africa, prices received by farmers are not optimal in the sense that they do not optimize government revenues. In this paper a dynamic model for optimal pricing of primary commodities is developed. The model and results demonstrate that optimal prices depend on marginal cost of the commodity stock, the exporting country's supply elasticity, the importing country's demand elasticity, the social rate of time discount. Therefore when the model is cast in a static framework, or the foreign elasticity of demand is not accounted for, the result could be biased.

INTRODUCTION

Virtually all African economies depend on a single or few primary export commodities. Despite the crucial role of primary commodities, government policies in many countries have slowed down their expansion and have in many instances contributed to their decline (Franco, 1981; Lutz and Scandizzo, 1980; Bale and Lutz, 1981). Policies have taken various forms, including the setting of producer prices below the international market price levels, direct or indirect taxation of commodity exports, and overvaluation of national currencies. In most developing countries prices received by farmers are not optimal in the sense that they do not optimize government revenues. Tax rates are often imposed on a cost-plus basis which does not take into account the foreign demand and export supply relationships in the world market.

Today, many developing nations face the challenge of how to set producer prices so as to maximize government revenues and without overly taxing producers. Governments must impose a tax on agricultural exports in order to generate revenues. However, inappropriate imposition of the tax can have deleterious effects on producers' welfare.

The purpose in this study is to develop a model for the optimal pricing of primary commodities in developing countries, taking into account the excess supply and demand relationships as well as the social rate of time discount and commodity storage costs. The model is applied to the cocoa subsector in Côte d'Ivoire and Ghana, two countries in Africa that depend heavily on the export of cocoa, and where the cocoa export trade is regulated through marketing boards (Gbetibouo and Delgado, 1984).

THE MODEL

Two models are considered: (a) the static approach and (b) the dynamic approach.

* United Nations Economic Commission for Africa, Ethiopia and International Livestock Centre for Africa, Ethiopia, respectively.

The Static Approach

The basic idea behind optimum taxation is that a nation facing a less than perfectly elastic demand curve can exploit its international market power via tax or export control to offset the combined deadweight losses caused domestically. As it faces the rest of the trading world, such a nation can select an optimal tax for its own benefit.

Mathematically, government total revenue R is defined as:

$$(1)\quad R = (P_w(Q) - P_d(Q))Q$$

Where $P_w(Q)$ and $P_d(Q)$ denote the inverse excess demand and supply curves, respectively. Totally differentiating Equation (1) gives:

$$(2)\quad dR = P_w^* dQ + Q^* dP_w/dQ^* dQ - P_d^* dQ - Q^* dP_d/dQ^* dQ = 0$$

This is equivalent to (after rearranging terms):

$$(3)\quad P_w + P_w^*(1/E_d) - P_d - P_d^*(1/E_s) = 0$$

Where $E_d = (dQ/dP_w)(P_w/Q)$ and $E_s = (dQ/dP_d)(P_d/Q)$ are the excess demand and supply elasticities. $P_w(1+1/E_d)$ is the marginal revenue (MR_f) and $P_d(1+1/E_s)$ is the marginal cost. Solving for the optimal producer price P_d^* gives:

$$(4)\quad P_d^* = (1+1/E_d)(P_w^* E_s/(E_s+1))$$

If the optimum export tax rate is expressed as a proportion of the world price P_w then Equation (4) can be written as:

$$(5)\quad P_w(1-T^*) = (1+1/E_d)(P_w^* E_s/(1+E_s))$$

The optimum tax rate becomes,

$$(6)\quad T^* = 1-[(1+1/E_d)(E_s/(1+E_s)]$$

Most often, prices are fixed by the marketing boards and do not vary with Q. In this case, the optimum tax rate is:

$$(7)\quad T^* = -1/E_d \text{ and } P_d^* = P_w - T^*$$

It is clear from Equation (7) that when the excess demand curve is perfectly elastic ($E_d = \infty$), the optimum tax rate is zero.

A Generalized Intertemporal Approach

So far the problem has been cast in a static framework. Governments normally manage stocks and have a long-run view of the welfare of their communities. The model proposed here has as its objective the maximization of the present value of the revenues derived from imposing an export tax subject to changes in the commodity stock over time.

Formally, the control problem over an infinite horizon can be stated as follows:

$$(8)\quad \text{Max}(W) = \int_0^\infty e^{-rt}\,(Q,S))dt$$

subject to:

$$(9)\quad R(Q,S) = (P_w(Q)Q - P_d(Q)Q) - C(S)$$

$$(10)\quad \dot{S} = -\dot{Q} = 0 \quad \text{if } \dot{S} = 0$$

$$(11)\quad Q,S > 0$$

Where, W is the measure of present value of government revenues; *r* is the social discount rate. $R(Q,S)$ represents the net government revenue and is defined as the difference between gross revenues from tax rate and the cost of managing the stock, $C(S)$, Equation (9). Equation (10) describes the changes in the commodity stock over time. Equation (11) gives the non-negativity conditions for the commodity stock, and the amount of commodity to be exported.

Assuming an interior solution, the current value Hamiltonian associated with the control problem described by Equations (8)–(11) is given by Equation (12):

$$(12)\quad H = P_w(Q)Q - P_d(Q)Q - C(S) + \lambda Q$$

where, λ is the current value costate associated with the equation of motion, Equation (10). Assuming an interior solution, the maximum principle requires that Equations (13)–(15) hold.

$$(13)\quad dH/dQ = Q(dP_d/dQ) + P_w - P_d - (dP_d/dQ)Q - \lambda = 0$$

$$(14)\quad r\lambda - \dot{\lambda} = H_s = -C_s$$

$$(15)\quad \lim_{t \to \infty} e^{-rt}\lambda(t)S(t) = 0$$

Equation (13) indicates that at any point in time, the quantity to be exported, Q, should be chosen so that the marginal revenue from imposing the tax is equal to the marginal cost of exporting Q plus the opportunity cost of holding the commodity stock (λ). Here, λ, measures the future benefits forgone by a decision to export quantity Q today. In other words, it is a measure of the marginal cost of 'harvesting' Q at time *t* rather than saving it for future generations. Equation (14) implies that the commodity stock services should be employed up to the point where the marginal benefit of the stock is equal to the social cost of the capital. The right hand side of Equation (14) represents the marginal benefit of the commodity stock while the left measures the cost of employing one unit of the commodity stock at any point in time. The cost includes both an interest charge $(r\lambda)$ and a capital gain $(-\dot{\lambda})$. Finally Equation (15) is the transversality condition.

Totally differentiating Equation (13) with respect to time and combining it with Equation (14) yields an expression for the time rate of change along the optimal path.

$$(16)\ \dot{Q} = Q\frac{r(P_w(1 + 1/E_d) - (P_d(1 + 1/E_s) + C_s}{P_w/E_d - P_d/E_s} = 0$$

where C_s is the marginal cost of the commodity stock.

In a steady state, the rate of change in the commodity stock is necessarily zero. Setting $\dot{S}_t = \dot{Q}_t = 0$ in equation (16), a steady state commodity stock S^* is uniquely defined by

$$(17)\ (P_w(1+1/E_d) - P_d(1+1/E_s)) = C_s$$

Solving for P_d^* in Equation (17) gives:

$$(18)\ P_d^* = (1+1/E_d)(P_w E_s/(1+E_s) + C_s E_s/(r(1 + E_s))$$

The optimum tax rate is obtained by solving $P_d^* = P_w(1-T^*)$

$$(19)\ T^* = 1-(1+1/E_d)(E_s/(1+E_s)) - C_s^* E_s/(rP_w(1+E_s))$$

It can be observed from Equations (18) and (19) that the optimal producer price and the export tax differ from those obtained under the static framework by the factor $C_s^* E_s/(rP_w(1+E_s))$. Comparative statics results can be obtained by taking the partial derivatives of P_d^* and T^* with respect to C_s and r.

$$(20)\ dP_d^*/dC_s = -E_s/(r(1+E_s)) < 0$$

$$(21)\ dT^*/dC_s = E_s/rP_w(1+E_s)) > 0$$

$$(22)\ dP_d/dr = C_s E_s/(r(1+E_s) < 0 \text{ and}$$

$$(23)\ dT^*/dr = C_s E_s/(rP_w(1+E_s) > 0$$

Two conclusions can be drawn from the analysis. (a) The optimum producer price depends on the marginal cost of commodity stock, the exporting country's supply elasticity, the import demand elasticity, and on the social rate. When the problem is cast in a static framework or when the foreign elasticity of demand is not taken into account, the results are biased. (b) An increase in the marginal cost of the stock leads to a decrease in the optimal producer price and an increase in the maximum tax rate. The social rate of time discount has the opposite effects. A higher value of *r* leads to a decrease in the optimal producer price and an increase in the optimal tax rate.

In the case where domestic price is fixed,

$$(24)\ T^* = -1/E_d - C_s/rP_w$$

It is clear from the results that a shortsighted trade policy that neglects commodity stock-flow relationships and the social rate of time discount will result in a serious over-taxation of the export sector. Too high a tax rate would result in considerable welfare losses through restrictions in the volume of trade, and shortfalls over time in export earnings.

Table 1 *Optimal Pricing in the Short and Long-run: Ghana and Côte d'Ivoire, Case I ($/ton)*

	Ghana				Côte d'Ivoire			
	P_w	P_d	P^*_{ds}	P^*_{dl}	P_w	P_d	P^*_{ds}	P^*_{dl}
1964	491.49	369.160	434.17	466.92	475.81	285.7	266.46	406.33
1965	380.48	369.60	336.34	361.45	349.21	322.34	195.56	298.22
1966	363.48	246.04	321.32	345.31	427.42	238.30	239.36	365.02
1967	453.73	194.04	401.09	431.04	533.33	284.63	298.67	455.46
1968	508.36	233.24	449.39	490.18	643.59	282.90	360.42	549.63
1969	684.35	251.86	604.96	650.13	823.53	251.87	461.18	703.29
1970	802.18	288.12	709.13	762.07	673.43	289.80	377.12	575.11
1971	603.82	161.70	533.77	573.63	670.07	325.30	375.24	572.24
1972	533.98	229.32	472.04	507.28	556.60	331.97	311.69	475.34
1973	788.24	318.92	696.80	748.83	875.52	352.52	490.30	747.69
1975	1489.13	478.82	1316.39	1414.67	1301.76	790.27	728.98	1111.70
1976	1366.77	510.97	1208.22	1298.43	1534.36	704.25	859.24	1310.34
1977	2290.70	638.72	2024.98	2176.16	2544.94	765.14	1425.16	2173.37
1978	3061.50	483.87	2706.36	2908.43	2920.90	1196.17	1635.70	2494.45
1979	3555.56	668.12	3143.12	3377.78	3196.49	1243.78	1790.03	2729.80
1980	3350.71	1452.00	2962.02	3183.17	2797.10	1328.61	1566.42	2388.78
1981	2063.38	1452.00	1824.03	1960.21	1675.64	1043.84	938.36	1430.99
1982	1596.69	1356.00	1411.47	1516.85	1530.33	892.19	856.98	1306.90
1983	1517.57	396.00	1394.57	1498.69	1474.51	718.77	825.73	1259.23
1984	2330.42	400.00	2060.09	2213.89	2027.61	729.77	1135.46	1731.58
1985	2078.31	480.00	1837.23	1974.39	2133.08	991.93	1194.53	1821.06
1986	2353.93	622.60	2080.87	2236.24	2177.56	1239.30	1219.43	1859.64
1987	2382.00	422.105	2105.68	2262.90	2382.00	1498.13	1335.82	2048.52
1988	1783.00	420.00	1576.17	1693.85	1783.00	1333.00	998.48	1533.38
1989	1795.00	396.00	1409.98	1515.25	1595.00	1333.00	893.20	1371.70
1989	1795.00	396.00	1409.98	1515.25	1595.00	1333.00	893.20	1371.70

Prices: P_w international; P_d domestic; P^*_{ds} short-run optimal domestic; P^*_{dl} long-run optimal domestic.

CALCULATION OF THE OPTIMAL PRICES AND EXPORT TAX RATES

In order to compute the optimal producer price and tax rate, import demand and excess supply elasticities were calculated using data from the top five exporters, including Côte d'Ivoire, Brazil, Ghana, Malaysia and Nigeria. Together these countries in 1988, exported 80 percent of the world cocoa to the top 4 importers; Germany, USA, The Netherlands and Italy. Results for optimal prices are reported in Table 1. In the short and long-runs, the optimal prices derived for Côte d'Ivoire are higher than the actual prices, in general, suggesting that farmers have been over taxed. Optimal producer prices are about 1.2 times greater than actual prices. Toward the end of the 1980s, however, the government objective of raising revenue became more rational than before in the short-run.

It is quite obvious that Ghana has been facing net social loss as optimal prices depart significantly from actual prices. By re-examining Table 1, it can be noticed that the estimated optimal prices are about 1.5 times greater than actual prices, for all years, and the gap was quite high in the 1980s. This clearly suggests that cocoa farmers were being over taxed in Ghana as well. Table 2 provides summary results of the optimal and actual tax rates for the period 1964–1988. A distinction is made between short-run and long-run. When government depends heavily on taxes for its revenue, it taxes on the basis of short-run elasticities. Otherwise, long-run elasticities are used. We see from Table 2 that when a government depends heavily on taxes for its revenue (short-run) and has a larger share (case I) the tax optimal tax rate is lower than the one which is heavily dependent on taxes (short-run) but has a small share of the market (case II). This is in line with our a priori expectations from the theoretical model. While the actual tax rates were about 48 and 60 percent in Côte d'Ivoire and Ghana, the suggested long-run optimal tax rates are about 14 and 5 percent for the two countries, respectively. The long-run case is the situation where the government has sources of revenue other than from cocoa.

Table 2 *Import Demand Elasticities Facing Côte d'Ivoire and Ghana and Their Optimal Export Taxes, 1964–1988, Cases I and II*

	Import demand elasticities		Actual taxes	Export tax (percent)			
Country	Short-run	Long-run		Short-run		Long-run	
Côte d'Ivoire				Case I	Case II	Case I	Case II
	−2.27	−6.84	48	44.0	62.5	14.0	54
Ghana	−8.56	−21.13	60	11.6	81	5.0	72

Notes: Case I: case of less than perfectly elastic situation; Case II: case of a highly elastic situation.

Table 3 presents the optimal tax rates using the dynamic model for Côte d'Ivoire alone. It shows that the tax rate varies with time. Also, the optimal tax rates are lower that the actual tax rates for the period 1980 to 1985. However during the last four years from 1986 to 1989, the actual tax rates were lower than the optimal. One should recall that the political situation in Cote d'Ivoire was a bit unstable and the world prices were going down. Therefore it was not politically feasible to reduce the prices that were given to the farmers. The only option that was left to the government was to reduce the actual tax that was perceived. The partial conclusion here is that if policy makers ignore the time factor, the discount rate and the stock-flow relationship, there would be risk of overtaxing producers.

Table 3 *Optimal Tax Rates: Dynamic Case (Percent): Côte d'Ivoire*

Year	Actual	Optimal
1980	61.08	45.0
1981	52.48	45.0
1982	47.70	46.5
1983	45.69	47.0
1984	51.27	46.0
1985	53.49	46.0
1986	43.08	47.0
1987	37.11	47.0
1988	25.23	47.0
1989	16.42	47.0

CONCLUSIONS

The results of the policy modelling exercise strongly suggest that, in general, the price and taxing behaviour of the two countries did not optimize net revenue. One issue that should be of interest to policy makers is the impact of the time factor in their taxation decisions. Since the estimate of the optimal tax is based on the price elasticity of demand and the price response of the commodity from other exporters, policy makers should take into account both short- and long-term demand and supply elasticities. This is especially true when there is a large gap between the two.

A comparison of the estimated optimal export tax rates for Côte d'Ivoire and Ghana with their current taxes show that when the government depends heavily on the tax for its revenue, it taxes on the basis of the short-run elasticities. This tax rate is much higher than if the long-run elasticities were used, which is usually the case when the taxes are a small proportion of government revenue. But the higher tax rate makes the country susceptible to loss of market share over time because it reduces the incentive to its own producers (while raising world prices) and encourages the substitution of the commodity by other producers. Actual export tax rates by Ghana on cocoa were much higher than the optimal rates even when based on short-run elasticity estimates. This may well have contributed to the reduction in the country's share of the world market.

Regardless of the reasons for the non optimal pricing and taxation behaviour, the policy framework presented in this study is of potential use to primary commodity producing countries as a yardstick against which to measure feasible policies. It should provide a basis for sound economic arguments to induce policy changes in the direction of optimal producer price.

REFERENCES

Bale, M. D. and Lutz, E., 1981, 'Price Distortions and Their Effects: An International Comparison', *American Journal of Agricultural Economics*, Vol. 63, No. 1, pp.8–22.

Franco, R., 1981, The Monopolistic Cocoa Pricing, *Journal of Development Economics*, No. 8, pp.77–92.

Gbetibouo, M. and Delgado, C., 1984, 'Lessons and Constraints of Export Crop-Led Growth', in Zartan, J.W. and Delgado, C. (eds.), *The Political Economy of the Ivory Coast*, Praeger, New York.

Lutz, E. and Scandizzo, P. L., 1980, 'Price Distortions in Developing Countries: A Bias Against Agriculture', *European Review of Agricultural Economics*, Vol. 7, No. 1, pp. 5–27.

GENERAL DISCUSSION — Yoav Kislev, Chairman *(Hebrew University of Jerusalem, Israel)*

Romeo M. Bautista provided the following reply to questions by the chairman and the discussant concerning taxation as an objective of government intervention. It is true that government interventions in developing countries are motivated by the need to raise revenue, among other important and well recognized objectives that also include income redistribution. However, as the title suggests, the paper is more narrowly concerned with the evaluation of the effects of government interventions on export price variability as it affects producer income and welfare. The political economy questions raises are interesting but are beyond the scope of the paper. One would like to see research in this area, more firmly based on intimate knowledge of the workings of developing country governments.

Dr Bautista argued that it is odd that the discussant found the conclusions of the paper to be 'good', but criticizes them for not being novel since the benefits of less government interventions have been known for some time. Criticism should be directed to the analysis done, not the conclusions reached. He noted that the calculated producer incomes are based not on 'instantaneous' supply response to price changes (as the discussant assumed) but on a distributed lag a la Koyck–Nerlove. Even if world commodity prices are distorted, policy analysis for 'small countries', to be useful, has to make use of expected or long-run world prices. It is not always the case that government intervention serves to reduce domestic price instability. Producers of copra (coconut) in the Philippines, for example, have faced a higher degree of price instability due to government intervention at the same time that the average copra price has been made lower (relative to no government intervention).

It was pointed out that the Egyptian government had heavily subsidized inputs to cotton producers, providing finance and sharing more than 50 percent of the costs of pest control. These subsidies were not considered by Bautista and Gehlhar (Amin I. Abdou). Quality degradation over an increasing proportion of the crop since the mid sixties explains much of the export-farm gate price gap.

Jean-Marc Boussard, commenting on the Gerrard and Spriggs paper observed that, in fact, the stabilization cost will be infinite. If we assume that agricultural production functions are homogenous and of degree 1, then the long-run marginal cost curve is flat. With a government buying any quantity supplied at fixed price, the demand is also parallel to the x axis. Then the production, stock and the cost of stabilization is infinite.

W.K. Asemso-Okyere (Ghana) suggested that in the Ehui and Ehui analysis the long-run dynamics of the cocoa industry should be taken into account. Since cocoa is produced from trees of different ages, modelling should have been with vintages so that the age-composition of the trees are taken into account. There are short-run supply responses but the government should maximize its revenues based on long-run supply response.

HARALD VON WITZKE AND ULRICH HAUSNER*

The Political Economic Myth and Reality of Agricultural Producer Price Support: The 'Agricultural Treadmill' Revisited

Abstract: The *myth* of agricultural price policy is that it can counteract the economic effect of the 'agricultural treadmill'. In this paper it is shown that this is not the case. The political economic *reality* of farm price programs is that a growth in agricultural supply leads to lower levels of price support, all other things bring equal. In US wheat and grain policy, the extent of endogenous policy adjustments has been in the same order of magnitude as price changes that would have occurred without price policy.

INTRODUCTION

In his book *Farm Prices: Myth and Reality*, the agricultural economist Willard W. Cochrane (1958) has characterized the economic mechanism that drives the long-term adjustment processes of agriculture in the course of economic development. The core of his argument is that in growing industrialized countries the growth in supply tends to outstrip the demand growth. Therefore, food and agricultural commodities become more abundant, and the long term trend of agricultural producer prices is negative. The growth in demand is limited because both the income elasticity of demand for food and the population growth tend to be low in developed countries. The growth in production is high because farmers are price takers and, therefore, the adoption of technological change is the most important way to increase individual incomes. However, collectively the race to increase output ultimately leads to lower prices and, given the low price elasticity of demand for food in developed countries, farm incomes tend to grow at lower rates than non-farm incomes.

Cochrane's treadmill theory is formulated in a closed economy framework. Hayami and Ruttan (1985) and Tyers and Anderson (1992) demonstrate that this phenomenon can, in principle, be observed on a global scale as well. As a consequence, the real world market prices of food and agricultural commodities tend to decline in the long run.

In most industrialized countries, government programs are in place which provide agricultural producers with prices above those prevailing on the world markets. Price support programs are maintained in an attempt to off-set or, at least, to alleviate the effects of the agricultural treadmill on relative farm incomes. Without government market intervention an increase in the supply of an agricultural commodity causes the market price to decline, whereby the price decline is determined by the extent of the supply growth and the price elasticity of demand, all other things being equal. The myth of farm price support programs is that a government set minimum producer price acts to change the effective demand elasticity faced by farmers to infinity. No matter what the supply is, farmers will always receive the minimum price, provided that the world market price is lower. This is typically reflected in textbook analyses of the social welfare effects of minimum producer price programs such as deficiency payments or variable levies. Government support is

* Centre for International Food and Agricultural Policy and Department of Agricultural and Applied Economics, University of Minnesota, respectively.

exogenously given. A change in supply does not affect the producer price and the resulting change in producer surplus is unambiguously positive.

However, public choice theory stipulates that policy decisions are endogenous rather than exogenously given. Agricultural economists have made a lot of progress in recent years analysing the determinants of agricultural policy decisions. One of the insights of this type of analysis is that not everything remains unchanged and that important variables may change when there is a growth in supply, some of which, in turn, may influence agricultural policy.

In the remainder of this paper we will develop a simple public choice model of agricultural producer price support. The model will be tailored to suit US wheat and corn policy, and it will be tested empirically for these two markets. We will then show that the reality of farm price support programs is that a growth in supply ultimately results in endogenous policy changes for US farmers which essentially lead to the same price reactions as would be observed in the absence of direct government market intervention.

A POLITICAL ECONOMIC FRAMEWORK: US CORN AND WHEAT TARGET PRICES

In the vast majority of developed countries, the government supports agricultural producer prices. In the United States, agricultural price policy is now almost six decades old. Since the early 1960s, US agricultural price support in wheat and corn has been characterized by two central mechanisms. One is the loan rate. This is the price at which the government provides loans to farmers. It enables them to hold crops for later sale. If the market price is below the loan rate farmers may forfeit the crops placed under loan to the government. The other mechanism consists of direct payments to farmers based on production or acreage planted to these crops. The resulting producer support price has been referred to as target price since the early 1970s. By setting the target price above and the loan rate at the expected world market price the government ran subsidize agriculture as much as desired while the commodities usually can be moved to the export markets without direct subsidy.

The following political economic analysis focuses on the target price. It is based on a straightforward public choice model where a single agricultural policy maker has preferences over agricultural producers and non-producers (that is, taxpayers). The policy maker's problem is:

(1) $\max U(Y, B)$

(2) $\text{s.t.} f_1(P) \geq Y$

(3) $f_2(P) \geq B$

where Y = producer income, B = budgetary expenditures of price policy, and P = target price.

Equation (1) is assumed to be continuous and concave, where $\partial U / \partial Y > 0$ and $\partial U / \partial B < 0$. The political economic constraints in Equations (2) and (3) are assumed to be continuous and linear. The target price is chosen to maximize utility (equation 1). The optimum condition of this maximization problem is:

$$(4)\quad (\partial U/\partial Y).(\partial f_1/\partial P) = (\partial U/\partial B).(\partial f_2/\partial P)$$

The interpretation of Equation (4) is straightforward. The policy maker sets the target price such that the marginal political economic benefits of raising the target price (via growing support from producers) equal its marginal political economic costs (via declining support from taxpayers).

Given the assumptions about the curvatures of Equations (1) through (3) it follows immediately from the Implicit Function Theorem that there is a solution for P in principle. However, unless the functional forms of Equations (1) through (3) are known there is no *a priori* information about its functional form. Let the (approximation for the) solution for t be linear:

$$(5)\quad P_t^0 = \alpha_0 + \alpha_1 Y_t + \alpha_2 B_t$$

In Equation (5), P_t^0 denotes the optimum price for t. Of course, in the real world policy makers are not perfectly free to adjust the target price from one year to the other. To account for policy inertia assume that the target price adjustments over time are Nerlovian:

$$(6)\quad P_t - P_{t-1} = \gamma\left(P_t^0 - P_{t-1}\right) + \theta_t$$

where $0 < \gamma \leq 1$ and the error term θ_t = NID.

From Equations (5) and (6) it follows:

$$(7)\quad P_t = \beta_0 + \beta_3 P_{t-1} + \beta_1 Y_t + \beta_2 B_t + \theta_t$$

where $\beta_0 = \gamma\alpha_0$, $\beta_3 = 1-\gamma$, $\beta_1 = \gamma\alpha_1$, and $\beta_2 = \gamma\alpha_2$.

EMPIRICAL EVIDENCE: 1962–63 — 1983–84

When the decisions on the target price in t are made, the policy makers do not know Y_t and B_t. Hence these variables have to be substituted by their expected values. If the policy maker has rational expectations then $Y_t = Y_t^* + v_t$ and $B_t = B_t^* + w_t$, where Y_t^* and B_t^* denote the expectations of Y_t and B_t respectively, and v_t and w_t are error terms which are NID. Hence, the empirical model is:

$$(8)\quad P_t = \beta_0 + \beta_3 P_{t-1} + \beta_1 Y_t^* + \beta_2 B_t^* + \varepsilon_t$$

Obviously, in developed countries one would expect the signs of both β_1 and β_2 to be negative. That is a relatively low (high) expected producer income as well as relatively low (high) expected budgetary expenditures will result in a relatively high (low) support price, all other things being equal. Moreover, $0 \leq \beta_3 < 1$, as $\beta_3 = 1 - \gamma$ and $0 < \gamma \leq 1$. Notice that $\varepsilon_t = \theta_t + \beta_1 v_t + \beta_2 w_t$, and, therefore, instrument variables have to be used for Y_t^* and B_t^*. The instruments have been estimated via auto regressions. The time lag was chosen for each time series based on the significance of the coefficients (see the appendix).

The empirical analysis covers the time period 1962–63 to 1983–84. The data used are from USDA (1984, 1989) publications. All monetary variables have been deflated by the CPI. As detailed information on US wheat and corn producer incomes is not available, the US share in total world exports was used as a proxy. The results of the regressions which are corrected for first order autocorrelation of the residuals are presented in Table 1. All coefficients have the expected signs and are highly significant.

Table 1 *The Determinants of the US Target Price in Wheat and Corn*

	Wheat	Corn
β_0	4.207 (2.90)	1.023 (3.90)
β_1	–0.0808 (–2.73)	–0.0090 (–3.04)
β_2	–0.6049 (–2.59)	–2.898 (–2.74)
β_3	0.6362 (5.21)	0.9313 (762)
$\overline{R}^2$	0.853	0.801
δ	–0.291 (–1.16)	–0.175 (–0.696)

Source: Own computations based on USDA (1984, 1989).
Notes: *t* values in parenthesis. The support price is in \$ per bushel; budgetary expenditures are in \$1000; the US share in world exports is in percent; and δ is the estimated autocorrelation correction parameter.

THE AGRICULTURAL TREADMILL WHEN POLITICAL DECISIONS ARE ENDOGENOUS

The analysis of endogenous agricultural producer price support has immediate implications for the agricultural treadmill. Technical change results in productivity growth in US agriculture which increases both policy determining variables, all other things being equal. This is illustrated graphically in Figure 1 for the small country case.

Technological change shifts the US supply curve from S to S'. At a given support price level (P_s) this increases producer surplus by ABO while budgetary expenditures grow by ABAFT. However, the growth in producer income and budgetary expenditures would result in a declining price support. This is shown in Figure 1 where the support price declines from P_s to P_s' The consequence is that the *effective* demand faced by producers when policy decisions are endogenous is less than perfectly elastic with regard to the price.

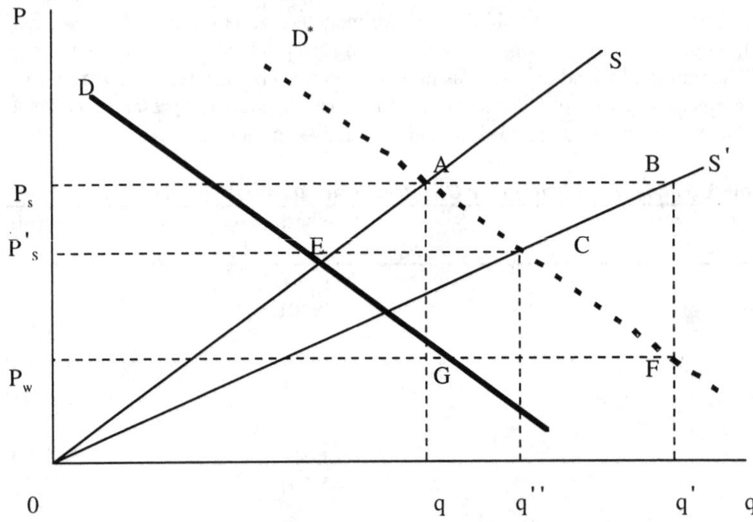

Figure 1 *The 'Agricultural Treadmill' when Price Policy is Endogenous*

Rather it is characterized by a movement from A to C which is extrapolated in Figure 1 to D^*.

As we have seen, the introduction of a minimum producer price does not render the agricultural treadmill dysfunctional. What price programs do, is they create temporary rents for landowners (be they farmers or not) which are eroded in subsequent periods via the endogenous adjustments of support prices, while the social welfare losses and adverse distributive effects continue for as long as the programs are in place. Obviously, the process discussed here can be offset when the political power of agricultural interest groups increases over time such that the minimum price would increase at any given level of agricultural income and budgetary expenditures. This is a phenomenon that has been observed in the course of economic development in many countries, and it explains part of the decline in real agricultural world market prices that has occurred in the last few decades (Tyers and Anderson, 1992). However, once agriculture has undergone major structural adjustments and it has become a small industry, the political power of agricultural interest groups does not grow much over time any more. Consequently, the *reality* of farm programs sets in, producer price support declines, and the agricultural treadmill begins to function again.

To illustrate the effects of the agricultural treadmill with government market intervention at given levels of political influence of agricultural interest groups, consider the empirical results of this study and assume an exogenous and permanent increase in US production each of corn and wheat. This will increase both x_1 and x_2 and will, thus, lead to a lower price in subsequent periods. Obviously, the dynamic nature of Equation (8) which was estimated for wheat and corn (see Table 1), implies that it may take several periods until the support price converges at its new equilibrium level. In addition to the parameters of these regressions, the extent of the producer support price reduction on each market depends on the domestic supply elasticity, international price transmission elasticities, the world market price elasticity of demand faced by the USA, policy adjustments in other countries, as well as changes in production and consumption in other countries.

Of course, the extent of the changes in producer support prices depends on the particular scenarios analysed and on the magnitude of the aforementioned parameters. For most of these parameters there exist econometric estimates on which a simulation of the effects of a growth in US production on producer price support can be based.

Table 2 exhibits the results of simulations of an exogenous and permanent 5 percent increase in the US production of wheat and corn respectively for the small and the large country case. Of course, the USA is a large country in both the wheat and the corn market. However, we have elected to analyse the small country case also, because only one additional parameter is needed for each commodity (the US supply elasticity), and there is some consensus about its order of magnitude. For the analysis of the producer support price changes resulting from an increase in production in the large country case, some additional assumptions and parameters are required[1]. As indicated by Table 2, both scenarios resulted in similar reductions of the producer support prices.

Table 2 *The Effect of a Five Percent Increase in US Wheat and Corn Production on the Real US Producer Support Prices in Wheat and Corn*[a]

Crop[b]	Wheat	Corn
x_{3t}	1.44	0.94
	(small country assumption)	
x_{3t+1}	1.36	0.91
x_{3t+5}	1.38	0.83
percent change t, t+5	–4.2	–11.7
	(large country assumption)	
x_{3t+1}	1.37	0.91
x_{3t+5}	1.38	0.82
percent change t, t+5	–4.2	–11.7

Source: Own computation based on USDA (1984, 1989). For details see the appendix.
Notes: [a] x_3 is the real producer support price deflated by the CPI; x_{3t} is the price in the base period.
[b] Base year t is 1983/84 for wheat and 1984–85 for corn.

In view of the nature of the empirical model and the variables used, it is not very surprising that the results of the large country scenario do not differ much from the small country case. Any given growth in production results in a relatively larger increase in budgetary expenditures in the large country case. The partial effect reduces the support price more than in the small country case. However, a growing production in the large country case reduces the world market price and thus stimulates domestic demand such that US exports increase less than in the small country case. Both partial effects happen to compensate each other in the scenarios analysed here and, therefore, the large country scenario leads to results which are very close to the small country case.

Given the dynamic nature of equations (13) and (14) we have reported the support prices for t+1 and t+5. Generally, the support price converged rather quickly. The price changes reported in Table 1 are in the expected direction. An increase in production reduces the producer support price for each commodity, as it acts to increase both support price determining variables x_1 and x_2. The extent of price reductions is reasonable; the resulting effective price elasticities actually faced by producers when US price support is endogenous was –1.19 for wheat and –0.43 for corn. These numbers are in the range of those reported for the world market demand elasticity faced by US wheat and corn producers (McCalla, Abbott and Paarlberg, 1986).

CONCLUSION

To our knowledge, our estimates of the extent of endogenous support price changes when there is an increase in production are the first of their kind. Further attempts at quantifying the effective producer price elasticity when price support is endogenous may result in estimates that differ from ours, depending on theoretical concepts used, time periods analysed, or scenarios simulated. In view of the fact that the analysis of the quantitative reaction of price support to changes in production is more complex than the more traditional analysis of supply or demand elasticities, it is likely that the range of estimates will be rather wide. Therefore, one must resist the temptation to over interpret the results reported in Table 2. Nevertheless, it is clear that during the time period analysed here, the agricultural treadmill has been functional in US wheat and corn production: An increase in production acts to reduce the level of producer price support and the price reduction is in the range to be expected without government market intervention.

NOTE

[1] The parameters used in the simulations in Table 2 are for each market: domestic US supply elasticity = 0.5; domestic US price elasticity of demand = –0.2; elasticity of transmission of world market to US consumer price = 1.0; effective export price elasticity faced by US producers = –1.65.

REFERENCES

Cochrane, W.W., 1988, *Farm Price: Myth and Reality*, University of Minnesota Press, Minneapolis.

Hayami, Y. and Ruttan, V.W., 1985, *Agricultural Development: An International Perspective*, 2nd ed., Johns Hopkins University Press, Baltimore, Maryland.

McCalla, F., Abbott, P. C. and Paarlberg, P.L., 1986, 'Policy Interdependence, Country Response, and the Analytical Challenge', in USDA-ERS, *Embargoes, Surplus Disposal and U.S. Agriculture*, Washington, D.C.

Tyers, R. and Anderson, K., 1992, *Disarray in World Food Markets*, Cambridge University Press.

USDA, 1984, *Background for 1985 Farm Legislation*, USDA-ERS, Washington, D.C.

USDA, 1989, *Background for 1990 Farm Legislation*, USDA-ERS, Washington, D.C.

APPENDIX

Estimates of Instrument Variables

$$Y_t^w = 23.09 + 0.4385\, Y_{t-1}^w$$
$$(2.79) \quad (2.21)$$
$$\bar{R}^2 = 0.151$$

$$B_t^w = 204\ 233 + 448.9\, B_{t-1}^w$$
$$(1.88) \quad (1.98)$$
$$\bar{R}^2 = 0.123$$

$$Y_t^c = 23.66 + 0.639\, Y_{t-2}^c$$
$$(2.96) \quad (1.46)$$
$$\bar{R}^2 = 0.374$$

$$B_t^c = 949\ 233 + 318.6\, B_{t-1}^c$$
$$(2.94) \quad (1.46)$$
$$\bar{R}^2 = 0.096$$

DISCUSSION OPENING — Paavo Makinen *(Ministry of Agriculture and Forestry, Finland)*

Let me start with a seemingly unrelated example from my own country, Finland. The development of agricultural policies had been relatively uneventful for the last 30 years until the latter part of the 1980s. It was generally accepted that the agricultural policies were rather costly, but the necessary funds were annually made available, anyhow, after normal political rethoric and bargaining.

Then along came the concept of PSE, which revealed to the general public and the MPs the agricultural policies actually may cost a lot more than the sum indicated in the budget. The whole concept was strongly disputed by the farmers but applauded by the critics of the policies. The main critical party, the social democrats, had incidentally been in the government for the previous 20 years.

With this added transparency one would have expected that a major change would have occured when the revision of the agricultural income legislation was due in 1990. In spite of big muscle flexing very little change actually took place, notwithstanding the fact that the centre party, the main farmers party, was not in the government. This certainly revealed well the preferences concerning agricultural policies in Finland.

For the last 35 years the centre party has been the leading party in the Government, but the agricultural sector has faced much bigger changes than ever before in the post war period.

Budget expenditures on agriculture have declined significantly, farmers pay a big part of the export subsidies, supply control measures have been tightened and Finland has accepted the GATT deal and negotiated the Treaty of Accession to the European Union, which both will tighten the economic environment of farmers even further.

All of these changes have been initiated exogenously, through outside events. I underline the word events, because no interest group or political party can claim a victory over agricultural policies through their own action. Due to a deep depression, the national budget became extremely tight and for general national economic and political reasons Finland had to make the deal in the GATT and with the EU.

I think that this example shows some of the complexities and interlinkages we are facing when attempting to model behaviour of policymakers. The discussion we have had so far in the conference has touched many of these issues, but the effects of general economic development and policies, such as fiscal, monetary and exhange rate policies, to agriculture and agricultural policy making have received little attention in our discussion on political economics.

This is also the case in the paper by von Witzke and Hausner. Unfortunately they have not been able to come here personally, and I thank Dr Kennedy for presenting their paper. I will confine here my comments to only the few which I found more important.

In building their model, the authors assume that there is a single agricultural policy maker and that political economic constraints are linear. They do not discuss the validity of these assumptions. Should we now accept that statistically nice results from the empirical part conform to these assumptions and that the specification of the model was right. Perhaps the 'nice' results were mostly due to the use of autocorrelated lagged variables.

I have some doubts to the both of these assumptions. To say that the USA has had a single policy maker over more than 20 years in spite of many changes of admininstration is confusing. We could not generalize this assumption to all countries, at least. This is, of course, an issue much debated here earlier on.

Furthermore, the linearity of the function concerning the budget may also be difficult to defend. Fiscal policies change over time and have an effect to agricultural spending. I am curious why the period for the study was extended only to 83–84 season. Surely the data is available. Some discussion on the validity of the US share of maize and wheat export as a proxy for an income variable would have been welcome. I was actually surprised that such statistics do not exist. Finally, no reference was made to set-aside schemes. Normally the decisions on support prices and set-aside programmes are made more or less simultaneously. This should have been taken into account.

MICHAEL SCHMITZ*

Cap and Food Security

Abstract: Although the food security discussion has given more emphasis to the individual (household) level as the proper unit of analysis, it still suffers from applying inappropriate indicators, which are mostly quantity oriented, instead of relying on more recent results of the literature that it is purchasing power or real income that matters. In addition, it has not been made clear so far how food security corresponds to the welfare status of agents. Since food security can more or less be associated with an uncertain world, this should at least be reflected in the value function of individuals who are generally risk averse. Therefore, it is proposed in the paper that the measurement of both food security and welfare should be based on the probability distribution of adjusted real household income over time on a daily basis. Food security can then be defined as the probability of any agent's real income exceeding a critical level, whereas the welfare status is measured as the agent's expected utility of this real income. Special formulas are developed in this context which allow one to calculate producer's and consumer's welfare under price uncertainty and risk aversion separating the risk response effect from the mean income moving effect of price fluctuations. In addition, an alternative measurement of protection in a stochastic world, the so called real protection rate, is proposed which simultaneously covers protection against low prices and volatile prices. All these indicators should be used when comparing and evaluating food security or food insecurity of any agent in whatever region. In the paper the concept is utilized to answer the raised question of how the EU contributes to worldwide food security.

INTRODUCTION

The representatives and advocates of the Common Agricultural Policy (CAP) of the European Union (EU), a major exporter of food and agricultural commodities, claim that (a) food security has already been achieved domestically for a long time as an unambiguous result of a well-defined and successful agricultural policy design, and that (b) their countries even provide abundant food for needy regions in the developing world, thus alleviating food insecurity abroad. Looking at the tremendous production, export, and stock volumes in these countries this statement seems to be supported at a first glance. In this paper it is argued that EU's agricultural policy has, in fact:

- contributed little if at all to domestic food security and is obviously not able to avoid newly arising poverty and hunger for some minorities;
- aggravated the efforts of providing people with enough food at reasonable prices in the developing world.

Before starting the discussion of these hypotheses in Section 3 it is worthwhile to give a precise definition of what is meant by food security, to develop an indicator with which one can measure food security, and finally to derive a conceptual framework for evaluating different degrees of food security. All three aspects will be discussed and analyzed as

* J.W. Goethe-University of Frankfurt, Germany.

general a way as possible in order to make the food security approach applicable for rural and urban poor in both developing (LDCs) and developed countries (DCs). The paper neither provides any quantitative estimates of food security levels (see Weber, 1993), nor discusses policy options for coping with the food security issue (see Koester, 1986; Thimm, 1993). Rather, it attempts to improve the theoretical foundation, to develop some alternative indicators, and to apply both to the mentioned hypotheses. More specifically, some more recent developments in the field of applied welfare economics are introduced which, in the author's view, have been underutilized in food security research. This kind of analysis might especially be useful for comparisons of food security levels between households, regions, and countries as well as for giving a basis on which national and supranational funds can be allocated to the poor.

DEFINITION, MEASUREMENT AND EVALUATION

'Food security is access by all people at all times to enough food for an active and healthy life' (World Bank, 1986). This definition which seems to reach the highest rate of acceptance among concerned researchers implies that (see Phillips and Taylor, 1990, p.1304):

- food is available, accessible, affordable — when and where needed — in sufficient quantity and quality;
- an assurance is given that this state of affairs to can be reasonably expected to continue.

Moreover, this widely accepted definition reflects the shifts from:

- a production orientation to a consumption and health focus;
- country-level, to household or individual-level analysis;
- a soley quantity point of view, to both quantity and quality issues;
- static or cross-section analysis, to dynamic analysis over time;
- merely transitory, to transitory and chronic malnutrition.

It has been noted that national food security does not imply household or individual food security (Staatz, D'Agostino and Sundberg, 1990, pp.1312–1316), that food security today does not imply food security tomorrow and that household food security does not automatically ensure nutritional security. Nutritional security is defined as the appropriate quantity and combination of inputs such as food, nutrition and health services, and caretaker's time needed to ensure an active and healthy life at all times for all people. Food security, therefore, is a necessary but not sufficient condition for nutritional security (Haddad, Hennedy and Sullivan, 1994, pp.329–330; Hahn and Bellin, 1993, p.21; Babu, 1994, pp.211–217; Babu and Pinstrup-Andersen, 1994, pp.218–233; Eele, 1994, pp.218–233). The most important result from previous research, however, has been the observation that hunger is caused by a lack of individual purchasing power or real income (see also Chisolm and Tyers, 1982, p.5) rather that by a deficiency in the total supply of food. Hence, individual poverty is the driving force behind hunger and malnutrition. This makes it clear, why food insecurity is not restricted to poor countries. Even in rich countries small but growing groups of the population do not have access to sufficient food (Allen and Thompson, 1990, pp.1162–1163; Phillips and Taylor, 1990, p.1304) because their real income falls below the poverty threshold.

With this causal relationship in mind, the question arises; under which preconditions could real individual income or real household income be an adequate basis for the measurement of food security? Obviously, some minimum income is required to meet an individual's needs. A minimum level of real income can also be interpreted as a minimum right to resources in the sense of Atkinson (1991, p.8) which enables individuals to participate in a particular society, as a guarantee of 'positive freedom'. As a rule of thumb the poverty or the food security line in developed countries is estimated to be that disposable household income which is less than 40 to 50 percent of the national average, thus implying a relative measure. In developing countries it would make more sense, however, to define a fixed amount of real purchasing power which would enable individuals to have access to enough healthy food.

When calculating this real purchasing power, it has to be kept in mind that income in-kind has to be added (i.e., home produced goods and services) and a discount for non-available or rationed food should be subtracted. But even when these problems are solved, three additional aspects warrant further attention; the relevant time period considered, the choice of equivalence scale in case of different household sizes and how food intake corresponds to income. Whereas the measurement of poverty is generally based on cross-section analysis (Atkinson, 1991, pp.5–17), the proposal here is to use time series analysis of real household income in order to capture seasonal variability and life cycle variations, including complete breakdowns of income (see also Ravallion and Huppi, 1991, pp.57–82). A further advantage of time series based food security measurement is that one can gradually and exactly measure food insecurity, thus overcoming the simple dichotomy between chronic and transitory malnutrition. The choice of the time unit (daily, weekly, monthly, annually) should depend on whether different options of dissaving, borrowing or participating in income streams of related people are available. If there aren't any risk sharing private or official institutions, then a daily-based income report would be the best. The required minimum household income (food security line) differs widely with the size of the household; the age structure of its members, the distribution between male and female, the degree of handicaps of people, and their nutritional health status. Buhmann *et al.* (1988, pp.115–142) therefore propose an adjusted income indicator (y_{adj}) to make food security or poverty levels of households comparable and to take into account the above mentioned aspects:

$$y_{adj} = \text{total real household income} / n^s$$

where n denotes the number of members of the household and s is the elasticity of family need with respect to family size. The equivalence scales are based on subjective evaluation and in the poverty literature this ranges from 0.25 to 0.72 (Atkinson, 1991, p.15). Finally, what can be said about the correlation of real income with food intake and the nutritional and healthy status of individuals? Fortunately, recent contributions in the literature show a strong positive relationship between income and nutrition implying that nutrition and health are improving with income growth (Schiff and Valdés, 1990, p.1320; von Braun, 1990, p.1323). Given a lack of data about the determinants of the nutrition and health production functions, real household income might therefore provide an acceptable basis for the measurement of food security (an example of how to calculate this real income indicator for sub-Saharan Africa is given in Sahn and Sarris, 1991, p.262).

So far only the level aspect of food security has been addressed. The level of real household income should not fall below a certain target or minimum level. However, food insecurity reflects the adverse effects of an uncertain world as well. Hence, we should also look at the fluctuations of real household income around its mean trend. Formally, it is the probability distribution of real income over time that matters and it should be the objective of any food security policy to keep the probability of real income falling below the target level as low as possible at reasonable opportunity costs. Then one can measure food insecurity *(FIS)* as the probability of real income falling below the critical level y^*:

$$(1)\quad FIS = F(y^*) = \phi\left[\frac{y^* - E[y]}{(\mathrm{var}[y])^{0.5}}\right] = \left[\frac{(\beta - 1)}{cv_y}\right]$$

where

ϕ	probability	E	expectation operator
var	variance	y	y_{adj} adjusted real income (random variable
cv	coefficient of variation	y^*	minimum income
β	y^* in percent of mean income		
$F(y)$	standard normalized cumulative distribution function		

For practical purposes the first (mean) and second (variance) moments of the probability distribution can be used to calculate the degree of food insecurity which ranges from zero to one. In that case the implicit assumption is made that real income fluctuations are normally distributed.

So far we have only addressed the positive questions of measurement. Nothing has been said about the evaluation of different probability distributions in welfare terms or how food security corresponds to individual welfare measures. Does the individual prefer one probability distribution over the other? The answer to this question depends on the weights the individual gives to mean, variance, skewness, and other moments in his/her preference function. The most common practice in economic analysis in such cases has been to apply the expected utility approach or the stochastic dominance approach (see Dillon and Anderson, 1990, pp.120–157). In the following analysis we'll use the former, assuming a normal (log-normal) distribution of real income which leads to a simple mean-variance (mean-coefficient of variation) formula of expected utility of income (Newbery and Stiglitz, 1981, p.85–89):

$$(2a)\quad E[U(y)] = E[y] - \frac{1}{2} A \,\mathrm{var}[y] \quad \text{normal distribution}$$

$$(2b)\quad E[U(y)] = E[y]\left[1 + cv_y^{\,2}\right]^{-1/2R} \quad \text{log-normal distribution}$$

A coefficient of absolute risk aversion

R coefficient of relative risk aversion

U utility

Alternatively, a safety first decision rule can be formulated, where a decision maker maximizes expected profits subject to the constraint that the probability (*FIS*) of real income falling below the critical level (y^*) does not exceed a certain level (Barry, 1984, p.63):

$$(2c)\quad E[U(y)] = E[y] - dFIS$$

where d is the absolute discontinuity of the utility function at $y = y^*$ which expresses the preference for food security or the risk aversion with respect to food insecurity.

These equations are especially useful as a complementary tool for the evaluation of food security because they:

- contain both mean and variance of income as arguments, thus considering the stochastic nature of the problem;
- can be applied to all types of vulnerable groups, i.e. producers, consumers, and other agents such as taxpayers and politicians (for the concept of vulnerability see Bohle, 1993, p.193–95);
- contain the risk attitudes of market agents;
- allow comparisons over time and among agents of situations with a different extent of food insecurity;
- provide a reasonable money measure of food security costs and benefits.

We are now in a position to define, to measure, and to assess food security or food insecurity, respectively. Hence, the question can be answered, what is the contribution of the CAP to domestic food security and to food security in LDCs?

Common Agricultural Policy and Food Security

Domestic food security Agricultural Price Policy in the EU implies an average increase of producer prices over their free market levels, a considerable stabilization of prices compared to the world market (see Table 1), and finally a distortion of the price pattern in favor of grains, milk, beef, and sugar beets, so-called northern products, at the expense of Mediterranean products. These market interventions will be evaluated from a producer's and consumer's point of view.

The impact of this price policy on producer's welfare can be measured by the expected utility of an indirect profit function (see Just, Hueth and Schmitz, 1982, p.349):

$$(3)\quad E[U(\pi)] = E[U(p\{\pi, v, K\})]$$

which is homogenous of degree 1 in prices and has the following properties (Hoteling's lemma):

$$\frac{\partial \pi}{\partial p} = q_s > 0; \ \frac{\partial^2 \pi}{\partial p^2} > 0; \ -\frac{\partial \pi}{\partial v} = x_D > 0; \ \frac{\partial^2 \pi}{\partial v^2} > 0$$

where

π	indirect profit	p	producer prices
v	factor prices	K	quantity vector of fixed inputs
q_s	output supply	x_D	input demand

Using the simple mean-variance approach of Equation (2a) and the approximation procedure for both moments following Mood, Graybill and Boes (1974, p.181) one can easily derive a money measure (certainty equivalent of indirect profit) for the expected utility of profits leaving the variance of input prices unaffected by policy.

Table 1 *Variability[a] of German Food Import Prices 1970 –1985*

Products	Price Variability (%) Imports from EC-Member Countries	Imports from Third Countries
Aggregates		
Grains and Cereal Products	5.6	17.9
Milk and Dairy Products	3.4	6.5
Swine and Pork	9.5	7.7
Cattle and Beef	7.3	16.4
Poultry and Poultry Meat	6.0	4.9
Eggs and their Derivatives	11.5	17.2
Single Products		
Wheat	5.8	24.5
Barley	6.4	21.3
Corn	6.1	17.9
Soymeal	18.3	21.4
Rice	9.3	21.6
Raw Sugar	4.3	62.2
Cattle	6.2	13.5
Swine	8.1	14.4
Butter	4.3	32.2

Source: Own calculation on basis of German Agricultural Statistics (see Schmitz, 1987, p.366).
Note: Measured as trend-corrected coefficient of variation following the approach of Cuddy and Della Valle, 1978, pp.79–85.

$$(4) \quad E[U(\pi)] \approx \pi(\bar{p}, \bar{v}, K) + \frac{1}{2} cv_p^2 \varepsilon Rev - \frac{1}{2} R \cdot cv_p^2 \frac{Rev^2}{\pi(\bar{p}, \bar{v}, K)}$$

where

$\bar{p}$, $\bar{v}$	mean prices	cv	coefficient of variation
ε	supply elasticity	Rev	Revenue

The first term on the RHS of Equation (4) is that level of profit where prices are at their mean. A mean preserving spread of producer prices, however, creates two additional terms in Equation (4). The second term on the RHS is equivalent to an increase of the expected profit under fluctuating prices from which the producer obviously benefits, whereas the third term addresses the producer's risk attitude. A risk averse producer, i.e., would face a loss of welfare under fluctuating prices. The producer gains from pure price stabilization under the Common Agricultural Policy if, and only if

$$(5)\quad R > \varepsilon \frac{\pi}{Rev}$$

which is likely to be the case assuming plausible parameter values. Since the mean profit change is also positive, the producer's welfare position has been clearly improved by the CAP.

Referring to the food insecurity status of producers under the CAP, it has to be stated that the probability of real profit to fall below the critical level has unequivocally been decreased since the mean is up and the variance is down. Hence, price support as well as price stabilization under the CAP have improved both the welfare position and food security of farmers although the benefits seem to be very unevenly distributed among different farms and regions (see von Witzke, 1979; Tarditi and Croci Angelini, 1982). Especially, farmers in the southern parts of the community producing Mediterranean commodities have benefitted less from the CAP since price support is lower and price stabilization takes place over a wider range between floor and ceiling prices compared to the case for northern products.

Unfortunately, traditional indicators of the rate of protection only refer to the level effect of price policies and ignore the price stabilizing effect. In fact, agricultural price policies in DCs aim at protecting farmers against both low world market prices and volatile world market prices. This kind of real world protection can only be calculated on basis of the expected utility approach, measuring the percentage increase of the expected utility of income or of the certainty equivalent of income, respectively. Using the mean-variance approximation again one can derive the following formula:

$$(6)\quad \text{Real Protection Rate} = (1+z)\left[\frac{1-RL_1}{1-RL_0}\right]-1$$

where

z	effective rate of protection
$RL = \frac{1}{2} Rcv_y^{\,2}$	relative risk loss (= relative risk premium)

Under certain assumptions the effective rate of protection in Equation (6) can be replaced by the nominal rate of protection and in the risk loss equation the coefficient of variation of prices can be used instead of incomes thus having an empirically sound indicator of real world protection.

Analogous to the producer case, the impact on consumers should be measured as the expected utility of equivalent income or money metric (MM). Money metric itself can be defined as that level of income needed at some vector of reference prices (p_0) in order for the consumer to attain the same utility of level he/she enjoys from income y_0 when faced with price vector (p_1). In other words money metric is the sum of the initial income (y_0) and the equivalent variation (EV). Since the equivalent variation from a pure price change can be derived from an expenditure function $(e[\cdot])$ as (see Boadway and Bruce, 1989, p.205):

$$(7)\ EV = e(p_0, u_1) - e(p_1, u_1)$$

for the money metric it follows:

$$(8)\ MM = Y_0 + \Delta\, e(p,\ u)$$

where the expenditure function is increasing with prices and utility, is homogeneous of degree 1 in prices, is concave in p, and has the following property (Shepard's Lemma):

$$\frac{\partial e(p,\bar{u})}{\partial p} = q_D{}^C \qquad \text{(compensated demand function)}$$

Using again the simple mean-variance approach of Equation (2a), the Mood, *et al.* (1974) approximation procedure for the mean and the variance of the money metric, and rearranging some terms, yields:

$$(9)\ E[U(MM)] \approx Y_0 + \frac{1}{2} cv_p^2 |\eta^c| EX - \frac{1}{2} R\, cv_p^2\, \frac{EX^2}{Y_0}$$

where

η^c compensated demand elasticity $(= \eta + s\lambda)$
s budget share of products with fluctuating prices
λ income elasticity
η (uncompensated) demand elasticity
EX mean expenditures for products with fluctuating prices

The interpretation of Equation (9) is analogous to that of Equation (4) for the producer. In accordance with the considerations of Helms (1985, pp.93–100), the expression in Equation (9) could be called the ex-ante equivalent income. The consumer finally gains from pure price stabilization if and only if:

$$(10)\ R > |\eta^c| / s$$

which is again likely to be the case as Turnovsky, *et.al.* (1980) state, although the relative gains seem to be negligible (Wright and Williams, 1988, pp.616–627) due to the low food share in consumer's budget. Thus, even with equal coefficients of risk aversion, producers might be more heavily affected by fluctuating prices than consumers.

Table 2 *Variability[b] of German Food Prices at Different Stages in the Food Chain 1970–1985*

Product	Price Variability (%)	Product	Price Variability (%)
Swine	8.1	Cattle	6.2
Roast pork	9.4	Roast beef	4.2
Lard	3.1	Fillet of beef	4.1
Ham	2.7		
		Poultry	5.3
Calf	6.5	Broiled chicken	3.6
Veal cutlet	8.4		
		Raw milk	4.8
Eggs from producer	6.4	Fresh milk	4.4
Eggs packing incl.	5.7	Butter	4.3
		Cheese	4.6
Wheat	5.8	Sugar beets	6.9
Wheat flour	3.2	White sugar	4.3
White bread	3.2		
Rye	6.4	White cabbage	33.1
Rye bread	2.5	Cabbage with trade-mark	14.0
		Cabbage in cans	4.9
Potatoes from producer	42.2	Red cabbage	42.8
Potatoes packing incl.	24.5	Cabbage with trade-mark	15.5
Potato salad	5.0	Cabbage in cans	4.8
Potato chips	2.4		
		Grape must	20.3
Apple from producer	36.6	Red wine	2.8
Apple with trade-mark	15.2	German champagne	6.8
Apple juice	7.2	Brandy	4.2
Apple purée	5.6		

Source: Own calculation on basis of German Agricultural Statistics (see Schmitz, 1987, pp.363–364).
Notes: [b]Measured as trend-corrected coefficient of variation following the approach of Cuddy and Della Valle, 1978, pp.79–85.

However, the central question of how the CAP affects mean and variance of consumer prices has been left unanswered so far. The answer depends on the transmission of price impulses from the wholesale to the retail level. Empirical studies show the EU consumers to shoulder the full burden of the price support at the wholesale level because the potential for replacing price increasing intermediate food or for substituting final food consumption is very limited (i.e., Schmitz, 1987, pp.368–370) and the CAP covers nearly the whole range of food items. In addition, the CAP contributes little to consumer's price stability. The statistically observed stability already exists due to high proportions of stable non-food inputs in food value added, to a partly anticyclical margin behaviour over time, and to risk transferring mechanisms for which consumers are obviously willing to pay. Surprisingly, the level of stability of final food prices hardly differs among products, irrespective of the fact that some wholesale prices or producer prices are the subject of the CAP and others not (see Table 2). Hence, the CAP has not only weakened the welfare position of consumers but has also increased the level of food insecurity.

This is in contrast to policymakers' claims. It holds especially for those consumers who spend a large portion of their budget on food, namely the older generation, families with many children, and unemployed people. The low real income of those minorities is eroded further by the CAP.

Nevertheless, some advocates might still argue that for a vast majority of people food security has already been provided. That is true. But this has not been caused by the food and agricultural policy. Rather, it originates from the overall performance and efficiency of the economy. Thus, it is fair to say that food security for most people exists despite the CAP.

Food Security in LDCs

How does the CAP affect food security and welfare of individual producers and consumers in developing countries? The answer to this question very much depends on:

- how the CAP distorts world market prices of agricultural commodities with respect to their level and volatility;
- how distorted world market prices are transmitted into domestic markets within the developing countries; and
- how this adjustment of domestic prices affects the real income of domestic agents.

Table 3 *Impact of Food Policy Liberalization in OECD Countries on World Market Prices of Selection Commodities*

Commodities	Change of Price Level (%)	Coefficient of Variation of Prices (%)	
		Before liberalization	After liberalization
Wheat	25	58	33
Coarse grain	3	53	47
Rice	18	38	28
Ruminant meat	43	24	7
Non-ruminant meat	10	8	8
Dairy products	95	26	11
Sugar	22	36	25
Weighted average	30	34	23

Source: Anderson and Tyers (1990), pp.67 and 70.

A vast literature exists on the impact of the CAP or similar agricultural policies of other industrialized countries on world markets and on developing countries (i.e. Anderson and Tyers, 1990; Hartmann and Schmitz, 1991, 1992). The focus has been on price level and price risk effects as well as on price level induced welfare effects in the third world. Less attention has been given to the risk benefits and risk losses of various policy options. Table 3 summarizes the world market price effects of food policy liberalization in OECD countries. The first result is that if food policies in those countries were completely liberalized, international food prices would rise by 30 percent on average and the degree of price instability would decline from 34 percent to 23 percent on average. Thus, the food policies of OECD countries are responsible for historically low world market prices and for about one third of the current price risk on international food markets, and considerably more in the wheat, beef and dairy product markets. The price level induced welfare effects in LDCs differ depending on:

- the level of protection and/or discrimination (which is most often the case) of the farming sector in developing countries;
- the degree of insulation of domestic agricultural markets from world markets, which is extremely high in LDCs as response to DCs food policies;
- the price responsiveness of productivity growth in agriculture;
- the extent to which LDCs liberalize their own trade and exchange rate policies and thereby remove indirect distortions affecting food prices.

In an optimistic scenario with a world-wide food policy liberalization and assuming incomplete price transmission in LDCs as well as price responsive productivity growth, developing countries would gain US$58 Billion (1985) per year and would in addition benefit from facing a reduced price volatility of about one-third (= 11 percent) of the current level; see Anderson and Tyers, 1990, p.66–70).

Using Equation (6) one can derive the percentage income gain from higher and stabilized world market prices for LDCs. The pure price level effect raises the income by about 33 percent whereas both effects together (price level increase and risk reduction) improve the income by 40 percent or 49 percent respectively depending on the relative risk aversion coefficient (R = 1 or R = 2). These figures may be convincing enough to prefer the real protection rate over the traditional rates of protection whenever there are price fluctuation effects by policy interventions.

Whereas uncertain world market prices affect exporting and importing countries' border prices more or less equally, the domestic price, welfare and food security effects differ with; the way LDCs transmit those fluctuations to their own domestic markets (see Schmitz, 1991 and Hammer and Knudsen, 1990), how risk averse consumers, producers, and taxpayers are, and how the world market price risk interacts with other risk sources within the country (see Valdés, 1981).

Considering an average elasticity of price transmission in LDCs of 0.39 (see Sullivan, 1990) under current food and non-food policies and assuming full price transmission (elasticity of 1.0) under liberalized policies, domestic producer and consumer prices in LDCs would significantly increase due to a liberalization and would fluctuate to a similar extent (one third of the current level). Hence, consumers would lose and producers would gain from free markets in welfare terms. In addition, some hidden benefits are likely to occur from reduced budget (tax) fluctuations which generally has been used as buffer for stabilizing domestic food prices and which is borne as risk burden by other members of the society. It is especially worth noting that external risks (i.e. world market price risks) do not simply disappear even if trade policy completely isolates the domestic market. Although consumers and producers are then prevented from facing external price risks, risk is nevertheless reflected in the government budget in that case, thus throwing the burden on taxpayers. Hence, market insulation generally implies simple redistribution of risk.

With respect to food security one can state that producers in LDCs suffer from the CAP since their mean income is lowered and the variance is raised, at least in cases where the price stabilization capacity of the domestic insulation policy is lower than the world market price destabilization capacity of the CAP. The rural poor are therefore most adversely affected by the EU policy. In contrast, the urban poor's food security increases due to the CAP unless price risks are fully transmitted to the domestic markets. In that case food insecurity might even increase depending on the magnitude of the variance term of real income and its adjustment. With high food shares in total household expenditures and a comparative low marketing margin as stabilizer the impact of price fluctuations on the income variance might be quite important.

Finally the question arises whether recent CAP reforms and other agricultural policy adjustments in DCs (i.e. GATT-results) reverse or at least weaken the above mentioned effects on food security and welfare in LDCs. At first glance one might get the impression that partial food policy liberalization and the tariffication of non-tariff trade barriers contribute a lot to an improvement of the situation. Going into more detail, however, one has to admit that:

- important surplus markets are excluded from the CAP reforms;
- new price distortions among agricultural commodities have been created;
- there is a tendency towards managed or regulated trade;
- special safeguard provisions (i.e. additional duties in case of declining world market prices) erode the stabilization potential of the tariffication strategy to a large extent.

Taking these aspects into account the recent agricultural policy reforms in DCs seem to be of limited value for developing countries, especially with respect to the risks engaging in international trade (see also Hartmann, 1995).

CONCLUSIONS

Although the food security discussion has given more emphasis on the individual (household) level as the proper unit of analysis, it still suffers from applying inappropriate indicators, which are mostly quantity oriented, instead of relying on the more recent result of the literature that it is purchasing power or real income that matters. In addition, it has not been made clear so far how food security corresponds to the welfare status of agents. Since food security can more or less be associated with an uncertain world, this should at least be reflected in the value function of individuals who are generally risk averse.

Therefore, it is proposed in the paper that the measurement of both food security and welfare should be based on the probability distribution of adjusted real household income over time. Food security can then be defined as the probability of any agent's real income exceeding a critical level, whereas the welfare status is measured as the agent's expected utility of this real income. Special formulas are developed in this context [Equations (4) and (9)] which allow one to calculate producer's and consumer's welfare under price uncertainty (assuming some degree of risk aversion and separating the risk response effect from the mean income moving effect of price fluctuations. In addition, an alternative measurement of protection in a stochastic world, the so callled real protection rate, is proposed [Equation(6)] which simultaneously covers protection against low prices and volatile prices. All these indicators should be used when comparing and evaluating food security or food insecurity of any agent in whatever region.

Applying this concept to the paper's question of how the EU contributes to food security one can conclude that despite recent agricultural policy reforms in DCs:

- EU producers are affected directly by higher and stabilized producer prices inducing an improved welfare and food security position of the small group of farm households;
- EU consumers, as a large group, suffer from EU's price policy in welfare and food security terms because the price increasing effect is fully transmitted from the wholesale to the retail level and stable consumer prices for food occur even without any producer price stabilization;
- the CAP with its strongly isolating character (low price transmission elasticities) has decreased and destabilized world market prices of agricultural commodities eroding at least potentially the most important source of real income earnings in LDCs, namely agricultural production;
- the CAP-induced negative income and food security effects for producers have been aggravated by the fact that most LDCs apply sector-specific and macroeconomic policies which, in addition, heavily discriminate against agriculture and severely endangers the access to enough and healthy food;
- the potential welfare and food security gains of price level reductions for consuming and for importing agents might be compensated to a certain extent by increasing price and income risks.

REFERENCES

Allen, J.E. and Thompson, A., 1990, 'Rural Poverty among Racial and Ethnic Minorities', *American Journal of Agricultural Economics*, Vol. 72, No. 5, pp.1161–1168.

Anderson, K. and Tyers, R., 1990, 'How Developing Countries Could Gain from Agricultural Trade Liberalization in the Uruguay Round', in Goldin, I. and Knudsen, O. (eds.), *Agricultural Trade Liberalization – Implications for Developing Countries*, Organisation for Economics and Co-operation and Development, Paris and World Bank, Washington, D.C., pp.41–75.

Atkinson, A.B., 1991, 'Comparing Poverty Rates Internationally: Lessons from Recent Studies in Developed Countries', *The World Bank Economic Review*, Vol. 5, No. 5, pp.3–21.

Babu, S.C., 'Food Security and Nutrition Monitoring in Africa; Introduction and Historical Background', *Food Policy*, Vol. 19, No. 3, 1994, pp.211–217.

Babu, S.C. and Pinstrup-Andersen, P., 1994, 'Food Security and Nutrition Monitoring. A Conceptual Framework, Issues and Challanges', *Food Policy*, Vol. 19, No. 3, pp.218–233.

Barry, P.J. (ed.), 1984, *Risk Management in Agriculture*, Ames, Iowa.

Boadway, R. and Bruce, N., 1989, *Welfare Economics*, Oxford, UK.

Bohle, H. G., 1993, '"Real" Markets and Food Security of "Real" People with a Case Study from Tamil Nadu/India', in Thimm, H.U. and Hahn, H. (eds.), *Regional Food Security and Rural Infrastructure,*

Vol. I (Schriften des Zentrums für regionale Entwicklungsforschung der Justus-Liebig-Universität Gießen, Band 50), Gießen, pp.191–202.

Buhmann, B., Rainwater, L., Schmaus, G. and Smeeding, T.M., 1988, 'Equivalence Scales, Well-Being, Inequality, and Poverty', *Review of Income and Wealth*, Vol. 34, pp.115–142.

Chisolm, A.H. and R. Tyers (eds.), 1982, *Food Security: Theory, Policy and Perspectives from Asia and the Pacific Rim*, Lexington, Massachusetts.

Cuddy, J.D.A. and Della Valle, P.A., 1988, 'Measuring Instability of Time Series Data', *Oxford Bulletin of Statistics*, Vol. 40, No. 1, pp.79–85.

Dillon, J.L. and Anderson, J.R., 1990, *The Analysis of Response in Crop and Livestock Production*, Third Edition, Pergamon Press, Oxford, UK.

Eele, G., 1994, 'Indicators for Food Security and Nutrition Monitoring: A Review of Experience from Southern Africa', *Food Policy*, Vol. 19, No. 3, pp.314–328.

Haddad, L., Hennedy, E. and Sullivan, J., 1994, 'Choice of Indicators for Food Security and Nutrition Monitoring', *Food Policy*, Vol. 19, No. 3, pp.329–343.

Hahn, H. and Bellin, F., 1993, 'Regional Food Security or Nutrition Security - What Difference Does It Make?' in Thimm, H. U. and Hahn, H. (eds.), *Regional Food Security and Rural Infrastructure*, Vol. I. (Schriften des Zentrums für regionale Entwicklungsforschung der Justus-Liebig-Universität Gießen, Band 50), Gießen pp.17–28.

Hammer, J.S. and Knudsen, O., 1990, 'Agricultural Trade Liberalization: Developing Country Responses' in Goldin, I. and Knudsen, O. (eds.), *Agricultural Trade Liberalization - Implications for Developing Countries*, Organisation for Economics and Co-operation and Development, Paris and World Bank, Washington, D.C., pp.391–414.

Hartmann, M., 1995, 'Neuere Entwicklungen im internationalen Agrarhandel - Gefahren und Chancen aus Sicht der Entwicklungsländer', Paper Presented at the 35th Annual Conference of the German Agricultural Economic Association, 5–6 October 1994, Hohenheim (Germany), in Grosskopf, W., Hanf, C. H., Heidhues, F. and Zeddies, J. (eds.), Die Landwirtschaft nach der EU-Agrarreform, Münster-Hiltrup.

Hartmann, M. and Schmitz, P.M., 1991, 'Impact of EC's Rebalancing Strategy on Developing Countries: The Case of Feed', Staff Papers Series, P 91-18, Department of Agricultural and Applied Economics, University of Minnesota, May.

Hartmann, M. and Schmitz, P.M., 1992, 'Free Trade Versus Supply Control – The Case of the EC', in Becker, T., Gray, R. and Schmitz, A. (eds.), *Mechanisms to Improve Agricultural Trade Performance Under the GATT*, Kiel.

Helms, L.J., 1985, 'Errors in the Numerical Assessment of the Benefits of Price Stabilization', *American Journal of Agricultural Economics*, Vol. 67, No. 1, pp.93–100.

Just, R.E., Hueth, D.L. and Schmitz, A., 1982, *Applied Welfare Economics and Public Policy*, Englewood Cliffs, New Jersey.

Koester, U., 1986, *Regional Cooperation to Improve Food Security in Southern and Eastern African Countries*, International Food Policy Research Institute, Research Report 53, Washington, D.C.

Mood, A.M., Graybill, F.A. and Boes, D.C., 1974, *Introduction to the Theory of Statistics*, Third Edition, McGraw Hill International, Tokyo.

Newbery, D.M.G. and Stiglitz, J.E., 1981, *The Theory of Commodity Price Stabilization, A Study in the Economics of Risk*, Clarendon Press, Oxford, New York.

Phillips, T.P. and Taylor, D.S., 1990, 'Optimal Control of Food Insecurity: A Conceptual Framework', *American Journal of Agricultural Economics*, Vol. 72, No. 5, pp.1304–1310.

Ravallion, M. and Huppi, M., 1991, 'Measuring Changes in Poverty: A Methological Case Study of Indonesia during an Adjustment Period', *The World Bank Economic Review*, Vol. 5, No. 1, pp.57–82.

Sahn, D.E. and Sarris, A., 1991, 'Structural Adjustment and the Welfare of Rural Smallholders: A Comparative Analysis from Sub-Saharan Africa', *The World Bank Economic Review*, Vol. 5, No. 2, pp.259–289.

Schiff, M. and A. Valdés, 1990, 'Poverty, Food Intake, and Malnutrition: Implications for Food Security in Developing Countries', *American Journal of Agricultural Economics*, Vol. 72, No. 5, pp.1318–1322.

Schmitz, P.M., 1987, 'Einfluß der Agrarmarktpolitik auf Lebensmittelmärkte und Ernährungsverhalten' (Impact of Agricultural Price Policy on Food Markets and Consumer Behavior), *Jahrbuch der Absatz- und Verbrauchsforschung*, Vol. 33, No. 4, pp.353–378.

Schmitz, P.M., 1991, 'Do Developed Exporting Countries Contribute to Food Security? - The Case of the EC', Staff Paper Series, P 91-34, Department of Agricultural and Applied Economics, University of Minnesota, July.

Staatz, J.M., D'Agostino, V.C. and Sundberg, S.,1990, 'Measuring Food Security in Africa: Conceptual, Empirical, and Policy Issues', *American Journal of Agricultural Economics*, Vol. 72, No. 5, pp.1311–1317.

Sullivan, J., 1990, 'Price Transmission Elasticities in the Trade Liberalization (TLIB) Database', Agriculture and Trade Analysis Division, ERS Staff Report No. AGES 9034, Economic Research Service, US Department of Agriculture, Washington, D.C.

Tarditi, S. and Croci Angelini, E., 1982, 'Regional Redistributive Effects of Common Price Support Policies', *European Review of Agricultural Economics*, Vol. 9, pp.255–270.

Thimm, H.U., 1993, 'Linkages of Rural Infrastructure to Food Security', in Thimm, H.U. and Hahn, H. (eds.), *Regional Food Security and Rural Infrastructure*, Vol. I. (Schriften des Zentrums für regionale Entwicklungsforschung der Justus-Liebig-Universität Gießen, Band 50), Gießen pp.53–64.

Valdés, A. (ed.), 1981, *Food Security for Developing Countries*, Westview Press, Boulder, Colorado.

von Braun, J., 1990, 'Food Insecurity: Discussion', *American Journal of Agricultural Economics*, Vol. 72, No. 5, pp.1323–1324.

von Witzke, H., 1979, 'Prices, Common Agricultural Price Policy and Personal Distribution of Income in West German Agriculture', *European Review of Agricultural Economics*, Vol. 6, pp.61–80.

Weber, A., 1993, 'Some Global Considerations to Food Production and Food Security', in Thimm, H.U. and Hahn, H. (eds.), *Regional Food Security and Rural Infrastructure*, Vol. I. (Schriften des Zentrums für regionale Entwicklungsforschung der Justus-Liebig-Universität Gießen, Band 50), Gießen, pp.13–15.

World Bank, 1996, *Poverty and Hunger: Issues and Options for Food Security in Developing Countries*, Washington, D.C.

Wright, B.D. and Williams, J.C., 1988, 'Measurement of Consumer Gains from Market Stabilization', *American Journal of Agricultural Economics*, Vol. 70, No. 3, pp.616–627.

JEAN-CHRISTOPHE BUREAU*

The CAP and the Unequal Public Support to European Agriculture

Abstract: In order to measure the effect of public support on production, aggregate measures are constructed as effective rates of protection, including all government interventions that affect supply. These measures are constructed considering effective protection rates as a superlative index number, which requires an econometric estimation of the price aggregator functions. This makes it possible to measure the effect of public intervention of 10 European countries, between 1973 and 1989. The unequal public support between EC countries is due to output price differences under the CAP regime. It is also caused by a very unbalanced protection and support across commodities.

INTRODUCTION

In spite of 30 years of Common Agricultural Policy (CAP), the agricultural sector does not benefit from the same level of protection and support in all European countries. An explanation is that the prices received and paid by producers are very different across countries. A study based on the construction of Purchasing Power Parities (PPPs) for the agricultural sector shows that output price differences are considerable across countries, whatever the exchange rate used (Barkaoui *et al.,* 1992). Not all these price inequalities are caused by protection related measures. Some are caused by inefficiencies in the marketing sector or the existence of surplus areas and importing areas. However, national subsidies, such as subsidies through Value Added Tax (VAT), increase output prices in certain countries. CAP regulations, such as the sugar regime, also induce large discrepancies in average prices. The effect of institutional prices set in ECUs combined with the discrepancies between the Green Exchange Rates and the rate of PPP create considerable differences in prices faced by farmers across countries (Bureau and Butault, 1992).

Another explanation of the unequal effects of the CAP is that protection and public intervention in markets are very different across commodities. The way countries benefit from the CAP depends on their output mix, but also on their input mix. For example, a tariff on wheat could offset the protective effect of a tariff on milk, depending on the importance of wheat input in milk production. Since some countries produce milk with land using techniques and other countries rely heavily on feedstuffs, the negative protection on the input mix varies across countries.

Measures of protection, while not measures of policy impacts, can be used to evaluate the magnitude of sectoral income transfers and distortions in resource allocation (Josling and Tangerman, 1989). Instead of dealing only with protection at the borders (that is, tariffs and import quotas), we measure public intervention which affects production decisions. We consider the effects on producers and we focus on protection and support which are supply response distortive. As a result, production decoupled transfers are not included. However, we include all policies that affect the price of a product and all payments which are tied to output, but not reflected in the market price. An aggregate measure is used that incorporates the wide variety of policy instruments affecting supply

* INRA-ESR, Gringon, France.

response including tariffs, import quotas, price support achieved through intervention, production quotas, export subsidies, consumption subsidies, subsidies and tariffs on inputs. Although we will use the term 'protection' in the text to remain consistent with a familiar literature, what we measure is the supply-distortive public intervention. For instance, a very small tariff is imposed on soybeans imported by the community. Nevertheless, our nominal rate of 'protection' for soybeans is very high, since a premium given to the crusher for using European oilseeds leads to a price received by the farmers that is much higher than the world price.

EFFECTIVE PROTECTION

The rate of effective protection is the appropriate indicator of the effects of protection on producers. The Effective Protection Rate (EPR) is the rate of protection provided to the value added in the production of a product (Corden, 1987). Nominal protection (that is, protection on the final output) is a relevant concept if the objects of interest are outputs which enter the consumers' choice function. Protection of value added is more appropriate as a measure of protection in the production process (Vousden, 1990). The EPR is the most satisfactory concept to capture the incentive impact of policy on production structure (Gruebel and Lloyd, 1972; Tsakok, 1990). EPR measures have a direct interpretation, which is that the producers of a country with an EPR > 1 are receiving a greater return on land, labour and capital, given intervention, than they would have without intervention. Thus, the EPR sums up the net result of several trade and non trade taxes, subsidies and policies.

Two basic definitions of an EPR have been developed in the literature. Corden (1966) defines the EPR as the proportionate increment in value added per unit of output brought about by the protection structure (over its free trade value). Leith (1968) defines the EPR as the proportional change due to the tariff structure in the 'price' of the value added, with the assumption that such a price can be defined meaningfully. Most studies assume a Leontief technology. In this case the Leith and Corden measures are equal. However, when substitutions between inputs and outputs occur, the Leith measure is superior to the Corden measure (Bhagwati and Srinivason, 1984; Gruebel and Lloyd, 1972).

A THEORETICAL INDEX OF EFFECTIVE PROTECTION

Aggregate measures of support such as Producer Subsidy Equivalents or PSEs (OECD, 1987; Webb, Lopez and Penn, 1989) are commonly used as indicators of barriers to trade and government intervention in agriculture. However, the inconsistency of these measures with economic theory generates numerous problems. Among many theoretical problems, the PSEs assume that quantities produced under government intervention are equal to the quantities produced without intervention. This assumption is particularly unrealistic for the agricultural sector because of high substitutions between crops and between inputs when prices vary. Using the Leith concept based on the price of the value added, one can take advantage of the work of Bruno (1973) and Woodland (1982), which provides a rigorous microeconomic foundation for this analysis. It is possible to take into account the substitutions between inputs and outputs that would occur if public intervention was removed. Therefore, measures of effective protection can be constructed as a 'superlative' index (Diewert, 1976) of the price of the value added.

Denote y a vector of outputs y_j, $j = 1, ..., N$; p is the vector of their prices. Denote x a vector of intermediate (variable) inputs x_i, $i = 1, ..., M$; w is the vector of their price. Denote $-z$ a vector of K primary factors $-z_k$, $k = 1, ..., K$. The technology can be represented by a revenue function:

$$(1)\quad R(p,w,-z) = \max_{y,x} \{py - wx : (y,x,-z) \in U\}$$

Effective protection requires a measure of the price of the value added. In order to ensure the existence of a unit value added function, it is necessary to assume separability (Bhagwati and Srinavasan, 1973) and constant returns to scale. We assume that the set of possibilities U is a cone and that the technology can be represented by a transformation function $T(y,x,-z) = 0$ which is of the form $T(y,x,-z) = T^*(y,x,-F(z)) = 0$, with F non decreasing, concave and linearly homogenous in z.

The interpretation of this separable form for T is that primary inputs combine to produce an amount $F(z)$ of a fictional intermediate product, real value added. This is then used along with other intermediate inputs to produce outputs (Woodland, 1982). Woodland (1977) shows that, under these assumptions, the revenue function, Equation (1), is multiplicatively separable. Therefore, the maximum value added, Equation (1), can be written as a product of two functions:

$$(2)\qquad \begin{aligned} V(p,w,z) &= \{R(p,w,\text{-}z):\ T^*(y,x,-F(z)) = 0\} \\ &= \max_{x,y} \{py - wx:\ T^*(y,x,-F(z)) = 0\} \\ &= \pi(p,w)\ F(z) \end{aligned}$$

$$\text{where } \pi(p,w) = \max_{x,y} \{py - wx:\ T^*(y,x,-F(z)) = 0\}$$

The nominal value added function is the product of a price index $\pi(p,w)$, the price of the value added, and a quantity index $F(z)$, the quantity of value added. The Leith measure of effective protection is the percentage change in the price of the value added due to protection. Denote p^p, w^p the price vectors under protection and p^w, w^w the world price vector, the EPR is:

$$(3)\quad \text{EPR} = \pi(p^p,w^p) / \pi(p^w,w^w) - 1$$

We assume that world prices are observable. This requires the assumption that they are not affected by the observed protection, that is, the small country assumption. If the technology is assumed to be Leontief, one can postulate input output coefficients which are constant in the two price situations, and the computation of EPR is straightforward. This would lead to a 'PSE type' measure of EPR, using the x and y observed in the protected situation. Since this assumption is unrealistic, the calculation of effective protection requires the knowledge of the function π.

In this particular case, we cannot avoid the estimation of the function π. The EPR, as defined above, can be seen as a price index for a composite good between two price situations. It is similar to the usual index numbers defined from a representation of the technology and used for time series comparisons (that is, the Konus, Allen, Malmquist, or Divisia indexes; see Diewert, 1981). In the theory of index numbers, one wants to approximate these 'true' theoretical indexes (e.g., Konus' true cost of living index) using only observable data. Here, we face exactly the same problem, since the EPR aims to approximate the 'true' price index of the value added. If we used only the x and y observed in the protected situation, we would get the equivalent of a Laspeyres index, which is a poor approximation of the true price index. In index number theory, it is well known that the Laspeyres index is an upper bound of the theoretical index (see Diewert 1981, 1986). Therefore, the 'PSE type' measure, which assumes that the quantities remain constant when shifting from a protected to a non protected situation introduces a considerable bias in the estimation of protection. In index number theory one can derive superlative indexes which do not cause such a bias (Diewert, 1976). However, all superlative prices indexes use data on quantities in both price situations, that is, protected and unprotected prices. Since quantities in the world price situation are not observed, econometric techniques must be used to estimate the price index of the value added as a parametric aggregator function. When a parametric aggregator function is estimated, the price index in the world price situation can be obtained from the world price of the individual commodities. The parametric form must be flexible in order to allow for substitutions between commodities.

THE ESTIMATION OF PRICE AGGREGATOR FUNCTIONS

A flexible functional form is specified for the valued added function. World prices are observed for homogenous commodities. This involves a very large number of goods. It is impossible to estimate a flexible functional form on a large number of commodities for practical reasons. A solution is to make further separability assumptions and to use nested aggregator functions, as proposed by Fuss (1977). This can be done using a two stage optimization procedure. The value added is a function of a limited number of aggregate commodities, that is, intermediate inputs X_h and outputs Y_s (for example, grains). Each of the X_h and the Y_s is itself a function of a subset of individual commodities x_i and y_j (for example, wheat, barley, etc.). The list of individual commodities includes 19 outputs and intermediate inputs. The nested structure of the nested price functions is described in Bureau (1993). This approach is valid under the assumption of homothetic separability between subgroups of commodities. The two stages are integrated through the estimation in a first stage of an instrumental variable for the aggregate price index of the separable group of commodities Y_s and X_h. The value added function is the upper stage of the model, and is estimated as the second stage in the optimization procedure. The practical implication of a separable form for the value added function is that we assume that the quantity of aggregate Y_s (and X_h) is chosen in a first step, and then the optimal mix of these aggregate quantities is chosen. Thus, the mix of the components of Y_s (that is, the relative level of the elements of the vector y_s) depends only on the price of the commodities included in the aggregate Y_s, and is independent of the level and the mix of other aggregates as well as the prices of commodities outside Y_s.

A Diewert and Ostensoe (1988)'s quadratic normalized restricted function was specified for π and for the aggregator functions defining the price P_s of the aggregate Y_s. This particular functional form has the advantage that curvature conditions can be imposed globally (and not locally as in the case of a translog function) without destroying the flexibility of the function (Diewert and Wales, 1987). Moreover, the imposition of multiplicative separability leads to a simple form of the function. The price aggregator functions for the aggregate Y_s and X_h were estimated by FIML, jointly with share equations. The fitted values of the prices are used as instruments in the estimation of the value added function. The value added function is estimated with an iterative Zellner procedure, which leads to a three stage iterative least squares. Curvature conditions are imposed as in Wiley *et al.* (1973). The specification of the function, the econometric procedure and the estimation results are described extensively in Bureau (1993). The result is a parametric expression of π as a function of prices p and w. This function gives a fitted value for $\pi\left(p^p, w^p\right)$. The fitted value of $\pi\left(p^w, w^w\right)$ is constructed by replacing the protected prices by the world prices in the function. The EPR is defined as in Equation (3), that is, as a ratio of fitted values minus one.

DATA

The data are described extensively in Bureau (1993). The ratio of the observed protected price and the world price of an individual commodity define a nominal protection rate. The protected price is a price at the farm gate level. The data come from various sources, such as Eurostat's price data base, the Farm Accountancy Data Network, and information on markets. In the case of beef and milk, the intervention price is used since other data sources were not consistent with the data available for the world prices. Milk is assumed to be composed of milk powder and butter, and the intervention price is also used. However, the common intervention price is corrected for price differences across countries that correspond to differences observed in the price of the raw product. World prices rely mainly on the unit value (FOB) of the exports outside the European Community (source Eurostat external trade data base). When a commodity is not exported in large quantities, the price is the CIF import price. In the case of beef, there are quality differences between the meat traded and produced, and the nominal protection rate was constructed from budget sources, that is, on the basis of unit refunds. In addition to the difference between world and protected prices, the nominal protection rates include the unit value of direct payments, and all forms of premiums. These data come from the detailed list of expenses of the European Guidance and Guarantee Fund provided by the EC Commission. A detailed list of the data and procedure used is available upon request. Rates of protection have been compiled since 1973, except for Greece where data are missing prior to 1980. Table I shows nominal rates of protection for selected commodities, average 1973–1989.

DIFFERENCES IN EFFECTIVE PROTECTION IN EUROPE

Table 2 presents the effective protection rates for the periods 1973–89 and for the periods 1985–89 and 1974–78 (the year 1973 is not very meaningful for the countries joining the European Community).

Table 1 *Nominal Rates of Protection, Selected Commodities: Average 1973–89 (1981–89 for Greece)*

	Germ	France	Italy	Neth	Bel-Lu	UK	Irel	Denm	Greece
Wheat	1.39	1.14	1.53	1.27	1.26	1.20	1.11	1.26	1.34
Barley	1.45	1.17	1.62	1.35	1.42	1.32	1.16	1.36	1.39
Corn	1.64	1.26	1.73	-	-	-	-	-	1.40
Sugar beets	2.04	1.70	2.28	1.87	2.04	2.01	2.08	1.85	2.37
Rapeseed	1.79	1.28	1.22	-	-	-	-	-	-
Soybean	-	-	-	-		-	-	-	1.49
Sunflower	-	1.10	1.40	-	-	-	-	-	1.39
Olive oil	-	1.22	1.29	-	-	-	-	-	1.16
Milk	1.14	1.10	1.21	1.10	1.12	1.08	1.07	1.12	1.13
Poultry	1.46	1.12	1.49	1.60	1.31	1.27	1.33	1.70	1.74
Pigmeat	1.18	1.20	1.29	1.18	1.35	1.06	1.10	1.14	1.22
Beef	1.62	1.63	1.75	1.75	1.71	1.48	1.34	1.43	1.83
Sheep	2.21	2.34	2.82	2.74	2.38	1.73	1.90	1.90	2.93

The EPR can be interpreted as the extra returns to an aggregate of primary inputs (that is, capital, land and labour) provided by public intervention. An EPR of 0.32 for example, means that the returns to these aggregate primary inputs is 32 percent larger than what it would have been under the world market price. Therefore, this indicator measures how much of the government support has ended up in the manager, worker, capital-owner and landowner's pockets. After that, some of this government support has generated returns to suppliers of intermediate inputs. These intermediate input suppliers include grain producers whose grain is purchased by some animal producers. The intermediate input suppliers also include foreign exporters. For example, it is well known that one effect of European public intervention is to contribute to financing the US ethanol program, through an increase in the returns to the corn gluten feed exported to the European Community. One step further would be unravel the effect of public intervention as returns to capital, land and labour in order to investigate how much public support contributes to higher returns to self-employed labour. However, in the typical European family farm, decisions regarding the household are not always separable from decisions regarding the production process. Land is most of the time owned by the manager. Returns to capital may differ from the market interest rate, even for long periods of time (which rules out an interpretation in terms of short term gaps between ex-ante and ex-post returns). This makes it difficult to single out the returns to the self employed labour provided by public intervention.

Belgium–Luxemburg, The Netherlands and Germany obtained the highest EPR over the 1973–89 period. This suggests that the support provided by the CAP has increased the returns to primary factors in those countries more than in the other European countries. Italy, France, Ireland and Denmark obtained a lower EPR over the 1973–89 period. The comparison between the 1974–89 period and the 1985–89 period shows that the EPR has decreased for Germany and The Netherlands, while it has increased for France, the United Kingdom and Ireland.

In the beginning of the period, Ireland and the UK had the lowest rates of protection in Europe, since UK and Irish prices were relatively low prior to the EC membership. In

Germany, Belgium and The Netherlands, the high rate of protection in the beginning of the period was mostly due to the high prices of beef and pigs relative to world market prices. French prices were low for grains and milk. Since France was a major European exporter, prices were close to the intervention price. Poultry prices were also low, since a large share of production consisted of frozen poultry for export in very competitive Middle East markets. Prices were much higher in Italy. However, the large production of vegetables, fruits, and olive oil contributed to a low rate of protection. In France, as well as in Italy, grains were significant components of feedstuffs. This also contributed to a low EPR since protection on inputs has a negative effect on the EPR.

During the 1970s, UK and Irish prices increased subsequent to EC membership. The level of protection in these countries peaked in the 1980s. World prices for pigs became very low when the EC stopped being a major importer. This caused the rates of protection in Germany, The Netherlands, Denmark and Belgium to peak in 1979.

The protection on grains and oilseeds increased more rapidly than the protection on other commodities in the 1980s. This was mainly due to a reduction in price for grains on the world market. The increase in oilseed production contributed to high EPRs in France and Italy. Direct payments also increased for some Italian crops such as olive oil and tobacco. As a result, major grain producers, such as France, the UK, and Italy show an increasing trend in the EPR over time. Concurrent with a decrease in pig and beef prices in the Netherlands, Germany and Belgium, the trend in the EPR is negative.

Table 2 *Effective Protection Rates*

Average	Germ	France	Italy	Neth	Bel-Lu	UK	Irel	Denm	Greece
1973–1989	0.32	0.21	0.16	0.34	0.43	0.28	0.24	0.25	-
1973–1978	0.35	0.14	0.15	0.36	0.42	0.10	0.10	0.6	-
1985–1989	0.28	0.35	0.17	0.20	0.37	0.39	0.30	0.25	0.23

Table 3 *Spatial Price Indices of Aggregate Agricultural Output*

Average	Germ	France	Italy	Neth	Bel-Lu	UK	Irel	Denm	Greece	EC
1973–1989	109	96	103	95	103	97	91	103	95	100

Source: Barkaoui *et al.* (1992).

Note: The spatial index is the ratio of the PPP for agricultural output to the nominal exchange rate. The base is 100 for the EC-10 aggregate.

At the end of the period (1985–89), major grain producers were among the most protected countries due to the very low world market prices for grains between 1986 and 1988, which led to a producer price which was up to two and a half times the world price. Although it is not clear in Table 2, this was no longer the case in 1989. After 1988, the nominal protection on grains had gone back to lower levels due a decrease in producer prices and negative levies. At the end of the period, nominal protection on pigs had become very low in all countries but Italy. Although nominal protection on milk was high after 1985, there is a considerable decrease in 1989, due to higher world prices and lower interior prices (levies). During 1981 to 1989, the UK, Belgium, France and Ireland were the countries with the highest EPR. Except for Belgium, these countries had the lowest EPR in the beginning of the period (1973–78).

CONCLUSION

Effective rates of protection provide a theoretical framework for measuring the level of public support to producers. EPRs can be used to measure various policies, including protection at the border and interior support. They can be expanded to include all forms of public intervention which distort the producer's supply response. In this case, they are more consistent with microeconomic theory than some other alternative aggregate measures of support such as the PSEs which include production decoupled support.

In this study, we focused on the unequal effects of protection and public support generated by the CAP. The results illustrate that the CAP increases returns to primary factors unequally among countries. The unbalanced structure of the protection in Europe is a major explanation. All commodities are not supported the same extent under the CAP. Countries like France and the United Kingdom have benefited from the considerable support on grains. France and Germany also benefited from the considerable support on beef. Meanwhile, countries where there are products with little support, such as flowers in The Netherlands and vegetables in Italy, have less benefited from the CAP support.

The unequal public support measured by the EPR also comes from price differences across countries. Bureau and Butault (1992) have pointed out the large discrepancies in prices received by European producers. The computation of PPPs for the agricultural sector by Barkaoui *et al.* (1992) illustrates the magnitude of price differences for the aggregate output (see Table 3). These differences are a major explanation of the ERP differences as measured in Table 1.

One should keep in mind the limitations of this study. The EPR results are conditional on the assumption that the European Community is a small country. This assumption is obviously heroic for products such as milk, since EC exports have a considerable influence on the world prices. These results show trends in the world prices that are sometimes exogenous to the CAP. For example, the decrease in EPR of some countries corresponds to changes in the world price of some important commodities, more than it corresponds to real policy changes. Another reason for the differences in EPRs is that each European country does not have the same input mix. The larger the share of intermediate input in the total input, the higher is the unit return to the primary factor. This contributes to an EPR which is higher in the Netherlands than in Ireland, even if the nominal protection on the outputs (that is, the returns to all inputs) are comparable in both countries.

REFERENCES

Barkaoui, A., Bureau, H.C. and Butault, J.P., 1992, *A set of Purchasing Power Parities for Comparing Prices and Productivity in European and United States Agriculture*, Wissenschaftsverlag Vauk, Kiel.

Bhagwati, J.N. and Srinivason, T.N., 1973, 'The General Equilibrium Theory of Effective Protection and Resource Allocation', *Journal of International Economics*, Vol. 3, pp.259–283.

Bhagwati, J.N. and Srinivason, T.N., 1973, *Lectures on International Trade*, MIT Press, Cambridge, Massachusetts.

Bruno, M., 1978, Duality, Intermediate Inputs and Value Added', in Fuss, M. and McFadden, D. (eds.), *Production Economics: a Dual Approach to Theory and Applications*, Vol. 2, North Holland, Amsterdam.
Bureau, J.C., 1993, 'Effective Protection and the Unequal Effects of the CAP', Paper presented at ERAE Seminar, Isola Capo Rizzuto, Italy.
Bureau, J.C. and Butault, J.P., 1992, 'Productivity Gaps, Price Advantages and Competitiveness in E.C. Agriculture', *European Review of Agricultural Economics*, No. 19, pp.25–48.
Corden, W.M., 1966, 'The Structure of a Tariff System and the Effective Protection Rate', *Journal of Political Economy*, Vol. 74, pp.221–37.
Corden, W.M., 1987, 'Effective Protection', in Eatwell, J., Milgate, M. and Newman, P. (eds.), *The New Palgrave, a Dictionary of Economics*, Vol. 2, Macmillan Press Ltd, London.
Diewert, W.E., 1976, 'Exact and Superlative Index Numbers', *Journal of Econometrics*, Vol. 4. pp.115–145.
Diewert, W.E., 1981, 'The Economic Theory of Index Numbers: A Survey', in Deaton, A. (ed.), *Essays In the Theory and Measurement of Consumer Behavior in Honour of Sir Richard Stone*, pp.163–208, Cambridge University Press, London.
Diewert, W.E. and Wales, T.J., 1987, 'Flexible Functional Forms and Global Curvature Conditions', *Econometrica*, Vol. 55, pp.43–68.
Diewert, W.E. and Ostensoe, L., 1988, 'Flexible Functional Forrns for Profit Functions and Global Curvature Conditions', in Barnett W.A., Berndt, E.R. and White, H. (eds.), *Dynamic Econometric Modelling*, Cambridge University Press.
Fuss, M., 1977, 'The Demand for Energy in Canadian Manufacturing', *Journal of Econometrics*, Vol. 5, pp.89–116.
Gruebel, H.G. and Lloyd, PJ., 1971, 'Factor Substitutions and Effective Tariffs Rates', *Review of Economic Studies*, Vol. 38, No. 113, pp.95–103.
Josling, T. and Tangermann, S., 1989, 'Measuring Levels of Protection in Agriculture: A Survey of Approaches and Results', in Maunder, A. and Valdes, A. (eds.), *Agriculture in an interdependent World*, Proceedings of the 20th International Conference of Agricultural Economists, International Association of Agricultural Economists, Buenos Aires, August, Queen Elizabeth House, Oxford, UK.
Leith, J.C., 1968, 'Substitution and Supply Elasticities in Calculating the Effective Protection Rate', *Quarterly Journal of Economics*, Vol. 82, No. 4, pp.588–601.
OECD, 1987, *National Policies and Agricultural Trade, Country study on the European Community*, Paris.
Tsakok, I., 1990, *Agricultural price policy, A Practitioner's Guide to Partial Equilibrium Analysis*, Cornell University Press, Ithaca, New York.
Vousden, N., 1990, *The Economics of Trade Protection*, Cambridge University Press.
Webb, AJ., Lopez, M. and Penn, R., 1990, *Estimates of Producer and Consumer Subsidy Equivalent. Government Intervention in Agriculture*, 1982–87, Economic Research Service, US Department of Agriculture, Statistical Bulletin 803, Washington, D.C.
Wiley, D.E., Schmidt, W.H. and Bramble, W.J., 1973, 'Studies of a Class of Covariance Structure Models', *Journal of the American Statistical Association*, Vol. 68, pp.317–23.
Woodland, A.D., 1977, 'Joints Outputs, Intermediate Inputs and International Trade Theory', *International Economic Review*, Vol. 18, No 3, pp.517–533.
Woodland, A.D., 1982, *International Trade and Resource Allocation*, North Holland, Amsterdam.

DISCUSSION OPENING – Elisbetta Croci-Angelini *(Siena University, Italy)*

It seems to me that the paper I am here to discuss is quite accurate and I do not have much to object to. The results — striking as they may appear and with the added characteristic of taking into account more elements than usual — are fairly much in line with the common knowledge that the CAP, while unable to avoid undesired side effects, has not managed of achieve its goals. However, I would like to attract your attention to a few points related to the subject of the paper.

At the very outset, the author argues that 'In spite of 30 years of Common Agricultural Policy (CAP), the agricultural sector does not benefit from the same level of protection and support in all European countries'. Some (I believe not rhetorical) questions arise from this sentence. (a) Why should they have benefitted from the same level of protection to the same extent? (b) How do you measure the benefits from protection? (c) Why is the member country's level of protection the relevant level?

I would like to discuss these issues and find out on what concepts they are based. The first question refers to a concept of competition widely shared by our profession. Since the very beginning of the experiment of economic integration in Europe, it was held among the 'founding fathers' that competition was to be granted within the EEC. This concept of competition often refers to a race (with some initial line up) and is based on the myth of equality of opportunities. In economics this can be likened to a comparative statics exercise involving a one-period economy, after which the winner of the competition is easily singled out and rewarded. Competition is deemed good because the rivalry implicit in it, by guaranteeing the survivial of the fittest, leads to an efficient allocation of resources. There is, however, a hypocritical side to it, as this idea of competition describes the world we experience in a grossly insufficient way. We live in a multi-period economy where the original line up does not usually take place, rules may change while running and many elements, forbidden in a proper race, are de facto either admitted or tolerated. History counts and the winner tends to keep winning.

The effective rate of protection (ERP) is certainly more accurate in pointing at bonuses, penalties and the like, but it still refers to this very short term concept of competition. No wonder that the common level of protection has benefitted the agricultural sector of the various countries to a different extent, as the author correctly proves in his paper. This is certainly due to differences in the prices paid and received by producers, in the efficiency of the marketing sector, in national subsidies and VAT rates, as well as in the Green Exchange Rates, as the author points out, but the importance of a host of long term elements, ranging from the behavioural to the insitutional, and for brevity referred to as 'different structures', should never be overlooked. Indeed, this requirement was acknowledged by the 'founding fathers' when stressing the need of a structural policy whose role was quickly forgotten. Did the unequal public support contribute to a more or to a less fair competition in agriculture? Did it foster convergence or divergence of the structural elements, or was it neutral?

A second point refers to how to classify the supply-distortive public interventions (i.e. public intervention which affects production decisions) and measure the benefits from protection. In principle, all public intervention could be regarded as supply-distortive, but we can limit our scope to those elements which are cost-distortive at the producer's level. However, in evaluating the benefits from protection, all costs involved should be taken into account, not only the most obvious fixed and variable costs, but also all transaction costs and externalities, to come up with some measure of the opportunity cost which is the relevant concept. Again, this concept is grounded on a short term idea of competitive markets, which in turn makes all the more blurred the picture of what should be understood as the benefits of protection.

This leads me to the third point. Why are we so obsessed with measures and findings at the member country level? The obvious reason, in addition to the availability of disaggregated data, is the Council of Ministers' decision-making process. Yet, the implication is that however 'common' we would like to call it, it can only be a sort of compromise among member counties, for which reason expecting even a faint level of economic optimality is far too unrealistic.

The member states supplement the CAP with their own national policies. Not only the CAP provides an unequal support to European agriculture, but national policies add to it and could have been modified, but have not been stopped, through the years. What does a map of national plus common public support reflect in terms of social equity and productive efficiency? What an ideal system would be, for stopping us short of pointing at these inequitable results? The common, as opposed to the national, attitude would suggest a public support which is equitable and efficient regardless of the (differing) benefits it may yield at the member state level. The national attitude, however, after over 30 years is still prevailing.

GENERAL DISCUSSION — R.M.W. Johnson, Rapporteur *(Ministry of Agriculture, New Zealand)*

Discussion flowing from Paavo Makinen's opening on the von Witzke and Hausner paper followed the line that there is no cure for the treadmill effect. Perhaps policy may delay the effect, lower farm prices should not be taken as a reason for automatic support. Questions were also raised about the realism of the authors' assumptions about the land market. Land markets may not be perfect.

Lynn Kennedy, who presented the paper, was questioned about the use of first order auto-regression on data (when trend is present) to test the model. This is not a rigorous test and will not reveal weaknesses in the model. Market conditions are not perfect for land (with regard to authors' market assumptions? He was also asked if there would be changes in consumer surpluses over time (Not so, said Dr Kennedy).

In opening the discussion on the Schmitz paper, Ewa Rabinowicz (Sweden) said that the paper is interesting but has some weak spots! He argued that the case for food security in Europe and developing countries is weaker than ever before and is not relevant to the issue of CAP reform. The measurement of a minimum standard should distinguish between supply and demand effects by separating the production and expenditure bases. The measure adopted of probability of falling below a critical level is too demand oriented. Account should be taken of whether there are physical limits to food availability in developing countries. Self-sufficiency in Sweden was no longer an issue. The stochastic properties of the model suggested should be explored further. There is a need to distinguish between real and nominal protection rates. In the case of developing countries, income distribution is important, and net importers could benefit from any reduction of prices following reform.

Further discussion of the paper centred on conditions faced by different LDCs and on breadth of the definition of food security. The paper states that effect of CAP is negative for LDCs because world market prices are lowered and are more volatile. However, there is a need to make a distinction between net food importing and net food exporting countries in LDCs. For importers, urban consumers have benefitted from low would market prices. Some of the audience thought that the price-lowering effect would be unlikely to be surpassed by the volatility effect. Regarding the impact of the reform of CAP, it was argued that the author should take account of substitutability of locally produced food (de Janvry and Sadoulet). If substitutability is high, higher world market prices induce higher domestic food production in LDCs. Food imports are lower. If substitutability is low, higher world food prices makes consumers in LDCs worse off.

It was also suggested that the gains net importing LDCs made from low world prices may have encouraged the large growth of the urban. It was also argued that the definition of food needs is too narrow. Two aspects that were raised concern the effect of transfers and food aid and the importance of distribution systems. When governments give aid in the name of food security, they look at shortages in production. Distribution systems are neglected. Sometimes, the crisis is caused by poor distribution systems and markets and not a failure in production.

Elizabetta Croci-Angelini (Italy), in opening the discussion on Bureau's paper said that paper has been carried out very carefully. It is interesting and informative that CAP has not guaranteed uniform protection to member countries. In terms of the conference agenda one should ask what effect this has on competition? It also raises the question of whether countries should be protected to the same degree? It does not seem possible to equalize income by present methods. The results suggest that there should not be a CAP at all! Public interventions are supply distorting and it appears transaction costs are often neglected in evaluations of this sort. Their inclusion should enable better estimates of opportunity cost of such policies.

In further discussion, it was argued that the suggestion that payments of set-aside be left out of protection calculations should be disregarded. They should be included, because the balance is weighted too much in favour of farmers as it is. It was also suggested that the EPR rate for Germany (0.32) looks too low considering the large transfers that are involved.

Discussion participants included D.Gale Johnson (USA), Oeivind Hoveid (Norway), K. Pilgram (Germany) and Eric Tollens (Belgium).

MELINDA SMALE AND PAUL W. HEISEY*

Grain Quality and Crop Breeding when Farmers Consume their Grain: Evidence from Malawi

Abstract: When farmers consume much of their grain output, end-use quality, in addition to standard production characteristics, affects farmers' seed choice and the economic returns to investment in crop breeding. Evidence from Malawi suggests that despite a lengthy research lag, emphasizing grain quality in recent years will amplify returns to research. Yet the story of that research breakthrough also suggests that when market signals are weak, physical and the social scientists who seek to play an informative role must be especially cautious in their assessment of research priorities.

INTRODUCTION

In some countries of sub-Saharan Africa, such as Malawi, markets for industrially processed grains are relatively unimportant. Farmers consume the grain they produce or grain obtained from other farmers through purchase or exchange. Farmers' cultivar preferences are then conditioned by a range of socio-economic factors that are related to both the production and the consumption characteristics of the grain. For example, farmers-cum-consumers are concerned about quality in end-use, such as the performance of the grain in home processing, cooking, and on-farm storage.

When farmers both produce and consume their grain, scientists' and farmers' assessments of new crop varieties can diverge because yield is the foremost criterion for research and development (R & D) in conventional crop breeding programs. Typically, scientists are not formally trained or encouraged to use farmer's knowledge or recognize the diversity of farmers' objectives. Further, the historical evolution of political and economic institutions in sub-Saharan Africa has usually meant that small farmers have no public voice as either consumers or producers. Their only market signal to researchers, observed dimly through a haze of regulated prices, structural adjustment policies and institutional variables, is the decision to adopt or not to adopt the new cultivar. Finally, nascent private seed companies, when they exist autonomously from parastatal organizations, have little money to expend on comprehensive marketing research.

There are two simple but important consequences for crop breeding. First, social scientists can serve a valuable function as intermediary market informants between farmers and breeders. At the same time, in an era of diminishing international funding sources for plant breeding, crop and social scientists must carefully evaluate the panoply of claims to the research dollar. Unless each farmer is willing to finance his or her own R&D, not every small farmer's idiosyncratic preference can be included in the research budget.

This paper highlights some grain quality and crop breeding issues in the context of a sub-Saharan agricultural economy where industrially processed grain occupies a small share of the active grain market. In Malawi, where most maize moves from the field to the farm household or between farm households, grain quality has played a pivotal role in determining the time-to-release of maize cultivars suitable for widespread adoption and the

* International Maize and Wheat Improvement Center (CIMMYT).

rate of economic returns to maize research. Here, we compare the farmers' rate of return to maize hybrids under various research strategy assumptions, and, in the absence of market data expressing quality differentials, use a simple method to estimate the rate of return to investment in grain quality research. Although evidence suggests that Malawi will obtain a substantial economic return to quality research in maize, the history of maize research there underlines the fact that when market signals are weak, both physical scientists and the social scientists who seek to play an informative role must be especially cautious in their assessment of research priorities.

ISSUES IN GRAIN QUALITY AND CROP BREEDING

Until recently, the emphasis in most conventional crop breeding programs was to select for cultivars with maximum harvest yields, although many programs have lent increasing importance to yield stability factors. When farmers consume a large portion of their crop output, the performance of the cultivar in on-farm processing and storage, as well as particular taste or cooking characteristics, may also be important. Improving the relevance of crop breeding for research clientele (and increasing economic returns to investment in crop breeding) therefore depends on incorporating selection criteria that are not related to harvest yield. Yet 'plant breeders cannot respond to every quirk of farmers' circumstances' because costs increase, and progress slows as the number of selection criteria increases (Haugerud and Collinson, 1990, p.357). In fact, costs are thought to increase exponentially with the number of traits for which breeders select (Arnold and Innes, 1984).

Assessing the problem of choosing selection criteria in markets for industrially processed grain, Brennan (1992) cautions that researchers much recognize the high opportunity costs of tailoring grain production to market requirements such as end-use quality characteristics. Necessary conditions for a change in breeding strategies in such markets are that breeders possess the technical and genetic means to achieve it, and the market niche is robust enough to sustain the research investment and stable enough over time to survive the initial research lag. A point of departure is to posit the same set of necessary conditions for a change in breeding strategies in markets for non-industrially processed grain. Two examples illustrate what can occur if only one or the other of the the necessary conditions noted by Brennan holds, or if one interest group controls too much of the market niche.

CIMMYT's effort to breed Quality Protein Maize (QPM) is an example of a research experience in which, at the outset, the constraints were believed to be technical and the 'market niche' robust. On the contrary, developing QPM was no more costly in terms of selection, evaluation, testing, and seed multiplication than other maize types but much more costly in terms of farmer and consumer information[1]. Based on the rapid diffusion of wheat and rice HYVs, physical and social scientists believed that maize with improved protein quality could dramatically alter the plight of undernourished farmers, and of rural and urban consumers. Yet there was little effective demand for QPM because quality was not observable to consumers (Cantrell, 1989). In the case of QPM, contrary to what was initially believed, breeders possessed the technical and genetic means to achieve the change in breeding strategy (condition 1), but the market niche was not robust (condition 2).

The case of barley breeding in Canada illustrates the dangers of emphasizing one grain trait (malting quality) even when a market niche (private brewing companies) is robust (Ullrich *et al.*, 1986). The relatively large sums of research money that were furnished by one important private interest group contributed to a shift in public research emphasis from yield to quality varietal research. Redirection of funds was associated with a high social opportunity cost.

GAUGING THE 'MARKET NICHE' FOR GRAIN QUALITY

Ex post or *ex ante* rates of return to quality research can be estimated, given that quality differentials are reflected in market prices. In developed countries, economists have used hedonic pricing models to test whether the implicit value of an attribute of an agricultural commodity, such as end-use quality, is adequately reflected in competitive market prices and/or grading systems (Espinosa and Goodwin, 1991; Perrin, 1980). Unnevehr's (1986) application of a hedonic prices model to the study of returns to research on improving the physical and chemical quality of rice in Southeast Asia is unique. Her findings implied underinvestment in quality improvement, although returns to quality improvement research were not as large as returns to rice yield improvements.

Many developing countries in sub-Saharan Africa have neither the market prices nor testing facilities to enable such research to be conducted systematically. Often, grain prices established by the official marketing boards are pan-territorial and uniform across cultivars. Price premia reflecting grain quality may appear in informal markets but because those markets are thin and irregular, they may be difficult to measure with reliability. Depending on the attribute and crop, laboratory tests may be required to accurately assign a quality rating. The propensity of maize to cross-pollinate, for example, probably contributes to relatively high variability in attributes even within one maize type. Under such circumstances, do farmers-cum-consumers recognize small quality differences when they exchange or purchase grain?

Viewed from the perspective of the issues raised above, the long gestation period before the release in Malawi of maize hybrids with improved grain quality is understandable. The next section interprets some of the factors contributing to the lengthy research lag.

GRAIN QUALITY AND MAIZE RESEARCH IN MALAWI

Flint and Dent Maize Types

From Malawi's independence in 1964 until 1990, all the maize hybrids imported or released by the national research system have been dents, a term that refers to grain texture. Denty, as compared to flinty, grains have a lower density of hard starch granules. The adoption of dent hybrids has been limited by the fact that with on-farm methods, the flinty, open-pollinated maize varieties Malawians call 'local maize' can be processed more efficiently into the fine white flour (*ufa woyera*) they prefer to use in preparing their staple food (*nsima*). The hard flinty varieties are also more resistant to weevils in storage than the denty hybrids that have been introduced or released in the past.

Given their preferences and the uncertainty of obtaining local maize for consumption through the marketing system, small farmers in Malawi have typically grown local maize for home consumption. The higher-yielding, denty hybrid varieties have been grown for sale — when they have been planted at all. In 1987, the national maize team initiated their flint hybrid program. Not until 1990, nearly thirty years after independence, were high-yielding flinty hybrids released by the national research system. Grain quality was not emphasized in hybrid maize research before 1987. In retrospect, this research lag can in part be understood by appplying Brennan's two basic criteria.

The Technical Feasibility of Flint Hybrids

Development of a conventional maize hybrid from scratch requires seven years or more, depending on the availability of germplasm collections. Suitable genetic material for developing flint hybrids in Malawi has not been easy to obtain. Inbred lines developed from Malawi's local flint landraces are too tall and their growing season is too long (Zambezi, 1992). Most breeding efforts for maize hybrids in other parts of the world have emphasized dents because of the belief that dent maizes have higher yield potential than flints (Blackie, 1989). Dents are also more suitable than flints for most industrial processes. Regional germplasm collections already consisted primarily of dent types by 1950. South African, Zimbabwean and Kenyan commercial farmers had begun mass selection and breeding programs with white, dent, open-pollinated maize types they introduced from the US in the early part of this century (Karanja, 1995; Rusike, 1994). Although Malawi's colonial agricultural department tested some materials imported from South Africa and Zimbabwe, the department concluded, on the basis of poor field performance, that improvement of local flint landraces was a better breeding strategy (Rusike, 1994.). By the time Malawi attained independence in 1964, the highest yielding materials in the region were white dents bred in South Africa, Zimbabwe and Kenya.

Despite the recognition of the need to improve local landraces, the colonial government in Malawi did not begin to devote resources to maize breeding and maize agronomy until after the Great Famine in 1949. The first breeder, R.T. Ellis, was posted to Malawi in 1953. Although several flint hybrids and synthetics were available for release to farmers on a pilot basis by the early 1960s, Ellis then took a position with Malawi's tea breeding organization and was subsequently able to devote only occasional time to the maintenance of maize breeding lines. From independence until 1970, the post of plant breeder in Malawi was filled intermittently by a series of expatriates on short-term contracts who split their research time between maize and tobacco. Breeding lines deteriorated because of vacancies, shortage of supplies, and funds (Zambezi, 1992). In 1967, the hybrid maize research program was officially 'discontinued'. Although the program was restored in 1977, all three national breeders left for advanced training in 1981, returning only intermittently through the next decade. Staffing discontinuities reduced the total breeding capacity and compounded technical difficulties.

When the decision was made to breed flinty hybrids in 1987, the national research team used non-conventional top-cross method to speed the development process. For each of the two flint hybrids they developed, an existing dent Malawi hybrid was bred with another parent from a flint population in CIMMYT's collection. The idea of using the top-cross breeding technique, having a national team with the qualifications and decision-making authority to use it, and access to public (CIMMYT) germplasm, relaxed the technical constraint to breeding flint hybrids in Malawi. An important factor in this process was the close, field-based collaboration with CIMMYT scientists after the establishment of the mid-altitude station in Harare in 1985.

A 'Market Niche' for Flint Hybrids

There are a number of reasons why the potential market for flint hybrids in Malawi has never been and is not yet adequately assessed. In the colonial period, officials in the agricultural department recognized the significance of the flint grain trait when they rejected the strategy of using exotic maize germplasm in part because of insect resistance problems (Rusike, 1994). However, neither the colonial administration nor commercial farmers in Malawi devoted resources to the improvement of local landraces, maize breeding, or maize agronomy until the 1950s. Two main causes of this can be identified.

First, Malawi never developed the settler economy or class of commercial farmers that emerged in Zimbabwe and Kenya during the early part of this century. In sheer numbers and composition, Malawi's European farmers were few relative to the African population and only a small proportion of them were engaged in staple crop production. Most ran large estates for the production of tobacco, cotton, and tea for export. Malawi's African farmers produced the major share of the tobacco crop from the late 1920s to independence, on customary land or as tenants.

Secondly, African farmers also produced the nation's maize. Even on the European estates, maize was cultivated by African tenants on land allocated to them for that purpose. Malawi's population remained predominantly rural throughout the colonial period, without an urban-based labouring and landless class to feed (Smale, 1994). After a brief flurry of interest over the potential of maize as a export crop before World War I (Rusike, 1994, op. cit.), maize remained a subsistence crop produced or exchanged by Africans to feed themselves. Questions of maize self-sufficiency and the need to invest in maize improvement did not assume policy importance until the Great Famine of 1949.

Following a brief period that was overtly supportive of smallholders (1962–65), the independent government embarked on a policy during the late 1960s and early 1970s to fuel economic growth through promoting estate production of export crops, including tobacco, tea, and sugar. A combination of pricing policies, marketing institutions and banking arrangements favoured these crops and their production by estates over smallholder cash crops and maize. On estates, maize was grown only as a secondary crop to feed labourers or sell to urban markets. The corporate estates established during this period were often managed by Zimbabweans hired on short-term contracts. The maize hybrid they knew and valued was Zimbabwe's high yielding, extremely popular, denty hybrid SR52. Malawi's estate owners had no interest in flint grain texture (Smale, 1994).

At the same time, the widely accepted perspective in international development organizations was that hybrids were too costly for small farmers. Breeding efforts in the IARCs have emphasized until recently the development of improved open-pollinated varieties. During the 1970s, a British Overseas Development Team led by Bolton was posted to the Malawi research system, with Bolton's time devoted exclusively to maize. In a series of trials comparing the performance of various hybrids and improved open-pollinated varieties, Bolton concluded that the dent Zimbabwean hybrid SR52 and the semi-flint composite UCA (of Tanzanian origin) were most promising. Bolton described SR52, the highest yielding cultivar in the trials, as appropriate for the few

Malawian commercial farmers who could produce it for sale under high-management conditions. National breeding efforts could then be concentrated on the development and adaptation of semi-flint composites for consumption or sale by small farmers (Bolton, 1974). During the late 1970s, the government adopted a two-pronged strategy of importing SR52 for commercial farmers and breeding flint open-pollinated varieties for small farmers. The two-pronged strategy reduced breeding costs through utilizing research 'spillover', and reflected the reigning wisdom about appropriate seed technology for small farmers, but also coincided well with the dualistic agricultural policies advocated by government during that period. Because smallholders were not considered as part of the market for maize hybrids, there was no perceived market for flint hybrids.

There were also arguments for promoting the consumption of dent rather than flint hybrids. Most nutritionists since the colonial period have insisted on the superiority of the coarse, whole-meal *mgaiwa* to the refined *ufa woyera*. Another argument was that the prevalence of mechanical mills in rural areas would change consumer preferences through reducing women's labour time in processing. Instead, rural women continue to use traditional hand-pounding methods, substituting the mill only in the final stage of processing. Some researchers assumed that with urbanization, roller mill operators, who prefer dents to flints as less injurious to their machinery, would become the major market for smallholder maize surpluses. By contrast, Malawi's population remains predominantly rural, most rural households are maize deficit producers, and a large proportion of marketed maize still circulates through small traders and farmer-consumer or farmer-farmer transactions.

Finally, the absence of the physical seed production and marketing infrastructure needed to diffuse flint hybrids among Malawi's several million smallholders was real. From the beginning of the maize breeding program until the organization of the National Seed Company of Malawi in 1978, seed multiplication and distribution were the responsibility of the Ministry of Agriculture and the Agricultural Development and Marketing Corporation (ADMARC). ADMARC was the sole official supplier of inputs and sole official buyer of smallholder produce, using a pan-territorial, uniform price for all maize grain types. The recent entry of profit-making seed enterprises and the gradual liberalization of the domestic grain trade have increased the incentives for hybrid seed production and marketing, although these incentives are still limited, particularly in some regions of the country.

In retrospect, it is not clear that either of Brennan's criteria for shifting breeding strategies to emphasize end-use quality have ever been met in Malawi. On the other hand, evidence suggests that emphasizing quality over yield in recent years is likely to amplify the economic rate of return to research. The next section provides rate of return estimates to illustrate this point.

THE ECONOMIC RATE OF RETURN TO GRAIN QUALITY RESEARCH

Farmer Objectives and the Rate of Return to Adoption

Table 1 shows how assumptions about farmers' objectives and the role of maize breeding in meeting those objectives affect whether or not hybrids appear worth the investment for

Table 1 *Marginal Rate of Return to Grain Quality for Malawi Farmers*

	Assumptions about Farmer Objectives							
	High Management Grain Sold		Low or Medium Management Grain Consumed					
Maize type	Local	Dent hybrid	Local	Dent hybrid	Local	Flint hybrid	Local	Flint hybrid
Fertilizer (kg/ha)	40–10		0	96–40	0	0	40–10	40–10
Benefits								
Yield (kg/ha)	1852	3788	1071	3788	1071	1578	1852	2484
Management adjustment (kg/ha)	1667	3409	857	3030	857	1262	1482	1987
Less processing losses (kg/ha)						2273		
Price	0.43	0.43	0.58	0.58	0.58	0.58	0.58	0.58
Less harvest/ transport cost	0.37	0.37						
Less insecticide costs					0.55			
Total	617	1261	497	1250	497	732	859	1153
Costs that vary								
Fertilizer	128.2	337.9		337.9				
Seed	9.25	91.25	14.5	91.25	14.50	91.25	14.50	91.25
Labour								
Land preparation	50.7	58.5	50.7	58.50	50.7	58.5	50.7	58.7
Fertilizer application	4.46	8.91		8.91				
Planting	1.60	1.87	1.60	1.87	1.60	1.87	1.60	1.87
Total	194.2	498.4		498.4	66.80	151.6	66.8	151.6
Net Benefits	422.6	763.0	430	751.6	430	580.6	792.5	1001
Marginal rate of return (percent)		112		75		177		246

Data sources: MOA/FAO/UNDP Fertilizer Demonstration Programme 1992–3; CIMMYT/MOA Maize Variety and Technology Adoption Survey 1989-90.

Note: Benefits and costs are in Malawi kwacha/ha.

small farmers, and why grain quality mattered in breeding Malawi hybrids. In Malawi, as in many other environments, both flint and dent hybrids outyield local maize varieties even when unfertilized (National Maize Variety Trials; MOA/FAO/UNDP Fertilizer Demonstration Program). The first panel compares the partial budgets for the medium and larger smallholder, to whom dent hybrids might have been promoted during the 1980s. As a rough indicator for purposes of comparison, a smallholder falling into the medium and largest size categories in Malawi would operate from 1.5 to 6 ha and would usually produce enough maize to market a surplus. About 26 percent of Malawian smallholders fell into these size categories in 1980, the year of the last National Sample Survey of Agriculture (NSSA). The farmer represented by the figures in the first panel applies recommended fertilizer rates, uses high management levels, produces a surplus of local maize and sells hybrid maize. In this case, even though the farmer produces maize for home consumption, the relevant maize price at the margin for both maize types is the producer price. The estimated marginal rate of return to the adoption of fertilized hybrid seed (111 percent) justifies the investment, especially for the well-informed 'model' farmer who is acquainted with the technology. In fact, however, only about 10–15 percent of Malawian smallholders were served by the credit and extension service in the mid-1980s (Sofranko and Fliegel, 1989), and less that 10 percent grew hybrid maize.

The figures in the second panel, composed of six columns, represent the vast majority of smallholders in Malawi. In all columns, the farmer produces maize for home consumption but does not market a surplus, and the relevant maize price is the consumer price. The first two columns of the second panel show why dent hybrids are not particularly attractive for smallholders with low management levels, who consume their maize and do not market a surplus. Given the heavy on-farm processing and storage losses associated with dent hybrids, the estimated marginal rate of return (75 percent) is probably insufficient to cover the costs and risk of investment in an unknown technology. By contrast, the third panel shows how even with low management and no fertilizer, adopting a flint hybrid is economic for smallholders who consume their maize. Unfertilized dent hybrid maize would have similar harvest yields, but by the time processing and storage losses were deducted, the farmer household would face a negative rate of return on the investment. The figures in the fourth panel illustrate the remarkable marginal rate of return (246 percent) associated with moderate management levels and the adoption of a flint hybrid. Clearly, with Malawi's maize hybrids, the emphasis on high-yielding dents requiring a great deal of management and high fertilizer levels limited the potential demand for research output.

ESTIMATED RATE OF RETURN TO RESEARCH ON GRAIN QUALITY

In the absence of market price information that reflects quality differentials, a set of assumptions about prices faced by farmers, management levels, and adoption paths to estimate the *ex ante* rate of return to quality research. The benefits associated with research investment in dent hybrids were substracted only from the benefits associated with investment in both dent and flint hybrids. Dent hybrid research simplistically represents investment in 'yield', while research on both dent and flint hybrids represents 'quality' as well as yield investments. The resulting benefits stream from adopting hybrids as a farmer-cum-consumer were compared to the weighted average of net benefits from fertilized and unfertilized local maize production. Some basic assumptions are listed in Table 2.

Table 2 *Assumptions Used in Calculating Internal Rates of Return to Maize Research in Malawi*

Variable	Assumed level
Benefits (Hybrid Maize Only)	
Proportion of aggregate maize planted in hybrids	25 percent dent hybrids only 75 percent flint and dent hybrids
Aggregate maize area	1.4 million hectares in year 2012
Population in 2002[a]	12.332 million
Maximum per capita consumption	230 kg/year
Maize yield	
hybrid	3.0 t/ha
local	1.1 t/ha[b]
Maize price	
Semi-flint hybrid	(i) 1992 ADMARC consumer price (ii) 1992 ADMARC producer price
Local maize	1992 ADMARC consumer price
Dent hybrid	1992 ADMARC producer price
Seed and fertilizer prices	1992 ADMARC smallholder prices
Initiation of adoption path with imported hybrids only	1985 (five year lag)
Ceiling adoption rate for imported hybrids only[c]	15 percent
Costs (All Maize Research)	
Per professional research officer	
1977–1984[d]	1977-1984 actual real level
1985–1990	1980-1984 average real level
Research implementation	average costs per maize researcher do not differ from DAR average
Number of maize researchers[e]	full-time weight 1; part-time weight 0.5
Conversion factors to 1992 prices[f]	GDP deflator

Notes : [a] House and Zimalirana (1992). Population increases are assumed to counteract possible downward pressure on maize prices caused by increased output.

[b] Weighted average of fertilized and unfertilized local maize yields under low management conditions, assuming, based on National Crop Estimates and survey data, that one third of local maize area is fertilized.

[c] Benefits from imported hybrids are deducted from total research benefits.

[d] Pardey and Roseboom (1989).

[e] GON; GOM/DOA; GOM/DAR.

[f] World Bank (1992); Reserve Bank of Malawi (1992).

In the first calculation, per hectare net benefits from adopting dent hybrids were determined by adjusting downwards the yield of hybrid maize fertilized at recommended rates by 20 percent, and valuing output at the producer price. In other words, dent hybrids are produced under low or medium management conditions but fertilized according to the package currently promoted[2], and sold rather than consumed. The adoption ceiling was projected by estimating a logistic function with data on the proportion of maize area planted to dent hybrids up to 1993. If adoption rates had continued to climb according to the observed pattern, about one-quarter of Malawi's maize area would eventually have been planted in dent hybrids. Per hectare net benefits from adopting flint hybrids were determined by the same yield adjustment and valuing output at the consumer price. The logistic function applied to the data through 1993 predicts that adoption of both flints and dents will reach 100 percent of all maize area in 2011. Forcing a lower adoption ceiling (75 percent of all maize area) to express unknown socioeconomic or institutional impediments[3], the total value of quality research is then the extra value of a 75 percent adoption ceiling to a 25 percent adoption ceiling, plus the assumed difference per hectare in the value to the farmer who is also a consumer.

In the second calculation, for a more conservative estimate of the per hectare benefit from adopting hybrids, the producer price was used to value output of both dent and flint hybrid maize. This assumption reflects the difficulty in generalizing farmer objectives and preferences when quality differentials are not expressed in market information. The only effect on research benefits from quality investments is then the higher adoption ceiling projected from the observed adoption pattern.

Direct and indirect costs of all maize breeding were calculated for each year from 1977 to 1990, overstating the costs of quality research by including yield research. The years of breeding adapted dent hybrids were necessary for developing local inbred lines that were suitable to use in the top-crosses. On the other hand, the flint germplasm for the top-cross was 'free' from the viewpoint of the national research system.

Given the assumptions invoked and the data up to 1993, the estimated internal rate of return to research investment in the grain quality of maize hybrids is 53 percent. With the more conservative pricing assumption, the estimate falls to 32 percent.

CONCLUSIONS

There seems no doubt that by emphasizing grain quality in recent years, the impact of Malawi's maize research program has been magnified, with some positive distributional consequences. That impact will depend over time on complementary investments in seed production and distribution systems, as well as continuity in the maize research program. The relevance of research output for Malawi's many smallholders is much greater than ever before — a laudable accomplishment for the scientists and institutions involved. Incorporating end-use quality in breeding objectives when farmers consume their maize makes economic sense.

On the other hand, the story of this accomplishment reveals some potential dangers associated with expanding selection criteria in crop breeding. Suppose Malawi's maize breeders had emphasized flint quality over yield in allocating their scarce research resources during the 1970s, using the money spent importing dent hybrids to developing flint hybrids or open-pollinated varieties. At that time, how long would it have taken them, with limited staff and fewer breeding techniques, to overcome the shortage of (a) exotic flint inbred lines and (b) suitable local material to breed inbred lines? Without a yield advantage, flinty, improved open-pollinated varieties would not have been attractive. In either case, the seed production and marketing system was not sufficiently developed to diffuse new seed types.

Even in 1987, the effective smallholder demand for hybrids was difficult to assess in Malawi's agricultural economy. Under pressure from the donor community, the research system gambled, and the opportunity cost of the gamble was reduced through utilizing a nonconventional breeding technique and public (CIMMYT) germplasm. The gamble appears to be paying off — but may not in other similar cases. Shifts in donor views on development priorities can become flights of imagination, and as Cantrell concluded with reference to the QPM program, 'imagination...is not necessarily a reliable guide to assigning priorities' in a crop breeding program. If any category of germplasm is to receive exceptional treatment, its special status must be based on a cool assessment of needs, benefits, and costs (Cantrill, 1989, p.9). In countries like Malawi, cool assessment requires special insights.

NOTES

[1] QPM seed was, however, more costly to produce commercially because of the need for isolation.

[2] Lower fertilizer levels may be more realistic as adoption of hybrid seed becomes more widespread and the distribution system becomes more flexible.

[3] For example, in the 1993–94 cropping season, credit was not disbursed because of repayment problems that accompanied major political changes in the previous year. As a result, the use of hybrid seed and fertilizer dropped precipitously after a seven-year pattern of rapid increase.

REFERENCES

Arnold, M.H. and Inness, N.L., 1984, 'Plant Breeding for Crop Improvement with Special Reference to Africa', in Hawksworth, D.L. (ed.), *Advancing Agricultural Production in Africa*, Commonwealth Agricultural Bureaux, Farnham Royal, UK.

Blackie, M.J., 1989, *Maize in East and Southern Africa*, Rockefeller Foundation, Mimeo, Lilongwe.

Bolton, A., 1974, 'Response of Maize Varieties to Various Environmental Factors', *Proceedings of the 5th East African Cereals Research Conference*, Lilongwe, 10–15 March.

Brennan, J.P., 1992, 'Economic Issues in the Establishment of Plant Breeding Programs to Meet Market Requirements', in Ahmadi, F. and Copeland, L. (eds.), *Grains End Uses, Quality Standards and Breeding Programs*, Proceedings of the Grains Research Symposium, Sydney, Australia.

Cantrell, R.P., 1989, 'Quality Protein Maize: A Better Lunch But Not a Free One', International Maize and Wheat Improvement Center (CIMMYT), Mimeo, El Batán.

Espinosa, J.A. and Goodwin, B.K., 1991, 'Hedonic Price Estimation for Kansas Wheat Characteristics; *Western Journal of Agricultural Economics*, Vol. 16, No. 1, pp.72–85.

Government of Malawi (GOM), 1964–1974, Department of Agriculture (DOA), *Annual Reports*, Zomba.

Government of Malawi (GOM), 1975–1978, Department of Agricultural Research (DAR), *Annual Reports*, Chitedze Research Station, Lilongwe.

Government of Malawi (GOM), 1979–1992, Maize Commodity Team, *Annual Reports*, Department of Agricultural Research (DAR), Lilongwe.

Government of Nyasaland (GON), 1954–1963, Department of Agriculture (DOA), *Annual Reports*, Zomba.

Haugerud, A. and Collinson, M.P., 1990, 'Plants, Genes and People: Improving the Relevance of Plant Breeding in Africa', *Experimental Agriculture*, No. 26, pp.341–362.

House, W.J. and Zimalirana, G., 1992, 'Rapid Population Growth and Poverty Generation in Malawi', *Journal of Modern African Studies*, Vol. 30, pp.141–161.
Karanja, D.D., 1995, *An Economic and Institutional Analysis of Maize Research in Kenya*, Michigan State University, International Development Paper, East Lansing, Michigan.
National Sample Survey of Agriculture (NSSA), 1980–81, 1984, Government Printer, Zomba.
Pardey, P.G. and Roseboom, J., 1989, *ISNAR Agricultural Research Indicator Series I*, Cambridge University Press, Cambridge.
Perrin, R.K., 1980, 'The Impact of Component Pricing of Soybeans and Milk', *American Journal of Agricultural Economics*, Vol. 62, No. 3, pp.445–55.
Reserve Bank of Malawi, 1992, *Financial and Economic Review*, Vol. 24, No. 3.
Rusike, J., 1994, Draft PhD. dissertation, Department of Agricultural Economics, Michigan State University, East Lansing.
Smale, M., 1994, 'Maize is Life: Malawi's Delayed Green Revolution', International Maize and Wheat Improvement Center (CIMMYT), Mimeo, El Batán.
Sofranko, A.J. and Fliegel, F.C., 1989, 'Malawi's Agricultural Development: A Success Story?' *Agricultural Economics*, Vol. 3, No. 1, pp.99–113.
Ulrich, A., Furtan, H. and Schmitz, A., 1986, 'Public and Private Returns from Joint Venture Research: An Example from Agriculture', *Quarterly Journal of Economics*, No. 100, pp.103–125.
Unnevehr, L.J., 1986, 'Returns to Research in Quality Improvement', *American Journal of Agricultural Economics*, Vol. 68, No. 3, pp.634–40.
World Bank, 1992, *World Tables 1992*, Johns Hopkins University Press, Baltimore.
Zambezi, B.T., 1992, Senior Maize Breeder, Malawi Department of Agricultural Research, Personal communication (March).

DISCUSSION OPENING — K.N. Ninan *(Institute For Social And Economic Change, Bangalore, India)*

Smale and Heisey's paper raises interesting issues concerning the Hobson's choice confronting plant breeders and policy makers in making research investment decisions given the conflicting needs for providing for future food requirements through emphasis on yield augmenting varieties in crop breeding research as against those emphasising quality improvement which cater specifically to farmers' tastes and preferences. This problem is not peculiar to Malawi but true of crop breeding research in most other countries as well. These questions assume importance since there are trade-offs involved between costs and benefits to farmers, plant breeders and country as a whole. Funding for crop breeding research being limited, there is need to make optimum and rational use of scarce research funds and other resources which also has to be justified by the expected returns. In evaluating research investment decisions the important question is to what extent the research priorities reflect development goals. Concerns about reducing poverty and attaining self sufficiency in food prompted many Asian and Latin American countries to emphasize yield augmentation in crop breeding programmes during the green revolution phase. Subsequent concerns about extending the benefits of growth to lagging regions and ecologically fragile areas led to research efforts in evolving location specific crop varieties that were tolerant of droughts and other environmental constraints.

Sub-Saharan Africa faces severe economic problems, with food production unable to keep pace with population growth. An idea of the projected demand for maize and other foods in Malawi and the demand-supply gaps would have indicated the broad parameters and constraints within which policy makers and plant breeders have to make decisions about priorities in crop breeding research. The paper doesn't shed much light on this.

Further, although the authors suggest some positive distributional consequences of quality improvement oriented crop breeding research in Malawi (in terms of wider participation by small farmers) the crucial questions are how far has this emphasis on quality improvement led to an improvement in nutritional levels of the poor and a reduction in poverty.

Secondly, allocations of available funds should be justified by the expected returns. The authors note that unlike in South-East Asia, where rates of return from quality improvement based research were lower than yield-based ones, in Malawi quality improvement based breeding research yielded high returns. The IRRs using alternate assumptions and sensitivity analysis ranged between 32 to 53 percent. It would have been interesting to know how changing prices and tastes and preferences, apart from other factors would alter these rates of return. Also it is important to know what are the social opportunity costs in terms of yields foregone or food imports required, etc.

Thirdly, the results obtained by the authors pertain to an economy like Malawi, characterized by weak market signals and a highly regulated market which have distorted the structure of incentives for plant breeding research. However, liberalization and structural adjustment policies in Malawi would change the incentives for plant breeding research and facilitate a greater role by private seed companies. The question then is what are the likely impacts of this changing policy environment on crop breeding research in Malawi, as also in other similarly placed countries.

Fourthly, the efficiency and viability of crop breeding research programmes also depends upon an effective extension system. In this connection the authors suggest a role for social and physical scientists in bridging the information gap between plant breeders and farmers. It would be interesting to discuss the parameters of this role and similarly of other agents like farm leaders, NGOs and local level institutions, and the media.

Lastly, as is the experience of many developing countries, in Malawi there is going to be greater commercialization of the food sector as the economy grows. That will change the incentives and policy environment for crop breeding research in Malawi. This is another issue which merits discussion. Thus there are both general issues and issues specific to Malawi which merit detailed discussion.

ROBERT TOWNSEND AND COLIN THIRTLE*

Dynamic Acreage Response: An Error Correction Model for Maize and Tobacco in Zimbabwe

Abstract: The paper presents an empirical investigation of the supply of maize and tobacco for commercial agriculture in Zimbabwe. The error correction model, which employs the concept of cointegration to avoid spurious regressions, is used in the analysis. The factors affecting percentage area planted to maize were shown to be expected real maize price, real price of tobacco, real price of fertilizer and government intervention. The factors affecting percentage area planted to tobacco were shown to be real price of tobacco, expected real price of maize and institutional factors. The own price elasticity for maize was 1.44 and 1.76 in the short and the long run, respectively, for tobacco these were 0.28 and 1.36 in the short and long run respectively.

INTRODUCTION

The study of agricultural supply response has long been one of the most fruitful approaches to determining the effects of policy on agricultural output. Nerlove (1958) was largely responsible for formalising the dynamic approach, based on lagged adjustments and expectations. However, agricultural time series tend to be trended and regressions of trended data, even though giving high R^2s and significant *t*-values, may be spurious (Granger and Newbold, 1974). The recent literature on cointegration analysis addresses the problem of spurious regressions, when analysing non-stationary data. Under certain conditions, these series may be modelled using dynamic error correction models, which take account of the dynamics of short run adjustment towards long-run equilibrium in a theoretically consistent manner. This study applies these techniques to the supply of maize and tobacco, which are Zimbabwe's main food crop and export crop respectively. Cointegration is used to test long run equilibrium relationships between the time series and provides a framework for the analysis of supply within an error correction framework.

The next section outlines the concepts of cointegration and error correction. The data, the model and results are then described, with policy implications considered in the concluding section.

THEORY

Cointegration

The concept of cointegration states that if there exists a long run relationship between two variables, then the deviations from the long run equilibrium path should be bounded, and if this is the case, then the variables are said to be cointegrated. Two conditions must be satisfied for variables to be cointegrated. Firstly, the series for the individual variables

* Birkbeck College, University of London and University of Reading, respectively. We thank the Development Bank of Southern Africa for financial support for this project.

must have the same statistical properties; that is, they must be integrated of the same order. If a series is stationary after differencing once, then it is said to be integrated of order one, or I(1). Stationarity tests are proposed by Fuller (1976) and Dickey and Fuller (1981), which determine if a series has a unit root (i.e., is non-stationary). These tests require the following regression

$$(1)\quad \Delta y_t = \alpha + \beta_t + (\rho - 1)y_{t-1} + \sum_{i=1}^{n} \lambda_i \Delta y_{t-i} + u_t$$

where Δy_t is the first difference in y_t, t is a trend term, n is the number of lags required to make the error term, u_t, white noise. The null hypothesis that the series has a unit root requires $(\rho-1) = 0$ or $\rho = 1$, indicating the process in nonstationary. In this case differencing y would yield a stationary process, that is: the process is difference stationary. The critical *t*-ratios are calculated by Fuller (1976). If the *t*-ratio for the coefficient $(\rho-1)$ is less than the critical value the hypothesis of a unit root is accepted and the series is non-stationary. If $(\rho - 1) < 0$ or $\rho < 1$ and the trend coefficient, β, is significant then y is trend stationary.

If the series are integrated of the same order, a static regression in the levels of the variables is run and tested to see if linear combinations of the variables are themselves integrated of the same order as the individual variables. If the variables are cointegrated, then there should exist a linear combination of these variables which is integrated of order one less than the individual variables. In the cointegrating regression

$$(2)\quad Y_t = a + bX_t + u_t$$

If Y~I(n) and X~I(n) then Y and X are said to be cointegrated if u_t~I(n–1). In Equation (2), b measures the long run relationship between Y and X, and u is the divergence from the equilibrium path. If there is a stable long run relationship between Y and X, then the divergence from it should be bounded. Engle and Granger (1987) argue that if cointegration holds, then the error correction model is a valid representation of the adjustment process (the Engle and Granger two step procedure).

Testing the order of integration of the cointegrating regression error term can be performed using the Dickey-Fuller (DF) test, the augmented Dickey-Fuller (ADF) test, or the cointegrating regression Durbin-Watson (CRDW) proposed by Sargan and Bhargava (1983). These tests are the same as those used for determining the order of integration of the variables, but here it is the residuals that are being tested. OLS ensures that the cointegrating regression will give residuals having the smallest possible sample variance, so the critical values must be adjusted. Some of these adjusted vales are presented in Banerjee *et al.* (1993), MacKinnon (1991) gives the most comprehensive set of critical values using response surfaces.

Another disadvantage of the OLS approach is that in the multivariate case, there may be more than one cointegrating vector. Thus, in the OLS approach there is no guarantee that a unique cointegrating vector has been estimated. Thus, the DF, ADF and CRDW tests have been superseded[1] by the Johansen Maximum Likelihood estimation method (Johansen, 1988; Johansen and Juselius, 1990). This approach allows the estimation of all the cointegrating relationships and constructs a range of statistical tests.

The Error Correction Mechanism

If two cointegrated variables y and x are in stable equilibrium then

$$(3) \quad Y = bX$$

but in the time series, $Y_t = bX_t$ may never be observed to hold. This discrepancy, $Y_t = bX_t$, contains useful information since on average the system will move towards equilibrium. If $Y_{t-1} - bX_{t-1}$ the previous disequilibrium, then the discrepancy should be useful as an explanatory variable for the next direction of movement of Y_t (Banerjee *et al.* 1993). Incorporating this observation into the variable changes model suggested by Granger and Newbold (1974) yields the error correction model. In effect, it reinstates the levels, and hence the long run considerations, into the differences specification which describes the short run relationships between variables.

The simplest error correction model involving X and Y takes the form

$$(4) \quad \Delta Y_t = \phi \Delta X_t - \alpha(Y_{t-1} - bX_{t-1}) + u_t$$

where ϕ captures the short run effect on Y of the changes in X, and b accounts for the long-run equilibrium relationship between Y and X. u_t is the disturbance term, with zero mean, constant variance and zero covariance. $(Y_{t-1} - bX_{t-1})$ is the divergence from long-run equilibrium, so measures the extent of correction of such errors by adjustment in Y. The negative sign indicates that the adjustments are in the right direction to restore the long-run relationship (Hallam and Zanoli, 1993).

In the context of Hendry's 'general to specific modelling' the error correction model (ECM) can be derived as a simple reparameterization of a general autoregressive distributed lag model (Hendry *et al.* 1984). With regard to the relevance to agricultural supply analysis Salmon (1982) and Nickell (1985) show how the ECM can be derived from the dynamic optimizing behaviour of economic agents, within this framework Hallam and Zanoli (1993) show that the ECM avoids the partial adjustments unrealistic assumption of a fixed target supply based on stationary expectations.

DATA, BACKGROUND AND MODEL

The principle sources of the data used were the Zimbabwe Agricultural Marketing Authority, the Central Statistics Office, the FAO Fertilizer Yearbooks, the Zimbabwe Tobacco Association, and Thirtle *et al.* (1993), who derived a production data set from the CSO Production Accounts of Agriculture, Forestry and Fisheries, various University of Zimbabwe working papers, the Statistical Yearbook of Zimbabwe 1987, and various published and unpublished papers from the Ministry of Agriculture, Lands and Rural Resettlement. Annual data, for the commercial sector, from 1970–1989 were used in the analysis.

The main food and cash crops in the Zimbabwean agricultural sector are maize and tobacco respectively. Maize has been the staple diet of the rural population for many years. The marketing of maize, over the sample period, was carried out under strict government control through the Grain Marketing Board (GMB) and the producer price is set by

Government. This is normally announced after planting. Tobacco makes a substantial contribution to the foreign exchange earnings, having earned over 967 million Zimbabwe dollars in 1990, or some 26 percent of estimated foreign exchange earnings for the year. Tobacco cultivation, being labour intensive, also generates large-scale rural employment and accounts for 15 percent of the total population engaged in agriculture. The tobacco crop, however, is marketed by the Tobacco Marketing Board on a free-auction system with no government support given. 97 percent of all tobacco grown in the commercial sector is flue cured. As maize and tobacco are of such primary importance, in terms of food security and foreign exchange earnings, it is worthwhile understanding the relationships governing farmers' responses to price policy changes in these enterprizes.

The supply function for an agricultural output can be expressed as

$$(5)\quad Q_i = f(P_i, P_j, P_k, I, T)$$

where Q_i = quantity of output of good i supplied, P_i = price of output i, P_j = price vector of competing outputs, P_k = price vector of inputs, I = institutional constraints, infrastructure etc., and T = the state of technology. However, the dependent variable used is the area planted, rather than output, because this is under the control of the farmer to a much greater degree than output, which is subject to the effects of exogenous variables like the weather. Thus, acreage planted is a better indicator of planned production, as has frequently been noted in the literature (see Askari and Cummings, 1977).

Difficulties arise in accounting for on-farm use of maize, when calculating the maize area planted. However a fairly consistent series was derived which represented the area planted to maize that was to be sold to the Grain Marketing Board. For tobacco, the area planted figures were available, and unlike maize, all the tobacco is sold off the farm. Both series were divided by the total land area available to the commercial farmers, to allow for land purchased by government for resettlement purposes. The resulting series are the percentage areas of the commercial farms planted to maize and tobacco.

The expected price of maize was estimated in the manner suggested by Lawrance and Jayne (1992). This is necessary since even though there is a so-called preplanting announced price, in almost all of the past years the price has been announced after planting. The producers' expected price for maize is assumed to be a function of recent price trends and the level of stocks held by the GMB. The expected price is estimated as

$$(6)\quad P_t^* = a_0 + a_1 P_{t-1} + a_2 (Endstock)_{t-1}$$

where P_t^* = the expected real price of maize, P_t = real price of maize in year $t-1$, $(Endstock)_{t-1}$ = stocks of maize in tons at the end of year $t-1$, or beginning stocks in year t. The maize price was constructed as the average price of grade A, B, and C maize, which accounted for about 97 percent of all deliveries to the GMB from the commercial farmers. The expected price of tobacco was taken as the price received by farmers in the previous year.

In deciding how much of the crop to plant, farmers also take into account the opportunity cost of producing that crop, as Equation (5) shows. The competing crops in the supply of maize were taken to be soyabeans and tobacco. Maize was assumed to compete with tobacco, in the tobacco supply equations.

The key production costs for maize and tobacco are fertilizer and labour. There is a minimum wage rate set by government, and is known at the beginning of the season, the wage in year *t* was used. The fertilizer price is not lagged either, as most farmers purchase fertilizer at the beginning of the season and the price is known. The fertilizer price was quality–adjusted to allow for changes in the nutrient content. The hedonic regression technique used assumes that the price of a heterogeneous product is a function of its quality characteristics (see Cooper *et al.* (1993) and Rayner and Lingard (1971)).

Lastly, a dummy variable was included in the maize supply model to explain the collapse in commercial plantings in 1987/1988 (Beynon 1993), when there was a threat of price cuts if there was excess production. A dummy variable was included in the tobacco supply equation to capture the effects of sales quotas imposed on tobacco growers during the years 1967–73, 1976–77 and 1981–83. A simple time trend variable was included to represent technical change.

ESTIMATION AND RESULTS

Cointegration

Following section two, we begin by examining the statistical properties of the series. All the variables are generated by an AR(1) process except expected real maize price and the real soya price which are generated by an AR(3) and AR(2) process respectively. The DF/ADF tests showed that all the variables are integrated of order one, I(1), except for the real price of soya which appears to be I(0) (see Table 1). This satisfies the first condition for variables to be cointegrated, namely that they are integrated of the same order, I(1). The second condition is that there must be some linear combination of the variables which are integrated of order one less than the individual variables. The tests for cointegration are similar to those used to test for the order of integration, but they are based on the residuals, as was explained in section two. These tests have been superseded by the maximum likelihood methods proposed by Johansen, which provide likelihood ratio tests for the existence of different numbers of cointegrating vectors.

Maize area planted, expected real maize price, real tobacco price, real fertilizer price and government intervention yielded a maximum eigenvalue test and trace test that rejected the null hypothesis of no cointegrating vectors at the 95 percent level. The maximum eigenvalue test statistic is estimated as 44.6 against a critical value of 34.4 and a trace test statistic is estimated as 86.7 against a critical of 76.1. Both tests reject the hypothesis of more than one cointegrating vector with an eigen test statistic of 23.5 against a critical value of 28.1 and the trace test statistic of 42.0 against a critical value of 53.1. Thus there is only one cointegrating vector.

Tobacco area planted, real tobacco price, expected real maize price and quotas similarly yielded a maximum eigenvalue test and trace test that rejected the hypothesis of no cointegrating vector at the 95 percent level. The maximum eigenvalue test statistic was estimated as 41.9 against a critical value of 28.3 and a trace test statistic of 72.2 against a critical value of 53.1. Both tests reject the hypothesis of more than one cointegrating vector yielding an eigenvalue test statistic of 21.0 against a critical value of 22.0 and the trace test statistic of 30.3 against a critical value of 34.9.

Error Correction Model

Where only one such vector exists it can be interpreted as an estimate of the long-run cointegrating relationships between the variables concerned (Hallam and Zanoli, 1993). Thus, the estimated parameter values from these equations are the long run coefficients. The Johansen normalized estimates for maize are

$$(7)\quad Q_m = 1.76P_m - 0.88P_t - 0.69P_f - 1.13Dum + 7.23$$

and for tobacco they are

$$(8)\quad Q_t = 1.39P_t - 1.03P_m - 0.48Quota - 2.13$$

The error correction model for a single explanatory variable is shown by Equation (4) of section two. The ECM for maize (tobacco is entirely similar), with the variables listed, would be

$$(9)\quad \Delta Y_t = \Sigma\phi_{Yi}\Delta Y_{t-i} + \Sigma\phi_{Mm}\Delta P_{Mt-m} + \Sigma\phi_{Tn} + \Delta P_{Tt-n} + \Sigma\phi_{Fk}\Delta P_{Ft-k} + \phi_D\Delta DUM$$
$$+\alpha(Y_{t-1} - b_M P_{Mt-1} - b_T P_{Tt-2} - b_F P_{Ft-1} - b_D DUM_{t-1})$$

The right hand side difference terms can be lagged a number of times, the length of lag being determined by the *t*-test. This model did not perform well with the limited number of observations available. However, as was explained in connection with Equation (4), ø captures the short run effect on Y of the changes in X, b accounts for the long-run equilibrium in the bivariate case. In order to reduce the number of variables to be estimated, thus increasing the degrees of freedom, the reduced form of the error correction model can be estimated. The residual term from Johansen cointegrating regressions in Equations (7) and (8) can be used to represent the bracket terms in Equation (9). The equation can thus be estimated as

$$(10)\quad \Delta Y_t = \Sigma\phi_{Yi}\Delta Y_{t-1} + \Sigma\phi_{Mm}\Delta P_{Mt-m} + \Sigma\phi_{Tn}\Delta P_{Tt-n} + \Sigma\phi_{Fk}\Delta P_{Ft-k} + \phi_D\Delta DUM + \alpha EC_{t-1}$$

This method only provides estimates for the short-run elasticities (the coefficients on the difference terms), but the parameters from the cointegrating regressions [Equations (7) and (8)] can be used as estimates of the long run elasticities.

The results reported in Table 2 are from models below chosen on the criteria of goodness of fit (variance dominance), data coherence, parameter parsimony and consistency with theory (Hendry and Richard, 1982).

The results in Table 2 show that percentage maize area planted is dependent on the real price of maize, the real price of tobacco, the real price of fertilizer and government intervention. The coefficient signs are consistent with *a priori* expectations. These results show that a 10 percent increase in the real price of maize will lead to an 14.4 percent increase in percentage area planted in the short run and a 17.6 percent increase in the long run. An increase in the expected real price of tobacco will cause a 8.8 percent decrease in maize area planted. A 10 percent increase in the real price of nutrient does not have a significant effect in the short run, but in the long run will decrease maize area grown by 6.8 percent.

Table 1 *Results of the DF/ADF Tests for Unit Root*

Variable levels	AR process	DF/ADF
Maize area	1	–2.6669
Tobacco area	1	–1.3921
Real fertilizer price	1	–1.9159
Real maize price	3	–2.7244
Real tobacco price	1	–2.7420
Real soya price		–3.8196
Real labour wage	1	–2.8658
Critical values		–3.0294
First differences		
Maize area		–4.4744
Tobacco area		–4.4857
Real fertilizer price		–4.4141
Real maize price		–7.4929
Real tobacco price		–6.4621
Real labour wage		–4.7642
Critical values		–3.0401

Notes: All the variables are in logarithms. The prices were deflated by the consumer price index.

Table 2 *Maize and Tobacco Supply: ECM Estimates*

Explanatory variables	Coefficients for Maize		Coefficients for Tobacco	
	Short-run	Long-run	Short-run	Long-run
Constant	-	7.23	-	–2.13
ΔP_{Mt}	1.44 (2.89)	1.76	-	–1.03
ΔP_{Tt-1}	–0.45 (–1.98)	–0.88	0.28 (3.93)	1.36
ΔP_{Ft}	-	–0.68	-	-
ΔDUM	–0.80 (–3.53)	–1.13	–0.17 (–5.10)	–0.48
EC_{t-1}	–0.79 (–2.64)		–0.34 (–5.83)	
R^2	0.76		0.79	
DW	1.8		2.2	

The result for tobacco show a similar degree of fit. Real tobacco price, real maize price and institutional factors, quotas, affected the percentage area allocated to tobacco. A 10 percent increase in the real price of tobacco will lead to a 2.8 percent increase in area planted in the short run and a 13.6 percent in the long run. The application of quotas will lead to a 1.7 percent decrease in area planted. Maize has a non significant effect in the short run but a 10 percent change in the real price will cause a reduction of 10.1 percent in area planted to tobacco in the long run.

The error correction coefficient (EC) measures the adjustments towards the long run relationship between maize area planted and maize price, tobacco price and fertilizer price, in the case of maize. In the case of tobacco, area planted, tobacco price, maize price and institutional constraints. The error correction term for maize is much larger (0.79) than for tobacco (0.34) indicating that the adjustment for maize area planted towards the long run relationship is almost completed in the current period while adjustment for tobacco is much slower. This is to be expected, as there is a larger infrastructure and human capital costs for tobacco cultivation, in terms of constructing curing barns and gaining managerial knowledge, whereas these requirements are less for maize.

All the tests for model adequacy yield satisfactory results when applied to the maize equation. The DW statistic indicates no residual serial correlation, further investigation using the Lagrange multiplier test for first and second order serial correlation yield an F-version of 0.0013 well below the critical values. The RESET test for functional form mis-specification yields a value of 0.88 which is below the critical value of 4.84, this indicated acceptance of the hypothesis of correct functional form. The Jarque–Bera test for normality in the residuals gives a value of 1.22 thus accepting the hypothesis of a normally distributed residuals. The heteroscedasticity test yields a value of 0.79 indicating no heteroscedasticity in the residuals.

The tobacco estimates also yield satisfactory results. The Lagrange multiplier test gave a value of 0.16, the Jarque–Bera test for normality yielded a value of 1.26, the test for heteroscedasticity yielded a value of 3.83 and the RESET test for correct functional form gave values of 1.41. All tests are accepted at the 95 percent level.

The error correction formulation of the model was tested against the more restrictive partial adjustment model, by imposing zero restrictions on the difference terms. The Wald test used yielded a x^2 of 46.04 for maize and 36.12 for tobacco. Both outcomes are above the critical values at the 95 percent level, so the additional restrictions imposed by the partial adjustment are rejected. Thus, the error correction model is preferred to the partial adjustment formulation.

CONCLUSION

These results show the commercial farmers to be highly responsive to output prices. The percentage area planted to maize depends on the expected real price of maize, the real price of tobacco, the real price of fertilizer and government actions. The percentage area of tobacco planted depends on the real tobacco price, the expected real maize price and institutional factors, such as quotas.

The government can have a strong influence on the cultivated area of maize, as the state controls the maize price. A 10 percent increase in the maize price will increase the cultivated area by 14 percent in the short run and over 17 percent in the long run. In the light of the recent debate on fertilizer price liberalization, the effect of fertilizer prices on food security is a major issue. These results show that a 10 percent increase in the fertilizer price will decrease maize cultivation by 6.8 percent in the long run, although the effect in the short run will not be significant. Although the commercial sector does not produce the majority of the maize its contribution is significant. The government also has the option of offsetting the decrease in maize area planted as a result of increased fertilizer prices, by increasing the maize price. However the opportunity costs of supporting commercial agriculture would need to be considered.

Input costs do not have a significant impact on the area planted to tobacco. This is probably due to the high returns to tobacco cultivation. The short run price response is small, due to the infrastructure costs described above, but in the long run farmers are extremely price responsive.

The insignificance of the wage rate variable also has implications. The minimum wage legislation may have decreased farm employment, but these results suggest that wages are not sufficiently high to influence production decisions.

The overall performance of the models suggest that these results provide useful information on the supply relationships. When considering policy analysis, however, additional limitations need to be considered. These include data limitations, partial analysis and long run macroeconomic effects such as the structural effects of the increased export earnings of tobacco on the rest of the economy. Zimbabwe has a dualistic agricultural sector, the large scale commercial sector and a small scale, basically subsistence sector therefore policy analysis should also consider distributional, equity and productivity effects.

NOTE

[1] They are discussed here because they are far more comprehensible than the Johansen approach that is actually used here.

REFERENCES

Askari, H. and Cummings, J.T., 1977, 'Estimating Agricultural Supply Response With the Nerlove Model: a Survey', *International Economic Review*, Vol. 18, No. 2. pp.257–92.

Banerjee, A., Dolado, J., Galbraith, J.W. and Hendry, D.F., 1993, *Cointegration, Error Correction and the Econometric Analysis of Non-stationary Data*, Oxford University Press Inc., New York.

Beynon, J., 1993, *Negotiating Maize Producer Prices in Zimbabwe*, Agricultural and Development Economics Seminar Series, Oxford University, Oxford, England.

Cooper, D., Rayner, A.J. and Greenway, D., 1993, 'Constant-quality price indices for agricultural inputs: tractors and fertilizer revisited', *Journal of Agricultural Economics*, Vol. 44, No. 1, pp.67–81.

Dickey, D.A. and Fuller, W.A., 1981, 'Likelihood Ratio Statistics for Autoregressive Time Series with a Unit Root', *Econometrica*, Vol. 49, No. 4, pp.1057–72.

Engle, R.F. and Granger, C.W.J., 1987, 'Cointegration and Error Correction: Representation, Estimation and Testing', *Econometrica*, Vol. 55, pp.251–76.

FAO, Fertilizer Yearbook (annual), Food and Agricultural Organisation of the United Nations, Rome, Italy.

Fuller, W.A., 1976, *Introduction to Statistical Time Series*, John Wiley and Sons, New York.

Granger, C.W. and Newbold, P., 1974, 'Spurious Regressions in Econometrics', *Journal of Econometrics*, Vol. 2, pp.111–20.

Hallam, D. and Zanoli, R., 1991, 'Error Correction Models and Agricultural Supply Response', *European Review of Agricultural Economics*, Vol. 20, No. 2, pp.151–166.

Hendry, D.F. and Richard, J.F., 1982, 'On the Formulation of Empirical Models in Dynamic Econometrics', *Journal of Econometrics*, Vol. 20, No. 1, pp.3–33.

Hendry, D.F., Pagan, A.R. and Sargan, J.D., 1984, 'Dynamic Specification', in Griliches, Z. and Intriligator, M.D. (eds.), *Handbook of Econometrics*, Vol II, Elsevier, Amsterdam, pp.1023–1100.

Johansen, S., 1988, 'Statistical analysis of cointegrating vectors', *Journal of Economic Dynamics and Control*, Vol. 12, pp.231–54.
Johansen, S. and Juselius, K., 1990, 'Maximum likelihood estimation and inference on cointegration - with applications to the demand for money', *Oxford Bulletin of Economics and Statistics*, Vol. 52, pp.169-210.
Lawrance, R. and Jayne, T.S., 1992, *Maize milling, market reform and Urban food security: The case of Zimbabwe*, Working Paper AAE 4/92, Department of Agricultural Economics and Extension, Faculty of Agriculture, University of Zimbabwe.
MacKinnon, J.G., 1991, 'Critical Values for Cointegration Tests', in Engle, R.F. and Granger, C.W.J. (eds.), *Long-Run Economic Relationships*, Oxford University Press, pp.267–76.
Nerlove, M., 1958, *The Dynamics of Supply: Estimation of Farmer Response to Price*, The Johns Hopkins Press, Baltimore.
Nickell, S., 1985, 'Error Correction Partial Adjustment and all that: an Expositionary Note', *Oxford Bulletin of Economics and Statistics*, Vol. 47, No. 2, pp.119–129.
Rayner, A.J. and Lingard, J. (1971), 'Fertilizer Prices and Quality Change: Construction of Fertilizer Price and Quantity Indices for Great Britain, 1956/57–1968/69', *Journal of Agricultural Economics*, Vol. 22, pp.149–162.
Salmon, M., 1982, 'Error Correction Mechanisms', *Econometric Journal*, Vol. 92, No. 3, pp.615–629.
Sargan, J.D. and Bhargava, A., 1983, 'Testing Residuals from Least Squares Regressions for Being Generated by the Guassian Random Walk', *Econometrica*, Vol. 51, No. 1, pp.153–174.
Thirtle, C., Atkins, J., Bottomely, P., Gonese. N, Govereh, J. and Khatri Y., 1993, 'Agricultural Productivity in Zimbabwe 1970–1990', *Economic Journal*, Vol. 103, No. 417, pp.474–480.
Zimbabwe Agricultural Marketing Authority (1983, 1989), *Economic Review of the Agricultural Industry of Zimbabwe.*

DISCUSSION OPENING — B.J. Revell *(Scottish Agricultural College and University of Aberdeen, UK)*

It is always heartening at an international conference to find a paper which is of more immediate relevance and application in the host country. The authors are thus to be congratulated for focusing their analysis of supply response on commercial production of maize and tobacco in Zimbabwe, which touches on fundamental issues underlying the wider questions of food security and foreign exchange earnings.

My comments on the paper cover three broad areas: methodology; model specification, estimation and interpretation and finally policy implications.

Methodology Co-integration analysis is something of the latest fashion in the analysis of economic time series, addressing specifically the problem of spurious regression relationships arising out of non-stationarity or trend in the variables. Traditionally, appropriate differencing of the data will ensure a stationary series. The difficulty arises in the estimation of equations specified purely in difference form (i.e. trend removed), since they only measure short-run responses. The error correction model (ECM) re-introduces variables in levels into the specification, thereby ensuring that there is a long-run equilibrium solution consistent with the hypothesized model.

In fact, the error correction model is only a special case of the ARMAX models, and ultimately, of the transfer function noise(TFN) models (Box and Jenkins 1976, Jenkins 1979) in which the generating process for the noise model is specified precisely, rather than modelled as an ARIMA process as in the TFN model. Indeed, since TFN models are capable of representing both partial adjustment processes and price expectations (adaptive and rational), then one wonders why they are not applied more in the context of supply response analysis. Certainly, the identification and estimation process is no more complex than that required to identify co-integrating vectors in the multivariate case, albeit that OLS can then be used for estimation of ECMs.

Furthermore, the impulse response function of the TFN will give both the short run and long-run responses(gain) of the system being modelled. Finally, the parameters of the noise model are estimated jointly with the 'structural' or economic parameters. In the ECM, the innovation series or deviations from equilibrium are generated through separate equation estimated in levels. The validity of the parameter on the error correction term thus depends upon having the right long run model.

Model Specification and Estimation The model specification is in terms of area shares, rather than area planted. Whilst this does enable the model to account for land redistribution from the commercial to the traditional sector, it does give rise to some confusion and errors in the exposition and interpretation of the results. The 'elasticity' estimates actually measure percentage changes in area shares resulting from percentage price changes, and not to changes in 'area planted' as the authors claim, nor even in the percentage points change in allocation of commercial land to maize and tobacco. It would have been helpful to have data on the maize and tobacco area shares to put in context the adjustments which might be implied both for these and other crops.

The authors do address price expectations formation, although the process for tobacco is given somewhat cursory treatment in view of the importance of tobacco to the economy. Since tobacco prices are determined outside an institutional framework, the nature of producer price expectations formation is likely to be more complex than that for maize, and surely deserves more consideration than a single period lag on the own price (change) variable. Is it not also likely that there is greater price uncertainty for tobacco than for maize, and this will also contribute towards the lower adjustment rate for this crop?

The ECM is a reversible supply function. I also wonder whether this is tenable in the case of tobacco, given the capital investment associated with its storage and processing.

Interpretation The authors draw some policy implications for the maize and tobacco sectors from their model. It is here that some reservations arise.

Whilst maize appears to respond to fertilizer prices, a 10 percent increase will decrease the area share by 6.8 percent in the long run, not the actual area planted as the authors state. Furthermore, since the traditional sector produces most maize, the question should perhaps more appropriately be examined through supply response analysis in this sector, and where the biggest impact of fertilizer price change will be on yields and production rather than area planted.

The interpretation of wage rate impact in the paper is also problematic. The authors conclude that wages 'are not sufficiently high to influence production decisions'. Given the scarcity of forex for capital investment in Zimbabwe over the period of estimation, might this not have inhibited the substitution of capital for labour, and thus made changes in production relatively invariant to wage rate changes?

Conclusions The authors have demonstrated an interesting application of the ECM and co-integration analysis in the context of supply response in the commercial sector of a developing country. The emphasis has been on modelling technique rather than on modelling to answer specific policy questions. The fundamental question is whether such sophisticated approaches are tenable in relation to the traditional agricultural sectors of sub-Saharan Africa.

References

Box, G.E.P. and Jenkins, G.M. 1976, *Time Series Analysis: Forecasting and Control*, Revised Edition, Holden Day, San Francisco.

Jenkins, G.M. 1979, *Practical Experiences with Modelling and Forecasting Time Series*, GJP, Jersey.

DANIEL C. CLAY AND THOMAS REARDON*

Determinants of Farm-Level Conservation Investments in Rwanda

Abstract: This paper analyzes the determinants of conservation investments at the farm level in Rwanda. The following tend to be important promoters of investment: (a) own-sources of liquidity, especially from off-farm employment; (b) smaller landholdings; (c) household labour; and, under certain circumstances (d) conservation knowledge (possibly from extension). But insecurity of land tenure (reflected in the share of rented land) tends to decrease investment. The policy implications are: (a) projects and policies aimed at developing off-farm enterprises by farm families can also indirectly promote soil conservation on-farm; this should be important to the Rwanda government and to external donors that are actively pursuing both to promote rural food security; (b) extension service's emphasis on conservation measures has clear pay-offs at the farm level, and also increases the compatibility of conservation and income diversification; (c) the nature of the land market and land tenure policy affect conservation investments.

INTRODUCTION

Declining productivity of farmland due to soil degradation poses an immediate threat to the livelihoods of farm families in Rwanda. Steep slopes, abundant rainfall, and intense demographic pressure have raised the spectre of food insecurity and have driven the country's smallholders to cultivate marginal lands once held in pasture and long fallow. Like many other highland countries in Africa, Asia, and Latin America, the problem of land degradation has for Rwanda become a matter of national concern. Rwanda's National Agricultural Commission now estimates that half the country's farmland suffers from moderate to severe erosion (Commission Nationale d'Agriculture, 1992); farmers report that the productivity of nearly half their holdings has declined in recent years from degradation (Clay, 1993).

The focus of Rwanda's national strategy to control soil erosion and restore productivity is the promotion of farm-level investments in soil conservation, notably grass strips, anti-erosion ditches, hedgerows and radical terraces. These investments require substantial household outlays of labour time and cash.

Conservation investments are crucial to the long-run interests of the country, as well as the individual farm household; they are found in varying degrees in no less than three-quarters of Rwanda's cultivable holdings. This paper examines the determinants of farmer investments in soil conservation. Specifically, we ask how economic incentives (e.g., risk due to insecurity of land tenure, and relative regional profitability of agriculture), household characteristics (e.g., non-farm income, wealth, human capital, and knowledge of conservation practices), and ecological attributes of farmers' operational holdings (e.g., steepness of slope, distance from the family compound) affect the investments that farmers make to ensure the continuing productivity of their land.

Though fundamental to the formulation of policies to promote conservation investments, there exists little empirical literature on these questions in developing

* Michigan State University, USA.

countries, particularly those of sub-Saharan Africa. Recent exceptions include Ehui *et al.* (1992) on land use determinants in Nigeria, and the impact of land tenure on land improvements in Rwanda, among other places (Blarel 1989; and Place and Hazell 1993). Research on the determinants of farm asset investments, e.g., Collier and Deepak (1980) in Kenya and Christensen (1989) in Burkina Faso, has been only slightly more prevalent. To contribute to this nascent literature in Africa, we pursue two objectives in this paper. The first is to describe the nature and extent of conservation investments in Rwanda; the second is to explain inter-household variations in conservation investments as a function of selected parcel, household, and regional variables.

CONTEXT

Ninety-three percent of Rwanda's population live in rural areas and nearly all rural households farm. On average, households cultivate slightly less than one hectare of land; the distribution of landholdings is inequitable by the standards of African smallholder agriculture (with a sevenfold difference in land per person between highest and lowest landholder quartiles). Pulses, roots and tubers, and grains are the main food staples, and coffee and tea are important cash crops. Farming is labour intensive. Hoes and machetes are the basic farm implements; animal traction is non-existent. Livestock husbandry is integral to the farming system, but the progressive conversion of pasture into cropland has caused a reduction in livestock production in recent decades, and a parallel decline in the amount of manure available for improving soil fertility. Rwanda's average population density is among the highest in Africa. Virtually all arable land is now used for agriculture; marginal lands once set aside for pasture or left in longfallow are now coming under more intensive cultivation. Rural informal and formal credit markets are severely underdeveloped.

Table 1 shows characteristics of the farm household sample. There is great variation over farm households in the degree to which they invest in soil conservation measures: grass strips are most common, followed by anti-erosion ditches, then hedgerows. Almost all operable land is either cropped or in woodlot. Little land is kept under fallow. Fields tend to be on slopes, and annual rainfall is high. These factors provide strong incentives for farmers to take appropriate measures aimed at controlling soil loss.

Non-farm income (wages from hired agricultural and non-agricultural work plus own-business income) constitutes on average about one third of total income, and about two-thirds of households earn some non-farm income. Operational holdings are very small, and are fragmented into many smaller plots. The vast majority of landholdings are owner-operated; only 9 percent are rented. Most households own a few small ruminants; less than a quarter own cattle. There is strong variation over households in their (self-reported) degree of knowledge of various soil conservation and productivity-enhancing practices. Agricultural profitability as well as price variability vary considerably over prefectures.

THEORY AND MODEL

Economic theory suggests conflicting hypotheses with respect to the determinants of conservation investments by smallholders in rural contexts such as Rwanda's. On the one

Table 1 *Conservation Investments Model Variables*

Model Variables	Overall mean	Coefficient of variation	Level of observation HH=1240 Mean Pref = 10
Conservation Investments			
A Grass strips (m/ha)	198	1.40	Parcel
B Anti-erosion ditches (m/ha)	157	1.72	Parcel
C Hedgerows (m/ha)	55	3.02	Parcel
Independent Variables			
A Monetary Incentive to Invest			
Agricultural profitability index	1.00	0.31	Prefecture
Mean agricultural wage (FRW)[a]	100	0.09	Prefecture
Mean non-agric. wage (FRW)	206	0.35	Prefecture
B Physical incentive to invest			
Erosivity of land use (C-value index)	0.13	0.46	Parcel
Share of operational holdings under fallow (ha)	0.17	1.47	Parcel
Slope (degrees)	16.92	0.64	Parcel
Location on slope (1=highest, 5=lowest)	3.11	0.33	Parcel
Distance from residence (minutes on foot)	7.61	2.14	Parcel
Size of parcel (ha)	0.77	1.03	Parcel
Mean annual rainfall (mm)	1214	0.14	Prefecture
C Risk of investment			
Ownership rights (1=own, 2=lease)	1.08	0.25	Parcel
Price variation (CV of agric. prices, 1986–92)	0.25	0.20	Prefecture
D Wealth and liquidity sources			
Landholdings owned (ha)	0.83	0.95	Household
Value of livestock (FRW)[a]	10 768	1.81	Household
Non-farm income (FRW)[a]	11 120	3.24	Household
Value of agri. production (FRW)[a]	22 150	0.83	Household
E Other household characteristics			
Number of adults (aged 15–65)	2.64	0.54	Household
Dependency ratio (econ. inactive/econ active)	121	0.74	Household
Number of literate household members	2.28	0.82	Household
Knowledge of conserv/prod techniques	3.59	0.55	Household
Age of head of household (years)	45	0.33	Household

Note: [a] 140FRW=1US$.

hand, a declining land base and weak credit markets (to insulate the household from food shortages) compels households to husband carefully their declining resource base, through conservation investments *inter alia* (Ehui *et al.*, 1992).

On the other hand, risk (from price and rainfall instability, or from insecurity of land tenure hence risk of appropriation of capital) is inimical to investment for risk-averse farmers (Newbery and Stiglitz, 1981). Rather than narrowly focusing on their land base, farmers diversify their asset portfolios and incomes (Binswanger, 1986; and Robison and Barry, 1987). Yet both from theory and empirical evidence for farm asset investment, off-farm income as a liquidity source would be critical to on-farm investments where there is failure of, or constraints in, the credit market (Reardon *et al.*, 1992). Moreover, Reardon and Vosti (1987) contend that where credit markets are underdeveloped, the least likely investments to receive credit are conservation measures.

Hence, there are competing forces (mirrored in competing theoretical hypotheses) encouraging and discouraging households from making these investments. But practical development policy choices depend on empirical evidence concerning these determinants in specific contexts. The model and hypotheses presented below are intended to address these practical needs.

Based on firm-level investment theory (see Christensen (1989) for review), we model farm-level conservation investments as a function of four sets of variables: (a) financial returns (incentives/disincentives) to investment; (b) physical returns to investment; (c) riskiness of investment; and (d) capacity to invest (human and physical capital, liquidity sources).

Following are the hypotheses related to each set of the above general determinants. The specific variables that comprise each group are listed in Table 1 along with their summary statistics.

Financial incentives to invest Agricultural profitability is expected to have a positive effect on conservation investments. The relative return to non-farm work, however, will have an ambiguous effect: better returns to non-farm investment mean competition with on-farm investment, but they may also raise the absolute amount of cash available to invest on the farm. In the presence of credit constraints, the latter (own liquidity) is critical.

Physical incentives to invest Greater steepness of slope increases the incentive to invest in soil protection as these slopes tend to be more susceptible to erosion. Farmers with greater holdings in fallow will be less likely to invest as their reliance on presently cultivated land is not as great. As fields become more dispersed and grow smaller, there is less incentive to build and maintain banks or apply fertility supplements because of higher travel/transaction costs. More erosive forms of land use (high C-values) will be associated with greater conservation investment; less erosive uses such as pasture, fallow and perennial crops will need, and receive, fewer investments.[1]

Riskiness of investment Holdings operated under lease rights (hence greater risk of appropriation of land conservation investments by owners of rented land), and those in areas of price and rainfall instability, will receive fewer investments than those for which the level of risk is lower. Though Blarel (1989) found no significant relationship between risk and conservation investments in Rwanda, we believe this to be due to the methodological and analytical limitations of that study.[2]

Physical and human capital, and own-liquidity sources With perfectly functioning credit markets and perfect information, household wealth and liquidity sources, such as cash crop sales and non-farm income, should not affect investment. Yet we suspect that gross imperfections in Rwanda's credit and information markets exist, and therefore hypothesize these own-liquidity sources to be crucial to investment. However, as noted earlier, non-farm income diversification is conceptually a 'two-edged sword,' providing liquidity for on-farm investments but also potentially competing (as a destination for such income) with these investments.

The installation and maintenance of conservation measures can be a very labour intensive endeavour, and will thus vary along with the availability of household labour. Larger households, *ceteris paribus,* will be more likely than smaller households to adopt conservation practices of all types. In addition to the amount of labour available, the quality of human capital can also make a difference. Higher levels of education and knowledge of conservation practices, particularly among household heads, should alert farm families to the long-run hazards of declining productivity, while also providing more information on specific countermeasures. These factors will exert a positive effect on conservation investments.

DATA

A reason for the dearth of empirical work on the determinants of conservation investments in Africa is the difficult data requirements. On one hand, such research requires data on the extent of farmers' conservation investments, implying either the physical measurement of terraces, for example, or on cash and labour time required to build them, or both. On the other hand, a broader set of data is needed to understand the farm management and household strategy context of these investments. Household farm and non-farm income, assets, demographic characteristics, and the ecological properties of farm holdings are examples of the kinds of information required. Such multi-level data are rare.

The data examined here, however, meet these varied requirements. They derive principally from a nationwide stratified-random sample of 1240 farm households (operating 6464 parcels) interviewed in 1991 by the Agricultural Statistics Division (DSA) of Rwanda's Ministry of Agriculture.[3] Interviews with heads of households and/or their spouses were conducted over a six-week period beginning in June 1991. The survey instrument treated both household-level variables (such as non-farm income) and parcel-level variables (such soil conservation investments, land tenure, and steepness of slope). To complete the dataset for our purposes, we integrated these data with those on farm and livestock enterprise management from the Ministry's ongoing national longitudinal survey on the same sample of households.

REGRESSION RESULTS

Ordinary least squares regressions on soil conservation investments are estimated using the variables described in previously, and the results are reported in Table 2. The results of these regressions are discussed below for each of the variable sets in our model. Because the OLS estimates are run at the parcel level, all estimates are weighted according to parcel size, as well as for the household's probability of selection.

Monetary incentive Agricultural profitability provides farmers with a strong incentive to invest in both grass strips and ditches, but it appears to be a disincentive for planting hedgerows. Non-agricultural wage rates, as expected, exert a negative effect on conservation investment, though only significant for grass strips and ditches.

Physical incentive More erosive forms of land use (high C-values), notably annual crops, are associated with greater conservation investment, though this relationship is not significant for anti-erosion ditches. Farmers are more likely to make investments in soil conservation if their holdings are closer to the family compound and if they are located higher on the slope. Historically, erosion has been the most severe on these upper slopes where farmers tend to grow beans and other important annual crops.

Holdings on steep slopes receive fewer investments in grass strips and ditches, but relatively greater investment in hedgerows. This seems paradoxical at first, but is likely a reflection of three factors: (a) Farmers tend to place these steep slopes under pasture, woodlot, and perennial crops because of their high susceptibility to erosion. Of the three types of investments examined here only hedgerows are commonly found in wooded parcels. Grass strips and ditches are almost always used in fields containing annual crops. (b) It is very costly to maintain investments on these slopes. (c) Population growth and land scarcity have pushed Rwandan farmers to occupy the very steep mid slopes where erosion problems are particularly common. The characteristic lightness and thinness of these soils make them especially prone to erosion; these characteristics also keep yields low and diminish returns to investments in soil conservation. Thus a downward spiral of low production and low investment is easily set into motion (Pingali and Binswanger, 1984) as these marginal lands are taken out of their traditional uses (forest, long fallow, rangeland, etc.) and put under more intensive cultivation.

Risk of investment As anticipated, for all forms of conservation investment, lands that are leased provide farmers with less incentive to invest, as the risk of appropriation is greater. This finding contradicts Blarel's (1989) conclusion, based on a smaller sample and bivariate analysis, that no such relationship exists. Price variation exerts a significant negative influence on the planting of hedgerows, yet, like agricultural profitability, there is a positive effect on the installation of anti-erosion ditches.

Wealth and liquidity Larger farms tend to invest less per hectare. This may confirm that credit (with land as collateral) is not important to these investments. Large holders also have more land under fallow and thus may feel less pressured to protect the soils of their operational holdings. It may also be that larger holders are not compelled to take conservation measures to meet daily food and cash needs. Many smallholders, on the other hand, appear to recognize that such investments are vital to their livelihoods, even in the short run.

Wealth in livestock does not have a strong effect on conservation investments, as it might have in countries where livestock play a larger part in the farm economy. Consistent with our expectations, non-farm income as a liquidity source for investments (hiring labour, buying materials) exerts a positive effect on investments in grass strips and hedgerows. However non-farm income exerts no significant effect on the installation of anti-erosion ditches.

Table 2 *OLS Regressions — Conservation Investments Model*

Independent Variables	Conservation Investment: Grass strips (m/ha)	Anti-erosion ditches (m/ha)	Hedge-rows (m/ha)
A Monetary incentive to invest			
Agricultural profitability index	0.18**	0.11**	–0.07**
Mean agricultural wage in prefecture	–0.02	0.12**	0.05**
Mean non-agricultural wage in pref.	–0.20**	–0.08**	0.01
B Physical incentive to invest			
Erosivity of land use (C-value index)	0.12**	0.01	0.07**
Share of operational holdings under fallow	–0.02	–0.02	0.02
Slope (degrees)	–0.06**	–0.06**	0.06**
Location on slope (1=lowest, 5=highest)	–0.16**	–0.11**	–0.09**
Distance from residence	–0.07**	–0.04**	0.02
Size of parcel	–0.00	0.10**	0.00
Mean annual rainfall	0.07**	–0.01	0.11**
C Risk of investment			
Ownership rights (1=own, 2=lease)	–0.07**	–0.03*	–0.07**
Price variation (1986–92)	0.00	0.08**	–0.07**
D Wealth and liquidity sources			
Landholdings owned	–0.15**	–0.17**	–0.15**
Value of livestock	0.02	0.04*	–0.01
Non-farm income	0.08**	–0.01	0.04**
Value of agricultural production	–0.01	0.04**	0.04**
E Other household characteristics			
Number of adults (aged 15–65)	0.09**	0.08**	0.05
Dependency ratio (econ inactive/econ active)	0.03	0.05	0.01
Number of literate household members	–0.06**	–0.03	–0.02
Knowledge of conserv/prod techniques	–0.05**	0.01	0.08**
Age of head of household (years)	0.02	–0.01	–0.01
R^2	0.13	0.10	0.06

Notes: *Significant $t \leq 0.05$. **Significant $t \leq 0.01$.

Human capital Household labour exerts a modest, positive effect on all three types of investment, suggesting the possibility of labour market constraints. Knowledge of conservation and productivity-enhancing technologies emerges as a positive and significant determinant of investments in hedgerows, but not of other conservation investments. Unlike grass strips and ditches, the use of hedgerows to control soil loss is a relatively new technology for Rwandan farmers, and its application is less widespread. As the extension service is an important vehicle for dissemination of this technology, it is perhaps for this reason that the positive effects of farmer knowledge are greater for hedgerows than for other, more traditional, conservation investments.

CONCLUSIONS AND POLICY IMPLICATIONS

The empirical analysis of conservation investments described in this paper provides us with five general conclusions. First, own sources of liquidity, especially from non-farm employment, are important determinants of capacity to invest in conservation measures. That non-farm cash sources are important is probably linked to failure of the credit market for cash outlays for labour and equipment. Yet increases in returns to non-farm employment, controlling for agricultural profitability, dampens the incentive to invest. Hence non-farm opportunities have a dual character of enabling but also sometimes competing with on-farm conservation investments.

Second, risk of appropriation of the investment (because of uncertain land use rights) decreases investment in conservation measures. This finding is inconsistent with those of Blarel (1989) and of Place and Hazell (1993) who conclude that land tenure status does not affect land improvements.

Third, smaller farms are more likely to invest in conservation measures, which makes sense given their dependence on the fertility of the small plots they intensively farm. Under conditions of rapid population increase, it is likely that the trend toward farm miniaturization will continue; our results suggest that this will not necessarily lead to unsustainable intensification.

Fourth, households with a greater supply of labour are more likely to take conservation measures than those with less household labour. An absence of household labour, coupled with low non-farm earnings (with which to hire labour), means that conservation investments will be few.

Fifth, conservation extension emerges as an important determinant of certain types of household conservation investment, notably those which have not yet been broadly disseminated and adopted among the farm population. Once techniques have become universally known and widely practiced, the impact of continuing extension appears to be negligible.

Several important policy implications emerge from these results. First, the Rwandan government seeks to achieve the following policy goals: to improve food security through increased farm productivity and profitability, to combat soil degradation, and to diversify rural household incomes (Commission Nationale d'Agriculture, 1992). We believe that the above results lend empirical support to the mutually-re-enforcing nature of these aims. This conclusion should also be important to external donor programming, as it implies that under certain circumstances, projects aimed at developing non-farm enterprises by farm families can indirectly promote soil conservation on-farm. Second, increasing the extension service's emphasis on new and appropriate conservation measures has clear payoffs at the farm level, and also increases the compatibility of the above policy goals. Third, the nature of land transactions and land tenure policy affect conservation investments.

NOTES

1 A well-known measure that reflects the protective quality of crops is the C-value. The C-value is defined as 'the ratio of soil loss from an area with a specific cover and tillage practice to that from an identical area in tilled continuous fallow' (Wischmeier and Smith, 1978). For any given field, the crop cover, canopy, and tillage practices can vary throughout the year. The C-value represents the average soil loss ratio resulting from these factors over the growing season.

2 Blarel's (1989) study was limited to just three of Rwanda's ten prefectures, and the analysis of tenure status and investments was conducted exclusively at the bivariate level.

3 The complete sample frame includes a total of 1248 households. However, due to military/political tensions in the prefecture of Byumba, along the Uganda border, interviewers were unable to conduct fieldwork in the region, and eight (0.6%) of the 1248 sampled households had to be omitted from this study. Sampling weights have been adjusted accordingly.

REFERENCES

Binswanger, H.P., 1986, 'Risk Aversion, Collateral Requirements, and the Markets for Credit and Insurance in Rural Areas', in Hazell, P., Pomareda, C. and Valdés, A. (eds.), *Crop Insurance for Agricultural Development*, Johns Hopkins University Press, Baltimore, Maryland.

Blarel, B., 1989, 'Land Tenure Security and Agricultural Production under Land Scarcity: The Case of Rwanda', Agricultural Policy Division, Agriculture and Rural Development Department, The World Bank, Washington, D.C.

Christensen, G., 1989, *Determinants of Private Investment in Rural Burkina Faso*, Ph.D. Dissertation, Cornell University, Ithaca, New York.

Clay, D.C., 1993, 'Fighting an Uphill Battle: Demographic Pressure, the Structure of Landholding, and Land Degradation in Rwanda', Forthcoming DSA Working Paper, Division des Statistiques Agricole, Rwanda.

Collier, P. and Deepak, L., 1980, *Poverty and Growth in Kenya*, World Bank Staff Working Paper No. 389 World Bank, Washington, D.C.

Commission Nationale d'Agriculture (CNA), 1992, 'Rapport de synthèse: rapport préliminaire', Government of Rwanda.

Ehui, S.K., Kang, B.T. and Spencer, D.S.C., 1992, 'Economic analysis of soil erosion effects in alley-cropping, no-till, and bush fallow systems in Southwestern Nigeria', in Moock, J.L and Rhoades, R.E (eds.), *Diversity, Farmer Knowledge, and Sustainability*, Cornell University Press, Ithaca, New York.

Newbery, D.M.G. and Stiglitz, J.E., 1981, *The Theory of Commodity Price Stabilization: A Study in the Economics of Risk*, Clarendon Press, Oxford.

Pingali, P. and Binswanger, H.P., 1984, 'Population Density and Farming Systems: The Changing Locus of Innovations and Technical Change', Discussion Paper No. ARU 24, World Bank, Washington, D.C.

Place, F. and Hazell, P., 1993, 'Productivity effects of indigenous land tenure systems in Sub-Saharan Africa', *American Journal of Agricultural Economics*, Vol. 75, No. 1, pp.10–19.

Reardon, T., Delgado, C. and Matlon, P., 1992, 'Determinants and Effects of Income Diversification Amongst Farm Households in Burkina Faso', *Journal of Development Studies* (January), Vol. 28, No.2, pp. 264–296.

Reardon, T. and Vosti, S.A., 1987, 'Issues in the Analysis of the Effects of Policy on Conservation and Productivity at the Household Level in Developing Countries', *Quarterly Journal of International Agriculture* (October), Vol. 31, No. 4, pp.381–396.

Robison, L.J. and Barry, P.J., 1987, *The Competitive Firm's Response to Risk*, Macmillan Publishing Co., New York.

Wischmeier, W.H. and Smith, D.D., 1978, *Predicting Rainfall Erosion Losses, A Guide to Conservation Planning*, Agricultural Handbook No.537, USDA, Washington, D.C., pp.1–58.

DISCUSSION OPENING — Eduardo Segarra *(Texas Tech University, USA)*

When I received Clay and Reardon's manuscript about conservation investments in Rwanda, I was looking forward to reading it for two reasons. The first reason was my personal interest in the topic. I have done quite a bit of work in the soil erosion and technology adoption/investment areas. The second was that I felt that this would be a good opportunity for me to learn more about a country and its people who happen to be currently under extreme hardship. After reading Clay and Reardon's manuscript, I am pleased to communicate to you that their manuscript lived up to my expectations and I learned more about Rwanda and its people.

Clay and Reardon do a good job in describing the nature and the extent of soil erosion problems and conservation investments in Rwanda. I believe that their research enhances the limited body of literature about soil erosion/conservation in sub-Saharan Africa. Also, their finding with respect to impacts of land tenure insecurity on conservation investments is right on target. However, I feel that some of the policy implications derived from their findings are not as straight forward, given the mixed significance (and in some cases the signs) of the independent variables across the three models estimated.

Given that the survey data are available to Clay and Reardon, I would encourage them to formulate a discrete choice model, most likely a tobit model, to calculate marginal probabilities of adoption of the conservation investments analyzed. This is because of the nature of the dependent variables used. In particular, tobit analysis is a hybrid of probit analysis and multiple regression which seeks to solve the problem of estimating coefficients in regressions with limited dependent variables. A limited dependent variable can be defined as a variable having a lower (or upper) limit which takes on the limit value in several observations and for the remaining observations the variable takes on a wide range of values above (or below) the limit. In Clay and Reardon's study the dependent variables, length of grass strips, anti-erosion ditches and hedgerows, have a lower limit of zero (I suspect that of the 6464 parcels there were some that did not have any conservation investments) and take on values over a wide range above that limit (see the overall means and the coefficients of variation of the dependent variables in Table 1).

Given the context of this paper, I feel that there are two steps involved in the adoption of conservation investments, the first being the existence or not of the investment itself on a particular parcel, and the second being the intensity of it (ie. the length of the particular investment). Also, I believe that the varied fixity nature of the conservation investments looked at by Clay and Reardon are influenced in varied degrees by the financial, physical, riskiness, and capacity to invest variables included in their analysis and this should be further investigated. The inclusion of a variable accounting for the difference of expected returns from a parcel with or without conservation investments should prove to be useful in the analysis. I believe that this study represents a good initial effort, but that there is a bit of room for improvement.

GENERAL DISCUSSION — Barry Shapiro, Rapporteur *(International Livestock Centre for Africa)*

Following K.N. Ninan's opening remarks on Smale and Heisey's paper, discussion moved to whether yield or quality should be emphasized in Malawi's breeding program. Local projected demand–supply conditions, however, often determine the manoeuvering room between such goals and the situation for Malawi was not addressed. The authors pointed out the difficulty of doing these *ex ante* projections. The decision criteria for allocation of scarce research resources promoted by the authors was expected returns. However, it was not clear how changing prices, storage and processing costs, and tastes and preferences alter these rates of return. The extent of improvement in nutritional levels of the poor and a reduction in poverty from emphasizing quality was also not clear. Other issues to consider include the social opportunity costs of breeding for quality in terms of yields forgone and of food imports required, the consequences of structural adjustment, and the role of changing incentives in the face of commercialization. Regarding the policy implications that zero fertilizer use gives higher yields with hybrids than with local maize, the presenter stated that farmers should be given more leeway to determine their own rates of fertilization in seed packages.

B.J. Revell, of the Scottish Agricultural College, Aberdeen, congratulated Townsend and Thirtle for focusing on the supply response of maize and tobacco in Zimbabwe since it touches on fundamental issues such as food security and foreign exchange earnings. Regarding methodology, the relation of the model to more general transfer function noise models was raised, leading to why partial adjustment processes and price expectations are not applied more in supply response analysis. Model specification was in terms of area shares, not area planted, leading to confusion regarding the interpretation of the results, including the elasticities. It was pointed out that data on area shares would have put into context the adjustments implied by the results. A single period lag for tobacco price expectations formation was called into question, as well as using a reversible supply function for tobacco given the capital investment associated with storage and processing. The usefulness of addressing the impact of fertilizer price change on yields and production rather than area planted in maize was pointed out.

Some doubts were raised about whether Thomson and Thirtle had actually estimated a supply curve. It was pointed out that, in the general VAR model which is represented with the ECM model, it is assumed that all of the variables are endogenous. If prices and areas sown are endogenous, the authors will have estimated a movement in equilibrium generated by movements in both supply and demand, rather than a supply curve.

Eduardo Segarra, in his comments on the Clay and Reardon paper about soil erosion and the adoption of conservation investments in Rwanda, called attention to the importance of the issues dealt with for all of sub-Saharan Africa. The negative relation between land tenure insecurity and conservation investment was highlighted as an important conclusion. However, the lack of other clear policy implications was mentioned given the mixed significance and in some cases the mixed signs of the explanatory factors across the models estimated. The authors were encouraged to formulate a discrete choice model, emphasizing the tobit model, to handle the limited dependent variable and to capture the two-stage nature of the adoption decision: the decision whether or not to adopt and then the intensity of adoption. The need to consider financial and risk variables to handle the fixed cost nature of the conservation choices was pointed out, as well as accounting for the difference in expected returns between investing or not investing in conservation.

Participants in the discussion included Richard Tiffin (University of Newcastle Upon Tyne, UK), Awudu Abdulai (Swiss Federal Institute of Technology, Zurich), Steve Franzel (ICRAF, Kenya), Duncan Boughton (Michigan State University), Jan W. Low (International Potato Centre, Kenya), I.N. Kumwenda (Ministry of Agriculture, Malawi), Thomas Engelhardt (GTZ, Germany) and Wilfred Mwangi (CIMMYT, Ethiopia).

ALBERTO A. FANTINO AND TERRENCE S. VEEMAN*

The Choice of Index Numbers in Measuring Agricultural Productivity: A Canadian Empirical Case Study

Abstract: The measurement of agricultural productivity is important in understanding growth in agriculture and in assessing competitiveness. In this paper, some difficulties related to the empirical measurement of productivity are analyzed using a Canadian case study. The paper focuses in particular on the choice of index number procedures, comparing traditional fixed base weight indexes with flexible or superlative indexes such as the Divisia and Fisher. Indexes of aggregate agricultural output, total farm input use, and total factor productivity are estimated for Canada and for the prairie region of western Canada from 1948 to 1991. Alternative productivity growth rates are reported and compared. The productivity results based on the Tornqvist–Theil approximation to the Divisia index and the chained Fisher index are very similar. Both these flexible weight index procedures are to be preferred over the Laspeyres, the most commonly used approach in Canada.

INTRODUCTION

The measurement and assessment of agricultural productivity is essential not only to a better understanding of agricultural growth but also to the issues of longer run competitiveness and economic sustainability. Comparisons of productivity over time are obviously important in assessing whether trends in the technical efficiency of production are increasing or decreasing. Productivity comparisons across regions, industries and nations are also critical to policy-makers. However, such comparisons, to be relevant, require more understanding and agreement on how productivity is to be measured.

In this paper, the appropriate choice of index numbers in aggregating outputs and inputs, which must underlie the measurement of productivity, is emphasized. In particular, the use of traditional, fixed base weight, indexing procedures, such as the Laspeyres and Paasche, is compared and contrasted to the use of improved, flexible index number approaches such as the Tornqvist–Theil approximation to the Divisia index and the Fisher index. More refined and up-to-date estimates of aggregate output, input, and productivity, based on the Tornqvist–Theil approach, are presented for Canadian agriculture and the prairie agricultural sector of western Canada. A more detailed comparison of the alternative index number approaches is then undertaken emphasizing western Canada as a case study. Finally, recommendations are drawn with respect to the relative merits of these alternative index number procedures in measuring productivity and in making productivity comparisons.

CONCEPTUAL ISSUES IN MEASURING PRODUCTIVITY

Much productivity discussion is based on partial productivity measures such as yield per acre (land productivity) or output per person (labour productivity). Such partial

* University of Alberta, Canada.

productivity measures can be seriously misleading if considerable input substitution is occurring. A conceptually superior way to estimate productivity is to measure total factor productivity (TFP) — the ratio of aggregate output over the aggregate of all inputs used in agricultural production. Such is the focus of this paper. There are two basic economic approaches to the measurement of productivity or technical change: the growth accounting or index number approach and the econometric approach in which the shift of the production or cost function is measured (Antle and Capalbo, 1988, pp.48–63). The productivity work reported in this paper is based on the first approach — the index number approach.

Among the most important and most difficult issues in measuring productivity by the index number route is the choice of an appropriate index number methodology to combine several agricultural outputs into an aggregate output index or to combine several farm inputs, suitably weighted, into an aggregate input index. Economists have shown that there is an exact correspondence between a given indexing procedure and the specific functional form of the aggregate production function which that index number procedure implies. We concentrate in this paper on the choice between traditional approaches such as the Laspeyres index or the Paasche index and flexible index procedures such as Divisia-related or Fisher indexes.[1] Most published works on agricultural productivity in Canada, particularly that done under the aegis of Agriculture Canada, has involved Laspeyres index number methods — for example, Brinkman and Prentice (1983) and Narayanan and Kizito (1992). Such indexing procedures, wherein base period prices are used as weights in aggregation, imply that the underlying production function is linear and that inputs in the production process are perfect substitutes.

Because of the restrictive nature of the production technology associated with the linear and Cobb–Douglas production functions, attention shifted in the 1970s to flexible form production and cost functions. A functional form or aggregator is called flexible if it is a second order approximation to an arbitrary twice differentiable homogeneous function. An indexing procedure which corresponds to a flexible aggregator is also flexible, or superlative in Diewert's (1976) terminology.

The most popular flexible indexing procedure employed during the past two decades in productivity analysis has been Divisia related. The continuous Divisia index has properties which make it advantageous in aggregation (Hulten, 1973). Moreover, the Tornqvist–Theil index, a discrete approximation to the Divisia index, was shown to be a superlative index and exact for a homogeneous translog production function (Christensen, 1975; and Diewert, 1976). In this flexible production technology, the elasticity of substitution between any input pair is flexible and inputs can be either substitutes or complements. In Tornqvist–Theil indexing, input cost shares (to be more specific, the arithmetic average of the input cost share in period t and the corresponding input cost share in period t–1) are used to weight respective input quantities in year t in constructing an aggregate input index. Analogously, output value shares, which are also flexible over time, are used to derive the Tornqvist–Theil aggregate output index. The practical cost of these conceptual improvements in indexing is that more data are required: price and quantity data are needed for each input and each output for every year in the time series period under examination.

The Fisher 'ideal' index, defined as the geometric mean of the Laspeyres and Paasche indexes, is also superlative, and corresponds to a quadratic mean of order two production function (Diewert, 1976). The Fisher index and its chained variant have not been employed in much empirical work on productivity. However, Fisher indexing enjoys certain interesting properties which induced us to include it in our study. These properties arise from the so called 'axiomatic approach' to index number construction. In this approach, desirable properties of indexing are defined, and the different indexing procedures are examined in this respect. The Fisher index is the only index that satisfies twenty relevant properties (Diewert, 1989a). The Tornqvist–Theil index, for example, fails the constant quantity test while the Laspeyres and Paasche indexes fail in regard to important properties, such as the time or region reversal tests (Diewert, 1989b). Recently, Bureau *et al.* (1994) used a Fisher-based index for the purpose of international productivity comparisons.

Finally, there is the issue of defining the base in the indexing procedure. Laspeyres, Paasche and Fisher are fixed-base procedures, the comparison year being fixed. The Tornqvist–Theil index involves a chaining procedure where the weights adjust every year in terms of the data for the current year and the previous year. A chaining procedure can also be applied to the Laspeyres, Paasche, and Fisher indexes to obtain 'chained' versions of each. There appear to be no clear theoretical reasons to prefer the chained index over the unchained, although intuitively the chaining appears to be preferable. In our empirical study all seven indexes are used.

ESTIMATION AND DATA

In using the index number approach to estimate productivity, TFP is derived as the ratio of aggregate output over aggregate input use. TFP growth in this framework is the residual difference between the rate of growth of aggregate output and the rate of growth of aggregate input. Therefore, the first step in estimating productivity is constructing indexes of aggregate output and aggregate input. To this end, data on production and average prices paid to farmers, as well as on input quantities or annual expenditures on input items by farmers, were collected for each year between 1948 and 1991. Data were obtained from several published and unpublished sources, the main sources being Statistics Canada and Agriculture Canada.

An aggregate output index comprising both crops and livestock was constructed for Canada and for the prairie region, comprising the provinces of Alberta, Saskatchewan, and Manitoba. Fourteen major crops were included: wheat, oats, barley, rye, mixed grain, corn, flax, soybeans, mustard, potatoes, hay, rapeseed, sunflower and sugar beets. The livestock items included were: cattle and calves, sheep and lambs, pigs, chicken, turkeys, eggs and dairy. The input side of the productivity equation included the input categories of capital, labour, and intermediate inputs or materials. More specifically, the aggregate input index included: land and buildings, summer fallow, machinery and livestock capital; labour comprising hired workers, unpaid farm operators and family workers; and material items including fertilizer, pesticides, fuel and oil, electricity, seeds, animal feeds and irrigation.

The construction of the index for aggregate inputs involves many conceptual and empirical problems. The major difficulty is that several 'durable' inputs, such as land and machinery, are used in production. The best measure of input use is represented by the service flows provided by the stocks, rather than the stocks themselves. Furthermore, not all input use involves actual cash outlay for the farmer so imputation is needed in the case of inputs such as land or unpaid operator and family labour. The annual service flows of the land, buildings and livestock capital items were assumed to be opportunity costs imputed as 4 percent of the respective nominal values. For machinery, depreciation and repairs were considered to be the relevant service flow and no opportunity cost was included. The labour input was derived in terms of man-hours data, although this required extrapolation for early years in the time period prior to 1966. For inputs with an imputed service flow or an actual annual expenditure (such as most material items), an implicit quantity index was computed by dividing the value of the service flow or expenditure by an appropriate price index.

Initially, the index number procedure used to derive aggregate output and aggregate input for Canada and for the prairie region of western Canada was the Tornqvist–Theil approximation to the Divisia index. The resulting output, input, and TFP indexes for agriculture in Canada are graphically portrayed in Figure 1. The same indexes for western Canada, also Divisia-based, are shown in Figure 2. Using the western Canadian data set, six further indexing procedures were implemented to measure aggregate output, input, and TFP in the prairie region: Laspeyres, Paasche, Fisher, Laspeyres chained, Paasche chained, and Fisher chained. The resulting productivity index numbers are plotted in Figures 3 and 4 and compared with the Divisia-based estimates of productivity.

EMPIRICAL RESULTS

Levels of agricultural output and productivity more than doubled in Canada (Figure 1) and the prairie region (Figure 2) between 1948 and 1991. Input use in Canadian agriculture actually declined over the entire period, led by sharp declines in labour employed in the 1950s as capital was substituted for labour. The time path of the productivity index closely follows that of the output index in both Canada and the prairies although from the mid-1970s onwards the two curves tend to diverge because output grows faster than productivity.

Estimated compound growth rates of output, input, and productivity for Canadian and prairie agriculture are briefly summarized in Table 1. These estimates are based on the Tornqvist–Theil approximation to the Divisia index. Canadian agricultural output, for example, grew by 1.86 percent per year over the entire period from 1948 to 1991, aggregate input use declined marginally by –0.02 percent per year, and productivity (TFP) increased by 1.88 percent per year.[2] In prairie agriculture, output increased more rapidly at 2.31 percent per year, input use rose moderately at 0.38 percent per year, and productivity increased at 1.92 percent per year between 1948 and 1991. Most output growth, therefore, was due to productivity growth rather than increased use of inputs. Since 1962, output and productivity have grown somewhat less rapidly in both Canada and the prairie region. Estimated rates are highly sensitive to the particular time period chosen. Both output and productivity exhibit large year-to-year variations mainly due to weather conditions. Using a drought year (1961 or 1974) as initial or final year biases growth rate estimation considerably. In previous research (Veeman and Fantino, 1985, 1990), about 80 percent of the variation in productivity is explained with a time trend and a number of weather variables. It is also possible to estimate 'weather-corrected' growth rates.

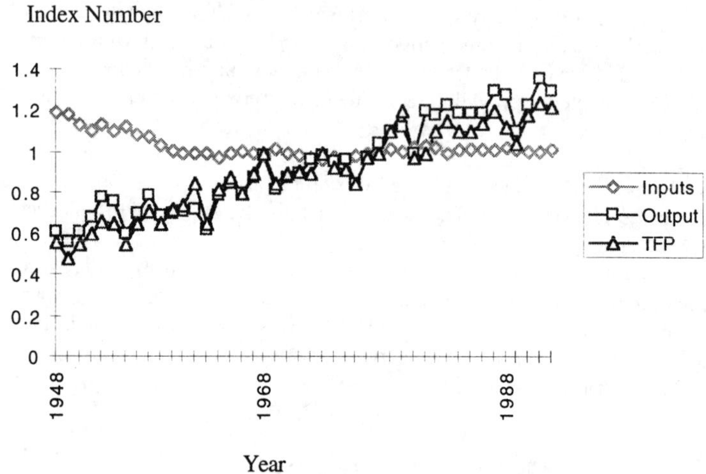

Figure 1 *Indexes of Output, Inputs and TFP — Canadian Agriculture, 1971=1*

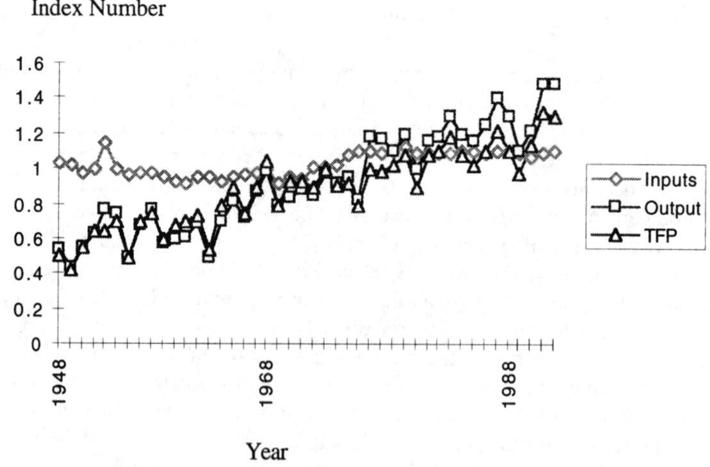

Figure 2 *Indexes of Output, Inputs and TFP — Prairie Agriculture, 1971=1*

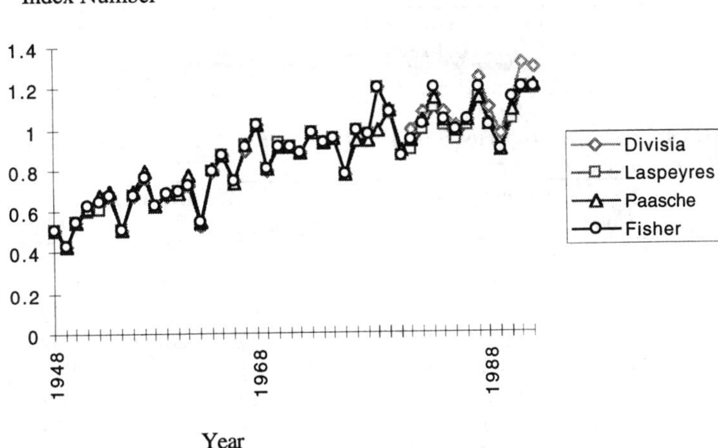

Figure 3 *Productivity Indexes — Prairie Agriculture, Base 1971 = 1*

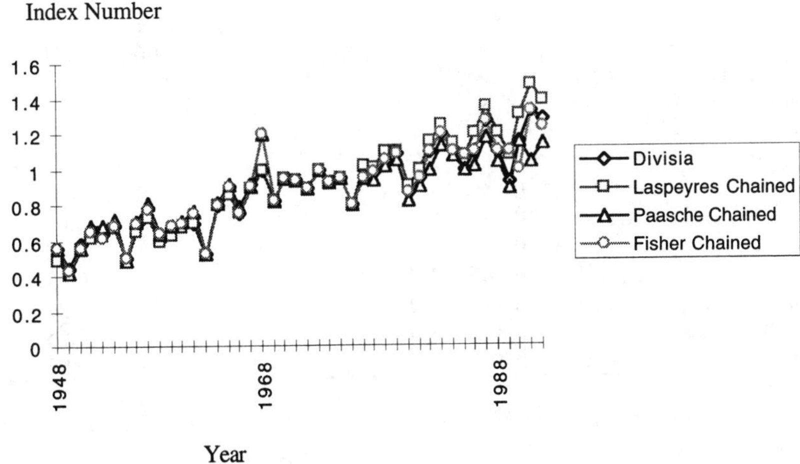

Figure 4 *Productivity Indexes — Prairie Agriculture, Base 1971 = 1*

Table 1 *Annual Growth Rates in Canadian and Prairie Agriculture, Divisa-Based: 1948–91 and 1962–91 (percent)*

	Canada		Prairies	
	1948–91	1962–91	1948–91	1962–91
Output	1.86	1.70	2.31	2.07
Inputs	–0.02	0.43	0.38	0.75
TFP	1.88	1.27	1.92	1.32

Table 2 *Output, Input and Productivity Growth Rates for Prairie Agriculture: Various Index Procedures*

	Percent per year			Relative to Divisia		
Index	Output	Input	TFP	Output	Input	TFP
1948–1991						
Divisia	2.31	0.38	1.92	1.00	1.00	1.00
Laspeyres	2.13	0.37	1.75	0.92	0.99	0.91
Paasche	2.16	0.49	1.66	0.93	1.29	0.86
Fisher	2.14	0.43	1.71	0.93	1.14	0.89
Laspeyres chained	2.73	0.42	2.30	1.18	1.12	1.19
Paasche chained	1.88	0.34	1.53	0.81	0.90	0.80
Fisher chained	2.30	0.38	1.91	1.00	1.01	0.99
1962–1991						
Divisia	2.07	0.74	1.32	1.00	1.00	1.00
Laspeyres	1.77	0.88	0.88	0.86	1.18	0.67
Paasche	1.82	0.79	1.02	0.88	1.05	0.78
Fisher	1.80	0.84	0.95	0.87	1.11	0.72
Laspeyres chained	2.58	0.80	1.77	1.24	1.06	1.34
Paasche chained	1.54	0.71	0.82	0.74	0.95	0.62
Fisher chained	2.06	0.75	1.29	0.99	1.01	0.98
1971–1991						
Divisia	2.01	0.45	1.55	1.00	1.00	1.00
Laspeyres	1.59	0.66	0.92	0.79	1.45	0.60
Paasche	1.62	0.47	1.15	0.81	1.04	0.74
Fisher	1.61	0.56	1.04	0.80	1.25	0.67
Laspeyres chained	2.51	0.49	2.01	1.25	1.09	1.29
Paasche chained	1.43	0.42	1.01	0.71	0.93	0.65
Fisher chained	1.97	0.46	1.51	0.98	1.01	0.97

The choice of a particular index number procedure is important to the magnitude of estimated growth rates. In Table 2, growth rates of output, input, and productivity in agriculture in the prairie region of western Canada over various time periods are presented for seven different index number procedures. In the right hand side of Table 2, these respective growth rates are indexed relative to the Divisia-based estimates. A relatively large discrepancy is evident between growth rates estimated from Divisia (Tornqvist–Theil) indexes and those estimated from Laspeyres or Paasche indexes. For example, over shorter time spans such as 1971 to 1991, the Laspeyres-based estimate of productivity growth is 40 percent below the Divisia-based estimate. A notable feature of these empirical results is that growth rates obtained from Divisia-based indexes are very similar to those generated from the Fisher chained index. In Figure 4, it is apparent that the productivity time paths for the Divisia-based (Tornqvist–Theil) index and the chained Fisher index are nearly the same.

Productivity growth rates under the seven alternative indexing procedures were also calculated for Canadian agriculture (not reported here), with generally similar results occurring, particularly for longer time periods. The Tornqvist–Theil and chained Fisher based rates of productivity growth diverge somewhat more than in the case of the prairies, a more agriculturally homogeneous region, but are still well within ten percent of each other.

CONCLUSION

In this paper, the choice of index number procedures in the empirical measurement of agricultural productivity has been analyzed using a Canadian case study. Measures of output, inputs, and total factor productivity vary considerably depending on the index number used in aggregation. Our empirical results for the Canadian prairies suggest there is little practical difference in estimates of productivity growth based on the Tornqvist–Theil approximation to the Divisia index as compared to the Fisher 'ideal' chained index. Either of these superlative indexes is to be preferred, for both conceptual and empirical reasons, over the Laspeyres index or its chained variant in the measurement of agricultural productivity.

NOTES

[1] Another option is geometric aggregation, following Solow, in which factor shares are used to construct an aggregate input index, and in which Cobb–Douglas production technology is implied.

[2] This productivity growth estimate for Canadian agriculture is quite similar to those calculated for agriculture in the United States over relatively similar time periods — for example, Ball's estimate (1992) of 1.83 percent per year over 1948–89 and Jorgenson and Gollop's (1992) estimate of 1.58 percent over 1947–85.

REFERENCES

Antle, J.M. and Capalbo, S.M., 1988, 'An Introduction to Recent Developments in Production Theory and Productivity Measurement' and Capalbo, S.M. and Antle, J.M. (eds.), *Agricultural Productivity: Measurement and Explanation*, Resources for the Future, Washington, D.C., pp.17–95.

Ball, E., 1992, 'Sources of Agricultural Economic Growth and Productivity: Discussion', *American Journal of Agricultural Economics*, Vol. 74, No. 3, pp.764–765.

Brinkman, G. L. and Prentice, B.E., 1983, 'Multifactor Productivity in Canadian Agriculture: An Analysis of Methodology and Performance, 1961–1980', Regional Development Branch, Agriculture Canada, Ottawa.

Bureau, J.C., Ball, V.E., Butault, J.P. and Barkaoui, A., 1994, 'Productivity Gaps Between European and United States Agriculture', in Narayanan, S. and King, J. (eds.), *Measuring Agricultural Productivity and Related Data for Regional, National and International Comparisons*, Policy Branch, Agriculture Canada, Ottawa, pp.68–79.

Christensen, L.R., 1975, 'Concepts and Measurement of Agricultural Productivity', *American Journal of Agricultural Economics*, Vol. 57, No. 5, pp.910–915.

Diewert, W. E., 1976, 'Exact and Superlative Index Numbers', *Journal of Econometrics*, Vol. 4, No. 2, pp.115–145.

Diewert, W. E., 1989a, 'Fisher Ideal Output, Input and Productivity Indexes Revisited', *The Journal of Productivity Analysis*, Vol. 3, pp.211–248.

Diewert, W. E., 1989b, 'The Measurement of Productivity', Discussion Paper 89-04, Department of Economics, University of British Columbia.

Hulten, C. R., 1973, 'Divisia Index Numbers', *Econometrica*, Vol. 41, No. 6, pp.1017–45.

Jorgenson, D.W. and Gollop, F.M., 1992. 'Productivity Growth in U.S. Agriculture: A Posterior Perspective', *American Journal of Agricultural Economics*, Vol 74, No. 3, pp.745–750.

Narayanan, S. and Kizito, E., 1992, 'Multifactor Productivity for Canadian Agriculture: Overview of Methodology', Farm Economic Analysis Division, Policy Branch, Agriculture Canada, Ottawa.

Veeman, T.S. and Fantino, A.A., 1985, 'Productivity Growth in Western Canadian Agriculture', Farming For the Future, Final Technical Report, Department of Rural Economy, University of Alberta, Edmonton.

Veeman, T.S. and Fantino, A.A., 1990, 'The Role of Fertilizer and Weather in Prairie Grain Production and Productivity', Farming For the Future, Final Technical Report 90-04, Department of Rural Economy, University of Alberta, Edmonton.

DISCUSSION OPENING — William Masters *(Purdue University, USA)*

It is often useful to begin discussion by asking, 'so what?' The question is especially apt for this paper, which I think does have very significant consequences for many of us. The authors are to be thanked for their attention to the kinds of methods that are actually used in practical policy analysis, and their well-balanced use of a little theory and a lot of evidence to argue for improved methods. This sort of work is often slighted in our profession, but is important to the real-world application of economic ideas.

The authors demonstrate clearly that the 'superlative' Divisia and Fisher ideal indexes give significantly different results than more common indexing methods, and so are preferable in practice as well as in theory. The empirical differences between these two superlative or 'flexible' methods, which require price observations corresponding to every quantity observation, appear to be very small, whereas the differences among conventional Laspeyres and Paasche methods, which use one quantity observation to weight many price observations, are quite large. This provides a very strong argument in favour of using either superlative index, in preference to any other method. The 'so what' consequences of the paper are therefore unusually clear.

I am not an expert in this field, but it does seem to me that the paper's central thesis is clearly presented and conclusively demonstrated. We therefore have the luxury of starting from where the authors left off, building on this excellent paper rather than criticizing it. I will just flag a few issues that seemed particularly important to me.

As a non-expert, I had thought that flexible forms were already dominant in empirical work in this field. If they are not, despite their theoretical advantages (and, as Fantino and Veeman show, significant empirical differences), why not? Fantino and Veeman clearly demonstrate the benefits of using the flexible methods. What of their costs? Clearly, government statistical services must now be persuaded of the need to collect and publish annual price series as well as quantities and in some cases the cost of doing so may well outweigh the benefits of better productivity measurement. In particular, it appears that conventional indexes often mismeasure the magnitude, but not the direction of TFP change. If this is the case, superlative indexes are needed mostly to compare TFP growth across countries or time periods — for an individual case, conventional measures may be acceptable. But if this is not the case, perhaps the authors could address the conditions under which directional errors would occur.

In general, we need to be sure we understand why a given result was obtained: this is not only important to the persuasiveness of our arguments, but also to their robustness. In this case, for example, it may be that index number results are so different because aggregate input use in Canada has in fact not grown much — so small errors due to input substitution over time have a big impact on measured TFP. In LDCs where input use has grown quickly (and where the cost of using better methods is greatest), perhaps conventional methods would be adequate — at least for the 'big picture' question of whether TFP is rising or falling. This is so particularly because the errors in conventional indexes appear to be fairly random, rather than systematic biases for or against particular kinds of technical changes.

Having raised these three points for discussion, we should perhaps not forget a logical next step for the authors: now that they have convinced us to use superlative indexes wherever possible, when will they come up with an add-on program for Lotus and Quattro, to help us calculate these things more easily, without having to spell Tornqvist–Theil?

K.P. KALIRAJAN AND R.T. SHAND*

Modelling and Measuring Technical Efficiency: An Alternative Approach

Abstract: In the literature, technical efficiency is measured as the ratio of observed output to potential output. Although there is no a priori theoretical reasoning, in the stochastic framework of measuring technical efficiency, the potential output is defined as a neutral shift from the observed output. The objective in this paper is to suggest a method to measure technical efficiency without having to consider the potential output as a neutral shift from the observed output.

INTRODUCTION

Technical efficiency, one of the two components of economic efficiency, is defined as the ability and willingness of any producing unit to obtain the maximum possible potential output from a given set of inputs and technology. In the literature, technical efficiency is measured as a ratio of actual output to the potential output (Aigner, Lovell and Schmidt, 1977; and Meeusen and van den Broeck, 1977). Based on techniques of estimating the potential output, the approaches to measuring technical efficiency generally vary from programming to statistical estimation[1]. In the latter approach, a firm-specific stochastic production frontier involving outputs and inputs is defined as follows:

$$(1)\quad y_i^* = f(x_i)\exp(v_i)$$

where, x_i is a vector of m inputs, v_is are statistical random errors with $N(0,\sigma_v^2)$, and y_i^* is the maximum possible stochastic potential output for the *i*th firm, which varies over time for the same firm and across firms in the same period.

It is rational to assume that firms may not know the parameters of their own frontier production function exactly for various reasons, and that this lack of knowledge is manifest principally as technical inefficiency. Therefore, the realized production function of the *i*th firm may be modelled as follows:

$$(2)\quad y_i = y_i^* \exp(u_i)$$

where exp(u) is defined as a measure of observed technical efficiency of the *i*th firm. It is further assumed that $u_i \leq 0$. When u_i takes the value zero, it means that the *i*th firm is technically fully efficient and realises its maximum possible potential output. On the other hand, when u_i assumes values less than zero, it means that the *i*th firm is not fully technically efficient and so produces output which is less than its potential output. Now, a measure of technical efficiency for the ith firm can be defined as:

$$(3)\quad \exp(u_i) = \frac{y_i, \text{given } u_i}{y_i^*, \text{given } u_i = 0}$$

* Australian National University.

To obtain the above measure the denominator has to be estimated, as the numerator is the observed output level. Assuming a functional form to represent the technology in Equation (1), and a density function for u in Equation (2), the denominator can be estimated by using the maximum likelihood methods.

There are three apparent limitations to this approach. First, the technology is parametized by some *ad hoc* functional forms involving outputs and inputs, which is restrictive. Second, assuming a density function for u_i is not based on any theoretical reasoning. Finally, and most importantly, the frontier production function defined in Equation (1) is assumed to be a neutral shift from the observed production function, Equation (2), which is questionable. Statistical tests are available and have been carried out to validate the selection of functional forms and the distributional assumption for u_i, but, the question as to why the frontier should be a neutral shift from the observed production function has not received much attention in the literature.

The objective in this paper is to suggest a method to estimate the frontier production function using cross-sectional data and to measure firm-specific technical efficiency for individual observations, when the frontier shifts non-neutrally from the observed production function. The following section explains the methodology which is followed by the estimation procedures.

FRONTIER WITH NON-NEUTRAL SHIFT

When technical efficiency is measured by using Equation (3), the underlying assumption is that the frontier is a neutral shift from the realized production function. This constant-slope, variable-intercept approach raises a basic question about the concept of technical efficiency. Where does technical efficiency come from? How does a firm achieve its technical efficiency? The literature indicates that a firm obtains its full technical efficiency by following the best practice techniques, given the technology. In other words, technical efficiency is determined by the method of application of inputs regardless of the levels of inputs. This implies that the different methods of applying various inputs will influence the output differently. That is, the slope coefficients will vary from firm to firm. Therefore, the constant-slope approach of measuring technical efficiency is not consistent with the definition of technical efficiency. The following specification of the production process which is consistent with the concept of technical efficiency, facilitates estimation of firm-specific technical efficiency for individual observations.

Assuming a Cobb–Douglas technology, the production relationship can be written as follows:[2]

$$(4) \quad \ln y_i = \beta_{i1} + \sum_{j=2}^{k} \beta_{ij} \ln x_{ij} + u_i \text{ for } i = 1,2,...,n$$

where y_i refers to the level of the output of the ith firm; x_{ij} refers to the level of the jth input used by the ith firm; β_{i1} is the intercept term for the ith firm; β_{ij}, $j>1$, is the actual response of the output to the method of application of the jth input by the ith firm, and u_i refers to the random disturbance term which is $N(0,\sigma_u^2)$.

Further, let, $\beta_{ij} = \beta_j + v_{ij}$, $\beta_{i1} = \beta_1 + v_{i1}$

$$E(v_{ij}) = 0, \quad E(v_{i1}) = 0, \quad E(\beta_{ij}) = \beta_j$$

$$\text{var}\left(\beta_{ij}\right) = \text{E}\left(\beta_{ij} - \beta_i\right)\left(\beta_{ik} - \beta_i\right)$$

$$= \sigma_{jj} \text{ for } j = k$$

$$= 0 \text{ for } j \neq k$$

$$= V$$

Now, with the above assumptions, following Swamy (1971), Equation (4) can be rewritten as:

$$(5) \quad \ln y_i = \beta_1 + \sum_{j=2}^{k} \beta_j \ln x_{ij} + w_i \qquad \text{for } i = 1,2,...,n$$

where $w_i = \sum_{j=2}^{k} v_{ij} \ \ln x_{ij} + v_{i1} + u_i$

$$E(w_i) = 0$$

$$\text{var}(w_i) = \sigma^2 + \sum_j \sigma_{jj} \ln x_{ij}^2 + \sigma_{11}$$

$$\text{cov}(w_i w_j) = 0 \text{ for } i \neq j$$

The assumptions underlying Equation (5) are as follows. (a) Technical efficiency is achieved by adopting the best practice techniques which involve the efficient use of inputs without having to increase their levels. Technical efficiency stems from two sources. First, the efficient use of each input which contributes individually to technical efficiency, and can be measured by the magnitudes of the varying random slope coefficients (β_{ij}s, excluding the intercepts). Second, when all the inputs are used efficiently, then it may produce a combined contribution over and above the individual contributions. This latter 'lump sum' contribution, if any, can be measured by the varying random intercept term. (b) The highest magnitude of each response coefficient and the intercept form the production coefficients of the potential frontier production function. Let $\beta_1^*, \beta_2^*, ..., \beta_k^*$ be the estimates of the parameters of the frontier production function:

$$\beta_j^* = \max\left\{\beta_{ij}\right\} \text{ for } i = 1,2,...,n \text{ and } j = 1,2,...,k$$

Now, the firm-specific potential frontier output for each observation can be worked out as:

$$(6) \quad \ln y_i^* = \beta_1^* + \sum_{j=2}^{k} \beta_j^* \ln x_{ij} \text{ for } i = 1,2,...,n$$

where x_{ij} is the actual level of the *j*th input used by the *i*th firm. The frontier output given by Equation (6) necessarily indicates the non-neutral shift of the frontier from the actual production function. Now, a measure of technical efficiency can be defined as follows:

$$(7)\quad E_i = \frac{y_i}{\exp(\ln y_i^*)}$$

where E_i = realized output/potential output and varies between 0 and 1.

ESTIMATION

Harville (1977) proposed a number of alternative estimators. Some of these, such as the maximum likelihood (ML) and the restricted ML, are only defined for legitimate values of v. Although procedures exist for guaranteeing the estimated v to be always non-negative at each iteration, the maximum may be at the boundary. Further, as the likelihood function is not globally concave, it allows for multiple local maxima (Maddala, 1971). The above problems can be eliminated by following the iterated GLS-likelihood maximization methods suggested by Breusch (1987) with some modifications.

The principles underlying Breusch's suggestions are as follows: the parameters are classified into two groups, of which, one represents the mean response coefficients and the other shows the variance parameters. The estimates are modified by maximising the likelihood over one classification with the other fixed at its estimated value from the previous step. The response coefficients are modified by GLS using v estimated from the previous step, and v is usually modified by using the residuals from the previous GLS estimates. The iterated GLS algorithm, which is computationally simple, usually provides feasible solutions (Breusch, 1987).

Now, following Griffiths (1972), the actual firm-specific and input-specific response coefficient predictor for the *i*th observation $\hat{\beta}_{ij}$, which is the best linear unbiased predictor (BLUP) can be obtained as follows:

$$(8)\quad \hat{\beta}_{ij} = \beta + \frac{vx_i}{x_i'vx_i}\hat{w}_i$$

The response coefficients representing the potential frontier production function can be identified as follows from the above estimates:

$$(9)\quad \hat{\beta}_j^* = \max\ \{\hat{\beta}_{ij}\}\ \text{for}\ i = 1,2,\ldots,n\ \text{and}\ j = 1,2,\ldots,k$$

Now, the firm-specific potential frontier output for each observation can be worked out as:

$$(10)\quad \ln y_i^* = \beta_1^* + \sum_{2}^{k} \hat{\beta}_j^* \ln x_{ij}$$

where x_{ij}s refer to actual levels of inputs used by the *i*th firm. Calculation of firm-specific technical efficiency for individual observation can then be calculated as follows:

$$TE = \frac{(y_i)}{\exp(\ln y_i^*)}$$

DATA AND RESULTS

Data for the present study were drawn from a random sample of 68 farmers growing high-yielding paddy variety IR 36 in the village of Solavanthan in Madurai district in Tamil Nadu State of India. The sample farms are well-irrigated and they are of medium size (between 5 and 10 acres), The selected village is visited frequently by the extension officials.

The following Cobb–Douglas type of production function has been assumed for the present study

$$(11)\ \ln y_i = \beta_{i1}\chi_{i1} + \sum_{j=1}^{k} \beta_{ij} \ln \chi_{ij} + u_i \text{ for } i = 1,2,...,68.$$

where,

y = high yielding (IR 36) paddy output in tonnes
χ_1 = 1,..a constant term
χ_2 = pre-harvest labour man days
χ_3 = fertiliser in kgs.
χ_4 = animal labour days
χ_5 = area in acres multiplied by a relevant soil fertility index
u = statistical 'white noise', which is $N(0,\sigma^2)$

The mean response coefficients of inputs are given in Table 1. All the coefficients are significant at the 5 per cent level and they all have theoretically acceptable signs and magnitudes. At the outset, the validity of the modelling of Equation (11) as a random coefficient specification for the present data set has been examined by following the testing procedures suggested by Breusch and Pagan (1979). They pointed out that the random coefficient specification, as described above, fits the class of heteroscedastic error models and have proposed a Lagrange multiplier test, which has the same asymptotic properties as the likelihood ratio tests in standard situations. The test results indicate that the random coefficient specification in Equation (11) could not be rejected for the present data set. This means that our modelling of the production process in the study area is appropriate. The Ramsey's (1969) RESET test for functional form was used and the calculated test Statistic $F_{(1,63)} = 2.72$. The tabulated $F_{(1,63)}$ value at the 5 per cent level was 3.65. Therefore, the Cobb–Douglas functional form could not be rejected for the data set.

Table 2 shows the range of actual response coefficients of inputs for individual observations. The variation in the farm-specific and input-specific elasticity coefficients is substantial. This means that the methods of application of different inputs vary among sample farms and, consequently, individual contributions of inputs to output differ from farm to farm. The estimates of the production coefficients of the frontier are derived using (9) and the results are given in Table 2. These estimates indicate the maximum possible contribution of each input to output when the inputs are applied efficiently following the best practices techniques. Further, these estimates are derived relaxing the conventional assumption that the frontier output is a neutral shift from the realised output.

Table 1 *Iterated GLS Estimates of the Mean Response Coefficients and the Variance Coefficients*

Inputs	Unit of measurement	Iterated GLS estimates: Variance coefficient	Iterated GLS estimates: Mean response coefficient
Constant	-	0.1216	0.3916 (0.1428)
Labour	Man days	0.1318	0.2012 (0.1065)
Fertilizer	kgs	0.1176	0.2584 (0.1265)
Animal labour	days	0.0820	0.0616 (0.0303)
Area	acres	0.1372	0.4763 (0.1329)

Notes: Figures in parentheses denote standard errors. Number of observations: 68. Log likelihood –118.34.

Table 2 *Range of Estimates of Actual Response Coefficients and Estimates of Frontier Production Function*

Inputs	Range of actual response coefficients	Estimates of the frontier production function
Constant	0.3896–0.3982	0.3982
Labour	0.1923–0.2106	0.2106
Fertilizer	0.2485–0.2615	0.2615
Animal power	0.0592–0.0678	0.0678
Area	0.4318–0.4682	0.4682

Table 3 *Frequency Distribution of Farm-Specific Technical Efficiency Measures*

Efficiency measures(%)	Number of firms	Percentage
71 – 75	0	29.4
76 – 80	16	23.5
81 – 85	14	20.6
86 – 90	13	19.1
91 – 95	5	7.4
Total	68	100

Following Equation (10), the potential frontier outputs for individual observations have been estimated and the calculated farm-specific technical efficiency measures for each sample farmer are shown in Table 3 in a frequency form. The efficiency measures range from 0.71 to 0.94.

CONCLUSIONS

The fixed coefficient frontier production function methodology hitherto used restricts measurement of efficiency to an overall measure. But, it is rational to argue that, depending on which farm uses which best practice technique with which input, production coefficients would vary from farm to farm. This provides the rationale and the necessity for the use of the variable coefficient frontier production function to measure firm-specific technical efficiencies. The results reveal substantial variations in the actual farm-specific and input-specific response coefficients, which means that methods of application of different inputs vary among farms, and consequently individual contributions of inputs to output differ from farm to farm.

In the light of the above findings, this method of measuring technical efficiency, which relaxes the conventional assumption of a neutral shift of the frontier function from the actual production function, provides valuable additional information to policy-makers. Not only can the analysis distinguish which farmers are more or less efficient, but also with respect to which inputs. This should, for example, give greater guidance as to the most appropriate direction for extension advice and calls for research on the reasons for variations in individual efficiencies.

NOTES

1 For a detailed discussion, see Bauer, 1990.

2 Equation (4) is a modification of the Hildreth–Houck (1968) random coefficient regression model. Unlike the Hildreth–Houck model, an additive disturbance term has been included in the proposed model, in addition to the random intercept term.

REFERENCES

Aigner, D.J., Lovell, C.A.K. and Schmidt, P., 1977, 'Formulation and Estimation of Stochastic Frontier Production Function Models', *Journal of Econometrics*, Vol. 6, No. 1, pp.21–37.

Bauer, P.W., 1990, 'Recent Developments in the Econometric Estimation of Frontier', *Journal of Econometrics*, Vol. 46, No. 1, pp.39–56.

Breusch, T.S.,1987, 'Maximum Likelihood Estimation of Random Effects Models', *Journal of Econometrics*, Vol. 36, No. 3, pp.383–389.

Breusch, T.S. and Pagan, A.R., 1979, 'The Lagrange Multiplier Test and its Application to Model Specification in Econometrics', *Review of Economic Studies*, Vol. 47, pp. 239–253.

Griffiths, W.E., 1972, 'Estimation of Actual Response Coefficients in the Hildreth-Houck Random Coefficient Model', *Journal of the American Statistical Association*, Vol. 67, No. 339, pp.633–635.

Harville, D.A., 1977, 'Maximum Likelihood Approaches to Variance Component Estimation and to Related Problems', *Journal of the American Statistical Association*, Vol. 72, No. 358, pp.584–595.

Hildreth, C. and Houck, J.P., 1968, 'Some Estimators for a Linear Model with Random Coefficients', *Journal of the American Statistical* Association, Vol. 63, No. 322, pp.584–595.

Maddala, G.S., 1971, 'The Use of Variance Models in Pooling Cross Section and Time Series Data', *Econometrica*, Vol. 39, No. 2, pp.341–358.

Meeusen, W. and van den Broeck, J., 1977, 'Efficiency Estimation from Cobb Douglas Production Functions with Composed Error', *International Economic Review*, Vol. 18, pp.435–444.

Ramsey, J., 1969, 'Tests of Specification Errors in Classical Linear Least-Squares Regression Analysis', *Journal of the Royal Statistical* Society, Series B, Vol. 31, No. 2, pp.350–371.

Swamy, P.A.V.B., 1971, *Statistical Inference in a Random Coefficient Regression Model*, Berlin, Springer, Verlag.

M.B. OBWANA, K.P. KALIRAJAN AND R.T. SHAND*

On Measuring Farmer-Specific and Input-Specific Allocative Efficiency

Abstract: The objective in this paper is to suggest an alternative method of estimating farmer-specific and input-specific allocative efficiency, taking into account the influence of the methods of application of inputs on output. Further, we compare the proposed measures with those calculated based on the existing conventional method using the same data set.

INTRODUCTION

The economic viability of a farmer depends on two important questions. First, how efficiently are the inputs used, given the technology, and secondly, how much of the inputs are utilized in the production process, given the technology and market prices. Examination of the above two questions is vital to the survival of farmers in the long run. There are several ways to answer these questions. The method most frequently used in the literature to answer the first question is to estimate the stochastic frontier output and to compare with the actual realized output popularized by Aigner *et al.* (1977) and Meeusen and van den Broeck (1977). The second question is usually answered by equating the marginal value product (MVP) calculated from the farm's realized production function with marginal cost (MC) of the variable inputs under the behavioural assumption of profit maximization.

While calculating the MVP, it is always assumed that the input-specific production response coefficients do not vary among farmers. However, as the magnitudes of coefficients reflect the 'contributions' of inputs which, in turn, are determined by the methods of their application, it is very unlikely that these coefficients are in fact constant across farmers. This can only occur when all the farmers are using the same methods of application of inputs. Empirical studies show that methods of application of inputs—and therefore the input-specific response coefficients—do vary among farmers (see, for example, IRRI (1979), Smith and Umali (1985), Kalirajan and Obwona (1994), among others). This means that testing of allocative efficiencies following the constant response coefficients approach may not produce reliable results.

The objective in this paper is to suggest a method of estimating farmer-specific and input-specific allocative efficiency, taking into account the influence of the methods of application of inputs on output. Further, we compare these measures with efficiency measures calculated based on the existing conventional method using the same data set.

MODELLING FARMER-SPECIFIC PRODUCTION BEHAVIOUR

Empirical evidence shows that with the same levels of inputs, different levels of outputs are obtained by following different methods of input application. This implies that the

* Australian National University.

different methods of applying various inputs will influence the output differently. Therefore, the existing stochastic frontier production function approach estimating constant slope but varying intercept coefficient does not appear to be meaningful. The random coefficient regression models popularized by Swamy (1971) and Hsiao (1986) facilitates modelling the differences in the methods of application of inputs by farmers by introducing variations not only in intercepts but also in slope coefficients of farmer-specific production functions. Furthermore, whether such modelling is valid with data can also be tested statistically.

The random coefficients regression model can be specified as:

$$(1)\quad y_i = x_i'\beta_i + \varepsilon_i; \qquad i = 1,\ldots,N$$

where y_i is an observed dependent variable and x_i is a $K \times 1$ vector of known non-random values of independent variables. ε_i is a random error term with mean zero and constant variance, σ_ε^2. We assume that each $K \times 1$ coefficients vector β_i varies from the mean response coefficient vector, $\overline{\beta}$, by a vector of random error terms, u_i, that is,

$$(2)\quad \beta_i = \overline{\beta} + u_i$$

When $x_{1i} = 1$, the additive equation error term cannot be distinguished from the randomly varying intercept. Consequently, ε_i is usually not explicitly included in Equation (1) (Hildreth and Houck, 1968).

For all the N observations, Equations (1) and (2) can be written more compactly as:[1]

$$(3)\quad y = X\overline{\beta} + w$$

where $w = D_x u$ and y is an $N \times 1$ vector, X is an $N \times K$ matrix of stacked X_i', D_x is an $N \times NK$ diagonal matrix of X_i', u is an $NK \times 1$ vector of u_i's. We assume that

$$(4)\quad E(u_i) = 0; \qquad i = 1,\ldots,N$$

$$E(u_{ki}u_{lj}') = \begin{cases} \Lambda_u & \text{if } k = l \text{ and } i = j \\ 0 & \text{otherwise} \end{cases}$$

An estimator which is best, linear and unbiased (BLU) of $\overline{\beta}$ in (3) is

$$(5)\quad \hat{\beta} = (X'\textstyle\sum_w^{-1} X)^{-1} X'\textstyle\sum_w^{-1} y$$

where

$$(6)\quad \textstyle\sum_w = D_x(I_N \otimes \Lambda_u)D_x'$$

and

$$\Lambda_u = \operatorname{diag}(\sigma_{u11},\ldots,\sigma_{uKK})$$

I_N in (6) is an indentity matrix of order N, $\otimes$ represents the Kronecker product and σ_{ukk}; ($k = 1,\ldots,K$) are elements of Λ_u. The ith diagonal element of $\sum_w$ in Equation (6) is

$$\sum_{wi} = \sum_{k=1}^{K} \sigma_{ukk} x_{ki}^2$$

Since Λ_u elements are not known, they have to be estimated. Hildreth and Houck (op. cit.) suggests several methods of estimating the elements of Λ_u. In this study, we follow the version of Hildreth and Houck procedure modified by Singh *et al.* (1976).[2]

After estimating Λ_u and obtaining the estimates of the mean response coefficients, $\overline{\beta}$ the individual response coefficient estimates of the β_is are given by

$$(7) \quad \hat{\beta}_i = \hat{\overline{\beta}} + \Lambda_u X_i' \left[X_i \Lambda_u X_i'\right]^{-1} \left(y_i - X_i \hat{\overline{\beta}} \right); \quad i = 1,\ldots,N$$

and are best linear and unbiased (Griffiths, 1972).

The validity of the application of the random coefficients specification to the data can be examined by following the test method suggested by Swamy (1971). If the production response coefficients in Equation (1) are random, then Λ_u will contain non-zero elements. Thus, the appropriate test for randomness is $H_o : \Lambda_u = 0$ against $H_a : \Lambda \neq 0$. Swamy (1971) developed a likelihood ratio test in the context of panel data models. The test statistic used here is a straightforward application of Swamy's test with only one period, that is, $T = 1$.

FARMER-SPECIFIC AND INPUT-SPECIFIC ALLOCATIVE EFFICIENCY

The criterion for determining the optimal levels of inputs used is to locate the point on the farmer-specific production function that has the highest associated isoprofit line. At this point, profits will be maximized. This point is characterized by a tangency condition: the slope of the farmer-specific production function should be equal to the slope of the farmer-specific isoprofit line. Since the slope of the production function is the marginal physical product, and the slope of the isoprofit line is the ratio of the price of the factor input to the price of the output, this condition can be written as:

$$(8) \quad MVP_k = MC_k; \qquad k = 2,\ldots,M$$

Now, considering a Cobb–Douglas production function with $M - 1$ variable inputs and ($K - M + 1$) fixed, denoted by x and z, respectively. The farmer-specific production function can be written as:

$$(9) \quad \ln y_i = \overline{\beta}_1 + \sum_{k=2}^{M} \beta_{ki} \ln x_{ki} + \sum_{j=M+1}^{K} \alpha_{ji} \ln z_{ji} + \varepsilon_i; \qquad i = 1,\ldots,N$$

The marginal productivity conditions in Equation (8) for profit maximization are

$$\beta_{2i}\frac{y_i}{x_{2i}} = \frac{p_{2i}}{p_{yi}}$$

$$(10)\quad \beta_{3i}\frac{y_i}{x_{3i}} = \frac{p_{3i}}{p_{yi}}$$

$$\vdots = \vdots$$

$$\beta_{\mathrm{M}i}\frac{y_i}{x_{Mi}} = \frac{p_{Mi}}{p_{yi}}; \qquad i = 1,\ldots,N$$

Equations (9) and (10) yield the following system of equations:

$$
\begin{aligned}
&\beta_{2i}\ln x_{2i} + \beta_{3i}\ln x_{3i} + \ldots + \beta_{Mi}\ln x_{Mi} - \ln y_i = -\sum_{j=M+1}^{K}\alpha_{ji}\ln z_{ji} - \ln\beta_{1i}\\
(11)\qquad &\ln x_{2i} \qquad\qquad\qquad\qquad - \ln y_{\mathrm{i}} = \ln\beta_{2i} - \ln p_{2i} + \ln p_{yi}\\
&\qquad\qquad\qquad\qquad\qquad\qquad = \vdots\\
&\qquad\qquad\qquad \ln x_{Mi} - \ln y_i = \ln\beta_{Mi} + \ln p_{yi}\\
&\qquad\qquad\qquad\qquad\qquad i = 1,\ldots,N
\end{aligned}
$$

These are *NM* equations in *NM* unknowns consisting of $x_2, x_3,\ldots,x_M$ and y. The parameters (βs) are estimates from Equation (9). The solutions to Equation (11) are the optimal output levels denoted by say, y^0, along with the optimal input levels $x_2^0,\ x_3^0,\ldots,x_M^0$.

Now a measure of farmer-specific and input-specific allocative efficiency (ISAE) to examine whether there is any under- or over-utilization of variable inputs can be defined as

$$(12)\quad ISAE_{ki} = \frac{x_{ki}}{x_{ki}^0};\ k = 2,\ldots,M \text{ and } i = 1,\ldots,N$$

where x_{ki} is the observed level of the *k*th input used by the *i*th farmer, and x_{ki}^0 is the optimal level of the *k*th input of the *i*th farmer obtained as solutions to the profit maximizing system, Equation (11). The above measure of *ISAE* can be equal to, greater or less than 1. When *ISAE* is equal to 1, it means that the farmer is efficiently allocating the particular input. On the hand, when *ISAE* is either greater or less than 1, this implies that the farmer is not efficient in choosing the level of the concerned input. More specifically, *ISAE* greater than 1 means that that particular variable input is being over-utilized, and *ISAE* less than 1 implies that the variable input in question is being under-utilized.

DATA AND EMPIRICAL ANALYSIS

Data for the present study came from a cost of cultivation project conducted by the Tamil Nadu Agricultural University in 1986. A random sample of 64 farmers growing the modern cotton variety MCU-5 in Madurai district, Tamil Nadu State in India was chosen for empirical analysis[3]. Sample farmers were operating between 5 and 10 acres of land. They may be named medium-sized farmers according to Indian standard.

The following Cobb–Douglas type of production function was estimated:[4]

$$(13)\ \ln y_i = \overline{\beta}_1 + \sum_{k=2}^{3} \beta_{ki} \ln x_{ki} + \alpha_{4i} \ln z_{4i} + \varepsilon_i;\ i = 1,2,\ldots,64$$

where

y = amount of cotton in tonnes
x_2 = labour in man days
x_3 = fertilizer in kilograms
z_4 = area operated in acres

βs are farmer-specific and variable input-specific response coefficients, α is the farmer-specific and fixed input-specific response coefficient, ε is the random disturbance term.

Table 1 *Mean Response Coefficients and the Range of Estimates of the Actual Response Coefficients*

Inputs	Coefficients	Mean response coefficients	Range of actual response coefficients
Constant	β_1	4.3072 (0.8765)	4.2813 – 4.3216
Labour	β_2	0.2518 (0.1204)	0.2316 – 0.2648
Fertilizer	β_3	0.2094 (0.0919)	0.1913 – 0.2216
Land	α_4	0.5206 (0.2582)	0.5004 – 0.5324

Note: Figures in parentheses are standard errors of estimates.

The mean response coefficients estimated as in Equation (5) are given in Table 1. These coefficients have theoretically acceptable signs and magnitudes and are significant at the 5 percent level. These coefficients can be considered as the production coefficients calculated based on conventional approach of using the weighted least squares estimation of production functions.

Table 2 *Farmer-specific and Input-specific Allocative Efficiencies of Variables Inputs*

	Number of farmers			
	Conventional method		Suggested method	
ISAE	Labour	Fertilizer	Labour	Fertilizer
<1	2	10	7	33
=1	43	30	11	14
>1	19	24	46	17
Total	64	64	64	64

Now, to arrive at the farmer-specific optimal levels based on the conventional approach, the above coefficients are substituted along with farmer-specific and input-specific prices in Equation (11). Then the farmer-specific and input-specific allocative efficiency measures are calculated as given in Equation (12) and the results are presented in Table 2.

Next, the hypothesis that the response coefficients are fixed across observations is tested by using the likelihood ratio test developed by Swamy (1971). The asymptotic $\chi^2_{\frac{1}{2}K(K+1)}$ chi-square test statistic was calculated to be 28.96 (with 10 degrees of freedom) which is significant at the 1 percent level. This means that the null hypothesis may be rejected and that the use of the fixed coefficients model is rejected in favour of the varying coefficients model of the present data set.

Actual response coefficients for individual observations are calculated using Equation (7) and the range of actual response coefficients is given in Table 1. The results show that there are variations in the farmer-specific and input-specific actual response coefficients. Thus, the results indicate that the conventional approach of modelling the production behaviour of sample farmers where the same response coefficients are assigned to each observation without first testing statistically is not appropriate.

Finally, using the above actual farmer-specific and input-specific production response coefficients along with farmer-specific and input-specific prices in Equation (11), the optimal input levels are calculated. The farmer-specific and input-specific allocative efficiencies are then calculated and the results are presented also in Table 2.

These results show that only about 17 percent and 22 percent of farmers appear to have efficiently allocated their labour and fertilizer inputs respectively. The corresponding figures from the conventional method are much higher, that is, 67 percent and 47 percent, respectively. In other words, when examined using our suggested approach, about 83 percent of sample farmers appear to be allocating the labour input inefficiently, while the corresponding figure for fertilizer is 78 percent. However, in the case of conventional approach which is based on the assumption of fixed input-specific production response coefficients for all sample farmers, only 33 percent of farmers seem to be allocating the labour input inefficiently and for the fertilizer, it is 53 percent. As the hypothesis of fixed production response coefficients for all the sample farmers has earlier on been rejected, in the light of the above results, it may be concluded that the conventional method of calculating allocative efficiencies is misleading.

CONCLUSION

Drawing on the principles of the random coefficient regression model, this paper suggests an approach to model the impact on allocative efficiency of different methods of application of a given technology at the farm level. The effect of different methods of applying a given technology on output manifests in the form of yielding different magnitudes of production coefficient across observations. The ratio of the actual level of input used to the optimal level of input calculated using the actual response coefficients and farmer-specific prices, provides a measure of farmer-specific and input-specific allocative efficiency.

The empirical results show that measuring allocative efficiency using the conventional method which does not take into account the possibility of variation in production response coefficients among farmers, may provide misleading results. This implies that any measurement of the allocative efficiencies should be preceded by testing whether the production response coefficients do vary among farmers.

NOTES

1 Without the random error term ε_i since $u_{1i} = \varepsilon_i$ by specification.

2 Hsiao (1975) shows that the Hildreth–Houck estimator is equivalent to the minimum-norm quadratic unbiased estimator (MINQUE) of Rao (1970).

3 Cotton is an important commercial crop in India, and Tamil Nadu is one of the major cotton producing states in India (Hitchings, 1983).

4 A translog functional form was estimated using the data set. But, the test based on translog estimates for a Cobb–Douglas functional form could not be rejected. Furthermore, a Cobb–Douglas production function has also been proved to be suitable in earlier empirical studies on cotton production in Tamil Nadu State (see, for example, Subramanian, 1986).

REFERENCES

Aigner, D.J., Lovell, C.A.K and Schmidt, P., 1977, 'Formulation and Estimation of Stochastic Frontier Production Function Models', *Journal of Econometrics*, Vol. 6, No. 1, pp.21–37.

Griffiths, W. E., 1972, 'Estimation of Actual Response Coefficients in the Hildreth–Houck Random Coefficient Model', *Journal of American Statistical Association*, Vol. 67, No. 339, pp.633–635.

Hildreth, C. and Houck, J.P., 1968, 'Some Estimates for Linear Model with Random Coefficients', *Journal of American Statistical Association*, Vol. 63, No. 322, pp.584–595.

Hitchings, J.A., 1983, The Economics of Cotton Cultivation in India — Supply and Demand for 1980–90, World Bank Staff Working Paper No. 68, Washington, D.C.

Hsiao, C., 1975, 'Some Estimation Methods for a Random Coefficients Model', *Econometrica*, Vol. 43, No. 2, pp.305–325.

Hsiao, C., 1986, *Analysis of Panel Data*, Econometric Society Monographs No. 11, Cambridge University Press, New York.

IRRI, 1979, 'Farm-level Constraints to High Rice Yields in Asia 1974–77', International Rice Research Institute, Los Banõs, Philippines.

Kalirajan, K.P. and Obwona, M.B., 1994, 'Frontier Production Function: The Stochastic Coefficients Approach', *Oxford Bulletin of Economics and Statistics*, Vol. 56, No. 1, pp. 87–96.

Meeusen, W. and van den Broeck, 1977, 'Efficiency Estimation from Cobb–Douglas Production Function with Composed Error', *International Economic Review*, Vol. 18, pp.435-444.

Rao, C.R., 1970, 'Estimation of Heteroscedastic Variances in Linear Models', *Journal of the American Statistical Association*, Vol. 65, No. 329, pp.161–72.

Singh, B., Nager, A.L., Chouldhry, N.K. and Raj. B., 1976, 'On the Estimation of Structural Changes: A Generalization of the Random Coefficients Regression Model', *International Economic Review*, Vol. 17, No. 2, pp.340–361.

Smith, J. and Umali, G., 1985, 'Production Risk and Optimal Fertilizer Rates: A Random Coefficient Model', *American Journal of Agricultural Economics*, Vol. 67, No. 3, pp.654–659.

Subramanian, G., 1986, 'Labour Demand and Supply Responsiveness of Cotton in Madurai District, Tamil Nadu', *Indian Journal of Agricultural Economics*, Vol. 41, No.2, pp.155–163.

Swamy, P.A.V.B., 1971, *Statistical Inference in Random Coefficient Regression Models*, Springer-Verlag, New York.

DISCUSSION OPENING — Steven A. Neff *(Economic Research Service, USDA)*

The paper uses a random coefficients technique to evaluate a 1986 study by G. Subramanian of farmer-specific and input-specific allocative efficiency for cotton farmers in Tamil Nadu, India. The present paper, following Subramanian, uses a Cobb–Douglas production function. I have no criticism of the application of the method. I do not find technical flaws.

Having said said, I will argue a bit with the premise, I will question the conclusion, and I will raise doubts about its applicability. The paper begins by asserting that a farmer's economic viability depends on the quantity of inputs and how effectively they are used, given technology and market prices. Of course technology and market prices are not given to farmers in many parts of the world, including Zimbabwe. Yesterday I heard a farmer in a communal area name the problems his group had encountered in the current growing season, including the breakdown of an irrigation pump. This intra-seasonal technology change was not a choice, but the technology was, for his farm, not a given. A large scale commercial farmer said that the Cotton Marketing Board is not guaranteeing the price of cotton in the coming year, so his viability depends crucially on his marketing results. I could give other examples for the United States, but I think I have made the point that the farmers' viability depends on many things, among which technology and market prices are not given. The paper is a bit oversold at the outset.

I promised to question the interpretation of the results. Applying the random coefficients technique, the authors find that only 17 percent and 22 percent of farmers are using labour and fertilizer inefficiently. Subramanian had found that 67 percent and 47 percent of farmers were using labour and fertilizer efficiently. Now I don't question that individual farmers' response coefficients are different, but I would question whether the difference can all be attributed to variations in the effectiveness of application of the inputs. I suspect that some of what is being called inefficiency is actually due to variations in labour and fertilizer quality. I might excuse the authors from responsibility for data quality because they are using an existing data set, but some of the 'inefficiency' may actually be due to data quality.

If I were the authors' student, I would see very dramatically the effect of taking into account the fact that response coefficients are not fixed. If I were the professor, I would have demonstrated very effectively that this point should be considered. If I were not a professor or student, but the state minister for agriculture in Tamil Nadu, my perspective would be quite different. If had seen the original study that concluded that my farmers are using their inputs efficiently, I might have concluded that there was no need to increase funding for my extension service. Now I have another study on exactly the same topic using exactly the same data, and it comes to an exactly opposite conclusion. What should I do? Should I rely on the one that favours my bias? Should I ask for a new study that looks at each assumption in a different way or uses another technique or a different functional form (after all, why use Cobb–Douglas?) that neither of these studies have considered? I am afraid that I am likely to ignore the studies and make my policy decisions based on other criteria. In short, it would have been helpful if the authors had offered some guidance on the applicability of the results.

GENERAL DISCUSSION — Claude Mehier, Rapporteur *(France)*

In the discussion of Fantino and Veeman's paper, the authors were asked several questions about how inputs were measured. The interest centred on capital components. Measures of multi-factor productivity are generally influenced by how the land input is measured. The authors were asked whether the results would change if account were taken of resource stocks and flows. There was further discussion of the importance the influence of changes in technology and the problem of measuring capital input as quality changed. A similar question was raised with regard to changes in labour quality over time. Other discussion concerned the influence of economies of scale and the tendency for total factor productivity measures to follow a cyclical pattern in the United States.

The authors of the other two papers were not present. A brief summary of Kalirajan and Shand's paper was presented by Oeivind Hoveid (Norway). Steve Neff (ERS, US Department of Agriculture) presented a brief outline of Obwana, Kalirajan and Shand's paper.

Participants in the discussion included Simeon Ehui (ILCA, Ethiopia), Franco Rosa (University of Udine, Italy) W. Huffman (Iowa State University) and Heinrich Hockmann (University of Gottingen, Germany).

DOUGLAS H. GRAHAM, GEETHA NAGARAJAN AND KOROTOUMOU QUATTARA*

Financial Liberalization, Bank Restructuring and the Implications for Non-Bank Intermediaries in the Financial Markets of Africa: Lessons from The Gambia

Abstract: Research on structural adjustment, liberalization and privatization in sub-Saharan Africa has not focused on the consequences of these policy initiatives on the financial sector. This paper documents and discusses the consequences of these reforms on the financial sector in The Gambia. Marked changes in the market structure and portfolio composition of the bank sector severely ration loan activity, particularly in rural areas. This creates a vacuum in which non-bank intermediaries currently operate with varying degrees of moral hazard and principal agent problems. The institutional design for non-bank intermediaries necessary to ensure a viable sustained supply of financial services for a rural clientele in Africa is discussed.

INTRODUCTION

Structural adjustment programmes and the liberalization of markets have traced a checkered path through recent African history. Documentation and analysis of the consequences of financial market liberalization, however, have been less evident in the literature on structural adjustment, which invariably focuses on fiscal and trade balances. At the same time, sub-Saharan African countries have become a laboratory for innovative approaches to reach a marginal clientéle with financial services. Although rarely analysed, there is a logical interrelationship between these two distinct macro and micro oriented developments in recent African financial history. This paper highlights the key consequences of structural adjustment on the financial sector and the implications for financial reforms and the emergence of client-owned non-bank financial intermediaries in the rural financial markets of The Gambia, as representative of the experience of many sub-Saharan African countries.

The Gambia serves as a revealing example of the impact of liberalization on institutional change in the financial sector. The country's experience illustrates how the private sector market demand has responded to the challenge of financial reform and draws out lessons for one increasingly travelled path of financial reform within structural adjustment efforts in Africa.

THE GAMBIA: FROM SUPPLY LEADING FINANCE TO PRIVATIZED FINANCIAL MARKETS

The principal macroeconomic parameters for The Gambia are presented in Table 1. Rising rates of inflation, negative real interest rates, growing budget deficits, and a low growth profile emerged by the mid-1980s. This state of affairs led the government to initiate the Economic Recovery Programme later reinforced by structural adjustment loans from the

* The Ohio State University, USA.

IMF and the World Bank (McPherson and Radelet, 1991). Increasingly rigorous stabilization policies have substantially reduced the rate of inflation from 1988 to the present. The thrust of liberalization in these programmes decisively reshaped the financial sector, which consists of a large public sector development bank and the branches of three international banks. Credit ceilings on the volume of credit were phased out as more traditional methods were established to control the money supply (i.e., open market operations in government securities). Interest rate ceilings were also removed and subsidized interest rates were eliminated, with positive real rates of interest emerging from 1988 onwards. In short, all the distortions and subsidies of the selective credit policies so characteristic of the former supply leading financial development strategy were removed.

Table 1 *Selected Macro-financial Indicators of Growth in The Gambia*

		Financial sector indicators			Real growth of bank credit (1981=100)	
Year	GDP growth rate	GDP deflator (%)	Real loan rate: agric. loans	Loan deposit ratio (private banks)	Agricultural credit	Total credit
1984	–4.5	17.2	–0.4	-	84	89
1985	3.1	8.6	–5.2	-	82	87
1986	2.5	42.9	–10.1	0.45	66	68
1987	2.8	29.9	–16.2	0.35	40	48
1988	1.7	6.4	6.4	0.25	44	47
1989	4.1	13.2	9.2	0.31	32	47
1990	5.6	14.6	9.8	0.31	19	40
1991	2.1	9.9	18.8	0.33	20	40

Source: Central Bank of The Gambia, various bulletins, reported in Graham, *et al.*, 1993.

Finally, a complete privatization of the supply of financial services emerged in July 1992 as the once dominant public sector Gambia Commercial and Development Bank (GCDB) sold its deposit base and a small part of its remaining non-delinquent portfolio to an international bank (Meridien). Instead of privatizing the GCDB itself, a small portion of its performing loans and an ample supply of treasury bills balanced out all its deposit liabilities and were transferred to this private international bank that agreed to enter the banking sector under these conditions. In effect, this buyout represented an implicit deposit insurance bailout vehicle for the government as it found an international bank to assume the deposit liabilities of a failing public sector bank it would otherwise have had to assume itself. Therefore, by late 1992, the banking sector consisted of the branches of four private international banks. The earlier experiment of creating a semi-specialized development bank came to an end as deregulation successfully privatized the country's entire supply of financial services.

Nevertheless, this path of liberalization created important consequences. Columns 5 and 6 of Table 1 highlight the substantial decline in total bank credit and, in particular, agricultural credit that accompanied this process of stabilization, liberalization and privatization. The ratio of agricultural credit to agricultural GDP declined from a range of

30 to 40 percent in the early to mid-1980s to 7 to 8 percent in the early 1990s as a result of the strong urban bias growing out of this financial market reform.

Two features of this decline merit comment. First, much of the decline in the outstanding credit balances, particularly for agriculture, is a reflection of the growing defaults in the GCDB that were finally written off as losses with the closure of this public sector bank in 1992. The decline in the credit balances for the performing loan portfolios of the private sector banks, though evident, was much less severe. Secondly, with the sharp decline in the supply of agricultural credit it is clear that groundnut producers and other rural clientéle have been substantially rationed out of the urban-biased portfolios of the remaining formal sector private banks. Given the high risk and high incidence of defaults in the agricultural portfolio, this is not surprising. Nevertheless, it is important to note that urban-based formal bank networks are not a viable institutional design for removing the dangers of moral hazard in the supply of rural credit in Africa. Other institutional innovations are required to service this missing market niche on a viable self-sustaining basis.

Table 2 *Asset Composition and Rates of Return on Loans and Non-loan Assets in the Gambian Private Banking Sector for Selected Years, 1986–91*

Year	1986	1987	1988	1989	1990	1991
	(1)	(2)	(3)	(4)	(5)	(6)
	A	Relative share of assets				
1. Cash	3.1	3.4	3.4	2.3	2.1	4.5
2. Government securities	25.2	31.4	45.9	45.5	50.4	42.8
3. Loans and advances	26.3	24.9	18.6	21.3	23.9	26.6
4. Other assets	45.4	40.7	32.1	30.9	23.7	26.1
5. Total assets	100.0	100.0	100.0	100.0	100.0	100.0
	B	Rates of return on loans and nonloan assets				
1. Return on loan assets			–3.9	10.3	7.9	-
2. Return on non-loan assets			14.4	14.2	15.2	-
3. Return on total assets			11.2	13.3	13.3	-

Source: Graham *et al.* (1993).

At the same time, an additional portfolio shift can be seen in the loan/deposit ratio for private banks, which declined from 45 percent in the mid-1980s to 31–33 percent by the early 1990s (Table 1, column 4). The low and declining loan/deposit ratio for private banks raises questions about the asset structure of the banking system. On the one hand, a sharp decline in loan activity has been recorded from the early 1980s. Clearly, some asset other than loans has risen in relative importance in the asset portfolio of the banking industry from 1986 to the present to absorb the excess liquidity in the banking system. The evidence in Table 2 is clear. Short term treasury bills (i.e., government securities) rose rapidly in the portfolios of the three commercial banks that eventually comprised the entire banking industry by the end of 1992. Whereas in 1986 treasury bills comprised only 25 percent of total assets, by 1990 they had increased to 50 percent of the asset portfolios of the private sector banks. This is far higher than the ratios typically recorded for government and corporate securities held by banks in developed countries (i.e., 20–25 percent).

From 1988 onwards the relative weight of treasury bills in total assets grew to roughly twice that of loans. In the final analysis, this risk-free return of T-bills clearly outweighed the risk-adjusted returns in the loan market. Table 2, panel B underlines this risk feature by comparing the rates of return to loan and non-loan activity for private commercial banks in the banking industry of The Gambia from 1988 to 1990. First, the risks of lending are apparent through both the negative returns recorded in 1988 and the greater variance in returns compared to non-loan activity (primarily returns from T-bills and foreign exchange transactions). The returns on non-loan activity are substantially higher and more stable through time, and unusually high by international standards. Rates of return on assets of only one to two percent are already considered high in the banking industry in developed economies. The high rates in The Gambia grow out of the wide gross intermediation margins of 15 to 16 points registered by banks in the country, which are three to four times higher than those characteristic of banks in more developed financial markets and clearly reflect the higher risks of lending and the lack of competition in the banking industry in The Gambia.

The challenge now facing the Gambian authorities is to expand and broaden financial intermediation beyond the mere transfer of the public deposits into securities to cover the government's budget deficits. More attention must be given to the encouragement of institutional innovations to increase the supply of financial services to the admittedly riskier rural clientéle that have been largely rationed out of bank portfolios through this path of deregulation and privatization. The degree to which NGOs can satisfactorily fill this vacuum and supply viable, self-sustaining financial services to their low-income constituencies is the challenge facing many African countries.

NONBANK FINANCIAL INTERMEDIATION: THE NGO OPTION

NGO services grow most rapidly in a liberalized economy and in a democratic policy environment. The relatively more liberal and open society in The Gambia has stimulated a response from several NGOs to create an alternative supply of financial services for their marginal constituencies. Their diverse operational philosophies, however, have resulted in heterogenous financial technologies that send mixed market signals and create market segmentation. Indeed, the entry of NGOs in the rural financial markets of The Gambia to overcome the lack of government services and the limited reach of formal financial services has led to a number of cases of market failure (Graham *et al.*, 1993). This raises the question of whether NGOs can develop into viable semi-formal financial institutions. An examination of the NGO experiences in The Gambia can shed some light on the role of NGOs as financial intermediaries and indicate possible policy implications for the financial sector in newly liberalized economies in Africa.

Principal-agent problems are allegedly low for NGOs compared to formal lenders such as banks due to information advantages gained from their operations at the grassroots level. However, problems inherent to rural financial markets remain in terms of developing incentive compatible contracts, contract enforcement and effective monitoring of agents. Lack of regulatory guidelines for NGOs in The Gambia, combined with lack of legal support to enforce contracts, offers weak incentives for the development of sustainable financial programmes by NGOs. The majority of these programmes are frequently designed as an opportunistic response to donor signals, with little emphasis on programme viability and sustainability. The problems can, however, be minimized through appropriate organizational design. The operational characteristics of four different NGO programmes that currently provide financial services in rural Gambia are reviewed. The evidence on their performance offers insights into the organizational features conducive to a sustainable supply of financial services.

NGOs became active participants in Gambian financial markets in the 1980s as a result of economic liberalization and the concomitant decline in formal financial services. Currently, 14 national and international NGOs provide financial services which supply nearly 20 percent of total agricultural loans (Graham *et al.*, 1993). The operational strategies of these several NGOs range from the classic supply leading model to more unsubsidized institutions. Table 3 summarizes the operational strategies and performance indicators of four representative designs which can be arranged in a continuum based on their level of subsidization.

At one extreme, in column one of Table 3, Action Aid, The Gambia (AATG), represents a typical supply leading model that is supported by external funds and offers subsidized loans to a targeted clientele. At the other extreme, in column four, the Village Savings and Credit Associations (VISACAs) offer untargeted loans at market rates using locally mobilized resources and attractive deposit services. The middle section of the continuum is composed of The Gambia Women's Financing Association (GWFA) that offers only unsubsidized loans using external funds and no deposit services, and the Association of Farmers, Educators and Teachers (AFET) that mobilizes local savings, to a large extent to provide unsubsidized loans that are linked to savings held by the beneficiaries.

In general, the evidence in Table 3 suggests that the sustainability of a programme depends largely on its ability to: generate internal funds through deposit mobilization by offering attractive interest rates to fund loans; cover operational costs without external subsidization; mitigate risks due to covariance in incomes through geographic and portfolio diversification; reduce agency problems through an increased stake of the depositor-savers and the local loan approval committee; develop appropriate collateral substitutes in the absence of tangible collateral held by the population, and recover loans. If performance indicators such as loan recovery rate, marginal clients served and services offered are a reflection of the efficiency of a programme followed by an NGO, the VISACA stands out as the best model to attain sustainability.

In summary, the emphasis on locally mobilized resources to supply loans and the use of local personnel to screen applicants have helped the VISACAs to reduce loan monitoring and contract enforcement costs. Furthermore, their attractive savings programmes that are flexible, remunerative and accessible with minimal transaction costs, provide incentives for savings mobilization and induce an incentive-compatible environment for contract enforcement on borrowers, as local saver-depositors closely monitor the use of their funds by borrowers. In addition, their use of both tangible collateral and effective collateral substitutes to supply loans to asset-poor members and enforce contracts contributes towards their success in loan repayment. The VISACA model is clearly a Pareto improvement over the other NGO models in The Gambia. As indicated in line 7, its agency problem of moral hazard is low in comparison to those of the

Table 3 *Operational Characteristics of Selected NGO Designs in Providing Financial Services and their Performance Indicators: The Case of The Gambia*

Items	NGOs			
	Action Aid The Gambia (AATG)	Gambian Women Financial Association (GWFA)	Association Farmers, Educators, Trainers (AFETs)	Village Savings and Credit Association (VISACAs)
	(1)	(2)	(3)	(4)
1. Status	International	National	National	Hybrid
2. Sponsors	UK[1]	WID of WB[1]	DANIDA[1], US embassy	CIDR/KFW[1]
3. Organizational design features				
a. Operational philosophy	Encourage income generating activities	Production loans	Improve access to financial services through village banks	Provide unsubsidized financial services
b. Source of funds for financial services	External	External	Local savings; some external	All local savings
c. Financial services offered	Credit, compulsory savings	Credit	Credit and savings	Credit and savings
d. Target clientele	Women and farmers	Women	Microbus, women and youth	Untargeted
e. Mode of reaching clientele	Mostly kafo groups	Individuals	Mostly kafo groups	Mostly individuals

Table 3 *Operational Characteristics of Selected NGO Designs in Providing Financial Services and their Performance Indicators: The Case of The Gambia* (continued)

Items	NGOs			
	Action Aid The Gambia (AATG)	Gambian Women Financial Association (GWFA)	Association Farmers, Educators, Trainers (AFETs)	Village Savings and Credit Association (VISACAs)
	(1)	(2)	(3)	(4)
4. Terms and conditions and instruments used				
a. Loan int. rate (%/yr)	12	24–25	24	40–60
b. Savings int. rate (%/yr)	0	-	15–18	20–40
c. Collateral	Group liability	Co-signers	Guarantors and savings	Animals, tools and jewelry
5. Subsidy component				
a. External technical assistance	High	Moderate	High	Moderate
b. Operational costs	High	High	Moderate	None
6. Performance Indicators (as of 1991)				
a. No. of loans issued	246 individuals; 53 groups	66 individuals	1343 individuals	1266 individuals
b. Ave. short term loan size ($)	25	580	28	37
c. Repayment rate (%)	42	75	72	95
d. Percent of women clients	63	100	82	52
7. Agency Problem	Severe	Moderate	Moderate	Low

Source: Graham *et al.*, 1993, chapters 1, 2 and 5.

Notes: UK: United Kingdom, WID of WB: Women in Development Division of the World Bank, DANIDA: Danish International Development Aid, CIDR/KFW: Centre International de Développement et de Recherce/Kreditanstalt fur Wiederaufbau.

other NGO designs. However, it is still susceptible to systemic failure due to its design as a village unit rather than as a broad network that could mitigate covariant income through geographic diversification. Furthermore, there are some limitations to locally available resources that can be mobilized in VISACAs. Hence, the VISACAs' loan portfolio is constrained by the economic activities of the region in which they operate. Nevertheless, in the end the model underlines the positive impact of local savings on the portfolio performance of the village banks.

CONCLUSIONS

Several conclusions may drawn from this study. First, it is clear that stabilization and deregulation was a necessary condition for The Gambia eventually to work itself out of growing economic stagnation from the late 1980s onwards. Secondly, it is also clear that deregulation of markets and a need to clean up the balance sheets of an insolvent development bank led to a decline in the real levels of outstanding credit from the levels established during the period of supply leading finance in the early to mid-1980s. This was, however, to be expected, given the high level of non-performing loans inflating the credit data for the earlier era. Thirdly, it is clear that there was a sectoral incidence in the reallocation of the portfolio of formal financial markets as agricultural lending declined relative to non-agricultural lending. In the meantime, riskier but potentially remunerative low-income clientele, particularly rural clientéle, were screened out of formal financial sector portfolios. In short, formal sector banking institutions have the resources, but not the information nor the contract enforcement mechanisms to service this clientéle.

Finally, it would appear that non-bank financial institutions can play a positive role in servicing the demand for financial services from this low-income rural clientéle. In The Gambia, several NGO initiatives are under way to fill the vacuum left by the downscaling and elimination of government subsidized credit delivery vehicles in rural areas. While local NGOs presumably have a comparative advantage over formal banks in the quality of local borrower information, they do not necessarily have the means to deal with effective monitoring and contract enforcement at this level. The evidence to date strongly suggests that local deposit-savings mobilization is essential to ensure a proper organizational incentive for effective monitoring and contract enforcement. Deposit services in village banks or savings and credit associations generate valuable services of safekeeping, liquidity reserves and returns on savings. Liquidity reserves are particularly important for rural clientele to manage risk and smooth consumption. Subsidization is legitimate in these cases for initial start-up costs and technical assistance support over a period of time. However, unsubsidized market rates should prevail for deposits and loans; otherwise, subsidized loan rates will come at the expense of a lower return for net savers in these institutions, weakening the base for local deposit mobilization.

In conclusion, it is necessary to document more fully the numerous NGO (non-bank) experiments currently operating in Africa. Some recent scholarship on the multiple roles and functions of informal contracts and the way in which they substitute for missing markets has enriched the literature (Udry, 1990; Eswaran and Kotwal, 1989), but it is more sparse on the recent experience of semi-formal financial intermediaries and the degree to which they can resolve the information and contract enforcement problems necessary to expand the frontier of finance in rural Africa and open the possibility for linking formal and informal financial markets.

REFERENCES

Eswaran, Muskesh and Kotwal, Ashok, 1989, 'Credit as Insurance in Agrarian Economies', *Journal of Development Economics*, No. 31, pp.7–54.

Graham, D. H. *et al.*, 1993, '*Financial Markets in The Gambia: 1981-1991*, A Report to the USAID Mission', The Ohio State Rural Finance Program, Banjul, The Gambia.

McPherson, M.F. and Radelet, S., 1991, 'Economic Reform in The Gambia: Policies, Politics, Foreign Aid and Luck', in Perkins, D.H. and Roemer, M. (eds.), *Reforming Economic Systems in Developing Countries*, Harvard University Press.

Udry, C., 1990, 'Credit Markets in Northern Nigeria: Credit as Insurance in a Rural Economy', *World Bank Economic Review*, Vol. 4, No. 3, pp.251–269.

DISCUSSION OPENING — Herbert I. Behrmann *(University of Natal, Republic of South Africa)*

This paper has been interesting to me in highlighting a particularly successful NGO form of credit Association, VISACA. It is reminiscent of the Raiffeisen system of cooperative credit that was developed in Germany in the nineteenth century. It is notable that the types of variable cost inputs that are financed with moveable collateral as security are those that realize high marginal returns but inputs that are not likely to be financed by banks because of the high risks. Simple, and not excessively punitive, rules are needed to administer such a form of credit.

A system of informal savings associations has developed on a large scale in South Africa called 'Stokvels' and there is apparently literature available on the functioning of this system.

RICHARD L. MEYER, GEETHA NAGARAJAN AND LEROY J. HUSHAK*

Segmentation in The Philippine Informal Credit Markets: A Multinomial Logit Analysis

Abstract: The paper explains the market segmentation that occurs in the Philippine informal credit markets through the matching of borrowers and lenders by their occupational specializations which internalizes transaction costs and facilitates economic activity. The regression results support a predictable pattern of matching farmer lenders with borrowers specialized in non-farm activities and trader lenders with borrowers specialized in farming.

INTRODUCTION

The informal credit market has reemerged in the 1980s as an important source of rural credit in the Philippines. The formal credit market was active during the 1970s but suffered a severe contraction in the 1980s due to the insolvency of many rural banks (Blanco and Meyer, 1989). The reemergence of the informal credit market has been accompanied by a change in the composition of informal lenders. Traditional moneylenders and landlords have been replaced by specialized farmer and trader lenders. Currently, they are the primary sources of credit in rice growing areas. They offer differentiated credit contracts usually involving linkages of credit with labour, land and product markets (Adams and Sandoval, 1992; Esguerra and Meyer, 1992; Floro and Yotopoulos, 1991; Geron, Nagarajan, 1988).

The existence of different credit contracts offered by various types of lenders would seem to imply competitive credit markets. It has been observed, however, that trader lenders tend to offer loan contracts to large, asset rich farmers, while farmer lenders tend to lend to small, asset poor farmers and landless labourers (Esguerra and Meyer, 1992; Floro and Yotopoulos, 1991). This paper argues that these observed patterns based on occupational specializations indicate a segmented market in which specialized borrowers and lenders are matched through loan contracts designed to internalize transaction costs. The two way matching of borrowers and lenders has two effects: (a) it reduces information problems inherent in credit markets and enhances borrower screening and contract enforcement mechanisms for lenders, and (b) it increases the quality of services received by specialized borrowers with specialized lenders rather than with non-specialized lenders. On the one hand, the risk and transaction costs associated with the contracts that suit the occupational specialization of utility maximizing lenders influence the type of borrowers preferred by them and hence the type of contracts offered to borrowers. On the other hand, the qualitative attributes of the contracts and the costs and risks involved in negotiating the contracts that suit the occupational specialization of utility maximizing borrowers determine their contract choice. Consequently, a one-to-one matching often occurs between specialized borrowers and lenders resulting in segmentation.

This paper rationalizes the observed segmentation based on occupational specialization and empirically tests the determinants that match informal lenders and borrowers in

* The Ohio State University, USA.

informal credit markets in a major rice growing area in the Philippines. These determinants help predict contract access and choice given lender and borrower characteristics, and provide evidence of market segmentation due to the occupational specializations of borrowers and lenders. The informal credit market is comprised of various types of lenders including traders, farmers, moneylenders, input dealers, rice millers, retail store owners, and friends and relatives. This paper concentrates on rice traders and farmer lenders because they are the primary sources of credit.

DESCRIPTION OF THE SAMPLE

The data used in this study were collected from two villages located in the major rice growing Nueva Ecija province in Central Luzon by the International Rice Research Institute during the period 1985–86 and 1989[1] The sample includes 127 randomly selected rice farming households and 29 lower income landless households that operated no farms. The majority of farms are irrigated by gravity irrigation systems and grow two rice crops a year. Furthermore, the farms are small and 83 percent of the land is under land reform beneficiary status[2]. Before land reform, the farms were large rice haciendas and the majority of farmers were share tenants. Land use and income source indicate that the occupational specialization of farm households is farming, but the observation of more than three non-farm employment sources per landless household suggests that their specialization is non-farm (Table 1).

Table 1 *Socio-Economic Characteristics of the Sample Households*

Items	FHH [a]	LHH[b]
Sample farm households (number)	127.0	29.0
Area irrigated (%)	72.0	-
Rice cropping intensity (%)	179.0	-
Average farm size (Ha.)	2.1	-
Area under beneficiary status (%)[c]	83.0	-
Area under non beneficiary status (%)[d]	15.0	-
Area under share tenancy (%)	2.0	-
Average farm income ('000 P/Yr)	17.4	-
Average no. of off and non-farm Employment sources/season	1.6	2.8
Average non and off farm income ('000 P/Yr)	8.20	3.28

Notes: FHH = Farm households; LHH = Landless households.

For the 156 households interviewed, 774 loan contracts were reported in three seasons from 191 different lenders; 131 different trader and farmer lenders accounted for 529 of the loans. In general, trader lenders specialized in agricultural trading while farmer lenders tended to be large, rich farmers specialized in farming. Table 2 shows that a higher proportion of farm households than landless households borrow from trader lenders and they provided larger sized loans to farm households than do farmer lenders. While the average seasonal interest rates were similar across both lender types, it was higher with trader than farmer lenders for landless households.

Collateral in the form of buildings, livestock, jewels etc., were seldom used to secure loans but a variety of collateral substitutes were used including tied contracts and guarantors. The majority of the loans were tied with product, labour and land markets. The frequency of linking credit with product markets was higher with trader than with farmer lender loans.

Table 2 *Loan Contracts of the Sample Farm and Landless Households, by Lender Type*

Item	Trader		Farmer	
	FHH[a]	LHH[b]	FHH[a]	LHH[b]
No. different lenders	26	8	85	19
No. of loan contracts	247	16	233	33
No. loans per lender	9.5	2.0	2.7	1.7
Ave. loan size ('000 P/contract)	6.01	1.03	2.11	0.72
Ave. seasonal interest rate (%/season)[e]	25.6	26.2	24.3	20.1
% Contracts with collateral	2	2	4	5
Contract linkages (% of contracts)				
Product link	84	47	58	14
Labour link	4	22	9	43
Land link	2	0	8	2
Land+labour+product links	0	11	1	14
No links	10	20	24	27
Information base for lenders (% of contracts)				
Friends and relatives	16	23	79	59
Business partners	55	28	3	17
Neighbours	29	2	16	14
None	0	47	2	10

Notes: [a] FHH = Farm households; LHH = Landless households; [b] Refers to land with Certificate of Land Transfer (CLT) or Leasehold (LH) tenurial status; [c] Refers to Owner Cultivator (OC) tenurial status;[d] Refers to Certificate of land transfer (CLT) or Leasehold (LH) tenurial status; [e] Season = 5 months.

Although the majority of loans received from farmer lenders were also linked with farm products, land and labour links were frequently used to secure these loans. The majority of loans made by traders to landless households involved product links while labour and land links were involved in farmer lender loans[3]. A typical loan contract from a trader lender required borrowers to repay with farm products, and a stipulation 'tampa' additionally required them to sell their entire marketable surplus to the lender so that economies of scale can be realized[4]. The trader lenders usually specialized in rice so their contracts were specified in terms of rice. On the other hand, since farmer lenders were directly involved in farming requiring land and labour, loan repayment was accepted in kind or linked to land and labour markets. They did not insist on 'tampa' and supplied loans to landless households by linking loans to labour and land markets[5] Land linked contracts involved the pawning of cultivation rights in which the borrower (pawner) temporarily transfers cultivation rights to the lender (pawnee) for a loan and redeems the rights upon loan repayment. In labour linked contracts, borrowers were required to provide lenders with permanent or temporary labour services.

There were many farmer loans, however, with no explicit factor market links, but with an implicit promise of reciprocity. This phenomena is explained by the large percentage of loans made to friends, relatives and neighbours. On the other hand, the majority of trader loans were made to business partners and borrowers with no familial ties. In the absence of formalized contracts, long term familial and business relations assure a well established informational base that enhances the lender's operational efficiency in loan screening and contract enforcement.

MATCHING OF BORROWERS AND LENDERS

The lenders use collateral substitutes to screen their borrowers and enforce contracts. However, a lender's technology to assimilate the information that a collateral substitute reveals about the borrower and his ability to enforce contracts varies with his occupational specialization. An occupation specific collateral substitute performs three functions: (a) it promotes a specialized lender's primary economic activity, (b) it provides a specialized lender with a relatively low cost technology to decipher information on borrower creditworthiness, and (c) it assists a specialized lender to more effectively enforce contracts compared to non-specialized lenders.

Let us assume two specialized lenders: trader lenders primarily specialized in agricultural trading and farmer lenders primarily specialized in farming. Trading is enhanced by marketing a large quantity at a low cost, while farming is facilitated by using enough land and labour to operate an economically viable farm. It can be postulated that trader lenders prefer to deal with farmer borrowers with the capacity to produce a marketable surplus large enough to help them to maximize their returns through economies of scale. Farmer lenders, on the other hand, require land and labour for farming. Therefore, they prefer to lend to farmer borrowers with secure land tenure status because cultivation rights can be transferred in the event of loan default. Also these households can offer family labour as collateral in labour linked contracts.

The supply of loans provided by trader and farmer lenders depends upon the information they have about borrowers that is obtained through long term business and familial relationships. This information is important in screening borrowers. Lenders have different technological abilities to acquire and utilize information. Although this information may be incomplete, the cost of obtaining it in the informal credit market is low compared to the formal credit market due to the physical proximity of the participants (Stiglitz, 1990). Related transactions in factor and product markets provide information that lenders can use to evaluate the borrower creditworthiness and repayment type[6].

Borrowers in rural areas tend to specialize in farming or in non-farm activities. Utility maximizing borrowers with access to multiple contracts tend to choose contracts perceived to be most advantageous. A borrower's occupational specialization provides resources that can be used as a collateral substitute with specialized lenders. For instance, we consider that a borrower has access to non-exclusive product linked contracts from both a trader lender and a farmer lender, and that there is no loan size rationing. The borrower can choose either contract to satisfy his loan demand. The majority of farmer lenders offer an advantage by charging lower interest rates than trader lenders, but trader lenders offer marketing services in addition to credit. These marketing services are especially important for farmers who specialize in farming and produce a large marketable surplus. Therefore, a farmer specialized in intensive farming and facing an imperfect product market will prefer borrowing from a trader lender rather than a farmer lender if product market access can be guaranteed.

Furthermore, in the absence of contingent markets, a risk averse borrower in an uncertain production environment will prefer a risk sharing contract. Trader lenders more often than farmer lenders offer loans with a built-in risk sharing mechanism in terms of loan rollover to the next season. A farmer lender would more likely request the borrower's cultivation rights in the event of loan default. In other words, there is a demand for risk-sharing contractual arrangements that act as insurance in the absence of contingent markets. Therefore, a borrower primarily specializing in farming will prefer a trader lender while a borrower specializing in non-farm activities will prefer a farmer lender because of his ability to offer land cultivation rights as collateral in exchange for loans.

The lender's flexibility in providing loans for borrower-specific purposes also influences contract choice. While the product tied loans from trader lenders allow little flexibility to divert loans to consumption purposes, farmer lender loans can be explicitly used for consumption provided the borrowers implicitly tie loans to land or labour services. Whereas loans are often fungible, the close monitoring by lenders or peers and penalties for default reduce fungibility in informal credit markets (Stiglitz, 1990).

For these reasons, the matching of lenders and borrowers can be explained by (a) the borrower's ability to offer collateral that is valued by lenders resulting in differential access to specialized lenders, and (b) the lender's ability to provide borrower specific services leading to the borrower's contract choice from among the accessible set of contracts. Consequently, a predictable pattern of loan contracts emerges that matches heterogenous borrowers and lenders. It can be posited that trader lenders are matched with borrowers who specialize in farming by operating larger farm sizes that produce a larger marketable surplus. Farmer lenders, however, tend to be matched with borrowers who specialize in non-farm activities, who operate smaller farm sizes and possess fewer total assets, but can provide more labour and secure land ownership rights to the lender. In the following section, these propositions are tested using the cross sectional data described above.

ECONOMETRIC ANALYSIS AND RESULTS

Since borrowers are matched with more than one type of specialized lender, a multinomial logit model is used to test the propositions stated above. The multinomial logit model helps predict the probability of matching heterogenous lenders and borrowers with particular characteristics. A general multinomial logit model with normalization of $\beta_1 = 1$ can be written as follows:

$$(1) \quad \frac{P_{ij}}{P_{i1}} = \alpha_0 + \beta_j' X_i + u_{ij}$$

for j = 2,3,4 outcomes, where, j = 4 observed outcomes including no matching (NB), or match with either traders (TL), farmers (FL) or other type of lenders (OT), $i = 1,2,....,n$ represents the borrower households, β is a vector of parameters to be estimated, and X is a vector of explanatory variables.

Table 3 *Matching of Informal Lenders and Borrowers: Multinomial Logit Estimates*

Variables	Multinomial Logit : FI/TI Model 1	Model 2	Model 3
	(Probabilities with respect to denominator)		
CONSTANT	1.934***	1.289*	2.049***
	(0.743)	(0.786)	(0.859)
ASSET	–0.204***	–0.210***	–0.146***
	(0.069)	(0.075)	(0.059)
EDUHH	0.149***	0.170***	0.104*
	(0.058)	(0.059)	(0.057)
CLTLH	–1.202**	–1.257**	–0.976*
	(0.554)	(0.558)	(0.603)
OC	–0.810	–1.067	–1.152
	(0.710)	(0.679)	(0.732)
DCUST	–2.63***	–2.388***	–2.989***
	(0.459)	(0.474)	(0.430)
REPUTE	0.985*	1.202**	0.566
	(0.542)	(0.561)	(0.522)
FSIZE	–0.148	–0.066	–0.055
	(0.185)	(0.186)	(0.173)
RETURNS	–0.257*	–0.277*	–0.252**
	(0.142)	(0.152)	(0.121)
LABOR	–0.079	–0.073	–0.025
	(0.102)	(0.102)	(0.101)
NONFARM	0.359	0.236	0.178
	(0.232)	(0.240)	(0.211)
Log-likelihood	–343.64	–327.38	–337.35
Chi-square	269.94	252.39	252.56

Notes: Asymptotic standard errors are reported in parentheses.
***, **, * represent significance at 1, 5 and 10 percent levels, respectively.
Model 1 uses interest rate as criterion for selecting marginal contracts.
Model 2 fixes trader lenders as marginal lenders.
Model 3 fixes farmer lenders as marginal lenders.

The independent variables are represented by the borrowing household's occupational specialization indicated by farm size in hectares (FSIZE), annual gross returns per hectare from rice farming (RETURNS) and annual nonfarm income (NONFARM). Human capital is denoted by the years of schooling of the household head (EDUHH) and the number of eligible labourers in the family (LABOR). The value of physical capital is measured by the market value of nonland assets (ASSETS) owned by the household. Security of tenure for land operated that can be used as collateral is captured by the proportion of total land operated by the household to land area under land reform beneficiary status (CLTLH) and under ownership status (OC). The ratio of number of years of residence in the village of the household head to his age (REPUTATION) and a dummy variable that captures the business customer relationship with the lender (DCUST) are proxies for the information available to the lenders. The variable DCUST refers to 1988-89, while all other variables refer to the year 1985 to avoid endogeneity problems[7].

A correctly specified multinomial logit model estimated by maximum likelihood methods gives consistent and efficient estimates. It is necessary, however, to ensure mutual exclusivity among the matching outcomes for correct model specification. This characteristic of the multinomial logit model is called Independence from Irrelevant Alternatives (Amemiya). Data indicate that about 23 percent of the FHH and 7 percent of the LHH were matched with more than one type of lender to satisfy their loan demand. An approximate mutual exclusivity among the outcomes can be ensured if matching observed only at the margin is considered for the analysis. Three criteria were used to select the marginal contract: contract with the highest implicit interest rate, trader lender as marginal lender, and farmer lender as marginal lender[8].

Three multinomial logit models were estimated, one for each criterion used to select the marginal contract. The results that compare traders with farmer lenders (FL/TL) are presented in Table 3. The results are consistent across the three models, and the significance of the likelihood ratios indicate a good fit[9]. The estimates are interpreted as the probability of observing the outcome in the numerator, FL, compared to the outcome in the denominator, TL. The negative and significant coefficients for ASSET and RETURNS variables show that poorer households with smaller marketable surplus tend to be matched with farmer rather than trader lenders. Conversely, borrowers who specialize in farming and have the ability to produce a larger marketable surplus are matched with trader lenders. The information variable REPUTE has a positive sign while DCUST has a negative sign. This shows that better reputation is more important than long-term customer relationships in a matching with farmer lenders, while it is the opposite with trader lenders. Farmer lenders use reputation as an information base when lending to poorer borrowers. This is not surprising since by their proximity the farmer lenders can accumulate better information about borrower creditworthiness through means other than customer relationships.

While the variable NONFARM is insignificant, a positive sign shows that borrowers who specialize in non-farm activities tend to be matched more with farmer than trader lenders. If the significant and positive coefficient for education, EDUHH, is an indication of borrower capacity to engage in education specific non-farm activities, there is some support for the borrower specialization hypotheses. The significant and negative coefficient for CLTLH indicates that land reform beneficiaries are matched with traders rather than farmers due to eviction risk but the negative sign for OC gives the opposite interpretation. This may imply that in practice there is little collateral specific risk due to tenurial status in the sample.

CONCLUSIONS AND POLICY IMPLICATIONS

The informal credit market is dominated by rice traders and farmer lenders in Philippine rice growing villages. They employ factor and product market ties and social relations to secure their loans with borrower households. We tested the argument that the matching of informal lenders with borrowers is based on their occupational specializations using primary data collected from rice growing villages. The regression results supported the argument. Trader lenders tend to be matched with borrowers who have a large rice production capacity, while farmer lenders tend to be matched with borrowers who use land, labour and product linked credit contracts and are engaged in non-farming activities.

This observed pattern in the matching of lenders with borrowers suggests that market segmentation occurs in rural informal credit markets based on occupational specialization. This segmentation limits the effective functioning of a particular type of lender to his/her specialized field where there exist adequate borrower screening technologies and contract enforcement mechanisms. Furthermore, access to loans from rice traders is limited to large farms specialized in rice production. There is a need for crop diversification due to environmental and income risks but these specialized lenders will find it difficult to service diversified farms. Lenders will have to incur high transaction costs to evaluate the creditworthiness of diversified farmers with whom they did not have other business transactions. Consequently, the core of eligible borrowers for the specialized lenders and the set of accessible lenders for diversified borrowers may be small unless the current specialized lenders develop information substitutes to service diversified farmers.

It would also be difficult to successfully introduce a formal credit institution to improve borrower access to credit. Formal institutions would have to solve borrower screening and contract enforcement problems in order to effectively compete with specialized lenders to provide borrower specific services. Since formal credit institutions cannot compete with informal lenders that specialize in trading, farming, etc., they must develop other mechanisms to provide borrower specific services at lower borrower screening and contract enforcement costs. The well documented failure of the Philippines rural banking system in the early eighties was due in part to its inability to develop financial technologies to meet this challenge. The experiments now underway in linking formal institutions with various types of informal financial arrangements may prove to be a more promising method to increase access to financial markets than the targeted credit approach of the earlier decades.

NOTES

1 The primary data on farm production, household income and demographic characteristics of the sample households were collected in 1985–86 and in 1988–89, while the data on the credit market transactions were collected in 1989.

2 Under the land reform of rice and corn lands in 1972, share tenants were supposed to be converted to Leaseholders (LH) by Operation Leasehold when the landlord owned less than 7 ha of land, or to Certificate of Land Transfer (CLT) holders under Operation Land Transfer when the landlord owned more than 7 ha of land (Hayami, Quisumbing and Adriano, 1990).

3 The majority of trader lenders owned and operated farms. Therefore, they provided loans to landless labourers who were employed on their farm. The loans were linked to either labour services or to earnings paid in rice.

4 While the 'tampa' condition is not explicitly stated in most of the product linked contracts from trader lenders, it is implicitly assumed by lenders and borrowers.

5 Although landless households in our sample refer to those that did not operate any land during the survey period, some previously owned land but pawned the land rights to the lender during the study period.

6 While familiar relationships and proximity reduce the endogenous risk of default due to borrower character, long term business relationships help a lender to form expectations about a borrower's ability to manage exogenous risks due to random shocks.

7 The variable DCUST is 1 if the borrower had a business customer relationship with the lender sometime during the previous 4 years and 0 otherwise.

8 See Nagarajan (1992) for details.

9 The Hausman and McFadden test (HM test) was performed on the above models to ensure absence of specification errors due to violation of the IIA property. The test statistic obtained for the three models was

4.99, 5.32 and 6.02, respectively. The null hypotheses that IIA holds could not be rejected at 0.90 confidence level indicating an absence of violation of IIA and confirming consistency of the estimates.

REFERENCES

Adams, D.W and Sandoval, V.N., 1992, 'Informal Finance in a Semi-rural Area of the Philippines', *Savings and Development*, Vol. 16, No. 2, pp.159–168.

Amemiya, T., 1985, *Advanced Econometrics*, Harvard University Press, Cambridge, Massachusetts.

Blanco, R. and Meyer, R.L., 1989, 'Rural Deposit Mobilization in the Philippines, 1977–1986', *Journal of Philippine Development*, Vol. 16, No. 1, pp.117–145.

Esguerra, E.F. and Meyer, R.L., 1992, 'Collateral Substitutes in Rural Informal Financial Markets: Evidence from an Agricultural Rice Economy', in Adams, D.W. and Fitchett, D. (eds.), *Informal Finance in Low Income Countries*, Westview Press, Colorado, pp.149–64.

Floro, S.L. and Yotopoulos, P., 1991, *Informal Credit Markets and the New Institutional Economics: The Case of Philippine Agriculture*, Westview Press, Colorado.

Geron, P., 1988, 'Microeconomic Behavior of Agents in a Credit-Output Market in an Agricultural Setting', unpublished Ph.D. dissertation, School of Economics, University of the Philippines.

Hayami, Y., Quisumbing, A. and Adriano, L., 1990, *Toward an Alternative Land Reform Paradigm: A Philippine Perspective*, Ateneo de Manila University Press, Quezon City.

Nagarajan, G., 1992, 'Informal Credit Markets in Philippine Rice Growing Areas', unpublished Ph.D. dissertation, The Ohio State University, Columbus, Ohio.

Stiglitz, J.E., 1990, 'Peer Monitoring and Credit Markets', *World Bank Economic Review*, Vol. 4, No. 3, pp.351–366.

DISCUSSION OPENING — John Sanders *(Purdue University, USA)*

This is a very nice paper showing how informal credit substituted for the breakdown of the formal Philippines rural sector financial institutions. This formal sector broke down at the start of the 1980s after a boom period in the 1970s. I had assumed that the bank failure was associated with the structural adjustment most developing countries were experiencing in the 1980s. At the end of the paper we are told that a principal factor in the insolvency of the formal rural financial sector were the high costs of the formal sector for borrower screening and contract enforcement. The informal sector could reduce the default risk and the transaction costs by knowing their borrowers and by tying loans to product delivery or to labour inputs to be provided by the borrowers. The emphasis of the paper then was on the identification of the characteristics of the borrowers associated with two principal types of lenders, larger farmers and traders. The statistical results then nicely separated the two classes of borrowers by farm and farmer characteristics.

As a discussant I would like to raise a conceptual issue in these types of studies and make a general observation about the evolution of institutions when there is rapid technical change in agriculture. First, is an important issue on diffusion studies in general. The theoretical underpinning of these studies is a demand function derived from the utility of credit, fertilizer, seeds or whatever is being evaluated, assuming that the supply is completely elastic. In many cases the price of the input is controlled in some way by the public sector and the input is then rationed to those demanding it. Diffusion studies identifying farmer characteristics are normally used in policy to attempt to facilitate the marketing of the input to the identified purchasers. With input supplies rationed the regressions can be identifying those able to obtain the rationed input. For example, larger farms would be expected to be able to work the system better to obtain subsidized inputs. The policy implications with input rationing then are very different. Rather than promote policies to facilitate those already getting the subsidized input, the results point to stopping the subsidies and letting the market function to allocate the input. And, if the government has equity goals, do something to increase the ability of the target group to purchase the input rather than subsidized inputs. By not specifying the theoretical assumptions in diffusion studies we can thus get into trouble when we get down to making policy recommendations. The Ohio State group is well aware of these issues of the inefficiency of subsidized inputs in resolving income equity problems. Moreover, the underlying assumption in this segmentation study is that credit costs are not controlled by the state. The segmented markets show who is able to get the credit and which market various types of borrowers access. The clear implication is that the segmentation then stresses the access problems and indicates the borrowers of choice in these informal markets.

Now there is a general issue of the role of credit in the process of rapid introduction of technological change. It is often argued that a fundamental requirement or even prerequisite for the technological change process is to have formal credit markets and some even argue for subsidized inputs. This study takes place in an area of rapid technological change in rice production and rapid technology introduction. It shows how when the formal credit markets broke down, the informal markets evolved and provided this input. This type of institutional evolution facilitating the process and responding to the new opportunities for increased income streams coming from technological change is exactly the types of operating mechanisms we would expect from the theory of induced innovation when it is also applied to induced institutional change.

Now if we could try to apply this to another region of the world which I know a little better, the Sahelian countries of West Africa. Here it is often argued that small farmers have no cash or access to formal or even to informal credit markets and therefore they cannot buy the new inputs associated with technological change. However, closer observation of these extended households shows that they receive remittances from relatives in other areas and that they acquire savings, which are kept in their animal stocks. They cash in these animal stock to use these remittances for certain consumption and social expenditures and could use them for input purchases. Hence, the problem of the failure to utilize technology does not appear to be associated with the supply of credit but with other factors discouraging them from investing in the new technologies. We treat these factors in some detail in a forthcoming book from Johns Hopkins Press entitled, *The Economics of Agricultural Technology in Semi-Arid Sub-Saharan Africa*. But the bottom line is that certain institutions such as the land tenure situation and the growth of the credit market are expected to evolve in the process of technological change with the pressure from the new income streams available with the use of these technologies. This makes the technological change processes much easier than if institutional credit and land reform from the communal system were prerequisites to the technological change process as is argued by some. This credit study in the Philippines illustrates nicely how institutions evolve and specialize to respond to the weaknesses in the previous system and by implication that there is substantial potential for institutional evolution where there is rapid technological change.

GEETHA NAGARAJAN, RICHARD L. MEYER AND DOUGLAS H. GRAHAM*

Institutional Design for Financial Intermediation by NGOs: Implications for Indigenous Self-Help Village Groups in The Gambia

Abstract: This paper examines the implications of the institutional designs employed by two types of NGOs for the functions performed by indigenous self-help village groups called *kafos* in The Gambia. NGOs were found to be only a partial substitute for the financial and insurance functions traditionally performed by these kafos. Institutional duality is, therefore, observed due to the coexistence of kafos alongside the NGOs providing the multiple services demanded by villagers. The design of NGO programs based on lessons learned from kafos tend to complement the kafos, and the villagers seem better served. These findings have implications for interventions which disrupt but only partially substitute for traditional village arrangements and institutions.

INTRODUCTION

Economists have begun to examine traditional informal village institutions and the implications of the coexistence of informal and formal institutions that provide services including a credit and insurance (Alderman and Paxon, 1992; Arnott and Stiglitz, 1991). Sub-saharan African (SSA) countries have a variety of multifunctional informal self-help groups that provide various services at the village level (Bouman, 1992). Such groups are called 'kafos' in The Gambia. Recently, non-governmental organizations (NGOs), frequently linked to international agencies, have rapidly expanded the scale and scope of their village-level operations in financial intermediation. While the operational designs of kafos are customized to suit the requirements of their members, the majority of NGO designs are conceived outside the village. Whereas some NGOs exert a *presence effect* by simply coexisting with kafos, others directly intervene into kafos, exerting an *intervention effect*[1]. While some NGOs follow the *savings first and untargeted credit approach*, others follow the classical supply-leading *credit first approach at subsidized rates*. The approach followed has profound effects on the functions performed and clientele served by the kafos.

The entry of NGOs into villages as financial intermediaries may cause the kafos either to disappear or to coexist with the NGOs leading to institutional duality. These developments have several distributional implications for the villages. This paper argues that the impact of introducing new institutions to resolve economic and social problems depends on their design that may either complement or substitute for indigenous village institutions. It provides insights about the implications of NGO institutional designs for kafos in The Gambia. The analysis is based on a purposive survey conducted in The Gambia on the functions performed by 41 kafos in 16 villages where two NGOs with different institutional designs are active.

* The Ohio State University, USA.

THE CONCEPTUAL MODEL

The kafos in The Gambia are multifunctional, voluntary and usually homogenous in terms of members' age, ethnicity, gender and occupation, but have various membership sizes. These kafos have evolved from simple age based groups to multifunctional self-help groups that provide multiple services including insurance, financial intermediation, labour exchange, and social and political services.[2]

Kafos traditionally fill in for missing markets by providing important village services. The recent emergence of NGOs with diverse approaches for providing village level financial intermediation may cause positive or negative externalities on kafos. For example, the NGOs may use external funds to make zero interest rate loans directly to individuals or may use the kafos as lending conduits. These loans may disrupt the traditional kafos that usually charge a positive interest rate on loans made from internally mobilized funds. This could destroy local savings mobilization if the villagers become dependent on cheap external funds.

The entrance of NGOs into villages may cause a shift in the relative importance *within and among the functions* performed by the traditional kafos depending on whether or not the NGO financial technologies complement or substitute for traditional kafo activities. Consequently, kafos may either disappear entirely due to a Darwinian process of complete substitution or institutional duality may occur. The NGOs will diminish or displace the kafos if their financial services are perfect substitutes for the financial, insurance and other services provided by kafos. Otherwise, institutional duality will occur with the kafos and NGOs simultaneously providing multiple services. Alternatively, the NGOs may only complement the insurance and financial services of kafos so they will continue to perform their traditional functions. As a result, institutional duality will emerge with a potentially healthy symbiotic relationship between kafos and NGOs resulting in a positive sum welfare game.

The emergence of NGOs as financial intermediaries provides an alternative financial system for villagers in a country where formal financial institutions provide few services in rural areas. Channelling financial services through kafos may increase their pool of resources and improve NGO loan recovery rates and reduce the transaction costs in mobilizing savings[3]. In this way, NGOs and kafos can be complementary resulting in a positive sum game. NGOs may also substitute for some or all of the kafo financial services leading to a more efficient use of kafo resources in alternative functions. Substitution, however, can be counterproductive if NGOs create negative externalities by providing financial services that destroy the carefully built institutional safeguards of the kafos. They may also contribute to the deterioration or discontinuation of traditional kafo insurance mechanisms that are especially useful to *marginal populations* (the elderly, women etc.) but are not offered by the NGOs. For these reasons, the specific approaches followed by NGOs in financial intermediation can influence traditional village institutions with a significant impact on villagers and their communities.

EMPIRICAL EVIDENCE FROM THE GAMBIA

The objective of this research was to examine the implications of NGOs providing financial services for the functions of traditional self-help village groups in The Gambia.

NGOs began offering financial services in the late 1980s and presently there are 14 NGOs using diverse institutional designs to supply financial services in rural and peri-urban villages (Graham *et al.*, 1992). We selected for study a total of 16 NGO and non-NGO villages, and two NGOs, Centre International de Development et de Recherche (CIDR) and Action Aid of the Gambia (AATG), that provide financial services. These two NGOs are active in rural areas where the majority of kafos are found, and their institutional designs are substantially different, allowing for interesting comparisons. Whereas Action Aid is a nationwide program, the CIDR provides only technical assistance to six villages in the Jahally-Pacharr area to set up and operate village savings and credit associations (VISACAs). Of the sixteen villages, five are serviced by both CIDR and Action Aid while the rest are serviced either by Action Aid alone or by no NGOs[4]. Data were gathered in two phases in 1991 and 1993 through the rapid appraisal approach and selected case studies of kafo activities in the sample villages.

Institutional Design Characteristics of the Action Aid and VISACAs

Action Aid uses external funds to provide subsidized loans to individuals through village kafos. The CIDR provides only technical assistance in the formation of VISACAs and encourages the village kafos to participate as clients in these savings and credit programs. We hereafter refer to CIDR activities as VISACAs. Action Aid does not mobilize local savings since it depends upon external donor funds to provide loans. In sharp contrast, the VISACAs rely almost exclusively on internally generated funds through village savings mobilization to supply loans to individuals and kafos at village determined interest rates. Furthermore, while Action Aid supplies loans only for production purposes and for women, the VISACAs do not target any specific loan purpose or clientele group. The VISACAs are owned and operated by the villagers and the savings and loan services are based on terms and conditions established in village wide assemblies. The terms and conditions for Action Aid loan programs, however, are set by external donors. Indeed, the institutional design of the VISACAs closely emulates the traditional village kafos. Therefore, the VISACAs can be considered endogenous to the village while Action Aid is an externally imposed institution. Furthermore, the VISACAs encourage the kafos to become members of their associations, while Action Aid directly uses kafos as conduits for loans to individual villagers. Therefore, the VISACAs influence kafos by their *presence* while Action Aid influences kafos by its *direct intervention* into their operations.

The Sample

A total of 41 kafos engaged in some form of financial intermediation and insurance functions were identified in the 16 villages and were examined for this study. The survey revealed that the kafos were fairly homogenous in member characteristics. Whereas 19 were comprised of only men and 14 were comprised of only women, eight were mixed gender. There were an average of three kafos per village and they were fairly large with an average membership size of 83 members, representing nearly 60 percent of the total adult village population (Table 1).

A classification based on level of NGO participation in the kafos showed that while 15 were not linked to any NGOs, 26 had some form of NGO involvement. Whereas 13 kafos functioned with no direct involvement with VISACAs and Action Aid but only subject to pure NGO presence effect in the region, three were subject to the intervention effect from Action Aid as conduits for its loans, and ten were subject to both the *presence effect* from VISACAs and the *intervention effect* from Action Aid through direct NGO involvement (Table 1). The kafo functions were clearly influenced by the degree of NGO participation in their activities as will be discussed later.

Table 1 *Characteristics and Activities Performed by Kafos, by NGO Activities*

Items	Total Sample	No NGOs Present	NGO Activity		
			Presence Effect	Intervention Effect	Presence and Intervention Effect
(1)	(2)	(3)	(4)	(5)	(6)
1. Number of kafos	41	15	13	3	10
2. Average number of members	83	46	116	57	104
a. male members	28	22	37	0	35
b. female members	55	24	79	57	69
3. Average age of kafos (years)	7	6	8	6	5
4. Activities performed (Number of kafos reporting)					
a. Insurance	31	12	8	3	8
b. Non-rotating savings and credit	31	13	9	3	6
c. Rotating savings and credit	6	0	2	0	4
d. Labour	11	2	4	0	5
e. Socio political	12	0	7	0	
5					
5. Total number of activities	91	27	30	6	28
6. Average number of activities/ kafo	2.2	1.8	2.3	2.0	2.8

Kafo Functions

The kafos generally were multifunctional and performed both economic and non-economic functions. These functions can be classified as four broad types:

Insurance In general, members (women, men or both) were engaged in a common activity such as jointly cultivating a plot of land and contributing the proceeds to a kafo fund primarily used to mitigate village level contingencies and, to a lesser extent, individual member contingencies. This type of group fund is often used to assist villagers who are economically disadvantaged to meet their emergency needs.

Financial intermediation Savings were mobilized without interest through regular fixed amounts of contributions to a group savings fund that was usually nonrotating in nature. Loans to kafo members for contingency needs were usually supplied from the fund at *a kafo determined interest rate*. Penalties for non-repayment of loans included social sanctions against the family of the borrower. The accumulated fund was equally divided among members at the end of a specified time (eg. ramadan feast). Rotating savings and credit associations (ROSCAs) are also increasingly found within kafos as a subset of their activities. Kafos used as conduits by Action Aid had an additional source of funds for lending from Action Aid. These kafos used part of these funds for production purposes on their common fields and lent out the rest to individual members.

Labour Labour was mobilized among kafo members and often hired out during periods of peak demand. The proceeds were divided among the members and, to a lesser extent, contributed to the kafo fund to meet member and kafo level contingencies.

Social and political These included the organization of soccer clubs, village festivals, political rallies, etc.

Based on the above classification, the activities of the kafos are presented in columns 3 to 6 in Table 1 by type of NGO participation in the village. Column 4 reports the number and characteristics of kafos that functioned with no direct involvement with VISACAs or Action Aid but only subject to pure NGO presence effect in the region. Column 5 provides details on kafos subject to the intervention effect from Action Aid as conduits for its loans. Column 6 describes the kafos that were subject to both the presence effect from VISACAs and the intervention effect from Action Aid through direct NGO involvement. The first important observation is that the traditional kafos did not disappear with the entry of NGOs into the villages but continued to coexist with them and continued to perform various activities including providing insurance and financial intermediation. This indicates that the financial services of the NGOs did not fully substitute for the traditional kafo activities. Secondly, the average number of kafo activities seems to have increased with the entry of NGOs into the village. The kafos in villages without NGOs primarily provided insurance and financial services, and temporary kafos were formed to provide labour and socio-political functions. With the emergence of NGOs as financial intermediaries, the kafos partially shifted from their traditional insurance and financial activities into labour and socio-political activities. In addition, since the NGOs were only a partial substitute, the kafos continued to perform some insurance and financial intermediation functions to provide the full range of services demanded by villagers. For example, the targeted production loans provided by Action Aid only partially satisfied the villager's demand for financial services, so kafos filled in the demand for contingency credit and savings services for their members. Thirdly, the observations on kafo sizes based on their type of NGO involvement shows no clear pattern. But, women's participation in kafos subject to the intervention effect from Action Aid is higher compared to other kafos because Action Aid specifically targets women.

Econometric Analysis and Results

Regression analysis was performed to explain the implications of NGO institutional design on kafo activities. While the VISACA is a village designed, non-interfering institution based on self-generated funds, the Action Aid is an externally designed program that directly intervenes into kafos with subsidized and targeted credit programs. It is difficult to separate the effects of terms and conditions from the intervention and non-intervention policies of the two NGOs. The limits on the tractability of the analysis, therefore, confine us to nest the presence and intervention effects along with terms and conditions such as the interest rate used by NGOs for providing financial services. Single equation logit models were estimated using the maximum likelihood method to examine the factors affecting the insurance and financial intermediation activities performed by kafos. The dependent variable is dichotomous, taking a value of 1 if the kafo performs insurance or financial intermediation, and 0 otherwise.

The independent variables include the ratio of number of kafo members to total population of the village, CONRATIO, and the gender composition of the kafo, GENDER, represented by the ratio of female members to total kafo members. The effect of NGO involvement is measured by four dummy variables where the value of one represents the following: NGOABS indicates absence of NGOs in the village, VISACA and AATG indicates involvement of VISACAs or Action Aid with the sample kafo, respectively, and VISAATG captures the interaction effect of both VISACA and Action Aid on the sample kafos. The regression analysis controls for the AATG dummy which is incorporated into the constant. The targeting of women kafos by Action Aid is represented by GENAATG calculated as the interaction between the GENDER and the AATG dummy.

Table 2 *Single Equation Logit Estimates for the Determinants of Insurance and Financial Activities of Kafos*

	Dependent Variable	
Independent Variables	Insurance	Financial Intermediation
(1)	(2)	(3)
Constant	1.209	0.629
	(1.181)	(1.071)
CONRATIO	–1.695	4.116
	(4.981)	(4.565)
GENDER	–3.096 *	–1.277
	(2.245)	(1.44)
NGOABS	0.374	1.278
	(1.154)	(1.222)
VISACA	–2.477 **	–0.457
	(1.529)	(1.072)
VISAATG	2.427 *	–1.506
	(1.673)	(1.275)
GENAATG	3.675 **	1.462
	(1.901)	(1.582)
Log-likelihood	–18.04	–20.78
Chi-square	9.47	6.84
Maddala R^2	0.21	0.17

Notes: Asymptotic standard errors given in parentheses.
**, * represent significance at 5 and 10 percent levels, respectively.

The regression results are presented in Table 2 and the corresponding weighted aggregate elasticities in Table 3. Significant chi-square values and good R^2 values confirm the explanatory power of this type of analysis of cross-section data. The signs of the variables are, in general, consistent with expectations. Column 2 presents the results for the insurance regressions. The negative and significant sign for the variable VISACA confirms the proposition stated earlier that the presence of the VISACAs in the villages tend to reduce the insurance functions performed by the kafos compared to Action Aid.

This indicates that the untargeted loan and saving services provided by the VISACAs partially substitute for the insurance functions performed by kafos. In contrast, since Action Aid loans were targeted towards production purposes, especially for women, kafos have continued to perform their traditional insurance role by providing contingency loan and savings services in the villages. The significant, positive and elastic coefficient for GENAATG compared to the significant but negative coefficient for GENDER further confirms the argument that by targeting women for production loans, the Action Aid fails to completely substitute for village insurance functions.

Table 3 *Weighted Aggregate Elasticities for the Determinants of Insurance and Financial Activities of Kafos*

	Dependent Variable	
Independent Variables	Insurance	Financial Intermediation
Constant	0.05	0.14
CONRATIO	–0.03	0.15
GENDER	–1.68	–0.16
NGOABS	0.01	0.07
VISACA	–0.04	–0.05
VISAATG	0.04	–0.11
GENAATG	1.71	0.09

The regression coefficients for financial intermediation presented in column 3 have the expected signs but are not significant because there is little variation in the financial services provided by kafos with various levels of NGO involvement. Table 1 shows that invariably all kafos provided financial intermediation services. However, there were shifts within the financial services provided by kafos based on the level of NGO involvement. The case studies revealed that the economically marginal members of kafos were not directly serviced by either the VISACAs or Action Aid. However, access by economically advantaged villagers to untargeted loans from the VISACAs may have reduced their crowding out of loans for marginal populations. On the other hand, the fact that Action Aid targeted production loans implied that villagers had to continue to depend on kafos for contingency loans. This reduced the access to loans for economically marginal kafo members. In addition, the borrower screening and contract enforcement techniques followed by VISACAs were also adopted by kafos to allocate their loan funds and this increased their loan repayment rates from 70 percent up to 95 percent. Meanwhile, loans made by kafos from funds provided by Action Aid carried few penalties so the recovery rate was less than 45 percent. While the untargeted loans from VISACAs did not substitute for financial services performed by kafos, they complemented the kafos because they are included as their members. Since the VISACAs do not intervene in kafo activities and they make untargeted loans from locally mobilized deposits at village determined interest rates, they are likely to produce positive benefits for kafos. Therefore, it is likely that the aggregate welfare of the village will at least not be reduced and may even increase because of the VISACA. In contrast, the targeted loans made by Action Aid at subsidized interest rates using external funds seem to negatively influence kafos by eroding their carefully built institutional safeguards. As a result, since Action Aid only partially substitutes for kafo activities, it may well reduce aggregate village welfare because the gains realized by some may not offset the losses of others.

CONCLUSION AND POLICY IMPLICATIONS

Kafos have traditionally provided a variety of services including insurance, financial intermediation, labour and social and political services in Gambian villages. Recently, NGOs following diverse philosophies have expanded rapidly into villages and some are providing financial services. Whereas some NGOs exert a *presence effect* by simply coexisting with kafos, others directly intervene into kafos, thereby exerting an *intervention effect*. While some NGOs follow the *savings first and untargeted credit approach*, others follow the classical *supply-leading, subsidized credit first approach*. This paper addresses the implications of the institutional designs followed by two different NGOs, Action Aid that intervenes in kafos with externally imposed terms and conditions for the credit program and VISACAs that do not intervene in kafos for functions performed by traditional village kafo groups. The study shows that the financial services provided by both Action Aid and VISACAs are only partial substitutes for kafo activities, but only VISACAs have positive externality effects on kafos in the sample villages. The implication is that institutional designs matters. An externally designed institution with a rudimentary financial technology that directly intervenes into traditional village structures may be inferior to a non-interfering institution that complements traditional village kafos. NGOs need to be cautious in designing their financial programs so that their actions do not damage the positive attributes of traditional village institutions.

NOTES

[1] It has been argued that targeting groups rather than individuals reduces transaction costs and repayment problems for lenders (Stiglitz, 1990; Varian, 1990). Empirical evidence from developing countries, however, shows mixed results in loan repayment performance with group lending (Huppi and Feder, 1990).

[2] See Nagarajan, Meyer and Ouattara (1993) for a discussion about the evolution of kafos in The Gambia.

[3] Rural households, especially women engaged in vegetable farming, often save in small quantities at frequent intervals (Shipton, 1992). The transaction costs involved in mobilizing these funds on an individual basis are often high for financial intermediaries. A group of savers, such as a kafo, can collectively deposit a larger amount and thus reduce transaction costs for the financial intermediaries.

[4] None of the sample villages was serviced by formal financial institutions, although three were eligible for production credit from the Gambia Cooperative Union.

REFERENCES

Alderman, H. and Paxson, C.H., 1992, 'Do the Poor Insure?: A Synthesis of the Literature on Risk and Consumption in Developing Countries', World Bank WPS 1008, Washington, D.C.

Arnott, R. and Stiglitz, J.E., 1991, 'Moral Hazard and Nonmarket Institutions: Dysfunctional Crowding Out or Peer Monitoring?', *The American Economic Review*, Vol. 81, No.1, pp.179–190.

Bouman, F., 1992, 'ROSCA and ASCRA: Beyond the Financial Landscape', Paper presented at the Seminar on Pioneers, Problems and Premises of Rural Financial Intermediation in Developing Countries, The Netherlands, November.

Graham, D.H., Meyer, R.L. and Cuevas, C.E. (eds.), 1992, 'Financial Markets in the Gambia: 1981-91', Department of Agricultural Economics and Rural Sociology, The Ohio State University, Columbus, Ohio.

Huppi, M. and Feder, G., 1990, 'The Role of Groups and Credit Cooperatives in Rural Lending', World Bank, *Research Observer*, Vol. 5, No. 2.

Nagarajan, G., Meyer, R.L. and Ouattara, K., 1993, 'Financial Intermediation by NGOs: Implications for Indigenous Village Groups in the Gambia', Paper presented at the Annual Meeting of the American Agricultural Economics Association, Orlando, August.

Shipton, P., 1992, 'The Rope and the Box', in Adams, D.W. and Fitchett, D. (eds.), *Informal Finance in Low-Income Countries*, Westview Press, Boulder, Colorado, pp.25–42.

Stiglitz, J.E., 1990, 'Peer Monitoring and Credit Markets', *World Bank Economic Review*, Vol. 4, No. 3, pp.351–366.

Varian, H.R., 1990, 'Monitoring Agents with Other Agents', *Journal of Institutional and Theoretical Economics*, Vol 146, No. 1, pp.153–176.

DISCUSSION OPENING Rekha Mehra *(International Centre for Research on Women, USA)*

The authors of this paper are to be commended for addressing an important and timely topic, namely, the role of non-governmental organizations (NGOs) in grass-roots development. Of late, the role of NGOs in development policy and programs has been growing in both developed and developing countries. Some of the impetus for their growth has come from the recent emphasis in development planning and policy-making to reduce the role of the government, whether in the marketplace or in implementing development programs. The implicit assumption generally is that NGOs' performance will be better.

The paper serves a very useful purpose in clarifying that NGOs are diverse organizations and that their performance can vary greatly. They represent a range of possibilities — some good, some bad. They can be effective or not, they can adopt sensible or inappropriate strategies. In particular, the authors focus on a key linkage, the relationship between indigenous and international orgznizations. This is an important area because donor aid is often channelled through international or developing country agencies to local NGOs. It is useful to know what works in these partnerships, and the authors highlight some of these points. They include learning from indigenous grassroots organizations, building on a base that is already in place, and complementing the work of local NGOs rather than crowding them out.

The paper is somewhat less effective in clarifying what *does not* work. The authors conclude that the relative 'success' of CIRD can be attributed to its non-interventionist approach while the failure of Action Aid is due to its interventionism. This is an intuitively appealing idea and generally makes sense. In this case, however, the data provided in the paper appear to support a somewhat different conclusion. Namely, the weakness of Action Aid lay in its failure to adopt sound financial strategies. The problem was compounded by its interventionist approach in that it forced these inappropriate financial strategies on its partners.

Clearly, Action Aid did not do its homework. It would have been interesting to learn why, when so much information is available about the elements of successful financial services, the organization still chose to go with 'cheap' credit. It would also be interesting to know why local NGOs accepted the offer of 'cheap' credit when they already seemed to be on the right track.

In a parallel vein, it was not simply the institutional factor of coexistence among the VISACAS that had a positive impact on the other local organizations, but rather that CIRD had something to offer, a positive example of borrower screening and contract enforcement that was worth emulating and made good technical sense.

I would also have been interested in knowing more about why Action Aid chose to target women with its poor financial strategies. I can only guess that it was because they thought the poor strategies would be easier to impose on a more marginalized group. It provides a good example of what *should not be done for women* and what donors should be wary of among NGOs who want to work in women-in-development.

CHARLES S. MATAYA AND MICHELE M. VEEMAN*

Trade Balance and the J-Curve Phenomenon in Malawi

Abstract: The effects of successive currency devaluations, since the 1980s, on Malawi's trade balance are analysed. The major hypothesis tested is that currency devaluation leads to an improvement in trade balance through changes in the real exchange rate. This hypothesis is not supported by the data for Malawi. Although there is evidence of a lagged adjustment yielding an improvement in the trade balance three years after devaluation, the magnitude of this improvement is insufficient to overcome the initial decline in the trade balance following devaluation. The extent of improvement is not consistent with that implied by the hypothesized J-curve effect. The analysis suggests that a one percent rise in real domestic income results in 0.5 per cent per reduction in the trade balance, whereas changes in real foreign income do not appear to have any effect on the trade balance. The lack of responsiveness of Malawi's trade balance to changes in foreign income may be associated with the unmanufactured nature of Malawi's export commodities and the relatively unfavorable market conditions for these exports in the major importing western countries. Other policy measures than those that have been relied on to date are evidently necessary for the desired improvements in trade balance to be achieved.

INTRODUCTION

Successive devaluations of the Malawi kwacha do not appear to have led to an improvement in the trade balance, in contrast to expectations based on international trade theory. Such apparent failures of the trade balance to respond positively to devaluation-induced relative price changes have often been attributed to a temporary lag in the adjustment of exports and imports, a hypothesized phenomenon termed the J-curve effect. Factors contributing to a possible J-curve effect include low trade elasticities, economic rigidities, contractual obligations, or lags in production cycles. The J-curve describes an initial post-devaluation decline in the trade balance, attributable to increased expenditures on import transactions contracted before the devaluation, and a lagged response in production adjustments, prior to overall trade balance improvement. This study seeks to determine, in a partial equilibrium framework, whether the J-curve phenomenon has applied in the adjustment of Malawi's trade balance after the series of currency devaluations that occurred, as part of the structural adjustment process, since the early 1980s.

In general, empirical evidence on the effects of currency devaluation on trade balance appears inconclusive. The results of one of the earliest studies (Laffer, 1973) of the time pattern of the trade balance following devaluation in the 1960s, showed that this led to an improvement in trade balance one year later in only eight of the fifteen countries considered. This improvement does not seem to have lasted longer than two to three years. There was evidence of a J-curve in four countries. A study by Salant (1975) also indicates that the effect of currency devaluation on trade balance in both developing and developed countries is unclear. Miles (1974) observes that the results obtained in some earlier studies may have been influenced by the failure to incorporate the effects of time and domestic

* University of Malawi and University of Alberta, Canada, respectively.

policy on trade flows and the use of annual data. Miles' use of quarterly data and residuals as indicators of trade flows does not support the hypothesis that devaluation improves trade balance, even after allowing for a time lag. However, the different approach applied by Himarios (1985) to Miles' data suggested that a devaluation generally improves the trade balance. The J-curve phenomenon has not been tested for Malawi or several other African countries. This study assesses whether the phenomenon may explain the apparent lack of response of the balance of Malawi's trade to successive devaluations.

CONCEPTUAL FRAMEWORK

Analyses of currency devaluation and trade balance should consider the specification of domestic demand for imports and foreign demand for domestic exports or excess supply. Domestic demand for imports is derived from the postulates of utility maximization which assume that a consumer chooses a bundle of goods that maximizes satisfaction subject to a given budget constraint. Summation over consumers yields aggregate demand. The aggregate domestic demand for imports can be presented as:

$$(1)\quad M_t = M_t\left(\frac{eP_M^*}{P_N}, Y_t\right)$$

where M_t is the quantity of imports, P_M^* and P_N are prices for imports and non-tradable goods, respectively (with P_M^* indicating the foreign currency denominated price of imports); Y_t is real domestic income; and e is the nominal exchange rate, expressed in units of domestic currency per unit of foreign currency.

The supply of domestic exports, derived from the theory of profit maximization, yields output supply as a function of input and output prices, giving domestic export supply as:

$$(2)\quad X_t = X_t\left(\frac{P_X}{P_N}, Y_t^*\right)$$

where P_X and P_N are prices of export and non-tradable goods, respectively, expressed in Malawi kwacha, and Y_t^* denotes foreign real income (in US dollars) which is included to account for shifts in the supply function resulting from external influences. The difference between Equations (2) and (1) constitutes the trade balance TB_t:

$$(3)\quad TB_t = X_t\left(\frac{P_X}{P_N}, Y_t^*\right) - M_t\left(\frac{eP_M^*}{P_N}, Y_t\right)$$

This reduces to:

$$(4)\quad TB_t = TB_t\left(\frac{P_T}{P_N}, Y_t^*, Y_t\right)$$

where P_T is a weighted average of export and import prices.

Assuming the Marshall–Lerner condition is satisfied, it is expected that: $\partial TB_t / \partial(P_T / P_N)$, $\partial TB_t / \partial Y_t^* > 0$, and $\partial TB_t / \partial Y_t < 0$. That is, an increase in the price of exports relative to imports is expected to have a positive effect on the trade balance and this balance is expected to increase with increases in real foreign income, and to decrease with increases in real domestic income.

The immediate effect of a currency devaluation is to increase the price of imported goods relative to domestic goods. The quantity of imports demanded is expected to fall as the quantity of domestic currency required to purchase the same unit of foreign currency rises. Further, the volume of exports is expected to rise as domestic producers expect to receive a larger quantity of domestic currency for the same unit of foreign currency. However, the J-curve effect relates to a time lag in the adjustment of exports and imports. An initial deterioration in trade balance is expected to arise from increased expenditure on import transactions that were contracted before the devaluation and a lagged response in production. Carbaugh (1980) observes that a lag in adjustment may be caused by failure to recognize a change in competitive conditions, uncertainty in forming new business connections and placing new orders, and a lag in delivery between the time new orders are placed and the time relative price changes have an impact on trade and payments flows, as well as replacement and production lags.

MODEL SPECIFICATIONS AND DATA

The basic model, from the preceding section, is:

$$(5) \quad TB_t = \alpha_0 + \alpha_1 RER_t + b_1 Y_t^* + b_2 Y_t + \varepsilon_t$$

where TB_t is the trade balance; RER_t is the real exchange rate, measured as a ratio of the price of traded and non-traded goods (P_T / P_N); Y_t and Y_t^* represent real domestic and foreign incomes, respectively; and ε_t represents a random error term. The effect of successive devaluations in Malawi may be underestimated if the partial market liberalization policy, part of the IMF-sponsored structural adjustment programme, and closure of the Mozambique trade route are not recognized in the analysis. The model is, therefore, modified as:

$$(6) \quad TB_t = \alpha_0 + \alpha_1 RER_t + b_1 Y_t + b_2 Y_t^* + b_3 LIB + b_4 PORT + \varepsilon_t$$

where *PORT* is a dummy variable that takes the value of one from 1978 (the period in which the Mozambique ports were constantly under military siege and eventually closed) and is otherwise zero; *LIB* is a partial liberalization dummy variable that takes the value one from 1985 and is otherwise zero.

Almon Distributed-Lag (ADL) Model

Based on the hypothesis that the adjustment process in Malawi's trade balance follows a J-curve, an Almon distributed-lag model is also applied. Consider an finite distributed-lag model of the following form:

$$(7)\quad TB_t = b_0 + b_1Y_t + b_2Y_t^* + b_3LIB + b_4PORT + \beta_0 RER_t + \beta_1 RER_{t-1} + \beta_2 RER_{t-2} + ... + \beta_k RER_{t-k} + \varepsilon_t$$

This may be expressed more compactly as:

$$(8)\quad TB_t = b_0 + b_1Y_t + b_2Y_t^* + b_3LIB + b_4PORT + \sum_{i=0}^{k} \beta_i RER_{t-i} + \varepsilon_t$$

From Weiestrass' theorem, Almon assumes that β_i can be approximated by a suitable-degree polynomial in *i*, the length of the lag (Gujarati 1988); i.e.,

$$(9)\quad \beta_i = \alpha_0 + \alpha_1 i + \alpha_2 i^2 + ... + \alpha_m i^m$$

where m is the degree of the polynomial. Substituting Equation (9) into (8) gives:

$$(10)\quad TB_t = b_0 + b_1Y_t + b_2Y_t^* + b_3LIB + b_4PORT + \sum_{i=0}^{k} (\alpha_0 + \alpha_1 i + \alpha_2 i^2 + ... + \alpha_i^m) RER_{t-i} + \varepsilon_t$$

which is the same as:

$$(11)\quad TB_t = b_0 + b_1Y_t + b_2Y_t^* + b_3LIB + b_4PORT + \alpha_0 \sum_{i=0}^{k} RER_{t-1} + \alpha_1 \sum_{i=0}^{k} iRER_{t-i} + \alpha_2 \sum_{i=0}^{k} i^2 RER_{t-i} + ... + \alpha_m \sum_{i=0}^{k} i^m RER_{t-i} + \varepsilon_t$$

Defining

$$(12)\quad Z_{0t} = \sum_{i=0}^{k} RER_{t-i}$$

$$Z_{1t} = \sum_{i=0}^{k} iRER_{t-i}$$

$$Z_{2t} = \sum_{i=0}^{k} i^2 RER_{t-i}$$

....

$$Z_{mt} = \sum_{i=0}^{k} i^m RER_{t-i}$$

Equation (11) may be rewritten as:

$$(13)\quad TB_t = b_0 + b_1Y_t + b_2Y_t^* + b_3LIB + b_4PORT + \alpha_0 Z_{0t} + \alpha_1 Z_{1t} + \alpha_2 Z_{2t} + \alpha_3 Z_{3t} + ... + \alpha_m Z_{mt} + \varepsilon_t$$

The Almon scheme specified in Equation (11) can be estimated by regressing the dependent variable *TB* on the constructed *Z* variables. As long as the disturbance term ε_t satisfies the assumptions of the classical linear regression model, Equation (13) can be estimated using the ordinary least squares (OLS) procedure and the estimates of β_i derived from the estimates of α_i (Gujarati 1988).

The static and the Almon distributed-lag models of Equations (6) and (13) are tested on annual data from 1965 through 1988. To facilitate data transformation into logarithms, trade balance is expressed as a ratio of export and import values. Values of exports and imports are from the Reserve Bank of Malawi. P_N is measured as the GDP deflator of the Government of Malawi; real domestic income is represented by GNP; real foreign income is proxied by the world production index (World Bank, 1990; Internatioanl Monetary Fund, 1993).

EMPIRICAL ESTIMATION, RESULTS AND DISCUSSION

Estimation of the Almon distributed lag model requires testing of the length and order of the lag structure. Gujarati (1988) notes that the degree of the polynomial should be at least one more than the number of turning points in the curve relating to the coefficients to be estimated. A full expression of a 'classical' J-curve has two turning points, suggesting that a third degree polynomial may be appropriate (Bahman-Oskooee, 1984). However, a simpler representation of the J-curve embodying a single turning point suggests a second degree polynomial. The minimum polynomial order and lag length tested was 2. Following Laffer's study, a five year lag was chosen as the upper bound and restricted models with reduced lag lengths were sequentially tested against this unrestricted upper bound model. The Akaike information criterion and Schwartz criterion statistic were used, as discussed in Judge *et al.* (1988) to assess lag length. Test results, presented in Table 1, suggest a three-year lag as an appropriate polynomial length.

Table 1 *Determination of Lag Length*

Variable	Two lags	Three lags	Four lags	Five lags
AIC	–3.678	–3.772	–3.717	–3.517
SC	–3.282	–3.323	–3.219	–2.971

Notes: AIC = Akaike information criterion statistic; SC = Schwartz criterion statistic.

Sequential testing to discriminate between second and third order polynomials also used the Akaike information criterion, which suggests that a second order polynomial better fits the data, although a log-likelihood ratio test does not reject the hypothesis that estimates from second and third order polynomial models are not significantly different from each other. These results are in Table 2.

To test the J-curve phenomenon, second and third order polynomial models with three lags were estimated using ordinary least squares procedures. A static model as specified in Equation (6) was also estimated to provide a basis for comparison. Results are in Table 3. Economic theory, and the empirical results, favour the dynamic models, relative to the static model. However, application of a log-likelihood ratio test to compare the two dynamic models, does not reject the hypothesis that their estimates are not significantly different.

Table 2 *Determination of Order of Polynomial*

Variable	2nd degree	3rd degree
LLF	18.022	18.683
LRT	1.322	
AIC	–3.756	–3.772

Notes: LLF = value of the log-likelihood function; LRT = log-likelihood ratio test statistic; AIC = Akaike information criterion statistic.

Table 3 *The Effect of Currency Devaluation on Malawi's Trade Balance 1965–1989*

	Static model		Three lags and 2nd degree polynomial		Three lags and 3rd degree polynomial	
Variable	Estimate	S.E	Estimate	S.E	Estimate	S.E
Constant	–3.888**	0.452	–3.152**	0.736	–3.132**	0.740
RGN	–0.314	0.209	–0.479*	0.248	–0.492*	0.254
RWP	0.039	0.056	–0.0136	0.066	–0.012	0.066
RER	–0.590**	0.180	0.109	0.236	0.149	0.294
LRER1	-	-	–0.706**	0.175	–0.807*	0.469
LRER2	-	-	–0.422**	0.163	–0.312	0.496
LRER3	-	-	0.960**	0.282	0.906**	0.361
LIB	–0.490**	0.066	–0.532**	0.051	–0.531**	0.051
PORT	–0.260**	0.072	–0.353**	0.095	–0.350**	0.096
DW	2.231		2.536		2.542	
Adj-R^2	0.887		0.910		0.902	
LLF	16.046		18.656		18.683	
LRT			0.054			
AIC	–3.680		–3.864		–3.772	
SC	–3.385		–3.466		–3.324	

Notes: RGN = real domestic income (GNP); RWP = real world production index; LIB = dummy for market liberalization policy; and PORT = dummy for closure of trade route through Mozambique; RER = real effective exchange rate; Adj-R^2 = adjusted R^2; S.E = standard error; LLF = log likelihood function; LRT = log likelihood ratio test statistic.
** and * = significantly different from zero at the 95 per cent and 90 per cent confidence levels, respectively.

Effect of the Real Exchange Rate on Trade Balance and the J-Curve Effect

The tested hypothesis is that currency devaluation leads to an improvement in the trade balance through changes in relative prices or the real exchange rate. The results of this partial equilibrium analysis suggest that a one per cent increase in the real exchange rate in the static model results in 0.59 per cent rise in trade deficit in the current year. However, the results of the distributed lag models suggest that following successive deteriorations in the first two years after a devaluation, a one per cent increase in relative prices results in slightly more than 0.90 per cent improvement in trade balance in the third year. Even so, the lagged improvement in the trade balance does not appear to be sufficient to offset the deterioration in the first two years after a devaluation, as required for full expression of the J-curve phenomenon.

The Real Income Effects

Both the static and the Almon distributed-lag models suggest that trade balance responds negatively to increases in domestic income, as expected. The responses are consistent with the aggregate import income elasticities reported for Malawi by Adu-Nyako *et al.* (1992). They fall within the ranges for a number of low income countries found in a study by Bahman-Oskooee. A relatively inelastic trade response to domestic income increase appears to reflect the dominance in imports of intermediate goods for infrastructural, industrial and agricultural development. However, changes in foreign income do not appear to have a significant effect on the behavior of Malawi's trade balance. The apparent lack of responsiveness of the trade balance to growth in world income highlights the problems Malawi faces from its dependence on raw material exports to western markets.

The Partial Market Liberalization Effect

The estimated effects of the partial liberalization of the domestic market, which included reduction in subsidies and partial price deregulation, imply a significant reduction in the trade balance. Interpreting the estimated coefficient on the dummy variable from the dynamic models as outlined by Gujarati (1988), implies a reduction of some 70 per cent in trade balance. The negative effect could be attributed to a rise in the expenditure on imports with removal of subsidies or as commodities assume their true opportunity cost. It can be expected to wane with a more efficient allocation of domestic resources following the reduction of price and non-price distortions. However, Wolf (1992) observes that liberalization would achieve the desired results only if a devaluation results in a reduction in domestic demand. In interpreting the anomaly in the sign of the liberalization parameter, the relatively recent date since the policy was implemented should be noted. The incomplete nature of the liberalization policies may also be a feature (Sahn *et al.*, 1990; Mtawali, 1993).

The Trade Route Effect

As expected, the closure of the Mozambique port had a significant negative impact on the trade balance, albeit less than that apparently associated with partial liberalization. Rerouting of cargo following the closure of the traditional trade route led to increased haulage cost and thus increased the cost of imports and reduced net export earnings for Malawi. A reduction in trade balance of some 40 per cent, according to the results of the dynamic models, can be inferred, following Gujarati (1988).

CONCLUSIONS

This paper tests the hypothesis that currency devaluation leads to an improvement in trade balance through changes in the real exchange rate. The results do not appear to support this hypothesis. The dynamic models indicate the existence of a lagged adjustment. The trade balance was adversely affected for two years after devaluation. A one percent change in the real exchange rate appears to be associated with a rise of about 0.90 per cent in the trade balance three years after the devaluation. Since the lagged trade balance responsiveness to a change in the real exchange rate does not offset the decline in the first two years, the full expression of the hypothesized J-curve effect does not apply.

The analysis suggests that a one percent rise in real domestic income results in approximately 0.5 per cent reduction in the trade balance whereas changes in real foreign income do not appear to have any significant effect on trade balance. The unresponsiveness of the trade balance to changes in foreign income may be attributable in part to the unmanufactured nature of Malawi's export commodities and also to the development of unfavorable market conditions in the major importing western countries. Tobacco, in particular, is a major source of export earnings and this commodity faces market problems in the west since it is classified as a health hazard. Sugar, another export, faces limited and distorted world markets. The effectiveness of the exchange rate policy appears to have been partly limited by the disturbance and eventual closure of the Mozambique port, a feature that highlights the difficulty for domestic policy of dealing with external factors and disturbances.

Evidently, an extended mix of domestic and external policy changes may be necessary to achieve the desired improvements in trade balance. Proposals have included regional integration (Koester, 1993), further domestic market liberalization (Valdes, 1993) and the need for more open importing policies in developed country markets.

REFERENCES

Adu-Nyako, Gottret, Weatherspoon and Seale, 1992, 'Macroeconomic Linkages Among Import Demand, Food Demand, and Foreign Debt', in Csaki, C., Dams, T.J., Metzger, D. and Van Zyl, J. (eds.), *Agricultural Restructuring in Southern Africa*, International Association of Agricultural Economists in association with the Association of Agricultural Economists of Namitsia, Windhoek, pp.163–76.

Bahman-Oskooee, M., 1984, 'Devaluation and the J-Curve: Some Evidence from LDC's', *Review of Economics and Statistics*, Vol. 67, No. 3, pp.500–504.

Carbaugh, R. J., 1980, *International Economics*, Winthrop Publishers, Inc., Cambridge, Massachusetts.

Gujarati, D., 1988, *Basic Econometrics*, 2nd Ed., McGraw Hill, New York.

Himarios, D., 1985, 'The Effects of Devaluation on the Trade Balance: A Critical View and Re-examination of Mile's **"New Results"**, *Journal of International Money and Finance*, No. 4, pp.553–563.

International Monetary Fund, 1993, *International Financial Statistics Yearbook*, Washington, D.C.

Judge, G.R., Griffiths, H.W., Lutkepohl, H. and Lee, T.C., 1988, *Introduction to the Theory and Practice of Econometrics*, 2nd Ed., John Wiley and Sons, New York.

Koestler, U., 1993, 'Agricultural Trade Between Malawi, Zambia and Zimbabwe: Competitiveness and Potential', in Valdes, A. and Muir-Leresche, K. (eds.), *Agricultural Reforms and Regional Market Integration in Malawi, Zambia, and Zimbabwe*, International Food Policy Research Institute, Washington, D.C., pp.32–76.

Laffer, A. B., 1973, 'Exchange Rates, The Terms of Trade, and the Trade Balance', Mimeo, University of Chicago.

Miles, M. A., 1974, 'Re-Evaluating the Effects of Devaluation', Mimeographed, University of Chicago.

Mtawali, K.M., 1993, 'Malawi', in Valdes, A. and Muir-Leresche, K. (eds.), *Agricultural Policy Reforms and Regional Market Integration in Malawi, Zambia, and Zimbabwe*, International Food Policy Research Institute, Washington, D.C.

Reserve Bank of Malawi, 1990, *Financial and Economic Review*, Vol. 22, No. 4.

Sahn, D.E., Arulpragasam, J. and Merid, L., 1990, *Policy Reform and Poverty in Malawi: A Survey of Decade of Experience*, Cornell Food and Nutrition Policy Program Monograph 7, Ithaca, New York.

Salant, M., 1975, 'Devaluations Improve the Balance of Payments Even if Not the Trade Balance', Mimeo, US Treasury Department, Washington, D.C.

Valdes, A., 1993, 'The Macroeconomic and Overall Policy Environment Necessary to Complement Agricultural Trade and Price Policy Reforms', Valdes, A. and Muir-Leresche, K. (eds.), *Agricultural Policy Reforms and Regional Market Integration in Malawi, Zambia, and Zimbabwe*, International Food Policy Research Institute, Washington, D.C., pp.11–31.
Wolf, P.; 1992, 'A Double-Edged Sword: Liberalization May Lead to Instability', *Development and Cooperation*, German Foundation for International Development, Berlin.
World Bank, 1990, *World Tables*, Johns Hopkins Press, Baltimore.

DISCUSSION OPENING — Christopher Gerrard *(World Bank)*

This paper addresses an important topic, namely optimal domestic policy — more specifically, structural adjustment policy — in small, open economies in response to external economic shocks. I have three major comments, two concerning the specification of the model and the third on the econometric results.

First, the authors surely know that a nominal exchange rate devaluation is not the only variable influencing the real exchange rate, and probably not the most important. Changes in the external terms of trade, changes in world real interest rates, and changes in capital flows, (e.g. foreign borrowing or foreign assistance) all influence the real exchange rate. Over the time period in question, 1965 to 1989, such factors have almost certainly had a greater impact on the real exchange rate than have nominal devaluations. It is not even clear to what extent nominal devaluations do influence the real exchange rate in small open economies. It depends upon what happens to the domestic price of non-traded goods. If the nominal devaluation is accompanied by increased foreign borrowing or foreign assistance, which is often the case, the domestic price of non-traded goods may rise by as much as that of traded goods, and the devaluation will have no impact on the real exchange rate. Thus, while the authors are estimating the impact of changes in the real exchange rate on the trade balance, they are not necessarily estimating the impact of nominal devaluations on the trade balance. They are more likely estimating the impact of some other factors that are influencing the real exchange rate.

Second, given the other influences on the real exchange rate, given the uncertain impact of nominal devaluations on the real exchange rate, and given the repetitive nature of the nominal devaluations, should one regard nominal devaluations as an exogenous or an endogenous variable? I would suggest that in Malawi during this time period, it should more appropriately be regarded as an endogenous variable. Changes in the real exchange rate that result from external economic shocks ultimately require an adjustment in some nominal domestic variables. For example, a real exchange depreciation will ultimately require either; a nominal exchange rate depreciation, a domestic deflation relative to the rest of the world or an overvalued exchange rate, manifested either in the existence of a parallel market or in increased foreign borrowing to accommodate the excess demand for foreign exchange resulting from the real exchange rate depreciation. Devaluations may be the result of real exchange rate depreciations. They may also be the result of expanding domestic credit in order to finance central government deficits.

Third, while I doubt that the authors have actually estimated the impact of nominal devaluations on the trade balance, they have nonetheless provided some estimates of the impact of changes in the real exchange rate on the trade balance, whatever it is that is causing the changes in the real exchange rate. In this regard, I think that their results are impressive and, maybe, quite accurate. They may indeed have uncovered a J-curve in response to changes in the real exchange rate. In the long term, we normally expect a real exchange rate depreciation caused, for example, by a deterioration in the terms of trade, to lead to an improvement in the real trade balance — since real imports will decline relative to real output. But, in the short term, the nominal trade balance typically worsens since import prices (and import expenditures) are increasing relative to export prices (and export receipts). As far as I can tell, not knowing precisely what data they are using for the trade balance and for the real exchange rate, this appears to be what they have estimated. If you consider that factors other than nominal devaluations are influencing the real exchange rate, I find the results quite plausible.

NICHOLAS W. MINOT*

Devaluation and Household Welfare in Rwanda

Abstract: One of the most common criticisms of currency devaluation is that it causes disproportionate suffering among the poor. This study examines the distributional impact of price changes associated with devaluation in Rwanda using a simplified household-firm model based on household budget data. The study approximates the welfare impact on each household in the sample, making use of 'willingness-to-pay' measures of welfare impact which are theoretically superior to the standard 'consumer surplus' measure. The results indicate that price changes associated with devaluation have a proportionately greater negative impact on the real income of urban households than rural, and within each sector a greater impact on high-income households than low-income. The main reason for this pattern is that rural and low-income households tend to be insulated from price changes by being less integrated in the cash economy.

INTRODUCTION

Since the early 1980s, an increasing number of less developed countries have been forced to implement macroeconomic adjustment programmes to deal with large current account deficits, inflation, and stagnant economic growth. One of the more controversial elements of these programmes is currency devaluation. In theory, devaluation addresses the problem of external deficits by stimulating exports and dampening the demand for exportable goods and imports. However, devaluation is unpopular in less developed countries and has been criticized by some researchers for being contractionary, inflationary, ineffective in reducing external deficits, and regressive in its impact on income distribution (Krugman and Taylor, 1978; Godfrey, 1985; Cornia, Jolly and Stewart, 1987).

This controversy has generated a significant body of theoretical and empirical research on the macroeconomic effects of currency devaluation (Edwards, 1989, reviews this literature). The distributional impact of devaluation, however, is more difficult to study. Economic theory yields ambiguous results. In the short run, devaluation should benefit both labour and capital-owners in tradeable goods sectors at the expense of those in the non-tradeable goods sector. In the long run, labour will gain if tradeable goods are more labour-intensive, while owners of capital will gain if the reverse is true (Johnson and Salope, 1980). Consumers of tradeable goods, generally presumed to be high-income households, lose relative to consumers of non-tradeables. Thus, the impact on income distribution depends on the factor-intensity of each sector, demand patterns, and the structure of production.

Empirical studies are hampered by the lack of regularly collected statistics describing income distribution. A frequently used proxy is real wages, which often decline after devaluation (Cooper, 1971; Edwards, 1989). Wage statistics, however, generally refer to the urban formal sector, which is not necessarily relevant to the bulk of the poor, located in the urban informal sector and in rural areas.

* Visiting Specialist at the Ministère du Plan in Kigali Rwanda, employed by Michigan State University with funding from the US Agency for International Development.

In a comparison of devaluation episodes in nine countries, Heller *et al.* (1988) conclude that that devaluation may reduce income disparities when the major export crop is produced by small farmers, while exacerbating inequality where export-oriented plantations dominate. Glewwe and de Tray (1988 and 1989), using household budget data from Peru and Côte d'Ivoire, suggest that the bulk of the poor, being rural and self-employed, should either benefit from higher farm prices or be unaffected, while the urban poor are more likely to be adversely affected. Sahn and Sarris (1991) calculate price and income indexes for the rural poor in five African countries before and after devaluation episodes. They find a mixture of gains and losses in the order of 5–10 percent, with no clear pattern in either direction. Studies using computable general equilibrium (CGE) models reveal that the effects of devaluation can vary widely, but the impact on the urban poor is generally negative, while the impact on the rural poor depends on the structure of agricultural production (Dervis, de Melo and Robinson, 1982; de Janvry, Fargeix and Sadoulet, 1988).

DATA AND METHODS

This study examines the impact of devaluation in Rwanda by combining price changes (both hypothetical and historical) and a simplified household-firm model based on household budget data[1]. The National Household Budget and Consumption Survey (ENBC) collected detailed information on income, expenditure, food consumption, and household characteristics from 570 households (see Ministère du Plan, 1988 and 1991).

Rural and urban demand models were estimated using a modified version of the Almost Ideal Demand System (AIDS)[2]. The urban and rural models had equations for 21 and 17 food categories, respectively, and nine non-food categories. The independent variables were total household expenditure, food prices, and the size and composition of the household. Non-food price elasticities could not be estimated directly and had to be derived under assumptions of strongly separable preferences (Frisch 1959).

The November 1990 devaluation raised the official price of foreign currency by 67 percent. Some simulations were run using the change in historical prices from six months before the devaluation to six months after. The interpretation of these simulation, however, is complicated by the fact that in October 1990 Rwanda was invaded by armed exiles based in Uganda. Restrictions on trade through Uganda and security measures within Rwanda affected prices even before the November devaluation.

In light of these complications, other simulations were run using hypothesized price effects of a 'pure' devaluation. The following assumptions were used.

- The designation of goods as tradeable or non-tradeable was done at the level of the ENBC product codes (400 in the rural survey, 825 in the urban). These were then aggregated to the level of the budget categories used in the regression.
- Based on Edwards (1989) study of 29 devaluation episodes, it was assumed that the ratio of tradeable prices to non-tradeable prices rises by 60 percent of the increase in the cost of foreign exchange.
- Again based on Edwards (1989), it was assumed that agricultural and non-agricultural real wages fall 3.5 percent and 8.5 percent, respectively.

The model simulates the effect of the changes in wages and prices on the demand for each good by each household in the sample, incorporating the income effect, the substitution effect, and the profit effect (the influence of output prices on income and hence demand). Changes in food consumption are combined with nutritional coefficients to estimate the impact of the price changes on caloric intake for each household. This information also allows us to estimate the welfare impact of the price changes for each household.

This study differs from previous studies of the welfare impact of devaluation in two respects. First, the welfare and nutritional impact is calculated for each household in the sample rather than for all households in a given region or income group. This allows the results to be aggregated to any desired sub-group of the population and provides information about the variability within each group. Second, the welfare impact is measured using equivalent variation and compensating variation. These measures represent the change in income equivalent to the price changes in terms of impact on household welfare and the change in income necessary to compensate the household for the price changes. These two 'willingness-to-pay' measures are theoretically superior to the standard 'consumer surplus' measure, yet require no more information about the demand function[3]. They are calculated using the method suggested by Vartia (1983) which involves numerical integration of the compensated (Hicksian) demand function[4].

RESULTS

The simulated impact of the hypothetical prices on caloric intake and household welfare are shown in Table 1. The first column shows the effect of wage and price changes on household income, the profit effect. Supply response is assumed to be zero in this simulation. Urban incomes fall 7.8 percent on average, less than the assumed fall in non-agricultural wage rates. In other words, reductions in wages (which constitute 44 percent of urban income) are partially offset by smaller reductions in non-wage incomes. Rural incomes fall by 3.8 percent on average. This figure reflects the fact that food crop sales (mostly nontradeable) are twice as important a source of income in rural areas as tradeable 'cash crop' sales. In addition, the importance of non-marketed output reduces the magnitude of the impact, measured as a percentage of total income.

The second and third columns provide the impact of consumer prices on purchasing power, as measured by equivalent variation and compensating variation, respectively. These figures are close to zero because consumer prices have been normalized.

The fourth and fifth columns show the net impact, combining the producer impact and consumer impact. The negative welfare impact (expressed as a percentage of total expenditure) is over three times greater for urban households than for rural households. The price changes associated with devaluation are equivalent to a 3 percent reduction in the income of rural households and a 10 percent drop in income for urban households. In addition, the reduction is twice as great for the richest 20 percent of households as it is for the poorest 20 percent. Households whose primary occupation is farming are least affected, while wage earners are most affected. Female-headed households are slightly more adversely affected than male-headed households, with devaluation being equivalent to 4.1 percent and 3.5 percent reductions in income, respectively.

The last column of Table 1 shows that, in spite of the reductions in real income, the impact of the price changes on caloric intake is either slightly positive for all groups considered. Two factors are at work. First, non-food items are more likely to have a large tradeable component and thus to experience greater price increases. Thus, the change in relative prices results in a shift from non-food to food consumption. Second, the food items with a large tradeable component (rice, bread, factory beer, and sugar) are relatively expensive sources of calories. Thus, relative price changes also induce a shift toward the cheaper sources of calories.

Table 1 *Effect of Hypothetical Devaluation on Rwandan Households*

	Producer impact (PS)	Consumer impact (EV–PS)	Consumer impact (CV–PS)	Net impact (EV)	Net impact (CV)	% change in caloric intake
Sector						
Rural	–3.8	0.7	0.6	–3.1	–3.2	1.3
Urban	–7.8	–2.7	–3.5	–10.4	–11.3	0.8
Mean	–4.0	0.5	0.4	–3.5	–3.6	1.3
Expenditure quintile						
1st	–4.0	1.5	1.4	–2.5	–2.6	0.4
2d	–4.0	1.0	0.9	–2.9	–3.0	0.7
3d	–2.6	–0.0	–0.1	–2.6	–2.8	1.9
4th	–4.3	0.7	0.6	–3.6	–3.8	0.7
5th	–5.1	–0.6	–0.9	–5.7	–6.0	2.6
Mean	–4.0	0.5	0.4	–3.5	–3.6	1.3
Principal occupation						
Farmer	–3.4	1.0	0.9	–2.5	–2.6	1.1
Artisan	–6.5	–0.2	–0.5	–6.7	–7.0	1.5
Merchant	–3.2	–1.6	–1.9	–4.8	–5.1	2.3
Employee	–6.9	–1.7	–2.2	–8.6	–9.1	2.7
Various	–4.8	–0.1	–0.3	–4.9	–5.1	1.0
Mean	–4.0	0.5	0.4	–3.5	–3.6	1.3
Sex of head of household						
Male	–3.9	0.5	0.4	–3.4	–3.5	1.5
Female	–4.5	0.5	0.4	–4.0	–4.1	0.5
Mean	–4.0	0.5	0.4	–3.5	–3.6	1.3

Source: Simulation based on Rwandan ENBC data.

Even after separating rural and urban households, the positive relationship between income level and the percentage reduction in real income due to devaluation remains. In rural areas, the impact on real income increases from –2.4 percent for the poorest quintile to –4.4 percent for the richest quintile. In the urban areas, the impact rising from –7.6 percent to –11.6 percent.

Other simulations were carried out using historical price changes from six months before the devaluation to six months after. Although the prices of tradeable goods did rise more than those of non-tradeables on average[5], the historical prices of individual goods bear little resemblance the hypothesized trends, due in part to the invasion and subsequent security measures. In spite of these differences, estimated nutritional and welfare impact of the historical prices is quite similar to that of the hypothetical prices, as shown in Table 2.

Table 2 *Effect of Historical Price Changes on Households*

	Producer impact (PS)	Consumer impact (EV–PS)	Consumer impact (CV–PS)	Net impact (EV)	Net impact (CV)	% change in caloric intake
Sector						
Rural	16.2	–20.3	–21.4	–4.1	–5.1	–2.5
Urban	1.4	–16.0	–19.1	–14.6	–17.8	0.8
Mean	15.5	–20.1	–21.3	–4.7	–5.8	–2.3
Expenditure quintile						
1st	16.7	–20.2	–21.2	–3.6	–4.5	–3.3
2d	16.7	–20.0	–20.8	–3.3	–4.1	–2.6
3d	15.8	–20.7	–22.0	–5.0	–6.3	–2.8
4th	16.0	–20.5	–21.6	–4.5	–5.6	–3.0
5th	12.1	–19.1	–20.6	–6.9	–8.5	–0.2
Mean	15.5	–20.1	–21.3	–4.7	–5.8	–2.3
Principal occupation						
Farmer	17.2	–20.7	–21.	–3.4	–4.3	–2.2
Artisan	10.6	–19.2	–21.2	–8.6	–10.6	–3.3
Merchant	12.1	–17.5	–18.8	–5.4	–6.7	–3.1
Employee	4.4	–16.4	–19.1	–12.0	–14.7	–2.2
Various	15.0	–20.4	–21.7	–5	–6.6	–2.1
Mean	15.5	–20.1	–21.3	–4.7	–5.8	–2.3
Sex of head of household						
Male	15.2	–20.0	–21.1	–4.8	–6.0	–2.3
Female	16.6	–20.7	–21.8	–4.1	–5.1	–2.4
Mean	15.5	–20.1	–21.3	–4.7	–5.8	–2.3

Source: Simulation based on Rwandan ENBC data.

Compared to the simulation using hypothetical prices, the simulation using historical prices yields a larger impact but one with similar distributional patterns. The welfare impact of the historical wages and prices was equivalent to a 4.1 percent reduction in income for the average rural household and a 14.6 percent decrease in income for the average urban household. The impact is almost twice as great, in proportional terms, for the richest quintile (–8.5 percent) as for the poorest quintile (–4.5 percent). As in the simulation using hypothetical prices, agricultural producers are relatively protected, while wage-earners are hardest hit. In contrast to the hypothetical price scenario, historical price data indicate that male-headed households were more seriously affected (–6.0 percent) than female-headed households (–5.1 percent).

Other experiments were carried out to determine the sensitivity of the result to changes in assumptions. Simulations were run assuming; (1) no change in real wage, (2) positive agricultural supply response, and (3) zero price elasticities of demand. In all of these simulations, the proportional impact of the devaluation was more adverse for urban households than for rural households and more adverse for low-income households than high-income households (see Minot, 1992).

Table 3 *Importance of Cash Expenditure by Rural and Urban Expenditure Quintiles*

Expenditure quintile	Home production as a % of food expenditure	Food consumption as a % of total expenditure	Home production as a % of total expenditure	Cash purchases as a % of total expenditure
Rural sector				
1st	77.1	86.0	67.8	32.2
2nd	74.8	85.3	64.3	35.7
3rd	77.4	83.7	65.9	34.1
4th	75.1	83.1	63.5	36.5
5th	74.9	80.0	62.0	38.0
Urban sector				
1st	38.0	80.7	32.4	67.6
2nd	24.2	73.2	19.5	80.5
3rd	18.3	66.0	13.7	86.3
4th	14.3	59.3	11.5	88.5
5th	9.6	53.7	6.2	93.8

Source: Rwandan ENBC.

DISCUSSION

The most intriguing aspect of these simulations is that the results are not sensitive to many of the assumptions used in the simulation. One hypothesis is that urban and high-income households spend a larger share of their income on imported (tradeable) goods. The data for Rwanda provide only weak support for this hypothesis. The share of cash expenditure allocated to tradeable goods rises with income in the urban areas (from 31 percent to 40 percent), but shows no pattern in the rural areas. Oddly, the share of tradeable goods in cash expenditure is barely larger in urban areas (39.2 percent) than in rural areas (36.6 percent). Urban households spend more on tradeable food (for example, rice, bread, sugar) as well as on transportation, which is largely tradeable. On the other hand, rural households' cash spending includes a significant share allocated to clothing, which is almost entirely tradeable. In fact, almost half of rural spending on tradeables is on clothing, particularly used clothing.

Another hypothesis is that the importance of home production isolates rural and low-income households from the effects of all price changes, including those associated with devaluation. Table 3 confirms that this is an important factor. Rural households and low-income households obtain a larger share of their food from home production and food is a larger share of overall expenditure. Thus, cash purchases account for just 32.2 percent of total expenditure for households in the poorest rural quintile, but 93.8 percent of total expenditure for the richest urban quintile. This helps explain why the hypothetical and historical price changes, which were quite different from each other, resulted in similar distributional effects in the simulations.

CONCLUSIONS AND POLICY IMPLICATIONS

In Rwanda, and, by extension, in similar semi-subsistence agricultural economies, the relative price effects of devaluation have a relatively moderate impact on rural households and the poor in general. In all the scenarios considered, the effect of a major devaluation on the poor was equivalent to a reduction in income of 4 percent or less. The impact on caloric intake was even less. The effect on urban and high-income households was two to three times as large in proportional terms. This study confirms the conventional wisdom that the urban poor are hit harder than the rural poor, but is at odds with the common perception that low-income urban households are affected more than higher-income households in the cities. These patterns are not caused by the differences in the propensity to purchase imports, but rather by the fact that rural and low-income households are insulated from price changes by the importance of home production.

These results suggest that, for economies similar to that of Rwanda, the distributional impact of devaluation should not be a major issue in weighing the advantages and disadvantages. Two caveats, however, should be mentioned in this context. First, the model simulates only the relative price (or 'expenditure-switching') effect of devaluation. It does not attempt to model the effect of devaluation on output, unemployment, or aggregate expenditure (the 'expenditure-reducing' effect). Second, without making assumptions about the marginal utility of money, it cannot be inferred that the 3 percent reduction in real incomes in rural areas is less 'painful' than the 10 percent reduction in real income in urban areas.

There is no simple way to alleviate the impact of devaluation on rural households. The same factor that protects them from devaluation, limited integration in the cash economy, also insulates them from the benefits of price policy. Manipulation of food prices, even if it were feasible, would leave many rural households unaffected and have mixed effects on the remainder. On the other hand, the simulation indicates that increased prices of clothing account for almost half of the negative effect of devaluation on low-income rural households. Reduction or elimination of import duties on clothing, particularly used clothing, could be considered.

With regard to research methods, this study shows that household budget data can be a rich source of information on distributional impact of policies such as devaluation. Furthermore, calculation of exact 'willingess-to-pay' welfare measures is feasible, even in the context of micro-simulation in which the impact of policy is simulated for each household in the sample. Finally, this study suggests that variation in the degree of market integration may be at least as important as variations in the propensity to consume imports in determining the distributional impact of currency devaluation.

NOTES

1 A household–firm model incorporates the effect of changing prices of goods and services produced by the household on household income and demand patterns (see Barnum and Squire, 1979). The version used here is simplified in that labour-leisure decisions are not explicitly modeled.

[2] The AIDS was developed by Deaton and Muelbauer (1980). This study follows Swamy and Binswanger (1983) by adding a squared income term so that budget share may rise and then fall with income.
[3] Perhaps the most common welfare measure, consumer surplus, is not well-defined in that, for multiple price changes, the result depends on the order in which the price changes are introduced in the calculations. In contrast, the two willingess-to-pay measures give consistent results.
[4] The Vartia method involves dividing the price changes into a large number of increments. After each increment, income is adjusted to compensate for the price change and new demand quantities are calculated. The sum of the income adjustments is the compensating variation (equivalent variation) if one starts at the original (final) equilibrium point for the calculations.
[5] From one month before the devaluation to seven months after, the price of tradeable rose 31 percent relative to that of non-tradeables (Minot, 1992).

REFERENCES

Barnum, H. and Squire, L., 1979, *A Model of an Agricultural Household: Theory and Evidence*, Occasional Paper No. 27, World Bank, Washington, D.C.

Cooper, R., 1971, *Exchange Rate Devaluation in Developing Countries*, Princeton Essays on International Finance No. 86, Princeton, New Jersey.

Cornia, G., Jolly, R. and Stewart, R. (eds.), 1987, *Adjustment with a Human Face: Protecting the Vulnerable and Promoting Growth*, Clarendon Press, Oxford, England.

de Janvry, A., Fargeix, A. and Sadoulet, E., 1990, 'The Welfare Effects of Stabilization Policies and Structural Adjustment Programs Analyzed in Computable General Equilibrium Framework', in Pinstrup-Anderson, P. (ed.), *Macroeconomic Policy Reform, Poverty, and Nutrition: Analytical Methodologies*, Food and Nutrition Program Monograph 3, Cornell University, Ithaca, New York.

Deaton, A. and Muelbauer, J., 1980, 'An Almost Ideal Demand System', *American Economic Review*, Vol. 70, No. 2, pp.312–26.

Edwards, S., 1989, *Real Exchange Rates, Devaluation, and Adjustment: Exchange Rate Policy in Developing Countries*, MIT Press, Cambridge, Massachusetts.

Frisch, R., 1959, 'A Complete Scheme for Computing all Direct and Cross Demand Elasticicities in a Model of Many Sectors', *Econometrica*, Vol. 24, No. 2, pp.177–196.

Glewwe, P. and de Tray, D., 1988, 'The Poor During Adjustment: a Case Study of Cote d'Ivoire', Working Paper No. 47, Living Standards Measurement Study, World Bank, Washington, D.C.

Glewwe, P. and de Tray, D., 1989, 'The Poor in Latin America During Adjustment: a Case Study of Peru', Working Paper No. 56, Living Standards Measurement Study, World Bank, Washington, D.C.

Godfrey, M., 1985, 'Trade and Exchange Rate policy in Sub-Saharan Africa', *IDS Bulletin*, Vol. 16, No. 3, pp. 31–38.

Heller, P., Lans Bovenberg, A., Catsambas, T., Chu, K. and Shome, P., 1988, *Implications of Fund-Supported Adjustment Programs for Poverty: Experiences in Selected Countries*, International Monetary Fund Occasional Paper No. 58, Washington, D.C.

Johnson, O. and Salope, J., 1980, 'Distributional Aspects of Stabilization Programs in Developing Countries', *International Monetary Fund Staff Papers*, Vol. 27, No. 1, pp.1–23.

Krugman, P. and Taylor, L., 1978, 'Contractionary Effects of Devaluation', *Journal of International Economics*, No. 8, pp. 445–456.

Ministère du Plan, 1988, *Consommation et Sources de Revenu des Ménages Ruraux*, Volume 3 of the National Household Budget and Consumption Survey (ENBC), Direction Générale de la Statistique, Kigali, Rwanda.

Ministère du Plan, 1991, *Consommation et Sources de Revenu des Ménages Urbains*, Volume U3 of the National Household Budget and Consumption Survey (ENBC), Direction Générale de la Statistique, Kigali, Rwanda.

Minot, N.W., 1992, 'Distributional Effects of Currency Devaluation on Households in Rwanda: an Application of Willingness-to-pay Welfare Methods', Ph.D. dissertation, Department of Agricultural Economics, Michigan State University, East Lansing.

Sahn, D. and Sarris, A., 1991, 'Structural Adjustment and the Welfare of Rural Smallholders: a Comparative Analysis from Sub-Saharan Africa', *World Bank Economic Review*, Vol. 5, No. 2, pp.259–89.

Swamy, F. and Binswanger, H.P., 1983, 'Flexible Consumer Demand Systems and Linear Estimation: Food in India', *American Journal of Agricultural Economics*, Vol. 6, No. 4, pp.675–684.

Vartia, Y., 1983, 'Efficient Methods of Measuring Welfare Change and Compensated Income in Terms of Ordinary Demand Functions', *Econometrica*, Vol. 51, No. 1, pp.79–98.

DISCUSSION OPENING — Godfrey Tyler *(University of Oxford, UK)*

I should like to congratulate Dr. Minot on his paper for the clarity with which it was written. By using sample household expenditure data in Rwanda, he was able to confirm the conventional wisdom that the relative price effects of devaluation hit the urban poor rather than the rural poor. It was comforting to see that the effect of a devaluation as high as 67 percent apparently decreases the income of the poor in general by 4 percent or less. Sadly, devaluation must now be the least of their worries. Higher income groups are hurt proportionally more, which he attributes not to higher propensities to purchase imports but to the fact that they rely much more on purchased rather than home produced goods. Low income and rural households are thus more insulated from price changes.

These results seem reasonable and I am mostly convinced by them, given the limitations of the study which Dr. Minot freely admits e.g., that it does not take into account the important effects of devaluation on output, employment and so on. However, I have a number of questions and comments.

Firstly, I was worried about how far the assumption (that following devaluation the real agricultural wage fell by 3.5 percent and the real non-agricultural wage by 8.5 percent) was driving the results. The author says that other simulations were carried out assuming no change in real wages; he still found that the impact was more adverse for urban than for rural households, but he was found that the impact was more adverse for low rather than high income households. But if most of the income of the urban poor comes from wages and the real wage is constant. Why should they suffer any adverse effects?

Secondly, I have a question about the breakdown of the overall effect of devaluation into the producer and consumer impacts and the different pattern between the hypothesized price changes and the historical price changes. Taking, for example, the farmer occupation in Table 1 (hypothetical prices) and using the compensating variation measure, the producer effect is –3.4 percent and the consumer effect +0.9 percent. In table 2 (historical prices) the producer effect is +17.2 percent and the consumer effect –21.5 percent. Could Dr. Minot explain these large differences and particularly why there is a switching in the signs of these effects?

This leads me on to my third point. The author says (page 6) that 'the historical prices of individual goods bear little resemblance to the hypothesized trends, due in part to the invasion and subsequent security measures'. He says only 'in part'. Would he therefore agree that a large part of the difference may lie in the fact that most goods and services lie on a continuous spectrum between the extremes of tradeable and non-tradeable, that they do not neatly fall into one or other categories (a convenient simplification for theoretical discussion) and that therefore their prices are likely to change in very different ways?

Finally, it appears Dr. Minot put transportation into the tradeable box, as he says on page 8 it is 'largely tradeable'. From what I have just said, it is obvious that I would not want to put it into any box but I understand that internal transport (buses, taxis, donkeys, camels?) is usually classified as a non-tradeable.

If buses and taxis are anything like those in Harare, I certainly would not put them in the tradeable category. I doubt whether any of them could get anywhere near the border!

J. EDWARD TAYLOR AND ANTONIO YÚNEZ-NAUDE*

Agricultural Policy and the Village Economy: A Computable General Equilibrium Analysis

Abstract: This paper explores the impacts of agricultural policy reforms on a Mexican village economy, using a village computable general equilibrium (CGE) model. In 1994, the Mexican government replaced staple price supports with direct income transfers to producers. Two scenarios are considered in this paper. The first is the case in which the elimination of price supports is transmitted directly to the village. The second is the case in which, due to high transactions costs in staple markets, the village is entirely insulated from the price change. In this case, the policy change consists only of an income transfer to crop producers. The more the reduction in controlled prices results in a decrease in local consumption prices, the more progressive the effect of the policy change is for household–farm incomes. The greater the transmission of the government price change to local producer prices, the greater the impact on local production activities and the greater the potential efficiency gain.

INTRODUCTION

The heterogeneity of Mexican agriculture has important implications for designing and implementing agricultural policies. Mexico is a country of many agricultures in two important respects. First, agricultural producers range in scale from small subsistence farmers to large commercial farmers. In between is an important middle sector of farmers, many of whom will be granted land title under the recent reform of Mexico's *ejido* (land reform) law but few of whom have access to credit, insurance and other resources necessary to be efficient producers. The middle sector of farm households tends to be income–diversified, so that a given percentage decrease in maize prices usually translates into a smaller decrease in total income. Migration by family members to urban areas in Mexico and to the USA is an important part of these households' strategy to reduce their income risk while acquiring liquidity, via income remittances from migration, to finance household–farm production activities.

Different household–farm groups tend to respond differently to changes in agricultural policy. For example, commercial farmers produce for markets, and producer prices (minus transactions costs) are important in shaping their production decisions. Other farmers produce for subsistence, where transactions costs create a gap between a (high) consumer price and a (low) producer price. In this case, consumer prices (plus transactions costs of buying) influence production decisions. These considerations may lead one to the conclusion that producer price supports influence production decisions on commercial farms but not on subsistence farms, which constitute perhaps one-half of all farms in Mexico.

This conclusion may be a reasonable first approximation but still erroneous because of a second respect in which there are many agricultures in Mexico: wide differences in transactions costs for producers and consumers that influence the ways in which changes in policy-set prices are transmitted to local producer and consumer prices. The effect of subsidized producer and consumer prices on local prices depends on the costs to producers and consumers of obtaining access to these prices.

* University of California, Davis and Centro de Estudios Económicos, El Colegio de México, respectively.

Two transactions-cost scenarios appear to be most common in rural Mexico. The first scenario is where producers have low-cost access to the government-guaranteed producer price, but rural consumers do not have access to the subsidized consumption price; that is, transactions costs for producers are low while transactions costs for consumers are high. Local consumers have to pay at least the guaranteed price for maize in order to bid harvests away from the government silos. Changes in the policy-determined producer price in this case can influence production incentives on both commercial and subsistence farms. A combination of low transactions costs for producers and high transactions costs for consumers is one of the most common situations in rural Mexico today. This is because of the limited number of government purchase points at which producers can receive the guaranteed staple price, and rural consumers' limited access to subsidized staples.

The second common scenario is where neither producers nor consumers have access to subsidized staple prices. In this case transactions costs for both producers and consumers are high, and prices are determined by equilibria in local staple markets without being directly affected by government prices.

In general, the lower the transactions costs are on the production side, the more changes in the government price of maize will be transmitted to local producer prices. The higher the transactions costs are on the consumption side relative to the production side, the higher the consumption price will be relative to the production price, and the greater the potential impact of changes in the government guaranteed price on consumer prices, as well.

The government-guaranteed producer price for corn (maize) rose to more than twice the world price in domestic currency in 1993, while the price to some consumers, primarily urban, has been maintained relatively close to the world price. Large price subsidies to producers have encouraged farmers — even on irrigated lands — to shift into maize production if they are within reach of a government grain silo. This recently has generated a highly subsidized surplus of corn together with a decline in the production of high-valued fruit and vegetable export crops. Because the subsidized consumer price of maize is generally not available in rural areas, the producer price support has resulted in high maize prices for rural consumers and large incentives for subsistence production.

The new agricultural policy will eliminate the guaranteed producer price for maize as a means of promoting a more rational and efficient allocation of resources in the agricultural sector. At the same time, subsidies in the form of income transfers to maize farmers, decoupled from maize production at the margin, will be used to support farmer incomes and perhaps also to reduce the distributional bias against small farmers that is inherent in the current price system. The size of these income transfers is determined by past staple production and not by the degree to which farmers participate in staple markets.

The present research considers some of the facts just described and explores the impacts of a combined price and income subsidy reform on a village economy in Mexico using a computable general equilibrium (CGE) framework. The village model is centred on a household farm of the type that is prevalent in rural Mexico, which is engaged in maize production but also in a portfolio of other economic activities, including migration. The general equilibrium model captures production and expenditure linkages within the village and between the village and the rest of Mexico, including village households' consumption and production demand for manufactured goods. Mexico-to-USA migration and internal migration are modelled explicitly as a function of the returns to migration and the returns to family labour in the village. The model is estimated using data from a 1989 survey of household farms in the central State of Michoacan (see Adelman, Taylor and Vogel, 1988, for a description of the village and an analysis based on a SAM model).

THE VILLAGE CGE MODEL

The Mexican village model consists of five blocks of equations: (1) a household–farm production block, (2) a household–farm income block, (3) an expenditure block, (4) a set of general equilibrium closure equations, and (5) a price block.

The household–farm production sector includes three production sectors and one commercial sector which serves to 'import' primarily manufactured goods into the village from the rest of Mexico. Production in each of these sectors is carried out with four factors: family labour, hired labour, physical capital and land. (In contrast to the traditional neoclassical household–farm model, it is not assumed that family and hired labour are perfect substitutes). The production technology in each sector is specified as Cobb–Douglas. The demand for non-factor (intermediate) inputs, including manufactured inputs imported into the village (e.g., fertilizer for maize production), is determined through the use of fixed input–output coefficients. Household farms are assumed to maximize utility from consumption goods and leisure. On the production side, this implies maximizing net farm income from the three production activities given market prices for output and market or shadow prices for factors of production and intermediate inputs. Physical capital and land inputs are fixed in the short run, but family and hired labour are variable inputs.

The household–farm sector consists of three groups: subsistence farm households, with fewer than 2 hectares of land; a middle group, with 2 to 8 hectares of land; and largeholder households, with more than 8 hectares of land. Household–farm income is the sum of wage income, capital, land and family labour value-added from household–farm production activities, and migrant remittances.

The expenditure block includes the consumption demand for village products and manufactured goods produced elsewhere in Mexico: leisure; savings, including investments in physical and human capital (schooling); taxes, including a 5 percent levy on maize production; and some household-to-household transfers.

Model closure includes equations for local factor-market equilibria, a village savings–investment balance, and a material balance equation. The factor equations ensure that village factor markets clear. The savings–investment balance constrains village investments in physical and human capital to be self-financed, that is, out of village household–farm savings. This is a reasonable specification given imperfect rural credit markets in Mexico. The material balance equation constrains total household–farm production in each sector to equal village demand plus net marketed surplus (village net exports).

The shadow wage of family labour is endogenous; it adjusts to ensure that family time allocated to village production activities, to migration and to leisure equals the family's total time endowment. Mexico-to-USA migration and internal migration are a function of the differential between household-group specific expected remittances per migrant and the shadow price of family labour in village production activities. The shadow prices of physical capital and land are also endogenous. The prices of hired labour, village output and intermediate inputs are exogenous; they are assumed to be determined in regional labour and commodity markets or, in the case of maize prices, by government policy, except where transactions costs are high. The simulations presented below explore, in a very stylized fashion, the sensitivity of policy outcomes to an imperfect transmission of the government-guaranteed staple price to villages, as would result from the presence of high transactions costs in maize markets.

Despite policy changes that have affected agricultural prices since 1989, simulations using the 1989 baseline village model are useful for experiments involving relative price changes and for a rural economy in which maize is the dominant crop. Most land in the survey area is *ejido* and most households are also farmers. Factor inputs and the prices of physical capital and hired labour were observed directly. Land rents were estimated econometrically from regressions of income from the various production activities on household–farm asset holdings. Family labour value-added was calculated as the value of production net of the costs of intermediate inputs, hired labour, physical capital and land rents. Household–farm savings and expenditure propensities were calculated directly from expenditure survey data, as were migrant-to-household remittances and migration elasticities.

It is most appropriate to view the CGE as a stylized model of a village economy in Mexico, estimated with real-world microeconomic data. Two major advantages of this model compared with national CGE models are, first, its detailed focus on the diversified household–farm economies that characterize rural Mexico, and second, the minimal number of assumptions that were needed to estimate and calibrate the model given the availability of detailed micro survey data.

POLICY SIMULATIONS

The estimated village model was used to explore the local impacts of a combined 40 percent reduction in the guaranteed price of maize and a compensating income transfer to maize-producing households, under two scenarios: Scenario 1, in which the full reduction in the guaranteed price is transmitted to producer and consumer prices in the village, and Scenario 2, in which the village is entirely insulated from the price change. The first case corresponds to low transactions costs on the production side (the cost of delivering the crop to the government silo is low) and high transactions costs on the consumption side (village consumers do not have access to the subsidized consumption price of maize). In the second scenario, neither producers nor consumers have access to the subsidized prices; that is, both the government silo and the government store are distant from the village. In both cases, the village receives an income transfer equal to 40 percent of the value of maize production before the price change. This transfer is distributed among the three village household groups in the same proportions as family labour value-added from maize production. This means that large-holder households directly benefit the most from the income subsidy.

Table 1 summarizes the village-wide impacts of the two policy experiments. Local maize production falls dramatically in Scenario 1, under which the full drop in the maize price is transmitted to the village. The 40 percent decrease in maize price results in a 33 percent decline in maize output. Although the income transfer is designed to just offset the loss in value of maize production as measured in market prices, total (nominal) household income increases by 2.6 percent. This is because, in response to the decreased profitability of maize, households reallocate their resources away from maize production towards other activities, the output of which increases from just under 1 percent in livestock to just over 7 percent in non-agricultural production.

In terms of household incomes, the policy is progressive. The real income of subsistence households increases by more than 11 percent, while those of medium and large-holder households increase by 3.5 percent and 7.9 percent, respectively. Subsistence households benefit both from the income transfer and from the lower local consumption price of maize resulting from the reduction in the guaranteed price. Because household–farm real income increases, the demand for leisure increases (by 6 percent) and the demand for manufactured goods in the village goes up slightly (by 0.09 percent). There is a very small increase in migration (0.16 percent).

Table 1 *Policy Simulation Results*

	Percentage Change	
	Scenario 1	Scenario 2
Household–farm production		
Staples	–33.44	–0.44
Livestock	0.77	–1.47
Non-agricultural production	7.12	–1.55
Household–farm incomes		
Total (nominal)	2.65	4.94
Real, by households group		
Subsistence households	1.2	2.80
Medium-holder households	3.56	3.21
Large-holder households	7.89	6.88
Migration	0.16	–2.47
Leisure	6.12	3.61
Demand for manufactured goods	0.09	2.80

Source: Estimates from Village CGE Model.

The results of the policy are different, particularly on the production and equity side, when the decrease in the guaranteed price of maize is not transmitted to the village. In this case, where there is no change in local prices but households receive the income transfer, household nominal income increases by a greater percentage than in Scenario 1 (by nearly 5 percent). Although there is no direct price incentive to reallocate production away from maize, the higher income induces households to demand more leisure, withdrawing some family labour from production. As result, output in all sectors falls slightly. A higher shadow price on family labour in the village discourages migration: in this scenario migration decreases by nearly 2.5 percent. The increase in income results in a relatively large linkage effect with the urban manufacturing sector; village demand for manufactured goods increases by 2.8 percent. The effect of the policy change on household–farm incomes in real terms is less progressive than before, because subsistence households do not benefit from a lower consumption price of maize. Real incomes in subsistence households increase by 2.8 percent, compared with 11 percent in the first scenario. By contrast, the changes in medium and large-holder households' real incomes are similar in the two experiments. In short, the more that the reduction in the guaranteed price results in a decrease in local consumption prices, the more progressive the effect on household–farm incomes. The greater the transmission of the government price change to local producer prices, the greater the impact on local production activities and the greater the potential efficiency gain.

CONCLUSIONS

The simulation results presented above suggest that Mexico can achieve both efficiency and income distribution gains by combining a reduction or elimination of price supports for maize with a compensating income transfer to maize farmers. In order to achieve both efficiency and equity objectives, it is important for the income transfer to be directed to subsistence farmers as well as to farmers who produce a marketed surplus of maize. Commercial farmers benefit from the compensating income transfer and from a more efficient allocation of resources among production activities. Subsistence farmers benefit from the income transfer and, where transactions costs on the consumption side are high, from lower consumption prices, as well.

Where imperfections in credit and insurance markets create liquidity and risk constraints on production, income transfers may stimulate production by alleviating these constraints. In this case, the positive effects of income subsidies on household–farm incomes may be understated by the simulation results presented above. There is econometric evidence that income transfers (in the form of migrant remittances) have a positive effect on local production activities in rural Mexico and elsewhere (Taylor, 1992; and Lucas, 1985). There is also evidence that migrant remittances influence input mixes in traditional crop activities (Fletcher and Taylor, 1992). It appears that, lacking access to credit and insurance, households in rural Mexico have engaged in migration in an effort to self-finance local production activities and/or to self-insure against local income risks. If income transfers enable household–farms to overcome these credit and insurance market failures, they may stimulate local production while offering an alternative to relying on migration income as a means to sustain rural production.

Finally, the role of transactions costs in shaping the local impacts of government price policies on production and household–farm real incomes underlines the importance of infrastructure development to increase market efficiency in rural areas, to enhance farmers' responsiveness to policy and market signals, and to ensure a more broad-based participation by farm households in economic growth.

REFERENCES

Adelman, I., Taylor, J.E. and Vogel, S., 1988, 'Life in a Mexican Village: a SAM Perspective', *Journal of Development Studies*, Vol. 5, pp.5–24.

Fafchamps, M., de Janvry, A. and Sadoulet, E. (1995), 'Transaction Costs and the State' in Peters, G.H. and Hedley, D.D. (eds.), *Agricultural Competitiveness: Market Forces and Policy Choice,* Proceedings of the Twenty-Second International Conference of Agricultural Economists, International Association of Agricultural Economists, Harare, Zimbabwe, 22–29 August 1994, Dartmouth, Aldershot, pp.343–354.

Fletcher, P.L. and Taylor, J.E., 1992, 'Migration and the Transformation of a Mexican Village House Economy', Paper presented at the 'New Perspectives on Mexico–U.S. Migration' Conference, University of Chicago, Chicago, 22–23 October.

Lucas, R.E.B., 1985, 'Emigration to South Africa's Mines', *American Economic Review*, Vol. 77, No. 3, pp.313–330.

Taylor, J.E., 1992, 'Remittances and Inequality Reconsidered: Direct, Indirect and Intertemporal Effects', *Journal of Policy Modelling*, Vol. 14, No. 2, pp.187–208.

DISCUSSION OPENING — Michel Benoit-Cattin *(Cirad-Montpellier, France)*

After a first examination, I feel a little bit frustrated. We need to know more concerning the village and the households. Referring to transaction costs, one must know where the village is located, how far from cities, infrastructure, main public facilities, etc.

As a CGE model is built on a social accounting matrix, the description of the local economy, the different types of households, the main activities, the relations with 'the rest of the world' could be easily derived from this social accounting matrix and have to be included in this kind of presentation. The reader is interested in knowing how many households of different types there are, what are their main activities, what were the prices paid to and by farmers as observed in 1989 compared with official prices. The information on prices gives an idea of the level of transaction costs and band prices.

In the CGE model, three types of household–farms are introduced according to their acreage: less than two hectares, between two and eight, and more than eight. I suppose that the smallest are net buyers of corn, those in the medium group are self-sufficient, and the largest are net sellers. If my deduction is correct, these three types correspond to three levels of shadow prices of production at the farm level, to be compared to bands of prices determined by official prices and high transaction costs, as explained in Fafchamps *et al.* (1995).

In the simulations, as official prices are affected, these price bands will change and the delimitation of types will be altered. I am not sure that the CGE model presented takes these fundamental aspects into account.

We know that elasticities play a key role within a CGE framework and that elasticities refer to marginal variations, but a 40 percent reduction in prices is not a marginal variation. Mathematical programming (linear or not) could be useful in such a context.

In the model, prices of village outputs are exogenous. One can derive policy implications only if Mexico as a whole is a price taker for these products; if not, you have to use prices given by a CGE (at least a multimarket) model for the country and, maybe, for the region.

KYRRE RICKERTSEN[*]

The Demand for Meat: Conditional and Unconditional Elasticities

Abstract: The demand for meat and other foodstuffs is estimated as a part of a four-stage demand system. Correction formulae for price and expenditure elasticities are used to calculate unconditional elasticities by the use of the estimated conditional elasticities. A static specification is rejected at a 5 percent level for each sub-system and a dynamic specification is used to take account of habit formation in consumption. The unconditional own-price elasticities for beef, lamb, pork and chicken are calculated as –0.48, –0.23, –0.66 and –1.14, respectively. The corresponding conditional elasticities are estimated to be –0.59, –0.25, –0.78 and –1.15. The unconditional expenditure elasticities are calculated to be 0.72 for beef, 0.42 for lamb, 0.81 for pork and 1.00 for chicken. The corresponding conditional elasticities are estimated to be 0.98, 0.57, 1.11 and 1.36. These results show the importance of correcting conditional elasticities before elasticities from different studies are compared or before the elasticities are used for policy purposes.

INTRODUCTION

Demand elasticities for meat are of practical interest for several reasons. Numerical values of price and expenditure elasticities are important for the formation of agricultural and other public policies. Furthermore, farmers, their marketing organizations, food processors and the food retailing industry need to forecast demand to plan future production and sales. As a result, elasticities are used in various models. Demand elasticities particularly have been estimated in several studies concentrating on the demand for meat. Some recent examples in various journals are Chalfant *et al.* (1991), Chen and Veeman (1991), Cashin (1991), Burton and Young (1992) and Mdafri and Brorson (1993).

Two questions are the focus of this paper. First, in the above mentioned studies, elasticities are estimated under weak separability assumptions within a system consisting of various meat products while other goods are excluded from the analysis. This is a very common practice in applied demand analysis when a rather limited number of observations is available. However, by only studying one sub-system, the interconnections among sub-systems are neglected. Consider the four-stage utility tree presented in Figure 1. A change in the price of pork will affect beef consumption directly within the meat sub-system at stage 4. But, in addition, the change in the price of pork will cause a change in the price of meat (at stage 3). This change will cause the consumers to change their consumption of meat and the total expenditure allocated to meat (at stage 4) will change. This change in meat expenditure will, in turn, cause an indirect change in the beef consumption. The total effect of the price change is the sum of the direct effect and indirect effects at the various stages.

* Agricultural University of Norway. This paper is a part of the Nordic project: 'Models and Projections of the Demand for Food in the Nordic Countries'. Financial support for this research is provided by the Agricultural Research Council of Norway. The author wishes to thank David Edgerton who wrote the TSP programme which was used for the estimations and Michael Farmer and the members of the Nordic project for useful comments.

Following Pollak and Wales (1992, p.47), the demand functions within a sub-system are called conditional demand functions. The estimated elasticities are then of course conditional elasticities. They will, in general, be different from unconditional elasticities calculated from a demand system that includes all goods. Since the unconditional elasticities are typically interpreted as being of greatest interest to policy-makers, it is an important to determine first, if we can expect large differences in the numerical values between the conditional and unconditional elasticities and, secondly, how we might correct for these differences by the use of estimates from a multi-stage demand system.

The second objective in this paper is to estimate the price and expenditure elasticities for disaggregate food commodities. These elasticities have rarely been estimated within a demand system framework in Norway; so the results are of intrinsic interest. One notable exception is Vale (1989) who applied household data. This implies a somewhat different interpretation of the estimated elasticities.

The outline of the paper is as follows. First, a dynamic version of the almost ideal demand system is presented. Second, weak separability and multi-stage budgeting are introduced. Approximate correction formulae for conditional elasticities derived in Edgerton (1992) are presented. Third, data and estimation procedures are briefly described. Finally, conditional and unconditional elasticities related to stage 1, stage 2, and the animalia part of stages 3 and 4 are discussed. Results for the complete utility tree described in Figure 1 are given in Rickertsen (1994).

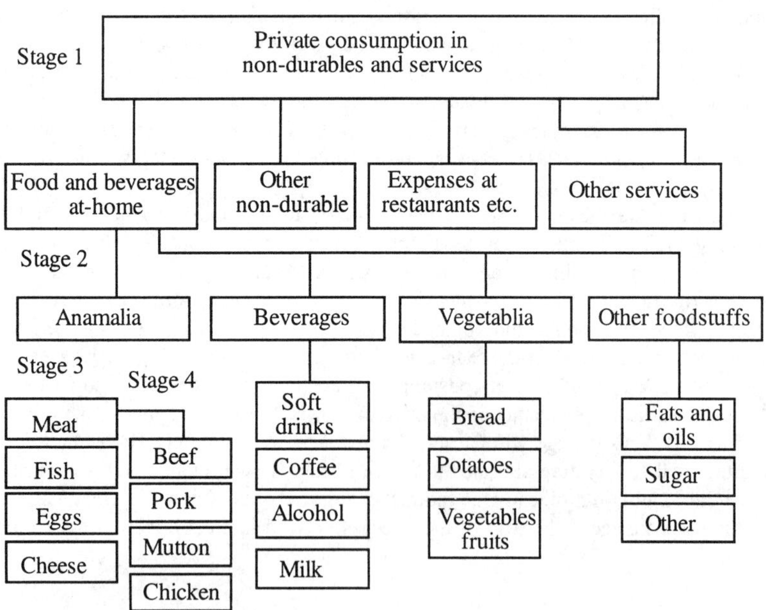

Figure 1 *Commodity Partitioning*

A DYNAMIC ALMOST IDEAL MODEL

The almost ideal demand system was first proposed in Deaton and Muellbauer (1980a). The *i*th good's budget share, w_i, is given by:

$$(1)\quad w_i = \alpha_i + \sum_{j=i}^{n} \gamma_{ij} \ln p_j + \beta_i \ln \frac{x}{P} \quad \text{for } i = 1,\ldots,n$$

where ln*P* is a price index defined by:

$$(2)\quad \ln P = \alpha_0 + \sum_{k=1}^{n} \alpha_k \ln p_k + \frac{1}{2} \sum_{k=1}^{n} \sum_{j=1}^{n} \gamma_{kj} \ln p_k \ln p_j$$

In Equations (1) and (2), p_i is the per unit price of good i and x is the total *per capita* expenditure on all goods included in the system.

The adding-up, homogeneity and symmetry restrictions may be expressed in terms of equality restrictions on the model's parameters of the form:

$$\Sigma_i \alpha_i = 1,\ \ \Sigma_i \beta_i = \Sigma_i \gamma_{ij} = 0 \ \ \text{(adding-up)}$$

$$(3)\quad \Sigma_j \gamma_{ij} = 0 \ \text{(homogenity)}$$

$$\gamma_{ij} = \gamma_{ji} \forall_{i,j} \ \text{(symmetry)}$$

Factors such as habit persistence suggest that consumers are unlikely to adjust fully in every time period. Consequently, a dynamic specification is desirable. Dynamics have been introduced into the almost ideal model in several ways, such as, to modify the intercept term of the price index, a_0 (e.g., Ray, 1985), to modify the intercept term of the share equations, a_i (e.g., Alessie and Kapteyn, 1991 or Assarsson, 1991), to estimate the model in difference form (e.g. Deaton and Muellbauer, 1980a) and to estimate the model within a general dynamic framework (e.g., Anderson and Blundell, 1983).

Following Assarsson (1991), the α_is are modified such that $\alpha_i = \alpha_{i0} + \Sigma_j \theta_{ij} w_{j(t-1)}$. This modification is quite simple and preserves the adding-up restrictions without increasing the numbers of parameters excessively. The *i*th good's budget share in period *t* is given by:

$$(4)\quad w_{it} = \alpha_{i0} + \sum_{j=1}^{n} \theta_{if} w_{j(t-1)} + \sum_{j=1}^{n} \gamma_{ij} \ln p_{jt} + \beta_i \ln \frac{x_t}{P_t}$$

where the price index $\ln P_t$ is defined by:

$$(5)\quad \ln P_t = \alpha_0 + \sum_{k=1}^{n} \alpha_{k0} \ln p_{kt} + \sum_{k=1}^{n} \sum_{j=1}^{n} \theta_{kj} w_{j(t-1)} \ln p_{kt} + \frac{1}{2} \sum_{k=1}^{n} \sum_{j=1}^{n} \gamma_{kj} \ln p_{kt} \ln p_{jt}$$

Equations (4) and (5) will be referred to as the dynamic true almost ideal demand model.

Adding up requires that $\Sigma_i \theta_{ij} = 0, \forall i$ in addition to the restrictions given by Equation (3). The restrictions $\Sigma_i \theta_{ij} = 0, \forall j$ are imposed to enable identification of the system.

The short-run own-price, cross-price and expenditure elasticities in period t are calculated as:

$$e_{iit} = -1 + \frac{\gamma_{ii}}{w_{it}} - \frac{\beta_i}{w_{it}}\left[\alpha_{i0} + \Sigma_k \theta_{ik} w_{k(t-1)} + \Sigma_k \gamma_{ik} \ln p_{kt}\right]$$

$$(6)\quad e_{ijt} = \frac{\gamma_{ij}}{w_{it}} - \frac{\beta_i}{w_{it}}\left[\alpha_{j0} + \Sigma_k \theta_{jk} w_{k(t-1)} + \Sigma_k \gamma_{jk} \ln p_{kt}\right]$$

$$E_{it} = 1 + \frac{\beta_i}{w_{it}}$$

WEAK SEPARABILITY AND UNCONDITIONAL ELASTICITIES

Let us divide our $m+n$ goods in two groups, A and B. The Marshallian demand function, $q^*_{A_i}$ for good i in group A is:

$$(7)\quad q^*_{Ai} = g^*_{Ai}(p_{A1},\ldots,p_{Am},p_{B1},\ldots,p_{Bn},x)$$

Weak separability allows us to divide the goods into sub-systems, such that a change in price of one good in one sub-system, A, affects the demand for all goods in another sub-system, B, in the same manner. Furthermore, weak separability makes it possible to divide the problem into several stages. Let us assume we have two stages.

At the first stage, the total expenditure is allocated between our two groups. This allocation is difficult because, in general, it is not possible to replace all the commodity prices and quantities within each group with a single price and a single quantity index. However, consider the following procedure based on Deaton and Muellbauer (1980b, pp.129–132) which is proposed in Edgerton (1992). Let the first-stage demand function for group A be approximated by:

$$(8)\quad q_A = g_A(P_A,P_B,x)$$

where q_A is expressed as real expenditure (at base year prices) and the Ps are true cost-of-living indexes. The indexes are themselves defined by $P_A = c_A(u_A{}^*,p_{A1},\ldots,p_{Am}) / c_A(u_A{}^*,p_{A1}{}^0,\ldots,p_{Am}{}^0)$ where c_A denotes the cost function associated with group A, $u_A{}^*$ the corresponding reference level of utility and $P_{Ai}{}^0$ the base period price of good i.

Weak separability is a necessary and sufficient condition for the second stage of the two-stage budgeting process. At the second stage, each group's expenditure function $x_A = c_A(u_A,p_{A1},\ldots,p_{Am})$ is minimized conditional on the utility level, u_A, implied by the first-stage demand functions (8). The resulting demand function for good i in group A is:

$$(9)\quad q_{Ai} = g_{Ai}(p_{A1},\ldots,p_{Am},x_A)$$

The demand functions, Equations (9) and (7), are conditional and unconditional demand functions, respectively. The two allocations, where stage one is defined by Equation (8) and stage two by Equation (9) yield identical results to an allocation made in one step, that is, Equation (7), given weak separability. However, the numerical values of the conditional and unconditional elasticities calculated by the use of Equations (9) and (7) are different. Edgerton (1992) derived formulae which recalculate the conditional to corresponding unconditional elasticities.

Let us concentrate on sub-system A. Following Edgerton (1992), let E_{AiA} denote the conditional expenditure elasticity for the ith good in group A, E_A the group expenditure elasticity for the Ath group, E_{Ai} the unconditional expenditure (= income) elasticity for good i within the Ath group, e_{Aij} the uncompensated conditional price elasticity between goods i and j in group A, e_{AA} the uncompensated own-price elasticity for group A and e_{AiAj} the uncompensated unconditional price elasticity for goods i and j in group A. The unconditional expenditure elasticities are calculated as:

$$(10)\quad E_{Ai} = \frac{\partial \ln g^*_{Ai}}{\partial \ln x} = \frac{\partial \ln g_{Ai}}{\partial \ln x_A}\frac{\partial \ln x_A}{\partial \ln x} = \frac{\partial \ln g_{Ai}}{\partial \ln x_A}\frac{\partial \ln g_A}{\partial \ln x} = E_{AiA}E_A$$

Note that $x_A \equiv P_A g_A(P_A, P_B, x)$. The relationship (10) is from a somewhat different line of arguments earlier suggested by, for example, Manser (1976, p.887).

The unconditional cross-price elasticity between goods i and j in group A is derived by the use of the chain rule on Equation (9)

$$(11)\quad e_{AiAj} = \frac{\partial \ln g^*_{Ai}}{\partial \ln p_{Aj}} = \frac{\partial \ln g_{Ai}}{\partial \ln p_{Aj}} + \frac{\partial \ln g_{Ai}}{\partial \ln x_A}\frac{\partial \ln x_A}{\partial \ln P_A}\frac{\partial \ln P_A}{\partial \ln p_{Aj}} = e_{Aij} + w_{AjA}E_{AiA}(1+e_{AA})$$

where $w_{AjA} = p_{Aj}q_{Aj} / x_A$ Note that $\partial \ln x / \partial \ln P_A = 0$ since income is given exogenously and $\partial \ln P_A / \partial \ln p_{Aj} = w_{AjA}$ by Shephard's lemma used on the true cost-of-living index which is proportional to an expenditure function. If the variation of prices with the utility level is rather small, other indexes may be good approximations to the true cost-of-living indexes. Paasche indexes are used here. The above formulae can by some notational difficulties be generalized to any number of stages and they are used to calculate unconditional elasticities for our four-stage utility tree described in Figure 1.

DATA, ESTIMATION AND TESTING

Annual National Accounts data from the Central Bureau of Statistics are used for the 1960–1991 period. At stage 4, disappearance data from the Agricultural Budget Commission and prices of representative goods are used. These prices are provided by various issues of Statistical Yearbook published by the Central Bureau of Statistics. It was impossible to construct a consistent data series for the consumer price of poultry and the producer price is used as a proxy variable.

The LSQ-procedure in the TSP-programme is used for estimation. This procedure iterates over the covariance matrix of the residuals and converges to the maximum likelihood estimators given the disturbances are multivariate normal. The method yields

Table 1 *Estimation Results: Stages 1 – 2 (t-values in parentheses)*

	α	θ				γ				β	w	R^2	BG
		1	2	3	4	1	2	3	4				
Stage 1													
Food	–0.119 (–2.22)	0.401 (4.48)	–0.674 (–4.06)	0.300 (3.50)	–0.027 (–0.39)	0.193 (5.09)	–0.005 (–0.43)	–0.143 (–6.70)	–0.044 (–1.79)	–0.092 (–6.18)	0.36	0.99	0.71
Restaurants	0.219 (5.20)	–0.144 (–2.57)	0.564 (4.70)	–0.157 (–2.82)	–0.263 (–5.57)	–0.005 (–0.43)	0.021 (2.96)	–0.003 (–0.21)	–0.013 (–1.15)	0.004 (0.43)	0.05	0.84	0.33
Other non-durables	0.426 (8.66)	0.116 (1.11)	0.268 (–1.41)	0.416 (7.54)	–0.264 (–2.66)	–0.143 (–6.70)	–0.003 (–0.21)	0.111 (4.48)	0.035 (1.48)	0.069 (4.12)	0.21	0.98	0.62
Services	0.474 (6.85)	–0.374 (–2.44)	0.378 (1.43)	–0.558 (–4.92)	0.554 (4.54)	–0.044 (–1.79)	–0.013 (–1.16)	0.035 (1.48)	0.022 (0.67)	0.019 (0.87)	0.38	0.96	0.37
	p-value for the hypothesis of no dynamics = 0.00												
Stage 2													
Animalia	0.327 (1.59)	0.419 (2.00)	–0.159 (–1.20)	–0.348 (–1.20)	0.088 (0.67)	0.023 (0.47)	–0.026 (–0.72)	0.046 (1.86)	–0.043 (–2.92)	0.005 (0.09)	0.32	0.89	0.96
Beverages	0.517 (2.94)	–0.286 (–1.70)	0.397 (3.10)	0.181 (0.65)	–0.292 (–3.09)	–0.026 (–0.72)	0.073 (2.36)	–0.057 (–2.57)	0.009 (0.66)	0.067 (1.53)	0.30	0.61	0.81
Vegetablia	–0.116 (–1.52)	–0.118 (–1.67)	–0.069 (–1.19)	0.139 (1.24)	0.048 (1.28)	0.046 (1.86)	–0.057 (–2.57)	0.054 (3.02)	–0.043 (–3.03)	–0.102 (–5.30)	0.24	0.96	0.17
Other	0.272 (2.30)	–0.014 (–0.13)	–0.170 (–2.51)	0.028 (0.16)	0.156 (1.58)	–0.043 (–2.92)	0.009 (0.66)	–0.043 (–3.03)	0.078 (4.26)	0.031 (1.02)	0.14	0.81	0.18
	p-value for the hypothesis of no dynamics = 0.02												

Table 1 (continued) *Estimation Results: Stages 3 – 4 (t-values in parentheses)*

	α	θ 1	θ 2	θ 3	θ 4	γ 1	γ 2	γ 3	γ 4	β	w	R^2	BG
Stage 3													
Meat	0.122 (0.44)	0.838 (6.51)	0.313 (1.39)	–1.316 (–4.88)	0.165 (0.56)	0.053 (1.41)	–0.007 (–0.40)	–0.013 (–0.77)	–0.033 (–1.67)	–0.014 (–0.26)	0.63	0.96	0.59
Fish	0.574 (2.74)	–0.527 (–5.21)	–0.077 (–0.41)	0.695 (3.05)	–0.091 (–0.46)	–0.007 (–0.40)	0.023 (1.44)	–0.007 (–0.48)	–0.009 (–0.84)	0.030 (0.76)	0.19	0.94	0.99
Cheese	0.163 (1.16)	–0.153 (–3.13)	–0.096 (–1.17)	0.588 (6.35)	–0.339 (–3.09)	–0.013 (–0.77)	–0.007 (–0.48)	0.017 (1.63)	0.004 (0.67)	–0.006 (–0.19)	0.11	0.90	0.22
Eggs	0.141 (2.31)	–0.158 (–4.23)	–0.140 (–2.22)	0.032 (0.47)	0.265 (2.18)	–0.033 (–1.67)	–0.009 (–0.84)	0.004 (0.67)	0.038 (3.38)	–0.010 (–0.87)	0.07	0.99	0.36
	p-value for the hypothesis of no dynamics = 0.00												
Stage 4													
Beef	–0.012 (–0.07)	0.585 (1.94)	0.022 (0.07)	0.384 (1.29)	–0.991 (–1.27)	0.164 (3.74)	–0.054 (–2.67)	–0.108 (–2.72)	–0.002 (–0.32)	–0.007 (–0.12)	0.40	0.63	0.03
Mutton	0.100 (1.40)	–0.073 (–0.63)	–0.068 (–0.37)	–0.287 (–2.20)	0.428 (1.12)	–0.054 (–2.67)	0.090 (4.15)	–0.032 (–1.77)	–0.042 (–0.80)	–0.050 (–2.22)	0.12	0.81	0.76
Pork	0.679 (3.70)	–0.312 (–0.97)	0.221 (0.79)	0.111 (0.38)	–0.020 (–0.03)	–0.108 (–2.72)	–0.032 (–1.77)	0.131 (3.10)	0.009 (1.20)	0.049 (0.78)	0.46	0.61	0.10
Chicken	0.233 (7.45)	–0.200 (–4.38)	–0.175 (–2.97)	–0. 208 (–4.30)	0.583 (4.41)	–0.002 (–0.32)	–0.004 (–0.80)	0.009 (1.20)	–0.003 (–0.58)	0.008 (0.98)	0.02	0.88	0.74
	p-value for the hypothesis of no dynamics = 0.03												

estimates which are invariant with respect to which equation is dropped. The homogeneity and symmetry restrictions are imposed on the various sub-systems.

The hypothesis of no dynamics is tested by a likelihood ratio test. This test has a bias towards rejection in small samples (e.g., Bewley, 1986) and a commonly used correction factor $(T–k)/T$ is used to calculate a corrected likelihood ratio test. Here T is the number of observations and k the average number of estimated parameters per equation.

ESTIMATION RESULTS

The parameter estimates with t-values of the parameters, the budget shares within the various sub-systems, the coefficients of determination (R^2), the p-values (the probabilities of rejecting a null hypothesis given that it is true) of a Breusch–Godfrey test (Godfrey 1978) for first-order autocorrelation (BG) and p-values for the hypothesis of no dynamics are shown in Table 1.

The four-stage system appears to have a high explanatory power. The R^2-values are above 0.8 for 13 of the 16 equations. However, the R^2-values can only be considered as indicators of the goodness of fit, since the measure is only truly applicable for a single linear equation. Nearly half the estimated parameters are significant at the 5 percent significance level which is used in this paper.

The Breusch–Godfrey test for autocorrelation is valid in the presence of lagged endogenous variables. Autocorrelation is rejected in each equation, except for beef. This is a major improvement compared with the corresponding static specification. Furthermore, the hypothesis of no dynamics is rejected for each sub-system.

ELASTICITIES

The numerical values of the estimated short-run uncompensated own-price and expenditure elasticities are shown in Table 2. The elasticities are of the expected sign and reasonable magnitudes. The conditional elasticities are calculated at mean and 1991 values of the input variables. There are only minor changes in the numerical values over time, with a possible exception for eggs.

The standard errors are approximated by the ANALYZ statement in TSP which computes the standard errors using the covariance matrix of the estimated parameters but treating the data as fixed constants. The elasticities are statistically significant, except for the own-price elasticity of lamb.

Expenditure data are mainly used in this study. The use of this data set has implications for the interpretation of the elasticities. Given expenditure data, the quantities will include effects of quality changes such as shifts from low to high processed foodstuffs. For example, expenditure data allow for the possibility that an increasing proportion of highly processed meats may increase the expenditure, even though the consumption of meat actually may decrease when measured by weight. This may be viewed as either an advantage or disadvantage depending on what part of the food chain is the primary focus.

The conditional and unconditional elasticities are identical for stage 1. The own-price elasticity of food and beverages is –0.4 and the expenditure elasticity is 0.7. The unconditional elasticities deviate substantially from the conditional for stage 2. These

Table 2 *Expenditure and Short-Run Uncompensated Own-Price Elasticities: Stages 1–4*

Variable	Own-price Conditional		Own-price Unconditional	Expenditure Conditional		Expenditure Unconditional
Stage 1						
Food and beverages	–0.44	–0.36	–0.44	0.74	0.69	0.74
	(0.10)	(0.12)		(0.04)	(0.05)	
Restaurants	–0.57	–0.52	–0.57	1.09	1.10	1.09
	(0.16)	(0.17)		(0.20)	(0.23)	
Other non-durables	–0.63	–0.65	–0.63	1.32	1.30	1.32
	(0.07)	(0.07)		(0.07)	(0.07)	
Services	–0.97	–0.97	–0.97	1.05	1.04	1.05
	(0.10)	(0.09)		(0.06)	(0.05)	
Stage 2						
Animalia	–0.94	–0.94	–0.76	1.01	1.01	0.75
	(0.15)	(0.15)		(0.15)	(0.15)	
Beverages	–0.88	–0.88	–0.68	1.22	1.22	0.90
	(0.09)	(0.09)		(0.14)	(0.14)	
Vegetablia	–0.83	-0.82	–0.75	0.56	0.53	0.41
	(0.05)	(0.06)		(0.09)	(0.09)	
Other foodstuffs	–0.48	–0.50	–0.38	1.23	1.22	0.91
	(0.12)	(0.11)		(0.22)	(0.21)	
Stage 3						
Meat	–0.90	–0.90	–0.74	0.98	0.98	0.73
	(0.08)	(0.09)		(0.08)	(0.09)	
Fish	–0.93	–0.95	–0.87	1.16	1.13	0.87
	(0.08)	(0.07)		(0.21)	(0.17)	
Cheese	–0.85	–0.88	–0.82	0.95	0.96	0.71
	(0.11)	(0.09)		(0.27)	(0.22)	
Eggs	–0.38	–0.22	–0.37	0.83	0.79	0.62
	(0.19)	(0.22)		(0.20)	(0.24)	
Stage 4						
Beef	–0.59	–0.60	–0.48	0.98	0.98	0.72
	(0.12)	(0.11)		(0.14)	(0.14)	
Mutton and lamb	–0.25	-0.21	–0.23	0.57	0.54	0.42
	(0.18)	(0.19)		(0.20)	(0.20)	
Pork	–0.78	–0.77	–0.66	1.11	1.11	0.81
	(0.13)	(0.13)		(0.14)	(0.14)	
Chicken	–1.15	–1.10	–1.14	1.36	1.25	1.00
	(0.22)	(0.16)		(0.35)	(0.26)	

Note: Standard errors in parentheses

deviations indicate the importance of correcting conditional elasticities used for policy purposes. The deviations are particularly large for the animalia and beverages groups. The unconditional elasticities both with respect to price and expenditure are inelastic at stage 3.

The unconditional own-price elasticities for beef, lamb, pork and chicken are calculated to be –0.48, –0.23, –0.66 and –1.14, respectively. The highly price inelastic demand for lamb may be somewhat surprising. The differences between conditional and unconditional own-price elasticities are of some importance for beef and pork which account for large budget shares within the meat sub-system.

The unconditional expenditure elasticities deviate substantially from the conditional ones. The unconditional expenditure elasticities for beef, lamb, pork and chicken are calculated to be 0.72, 0.42, 0.81 and 1.00, respectively.

CONCLUSIONS

The hypothesis of no dynamics is rejected for each stage. Furthermore, the dynamic specification removes autocorrelation to a large extent. These findings indicate the importance of a dynamic specification.

The estimated elasticities are of the expected sign and reasonable magnitudes. The correction from conditional to unconditional elasticities proved to be empirically important for many goods. This emphasizes the importance of correcting conditional elasticities before results from different studies are compared or before the elasticities are used for policy purposes. This is not the current practice in the literature. The demands for beef, lamb and pork are inelastic with respect to own-price as well as expenditure while the demand for chicken is price elastic.

REFERENCES

Alessie, R. and Kapteyn, A., 1991, 'Habit Formation, Interdependent Preferences and Demographic Effects in the Almost Ideal Demand System', *The Economic Journal*, Vol. 101, No. 407, pp.404–419.

Anderson, G. and Blundell, R., 1983, 'Testing Restrictions in a Flexible Demand System: An Application to Consumers' Expenditure in Canada', *Review of Economic Studies*, Vol. 50, No. 162, pp.397–410.

Assarsson, B., 1991, 'Alcohol Pricing Policy and the Demand for Alcohol in Sweden 1978–1988', Working Paper, Department of Economics, Uppsala University, Sweden.

Bewley, R., 1986, *Allocation Models: Specification, Estimation and Applications*, Ballinger, Cambridge, Massachusetts.

Burton, M. and Young, T., 1992, 'The Structure of Changing Tastes for Meat and Fish in Great Britain', *European Review of Agricultural Economics*, Vol. 19, No. 2, pp.165–180.

Cashin, P., 1991, 'A Model of the Disaggregated Demand for Meat in Australia', *Australian Journal of Agricultural Economics*, Vol. 35, No. 3, pp.263–284.

Central Bureau of Statistics, various years, 'National Accounts', Oslo-Kongsvinger.

Chalfant, J.A., Gray, R.S. and White, K.J., 1991, 'Evaluating Prior Beliefs in a Demand System: The Case of Meat Demand in Canada', *American Journal of Agricultural Economics*, Vol. 73, No. 2, pp.476–490.

Chen, P.Y. and Veeman, M.M., 1991, 'An Almost Ideal Demand System Analysis for Meats with Habit Formation and Structural Change', *Canadian Journal of Agricultural Economics*, Vol. 39, No. 2, pp.223–235.

Deaton, A. and Muellbauer, J., 1980a, 'An Almost Ideal Demand System', *The American Economic Review*, Vol. 70, No. 3, pp.312–326.

Deaton, A. and Muellbauer, J., 1980b, *Economics and Consumer Behaviour*, Cambridge University Press, Cambridge, UK.
Edgerton, D. L., 1992, 'Estimating Elasticities in Multi-Stage Demand Systems', Paper presented at AAEA-NAREA Annual Meeting, Baltimore.
Godfrey L.G., 1978, 'Testing Against General Autoregressive and Moving Average Error Models When the Regressors Include Lagged Dependent Variables', *Econometrica*, Vol. 46, No. 6, pp.1293–301.
Manser, M. E., 1976, 'Elasticities of Demand for Food: An Analysis Using Non-Additive Utility Functions Allowing for Habit Formation', *Southern Economic Journal*, Vol. 43, No. 4, pp.879–891.
Mdafri, A. and Brorsen, B.W., 1993, 'Demand for Red Meat, Poultry, and Fish in Morocco: An Almost Ideal Demand System', *Agricultural Economics*, Vol. 9, No. 2, pp.155–163.
Pollak R.A. and Wales, T. J., 1992, *Demand System Specification & Estimation*, Oxford University Press, New York.
Ray, R., 1985, 'Specification and Time Series Estimation of Dynamic Gorman Polar Form Demand Systems', *European Economic Review*, Vol. 27, No. 3, pp.357–374.
Rickertsen, K., 1994, 'Static and Dynamic AIDS Models of Demand for Food in Norway', forthcoming Report, Department of Economics and Social Sciences, The Agricultural University of Norway, Ås.
Vale, P.H., 1989, 'Etterspørsel etter matvarer', Report No. 59, Department of Economics and Social Sciences, The Agricultural University of Norway, Ås.

DISCUSSION OPENING — Wen S. Chern *(The Ohio State University, USA)*

This paper presents the econometric results of estimating a four-stage dynamic almost ideal demand system in Norway. The study was rigorously done and the paper was well written. The author made two important contributions. One is to demonstrate the differences between the conditional and unconditional demand elasticities. The other is to show that the full AIDS model can be easily estimated with a widely accessible computer package. Rickertsen defines conditional elasticities as those typically obtained from a demand system estimated for a subset of commodities such as beef, lamb, pork, and chicken in his model. The unconditional elasticities are defined as those obtained from a demand model including all non-durable goods and services in the consumer's budget. Estimates of unconditional elasticities are important because they are the elasticities needed in welfare analysis. The second contribution is important because most of applications of the AIDS were based on the linear approximate form. Few empirical applications estimated the full AIDS.

I have several comments on the paper. First, the unconditional elasticities as defined in the paper are not perfectly unconditional. In fact, they are still conditional upon the assumption of weak separability among non-durable goods and services, and the assumption of the independence of non-durables from the demand for durable goods. Specifically, the correction formulae are derived from the specification of various stages of utility maximization. For example, if the author reduces his four stages to three or extends it to five stages, the estimates of unconditional elasticities are likely different. In fact, with the data on hand, one can estimate a truly unconditional one-stage model (with some demand components highly aggregated). It would be very interesting to compare the unconditional elasticities obtained in the paper with those obtained from the one-stage model.

My second comment is on dynamic specification. The author used the lagged budget shares and the demographic translation to incorporate these lagged variables. There is not a single most acceptable way to capture the habit formation. Personally, I would prefer use of the lagged quantity variables to budget shares. Still the general dynamic framework developed by Anderson and Blundell should be explored. In any case, when the lagged variables are included, short-run and long-run elasticities are distinguishable in the model. Unfortunately, in the highly non-linear AIDS model, the long-run elasticities can not be derived analytically. However, they can be estimated by a simulation technique. In the present model, there are no theoretical and statistical criteria available for evaluating the magnitudes or signs of the estimated coefficients of lagged variables. Currently, there are negative and positive coefficients, some smaller than one and others greater than one. There are no clues about what the long-run elasticities would look like. A few notes on the long-run elasticities would be useful in the paper.

The empirical estimates offer interesting insights into consumer behaviour in Norway. First, there appears to be no inferior good in Norway. The demand for food consumed at home is inelastic with respect to both own price and income. All foods appear to be necessities except chicken whose demand is elastic with respect to price and income. It would be useful to report the budget shares of the goods included in all four stages in the model so that one could try to further explain what these estimated elasticities imply when changes in prices or income occur. Overall this is an excellent paper. I congratulate the author on a job well done.

JEAN-MARC BOUSSARD*

A Risk Generated Non-Linear Cobweb

Abstract: With risk averse producers, the traditional cobweb model becomes non-linear. The currently produced quantity is an homographic function of previous years' quantities. This may result in the market generating chaotic price and quantity series, especially if demand is rigid. Hedging facilities are unable to reduce the magnitude of fluctuations, which are socially detrimental, especially from the consumers' point of view. This justifies public intervention in markets such as those for staple food commodities or health care.

INTRODUCTION

The 'cobweb' dynamic market model is well known (Ezekiel, 1938):

$$(1)\quad \begin{cases} p_t^* = aq_t + b & \text{(supply)} \\ p_t = \alpha q_t + \beta & \text{(demand)} \\ p_t^* = p_{t-1} & \text{(expectations)} \end{cases}$$

Here, q_t and p_t are quantities and prices, respectively at period *t*, whereas p_t^* is the expected price, and *a, b,*α*,* β, are constant scalar coefficients. Then:

$$(2)\quad q_t = \frac{\alpha}{a} q_{t-1} + (\beta - b)/a$$

Since $\alpha < 0$, and $a > 0$, this implies that q_t bounces up and down throughout time. If $\left|\frac{\alpha}{a}\right| < 1$, then $|q_t - q_{t-1}| < |q_{t-1} - q_{t-2}|$. Thus, the amplitude of oscillations is always decreasing, and the optimal market equilibrium situation will be reached after a while. On the contrary, when the opposite situation arises, $\left|\frac{\alpha}{\mathrm{a}}\right| > 1$ and the cycles 'explode'. Finally, for $\left|\frac{\alpha}{a}\right| = 1$, cycles of constant amplitude continue indefinitely, but this situation is unstable, for any change in a or α will toggle toward damped or exploding cycles.

This model was originally designed as an explanation of the 'hog cycle'. It has also been used for evaluating consumers' and producers' losses from the cycle, in partial equilibrium analysis (Waugh, 1944). Yet, because of its too obvious defects, it has never been considered as a very useful tool. Nobody saw an 'exploding' market (with negative prices and quantities). The permanent cycle regime is unstable, as we have seen. Above all, the naive expectation scheme has been criticized, on the grounds that well informed producers could easily make a profit by introducing a lag into their production plans, behaviour which should eliminate the very causes of the cycle.

* INRA-ENGREF, Paris.

For these reasons, the cobweb model has been neglected during recent years. The literature devoted to price stabilization (Oi, 1961; Massel, 1970; Newbery and Stiglitz, 1981) is in general based on the idea that market fluctuations are caused by exogenous random shocks. In addition, the latter are assumed to be geographically distributed in such a way that increasing the size of market basins should dampen variability, as a consequence of the 'law of large numbers'[1].

One may nevertheless be puzzled by the fact that fluctuations continue to occur, and seemingly without the size of market having very much effect on the extent of movement. Can this fact be a consequence of an endogenous market generated mechanism, which would produce apparently random series, against any counter cyclical policy of the usual kind?

This paper brings an hypothetical positive answer to this question. It is based on the non-linearities introduced by introducing risk aversion into the traditional cobweb model. Of course, this mechanism is not the only one likely to generate pseudo random market fluctuations. However, it is one of them, and for that reason only, deserves a modest amount of attention.

A CHAOTIC MOTION GENERATED FROM RISK EXPECTATIONS

Let us suppose that actual price p_t is uncertain in Equation (1), so that p_t^* has mean $\overline{p}_t^*$ and variance $\overline{v}_t^*$. Notice that $\overline{p}_t^*$ and $\overline{v}_t^*$ are subjective expectations, the outcomes of producers' guesses. The certainty equivalent of the outcome $r = pq$ is $\overline{r} - A\,\sigma_r^2 = \overline{p}_t^*\, q_t - A\,\overline{v}_t^*\, q_t^2$ and thus, the marginal revenue certainty equivalent is[2]:

(2) $\tilde{p} = \overline{p}_t^* - 2A\overline{v}_t^* q_t$

where A is the producer's absolute risk aversion coefficient. Let us also assume a linear marginal cost, as in Equation (1), so that the supply equation is:

(3) $\tilde{p} = aq + b$

Combining Equations (2) and (3) gives:

(4) $\left(\overline{p}_t^* - b\right)/\left(a + 2A\overline{v}_t^*\right)$

In addition, suppose $\overline{p}_t^* = \hat{p}$ is constant (producers expect a constant, 'normal' price), but v_t^* can vary according to past experience (when the magnitude of market fluctuations increases, producers become more cautious). More precisely, assume $v_t^* = (p_{t-1} - \hat{p})^2$. Then, replacing v_t^* and p_t^* in Equation (5) gives:

(5) $q_t = \dfrac{\hat{p} - b}{a + 2\,A\left(p_{t-1} - \hat{p}\,\right)^2} = \dfrac{\hat{p} - b}{a + 2\,A\left(\alpha\, q_{t-1} + \beta - \hat{p}\,\right)^2}$

In this way, q_t is shown to be an homographic function of q_{t-1}. With

$$(6)\quad \begin{cases} x_t = \hat{p} - \beta - \alpha q_t \\ \gamma = (\hat{p} - \beta)\sqrt{\dfrac{2A}{a}} \\ \delta = -\dfrac{\alpha}{a}(\hat{p} - b)\sqrt{\dfrac{2A}{a}} \end{cases}$$

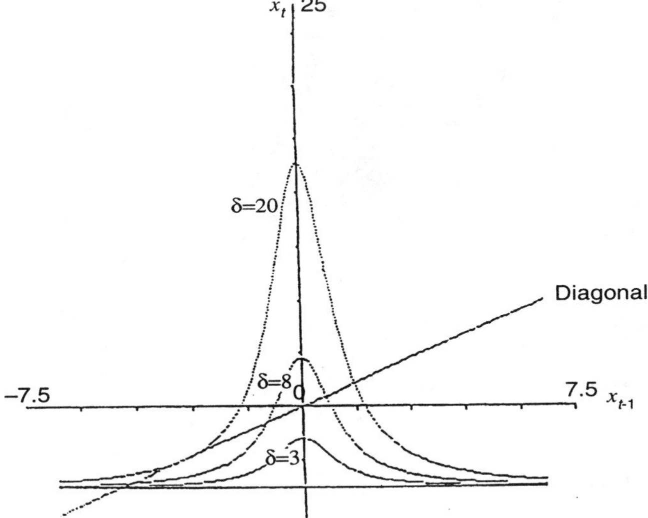

Figure 1 *Plotting of x_t versus x_{t-1} for $\delta = -5$*

Equation (5) can be transformed as:

$$(7)\quad x_t = \gamma + \frac{\delta}{1 + x_{t-1}^2}$$

(notice that x_t is now a magnitude related to prices rather than to quantities, but insofar as prices and quantities are linked by linear relations, this is not a problem).

It is possible to plot x_t versus x_{t-1}. One gets a hat-shaped curve, the precise setting of which depends upon the parameters γ and δ (Figure 1). This is the kind of configuration which is likely to generate chaotic behaviour for the series $X = x_0, \ldots, x_t$.

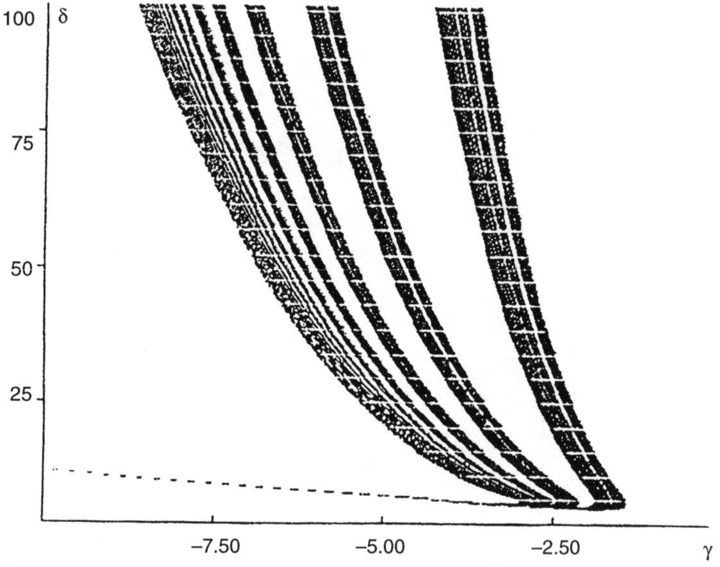

Figure 2 *Regions of the γ, δ Plane Where Chaotic Motion Occurs, for* $x_0 = 0$

There is no simple way to predict from the values of parameters whether any actual realization of X will or will not be chaotic. But it is possible to try a number of such values, and to infer the nature of the corresponding orbits from the magnitude of the associated Lyapounov exponent, that is, $\lim_{T \to \infty} \frac{1}{T} \sum_{t=1}^{T} \ln h_t$. Figure 2 illustrates the result of such trials, for $x_0 = 0$, $-10 < \gamma < 0$, and $0 < \delta < 100$. Black points are those for which the corresponding Lyapounov exponent is positive. The corresponding set in R^2 seems to be a fractal object, with the black points never completely covering a given area of the (γ, δ) plane.

It is difficult to say much more about this map. Yet, the preceding discussion shows how and why, for some values of the parameters, chaotic motion may result from market operation. Returning to the original parameters, as given by Equation (6), one can understand that steep demand and flat supply curves are likely to produce such situations.

MORE COMPLICATED MODELS

What could happen with more realistic models, better expectation schemes, non-linear supply and demand curves, etc...? Answering such questions is not easy, since any 'more complicated' model will be just as discussable as the present one in some aspect. Yet, a few variants of the basic model have been investigated.

Expectation Schemes

The most discussable assumption of the basic model is the constancy of $\hat{p}$, the expected price. In this context, the model which seems to stay as close as possible to the original Ezekiel model comes from:

$$(8)\quad \begin{cases} \overline{p}_t^* = p_{t-2} \\ v_t^* = \left(p_{t-1} - \overline{p}_t^*\right)^2 \end{cases}$$

Here, p_{t-2} is chosen as an estimate for $\overline{p}_t^*$ rather than p_{t-1} because of the obvious existence of a pseudo period 2, which should induce the producer to base expectations on the same lag. With these specifications, the model is a map of order 2, defined by:

$$(9)\quad \begin{cases} x_{1t} = q_t = \dfrac{\alpha x_{2t-1} + \beta - b}{a + 2A\,\alpha^2\left(x_{1t-1} - x_{2t-1}\right)^2} \\ x_{2t} = q_{t-1} = x_{1t-1} \end{cases}$$

In fact, the series generated in that way are quite similar to those generated by Equation (7). Thus, the constancy of $\hat{p}$ is not really the main reason for this behaviour. But is this result a consequence of the arbitrary choice of p_{t-2} as the basis for price expectation, and of p_{t-1} for the variance expectation? Would the outcome be different if the two had been permuted? Especially, would it be more rational to treat both prices and quantities as symmetrical, and then:

$$(10)\quad \begin{cases} \overline{p}_t^* = \dfrac{1}{2}(p_{t-1} + p_{t-2}) \\ \overline{v}_t^* = \dfrac{1}{2}\sum_{i=1,2}(p_{t-i} - \overline{p}_{t-i}^*)^2 \end{cases}$$

Again, the main conclusions remain approximately the same: convergence occurs frequently when α/a is small. Large α/a produces cycles, chaotic motion, or even divergence (that is, cycles of increasing extent). Divergence occurs, for instance, with adaptive expectations:

$$(11)\quad \begin{cases} \overline{p}_t^* = \overline{p}_{t-1}^* + \varepsilon_a(\overline{p}_{t-1}^* - p_{t-1}) \\ \overline{v}_t^* = (\overline{p}_{t-1}^* - p_{t-1})^2 \end{cases}$$

where ε_a is a 'coefficient of error correction'. In that case, nothing prevents $\overline{p}_t^*$ from growing to infinity, with detrimental consequences.

Futures Markets

A strong objection to the relevance of the above models is the absence of hedging facilities. Actually futures markets constitute the liberal answer to the kind of irregular behaviour described above, especially because, at least from the point of view of the producers, they provide a simple way to partially or totally remove risk interference with production decisions. Yet, futures markets are unable to remove market instability. Let us assume that:

- all identical farmers maximize a Freund–Markowitz utility function, with constant risk aversion coefficient *A*, and a linear marginal cost, as in Equation (1).
- all identical speculators (traders) maximize the same kind of function, with constant risk aversion coefficient *B*.
- farmers can choose to sell at planting time on the futures market, or to sell at harvest time on the spot market.

Then it can be shown (Newbery and Stiglitz, 1981; Boussard, 1993) that the market equilibrium is the same as with an average risk coefficient *C*, such that:

$$(12)\quad \frac{1}{C} = \frac{1}{A} + \frac{1}{B}$$

This means that the above reasoning is still valid, and that futures markets will generate the same kind of fluctuations as with a spot market only, under suitable conditions.

The welfare consequences of this situation need to be examined, but since the mean values of quantities are in general lower than those corresponding to the long-run equilibrium, it can be confidently assumed that they are detrimental.

Constant Elasticity Supply and Demand Curves

The existence of negative values for prices and quantities is a natural consequence of making use of linear supply and demand curves. In the case of the original cobweb model, a straightforward solution to this problem was to change the units on the axis. Replacing p and q in Equation (1) by their logarithms does not formally modify the model, and guarantees positive prices and quantities. In addition, a and α can then be interpreted as constant elasticities, which may make many applied economists feel more comfortable.

When risk is taken into account in the model, the trick is no longer possible, at least without modifications of some of the basic equations. Replacing the demand Equation in (1) by:

$$(13)\quad p_t = \beta q_t^{\alpha}$$

and Equation (3) by:

$$(14)\quad \tilde{p}_t = b q_t^{a}$$

adds new kinds of non-linearities to market equilibrium equations. In practice, the general behaviour of models built along that line is not very different from what has been seen above.

CONCLUSION

The above models are very simple, even simplistic. Yet, they are not without far reaching implications. First, it is ironic to see risk and fluctuations stemming from risk aversion. In fact, other mechanisms than those reviewed above are likely to be involved in risk generation: for instance, all consequences of capital accumulation have been ignored in this paper although most analysts seeking sources of chaotic motion in economics would probably make it the basic ingredient for such models[3]. Yet, the above model provides a plausible explanation for the existence of irregular cycles that previous cobweb models failed to account for, in general, and which are nevertheless persistent, as is demonstrated by recent empirical studies (Holzer and Precht, 1993).

It is important to notice that the above results are independent of market size. This is the main difference between endogenous (chaotic) or exogenous (climatic or random) sources of uncertainty. With fluctuations occurring as results of a large number of independent shocks, increasing the size of market would probably reduce the magnitude of risks (Blandford, 1983; Tyers, 1991, op. cit.; Tyers and Anderson, 1992, *op. cit*, in the case of staple food commodities. But with endogenous fluctuations such as those reported above, no such damping mechanism is to be expected.

The models just presented also explain the basic inability of hedging to reduce the detrimental effects of fluctuations. In that context, it is illusory to hope that futures markets could significantly alleviate the social cost of economic fluctuations, especially on the consumer's side.

Finally, the above discussion casts new light on expectations. Not only are expectations pertaining to *mean values* important for market outcomes, those pertaining to *variability* can be just as crucial. Of course, anybody acquainted with risk decision theory can say the same. Yet, while a large body of literature has been devoted to the elicitation of mean values expectation schemes, much less is concerned with variance expectation schemes. This is perhaps a new field to be considered[4].

NOTES

1 This aspect has been extensively discussed for agricultural commodities (Tyers, 1990; Tyers and Anderson, 1992).

2 This is a very classical result, which easily generalises to the multiproduct case (Hazell and Scandizzo, 1977, among others).

3 As examples of such research, in the spirit of Goodwin (1951), see; Puu (1991), Chavas and Holt (1993) or Gerard (1990).

4 Can it be said that little progress has been made in this direction since Shackle (1961)? However, see Chalfant *et al*, (1990).

REFERENCES

Blandford, D., 1983, 'Instability in World Grain Markets', *Journal of Agricultural Economics*, Vol. 34, No. 3, pp.379–392.

Chalfant, J.A., Collender, N. and Subramania, S., 1990, 'The Mean and Variance of the Mean Variance Decision Rule', *American Journal of Agricultural Economics*, Vol. 72, No. 4, pp.966–974.

Chavas, J.P. and Holt, M.T., 1993, 'Market instability and non linear dynamics', *American Journal of Agricultural Economics*, Vol. 75, No. 1, pp.113–120.

Ezekiel, 1938, 'The Cobweb Theorem', *Quarterly Journal of Economics*, Vol. 53, pp.225–280.

Fulponi, L., 1993, *Commodity Price Variability: Its Nature and Causes*, OECD, Paris.

Gerard, F., 1991, 'Instabilité des Prix Agricoles et Influence de L'incertitude sur les Comportements Economiques, Thesis, Paris I Université, Paris.

Goodwin, R.M., 1951, 'The Non Linear Accelator and the Persistence of Business Cycle', *Econometrica*, No. 19, pp.1–17.

Hazell, P.B.R. and Scandizzo, P., 1977, 'Farmers' Expectation, Risk Aversion and Market Equilibrium Under Risk', *American Journal of Agricultural Economics*, Vol. 59, No. 1, pp.204–209.

Holzer, C. and Precht, M., 1993, Der chaotische Schweinezyklus, Agrarwirtchaft, Vol. 42, No. 7, pp.276–283.

Massel, B.F., 1970, 'Some Welfare Implications of International Price Stabilization', *Journal of Political Economy*, Vol. 78, No. 2, pp.404–417.

Newbery, D.M.G. and Stiglitz, J.E., 1981, *The Theory of Commodity Price Stabilization*, Clarendon Press, Oxford, England.

Oi, W., 1961, 'The Desirability of Price Instability Under Perfect Competition', *Econometrica*, Vol. 27, pp.58–64.

Puu, T., 1991, *Non Linear Economic Dynamics*, Springer, Verlag, Berlin.

Schackle, G.L.S., 1961, *Decision Order and Time in Human Affairs*, Cambridge University Press, Cambridge, England.

Tyers, K., 1990, 'Implicit Policy Preferences and the Assessment of Negotiable Trade Policy Reforms', *European Economic Review*, Vol. 34, No. 1, pp.319–1426.

Tyers, R. and Anderson, J.K., 1992, *Disarray in World Food Markets: A Quantitative Assessment*, Cambridge University Press, Cambridge.

Waugh, F.V., 1944, 'Does the consumer benefit from price instability?', *Quarterly Journal of Economics*, Vol. 58, pp.602–614.

DISCUSSION OPENING — Benedict White *(University of Newcastle Upon Tyne, UK)*

This was an interesting and stimulating paper. It takes the cobweb model as a starting point and modifies the model structure to involve risk aversion and the assumption that producers have fixed expectations about the mean price and naive expectations about price variance. On this basis, equilibrium output and price may show chaotic behaviour. That is, behaviour which is apparently random, but is in fact generated by a deterministic non-linear difference equation.

Such models may also show cyclical behaviour or converge. It is proposed that markets which show persistent cycles may be represented by non-linear difference equations, instead of the usual alternative explanations which focus on lags in the supply response.

It is now a well known result that some models of markets, for particular parameter sets, may show either chaotic or complex cyclical behaviour.

My questions about this paper concern the implications of this result for applied market analysis. First, the main model presented in thepaper assumes producers are risk averse and have a constant absolute risk aversion. Mean price expectations are constant, but the expectation of variance is formed by the lagged variance. These assumptions are restrictive and quite unrealistic. Is it possible to show that chaotic behaviour occurs under a more general – and realistic – set of behavioural assumptions or mathematical forms? Second, continuing on the theme of the realism of the assumptions, could market agents determine the form of the underlying non-linear difference equation and use this equation to form rational expectations and eliminate chaotic market behaviour? In this context, the market price may settle at a constant value. Third, can we identify and estimate these equations from market quantity data? It may be that stochastic effects, such as yield variations, may overwhelm chaotic effects. Is it perhaps the case that we will be able to estimate non-liear difference equatins which predict the price and quantity series, but cannot be directly related to a single structural economic model?

In summary, this paper and others establish that chaotic behaviour can be exhibited by dynamic market models. What is unclear is where this result takes us. Do we ignore the possibility of chaotic behaviour and continue to estimate maket models based on dunctional forms which preclude chaotic behaviour? Or do the econometric tools exist to estimate econometric models which show chaotic behaviour?

CATHERINE HALBRENDT, JOHN PESEK, APRIL PARSONS AND ROBERT LINDNER*

Analysis of Australian Consumer Preference for pST-Pork Products

Abstract: Conjoint measurement was used to determine consumer preference for pork produced with genetically engineered porcine somatotropin (pST). A preference model was constructed based on three pork attributes, fat reduction, price and technology, which allowed for estimable interactions between attributes. Interview surveys were used to collect conjoint data in several shopping centres in three cities. Respondents generally preferred leaner pST-produced pork, but only at fat reduction levels greater than currently attainable with conventional technology.

INTRODUCTION

The Australian meat industry is facing changes in consumer preferences toward the types and amount of meat in their diets. Per capita consumption of red meat (beef, veal, lamb and mutton) has fallen over the last several decades, while white meat (poultry), pork and seafood consumption have increased. One of the main reasons for the changing trend in meat consumption is the perceived health risks of red meat consumption (Gardner, 1990; and Bartley *et al.,* 1988).

Currently, there is an opportunity for expansion of the pig industry by promoting pigmeat as a healthier alternative to beef, chicken and other meats, with leaner pork produced with genetically engineered porcine somatotropin (pST), a protein that occurs naturally in pigs. Produced in the anterior pituitary gland, pST regulates pig growth and controls pig metabolism. Metabolic activity involves the decrease of fat storage and the increase in development of muscle (i.e., lean meat) (Turman and Andrews, 1955).

Through advances in genetic engineering technology, it is now possible to manufacture pST economically. Experiments have shown that pigs supplemented with man-made pST experience increases in growth rates and feed efficiency, and carcass fat reduction.

The implications of the successful adoption of pST by the pork industry include: benefits to consumers in the form of healthier, leaner pork products at lower prices; benefits to producers in the form of lower production costs and more lean meat per carcass, and; benefits to the environment in the form of more efficient feed use by pigs and less waste.

The successful adoption of pST by the Australian pork industry will depend on the extent to which Australian pork consumers will accept pST technology in pork production. In 1990, Taverner summarized the results of a survey conducted by Couchman and Fink-Jenson of over 2000 New Zealand residents. Respondents said their highest level of concern over the use of genetic engineering was in the case of meat products, and 27 percent said their main concern over eating genetically engineered meat was that it is 'unnatural'. This study's objective is to determine Australian consumers' preferences for pork produced with/and without genetically engineered pST, using conjoint measurement.

* University of Delaware, USA, University of Delaware, USA and University of Western Australia, respectively.

METHODOLOGY

Conjoint measurement is a multivariate market research technique which can aid in sorting out the relative importance of a product's multi-dimensional attributes (Green and Wind, 1975). Conjoint measurement refers to any decompositional method that estimates the structure of consumers' preferences given the consumers' overall evaluations of a set of alternative products that are pre-specified in terms of levels of different attributes.

Conjoint Measurement

Two especially useful results yielded by conjoint measurement include the ability to determine a hypothetical 'ideal' product design that would maximize overall consumer utility, and the ability to construct a set of competitive product profiles for any specified level of utility (Green and Wind, 1975). To conduct the conjoint experiment, the product is presented to the respondent in the form of several product profiles, each comprised of several attributes which vary simultaneously. The respondent rates each profile according to preference, the rating representing the level of utility provided by each product profile.

More recently, the theory of consumer utility is increasingly considered a two-stage process that goes a step beyond the traditional economic theory of consumer demand. For example, based on Lancaster's model of consumer behaviour, the theory of brand preference states that goods are valued for the attributes they possess, and that differentiated products are essentially different packages of attributes (Ratchford, 1975). In other words, utility is determined not by the goods themselves, but by the consumer's preference for attributes which the goods possess. This two-stage theory of consumer utility is described according to Ratchford:

> A consumer maximizes an ordinal preference function for characteristics U(z), where z is a vector of characteristics 1,...,r, subject to the usual budget constraint $px \leq k$, where p is a vector of prices for each of these goods and k is income. Goods, x, are transformed into characteristics, z, through the relation $z = Bx$, where B is an r x n matrix which transforms the n goods into r characteristics. The model may therefore by written succinctly as:
>
> Maximize U(z)
> Subject to: $px \leq k$
> With $z = Bx$.

Conjoint measurement comes into play as a method for determining the level of consumer preference for these characteristics (product attributes).

The steps taken to implement the conjoint measurement of consumer preference for pST pork were: the selection of pork product attributes and their levels; construction of a set of pork product profiles for evaluation; specification of a preference model; selection of an appropriate estimation method; design of a survey instrument; administration of the survey and conjoint analysis; and evaluation of results.

Pork Product Attributes and Attribute Levels

Pork product attributes were chosen based on their importance to consumers in making pork purchasing decisions (according to past studies) and their ability to meet the main objective of the study (i.e., to evaluate preference for pST pork). A review of past pork studies revealed that the most important attributes to consumers are fat content and price. Technology was used as a pork attribute (pST or current technology) to meet the main objective of the study.

Attribute levels corresponded to points along a represented range of an attribute. Consultation with researchers on pig breeding indicated that fat reduction from 0 to 20 percent was attainable with conventional technology. Fat reduction ranging from 10 to 40 percent was attainable using pST (see Table 1). Price ranged from $A6.99 to $A8.99 per kilogram, which was in line with the Australian price for pork chops at the time of survey. Given the limitations of conventional technology and the high fat reduction potential of pST, the attribute combinations of some product profiles were unrealistic (e.g., a pork profile of zero fat reduction at the higher price of $A8.99/kg produced with pST) and they were eliminated. Once attributes and levels were selected, hypothetical products were formed for respondents to evaluate and assign preference ratings.

Table 1 *Pork Product Attributes and Attribute Levels*

Attributes	Attribute Levels
Price	$A6.99/kilogram
	$A8.99/kilogram
Fat reduction level	0% (current technology)
	10% (current technology, pST)
	20% (current technology, pST)
	40% (pST)
Fat reduction technology	Current technology/Trimming
	pST

Interactions Among Attributes

It is common in conjoint studies to assume no interactions between attributes (Halbrendt, *et al*; 1990; and Green and Wind, 1975). When the design of this conjoint experiment was being planned, the possible complex relationships between the attributes (price, pST and fat reduction) strongly suggested the design should allow for interactions between attributes.

Therefore, the product profiles in this study were designed to allow for estimable interactions between each of the attributes. The allowance of attribute interactions resulted in a large, automatic increase in the number of product profiles. To overcome this situation, the numbers of attributes and ranges of attribute levels were limited.

Attribute Levels and Utility Functional Form

Initially, two attribute levels for technology (pST or current), four levels for fat reduction: (0, 10, 20) percent for current technology and (10, 20, 40) percent for pST technology, and three levels for price were considered. Using three-level attributes would have allowed for the estimation of quadratic functional forms such as those for the fat reduction and price attributes. However, this would have yielded too large a number of product profiles for the respondents to evaluate. Pre-tests and past studies have shown that rating more than about nine product profiles becomes unmanageable for most respondents. However, the number of product profiles must be at least equal to the number of estimated parameters specified in the empirical model (see equation 1). Otherwise, the design matrix used in the analysis will not have full rank. Therefore, this study needed at least ten profiles. The price attribute was reduced from three to two levels, suggesting a linear functional form for price. A past conjoint study (Halbrendt *et al.,* 1990) in which three price levels were used revealed that the the price variable response was linear. In addition, given the modest nature of food price changes, a linear price response seemed very reasonable.

Product Profile Selection

The two-level price and technology attributes and the four-level fat reduction attribute resulted in a design with 16 profiles (2x2x4). The authors decided to use ten profiles to satisfy the requirements of the model and to reduce the possibility of respondent fatigue (ten profiles being close to the ideal number of nine). To collapse the number of profiles from 16 to 10, four infeasible profiles were first logically deleted (two current technology profiles with 40 percent fat reduction; and two pST-produced profiles with zero percent fat reduction. Forty percent fat reduction is not attainable using current technology and pST-produced pork must have some level of fat reduction). From the remaining 12 profiles, two more needed to be deleted. The D-optimality design criterion was used to determine which of the two profiles to exclude. From the work of several authors (see Box and Draper, 1971), this criterion is known to have excellent properties such as low variances for the parameters, and low correlations among parameters (Mitchell, 1974). The ten profiles yielded by the D-optimality design process are shown in Table 2.

Table 2 *Pork Product Profiles used for Evaluation by Respondents*

Profile	Technology	Fat Reduction %	Price $A/kg
1	Current	10	6.99
2	Current	20	8.99
3	pST	40	6.99
4	pST	20	8.99
5	pST	20	6.99
6	Current	20	6.99
7	pST	10	6.99
8	pST	40	8.99
9	Current	0	8.99
10	Current	0	6.99

MODEL ESTIMATION TECHNIQUE

Conjoint experiments are usually 'repeated measures' designs. In other words, the same experimental unit (respondent) is measured (asked to rate product profile) several times. The advantages of repeated measures are lower costs and variance reduction. It is generally less expensive to ask 500 people to rate 10 profiles than to ask 5000 people to rate one profile each. The other major advantage of repeated measures designs is variance reduction. Even ignoring costs, 5000 people would be more heterogeneous, resulting in a likely loss of precision.

However, because measurements by the same respondent are apt to be correlated, an analysis of a repeated measures study should correct for the within-respondent correlation. Ignoring the correlation structure may lead to inaccurate estimates, standard errors and tests. In this paper the weighted least squares approach of Grizzle, Starmer and Koch (1967) was used to correct for possible within-respondent correlation.

Sampling

The population to be surveyed consisted of Australian consumers who eat pork. The surveys were conducted in shopping centres. A commonly encountered feature of survey sampling is that a certain amount of information is known about the elements of the population to be studied. Supplementary information (e.g., income or an area) can be used either at the design stage to improve the sample estimators or both. Because information on respondents' attitudinal responses on genetic engineering has revealed that various socio-demographics can have an effect, the sample should adequately represent various socio-demographic groups. This study's data were collected in shopping centres around the country.

Surveys were conducted in June and July, 1992. Survey interviews were administered in three cities: Perth, Sydney and Brisbane. According to census data, the combined populations of the three cities make up one-third of Australia's total population.

Model Specification

Unlike most conjoint experiments in which the importance of the main effects of product attributes are emphasized, the model for consumer preference of pST-supplemented pork products was specified to include interactions among the attributes. Interactive models imply that there is variation in the dependent variable (rating) associated with two or more of the independent variables (product attributes) working together. Although results are easier to interpret, main effects models could be misspecified, especially with attributes having negative correlation (i.e., price and leanness), and often do not provide as good a fit as models including interactions (Forthofer and Lehnen, 1981). The conjoint model was specified to include attribute interactions as:

(1) $$\text{RATING} = \beta_0 + \beta_1\text{PST} + \beta_2\text{RED} + \beta_3\text{RED2} + \beta_4\text{PST*RED} + \beta_5\text{PST*RED2} + \beta_6\text{PRICE} + \beta_7\text{PST*PRICE} + \beta_8\text{PRICE*RED} + \beta_9\text{PRICE*RED2}$$

where: RATING = 1 to 6; 1 is least preferred and 6 is most preferred

PST = dummy variable for technology; 1 if pST, 0 if current technology

RED = Level of fat reduction; 0, 10, 20, or 40 percent

PRICE = Price for pork products; $A8.99/kg or $A6.99/kg.

The model was estimated using Weighted Least Squares (WLS), a regression technique which gives more weight to the product profiles that have smaller variances than those with larger variances (Forthofer and Lehnen, 1981). This technique was appropriate given the potential problems of correlation among responses by each respondent and unequal variances among product profiles.

RESULTS

Socio-Demographics Responses

A total of 600 surveys was completed, of which 557 were usable. Of the 557 respondents, 74 percent were the primary shopper for the household and 26 percent were not. The majority of respondents were female (68 percent). Over half of the respondents lived in households with 2–3 members (52 percent). There was also a large majority of married or defacto respondents, totalling 60 percent. Fifty-one percent of the respondents were over 39 years of age. Twenty-eight percent of the respondents completed secondary school, 19 percent had some tertiary education, and 21 percent completed tertiary education. Sixty-one percent of the respondents who answered the income level question had incomes of over $A25 000. Australia was the most-represented birthplace, with 66 percent of the respondents being born there. The occupations of respondents varied over the list of categories, but there was a fairly large representation of retired and professional respondents (40 percent). After testing for socio-demographic effects on pork product profile ratings, it was found that the model was homogeneous in response. In other words, ratings of pork product profiles across different socio-demographic groups of respondents were not significantly different.

Table 3 *Mean Utility Values for Survey Product Profiles*

Profile	Technology	Fat Reduction %	Price $A/kg	Mean Utility	Standard Deviation	Standard Error
1	Current	10	6.99	2.44	1.34	0.06
2	Current	20	8.99	3.55	1.30	0.06
3	pST	40	6.99	4.97	1.70	0.07
4	pST	20	8.99	3.02	1.26	0.05
5	pST	20	6.99	3.57	1.37	0.06
6	Current	20	6.99	4.18	1.29	0.05
7	pST	10	6.99	2.12	1.13	0.05
8	pST	40	8.99	4.36	1.67	0.07
9	Current	0	8.99	1.41	1.04	0.04
10	Current	0	6.99	1.57	1.19	0.05

Conjoint Experiment Results

The conjoint analysis allowed respondents to choose among several products, each being a unique combination of attributes. Respondents were asked to evaluate each product in terms of the level of utility they would gain from the purchase of a particular product. The ten product profiles and their mean utility values are presented in Table 3. The product with the highest mean utility of 4.97 was profile 3, which was pST-supplemented, 6.99/kg, and has a fat reduction level of 40 percent. The higher-priced profile 8 also pST supplemented with the 40 percent fat reduction level had the second-highest utility of 4.36. Profile 6, which is current technology, 6.99/kg, and 20 percent fat reduction also had a fairly high mean utility of 4.18. Respondents considered leanness an important attribute to pork products. This can be seen at the 40 percent fat reduction points at which utility was the highest. However, at the 20 percent reduction points, respondents preferred the pork produced with current technology. They were getting roughly the same utility for the high-priced current technology pork as the low-priced pST-produced pork when fat reduction was 20 percent. The profiles with the lowest utilities were those with the 0 percent fat reduction. These are profiles 9 and 10, and have utilities of 1.41 and 1.57, respectively.

Table 4 *Estimated Conjoint Model Parameters*

Variable	Parameter Estimate	Standard Error	Chi-Square
Intercept	2.1135	0.1423	220.52*
PST	–16879	0.2418	48.74*
RED	0.1632	0.0194	71.02*
RED2	0.0025	0.0006	20.30*
PST*RED	0.1771	0.0178	99.41*
PST*RED2	–0.0069	0.0006	138.95*
PRICE	–0.0777	0.0158	24.26*
PST*PRICE	0.0411	0.0321	1.64
PRICE*RED	–0.0172	0.0023	54.89*
PRICE*RED2	0.0003	0.0001	27.95*

Note: * Implies significance at the 1 percent level.

The weighted-least-squares estimated parameters are presented in Table 4. Nine of the ten parameters were significant at the 1 percent level, indicating the interactive model was well-specified. Consistent with economic theory, the price parameter estimate was negative, indicating an inverse relationship of price with utility. The estimated pST parameter alone was negative, suggesting pST has an adverse impact on utility. However, when pST interacts with either leanness or price, the overall effect was positive indicating pST that could produce leaner pork at a competitive price increases which respondents' utility. The fat reduction parameters generally were positive, confirming that higher fat reduction translates to higher utility. As shown in Table 3, current technology products at a fat reduction level of 20 percent even at a higher price of $A8.99 per kilogram can compete with pST pork with the same amount of fat reduction at a lower price of $A6.99 per kilogram. Only at greater levels of fat reduction was pST-produced pork preferred over non-pST pork. Table 5 shows the combinations of fat reduction levels and price of pST products that yield the same level of utility (4.18) to respondents as the current technology products at the 20 percent fat reduction level, assuming a price of $A6.99/kg. For consumers to accept pST pork, the pork sold has to be comprised of attribute levels better than the combinations presented in Table 5.

Table 5 *Hypothetical pST Products that Yield the Same Utility as Current Technology at 20 Percent Fat Reduction*

Current Technology	Competitive pST Products			
	Price $A/kg	Fat Reduction %	Price $A/kg	Fat Reduction %
Price = $A6.99/kg	6.04	23	8.45	32
Rating = 4.18	6.40	24	8.63	33
	6.73	25	8.80	34
Fat Reduction =	7.04	26	8.96	35
20 percent	7.32	27	9.10	36
	7.58	28	9.24	37
	7.82	29	9.36	38
	8.05	30	9.47	39
	8.26	31	9.58	40

SUMMARY

In general, respondents appeared to be in favour of pST-produced pork at the higher fat reduction levels. Utility was greatest for pST products where fat reduction is at a very high level, e.g. 40 percent. When given a choice between pST or current technology when both were available (10 or 20 percent fat reduction levels), respondents preferred the current technology pork products.

Also, as fat reduction increases, consumers were found to be more price sensitive. Respondents were not as willing to pay for fatty pork products, but exhibit high levels of utility with high levels of fat reduction combined with a low price.

For the successful adoption of pST, the price of pork products produced with pST will have to remain very competitive, and the level of fat reduction will have to be higher than current technology can attain. Therefore, with a combination of leaner pork at competitive prices, consumers will be willing to consume pST pork, but not willing to pay a premium unless they achieve leanness beyond that which current technology can achieve.

REFERENCES

Bartley, S., Ball, K. and Weeks, P., 1988, *Household Meat Consumption in Sydney and Melbourne*, Australian Bureau of Agricultural and Resource Economics, Discussion Paper 88.2, AGPS, Canberra.

Box, M.J. and Draper, N.R. (1971), 'Factorial Designs, the |X'X| Criterion, and Some Related Matters', *Technometrics*, Vol. 13, No. 4, pp.731–742.

Forthofer, R.N. and Lehnen, R.G., 1981, *Public Program Analysis: A New Categorical Data Approach*, Wadsworth, Gelmont, California.

Gardner, J.A.A., 1990, 'Industry Structure and Trends', in Gardner, J.A.A., Dunkin, A.C. and Lloyd, L.C. (eds.), *Pig Production in Australia*, Butterworths Pty Limited, Sydney, Australia, July–August, pp.107–117.

Green, P.E. and Wind, Y., 1975, 'New Ways to Measure Consumers Judgments', *Harvard Business Review*, pp.89–108.

Grizzle, J.E., Starmer, C.F. and Koch, G.G., 1969, 'Analysis of Categorical Data by Linear Models', *Biometrics*, Vol. 25, No. 3, pp.489–504.

Halbrendt, C.K., Wirth, F. and Vaughn, G., 1990, 'Conjoint Analysis of the Mid-Atlantic Food-Fish Market for Farm-Raised Hybrid Striped Bass', *Southern Journal of Agricultural Economics*, Vol. 23, No. 1, pp.155–163.

Mitchell, T.J, 1974, 'An Algorithm for the Construction of 'D-Optimal' Experimental Designs', *Technometrics*, Vol. 16, No. 2, pp.203–210.

Ratchford, B.T., 1975, 'The New Economic Theory of Consumer Behavior: An Interpretive Essay', *Journal of Consumer Research*, Vol. 2, No. 2, pp.65–75.

Taverner, M., 1990, 'Determinants of Public Acceptance in Australasia of Biotechnology for the Control of Growth and Product Quality in Pig Meat Production', Paper presented for a symposium organised by The American Society of Animal Science and The European Association of Animal Production, 'Biotechnology for Control of Growth and Product Quality in Meat Production: Implications and Acceptability'.

Turman, E.J. and Andrews, F.N., 1955, 'Some Effects of Purified Anterior Pituitary Growth Hormone on Swine', *Journal of Animal Science*, Vol. 14, No. 1, pp.7–18.

DISCUSSION OPENING — Eugene Jones *(The Ohio State University, USA)*

This paper addresses an important and very timely subject. It is widely recognized that farms groups must become more market oriented if they are to compete successfully in the market place. Heretofore, many producers have pursued a production-orientated strategy, expecting consumers to purchase whatever they produce. Producer groups pursuing production-oriented strategies are facing marketing challenges, particularly as the variety of products available to consumers continues to increase. Fortunately, this paper focuses on a market-oriented strategy, attempting to identify product attributes demanded by consumers and then communicating these desired product attributes to producers for incorporation into the production decisions. Such an approach is much needed and I commend the authors for this very interesting paper.

As a discussant, I simply want to highlight a few things to help initiate discussion from the audience. First, information communicated to pork producers regarding consumer preferences needs to reflect the preferences of the 'true' population. That is, a representative sample of the population must be surveyed. As presented, it is not clear if the authors have conducted a random sample of the population. Although the survey method included a diverse group with respect to income, it still appears as though those surveyed included anyone who would spend time with the survey conductors. Secondly, it seems that the range of fat reduction offered to the consumer includes an irrelevant range. With studies suggesting that the current technology can achieve up to 20 percent fat reduction, it seems unreasonable for consumers to express a preference for pST treated products that obtain fat reduction of only 20 percent. That is, with the pST treated pork considered 'unnatural' it seems unreasonable to expect consumers to purchase it if they can get the same product in its 'natural' form.

Some additional points related to this paper are also noted. If we can assume that consumers have clearly expressed their preferences to researchers, it is still important for the researchers to recognize the gap that most often exists between consumers' expressed preferences and preferences revealed in their market purchases. That is, it is important for the researchers to communicate to farm producers that consumers' stated preferences will likely overstate their revealed preferences. Fourthly, with respect to interaction variables in the model, it would have been helpful to this reader if the authors had provided a theoretical discussion of the expected effects of these variables. For example, what is the expected effect on utility of pST interacting with fat reduction or price interacting with fat reduction? Clearly, Weighted Least Squares regression will yield some signs that can be rationalized, but it would be useful to have some *a priori* expectations regarding the effects of these variables.

Finally, I wish to comment on the use of 'product attributes' as opposed to 'products' in empirical studies. Although I am convinced that the use of product attributes is the right approach, it seems inappropriate to evaluate them in isolation. For example, with respect to the current study where fat reduction appears to be the dominant product attribute, it is quite likely that one's preference for fat reduction is a function of one's taste for the product and frequency of eating the product. In general, one who eats pork twice a month is likely to have a lower preference for pST-treated pork than one who eats pork twice per week. In short, it seems that other socio-economic factors must be integrated with the product attributes.

In summary, the authors have presented an interesting and thought provoking paper. Anyone interested in consumer research related to product attributes is likely to gain tremendous insights from reading this paper. The authors are certainly to be applauded.

STEPHAN J. GOETZ, DAVID L. DEBERTIN AND ANGELOS PAGOULATOS*

Linkages Between Human Capital and the Environment: Implications for Sustainable Economic Development

Abstract: An empirical analysis reveals that US states with a more highly educated population have better environmental conditions, after controlling for income and industrial composition. The strategy of raising human capital stocks to maintain or improve environmental quality is proposed as a complement, if not an alternative, to direct government intervention which consists of command and control, market incentives and moral suasion. Under this approach, general education becomes the control variable which guides economic behaviour in a manner consistent with long-term environmental sustainability.

INTRODUCTION

Past public efforts to guide economic activity in directions compatible with environmental quality have involved one of two strategies. The first has been to internalize externalities using a combination of tax and market incentives. Originating in the work of Pigou (1920), and developed primarily by resource economists, this strategy is exemplified by trading of pollution rights between two or more polluting firms. The second strategy has been to educate private sector decision-makers about harmful effects of specific chemicals and pollutants including fertilizers, pesticides, herbicides and, more recently, refrigerator coolants. This strategy relies on moral suasion rather than explicit market incentives, and generally falls into the domain of consumer and home economics.

Our paper is motivated by the question of whether there are public policies that complement these narrowly conceived strategies for addressing issues of environmental quality. We propose that economic agents with larger human capital endowments derive greater utility from a clean environment and, when confronted with multiple options, will most likely choose the option consistent with environmental quality. This hypothesis is developed conceptually and tested empirically. The focus is on environmental impacts of additional general education, not issues-specific education about the environment by public or private agencies. This distinction is analogous to that between general and specific human capital in the earnings literature. Increasing the population's general education, while an indirect and medium- to long-run approach, may increase the efficiency of market intervention — that is, employing tax penalties for polluting and rewards for not polluting — and spending on educational campaigns directed at specific types of pollution and their probable consequences. While the importance of human capital has been widely recognized in economics, including the economic development, wage-earnings and health economics literatures, its potential role in maintaining environmental quality has largely been ignored. We argue that this approach may be particularly effective in developing countries, where enforcement of pollution standards is difficult and sometimes impossible. Literacy is, of course, a prerequisite to using printed media for disseminating information about pollutants and environmental hazards.

* University of Kentucky, USA.

PUBLIC POLICY TOWARD THE ENVIRONMENT

Examples of US legislation designed to maintain or improve environmental quality include the Clean Air and Water Acts, the Toxic Substance Control Act, the Federal Insecticide and Rodenticide Acts, and the Comprehensive Environmental Response, Compensation and Liability Act (the 'Superfund'), which contributes public monies as a last resort to clean up toxic sites (e.g., Cropper *et al.*, 1992). In agriculture, Turvey (1991, p.1399, citing Hamilton, 1990) writes:

> ...legislatures and courts now recognize that it is the responsibility of farmers to establish and maintain soil and water conservation practices as well as erosion control practices, and these practices are in the interest of the public good and within the domain of state power.

Clearly, direct public intervention to control environmental quality is widespread, and under the 'New Federalism' the burden of intervention is falling increasingly onto states. At the same time, pollution is a global rather than a national problem, and it is unclear whether incentive-based programmes will succeed in developing nations, which do not have a '... reasonably sophisticated environmental control agency' (Hahn and Stavins, 1992, p.467).

Educational campaigns directed at improving environmental conditions include activities by consumer awareness groups, labels on hazardous materials indicating how they should be disposed of, and chemical-specific educational efforts by the USDA's Cooperative Extension Service for farmers and farm workers. The National Research Council (1991) recently published a volume addressing educational aspects of specific topics in sustainable agriculture. McConnell (1983, p.88) suggests 'that information about soil depth and its economic value be disseminated' to farmers so soil loss can be reduced and land values maintained. Braden *et al.* (1989) argue that reducing the movement of agricultural pollutants can be as effective as containing emissions; this requires education of and co-operation among farmers. These indirect approaches to influencing behaviour appeal to producers' moral responsibility; they affect market outcomes by influencing decision-makers' tastes and preferences. In addition, they influence profit-maximizing calculations by changing decision-makers' knowledge about how to combine specific inputs optimally (that is, the production function). Producer education about potentially hazardous environmental effects of their actions is complemented with consumer information about benefits of using chemicals. Babcock *et al.* (1992, p.171), for example, write that 'improved information about damage control agent productivity is vital' to balance 'public concerns about chemical residues and ecological damage with the need to maintain food and fiber production'.

The moral suasion/information-based strategy and the incentive-based strategy both assume that externalities can be reduced through carefully directed public interventions and, more importantly, that social benefits exceed the long-run costs. The question is whether and how markets can be made to function more perfectly with respect to the pricing of environmental services (Howarth and Norgaard, 1992). In terms of globally reducing environmental pollution, Batie (1989, p.1096) warns of 'the enormity of the transactions costs of orchestrating a coordinated international response to achieve sustainability goals through programs such as the reduction of certain gas emissions or the reforestation of vast areas.' We are unaware of any studies that have evaluated or compared the long-run relative effectiveness of either of these two strategies.

HUMAN CAPITAL AND ENVIRONMENT: CONCEPTUAL ASPECTS

Casual empiricism in both developing and developed countries suggests that countries, regions, and communities with lower educational attainment often experience greater environmental problems. This link could mask a more fundamental causality: that higher incomes obtained through more education increase economic agents' willingness and ability to pay for a clean environment (given a positive income elasticity of demand), and vice versa. Thus, when the Environmental Protection Authority recently coined the term 'environmental racism' in reporting that US minorities bear a disproportionate share of environmental decay and health hazards from pollution, some argued that the problem was one of poverty rather than race.

We suggest that human capital has a positive relationship to environmental quality that is independent of income. Higher education levels are associated with environmental awareness, which leads to improved long-term environmental quality for a number of reasons. They can be separated into: (a) those affecting perceived benefits of environmental quality; and (b) the costs of achieving the quality (including learning about alternatives). In terms of perceived benefits, investment in education requires sacrificing present benefits for higher expected future returns. That is, educated decision-makers are also more likely to attach greater utility to future environmental pay-offs (they have longer time horizons and lower discount rates). This includes reducing pollution along highways and in parks and other recreational areas, which can otherwise deter tourists and reduce earnings from tourism in the future. Similarly, the highly educated are more likely to be aware of detrimental consequences of environmental degradation to their health. For these reasons, educated decision-makers may be more likely to become involved in community activities designed to improve the environment, more likely to pressure state legislators to commit proportionately more funds to environmental programmes, and more likely to persuade manufacturers to reduce pollution. On the cost side of achieving environmental protection, educated decision-makers may be better able to absorb, interpret and comprehend information (Nelson and Phelps, 1966; and Schultz, 1975), particularly abstract concepts such as those related to long-term harmful effects of depleting the ozone layer, or consequences of global warming, acid rain and soil erosion. They are also more likely to learn about and understand complex, long-term issues associated with environmental conditions. Thus, economic agents with a higher general education level face lower transaction costs of collecting and assimilating information about which activities result in various degrees of environmental damage. Because the (perceived) benefits of environmental protection are higher, and the costs of acting accordingly lower, a more highly educated agent faces a higher benefit–cost ratio than a less highly educated agent, and is therefore more likely to choose options that are consistent with environmental protection. These effects are in addition to any impacts of special educational programmes created by federal and state governments that specifically target environmental awareness.

In agriculture, highly educated farmers may be more likely to follow label recommendations for pesticide applications and understand the need for adopting production practices to reduce harmful effects of wind and water on soil, even though conservation benefits may not appear for many years (Pagoulatos *et al.*, 1989). Several farm-level studies reveal a positive relationship between education and adoption of new technology. Lin (1991), for example, shows that educated Chinese farmers more rapidly adopt hybrid rice varieties. Rahm and Huffman (1984) demonstrate that greater schooling facilitates the adoption of erosion control practices by farmers, while Norris and Batie (1987, p.87) write: 'education will continue to be an important component of a successful conservation program'. Similarly, Ervin and Ervin (1982) find positive relationships between farmers' educational attainment and the perception that erosion is a problem, number of control practices adopted, and effort made to conserve soil. Lynne *et al.* (1988) stress the importance of fostering attitudes favourable towards conservation as alternatives to farm income-increasing programmes and taxation.

We test the following hypothesis: US states with larger stocks of human capital perform better on a variety of environmental quality measures. More specifically, the condition of the environment in state i (E_i) at any moment in time can be thought to depend on the stock of human capital h_i, state income per person y_i and the percentage of the population that is a minority m_i. In addition, we control for industrial mixes in each state using the relative contribution of different economic sectors j to gross state product G_j. Finally, we add a random error term, ε_i which is assumed to exhibit standard Gaussian properties:

$$(1) \quad E_i = \Phi(h_i, y_i, m_i, G_{ji}) + \varepsilon_i$$

The percentage of population 25 years or older with a high school diploma is used to measure human capital.

EMPIRICAL EVIDENCE

The relationship between water pollution scores and the percentage of residents 25 years and older having a high school diploma for the 50 states is illustrated in Figure 1; the scores are based on Hall and Kerr (1991) and represent different measures of water pollution, most of which are observed in the year 1988. States with a more highly educated population tend to have fewer pollution problems. Clearly, water pollution depends not only on residents' education, but also on other features such as population density and its geographic distribution, major types of industry, and general geophysical conditions. Thus, it is not surprising that Western states are below the trend line whereas mid-Western industrial states, and certain states where chemical-intensive farming patterns prevail, are above.

Figure 2 shows how overall environmental conditions in each state relate to human capital. These conditions are the sum of each state's ranking on 179 environmental indicators, including water pollution (a higher rank indicates better environmental conditions). However, additional factors such as the number of farms per 1000 population, number of farms gained or lost between 1974 and 1987, workplace deaths per 100 000 jobs, population share without health insurance, etc., are included so the index has to be viewed with some caution for the purposes of this study. Nevertheless, the general conclusion about the effect of human capital on environmental quality remains valid when disaggregate measures (such as water or air pollution) are used.

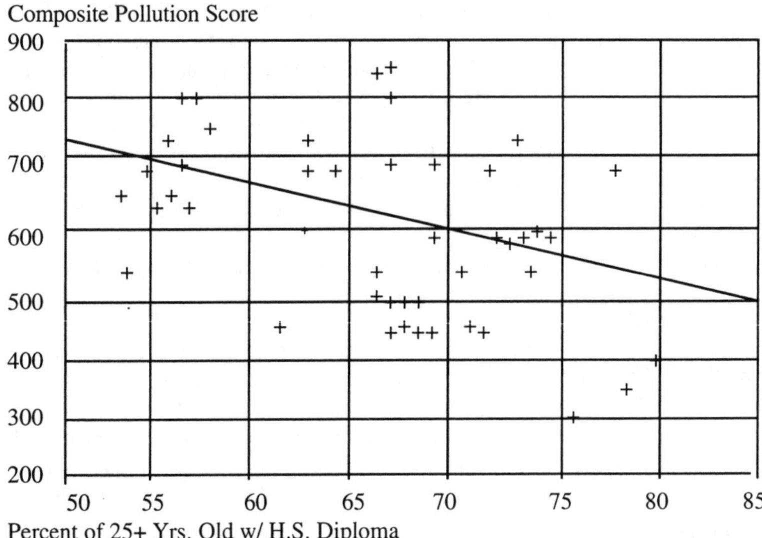

Figure 1 *Composite Water Pollution as a Function of Human Capital, US States*

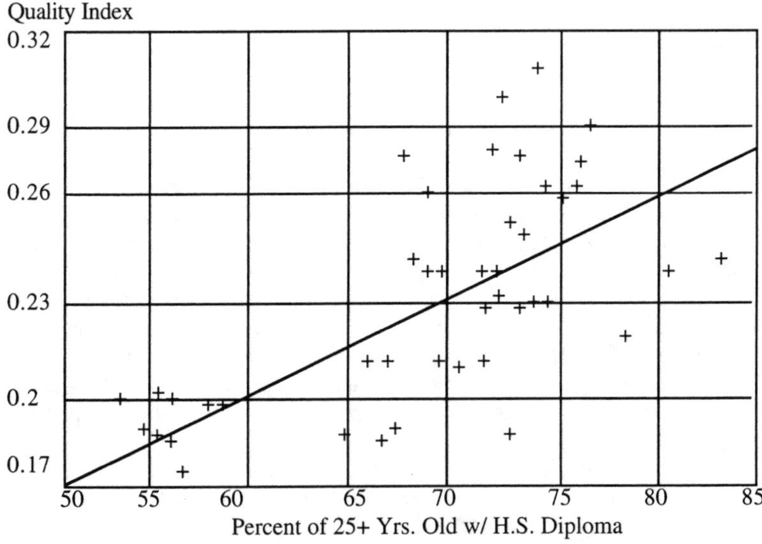

Figure 2 *Environmental Quality versus Human Capital, US States*

Regression results for Equation (1) are reported in Table 1. Higher levels of h_i are associated with significantly better environmental conditions. The coefficient for income per person does not differ significantly from zero, conceivably reflecting the offsetting effects of greater willingness and ability to pay for a clean environment, on the one hand, and consumption of polluting goods such as large and inefficient automobiles, on the other. Table 1 also suggests states with proportionally more minorities have worse environmental conditions, other things being equal. These results hold even when the percentage of gross state product derived from different sectors is included in the regression. Greater shares of farming, mining, construction, manufacturing, transportation and services (relative to government), are associated with worse environmental conditions in a statistically significant manner. With the possible exception

Table 1 *Determinants of States' Environmental Conditions*[a]

Variable	Parameter estimates (*t*-statistic)
Constant	–433.1
	(0.14)
1988 income/capita	–0.0278
	(0.62)
Percent minority	–14.8*
	(1.95)
1980 Human capital[b]	32.2*
	(2.66)
1988 Gross State Product (%) from:[c]	
Farming	–80.3*
	(2.03)
Mining	83.6*
	(2.29)
Construction	96.3*
	(1.68)
Manufacturing	–101.8*
	(3.29)
Transportation	–225.8*
	(3.58)
Wholesaling	–106.2
	(1.53)
Retailing	–70.8
	(0.69)
Fire, insurance and retail services	23.0
	(0.51)
Services	–61.7*
	(1.84)
Adjusted R-squared	61.5

Notes: [a] Environmental conditions are based on each state's ranking — a higher index value indicates better environmental conditions. [b] Percentage of population 25 years and older with a high school diploma. [c] Government is the excluded category. * Significant at 10 percent or lower.

of services, these latter results are not surprising. The coefficient estimates for education retain the expected signs and remain significant when air pollution, air quality control and fish, wildlife and forestry spending per capita are used as dependent variables in Equation (1).

CONCLUSION

Increasing the human capital endowment of economic agents has four advantages over conventional methods for addressing environmental problems. First, it would be supported by those arguing that environmental policies which increase environmental quality with less government intervention are superior. Because there is no intervention via pollution taxes or specific economic incentives for not polluting, market signals and solutions are not distorted; market outcomes change *endogenously* as tastes and preferences of private decision-makers change.

Second, the long-term benefit–cost ratio of public expenditures for general education may be greater than benefit–cost ratios for public spending to alleviate specific environmental problems. Third, while we are uncertain of the comparative effectiveness of expenditures on education directed toward upgrading the population's general educational level, reducing high school drop-out rates, etc. versus expenditures for educating (not-in-school) adults about specific environmental problems, it appears that education about environmental issues is not independent of general public education. For example, discussion and instruction about environmental issues could take place in elementary and secondary natural sciences courses.

Fourth, positive externalities accrue to efforts designed to increase educational levels that have implications for economic growth and development. Unemployment in depressed rural regions of the United States is often associated with low human capital stocks. Communities and states with high average human capital stocks will be more capable of attracting high technology, skill-intensive firms and industry that are less polluting. This is consistent with the position that economic development can be compatible with long-run environmental quality (e.g., Hutchinson, 1990, p.xvi; and Bromley, 1992). More generally, increasing human capital stocks will entail additional tangible and intangible benefits which need to be incorporated into long-run benefit–cost calculations involving environmental benefits.

This analysis can be extended to a cross section of countries or regions within countries at different stages of development. An hypothesis is that environmental problems increase as countries make the transition from hunting and gathering to agrarian and industrial societies. Later, as incomes and education increase, the willingness and ability of residents to reduce pollution levels also increase. Eastern European countries face similar transitional problems as they introduce market reforms. More generally, in deciding whether to use specific educational programmes or market-based incentive schemes to improve environmental conditions, governments may consider allocating incremental funds to increasing the population's general education as a more cost-effective alternative.

REFERENCES

Babcock, B.A., Lichtenberg, E. and Zilberman, D., 1992, 'Impact of Damage Control and Quality of Output: Estimating Pest Control Effectiveness', *American Journal of Agricultural Economics*, Vol. 74, No. 1, pp.163–172.

Batie, S.S., 1989, 'Sustainable Development Challenges to the Profession of Agricultural Economics', *American Journal of Agricultural Economics*, Vol. 71, No. 5, pp.1083–1101.

Braden, J.B., Johnson, GV., Bouzaher, A. and Miltz, D., 1989, 'Optimal Spatial Management of Agricultural Pollution', *American Journal of Agricultural Economics*, Vol. 71, No. 2, pp.405–413.

Bromley, D.W., 1992, 'Balancing Policy for Environment and Economic Development', in *Increasing Understanding of Public Problems and Issues — 1991*, Farm Foundation, Illinois, pp.97–106.

Cropper, M.L., Evans, W.N., Beradi, S.J., Ducla-Soares, M.M. and Portney, P.R., 1992, 'The Determinants of Pesticide Regulation: A Statistical Analysis of EPA Decision Making', *Journal of Political Economy*, Vol. 100, No. 1, pp.175–197.

Ervin, C.A. and Ervin, D.E., 1982, 'Factors Affecting the Use of Soil Conservation Practices: Hypotheses, Evidence and Policy Implications', *Land Economics*, Vol. 58, No. 3, pp.277–292.

Hahn, R.W. and Stavins, R.N., 1992, 'Economic Incentives for Environmental Protection: Integrating Theory and Practice', *American Economic Review*, Vol. 82, No. 2, pp.464–468.

Hall, B. and Kerr, M.L., 1991, *1991–1992 Green Index: A State-by-State Guide to the Nation's Environmental Health*, Island Press, Washington, D.C.

Hamilton, N.D., 1990, 'Adjusting Farm Tenancy Practices to Support Sustainable Agriculture', *Journal of Agricultural Taxation Law*, Vol. 12, pp.226–252.

Howarth, R.B. and Norgaard, R.B., 1992, 'Environmental Valuation under Sustainable Development', *American Economic Review*, Vol. 82, No. 2, pp.473–477.

Hutchinson, F.E., 1990, 'Introduction' in Edwards, C.A., Rattan, L., Madden, P., Miller, R.H. and House, G. (eds.), Soil and Water Conservation Society, Ankeny, Iowa.

Lin, J.Y., 1991, 'Education and Innovation Adoption in Agriculture: Evidence from Hybrid Rice in China', *American Journal of Agricultural Economics*, Vol. 73, No. 3, pp.712–723.

Lynne, G.D., Shonkwiler, J.S and Rola, L.R., 1988, 'Attitudes and Farmer Conservation Behavior', *American Journal of Agricultural Economics*, Vol. 70, No. 1, pp.12–19.

McConnell, K.E., 1983, 'An Economic Model of Soil Conservation', *American Journal of Agricultural Economics*, Vol. 65, No. 1, pp.83–89.

National Research Council, 1991, *Sustainable Agriculture Research and Education in the Field* (Proceedings), National Academy Press, Washington, D.C.

Nelson, R.R. and Phelps, E.S., 1966, 'Investment in Humans, Technological Diffusion, and Economic Growth', *American Economic Review*, Vol. 56, No.2, pp.69–75.

Norris, P.E. and Batie, S.S., 1987, 'Virginia Farmers' Soil Conservation Decisions: An Application of Tobit Analysis', *Southern Journal of Agricultural Economics*, Vol. 19, No. 1, pp.79–90.

Pagoulatos, A., Debertin, D.L. and Sjarkowi, F., 1989, 'Soil Erosion, Intertemporal Decisionmaking, and the Soil Conservation Decision', *Southern Journal of Agricultural Economics*, Vol. 22, No.2, pp.55–62.

Pigou, A.C., 1920, *The Economics of Welfare*, Macmillan, London, UK.

Rahm, M.R. and Huffman, W.E., 1984, 'The Adoption of Reduced Tillage: The Role of Human Capital and Other Variables', *American Journal of Agricultural Economics*, Vol. 66, No. 4, pp.405–413.

Schultz, T.W., 1975, 'The Value of the Ability to Deal with Disequilibria', *Journal of Economic Literature*, Vol. 13, No. 2, pp.827–864.

Turvey, C.G., 1991, 'Environmental Quality Constraints and Farm-Level Decision Making', *American Journal of Agricultural Economics*, Vol. 73, No. 5, pp.1399–1406.

DISCUSSION OPENING — Chamhuri Siwar *(University Kebangsaan, Malaysia)*

This paper deals with the relationship between human capital and the environment. In general, it concludes that better environmental conditions are positively related with a more highly educated population. More specifically, the writers test the hypothesis that 'US states with larger stocks of human capital perform better on a variety of environmental quality measures'. The writers tested environmental conditions (E_i) with stock of human capital (h_i) represented by the percentage of residents 25 years and older having a high school diploma, state per capita income (Y_i), minorities as a percentage of the population (m_i) and the relative contribution of different economic sectors to gross state product (G_i). The result showing a positive relationship between human capital and environmental quality is expected. One may question the use of the percentage of residents 25 years and older having a high school diploma as a proxy for human capital. It seems that the larger the population, the higher will be the percentage of residents having a high school diploma. It may be useful to use the quality of human capital variable intead of just the stock of human capital. The percentage of residents with college or university degrees or the state expenditure on higher education may be a proxy for quality of human capital.

The association between higher per capita income and better environmental conditions is not very significant. One would expect the result to be significant, probably due to higher expenditures for environmental protection, enforcement measures and environmental awareness programmes. The assumption that higher incomes bring along higher consumption of polluting goods such as large, inefficient automobiles, offsetting the effects of greater willingness and ability to pay for a clean environment, seems to be contrary to the initial results that educated residents (higher human capital stock) are related to better environmental conditions. The association between minorities and worse environmental conditions may be disturbing for minorities. One would have thought that environmental problems are race neutral. The association between minorities and worse environmental conditions may be traced to poverty and lower educational levels. It is not surprising also that the major industries (farming, mining, construction, manufacturing and transportation) are the major contributors to worse environmental conditions.

Three questions may be raised here. What is the role of higher human capital in offsetting these effects? Have higher per capita incomes not been translated into improved environmental measures, enforcements and other direct measures to improve the environment? What is the contribution of the major industries (farming, mining, manufacturing, construction and transportation) to conservation, improving the enviromental and sustainable economic development. Are not the industries more concerned for environmental and sustainable development?

Finally, there is no denying that higher educational and human capital levels contribute to better environmental conditions in the long run. But it is also the educated, prompted by greed and profit motives, who plunder and exploit valuable resources (timber, mining) causing environmental degradation. The result of long-term educational programmes on environmental awareness may be less tangible than continuous efforts and measures to deter industries and consumers from polluting the environment. At best, the role of education and human capital towards a more sustainable economic development is complementary.

THOMAS C. PINCKNEY*

Does Education Increase Agricultural Productivity in Africa?

Abstract: Past published studies establishing a significant, positive link between education and agricultural productivity have used Asian data almost exclusively. With one exception, these studies have not checked to see if the positive impact of education comes about only by screening for ability. Using household level data from coffee regions of Kenya and Tanzania, this study finds that households in which the agricultural decision-maker is numerate and literate produce 30 percent more agricultural output, holding other variables constant. This estimate of the impact of education is markedly higher than those made using years of schooling as an independent variable. Increasing cognitive skills beyond basic numeracy and literacy has no additional impact on production. Evidence from Kenya (but not from Tanzania) suggests that reasoning ability and the presence of at least one educated person in the household also increase productivity substantially.

INTRODUCTION

Increasing labour and total factor productivity in agriculture is widely acknowledged as one key to achieving growth with equity in Africa (Mellor *et al.*, 1987). Rapid expansion of education systems in the post-independence period has increased the size of the educated labour force dramatically. An increasing number of educated workers are remaining in or returning to rural areas as public sector employment stabilizes or even declines in most African countries. For example, in Kenya the number of persons over 20 years of age residing in rural areas who had completed at least one year of secondary education rose from about 147 000 in 1969 to 576 000 in 1979 to over 1.2 million in 1988.[1]

Most observers would expect this increase in the education of the rural labour force to have a positive impact on agriculture. Indeed, the World Bank's (1989, p.64) most recent perspective study on Africa states categorically that 'raising educational levels enhances agricultural productivity'. The evidence for this statement comes primarily from Jamison and Lau (1982), who compiled and analyzed 37 earlier studies relating education to agricultural productivity. They conclude that, on average, four years of education increase output by 7.2 percent, and that this percentage is higher in rapidly changing agricultural environments. More recent studies have confirmed a positive relationship between education and productivity (Pudasaini, 1983; Jamison and Moock, 1984; and Azhar, 1991) or education and adoption of new technologies (Lin, 1991).

There are at least three reasons to question the sanguine view of the World Bank report. First, of the 37 studies cited by Jamison and Lau only two are from Africa: Hopcraft

* Williams College, Williamstown, Virginia. Special thanks to Kaye Husbands and Tobias Konyango, co-authors on a related paper; Peter Kimuyu and Wilbald Maro, the other principal researchers on this project; Henry Bruton, Cappy Hill, and participants at workshops in Nairobi, Dar es Salaam, and USAID where a related paper was presented. This research was funded by the United States Agency for International Development Africa Bureau, with additional funding from the African Economics Research Consortium and the United States Information Agency. The opinions and conclusions here expressed are those of the author and do not necessarily reflect those of the sponsoring institutions.

(1974) and Moock (1973, 1981), both from Kenya. All of the more recent studies cited above are from Asia. Hopcraft finds negative, significant effects of education on output, while Moock finds an almost-significant, positive impact of four or more years of education, but a negative impact of fewer than four years. These results, combined with the slower pace of technological advance in Africa compared to Asia, cast considerable doubt on the relevance of results from Asia for African agriculture.

Second, results for Africa outside of Kenya are not available. Kenya is rather unique both in terms of cropping systems and educational history. Comparative evidence between similar locations in Kenya and another country in Africa would be informative.

Third, all of the studies cited in Jamison and Lau (1982) use the number of years of schooling (either of the head of the household or an average for the household) as indicators of education. It is possible, however, that the positive impact of this variable on agricultural productivity results because education screens more able from less able persons (Knight and Sabot, 1990); the significant coefficient could be a reflection of the higher ability of more educated persons, but those persons did not gain that ability through education. If education only serves to screen persons by ability, we would not expect an increase in agricultural productivity to follow increases in rural education.

This study tests for the impact of education on agricultural productivity in similar villages in coffee-growing areas of Kenya and Tanzania, controlling for ability. Tests of cognitive skills — numeracy and literacy skills learned in school — gauge how much of the knowledge learned in school is retained by household heads. Results for the two sites are striking. First, in both locations, basic literacy and numeracy skills increase output much *more* than estimates from elsewhere would suggest. Holding other inputs constant, output is more than 30 percent higher when agricultural decision-makers can add and subtract two-digit numbers and read and comprehend simple paragraphs. These estimates are much larger than those found in Jamison and Lau (1982) and other studies. Additional cognitive skills beyond basic numeracy and literacy, however, have no significant impact on output in either site.

Other results differ between the sites. In the Kenyan site, education of another household member compensates partially for the lack of cognitive skills in the agricultural decision-maker. In addition, reasoning ability of the agricultural decision-maker is correlated with increased output. Finally, holding cognitive skills and reasoning ability constant, having attended primary school *decreases* output. None of these results carry over to Tanzania.

The next three sections discuss the data, the empirical results, and conclusions.

THE DATA

Data for this study were collected in crop year 1991–92. Two similar communities were selected in coffee-growing areas of Murang'a District in Kenya and Kilimanjaro Region, Tanzania, based on their participation as sampling clusters in national surveys in the late 1970s.[2] There was only one such cluster in Murang'a; of the two in Kilimanjaro, one was deemed too near the town of Moshi. The selected clusters are each about 25km from a major town (Thika and Moshi). Both areas receive annual rainfall of about 1500mm. The Kenyan site is somewhat higher in elevation, ranging from 1680m to 1800m, while the Tanzanian site is between 1200m and 1540m. In addition to coffee, dairy, bananas, maize and beans are important in both locations; dairy is relatively much more important in the Kenyan site, bananas in the Tanzanian site. Both areas are densely populated in highland areas. In Kilimanjaro, where the slopes up the mountain are steeper, most households own or have access to a second parcel of land at an elevation of 800m to 1100m where they grow maize and beans during one season a year. These lower plots are on average about 8km from the upper household coffee/banana plots. Virtually all households in both locations are members of coffee co-operative marketing societies. The societies in Kenya also provide seasonal credit for purchased inputs used on other crops; the Tanzanian society only provides such credit for coffee inputs.

Approximately one-quarter of the households in each community were sampled (120 in Kenya, 116 in Tanzania), including about twenty in each community which had taken part in the national surveys in the late 1970s; the remainder were chosen randomly. Unfortunately, in Tanzania the sampling cluster for the national survey stretched all the way from 800m to 1800m elevation; the production functions for some of these households were thus significantly different from those for the households in the 1200–1540m range. Households living outside this range were therefore excluded for the purposes of this paper. After dropping these households plus a few more with incomplete or obviously incorrect data, this analysis includes 95 households in Tanzania and 103 in Kenya. Each household was visited at least five times during the crop year. In Kenya, participants' reports of coffee deliveries were checked and corrected by data directly from the local co-operative societies.

After two rounds of surveying, the agricultural decision-maker for each household was determined subjectively through discussions with enumerators. In most cases we accepted the household's designation of such a decision-maker, but for a few households it was obvious that, say, a husband who worked in town and was only home once a month could not be such a decision-maker, regardless of what his wife reported. Each agricultural decision-maker took three tests as measures of human capital. Raven's Coloured Progressive Matrices (CPM) is a 36 question test of reasoning ability; literacy is not an asset in taking the test (Raven *et al.*, 1991). Knight and Sabot (1990) use the same test to control for ability in their study of education and urban labour markets in East Africa. Jamison and Moock (1984) also use this instrument as a control for ability in their study of education and agricultural productivity in Nepal (although it is insignificant in that study).

In addition to the CPM, agricultural decision-makers took two tests of cognitive skills, one of numeracy and one of literacy. These tests were slightly modified versions of those used by Knight and Sabot (1990). The tests were originally developed by the Educational Testing Service. The simplest questions on the literacy test consist of reading a paragraph about, say, a fish market, and then choosing whether the paragraph is about a fish, vegetable, meat, or fruit market. The simplest questions on the numeracy test consist of adding and subtracting two-digit numbers. In all, there were 63 multiple choice questions, with four possible answers for each; those respondents who were illiterate, or scored less than 16 (the expected value of random guessing) on the test were assigned a score of 16.

EDUCATION AND PRODUCTIVITY

Total value of output for both agricultural and livestock activities is assumed to be a function of labour inputs, land, other fixed inputs, purchased variable inputs and human capital. Total value of output is used rather than output of individual crops or products for two reasons. First, agricultural and livestock activities in these areas are highly integrated, usually in unmeasurable ways. Manure from the livestock is placed on the permanent and field crops. Crop residues such as banana and maize stalks are fed to livestock. Nappier grass is grown specifically for livestock feed, but measuring amounts harvested and fed is highly problematical. Intercropping is prevalent: maize and beans in both sites, coffee and bananas in Tanzania, coffee and beans in Kenya.[3] In such an agricultural economy, attempting to separate out one crop or product is likely to lead to major measurement errors.

Secondly, one way that education should affect productivity is through the educated operator choosing a more appropriate crop mix. This cannot be estimated with single-crop production functions (Welch, 1970).

Of the total value of agricultural production in the Kenyan sample, 41 percent consists of livestock products, primarily milk. The corresponding percentage for the Tanzanian sample is only 12 percent. Coffee production constitutes 25 percent of the total value for Kenya, while only 15 percent for Tanzania. Bananas for both cooking and brewing alcohol make up 27 percent of the value of Tanzanian production. Overall, 47 percent of the value of production in the Kenyan sample is consumed on-farm, while 69 percent is consumed on-farm in the Tanzanian sample.[4]

The labour variable includes all reported labour on the farm, whether adult, child, hired, or donated. Land includes all land operated by the household. The primary fixed input is dairy cattle, particularly in Kenya. Purchased variable inputs include fertilizers and sprays for coffee.

Several variables make up the human capital component. Experience is approximated by subtracting years of education from age minus six (as is common in labour market studies). Years of schooling could also be important if some aspect of school other than acquiring numeracy and literacy skills has an impact on agricultural productivity. Finally, schooling of household members other than the agricultural decision-maker could have an influence on productivity (unfortunately, no CPM or cognitive skills tests were administered to other household members, so years of schooling or a dummy must be used).

As with most of the previous studies of education and agricultural productivity, this study uses a modified Cobb–Douglas production function.[5] The human capital variables enter in levels rather than logarithms, implying that a unit change in these variables produces a constant change in the logarithm of the value of agricultural production. The impact of experience is hypothesized to decrease with increasing experience, and thus the usual squared term is included. Appropriate functional forms for the CPM and cognitive skills variables are unknown; there is no reason to believe, for example, that correctly recalling and using the Pythagorean theorem will have the same impact on output as correctly adding and subtracting two-digit numbers. Consequently, dummy variables for four different ranges of scores on each test were included in an exploratory regression. For both the CPM and the cognitive skills variables, estimates for test scores above a particular level of achievement had no significant impact on output. This 'threshold effect' is common to several of the earlier studies of education and agricultural productivity (Jamison and Moock, 1984; Moock, 1981; and Azhar, 1991). Thus, for the regression reported here, dummy variables only are included for the CPM and cognitive skills variables. For the CPM, the dummy equals 1 for a score of 13 or above (achieved by 75 percent of the Tanzanian sample and 76 percent of the Kenyan sample). For the cognitive skills tests, the dummy equals 1 for a score of 22 or more (achieved by 50 percent of the Kenyan sample and 43 percent of the Tanzanian sample). A respondent who could add and subtract two-digit numbers, answer simple questions about the content of a paragraph, and randomly guess at the remaining questions would have an expected score on the test of about 22.

Similarly, the years of schooling variables are entered as dummies since there is no reason to believe that the relationship between years of schooling and productivity will be linear. For the agricultural decision-maker, dummies for attending two or more years of primary school and at least one year of secondary school are included.

A dummy variable is also included to proxy for the impact of the presence of other educated persons in the household. In some households, the agricultural decision-maker may not be educated, but may depend on another educated person in the household to read recommendations and make calculations, while he or she retains overall decision-making authority. If this is so, education of those other than the decision-maker will have the largest effect when the decision-maker is uneducated. This variable is therefore set equal to 1 when someone in the household has completed primary school, but the decision-maker scores less than the threshold of 22 on the cognitive skills test.

Several of the earlier studies of education and productivity include an agricultural extension variable. In most cases the specification is simply the number of recent contacts with extension agents. We administered a short test of knowledge of extension recommendations, as did Jamison and Moock (1984). The coefficient of this variable is neither large nor significant under any circumstances and was left out of the equations reported in this paper. Jamison and Moock also find no significance for this variable, but in the same equation have a significant positive impact of extension contacts. If extension contacts do not increase agricultural knowledge, it seems more likely that their significant result is related to unobserved characteristics of the farmers who seek out or receive more extension visits, rather than the impact of the contact itself. We attempt to sort out some of these unobserved characteristics below.

EMPIRICAL RESULTS

Table 1 presents results from both Kenya and Tanzania. The usual factor variables all have the correct sign, although the estimates of the coefficient of land are surprisingly small and not significantly different from zero. Coefficients of labour are strongly significant and of reasonable size. The coefficient of assets is much larger in Kenya — 0.19 versus 0.07 — reflecting the greater importance of livestock assets in total production in that location. Variable inputs are significant and of reasonable size in both equations. However, the Cobb–Douglas form hides an important distinction between them. Translating into levels, at the mean a 100 shilling increase in inputs is estimated to increase output by about 98 shillings in Kenya, implying that purchased inputs are used until their marginal product approximately equals their cost. In Tanzania, on the other hand, a 100 shilling increase in inputs is estimated to increase output by 280 shillings, implying gross underutilization of such inputs. This difference may result from the varying co-operative society policies towards providing seasonal credit for crops other than coffee.

The human capital variables produce striking results. Of most importance, the coefficient of the cognitive skills dummy is quite large and highly significant in both equations. Agricultural decision-makers with scores on the cognitive skills tests of 22 or higher produce over 30 percent more output than those with lower scores, holding other variables constant. These estimates are much higher than the Jamison and Lau (1982) meta-estimate of four years schooling increasing output by 7.2 percent. Since these tests measure skills learned almost exclusively in formal educational settings, the results provide strong support to the hypothesis that in Africa, too, educational achievement enhances agricultural productivity.

Table 1 *Production Function Estimates*

	Kenya		Tanzania	
Variables[a]	Coefficient	*t*-statistic	Coefficient	*t*-statistic
Constant	4.61		8.51	
Logarithm of labour used	0.305	4.48	0.231	1.94
Logarithm of land operated	0.00837	0.15	0.0917	1.50
Logarithm of agricultural assets	0.191	3.58	0.0723	1.39
Logarithm of purchased inputs	0.160	3.03	1.107	3.28
Human capital variables:				
Experience	0.0159	1.51	0.0058	0.54
Experience squared	–0.000126	–0.80	–0.0000378	–0.25
Raven CPM score >=13[b]	0.227	2.28	-0.0488	–0.50
Cognitive skills test score >=22[c]	0.352	2.90	0.294	2.36
Primary education[d]	–0.178	–1.78	–0.00586	–0.05
Secondary education[e]	–0.0487	–0.41	0.0814	0.50
Educated person in household[f]	0.273	2.49	0.0369	0.32
R-squared	0.757		0.500	
Adjusted R-squared	0.727		0.434	
Observations	103		95	
Breusch–Pagan Chi-squared (11)[g]	9.28		3.78	

Notes: [a] The dependent variable is the logarithm of the gross value of production.

[b] The Raven CPM test is a measure of reasoning ability.

[c] The cognitive skills tests measures numeracy and literacy.

[d] 'Primary education' is a dummy variable equaling 1 when the agricultural decision-maker attended two or more years of primary school.

[e] 'Secondary education' is a dummy variable equaling 1 when the agricultural decision-maker attended at least one year of secondary school.

[f] 'Educated person in household' is a dummy variable equaling 1 when the agricultural decision-maker scored less than 22 on the cognitive skills test and at least one other member of the household had completed primary school.

[g] The number appearing in parenthesis is the degrees of freedom for the Breusch–Pagan chi-squared test for heteroscedasticity. The Breusch–Pagan statistics for both regressions are insignificant.

If this study had been concerned only with the Tanzanian sample, the human capital story would have stopped there. All other human capital variables give no evidence of affecting agricultural output. The coefficient of the secondary school dummy is reasonably large in size — secondary schooling is estimated to raise output by over 8 percent — but the estimated standard error is double the point estimate of the coefficient. Most notably, the Raven CPM test has no impact on output, indicating that for this sample the returns to schooling are related to what was learned in school and not to ability. In addition, having an educated person in the household when the decision-maker is uneducated does not raise agricultural productivity.

In the Kenyan sample, however, all human capital variables other than the secondary school dummy are important in size and significantly different from zero.[6] Decision-makers who score 13 or higher on the Raven CPM test produce 25 percent more output than those who do not, holding schooling and cognitive skills constant. Having an educated person in the household, whether or not that person is the agricultural decision-maker, appears to raise output by close to 30 percent. Most surprisingly, having a decision-maker who attended primary school *lowers* output by about 19 percent, holding cognitive skills, reasoning ability, and the presence of other educated persons constant.

Our expectation had been that the education dummies were proxying for *positive* impacts of education on productivity other than those that arise through the literacy and numeracy learned in school. We had thought that this might include a willingness to try new methods, or a greater likelihood of accepting the advice of an extension agent. These effects, however, if they are important at all, are overwhelmed by some other effects. Recall that our evidence suggests that cognitive skills over and above basic numeracy and literacy have no additional impact on productivity. Furthermore, the CPM test controls for one type of reasoning ability, but certainly does not control for all personal characteristics that have an impact on either success in school or agricultural productivity. Because we control for literacy and numeracy in the regression, the primary school dummy is picking up the impact of having attended school and *not* becoming reasonably literate and numerate. It seems most likely, then, that this negative dummy is a proxy for personal characteristics unrelated to reasoning ability that lead to both a lack of learning in school and failure to be on the production frontier as a farmer. Having a poor work ethic may be one such characteristic.[7]

DISCUSSION

If the similarity in the magnitudes of the cognitive skills coefficients in the two equations is encouraging, the large differences between coefficients of other human capital variables is somewhat disturbing, particularly given the similarities between the two production systems. Moreover, these results are not fragile; although space does not permit reporting more equations, other functional forms and specifications change the magnitudes, but yield the same set of significant coefficients for the two locations.

Presumably the difference relates to different production systems. The relative importance of dairy production is the most striking difference between the two communities. A much higher percentage of the dairy cattle in the Kenyan site are pure-bred exotics or improved varieties. Although the ancestors of these farmers have kept cattle for generations, zero-grazing high quality dairy cows is a new technology that has expanded rapidly in the past 15 years. It is reasonable to expect that farmers with more human capital would be more likely to adopt and then be more successful at managing this enterprise. However, there is no obvious reason to expect that this would show up as a larger coefficient on the Raven CPM test, or increased impact of other educated persons on agricultural productivity.

Even though it was not significant in Tanzania, the significant Raven CPM test for Kenya indicates the potential usefulness of this instrument in controlling for reasoning ability. It is reasonable to conclude that the earlier studies that found a positive impact of education on agriculture were reporting screening effects in part. Future studies should investigate this relationship further, and expect threshold effects of this variable.

The other important human capital variable, the presence of an educated person in the household when the decision-maker has poor cognitive skills, is particularly important when gauging the timing of the impact of education on productivity. At present, the large increases in education in much of Africa have had only small effects on the average education of agricultural decision-makers because of the age composition of those decision-makers. If educated persons in the household have an impact as soon as they receive that education, returns to society from education will come much sooner and, by aggregating over time, will be much larger. Sorting out why in some systems this seems to occur, while in others it does not, would be a useful piece of research.

CONCLUSIONS

Finding large, highly significant coefficients on cognitive skills in both sites strengthens considerably the contention that increases in education will lead to improved agricultural productivity in Africa. Indeed, the size of the estimated impact dwarfs earlier estimates from any continent based on schooling alone. These results indicate that we can expect the large educated cohort beginning to permeate rural areas in Africa to have a substantial impact on productivity in the years ahead.

This study, however, concerns only coffee-producing, high-potential areas. The Kenyan sample also includes a large amount of income from dairying, which has a rather complex production function and is a relatively new technology. The earlier, more ambiguous results from Kenya were for annual crops (Moock, 1981; and Hopcraft, 1974). Certainly further research is required to see if these strong predictions of increased productivity hold for the large number of farmers engaged primarily in annual crop production in lower potential areas, and in other parts of the continent.

Furthermore, these results do not imply that increases in cognitive skills always improve agricultural productivity. After achieving rather rudimentary levels of literacy and numeracy, further advances did *not* improve productivity, even in the more technologically complex production environment in Kenya. This is in stark contrast to the wage market conclusions of Knight and Sabot (1990). Thus, investments in education beyond basic literacy and numeracy cannot be justified by the potential impact of these investments on agriculture, even in high-potential areas.

Nevertheless, the primary conclusion of this study is positive: past investments in education are beginning to have an impact on African agriculture today, and this impact should expand dramatically in the next decade as numerate and literate individuals control an increasing number of African farms.

NOTES

[1] Derived from the 1969 and 1979 Census reports and the 1988 Rural Literacy Survey. The percentage of the rural population 20 and over with some secondary education increased from 3.6 per cent to 17 per cent during the same period.

[2] This paper is part of a larger study on the determinants of long-run growth in rural areas of these countries, thus the links to the previous household surveys.

[3] Such intercropping with coffee remains illegal in Kenya, but after the 1989 fall in coffee prices these restrictions have not been enforced.

[4] Note that the percentages given for livestock products and bananas include the value of both sales and on-farm consumption.

[5] Translog production functions produce the same pattern of results for the human capital variables; the hypothesis that the true functional form is Cobb–Douglas cannot be rejected.

[6] The experience variables are not significant individually, but are significant at the 90 per cent level jointly.

[7] It is conceivable that attending school itself leads to negative attitudes towards agriculture. A number of observers of education in Kenya have suggested that this is the case; this supposed anti-agriculture bias was one of the rationales for a change in the education system implemented in the mid-1980s. Possibly, these attitudes lead to lower productivity by those who do, despite their wishes, become farmers. In order to be significant, however, this impact would have to continue to exist decades after leaving school. This persistence seems much less likely than the persistence of the unobserved personal characteristics hypothesized in the text.

REFERENCES

Azhar, R.A., 1991, 'Education and Technical Efficiency during the Green Revolution in Pakistan', *Economic Development and Cultural Change*, Vol. 39, No. 3, pp.651–665.

Hopcraft, P.N., 1974, 'Human Resources and Technical Skills in Agricultural Development', Ph.D. dissertation, Food Research Institute, Stanford University, Stanford, California.

Jamison, D.T. and Lau, L.J., 1982, *Farmer Education and Farm Efficiency*, Johns Hopkins University Press, Baltimore, Maryland.

Jamison, D.T. and Moock, P.R., 1984, 'Farmer Education and Farm Efficiency in Nepal: The Role of Schooling, Extension Services, and Cognitive Skills', *World Development*, Vol. 12, No. 1, pp.67–86.

Knight, J.B. and Sabot, R.H., 1990, *Education, Productivity and Inequality: The East African Natural Experiment*, Oxford University Press, Oxford, UK.

Lin, J.Y., 1991, 'Education and Innovation Adoption in Agriculture: Evidence from Hybrid Rice in China', *American Journal of Agricultural Economics*, Vol. 73, No. 3, pp.713–723.

Mellor, J.W., Delgado, C.L. and Blackie, M.J., 1987, *Accelerating Food Production in Sub-Saharan Africa*, Johns Hopkins University Press, Baltimore, Maryland.

Moock, P.R., 1973, 'Managerial Ability in Small Farm Production: An Analysis of Maize Yields in the Vihiga Division of Kenya', Ph.D. dissertation, Columbia University, New York.

Moock, P.R., 1981, 'Education and Technical Efficiency in Small Farm Production', *Economic Development and Cultural Change*, Vol. 29, pp.723–739.

Pudasaini, S.P., 1983, 'The Effects of Education in Agriculture: Evidence from Nepal', *American Journal of Agricultural Economics*, Vol. 65, No. 3, pp.509–515.

Raven, J., Raven, J.C. and Court, J.H., 1991, *Raven Manual: Section 1, General Overview*, Oxford Psychologists Press.

Welch F., 1970, 'Education in Production', *Journal of Political Economy*, Vol. 78, No.1, pp.32–59.

World Bank, 1989, *Sub-Saharan Africa: From Crisis to Sustainable Growth*, Washington, D.C.

JIKUN HUANG AND SCOTT ROZELLE*

Technological Change: The Re-Discovery of the Engine of Productivity Growth in China's Rural Economy

Abstract: The purpose of the paper is to explain the determinants of technological adoption and demonstrate the importance of technological change in rice yield growth during China's reform period. Using a unique data set on the nation's rice economy, in the first part of a two stage econometric model, adoption of new technologies (hybrid rice and single/double cropped rice) is shown to be chosen on the basis of two basic factors: the availability of a new technologies and the willingness of producers to adopt them. Treating technology as an endogenous factor, a set of rice supply and derived demand equations is subsequently estimated, and the parameters are used in a decomposition analysis. While institutional and environmental factors are found to be significant determinants of post-reform productivity increases, technological change has been shown to be the greatest across all periods, and can account for most of the growth in recent years.

INTRODUCTION

Since the mid-1970s, rapid growth throughout the economy has created rising incomes in many parts of China's rural sector. Economists have focused much of their attention on understanding the implications of the bold moves to decollectivize agricultural production and to liberalize rural markets (Sicular, 1991). The earliest empirical investigations centred on measuring the contribution of organizational and marketing reforms to agricultural growth (McMillan, Whalley and Zhu, 1989; and Lin, 1992b). The results of these investigations showed that implementation of the household responsibility system created most of the increase in productivity in the early reform years.

In part due to the influence of these works, few researchers have seriously considered the role of technical change in agricultural productivity growth. Even in these studies, technology is either assumed to be static (e.g., McMillan, Whalley and Zhu, 1989), or is measured by a time trend (e.g., Fan, 1991; and Lin, 1992b). Two notable exceptions empirically explore the determinants of technological change (Lin, 1992a) and try to develop a better understanding of its role in the growth of agricultural productivity (Fan and Pardey, 1992). These works expand the understanding of factors which influence technology adoption and provide an introduction to many issues facing research decision-makers in China. Even these studies, however, adopt restrictive assumptions: technology is exogenously given, and the analyses use aggregate data on agricultural value or total grain production. The observations of Stone (1988) and Huang and Rosegrant (1993)

* China National Rice Research Institute and Stanford University, respectively. The authors thank Scott Pearson, Pan Yotopoulos, Wally Falcon, Ramone Myer, Jeffrey Williams, Marcel Fafchamp, Mahabub Hossain, Mark Rosegrant and Shenngen Fan for comments on this paper. This paper is one of a series of studies written as part of the Chinese Rice Economy Project, a collaborative research programme between China National Research Institute and Stanford University. The authors acknowledge the support of the International Development Research Centre (IDRC), the International Rice Research Institute (IRRI) and the International Food Policy Research Institute (IFPRI). The Rockefeller Foundation's support is also gratefully acknowledged.

suggest that technology may not be exogenous and that using disaggregated data is preferable since the changing structure of China's crop and variety mix may be one of the main determinants of agricultural growth.

In this paper, two important technology decisions — the adoption of hybrid rice and the choice of single or double cropped rice — are explained. As an integral part of the producer's decision-making process, the decision to adopt these two technologies is then used to explain changes in yields and the patterns of input use. After estimating this new set of technology-endogenous, supply and demand equations, a decomposition of productivity changes seeks to assess the relative importance of the role of technological change (versus that of institutional reform or other factors) in China's recent productivity growth. Based on a unique set of data made available to the authors by the State Price Bureau (SPB) in China, the paper provides the first sectoral analysis of the impact of technology, price changes and other fixed factors on the use of labour, chemical fertilizer and organic manure for rice production.

RICE PRODUCTION IN CHINA

Rice has long been the most important food crop in China's agricultural economy. Over the past decade rice has contributed nearly 40 percent of the nation's caloric intake. China's rice sector is the largest component of the world's rice economy, accounting for some 37 percent of world rice production. The performance of China's rice sector, in terms of yields, has also been impressive during most of the past four decades, growing at rates of 1.5 to 5.2 percent, with technology playing a major role. China developed and extended fertilizer-responsive, semi-dwarf rice varieties in the early 1960s before the rest of the world had been introduced to 'green revolution' technology (Stone, 1988).

Understanding the role of technological change during the reform period requires a close examination of the spread of hybrid rice and fundamental shifts in single and double-rice cropping patterns. In 1976, China began to extend F_1 hybrid rice varieties for use in farmer's fields (He *et al.*, 1984). With a potential 15 to 20 percent yield advantage over conventional high yielding varieties, the area under hybrid rice expanded rapidly from 4.3 million hectares in 1978 to 15.9 million hectares in 1990, increasing from 12.6 percent of rice sown area to 41.2 percent. However, significant differences among the provinces exist in rates of adoption over time (Huang and Rozelle, 1993b).

With the exception of Lin (1992a), surprisingly little formal attention has centred on explaining the differences in these adoption rates. Lin identifies a number of variables that are important in facilitating the availability of new varieties, including the size of the rice market in a region (as it induces higher research expenditures on new technologies), and the level of development of hybrid rice seed production capacity. In addition, factors which make hybrid rice attractive for producers must still be considered, such as profitability (which during the reform era is more tied to the yield gap between conventional and hybrid varieties, rather than the price differential which has emerged only recently (He *et al.*, 1984)). These yield gaps have been thought to play an important role in the determination of inter-provincial levels of adoption. Sichuan Province, for example, which has the highest level of adoption (55 percent), also has one of the highest yield gaps (7.3 tonnes per hectare for hybrid varieties versus 4.7 tonnes per hectare for conventional varieties). In contrast, Zhejiang producers use hybrid rice on 26.1 percent of their rice area but their yield gap is less than 3 percent. On the input side, there is no discernable pattern of differences in the amount of labour required for hybrid rice (SPB, 1976–91).

The shifts in single and double-rice cropping patterns over the past four decades have played an equally important role in grain productivity. During the 1960s and 1970s, China's agricultural leaders set high grain production targets in order to achieve regional self-sufficiency. Officials had strong incentives to maximize their grain output, and researchers developed varieties facilitating the switch from one to two crops (Lin and Min, 1991). The development of photo-period insensitivity technologies made it possible for breeders to create rice varieties that could be planted earlier and those that could be harvested later in the season; breakthroughs in the average maturation time and cold tolerance were also important.

Just as with hybrid rice, yield difference between the crops is claimed by leaders to be the most important determinant of adoption. These gaps induced agricultural leaders during the 'Agricultural First' campaigns of the 1960s and 1970s to push the level of adoption of double-cropping technology to 71 percent of rice sown area in 1975 (Huang and Rozelle, 1993b). Unlike hybrids, however, these gains only come at the expense of sharply increased labour and chemical fertilizer use on a cultivated area basis (SPB, 1976–91). The opportunity cost of labour can be expected to be associated (negatively) with the use patterns of single and double cropped varieties.[1]

A RICE SUPPLY MODEL WITH ENDOGENOUS TECHNOLOGICAL CHANGE

In order to test the importance of the technology decision in the productivity rises during the reform period, a model is specified where rice cultivators in China are assumed to make decisions in a two-step process. At the beginning of the cropping season, farmers and local leaders agree on their planting strategy, deciding what proportion of their fixed paddy area to commit to hybrid rice, and what proportion to put into a two-season rice rotation. Producers subsequently make their variable input decisions, choosing the level of labour, fertilizer and organic manure that they will apply to their rice crops (which, in turn, determines their yield response).

Technology Adoption Equations

The specification of these equations, which are to be empirically estimated, depends on the observations made in the previous section, as well as a number of theoretical considerations based on profit-maximizing behaviour of producers.[2] The adoption of hybrid rice can be explained by the following equation:

Hybrid Rice Adoption = f_1(Rice Market Size; Yield Gap (between Hybrids and HYVs); Income; Institutional Factors; Time Trend; Provincial Dummies)

The double-cropped rice equation contains the same set of variables as the hybrid rice equation except for the income variable which is not included since there is no reason to expect that quality of rice is connected with double cropping. Instead the wage level of each province is included to account for the observed fact that double cropping seems to be negatively related to the opportunity cost of labour. The decision to cultivate rice in two seasons is described as follows:

Double-Cropped Rice Technology Adoption = f_2(Market Size; Yield Gap (between Single and Double-Cropped Rice); Wage; Labour-to-Land Ratio; Institutional Factors; Time Trend; Provincial Dummies).

Since the dependent variables in these equations are restricted (between zero and one), ordinary least squares estimators produce biased and inconsistent parameter estimates (Maddala, 1983). To correct for this problem, a Tobit model are used to estimate the parameters.

Yield Response and Input Demand Equations

After the varieties and cropping patterns have been chosen, producers then must choose their inputs levels, which in turn determine the yield response. It is assumed that the input allocative behaviour of profit-maximizing producers are consistent with Diewert's generalized Leontief profit function[3]:

$$(1)\quad \Pi^* = \Sigma_i^m \Sigma_j^m \beta_{if} p_i^{\frac{1}{2}} p_j^{\frac{1}{2}} + \Sigma_i^m \Sigma_k^n \beta_{ik} p_i z_k$$

where Π^* is maximized profits, p_i represents output and input prices, z_k are shifter variables (including technology, fixed inputs, and other institutional and environmental factors), and β_{ij} is a set of parameters to be estimated.

Using Shephard's Lemma, the yield response and input demand system can be derived from Equation (1). The equations to be estimated take the form:

$$(2)\quad x_i = a_i + \Sigma_{i \neq j}^m \beta_{if} \left(p_j / p_i\right)^{\frac{1}{2}} + \Sigma_k^n \beta_{ik} z_k$$

In this application, x_i represents the optimal yield response and the factor demands for labour, chemical fertilizer and organic manure. Because prices are normalized, homogeneity is imposed in the system.

In addition to prices, a number of other 'fixed' and 'quasi-fixed' factors affect the supply and derived demand decisions of producers. As discussed above, rice yields and factor demands are affected by the choice of hybrid rice technology and the double-cropping decision. Predicted values from the stage one equations are employed to avoid simultaneity bias. To capture the impact of institutional reform, the variable representing the implementation of the household responsibility system (also used in the technology equations) is included in each of the equations. Huang and Rozelle (1993a) demonstrate the increasingly important role of environmental factors in determining China's overall grain yields, and two variables which are most likely to affect rice yields are included.

The four yield and factor demand equations are estimated as a system to take into account the contemporaneous correlation among the error term which is added to each equation. Provincial dummies help guard against heteroskedasticity. Predicted values of hybrid rice and double-cropping adoption levels are used in the estimation. Using the estimated parameters from Equation (2), own- and cross-price elasticities can be computed as in Huang and Rosegrant (1993).

Data

Provincial cross-sectional, time-series data for China's 13 southern rice growing provinces from 1975–90 are used in the analysis. Hybrid rice adoption rates and information on rice sown area by season come primarily from a data base managed by the China National Rice Research Institute. Missing data for earlier years were collected by the authors through a mail survey sent to officials in the Bureaus of Agriculture of each province. The rest of the standard input and output data as well as information on the environmental variables come from secondary sources (ZGTJNJ and ZGNYNJ, 1980–92; the Ministry of Agriculture; and the Ministry of Water Conservation). The HRS variable, which is the proportion of households which had implemented decollectivization policies in a year, comes from Lin (1992b).

The most unique part of the data comes from the 'Cost of Production Survey', a data collection programme that has been run by the State Price Bureau since the mid-1970s. Based on annual household surveys conducted by county Price Bureau personnel, detailed by-crop and by-variety information are available for over 50 variables, including both expenditure (in value terms) and quantity data. Labour and fertilizer use, the organic manure variable, and wages and prices are all taken directly from the data set or are derived by manipulating total expenditure and quantity of a good.

THE RESULTS

Determinants of Technological Change

The results of the Tobit estimates for the normalized coefficients of the technology adoption equations are reported in columns 1 and 3 of Table 1. Given the log form of the market size, income, wage, and population density variables, the coefficients on the untransformed form of these variables (columns 2 and 4) can be interpreted as changes in adoption levels due to percentage changes in these variables. The estimates of the provincial dummies are not presented. The coefficients are nearly all as expected and significantly different from zero. The R^2 between the predicted values of technology adoption variables and those actually observed are 0.87 and 0.96, indicating the strong explanatory power of the specifications. The results are robust to specification changes and functional form selection.

The results strongly show that profit-seeking farmers and cost conscious local leaders in China only adopt these newly available varieties if they are technically more efficient, overcome production constraints or save on scarce resources. One compelling reason for adoption is seen in the yield gap variable in both equations. Given the small difference between the prices of rice during much of the sample period, the positive sign in the hybrid rice equation shows that producers choose new technologies based on the higher expected yields and revenues. Likewise, as the yield of single-season rises relative to double-cropped rice, there is a movement away from cultivating rice in two seasons. The high *t*-ratios in both equations point to the importance of this variable in the adoption decision.

Table 1 *Tobit Estimations for Hybrid Rice Adoption and Double-Cropped Rice Equations in China, 1975–90*

		Hybrid rice adoption rate		Double-cropped rice ratio	
		HYBRID ADOPT		DOUBLE ADOPT	
Variables	Code name	Normalised coefficient	Regression coefficient	Normalised coefficient	Regression coefficient
Intercept		–37.83 (–2.44)	–2.88	–96.28 (–4.54)	–7.09
Ln(market size)$_{t-1}$	TECHAVAIL	5.34 (2.96)	0.41	11.04 (5.60)	0.81
Hybrid–CV yield gap$_{t-1}$	YIELDGAP (Hybrid rice)	0.68 (4.33)	0.05		
Single–double-cropping Yield gap$_{t-1}$	YIELDGAP (Double crop)			–0.90 (–5.45)	–0.70
Ln (income)$_{t-1}$	INCOME	–1.17 (–1.66)	–0.09		
Ln(wage)$_{t-1}$	P_w			–1.33 (–2.04)	–0.10
Ln(population density)	POPDENSITY			0.17 (2.81)	0.67
Household responsibility	HRS	–0.83 (–1.61)	–0.06	0.66 (1.34)	0.05
Time trend	TREND	0.61 (10.92)	0.05	–0.19 (–2.77)	–0.01
Log-likelihood value		217.52		241.09	
R^2 between observed and predicted		0.87		0.96	

Notes: Figures in parentheses are absolute asymptotic *t*-values. Provincial dummies are not shown. Normalized coefficients calculated by method used in Tobin (1958).

Income and wages are also found to be important adoption determinants. The role of taste preferences in the hybrid rice adoption decision is demonstrated by the negative sign on the coefficient of the income variable. As observed during field visits to east coast provinces in the early 1990s, producers in economically better off areas can afford to forego the additional yields provided by hybrid varieties. The negative (and significant) signs on the wage coefficients, however, point to the influence that wages exert on cropping pattern selection. Rising wages in the east coast provinces (in some areas by several times) are responsible for the movement to single cropping in these areas. The magnitude of the coefficient (–0.10) means that as wages double, the proportion of area sown to two-season rice drops by 10 percent.

Table 2 *Rice Yield and Input Demand System, Estimated by Zellner's Seemingly Unrelated Regression, 1975–90*

			Input Demand Equations		
		Rice Yields	Chemical Fertilizer (kg/ha)	Labour (day/ha)	Organic Fert. Ratio
Variables	Code name	RICEYIELD	CHEMFERT	LABOUR	ORGANIC/ CHEMICAL
Intercept		7.12	0.29	60.49	342.79
		(9.56)	(3.73)	(0.46)	(4.73)
$(P_f/P_r)^{0.5}$	Price Ratios	–1.32			
		(–4.63)			
$(P_w/P_r)^{0.5}$	"	0.02			
		(2.70			
$(P_r/P_f)^{0.5}$	"		–39.32		
			(–0.25)		
$(P_w/P_f)^{0.5}$	"		10.56		
			(3.98)		
$(P_r/P_w)^{0.5}$	"			3103.60	
				(0.86)	
$(P_f/P_w)^{0.5}$	"			6264.70	9.91
				(2.49)	(3.23)
Hybrid rice adoption[a]	HYBRID_ ADOPT	2.68	304.28	–110.59	
		(8.42)	(1.22)	(–2.01)	
Double-rice adoption	DOUBLE_ ADOPT	–2.32	121.66	92.76	
		(–5.05)	(0.70)	(1.11)	
Organic fertilizer	ORGANIC/ CHEMICAL	0.06			
		(0.24)			
Severity of disaster	DISASTER	–1.99			
		(–4.07)			
Salinization	SALINITY	–9.19			
		(–2.52)			
Household	HRS	0.47	5.08	–162.00	–0.18
		(3.96)	(0.09)	(–6.78)	(–7.19)
Time	TREND		10.62		
			(0.99)		
R^2		0.91	0.65	0.79	0.84

Notes: Figures in parentheses are *t*-values. Provincial dummies are not shown.
[a] Estimated values from the equations in Table 4.

The signs on the time trend and population density variables in the double-cropping equation are consistent with the results implied by the wage variable, and support the predictions of the Hayami and Ruttan induced innovation hypothesis. The negative sign on the time trend variable may in part be measuring the success breeders have had in creating higher yielding and better quality single-season rice varieties. Breeders have been responding to rising wages in these localities which signal the shortage of labour in local markets. Newer varieties of single-season rice, which are used to replace labour-intensive double-cropping systems, help producers economize on labour.

Likewise, given equal levels of wages, areas with scarce land resources require technologies that conserve land, which is exactly the role of double cropping technologies. Apparently these demands have been satisfied by research staff (in areas where labour is more abundant), as adoption rates of two-season rice are higher in more densely populated areas. Finally, the spread of the household responsibility system in the early 1980s slowed the spread of hybrid rice, although only by a total of six percent. The relationship was relatively weak with a *t*-ratio of only –1.61. Meanwhile, decollectivization had less effect on double-cropped area. (The magnitude of its coefficient, — 0.66, is small relative to its standard error.)

Rice Yield and Factor Demand

The four-equation rice sector model has produced remarkably robust results which are consistent with most of the *a priori* expectations (Table 2). The R^2 for the rice yield equation is 0.91; those for the factor demand equations range from 0.84 to 0.65. The provincial dummies are omitted for simplicity. The coefficients of the price variables with relatively high *t*-ratios have the expected signs except for the wage variable in the yield equation.[4] The price elasticities implied by these estimates, in general, have the expected signs and magnitudes consistent with those expected in a labour-intensive, East Asian setting (Table 3).

Table 3 *Yield and Input Demand Elasticities Evaluated at the Sample Mean, 1975–90*

		Fertilizer		
Variables	Rice Yield	Chemical	Organic	Labour
Rice price	0.039	–0.031		0.074
Fertilizer price	–0.140	0.370	0.285	0.150
Wage	0.102	0.401	–0.285	–0.224
Hybrid rice adoption	0.116	0.097		–0.050
Double cropping rice adoption	–0.300	0.116		0.126
Ratio of organic fertilizer	0.005			
Severity of disaster	–0.030			
Severity of salinization	–0.063			

The coefficients of the shifter variables in the rice yield response equation have the expected signs and most are significant (except for the soil fertility variable in the yield equation and several variables in the fertilizer equation). The importance of the technology variables in the determination of China's rice yields can be seen from the value of their elasticities (Table 3). If the adoption rates of hybrid rice and single-season rice simultaneously increase by 10 percent, rice yields increase by 4.16 percent (the sum of the elasticities, 0.116 + 0.300). The significance of these variables shows the importance of the technology decision in the determination of rice yields.

Technological choice also influences the optimal use of fertilizer and labour for rice production. Hybrid rice is fertilizer-using, a characteristic of hybrid varieties for all crops (SPB, 1976–91). The positive net regression coefficient for the hybrid rice variable in the labour equation suggests that the technology is labour saving. Although the elasticity is small, this result is of interest; published statistics and field research on this issue have generated mixed outcomes prior to this study.

Table 4 *Decomposition Changes in Rice Productivity in China by Source, 1975–90*

Sources of rice yield change	Yield changes 1975–90[a]	1975–84[a]	1985–90[a]
Technologies	1.391 (66.8)	0.842 (49.3)	0.549 (146.6)
Hybrid rice	1.118 (53.7)	0.625 (36.6)	0.493 (131.7)
HRS	–0.158 (–7.6)	–0.158 (–9.3)	0.000 (0.0)
Cropping system	0.273 (13.1)	0.217 (12.7)	0.056 (14.9)
HRS	–0.114 (–5.5)	–0.114 (–6.7)	0.000 (0.0)
HRS	0.465 (22.3)	0.464 (27.2)	0.001 (0.4)
Environmental effects (Disaster and salinity)	–0.225 (–10.8)	–0.132 (–7.7)	–0.093 (–24.8)
Residuals (inputs and others)	(21.7)	(31.3)	(–71.8)
Total	2.082 (100)	1.708 (100)	0.374 (100)

Notes: Figures in the parentheses are the contributions to growth in percentage terms. Beginning and ending yields used to calculate changes in rice yields are three-year means — 1975 is the average of 1975–77; 1984 is the average of 1983–85; 1985 is the average of 1984–86; 1990 is the average of 1988–1990.

Environmental and institutional factors are also important determinants of yields and factor demands. The incentive effect of decollectivization on agricultural productivity, which has been reported for aggregate crop production (Lin, 1992b) and on the aggregate output of the non-industrial rural economy (McMillan, Whalley and Zhu, 1989; and Fan, 1991), is also clearly present in rice productivity. The negative impact of HRS on the use of labour and organic manure use, and the insignificant effect on fertilizer use, demonstrates the incentive effect of decollectivization.

Sources of Yield Growth

The results of this paper have identified a number of factors which have been influential in the determination of rice yields. In this section, the relative magnitudes of their impact are decomposed. Between 1976 and 1990, rice yields increased by a total of 2.08 tonnes per hectare (Table 4, column 1). Improvements in technology contributed 66.8 percent of this growth, accounting for 1.39 tonnes per hectare. Hybrid rice adoption can account for most of the technical change component (and 53.7 percent of the total change), increasing rice yields by 1.12 tonnes per hectare; the expansion of single-season area (with improved varieties) contributed 13.1 percent of the yield increase. In addition to technological factors, institutional changes have augmented rice yields by 22.3 percent. In contrast, decreasing soil fertility, natural disasters and salinization (reported in Table 4 as 'Environmental effects') led to a 225 kilogram per hectare loss in rice yields. The rest of the growth is accounted for by increases in inputs and non-hybrid rice related technological change.

To facilitate comparisons of these results with those of previous research, a separate breakdown identifies the sources of growth in rice yields between 1976 and 1984 (Table 4). Even during this period, which was undergoing rapid institutional change, 49.3 percent of the 1.71 tonnes of rice yield increase was contributed by technological factors. The decomposition exercise shows that 27.2 percent of the rice yield improvements was due to the implementation of HRS. Over a similar time period Lin (1992b) estimates the shift from collective production to the HRS created 47 percent of agricultural output growth and over 90 percent of agricultural productivity growth. McMillan, Whalley and Zhu (1989) use a growth accounting procedure and estimate that over 60 percent of agricultural productivity increases can be attributed to decollectivization. When technology is explicitly specified and modelled as an endogenous decision, as has been done in this paper, the importance of technological change rises dramatically.

CONCLUSIONS

The purpose of the paper is to explain the determinants of technological adoption and to demonstrate the importance of technological change in rice yield growth during China's reform period. Adoption of new technologies depends on two basic factors: the availability of a new technologies and the willingness of producers to adopt them. Both sets of factors have been shown to be important in this analysis. While institutional and environmental factors are significant determinants of post-reform productivity increases, technological change has been shown to be the greatest across all periods, and can account for most all of the growth in recent years.

These results are evidence of the great contribution of China's agricultural research system to the increase in productivity. To the extent that future growth will depend primarily on continuing technological breakthroughs, the outcome of the recent efforts to reform the research sector are critical. On the one hand, there have been policies to make institutes more responsive to the needs of society (which has typically been carried out by allowing institutes to set up consultancy enterprises or seed distribution outlets whose services are 'bought' on a free market basis). On the other hand, severe cut backs in research funding may be keeping scientists from being able to work in areas of fruitful research. Under these conditions, researchers and breeders may reduce their efforts to produce new technologies. Chinese leaders should carefully and continually review the health of the agricultural research system to ensure that in the future, the nation can still rely on technology as an engine of growth.

NOTES

1 In the dynamic coastal regions, two-season rice was shown to be economically inefficient in the early 1980s due to the high wage levels (Wiens, 1982). Following the rural industrialization boom of the reform era, the area planted to two-season rice fell sharply in the east coast areas, and nationwide fell from 66 percent in 1980 to 58 percent in 1990 (Huang and Rozelle, 1993b).

2 For a full discussion of the specification and functional form choice, see Huang and Rozelle (1993).

3 The assumption of constrained profit-maximizing behaviour can be justified on several grounds. For most of the sample period China has been operating under the household responsibility system, and producers have faced a two-tiered pricing system. The higher price in this system is typically closely pegged to the market price. Even though the government intervenes, the farm household is still the residual claimant on profits and is facing output and input prices which are, in part, reflective of supply and demand forces (Tian, 1992; and Huang and Rosegrant, 1993).

4 It may be at certain income levels, as wages rise, the demand by households for rice could lead farmers to increase yields to satisfy such demand. It may also be that as wages rise, binding liquidity constraints are relaxed allowing producers to increase yields through use of more material inputs.

REFERENCES

Fan, S., 1991, 'Effects of Technological Change and Institutional Reform on Production Growth in Chinese Agriculture', *American Journal of Agricultural Economics*, Vol. 73, No. 2, pp.266–275.

Fan, S. and Pardey, P., 1992, *Agricultural Research in China: Its Institutional Development and Impact*, International Service for National Agricultural Research, The Hague, The Netherlands.

He, G., Te, A., Travers, L., Lai, X. and Herdt., R., 1984, 'The Economics of Hybrid Rice Production in China', *IRRI Research Paper Series*, No. 101, Los Banos, The Philippines.

Huang, J. and Rosegrant, M., 1993, 'Grain Supply Response in China: A Preliminary Analysis', Paper presented at the Second Workshop on Projections and Policy Implications of Medium and Long Term Rice Supply and Demand, International Rice Research Institute, Los Banos, The Philippines, April.

Huang, J. and Rozelle, S., 1993a, 'Sustainable Agriculture in China: An Evaluation of Grain Yields', Paper presented at the International Symposium on Sustainable Agricultural and Rural Development, Beijing, China, May.

Huang, J. and Rozelle, S., 1993b, 'Technological Change: Decomposing Productivity Change in China's Post-Reform Rice Economy', Working Paper, Food Research Institute, Stanford University.

Lin, J.Y., 1992a, 'Hybrid Rice Innovation in China: A Study of Market-Demand Induced Technological Innovation in a Centrally Planned Economy', *Review of Economics and Statistics*, Vol. 74, No. 1, pp.14–20.

Lin, J.Y., 1992b, 'Rural Reforms and Agricultural Growth in China', *American Economic Review*, Vol. 82, No. 1, pp.34–51.

Lin, S. C. and Min, S. K., 1991, *Rice Varieties and Their Geneology in China*, Shanghai Science and Technology Press, Shanghai, China.

Maddala, G.S., 1983, *Limited Dependent and Qualitative Variables in Econometrics*, Cambridge University Press, Cambridge, UK.

McMillan, J., Whalley, J. and Zhu, L., 1989, 'The Impact of China's Economic Reforms on Agricultural Productivity Growth', *Journal of Political Economy*, Vol. 97, pp.781–807.

Sicular, T., 1991, 'China's Agricultural Policy During the Reform Period', in Joint Economic Committee Congress of the United States (ed.), *China's Economic Dilemma in the 1990s: The Problems of Reforms, Modernization and Interdependence*, Vol. 1, pp.340–364.

SPB, 1988-90, *Quanguo Nongchanpin Chengben Shouyi Ziliao Huibian* (National Agricultural Production Cost and Revenue Information Summary), China Price Bureau Press, Beijing, China.

Stone, B., 1988, 'Developments in Agricultural Technology', *China Quarterly*, Vol. 116.

Tian, J.Y., 1992, 'Jiakuai Gaige Kaifang Bufa Shixian Nongye Xiang Gaochan Youzhi Gaoxiao De Zhuanyi' ('Accelerate the Pace of Reforms: Strive for Higher Quality and Higher Efficiency in Agriculture'), *Renmin Ribao* (People's Daily), 3 July, p.3.

Tobin, J., 1958, 'Estimations of Relationships for Limited Dependent Variables', *Econometrica*, Vol. 26, pp.24–36.

Wiens, T., 1982, 'The Limits to Agricultural Intensification: The Suzhou Experience', *China Under the Four Modernization, Part I*, US Government Printing Office, pp.462–474.

ZGNYNJ, 1981–92, *Zhongguo Nongye Nianjian* (China Agricultural Yearbook), China Agricultural Press, Beijing.

ZGTJNJ, 1980,1986–92, *Zhongguo Tongji Nianjian* (China Statistical Year Book), China Statistical Press, Beijing.

P. LYNN KENNEDY, HARALD VON WITZKE AND TERRY L. ROE*

International Strategic Agricultural Trade Policy Interdependence and the Exchange Rate: A Game Theoretical Analysis

Abstract: International strategic agricultural trade policy interdependence is modelled using a game theoretical framework. The model distinguishes between the European Community, the United States and a politically passive rest-of-the-world. Particular emphasis is placed on the effect of the exchange rate on the equilibrium outcome of this game.

INTRODUCTION

In most countries, agriculture has become increasingly open, as evidenced by the dramatic increase in the volume of international trade since the end of World War II. One of the consequences of the growing openness of agriculture is a growing international interdependence. Around the globe, agricultural trade policies are determined by political processes which in turn are influenced by the linkage of their agricultural sectors to world markets, and hence to the polity in other major trading nations. Any large country's agricultural trade decisions can affect world market prices and international trade flows and thus other countries' agriculture. This in turn may lead to changes in other countries' policy adjustments.

It has been shown that in many countries, including the USA and the European Community (EC), the level of agricultural producer price support is determined to a large extent by agricultural incomes and budgetary expenditures caused by farm programmes (e.g., Riethmueller and Roe, 1986; and von Witzke, 1986, 1990). Typically, the functional relationship is such that relatively low (high) agricultural incomes, and relatively low (high) budgetary expenditures result in relatively high (low) levels of price support.

In the 1980s, the budgetary expenditures of farm programmes skyrocketed in many countries, inducing political demands for agricultural and trade policy reform. However, the growing international interdependence had made unilateral reform a politically unattractive option. Under these circumstances policy-makers face a classical 'prisoner's dilemma' as they have to expect that unilateral policy reform would be counteracted by other countries' endogenous policy adjustments.

To illustrate this, consider a world of two large countries, the USA and the EC. Suppose that the USA discontinued agricultural price support. Of course, this would lead to price increases on the world markets. This, in turn, would reduce EC budgetary expenditures, as it reduces the export subsidies the EC pays to dispose of its surplus production. The budgetary savings would be used by the EC to increase agricultural price support further. This would result in growing EC exports which would reduce world market prices, all other things being equal, and lead to additional structural adjustment of US agriculture.

* This research was supported by the University of Minnesota Agricultural Experiment Station.

To model this international strategic agricultural policy interdependence, we will develop a non-co-operative game of a three-country world consisting of the USA, the EC, and a politically passive rest-of-the-world. In our model each country chooses its policy strategies based on a *political pay-off function* (PPF). Particular emphasis is placed on the role of the exchange rate between the two countries in determining policy strategies. First, we discuss the role of the exchange rate in determining the choice of policy strategies. Then the theoretical framework is outlined, and third, we discuss the empirical results of the game. Comments on the stability of international agreements on agricultural and trade policy reform in the presence of exchange rate fluctuations conclude the paper.

THE ROLE OF THE EXCHANGE RATE

The measurement of the extent of agricultural trade protection has been a popular area of agricultural economic research in recent years, and it has played an important role in the multilateral trade negotiations in the Uruguay Round of the General Agreement on Tariffs and Trade. One of the problems involved is that measures of trade protection, such as the Nominal Protection Coefficient (NPC) or the Producer Subsidy Equivalent, are influenced not only by domestic price support and international price levels but also by exchange rates which have the tendency to fluctuate over time.

Consider the ECU/US$ exchange rate and price support in wheat. During the mid-1980s the US$ was rather strong relative to the currencies that form the ECU. In 1985, when the ECU/US$ exchange rate peaked the ECU world market price of wheat was at about the same level as EC support prices. Consequently, the NPC of wheat in the EC approached unity and the EC could export at zero or very low export subsidies.

By 1992 the value of the US$ had declined relative to the ECU to 0.76 ECU/US$ (Commission of the EC, 1992). Although wheat price support in the EC had declined by about 30 percent since 1985, the change in the exchange rate together with world market changes had resulted in an NPC in the EC of 1.94 (OECD, 1993).

This phenomenon has a number of implications. For instance, in 1985 it was difficult for the USA to claim that the EC's Common Agricultural Policy (CAP) was protectionist and distorting international agricultural trade. But it was not a change in the CAP towards a more liberal policy that had resulted in such a low NPC; it was a temporarily high value of the US$ relative to the ECU. Likewise the growing NPC in the EC since 1985 was not the consequence of more protectionist tendencies in EC agriculture. Quite the opposite, the real support price has declined considerably. For the most part it was the consequence of a declining value of the US$.

THEORETICAL FRAMEWORK

Our analysis is based on a multi-commodity model of agriculture. The initial model was developed by Mahé, Tavèra and Trochet (1988). Subsequently a political economic sub-model was added (Johnson, 1990; and Johnson, Mahé and Roe, 1993) and other modifications were made (Kennedy, 1994).

In our model, N commodities are produced, consumed, and traded by two main countries, the EC and the USA, and the rest-of-the-world. Governments intervene in domestic markets either through the use of price (π) or supply/demand shift (θ) instruments. Price instruments, denoted as $A_{ik}^{\pi S}$ for producers and $A_{ik}^{\pi Q}$ for consumers of commodity i in country k, affect the prices observed by the supply and final demand sectors. With the world price of commodity i represented as P_i^W the domestic price functions for country k are:

$$(1)\quad P_{ik}^S = P_{ik}^S(A_{ik}^{\pi S}, P_i^W) \text{ and } P_{ik}^Q = P_{ik}^Q(A_{ik}^{\pi Q}, P_i^W), \text{ for } i = 1,2,...,N$$

Supply/demand shift instruments, denoted as $A_{ik}^{\theta S}$ for producers and $A_{ik}^{\theta Q}$ for consumers of commodity i in country k, are implicit elements of exogenous variable vectors X_k^S and X_k^Q.

Throughout the process of agricultural policy formulation the welfare effects of various actions are taken into account by the government. Policy-makers behave as though they are using a weighing system to compare the gains of certain groups versus the losses of others. In order to model this behaviour, a political pay-off function (PPF) is used. The PPF, a weighted, additive function of producer quasi-rents, consumer utility, and budget costs, is the objective function which, through their policy choices, policy-makers behave as though they seek to maximize. The weights are determined empirically in the model, based on observed policies.

Let $-k$ denote the other main country while the actions of country k are represented by $A_k = \{A_k^{\pi S}, A_k^{\pi Q}, A_k^{\theta S}, A_k^{\theta Q}\}$. Producers are grouped according to commodities with their welfare defined as the profit obtained through the production and marketing of that commodity. Producer quasi-rents, consumer utility, and the budget of country k are expressed as functions of government policies in the following equations:

$$(2)\quad \tilde{\Pi}_k(A_k, A_{-k}) = \Pi_k\{P_k^S[A_k^{\pi S}, P^W(A_k, A_{-k})], A_k^{\theta S}\}$$

$$(3)\quad \tilde{U}_k(A_k, A_{-k}) = U_k\{P_k^Q[A_k^{\pi Q}, P^W(A_k, A_{-k})], A_k^{\theta Q}\}$$

$$(4)\quad \tilde{B}_k(A_k, A_{-k}) = B_k\{P_k^S[A_k^{\pi S}, P^W(A_k, A_{-k})], P_k^Q[A_k^{\pi Q}, P^W(A_k, A_{-k})], P^W(A_k, A_{-k})], A_k^{\theta S}, A_k^{\theta Q}\}$$

The budget weight is normalized to one and the PPF, expressed as a function of government policies, is shown as:

$$(5)\quad V_k(A_k, A_{-k}) = \tilde{\Pi}_k(A_k, A_{-k}) \cdot \lambda_{Sk} + \tilde{U}_k(A_k, A_{-k}) \cdot \lambda_{Qk} + \tilde{B}_k(A_k, A_{-k})$$

where λ_{Sk} is a strictly positive, N x 1 vector which represents the relative political weights of the producer groups in country k, and λ_{Qk} is a strictly positive scaler representing the relative political weight of the consumer group in country k.

If the policy decision process of interdependent countries is to be modelled, a Nash equilibrium occurs where each country chooses its policy which maximizes its PPF given the policy choice of the other. This equilibrium is defined using a *best response correspondence*. For a given A_{-k}, government k chooses A_k^* one possible best response to A_{-k}, such that:

(6) $V_k(A_k^*, A_{-k}) \geq V_k(A_k, A_{-k})$, for all $A_k \in \mathbf{A}_k$

where $\mathbf{A}_k$ is the set of all possible actions which can be employed by government k. Every A_{-k} element of $\mathbf{A}_{-k}$ has at least one A_k^* element of $\mathbf{A}_k$ which is a best response for country k. A Nash equilibrium is defined as the set of actions A_k^*, A_{-k}^* where A_k^* is a best response to A_{-k}^* for country k, and A_{-k}^* is a best response to A_k^*, for country $-k$.

Differentiating Equation (5) with respect to A_k^S and A_k^Q, the first-order necessary conditions for a maximum are

$$(7)\quad \begin{bmatrix} \dfrac{\delta V_k}{\delta A_k^S} \\ \\ \dfrac{\delta V_k}{\delta A_k^Q} \end{bmatrix} = \begin{bmatrix} \dfrac{\delta \tilde{\Pi}_k}{\delta A_k^S} \dfrac{\delta \tilde{U}_k}{\delta A_k^S} \\ \\ \dfrac{\delta \tilde{\Pi}_k}{\delta A_k^Q} \dfrac{\delta \tilde{U}_k}{\delta A_k^Q} \end{bmatrix} \cdot \begin{bmatrix} \lambda_{Sk} \\ \\ \lambda_{Qk} \end{bmatrix} + \begin{bmatrix} \dfrac{\delta \tilde{B}_k}{\delta A_k^S} \\ \\ \dfrac{\delta \tilde{B}_k}{\delta A_k^Q} \end{bmatrix} = \begin{bmatrix} 0 \\ \\ 0 \end{bmatrix}$$

Under the assumption that V_k is concave in A_k given A_{-k}, any A_k^* which solves Equation (7) maximizes V_k. Thus, by definition, A_k^* is a best response to A_{-k}. In the situation where the two countries negotiate with one another, no agreement will be reached or kept unless both countries are made at least as well off as they were prior to the agreement. A necessary condition for a treaty is that there exist at least one pair of actions (A_k^+, A_{-k}^+) satisfying

(8) $V_k(A_k^+, A_{-k}^+) \geq V_k(A_k^*, A_{-k}^*)$ and $(V_{-k}(A_k^+, A_{-k}^+) \geq V_{-k}(A_k^*, A_{-k}^*)$

Actions (A_k^+, A_{-k}^+) satisfying Equation (8) are called treaty actions. The *treaty action space* is the set of all treaty actions. In order to achieve an agreement in which both governments are made at least as well off as prior to negotiations, the settlement must lie within the treaty action space.

EMPIRICAL ANALYSIS

This analysis is based on 1990 as the base year. We distinguish 7 commodity groups consisting of cereals, oilmeals, feed grain substitutes, beef, pork and poultry, milk, and sugar. The PPFs for the USA and EC were generated through the evaluation of small changes in the observed policies from their base year levels. These changes were then used to approximate the partial derivatives in Equation (7). When Equation (7) is solved for λ_{Sk} and λ_{Qk} one obtains approximations of the PPF weights. These weights are normalized such that the budget weight is one. They are presented in Table 1.

In this two-player, normal-form, non-co-operative game, defined by $G = \{\mathbf{A}_{US}, \mathbf{A}_{EC}; \mathbf{P}_{US}, \mathbf{P}_{EC}\}$ each country k chooses some action $A_k \in \mathbf{A}_k$ in order to maximize its PPF, given the action choices of the other country. The policy strategies analyzed here are several different degrees of across-the-board trade liberalization. The action space $\mathrm{A}_k = \{SQ_k, 75_k, 50_k, 25_k, FT_k\}$ for k = USA, EC. Actions of the USA and

EC are status quo (SQ), protection at 75 percent of the status quo level (75), protection at 50 percent of the status quo level (50), protection at 25 percent of the status quo level (25), and free trade (FT). Game simulations are conducted in which compensation is not allowed (NC) and in which governments provide compensation to losers (BC).

In the BC scenarios, government budget savings, resulting from liberalization, are transferred to producers. In order to receive this transfer, the PPF weight of a sector must be greater than one.

Table 1 *Political Pay-Off Function Weights and Their Ranking by Interest Group for the USA and the EC, Based on 1990 Data*

	United States		European Community	
Interest group	Rank	Weight	Rank	Weight
Sugar	1	1.32	1	1.49
Milk	2	1.31	2	1.41
Cereals	3	1.15	3	1.37
Oilmeals	4	1.04	4	1.35
Budget	5	1.00	7	1.00
Beef	6	0.89	5	1.29
Consumers	7	0.85	8	0.90
Pork and poultry	8	0.84	6	1.01

Source: Kennedy (1993).

Table 2 *PPF Values for US and EC Protection Reductions without Budget Compensation, 1990*

	EC actions				
US actions	SQ_{EC}	75_{EC}	50_{EC}	25_{EC}	FT_{EC}
SQ_{US}	0, 0	97, 120	210, –441	323, –1 716	461, –4 174
75_{US}	434, 168	545, 242*	683, –335	854, –1 662	1093, –4 181
50_{EC}	132, 359	239, 453	378, –150	548, –1 469	791, –4 004
25_{US}	–531, 577	–442, 680	–320, 116	–151, –1 238	56, –3 772
FT_{US}	–1675, 844	–1552, 957	–1486, 392	–1384, –915	–1216, –3 479

Notes: The pair (P_{US}, P_{EC}) are the PPF for the USA and EC respectively. * The unique Nash equilibrium occurs at $(75_{US}, 75_{EC})$.

The base solution for 1990 without direct compensation of producers is presented in Table 2. The Nash equilibrium in this, as well as in all other scenarios analyzed here, is unique. It is marked by a star (*). As can be seen, without use of budgetary savings to compensate producers, only limited liberalization can be expected in both the USA and the EC. If budget savings are used to compensate producers, both countries are willing to liberalize more (Table 3). However, the USA is willing to reduce trade protection more than the EC. This is consistent in principle with the strategies both countries have pursued in the GATT negotiations.

Table 4 depicts the Nash equilibria at alternative exchange rates. We use the maximum and minimum US$/ECU exchange rate since the introduction of the ECU in 1978 (1.39 US$/ECU in 1980; 0.76 US$/ECU in 1985). This implies that compared with 1990 (1.27 US$/ECU) we simulate the effect of a 9.4 percent devaluation and a 40.2 percent revaluation of the dollar. A devaluation of the dollar results in the same Nash equilibrium for NC^D as that found for the actual 1990 exchange rate, NC^A. However, BC^D occurs at a point where the USA chooses free trade while the EC once again picks a 50 percent reduction of its protection levels. The results of a revaluation of the dollar show both countries retaining the status quo in NC^R, while the solution BC^R finds the USA choosing the status quo and the EC reducing its protection levels by 50 percent.

Table 3 *PPF Values for US and EC Protection Reductions with Budget Compensation, 1990*

	EC actions				
US actions	SQ_{EC}	75_{EC}	50_{EC}	25_{EC}	FT_{EC}
SQ_{US}	0, 0	101, 2235	221, 3331	341, 2911	490, 493
75_{US}	1522, 191	1463, 2287	1383, 3455	1320, 2969	1354, 479
50_{US}	2112, 409	2182, 2306	2203, 3557	2178, 3169	2129, 1636
25_{US}	2280, 657	2348, 2343	2399, 3681*	2495, 3339	2610, 853
FT_{US}	1745, 961	1852, 2399	1915, 3856	1989, 3532	2087, 1112

Notes: The pair (P_{US}, P_{EC}) are the PPF for the USA and EC respectively. *The unique Nash equilibrium occurs at $(25_{US}, 50_{EC})$.

Table 4 *Nash Equilibrium Solutions to Games Using Various Exchange Rate Levels*

	EC Actions				
USA Actions	SQ_{EC}	75_{EC}	50_{EC}	25_{EC}	FT_{EC}
SQ_{US}	NC^R		BC^R		
75_{US}		NC^A, NC^D			
50_{US}					
25_{US}			BC^A		
FT_{US}			BC^D		

Note: Game solutions with no budget compensation and with budget compensation are represented by NC^E and BC^E, respectively for $E = A, R, D$, where A denotes actual exchange rate, R denotes a revalued dollar, and D denotes a devalued dollar.

Without budget compensation, both countries are induced to choose policies at or near the status quo regardless of the exchange rate. If compensation is allowed, the EC reduces its protection levels by 50 percent. Solutions involving compensation indicate that the USA loses incentive to reduce protection given a revaluation of the dollar, while incentive to liberalize trade policies increases as the dollar is devalued, due to the relative change in prices of traded goods.

CONCLUSION

Knowledge of the state of economic policy is typically sufficient for economists to suggest numerous policy alternatives that, even in the presence of second best, can lead to Pareto superior outcomes. The problem of course is that the policy alternatives which are politically acceptable are typically a small or a null subset of those that lead to these outcomes. The approach utilized here narrows the policy set to the level of reform that seems politically acceptable, and then shows the sensitivity of this set to compensatory payments from budget savings, and to fluctuations in the value of the US$ relative to the ECU. Without compensatory payments to those with the highest political influence, the results suggest that only modest reform is possible. With compensation, liberalization occurs but free trade is not obtained.

These results are not surprising in light of the concerns expressed by EC negotiators; clearly, the linkage between the value of the dollar and the influence of special interests serves to link broader economic policy to possibilities for reform at the sectoral level. The GATT plays a unique role in this regard because bringing agriculture under its discipline leads to pressures for macroeconomic stability as well.

We suggest that as the world moves in the direction of regional trading blocks, more in-depth and sophisticated analysis of the type presented here will be needed in order to focus attention on those reforms that are politically feasible and Pareto superior. Economists will need to analyze the design of various institutional mechanisms that can minimize the tendencies for prisoners dilemma outcomes.

REFERENCES

Commission of the European Communities, *The Agricultural Situation in the Community*, Brussels, various issues, including 1992.

Johnson, M.A., 1990, *Agricultural Policies as Nash Equilibria*, Ph.D. dissertation, University of Minnesota, St. Paul.

Johnson, M.A., Mahè, L. and Roe, T.L., 1993, 'Trade Compromises Between the European Community and the USA: An Interest Group – Game Theory Approach', *Journal of Policy Modelling*, Vol. 15, pp.199–222.

Kennedy, P.L., 1994, 'Agricultural Policy Decisions in the Uruguay Round: A Game-Theoretic Examination', Ph.D. dissertation, University of Minnesota, St. Paul, Minnesota.

Mahè, L., Tavèra, C. and Trochet, T., 1988, *An Analysis of Interaction Between EC and USA Policies with a Simplified World Trade Model: MISS*, background paper for the Report to the Commission of the European Communities on Disharmonies in EC and US Agricultural Policies.

OECD, 1993, *Agricultural Policies, Markets and Trade*, OECD, Paris.

Riethmueller, P. and T. Roe, 1986, 'Government Intervention in Commodity Markets: The Case of Japanese Rice and Wheat Policy', *Journal of Policy Modelling*, Vol. 8, pp.327–349.

von Witzke, H., 1986, 'Endogenous Supranational Policy Decisions: The Common Agricultural Policy of the European Community', *Public Choice*, Vol. 48, pp.157–174.

von Witzke, H., 1990, 'Determinants of the USA Wheat Producer Support Price: Do Presidential Elections Matter?', *Public Choice*, Vol. 64, pp.155–165.

DISCUSSION OPENING — Stephan von Cramon-Taubadel *(Institut für Agrarökonomie, Christian-Albrechts-Universität, Germany)*

Kennedy, von Witzke and Roe are to be congratulated for producing a very concise, topical and interesting paper. Along with their focus on interdependence, their explicit consideration of the exchange rate is particularly pertinent. Recall that the first agricultural market organization in the EU was completed in mid-1967. As a consequence, intra-EU agricultural trade was liberalized — at the cost of much trade diversion — and EU farm prices were exposed to exchange rate movements. Due to Bretton Woods, this exposure seemed harmless. However, less than two years later, as Bretton Woods began to crumble and exchange rate fluctuations increased, EU policy makers were scrambling to reinstate barriers to intra-EU trade. The resulting agri-monetary system (AMS) of tariffs spelled the end of the EU's common agricultural market. Any agricultural trade liberalization that would expose EU farm prices to exchange rate induced fluctuations like those that would have resulted from the US$'s gyrations during the 1980s, would likely be just as short lived as the EU's common agricultural market. Hence, Kennedy, von Witzke and Roe are right to stress the link between agricultural liberalization and macroeconomic stability.

The AMS continues to play an important role in EU agriculture. Because of the 'green' ECU, a particularly byzantine aspect of the AMS that is designed to keep the strength of the DM from depressing German farm prices, EU agricultural prices in US$ are actually 21 percent higher than the US$/ECU exchange rate would suggest. Kennedy, von Witzke and Roe do not mention the green ECU in their paper, but I assume that their calculations account for this hidden protectionism.

Several aspects of the paper merit closer examination. First, the empirical analysis is based on 1990 data. Since 1990, the EU and the USA have come to terms on agriculture and the EU has reformed its cereals and oilseeds market organizations. Do Kennedy, von Witzke and Roe feel that these developments bear out the results of their model? I suspect that the answer to this question would hinge on the fact that they analyze across-the-board liberalization while the EU's recent changes are product specific. The authors stress that economists should pay more attention to politically feasible alternatives; given the differences in the PPF weights reported in Table 1, across-the-board liberalization does not appear to be such an alternative.

Second, while Kennedy, von Witzke and Roe refer to the prisoner's dilemma in their paper, I do not see a classic prisoner's dilemma in their results. There is a strategy available to each country that maximizes its PPF regardless of the other's action. For example, in Table 3, the USA should move to 25 percent of status quo protection no matter what the EU does. Of course, each would like to see the other liberalize more, but this is not a prisoner's dilemma outcome in which strategic behaviour precludes a solution that both would prefer.

Indeed, my first reaction to Tables 2 and 3 was: why haven't we seen the suggested solutions? Is it because politicians haven't been asking economists for advice on how to increase political pay-offs? Note that this also casts doubt on the derivation of the PPF weights in Table 1. If the US PPF increases following a move to 75 percent of status quo protection regardless of the EU's action (Table 2), the status quo cannot represent an optimum. In this case, the PPF has not been maximized, and the first order conditions used to derive PPF weights do not hold. Combined with other problems surrounding the estimation and use of PPF weights — for example, that they are endogenous and may vary with major policy changes such as total liberalization, or that they are conditional on the stochastic elasticity estimates used to derive them — this suggests that Kennedy, von Witzke and Roe's empirical results must be considered illustrative and preliminary.

MARY E. BURFISHER, SHERMAN ROBINSON AND KAREN THIERFELDER*

Migration, Prices and Wages in a North American Free Trade Agreement

Abstract: Much of the debate over potential wage changes under a North American Free Trade Agreement (NAFTA) reflects views about the links between output prices and factor prices as described in the Stolper–Samuelson theorem. But the Stolper–Samuelson theorem does not fully describe the likely labour market effects of NAFTA because it includes the assumption that factors do not migrate. There are two forces at work that will affect US-Mexican wages under NAFTA; (a) indirect links between prices and wages as described in the Stolper–Samuelson theorem, and (b) direct effects of migration on labour supplies in the two countries. We use an 11-sector computable general equilibrium model of Mexico and the USA with both price changes and migration to determine which wage effect dominates following trade liberalization. We find that migration effects generally dominate Stolper–Samuelson effects on wages. Empirically, Stolper–Samuelson effects are very small.

INTRODUCTION

Much of the debate over the establishment of a North American Free Trade Agreement (NAFTA) concerns its impact on wages, and the potential for NAFTA to result in higher wages for unskilled labour in Mexico, but lower wages for unskilled labour in the USA. This view can be derived from the Stolper–Samuelson theorem, which links changes in wages and rents to the changes in product prices caused by trade liberalization. Mexico is abundant in unskilled labour relative to the USA, and trade reform will increase Mexico's relative price of manufactured goods which it exports to the USA. According to the theorem, unskilled wages will fall in the USA and rise in Mexico as Mexican exports displace US production of labour-intensive goods.

But the Stolper–Samuelson theorem does not fully describe the likely labour market effects of a NAFTA for several reasons. First and foremost, is the direct effect of US-Mexico labour migration on labour supply and wages in the two countries. When using the Stolper-Samuelson theorem, aggregate factor supplies are assumed constant and shifts in labour demand curves determine wage changes. However, the effects of trade liberalization on wages can be ambiguous when there is international labour mobility which shifts the labour supply curve as well.[1]

Secondly, Mexico strongly protects agriculture, especially the food maize sector, and agriculture uses rural labour relatively intensively. The Stolper–Samuelson effects are then more complex, with trade liberalization helping manufacturing, which uses unskilled labour intensively, and hurting agriculture, which uses rural labour intensively. As Mexico eliminates barriers to food maize imports, the rural wage should fall. Given rural-urban migration within Mexico, the fall in rural wages will lead to an increase in the supply of labour to Mexican urban areas and to the manufacturing sectors. This will offset the increase in urban unskilled wages as the manufacturing sectors expand. There will also be

* US Department of Agriculture, University of California, Berkeley and US Naval Academy, respectively.

an increase in migration pressure to the USA. The net wage changes in both the USA and Mexico will thus depend on a mix of Stolper–Samuelson and migration effects, and these can have offsetting effects on wages.

Finally, there are many existing distortions in both countries which will not be eliminated by NAFTA. For example, NAFTA does not affect trade barriers that Mexico and the USA maintain against other countries. In addition, there are other distortions, including existing taxes, subsidies and intersectoral differences in wages and profit rates. All these complicate trade theory, requiring analysis of trade liberalization in a 'second best' environment.

In this paper, a computable general equilibrium (CGE) model of the USA and Mexico is used which allows for both Stolper–Samuelson and migration effects to assess the wage changes that will accompany NAFTA. When specifying migration, it is assumed that workers migrate between rural and urban areas in Mexico, as well as to the rural and urban labour markets in the USA, to maintain constant real wage differences. In addition to migration, the empirical model captures other aspects of the US and Mexican economies that violate the assumptions used to analyse the links between output prices and factor prices in neoclassical trade theory. A number of existing distortions, such as indirect taxes and sectoral wage differentials, are incorporated in the model. It is also assumed that Mexico and the USA have different production technologies in the use of both intermediate inputs and primary factors.

The remainder of the paper is organized as follows. A three-country, eleven-sector, computable general equilibrium (CGE) model is described. Since most of the migration anticipated under NAFTA will come from rural Mexico, farm sectors are modelled in detail, giving attention to the rural and unskilled labour markets, and to the structure of agricultural programs.

Model simulations are presented which are designed to explore the two mechanisms, price changes and migration, through which trade reform leads to wage changes; in particular, we ask whether migration has a bigger impact on relative wages than do changes in relative output prices, the driving mechanism in the Stolper–Samuelson theorem. It is found that migration generally has the dominant effect on wages under NAFTA.

THREE-COUNTRY CGE MODEL

The CGE model is an eleven-sector, three-country, computable general equilibrium model. The production and consumption behaviour in the USA and Mexico is modelled in detail, and the two countries are linked through trade and migration flows. Production and consumption details are not specified for the rest of the world. Rather, world demand and supply functions for traded goods are specified[2] largely by assuming fixed world prices. The model's 11 sectors include four farm and one food processing sector. The food maize sector refers to maize used for human consumption. The program crops sector is composed of the other crops eligible for US deficiency payments — feed maize, food grains, soybeans and cotton. Other agriculture includes livestock, poultry, forestry and fisheries, and other miscellaneous agriculture.[3]

The model is in the theoretical tradition of neoclassical, trade-focused, CGE models. Each sector produces a composite commodity that can be transformed according to a constant elasticity of transformation (CET) function into a commodity sold on the domestic market or into an export. Output is produced according to a constant elasticity of substitution (CES) production function in primary factors, and fixed input-output coefficients for intermediate inputs.

The model simulates a market economy, with prices and quantities assumed to adjust to clear markets. All transactions in the circular flow of income are captured. Each country model traces the flow of income (starting with factor payments) from producers to households, government, and investors, and finally back to demand for goods in product markets. Consumption, intermediate demand, government, and investment are the four components of domestic demand. There are three key macro balances in each country model, the government deficit, aggregate investment and savings, and the balance of trade.

The model includes six primary factors: rural labour, urban unskilled labour, urban skilled labour; professional labour, capital and agricultural land. Full employment for all labour categories is assumed and aggregate supplies are set exogenously. In the experiments reported here, it is assumed that agricultural land is immobile among crops, but that all other factors are intersectorally mobile.

Agricultural trade policies and domestic farm programs are modeled explicitly, including tariffs, import quotas, input subsidies to producers and processors, Mexico's tortilla subsidies to low income households, and the US deficiency payment program. Deficiency payments and the tariff-equivalents of quotas are determined endogenously and are not treated as fixed *ad valorem* wedges.

In the CGE model, three migration flows are specified: rural Mexico to rural US labour markets, urban unskilled Mexico to urban unskilled US labour markets, and internal migration within Mexico from rural to unskilled urban labour markets.[4] In equilibrium, international migration adjusts to maintain a specified ratio of real average wages, for linked labour markets in the two countries, measured in a common currency. Similarly, internal migration in Mexico maintains a specified ratio of average real wages between the rural and unskilled urban markets. The domestic labour supply in each skill category in each country is adjusted by the migrant labour flow.

Migration flows generated by the CGE model refer to changes in migration from a base of zero. They should be seen as additional migration flows due to the policy change, adding to (or reducing) current flows.

To determine migration levels, one must evaluate the labour market equilibrium in each country as well as the migration equation. The system of labour demand and labour supply equations by country, including migration between countries, is solved simultaneously. Labour demand in each country is a function of the output price and the relative wage. The vertical labour supply curve shifts when labour migrates.

To identify sources of the wage change in a simple general equilibrium model with migration, one can consider the forces affecting labour supply and demand independently. Labour demand shifts depend on changes in the relative output price given factor intensities in production. For example, an increase in the output of the labour intensive good means that labour demand will increase. The magnitude of the labour demand shift depends on the output elasticity to a relative price change and on the elasticity of labour demand to an output change. Given a fixed aggregate labour supply, the wage will increase following an increase in the price of the labour intensive good.

When one allows labour to migrate, and assumes workers migrate to maintain fixed wage differentials, labour moves into the country that experiences the wage increase under no migration. The increase in labour supply reduces the wage. Since the supply curve shifts, the wage elasticity of labour demand matters in determining wage changes in the home country. Migration occurs until the initial wage differential has been re-established. When the labour demand curve is inelastic, a small amount of migration is needed to affect wages and restore the initial differential. More migration occurs when the labour demand curves in each country are more elastic. In an empirical model, the magnitude of the labour demand and labour supply changes will depend on the elasticities implicit in the observed base-year equilibrium.

MODEL RESULTS

Three scenarios are specified which are designed to explore wage and migration changes that accompany bilateral tariff and quota elimination between the USA and Mexico. In the scenarios, alternative assumptions are made about labour migration to decompose the effects of relative price changes and migration on wages. Scenario 1, considers bilateral trade liberalization between the USA and Mexico when there are no migration flows.

Table 1 *Real Factor Returns Under a USA-Mexico FTA, With and Without Migration*

	No migration	Internal migration	Internal and international migration
Migration		— '000 persons —	
US rural	0	0	20
US urban unskilled	0	0	400
Mexican rural-urban	0	180	340
US factor prices		–Percent change from base–	
Rural	0.8	0.9	–1.0
Urban unskilled	–0.1	–0.1	–1.0
Union	0.0	0.0	0.1
Professional	0.0	0.0	0.0
Agricultural land	0.5	0.5	0.7
Capital	–0.1	–0.1	0.0
Mexican factor prices			
Rural	–5.3	–1.9	1.0
Urban unskilled	0.4	–1.9	1.0
Union	0.6	0.6	0.4
Professional	0.5	0.5	0.3
Agricultural land	–6.6	–6.7	–7.6
Capital	0.2	0.3	0.2

To evaluate internal migration effects, Scenario 1 is extended and migration within Mexico between its rural and urban unskilled labour markets is allowed in Scenario 2. Finally, in Scenario 3 both internal Mexican migration and international migration flows between the rural and urban unskilled labour markets in Mexico and the USA are allowed, in conjunction with bilateral trade liberalization. In the scenario with full migration, the sensitivity of migration to different model assumptions is considered, focusing on the role of exchange rates and fixed wage differentials. In all three scenarios, no change in domestic policies is assumed.

With no migration, trade liberalization causes Mexico's rural wage to decline over 5 percent, while the US rural wage rises 0.8 percent, consistent with the Stolper–Samuelson theorem (Table 1). Increasing the mobility of rural labour diminishes the effects of falling Mexican farm prices on rural wages. When it is assumed labour can migrate between rural and urban areas in Mexico, Mexican rural wages decline by only 2 percent. As 180 000 workers migrate to urban areas, the decline in the rural labour supply partially offsets the effect of a decline in labour demand on the rural wage.

In Mexico's urban labour market, unskilled wages rise 0.4 percent when there is no migration, reflecting the increase in the demand for labour as the manufacturing sectors expand. With internal migration, the migration effect dominates the labour demand effect on wages. The increase in labour supply due to urban migration causes urban unskilled wages in Mexico to decline by 2 percent, despite the increase in labour demand as output expands under NAFTA.

Table 2 *Aggregate Effects of a USA-Mexico FTA, With and Without Migration*

	Scenario 1 No migration	Scenario 2 Internal migration	Scenario 3 Internal and international migration
		— Percent change from base —	
Real GDP – USA	0.0	0.0	0.1
Real GDP – Mexico	0.5	0.6	0.3
Exchange rate – USA	0.0	0.0	0.0
Exchange rate – Mexico	2.1	2.2	2.0
US exports to Mexico	8.4	8.7	8.6
US exports to rest	0.0	0.0	0.2
US imports from rest	0.1	0.1	0.2
Mexican exports to USA	5.0	5.0	5.1
Mexican exports to rest	4.7	5.0	4.6
Mexican imports from rest	–0.6	-0.6	–0.8
Farm program expenditure:			
USA	–0.7	–0.7	–0.5
Mexico	–1.5	–1.9	–2.6
Terms of trade:		— Index, base = 1.0 —	
USA to Mexico	1.01	1.01	1.01
USA to world	1.00	1.00	1.00
Mexico to USA	0.99	0.99	0.99
Mexico to world	0.99	0.99	0.99

Notes: The 'real exchange rate' is the price-level-deflated exchange rate using the GDP deflator. A positive change represents a depreciation. Exports are valued at world prices (in dollars).

In Scenario 3, it is found that international migration reverses the effects of NAFTA on rural wages in the USA and Mexico, compared to the scenario with no migration. When is international migration is assumed, 360 000 rural Mexican workers (6 percent of the farm labour force) migrate to either urban Mexico or to the USA. This decline in the supply of rural workers causes Mexican rural wages to rise by 1.0 percent, dominating the agricultural price decline which works to reduce farm wages. In the USA, the increase in rural labour supply causes rural wages to fall by 1.0 percent, despite the upward pressure of rising farm prices on rural wages.

With international migration, the changes in the labour supply in Mexico's urban labour market depend on the net effect of labour entering from the rural areas and labour leaving for the US urban areas. Under NAFTA, migration to the USA dominates and the Mexican urban labour supply declines. The decrease in labour supply and the increase in labour demand associated with output changes following NAFTA complement one another in terms of the effect on the urban wage in Mexico. The Mexican urban wage increases 1 percent, compared to an increase of 0.4 percent when only labour demand changes affect the wage in Scenario 1.

In the USA, the urban wage declines further with international migration than in scenario 1, with no migration. With no migration, the decline in the demand for urban unskilled labour (following the price changes associated with NAFTA) reduces the urban unskilled wage by 0.1 percent. This Stolper–Samuelson effect is quite small. The increase in the supply of urban unskilled labour, in the scenario with migration, reduces the urban unskilled wage further. It declines by 1.0 percent in the USA — still small, but an order of magnitude larger than the Stolper–Samuelson effect.

In Mexico's urban labour market, unskilled wages rise 0.4 percent when there is no migration, reflecting the increase in the demand for labour as the manufacturing sectors expand. With internal migration, the migration effect dominates the labour demand effect on wages. The increase in labour supply due to urban migration causes urban unskilled wages in Mexico to decline by 2 percent, despite the increase in labour demand as output expands under NAFTA.

Aggregate effects of NAFTA are reported in Table 2. Unlike the case of factor prices, aggregate results of NAFTA are almost unchanged by varying the migration assumptions in Scenarios 1–3. For the USA, there are no measurable aggregate efficiency gains from trade liberalization with Mexico in Scenarios 1 and 2, and migration largely accounts for the small increase in GDP in Scenario 3. In Mexico, real GDP increases slightly in all scenarios, but is lowest in Scenario 3, because labour migration to the USA reduces its labour endowment.

Bilateral trade increases significantly in all three NAFTA scenarios. For the USA, NAFTA is trade creating in all three scenarios, with imports rising from both Mexico and the rest of the world. For Mexico, NAFTA causes some trade diversion.

Both countries' farm program expenditures fall under all three scenarios. In the USA, the decline in expenditure reflects a decline in the deficiency payment because farm prices rise with export growth to Mexico. In Mexico, farm program expenditures fall because of the decline in farm output. Bilateral trade expansion occurs with virtually no effect on the international terms of trade. Sectoral results are presented in Table 3. Bilateral export growth of both countries under NAFTA is highest in the farm sectors, reflecting that both countries have provided relatively high trade protection to agriculture. Agricultural trade growth is accomplished mostly through changes in crop mix, with little change in total farm output.[5]

Table 3 *Sectoral Effects of an FTA on the USA and Mexico, With and Without Migration*

	No migration		Internal migration		Internal and international migration	
	Output	Exports	Output	Exports	Output	Exports
United States	— percent change from base —					
Farm	0.2	44.5	0.2	47.9	0.4	51.3
Maize	4.9	128.4	5.2	134.9	6.7	141.8
Program crops	0.3	36.8	0.3	41.0	0.7	44.0
Fruit/vegetables	0.1	13.3	0.1	13.1	0.4	11.9
Other agriculture	0.1	8.9	0.1	9.3	0.2	8.8
Food processing	–0.1	8.7	–0.1	9.0	0.1	8.5
Other light mfg.	0.0	7.4	0.0	7.6	0.1	7.1
Oil/gas	0.0	17.8	0.0	18.0	0.0	17.7
Intermediates	0.1	8.4	0.1	8.4	0.2	8.0
Consumer durables	0.0	9.5	0.0	9.5	0.2	9.3
Capital goods	0.1	9.5	0.1	9.5	0.1	9.2
Services	0.0	–2.4	0.0	–2.4	0.1	–2.6
Mexico						
Farm	0.1	10.2	–0.3	9.4	–1.1	8.8
Maize	–8.8	0.0	–10.8	0.0	–13.1	0.0
Program crops	–3.7	0.0	–4.5	0.0	–5.5	0.0
Fruit/vegetables	7.7	21.7	6.5	21.2	5.2	21.1
Other agriculture	0.6	2.2	0.5	2.0	0.0	2.0
Food processing	0.1	7.7	0.0	7.6	–0.5	7.7
Other light mfg.	0.7	8.8	0.8	8.9	0.6	9.0
Oil/gas	0.0	4.3	0.0	4.3	0.0	4.5
Intermediates	1.5	4.0	1.6	4.1	1.4	4.2
Consumer durables	4.3	5.5	4.7	5.8	4.7	5.8
Capital goods	2.8	7.7	2.9	7.8	2.8	7.7
Services	–0.2	0.1	-0.1	0.2	–0.3	0.2

Note: Real output and exports. Exports are to partner country (USA or Mexico).

CONCLUSION

Much of the debate over potential wage changes under NAFTA reflects views about the indirect links between output prices and factor prices as described in the Stolper–Samuelson theorem. The model underlying the theorem assumes no international factor mobility, which is unrealistic for the USA and Mexico, where there is significant labour migration. An eleven-sector CGE model of the USA and Mexico is developed that includes both relative-price and migration effects, to analyse the empirical importance of the two mechanisms. It is found that Stolper–Samuelson effects occur, but that they are very small, and have perhaps been given too much emphasis in the debate over the wage effects of NAFTA. Furthermore, migration effects largely dominate indirect price effects, generating wage changes under NAFTA that are contrary to expectations based on the Stolper–Samuelson theorem alone.

In the farm sector, for example, when we assume no migration, we find that removing protection causes rural wages in Mexico to fall (and rural wages in the USA to rise), reflecting Mexico's current high levels of protection to agricultural sectors. These results are consistent with the Stolper–Samuelson theorem. When migration is allowed, the wage effects are reversed. The decline in the rural labour supply in Mexico causes the rural wage to rise rather than fall. Conversely, in the USA, the rural wage falls, due to the increased rural labour migration from Mexico.

NOTES

1 In the Heckscher–Ohlin model, trade in factors can be a substitute for trade in commodities. Both can have an identical effect on wages under certain assumptions such as unrestricted factor flows and incomplete specialization under free trade. The issue becomes more complex in US-Mexico relations because technologies are very different and there are migration restrictions. One does not necessarily expect migration to have the same effect on wages as the labour demand changes described in the Stolper–Samuelson theorem.

2 In two sectors, maize and program crops, downward sloping world demand curves for US exports are assumed, and hence world prices are not fixed for these sectors.

3 The base year for Mexico is mostly 1988. The USA uses a 1987 base year because of the severe contraction of agricultural output following the 1988 drought. Bilateral trade flows are from 1988. Because of the volatility in USA 1987–88 agricultural output, the model follows Adams and Higgs (1986) in the use of a 'synthetic' base year for the USA, imposing 1988 US-Mexican bilateral trade flows on a 1987 base USA economy. The data base is documented in Burfisher, Thierfelder, and Hanson (1992). Unpublished data on Mexican employment were compiled by Dolores Nieto, Colegio de Mexico.

4 There is no internal migration between the urban and the rural labour market in the USA, but the two labour markets are implicitly linked, given the other migration flows.

5 Since migration effects largely determine the wage changes following NAFTA, we do sensitivity experiments of our specification of migration against Scenario 3. First, we eliminate the exchange rate effects on the migration decision by fixing the exchange rate in the migration equation at the base year level. We find that migration from Mexico to the USA falls compared to Scenario 3, in which the depreciating Mexican peso stimulates migration. In Mexico's rural labour market, migration effects no longer dominate the effects of relative price changes on the rural wage. In Mexico's urban unskilled labor market, and in the US labour markets, migration effects on wages still dominate, but have less of an impact. Second, we explore the sensitivity of migration to our assumption that wage differentials between the USA and Mexico are held constant at their base year levels. We find that the results are sensitive to this assumption. If Mexico grows more rapidly than the USA, the model will generate a large decrease in migration in order to maintain the wage differential. Over the long run, with increased Mexican growth, one expects to observe growth in wages, a narrowing of the wage differential between the two countries, and a reduction in migration pressure. We have not sought to capture this mix of effects in the model because these long-run trends are not directly related to NAFTA. Finally, three key elasticities affect the magnitude of migration: output elasticity to a relative price change, labour demand elasticity with respect to output change, and the wage elasticity of labour demand. While we do not do sensitivity tests around elasticities, we can define and evaluate the values implicit in our data on the US and Mexican economies. The differences in elasticities help to explain the patterns of migration changes we observe in the empirical model.

REFERENCES

Adams, P.D. and Higgs, P.J., 1986, 'Calibration of Computable General Equilibrium Models from Synthetic Benchmark Equilibrium Data Sets', *IMPACT Preliminary Working Paper*, No. OP-57, Melbourne, Australia.

Burfisher, M.E., Thierfelder, K.E. and Hanson, K., 1992, 'Data Base for a Computable General Equilibrium Analysis of a US–Mexico Free Trade Agreement', Staff Paper, Economic Research Service, US Department of Agriculture, Staff Report No. AGES-9225, Washington, D.C.

DAVID R. LEE AND KRISTIN A. MARKUSSEN*

Structural Adjustment and Agricultural Export Response in Latin America

Abstract: Expanding exports has been one of the principal goals of structural adjustment programs aimed at restoring external balance of payments equilibria in many developing countries. This paper analyzes agricultural export response for selected crops in 8 Latin American countries over the period 1961–1990 in an attempt to confirm the export-enhancing effects of structural adjustment. The results show that: (a) commodity and country disaggregation in estimation generates much higher export response elasticities than previously estimated; (b) variations in the real exchange rate have a dominant effect in stimulating export response, compared to commodity price changes; and (c) statistical tests confirm structural change in export response elasticities in over half of the equations estimated. Overall, the evidence suggests that stabilization and adjustment reforms have had a significant though non-uniform effect in stimulating agricultural export expansion in Latin America.

INTRODUCTION

Increasing exports as an intermediate step toward restoring external balance of payments equilibrium has been a central component of most economic stabilization and structural adjustment programs initiated in the 1980s and 1990s. Export promoting policies and programs have been particularly extensive in Latin America, where the largest proportion of adjustment lending has occurred (44 percent of adjustment lending in 1989, for example). Though agriculture's relative contribution to GDP declined in most Latin America countries prior to the 1980s, agriculture has maintained an important role in terms of export and employment generation and in providing 'the lead to the rest of the economy in the process of adjustment and economic recovery' (Chhibber, 1988).

This paper assesses agricultural export performance in response to changes in two key determinants of export supply — exchange rates and producer prices — which were influenced by structural adjustment programs of the 1980s. Export responsiveness is estimated for selected export crops in eight Latin American countries in the period through 1980. In each case, export response is estimated prior to the initiation of structural adjustment programs and for a longer time series incorporating the post-adjustment period. Changes in export responsiveness to price and exchange rate variation under both regimes are tested statistically. The results demonstrate the key role played especially by exchange rate policy in determining export responsiveness, as well as differing country and commodity experiences.

STRUCTURAL ADJUSTMENT AND AGRICULTURE IN LATIN AMERICA

Though experiences differed from country to country, the economic developments of the 1970s and early 1980s which precipitated the economic stabilization and structural adjustment programs of the 1980s are depressingly familiar: the collapse of the Bretton

* Cornell University, USA, and National Bank of Alaska, formerly Cornell University, respectively.

Woods Agreement and increased exchange rate variability; OPEC's formation and subsequent oil price shocks in the early and late 1970s; the flood of petro-dollars and increasing debt burdens assumed by many countries in the late 1970s; and finally, increases in real interest rates and threats of default in the late 1970s and early 1980s. The results of these developments are equally familiar: chronic inflation stimulated by oil and commodity price shocks and reinforced by lax or ineffective monetary and fiscal policy; depletion of international currency reserves; increases in debt service payments; and low or negative real economic growth caused by the above factors and exacerbated by the worldwide recession of the early 1980s.

In response to these developments, 13 Latin American countries engaged in economic stabilization programs with the IMF and structural adjustment programs with the World Bank in the period through 1990. Due largely to data constraints (discussed below), 8 of these countries are included in this analysis: Argentina; Bolivia; Brazil; Chile; Colombia; Costa Rica; Ecuador and Mexico. In these 8 countries, IMF loans amounting to 21.6 billion SDR's and structural adjustment loans totalling $9.0 billion were approved in the 1980–90 period (World Bank, 1990). These loans supported a wide variety of macroeconomic and sectoral reforms, including stricter monetary and fiscal policies, public sector reforms, privatization of public enterprizes, tax reforms, subsidy reduction and elimination, and, perhaps most importantly, devaluation of domestic currencies.

The effects of these reforms have varied widely from country to country. In spite of the goal of generating overall economic growth, real per capita GDP increased from 1980 to 1990 in only 2 of the 8 countries, Chile (3.8 percent) and Colombia (6.3 percent) (Table 1). Inflation abated in several countries (Bolivia, Costa Rica, Mexico), but remained at excessive levels in others (Argentina and Brazil, most notably). The terms of trade declined sharply in all 8 countries over the 1980s. Yet, in many countries, the macroeconomic preconditions for improved economic performance were created. Except for Brazil, each of the countries experienced a real devaluation over the late 1980s, making their exports more globally competitive. Export growth, in most cases, responded to these and other economic incentives by expanding at rates well above early 1980s levels (Table 1). Current account balances, in turn, responded in 7 of the 8 countries, registering improved performance by the end of the decade. Other details are provided in Markussen (1993).

Because of the importance of the agricultural sector in employment and GDP in many of these countries and the prominence of agricultural exports among tradable goods, macroeconomic and structural reforms such as currency devaluation have particularly important implications for this sector. In 6 of the 8 adjusting countries, agriculture's proportion of GDP increased over the 1980s. In 4 countries, agriculture's share of total country exports increased, while in the other 4 countries, the proportion of agricultural exports remained high, ranging from 15–20 percent (Brazil) to nearly 60 percent (Costa Rica). Real annual growth in agricultural exports between 1980–82 and 1990–92 averaged 9.1 percent across the eight countries, ranging from 3.6 percent in Brazil to 18.9 percent in Chile (Table 2). Clearly, the performance of agriculture has remained crucial in determining the outcomes of adjustment in both the tradable sector and the overall economy.

Recent Literature on Agricultural Export Response

A number of studies over the past decade have examined export behaviour as it relates to the structural adjustment policies of the 1980s. Hazell, Jaramillo and Williamson (1990) estimate price variability for 15 commodities and 22 countries and find that real exchange rates, domestic marketing arrangements and other government interventions have played a major role in buffering variability of price transmission to producers. They foresee increased export price variability arising from structural adjustment programs impeding the expansion of agricultural exports in many countries. Gersovitz and Paxson (1990) specify the conditions under which export response may differ from production response to output price changes.

Table 1 *Macroeconomic Indicators for Selected Latin American Countries*

	GDP per capita (1987 $)		Average annual inflation (%)		Real Effective Exchange Rate 1985=100
	1980	1990	1980-82	1989-91	1990
Argentina	2990	2170	142.5	2117.2	134
Bolivia	850	600	115.2	16.4	191
Brazil	2000	1820	94.8	1307.3	70
Chile	1580	1640	20.5	22.5	142
Colombia	1110	1180	26.0	28.4	160
Costa Rica	1740	1660	54.9	20.9	126
Ecuador	1310	1080	18.9	50.9	159
Mexico	1920	1750	52.4	22.8	107

	Terms of Trade (Index:1980=100)	Average Annual Growth in Exports (volume)		Current Account balance ($ million)	
	1990	1979-81	1989-91	1980	1990
Argentina	67	1.0	25.0	–4774	1789
Bolivia	74	–1.5	13.0	–6	–194
Brazil	82	19.8	11.1	–12 806	–2983
Chile	84	9.0	11.1	–1971	–790
Colombia	80	0.5	–3.9	–206	391
Costa Rica	70	4.5	4.2	–664	–514
Ecuador	66	–2.1	7.6	–642	–136
Mexico	70	18.1	21.2	–10 750	–5255

Source: ECLAC, *Economic Survey of Latin America*, various years; World Bank, 1992.

Several papers analyze export response under structural adjustment using variations of traditional supply response methodologies, though each of these studies is characterized by significant limitations. Bond (1985) estimates primary commodity export supply as a function of prices, exchange rates, and supply shifters. Results for Western Hemisphere food crops and agricultural raw materials demonstrate negative current period price elasticities of supply and very low one-period lagged supply elasticities (0.07 and 0.03, respectively). The empirical results provide weak support for the author's claim that 'export supply in developing countries does indeed respond to improved price incentives', though rather more support for the conclusion that 'this evidence lends support to a developing country's use of the exchange rate as a policy tool to improve the trade balance' (p.227). Bond's analysis, though, omits the structural adjustment years of the 1980s.

Balassa (1988) estimates the response of agricultural export/output ratios in 16 sub-Saharan African countries though 1982. Like Bond, he finds that real exchange rates were a significant determinant of export response, particularly so for agricultural exports compared to exports of goods and services. Countries with 'market-oriented economies' are shown to have performed especially well. Belassa's analysis extends only through 1982, however, early in the structural adjustment process, and is confined only to African countries.

Wattleworth (1988) examines the collective effects of simultaneous export expansion among developing countries on selected export markets. He confirms the importance of the real exchange rate in accounting for export response, but uses output supply elasticities as a proxy for export supply elasticities, which he notes are often unavailable.

Finally, Islam and Subramanian (1989) estimate developing country agricultural export response as a function of a number of supply and demand-side variables influencing export behaviour. Their empirical results are mixed, with only variables representing a time trend and a dummy variable for oil price shocks consistently significant. In addition, the mixture of demand and supply-side explanatory variables raises questions as to whether the estimation equations are properly identified, while the time series used (1962–1983) yields few insights relevant to export behaviour under structural adjustment.

ESTIMATING AGRICULTURAL EXPORT RESPONSE FOR LATIN AMERICA

This paper analyzes agricultural export response in 8 Latin American countries in the period through 1990. The central question that is addressed and tested statistically is whether price and exchange rate changes accompanying structural adjustment have resulted in changes in export responsiveness due to the improved economic incentives created for producers and exporters. This hypothesis is tested by estimating export supply response equations for 22 country—commodity combinations, first, for periods prior to structural adjustment (unique to each country), and then, for complete time series extending through 1990. Chow tests are employed in each case to formally test for structural change in the estimated coefficients between the pre-adjustment and entire time series following the standard methodology outlined in Kennedy (1985).

The countries and commodities used in this analysis were chosen based on 3 criteria: first, data availability; second, that the export crops represented major exports of the country in question; and third, on enough time having elapsed since the initiation of structural adjustment for potential effects on exports to be realized. The result was the set of 22 country-commodity combinations given in Table 3. For 17 of these cases, crop exports increased between 1980 and 1990 (Table 2). Five other Latin American countries which had initiated stabilization and adjustment programs in the 1980s (Honduras, Jamaica, Panama, Uruguay, and Venezuela) were excluded.

Table 2 *Exports of Selected Latin American Countries, 1980–82 and 1990–92*

Country	Total Exports) (annual average) 1980–82	1990–92	Total Agricultural Exports (annual average) 1980–82	1990–92
Argentina ($ million)	5489	12 188	3771	7054
Maize ('000 tonnes)			957	4329
Soybeans ('000 tonnes)			268	3588
Wheat ('000 tonnes)			021	5807
Bolivia ($ million)	94	828	54	155
Coffee (tonnes)			5777	6069
Brazil ($ million)	14 093	32 841	6027	8553
Cocoa (tonnes)			130 763	95 566
Coffee (tonnes)			832 644	989 994
Soybeans ('000 tonnes)			1167	3265
Chile ($ million)	2715	9251	253	1431
Apples (tonnes)			191 719	374 711
Grapes (tonnes)			89 665	439 715
Peaches (tonnes)			10 587	73 279
Pears (tonnes)			26 402	112 147
Colombia ($ million)	2407	7022	1608	2439
Bananas ('000 tonnes)			766	1374
Coffee (tonnes)			573 734	827 197
Costa Rica ($ million)	637	1625	438	962
Bananas ('000 tonnes)			1022	1587
Cocoa (tonnes)			2068	519
Coffee (tonnes)			87 983	143 276
Ecuador ($ million)	1647	2858	374	891
Bananas ('000 tonnes)			1261	2494
Cocoa (tonnes)			26 217	51 410
Coffee (tonnes)			61 914	85 731
Mexico ($ million)	12 725	27 219	1014	2996
Coffee (tonnes)			159 308	208 378
Cotton (lint; tonnes)			160 037	45 792
Tomatoes (tonnes)			472 101	336 007

Note: Export values are real 1990–92 $.

Data on the dependent variables, annual export volumes, in each estimated equation were from FAO (1992). Data on annual producer prices were obtained from the SIAPA datbase on the International Institute for Cooperation in Agriculture (IICA), and were used in current and one period lagged forms. Exchange rates were calculated using data from the

International Monetary Fund (1990, 1992), based on Edward's (1989) standard definition of the real exchange rate. This calculation adjusts the nominal dollar exchange rate by the ratio of the wholesale price index in the USA to the consumer price index in the domestic economy to account for relative rates of inflation. In the results reported here, price and exchange rate variables were used in composite form as regressors; in other estimates (not shown), they were used singly. Both formats have been employed in the literature. A linear time trend, intercept dummy variables, and slope interaction variables were included as regressors in preliminary estimation equations but did not prove consistently significant. Further details regarding the variables, data, and tests for structural change are contained in Markussen (1993).

Table 3 *Countries, Crops and Years Analyzed*

Argentina	Bolivia	Brazil
Maize (1961–1990)	Coffee (1970–1990)	Cocoa (1966–1990)
Soybeans (1965–1990)		Coffee (1966–1989)
Wheat (1961–1990)		Soybeans (1970–1989)
Chile	**Colombia**	**Costa Rica**
Apples (1969–1990)	Bananas (1968–1990)	Bananas (1968–1990)
Grapes (1969–1990)	Coffee (1968–1990)	Cocoa (1968–1990)
Peaches (1968–1990)		Coffee (1968–1990)
Pears (1968–1990)		
Ecuador	**Mexico**	
Bananas (1968–1990)	Coffee (1968–1990)	
Cocoa (1968–1990)	Cotton (lint) (1968–1990)	
Coffee (1968–1990)	Tomatoes (1968–1990)	

The present analysis addresses a number of the limitations of previous research. First, by estimating the responsiveness of individual export crops in specific countries, the aggregation problem faced by Bond is overcome. Aggregation of crops in estimating export response not only obscures the effects on specific commodities, but can be expected *a priori* to generate a low aggregate elasticity of supply, given the substitution relationships commonly existing among agricultural commodities. (Conversely, as Lele 1992, argues, examining export response gives only one part of the story with respect to adjustment, given the substitution relationships that exist between crops for domestic consumption.) Second, the time series used in each country–commodity combination analyzed here ends in 1990, thus incorporating up to a decade's experience with structural adjustment, depending on the country. Finally, the analysis generates estimates of export supply response to changes in solely supply-side variables (prices and exchange rates), thus addressing the need for export supply elasticities identified by Wattleworth (1988) and avoiding the potential identification problems raised in the study of Islam and Subramanian.

Table 4 *Regression Results Using Composite Variable (Price and Exchange Rate)*

Country, and Initial Year of Adjustment	Crop	Pre-Adjustment			Whole Period			F-Statistic
		β	s	ε	β	s	ε	
Argentina (1983)	Maize	0.203	0.299	0.203	0.059	0.186	0.059	1.198
	Soybeans3.176	2.038	3.176	3.015**	1.376	3.015	0.930	
	Wheat$_l$	–148.077	1803.930	–0.017	2249.440	1970.980	0.238	4.221***
Bolivia (1980)	Coffee$_l$	229.480	182.663	0.276	309.186	192.082	0.329	2.834
Brazil (1983)	Cocoa	0.198***	0.068	0.198	0.201***	0.051	0.201	0.362
	Coffee	–0.289***	0.045	0.289	–0.192***	0.048	–0.192	4.360***
	Soybeans	1.796***	0.561	1.796	1.734***	0.444	1.734	0.814
Chile (1985)	Apples$_l$	6.724***	1.716	0.780	10.854***	1.443	1.030	6.108***
	Grapes$_l$	2.044***	0.645	0.840	4.115***	0.818	1.090	19.999***
	Peaches$_l$	0.317***	0.062	0.815	0.802***	0.147	1.224	23.071***
	Pears$_l$	1.102***	0.128	0.900	1.626***	0.285	1.093	29.807***
Colombia (1985)	Bananas$_l$	104.746***	11.014	1.153	45.823***	8.219	0.602	6.359***
	Coffee$_l$	4.122	4.128	0.086	8.602**	3.282	0.200	3.378**
Costa Rica (1985)	Bananas$_l$	80.463	176.629	0.092	57.173	51.651	0.109	1.814
	Cocoa$_l$	–0.120	0.100	–0.161	–0.169**	0.079	–0.435	0.573
	Coffee$_l$	3.810	3.456	0.073	7.017*	3.536	0.166	6.769***
Ecuador (1986)	Bananas$_l$	–20.943	39.289	–0.044	88.345***	22.836	0.250	3.823***
	Cocoa	–0.412**	0.419	–0.412	–0.116	0.190	–0.116	4.759***
	Coffee$_l$	6.121***	1.607	0.394	7.306	1.158	0.503	1.534
Mexico (1983)	Coffee$_l$	3.560	2.390	0.127	4.568	2.757	0.163	5.360***
	Cotton	–0.583***	0.153	–0.583	–0.888***	0.200	–0.888	4.877***
	Tomatoes$_l$	29.973***	7.783	0.749	9.481**	3.501	0.271	1.595

Notes: *, **, *** denote statistical significance at 10 percent, 5 percent and 1 percent levels, respectively. $_l$ linear regression; all others in double logarithmic form.

Source: Markussen, 1993.

EMPIRICAL RESULTS

Export response equations were estimated for each commodity–country combination and, in each case, for two time periods: 1961 (or another proximate initial year) through the year prior to the initiation of stabilization and or adjustment programs, and then for the entire time series through 1990. Equations were estimated by OLS, adjusted for autocorrelation wherever necessary. A seemingly unrelated regression (SUR) approach was not followed due to the different years in which adjustment programs were initiated across countries, and thus the different time series estimated.

Due to the number of equations estimated, the full set of regression estimates is not reported here, but is discussed in detail in Markussen, 1993. Table 4 summarizes the estimated coefficients, standard errors, and elasticities derived using the composite price and exchange rate variable specification, similar to Bond and Wattleworth. The estimates, however, are generally much stronger. Several negatively signed elasticities are estimated, though these are mostly for perennials, whose price response behaviour is considerably complicated than that for annual crops. However, it is clear that disaggregation of agricultural exports at the individual crop level generally results in export supply elasticities which are higher, in some cases much higher, than the low elasticities reported by Bond. In addition, in 15 of 22 cases, the export elasticity increases in the sample period including adjustment years, compared to the pre-adjustment period. In 11 of those cases, the change is statistically significant using a Chow test.

When variables representing exchange rates and prices are included separately as regressors (not shown), the econometric results are somewhat weaker and include more negatively signed coefficients (particularly for the price variables for perennials). Two conclusions are evident, however. First, the responsiveness of exports to changes in the real exchange rate, particularly for the longer sample period incorporating the post-adjustment years, tends to dominate responsiveness to price changes. Second, Chow tests confirm structural change in fewer cases, in part reflecting the more limited explanatory ability of this specification compared to use of the composite price-exchange rate variable.

CONCLUSIONS

This analysis builds on previous research by estimating agricultural export response under structural adjustment for 8 Latin American countries, disaggregated at individual country and commodity levels, for years extending through 1990. The results permit several conclusions. First, disaggregation at the country/commodity level results in much higher export response elasticities — with respect to both price and exchange rates — than those previously estimated (e.g. Bond). Second, real exchange rate variation is shown to dominate variations in commodity prices in determining export supply response. There appear to be significant returns to macroeconomic reforms which include currency devaluation and increase economic incentives for producers and exporters. Third, structural change in export responsiveness after the initiation of adjustment is confirmed in well over half the cases in which a composite variable (incorporating price and real exchange rate effects) is the primary explanatory variable.

These results suggest that exchange rate and price reforms under structural adjustment are, in many cases, having their intended effects in stimulating agricultural exports. One qualification to this conclusion is that since many countries had previously experienced seriously overvalued exchange rates, the effects of initial large-scale currency devaluations in stimulating exports may overstate the effects to be expected from subsequent or continuing devaluations.

REFERENCES

Balassa, B., 1988, 'Incentive Policies and Agricultural Performance in Sub-Saharan Africa', PPR Working Paper Series, World Bank, Washington, D.C.

Bond, M.E., 1985, 'An Econometric Study of Primary Commodity Exports from Developing Country Regions to the World', *IMF Staff Papers*, Vol. 34, pp.191–227.

Chhibber, A., 1988, 'Raising Agricultural Output: Price and Nonprice Factors', *Finance and Development*, June, Vol. 25, No. 2, pp.44–47.

Edwards, S., 1989, *Exchange Rate Misalignment in Developing Countries, 1988*, World Bank Occasional Paper No. 2, New Series, The Johns Hopkins University Press, Baltimore, Maryland.

Food and Agricultural Organization of the United Nations (various years), *Trade Yearbook*, Rome.

Gersovitz, M. and Paxson, C.H., 1990, *The Economies of Africa and the Prices of Their Exports*, Princeton Studies in International Finance No. 68, International Finance Section, Department of Economics, Princeton University, Princeton, New Jersey.

Hazell, P.B.R., Jaramillo, M. and Williamson, A., 1990, 'The Relationship Between World Price Instability and the Prices Farmers Receive in Developing Countries', *Journal of Agricultural Economics*, Vol. 42, pp.227–241.

International Monetary Fund, *International Financial Statistics Yearbook* (various years), International Monetary Fund, Washington, D.C.

Islam, N. and Subramanian, A., 1989, 'Agricultural Exports of Developing Countries: Estimates of Income and Price Elasticities of Demand and Supply', *Journal of Agricultural Economics*, Vol. 40, pp.221–231.

Kennedy, P., 1985, *A Guide to Econometrics*, 2nd ed., MIT Press, Cambridge, Massachusetts.

Lele, U., 1992, 'Structural Adjustment and Agriculture: A Comparative Perspective on Performance in Africa, Asia, and Latin America', International Working Paper Series IW92-30r, Food and Resource Economics Department, University of Florida.

Markussen, K., 1993, 'An Econometric Analysis of Agricultural Export Supply Response and Structural Adjustment in Latin America', Unpublished M.S. Thesis, Department of Agricultural Economics, Cornell University, Ithaca, New York.

Wattleworth, M., 1988, 'The Effects of Collective Devaluation on Commodity Prices and Exports', *IMF Staff Papers*, Vol. 35, pp.166–180.

World Bank, 1990, *Adjustment Lending Policies for Sustainable Growth*, Country Economics Department, PRS14, Washington, D.C.

World Bank, 1992, *World Tables*, Washington, D.C.

DISCUSSION OPENING — Paulo F. Cidade de Araujo *(University of Sao Paulo, Brazil)*

Markussen and Lee undertake the important, challenging and worthwhile task of investigating the effect of structural macroeconomic adjustment processes on the agricultural exports of selected crops and countries in Latin America. Their main tool is a regression analysis of exports against a variable constructed from the exchange rate and producer prices over the period from the 1960s to 1990. Their statistical results seem to indicate that there exists a mixed result, at best. Roughly half of the parameters estimated are non-significant and some are significant in the 'wrong' direction. The same applies to the test of structural change.

Unfortunately, the theoretical and empirical models used are not presented in the paper. This precludes a deeper analysis of specific issues and I would like to keep this discussion on general problems only. Two main questions arise from the paper. First, does it indicate that the export of agricultural commodities in Latin American countries is not responsive to economic variables? Second, do the macroeconomic adjustment plans undertaken by several Latin American countries have a positive impact on the agricultural exports? I would like to claim that these are complex questions and that the study presented gives a partial view of the whole picture. I will limit my consideration to two main points.

First, it seems to me that exports of a given crop in a given country are determined by several economic and exogenous variables which cannot be summarized by the exchange rate and the producer prices. Ceteris paribus, it is reasonable that exports do respond to exchange rate devaluation. However, their response to producer prices is less clear. Instead, export/international prices of that commodity seems to be more appropriate. And, if that country is dependent on the international markets in terms of agricultural inputs then the exchange rate net effect is not that clear, exante (however, the above price effect is!). Adding their effect in a composed variable may make the analysis difficult.

If the crop considered faces an important domestic market, then the effect of exchange rate and international prices may be influenced by the performance of the country's economy. This is an important issue when dealing with adjustment processes. They usually have strong effects on the macroeconomic environment which influences the domestic demand.

In the specific case of perennials, it is well known that due to their biological characteristics, the output does not respond significantly in the short run. In these cases, it seems difficult to believe that the model used can capture the real effect of exchange rate and prices on the exports. More than half of the cases are of this type of crop.

Second, there are several exogenous variables that affect the incentives for exporting in Latin American countries. In the specific case of Brazil, exports of the crops considered (coffee, cocoa and soybean) have been significantly controlled by the government. Export taxes and quotas have been imposed and altered quite considerably in the period analyzed. Many of these interventions were implemented in response to (or as part of) changes in the macroeconomic environment!

More recently, there seems to exist a trend of processing these commodities in the producer countries and exporting processed products and byproducts. This is the case of coffee and soybean in Brazil. It seems reasonable to suspect that the effect of them may explain part of the difficulties faced by the researchers in this area.

Coming from one of the countries considered in the study, I understand how hard it is to overcome difficulties related to good data and reliable information regarding export procedures and government policies. However, I'd like to praise their effort and encourage both authors in further deepening their study.

GENERAL DISCUSSION — Ian Jarratt (*Queensland Department of Primary Industries, Australia)*

The Kennedy, von Witzke and Roe paper was considered by the discussion opener to be very relevant because the effects of the GATT agreement will be significantly influenced by exchange rates. The use of 1990 data was questioned. It was agreed that 1994 weights should be used to reflect changes in policies. The PPF will change over time. John Freebairn questioned the exogenous exchange rate assumption but it was defended as the grounds of the likely limited influence of agricultural exchange rates.

The discussant for Burfisher, Robinson and Theirfelder's paper considered that the assumptions for the Stolper–Samuelson theory were not met by NAFTA and the conditions in the USA and Mexico. It was emphasized that NAFTA does not provide for labour mobility. The main factor influencing this in part of NAFTA will be capital mobility and this should be the main focus of analysis.

The opener for Lee and Markussen's paper noted that the results were mixed because the study deals only with some of the influences on export volumes and there are major data availability problems. Issues raised included: the influence of exchange rates on farm input prices, the importance of domestic demand for some commodities, the effects of exogenous variables such as export taxes/quotas and policies to encourage processed exports. The special situation of perennial and storable crops was also highlighted as a problem for modellers. However, the study was considered useful. William Amponsah also contributed to the discussion.

WILLIAM A. MASTERS AND ALEX WINTER-NELSON*

Evaluating the Economic Efficiency of Agricultural Activities in Developing Countries: Domestic Resource Costs and the Social Cost–Benefit Ratio

Abstract: This paper demonstrates that the conventional Domestic Resource Cost (DRC) indicator is biased against factor-intensive, low-input techniques, and that a simple Social Cost–Benefit (SCB) ratio is generally a more appropriate measure of economic efficiency. The potential policy significance of improved measurement is shown with data from Zimbabwe and Kenya. In Zimbabwe, the DRC is shown to incorrectly rank high-input large-scale farming systems above more labour-intensive smallholder systems; in Kenya, the DRC incorrectly ranks high-input horticultural crops above more labour-intensive food grains and traditional export crops.

INTRODUCTION

During the 1980s the Domestic Resource Cost (DRC) became a standard measure of economic efficiency used in developing countries, has been prescribed in texts, used in academic research, and in policy studies for FAO CIMMYT, IFPRI, OECD; (World Bank, 1984a, 1984b; Monke and Pearson, 1989; Tsakok, 1989; Nelson and Panggabean, 1991; Williams, 1992; Appleyard, 1987; Morris, 1988; Gonzales *et al.*, 1993; Alpine and Pickett, 1993).

In this paper it is shown that the DRC is often significantly biased and should generally be replaced with a broader social cost–benefit (SCB) ratio, using exactly the same data but in a different formula. The bias in the DRC arises because it exaggerates the costs of domestic factors relative to tradeable inputs. In particular, it understates the profitability of land and labour-intensive smallholder farming, relative to more input-intensive activities. The SCB ratio treats all costs equally, which eliminates this bias.

The DRC ratio was originally developed for use where there was no shadow exchange rate at which to convert the values of non-tradeable and tradeable goods into a common currency. The fundamental rationale for the DRC was that the shadow prices of tradeables and non-tradeables were denominated in different currencies, and therefore must be kept separate (Bruno, 1978; Krueger, 1966). But in the intervening 25 years, considerable progress has been made in estimating shadow exchange rates. Today, they can be measured at least as accurately as the shadow prices for labour, land, capital or other domestic factors. Where a shadow exchange rate has been measured, the fundamental justification for using DRCs is lost and the more general SCB ratio is more appropriate.

To construct measures of economic efficiency such as the DRC or SCB, the input and outputs for each activity must be valued at their economic opportunity cost or shadow price, which is found in the international market for traded goods, and in the domestic market for non-tradeables (Srinivasan and Bhagwati, 1978; Tower, 1984; Dręze and Stern, 1987; Monke and Pearson, 1989). It is assumed here the best available estimates of shadow prices are used, to focus on the appropriate ratio with which to value farm activities.

* Purdue University and University of Illinois, USA, respectively.

For a given set of budget data and estimated economic opportunity costs, the DRC exaggerates the cost of domestic factors such as land and labour, as opposed to tradeable inputs. This leads the DRC to discriminate against factor-intensive activities, which is particularly important in developing countries where use of the DRC consistently understates the contribution of traditional smallholder farming systems relative to more 'modern' input-intensive production. The DRC exaggerates the benefits of using herbicides and mechanical equipment to substitute for labour, as well as the benefits of using fertilizer and other inputs to raise yields and substitute for land. The next section investigates the policy significance of these biases, using recent data from Zimbabwe and Kenya.

The next section of the paper analyzes the source of bias in the DRC, and the rationale for preferring the SCB. The final section uses data from Zimbabwe and Kenya to illustrate the potential policy significance of the biased rankings. These data reveal the expected tendency of the DRC to exaggerate the benefits of activities using purchased inputs intensively, and to discriminate against factor-intensive low-input systems.

THEORETICAL PROPERTIES OF ALTERNATIVE INDICATORS

Indicators of economic efficiency are used primarily when the elasticities and other parameters of supply and demand functions are not known, and cannot be estimated in the available time. Nonetheless, indicators of efficiency can be constructed using average cost budgets, in which inputs and outputs are valued at shadow prices. Indicators typically use fixed input-output coefficients (thereby ignoring input substitution effects) and estimate the shadow price of each budget item separately (thereby ignoring cross price effects). Such simplifications imply that the resulting estimates are valid only for relatively small changes in activity levels; better estimates for larger changes would require an economic model showing equilibrium adjustments in production and consumption.

Definitions of the DRC and SCB

Budget data are normally presented in the form of revenues (R) and costs (C); because they are initially measured in different currencies, costs are often disaggregated into tradeable inputs (T) and non-tradeable domestic factors (D) such as labour and land. Also, because outputs are typically tradeable, tradeable costs (T) may be subtracted from revenue (R) to obtain tradeable value added (V).

Where no shadow exchange rate is available, Krueger (1966) and Bruno (1967) demonstrated that activities can be compared through the domestic currency cost of primary factors (D) used to generate a unit of foreign currency (V):

$$(1)\quad DRC = D/(R - T) = D/V$$

The units of such a 'relative' *DRC* are domestic currency per unit of foreign currency; this sort of measure can be used to rank alternative activities, but the cut-off between profitable and unprofitable activities is the unknown shadow exchange rate.

Warr (1983) demonstrated that the rankings produced with such a *DRC* may be incorrect unless a shadow exchange rate (e^*) is used to convert all values into a common currency, and all costs subtracted from all benefits to form a Net Present Value (*NPV*) or Net Social Benefit (*NSB*) measure. But the *NSB* measure would have specific units (for example, dollars per ha or per tonne of product), and therefore tends to favour more input-intensive, higher cost/higher benefit activities, even if a larger number of smaller activities would be more profitable. For activities that can be replicated at roughly constant returns to scale, like most farming enterprizes, a unit-free cost–benefit ratio is preferable.

Among cost–benefit ratios, using the shadow exchange rate in the *DRC* formula does not affect rankings; it merely re-scales the measure to allow the use of the *DRC* as a yes-no criterion, as all activities whose *DRC* is below one are socially profitable. The resulting 'absolute' *DRC* is:

$$(1') \quad DRC = D/e^*(R-T) = D/e^*V$$

In this paper the term '*DRC*' is used to refer to the absolute version of the *DRC*, since it is now far more commonly used than the relative one. The objective is to show that once all costs are converted into the same currency, the separation of domestic factor costs from tradeable inputs is no longer justified, and it is preferable to use a general social cost–benefit ratio (*SCB*):

$$(2) \quad SCB = (D + e^*T)e^*R$$

The *SCB* and the *DRC* are very similar measures. They use identical data, so there is no difference in terms of ease of calculation. Both are unit free ratios, unaffected by the scale of the activity and therefore preferable to measures such as net present value or net social profits which are denominated in scale specific units. But when choosing between the DRC and SCB, there are two fundamental reasons why the SCB is generally more accurate; one is well known, but to our knowledge the other has not been noted previously.

The first possible source of error in the *DRC* was highlighted by Bruno (1967), who noted that because the *DRC* requires separation of tradeable inputs (*T*) from domestic factors (*D*), it is subject to classification errors. If a tradeable input is mis-classified as non-tradeable, the *DRC* will be overstated, and vice versa. The *SCB* uses a shadow exchange rate to aggregate tradeable and non-tradeable costs and thereby avoid such errors, thus producing more accurate rankings[1].

The second source of error arises even if all costs and benefits are correctly measured and correctly classified. In this case, the two indicators are equivalent criteria for distinguishing efficient from inefficient activities: both the *DRC* and *SCB* will be greater than one for efficient activities, and less than one for inefficient ones. But the *DRC* and *SCB* can still rank activities differently, so the choice of indicator can have an influence on policy makers' priorities wherever all socially desirable activities cannot simultaneously be expanded.

Activity Rankings Under the DRC and the SCB

The *DRC* measures domestic factor costs per unit of tradeable value added. Choosing activities with the lowest *DRC* will produce the highest return to the domestic factors in terms of value added. But this is a true measure of national income or welfare only if domestic factors are fixed in supply. In fact, land and labour can move between activities, so that the supply of domestic factors to individual farm activities is not fixed — even though aggregate supply may be limited. At the margin, the opportunity cost of supplying domestic factors is captured by their shadow prices. Thus, as long as the best available estimate of these opportunity costs is used, the best available measure of the economic gains (or losses) from expanding a particular cropping activity is the returns to all inputs, both non-tradeable and tradeable. This is captured by the ratio of total social costs to total social benefits: the *SCB* rather than the *DRC*.

The possibility that the SCB will produce a different ranking than the *DRC* can be seen in Figure 1. To display the input mix in two dimensions we have normalized all activities to a common level of revenue ($\breve{R}$). These activities are mapped in terms of their domestic resource costs (*D*) along the vertical axis and tradeable input costs (*T*) along the horizontal axis, evaluated in a common currency. Along the diagonal 'break-even' line going from upper left to lower right costs exactly equal revenues so that the *DRC* and *SCB* ratios equal one. This line intersects the axes at the normalized level of revenues, $\breve{R}$. All activities that fall above the breakeven line have total costs greater than $\breve{R}$, and *DRCs* and *SCBs* greater than one, so the two measures are equally able to distinguish efficient from inefficient activities. Errors arise only in ranking activities with different input combinations: when, for example, comparing activity A with more factor-intensive activities that lie above and to the left of it, or more input-intensive activities that lie below and to the right. The *DRC* and *SCB* levels for A are different from one another; they are defined by:

(3) $DRC_A = D_A/(\breve{R} - T_A)$, and

(4) $SCB_A = (D_A + T_A)/\breve{R}$

Since revenues are fixed at $\breve{R}$, we can rearrange terms to find the sets of all activities sharing DRC_A and SCB_A. These sets are defined by the following equations:

(5) $D_A = DRC_A \cdot \breve{R} - DRC_A \cdot T_A$, and

(6) $D_A = SCB_A \cdot \breve{R} - T_A$

Thus a line through point A with the slope of minus DRC_A traces the set of all activities having DRC_A; a line through point A with a slope of minus one traces the set of all activities with SCB_A since these sets intersect only at A, conflicting rankings are possible. Algebraically, one set of activities for which *DRC* and *SCB* rankings conflict is the set of all X such that:

(7) $D_X/(\breve{R} - T_X) < D_A/(R_X - T_A)$ and $(D_X + T_X)/\breve{R} > (D_A + T_A)/\breve{R}$

Such activities would be ranked as more efficient than A using the *DRC*, but the *SCB* shows them to be less efficient. An example is activity B, in the shaded area below point A; relative to A such activities use tradeable inputs intensively.

Similar ranking conflicts arise for the set of all X such that:

(8) $D_X / (\breve{R} - T_X) > D_A / (\breve{R} - T_A)$ and $(D_X + T_X) / \breve{R} < (D_A + T_A) / \breve{R}$

These activities are judged to be less efficient than A using the *DRC*, but the *SCB* shows them to be more efficient. An example is activity C, in the shaded area above A; such activities are factor-intensive relative to A.

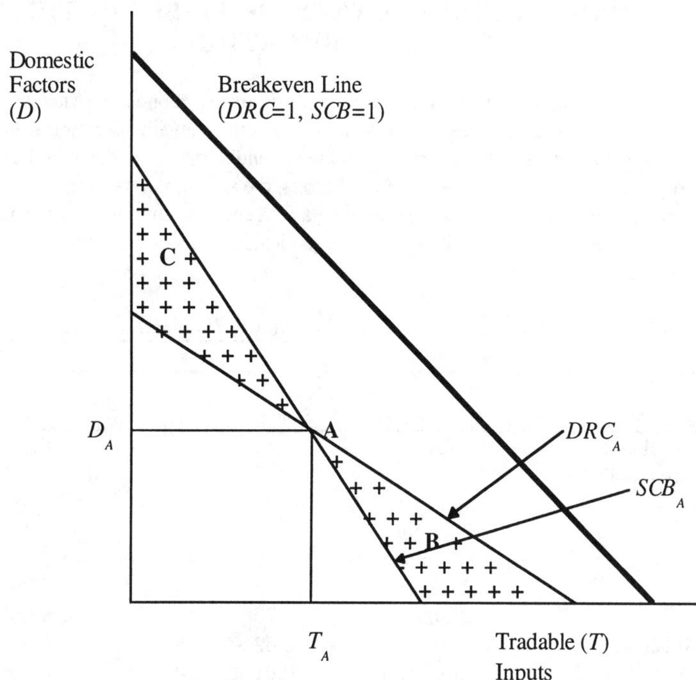

Figure 1 *Potential Ranking Conflicts Between DRCs and SCBs*

If policy makers are to choose among more than one socially desirable activity, the possibility of conflicting rankings makes it necessary to choose one ranking method over the other. In this context *SCB* rankings are more accurate than *DRC* rankings because transfering a given level of costs from tradeable and to non-tradeable inputs does not change total costs or total revenue and hence cannot affect welfare or economic growth. The marginal rate of substitution between tradeable and non-tradeable inputs is captured by the shadow exchange rate; as long as the rate used is the best available estimate, the *SCB* is the best estimate of economic efficiency, and the SCB_A line traces a true social 'indifference curve' among alternative activities.

For a given set of budget data and estimated economic opportunity costs, the *DRC* exaggerates the cost of domestic factors such as land and labour, as opposed to tradeable inputs. This leads the *DRC* to discriminate against factor-intensive activities, which is particularly important in developing countries where use of the *DRC* consistently understates the contribution of traditional smallholder farming systems relative to more 'modern' input-intensive production. The *DRC* exaggerates the benefits of using herbicides and mechanical equipment to substitute for labour, as well as the benefits of using fertilizer and other inputs to raise yields and substitute for land. In the next section we investigate the policy significance of these biases, using recent data from Zimbabwe and Kenya.

POLICY SIGNIFICANCE OF BIASES IN THE DRC INDICATOR

Data for Zimbabwe are taken from an analysis of the economic efficiency of nine crops across the country's three major farming systems: smallholder farms in low potential areas, smallholders in high potential areas, and large-scale commercial farms in high potential areas (Masters, 1994). For all crops, the smallholder systems use few purchased inputs, rely heavily on family labour, and generate low yields, whereas large-scale commercial farms use fertilizers, crop chemicals and machinery to achieve higher yields and reduce labour requirements.

Table 1 *DRC and SCB Indicators for Zimbabwe, 1989 Harvest Year*

Cropping activity		*SCB*		*DRC*	
System	Crop	Value	Rank	Value	Rank
Small scale	Maize	0.59	4	0.52	4
Low potential	Groundnuts	0.57	3	0.52	5
	Sunflower	0.99	11	0.99	11
	Pearl millet	2.79	16	4.34	16
	Sorghum	2.29	15	2.63	15
	Finger millet	1.18	14	1.20	14
	Whole farm	**0.73**		**0.68**	
Small scale	Maize	0.62	6	0.53	6
High potential	Groundnuts	0.91	10	0.89	10
	Sunflower	1.05	12	1.06	12
	Finger millet	1.17	13	1.19	13
	Cotton	0.77	9	0.72	9
	Whole farm	**0.67**		**0.60**	
Large scale	Maize	0.75	8	0.63	7
High potential	Groundnuts	0.53	1	0.42	1
	Cotton	0.56	2	0.43	2
	Wheat	0.74	7	0.65	8
	Soybeans	0.61	5	0.48	3
	Whole farm	**0.67**		**0.54**	

Table 1 shows the *DRC* and *SCB* values for each crop and each production technology, along with the relative ranking of each activity. Both measures agree that all three farm types are economically efficient on a whole-farm basis, and that only a few individual crops are not. But the rankings among crops differ. Since there is generally an elastic

Table 2 *DRC and SCB Indicators for Kenya, 1989–1990 Crop Year*

	Social Cost–Benefit Ratio (SCB)			Domestic Resource Cost Ratio (DRC)		
Rank	Class[a]	Crop[b]	Value	Class	Crop	Value
1	h	French Beans (KAK)	0.20	h	Oranges (NKU)	0.10
2	h	Irrigated Tomato (NYE)	0.20	c	Large-scale wheat (NKU)	0.12
3	h	Oranges (NKU)	0.22	h	Irrigated tomato (NYE)	0.12
4	h	Canning Tomato (NKU)	0.23	h	French Beans (KAK)	0.14
5	c	Maize-beans (KIS)	0.24	h	Canning tomato (NKU)	0.15
6	h	High Tomato (NKU)	0.31	c	Maize-beans (KIS)	0.19
7	te	Coffee (KIS)	0.33	c	Wheat (NKU)	0.19
8	te	Cotton (SIA)	0.35	h	High tomato (NKU)	0.21
9	c	Wheat (NYE)	0.37	c	Wheat (NYE)	0.25
10	c	Maize-beans (SIA)	0.40	h	Irrigated cabbage (NYE)	0.25
11	c	Maize-beans (KAK)	0.40	h	Potato (NYE)	0.29
12	te	Pyrethrum (KIS)	0.41	c	Maize-beans (NKU)	0.32
13	c	Maize (NYE)	0.41	te	Coffee (KIS)	0.33
14	c	Maize-beans (NKU)	0.41	te	Cotton (SIA)	0.33
15	te	High pyrethrum (NKU)	0.42	c	Maize-beans (KAK)	0.34
16	h	Irrigated cabbage (NYE)	0.43	c	Maize (NYE)	0.34
17	c	Tractor maize (NKU)	0.43	c	Tractor maize (NKU)	0.35
18	te	Tea (NYE)	0.43	c	Maize-beans (SIA)	0.36
19	c	Lg.-scale wheat (NKU)	0.45	te	Tea (NYE)	0.37
20	h	Tomato (NYE)	0.47	c	Maize-beans (NYE)	0.38
21	c	Maize-beans (NYE)	0.47	h	Tomato (NYE)	0.39
22	h	Potato (NYE)	0.49	te	Pyrethrum (KIS)	0.40
23	te	Pyrethrum (NKU)	0.52	h	Potato (NYE)	0.40
24	c	Wheat (NKU)	0.54	te	High pyrethrum (NKU	0.42
25	c	Ox-plough maize (NKU)	0.58	h	Tomatoes (NKU)	0.44
26	h	Tomato (NKU)	0.60	te	Pyrethrum (NKU)	0.52
27	c	Improved sorghum (SIA)	0.62	c	Ox-plough maize (NKU)	0.53
28	h	Potato (NKU)	0.62	h	potatoes (NKU)	0.56
29	h	Irrigated potato (NYE)	0.64	te	Lg.-scale coffee (NKU)	0.59
30	te	Tea (KAK)	0.82	c	Improved sorghum (SIA)	0.59
31	te	Lg.-scale coffee (NKU)	0.82	te	Tea (KAK)	0.78
32	te	Coffee (NKU)	0.92	te	Coffee (NKU)	0.77
33	te	Coffee (NYE)	1.03	te	Coffee (NYE)	1.05
34	c	Finger millet (KIS)	1.13	c	Finger millet (KIS)	1.13
35	c	Local sorghum (SIA)	1.40	c	Local sorghum (SIA)	1.45
36	te	Tea (KIS)	1.94	te	Tea (KIS)	3.96

Notes: [a] Crop classifications are: h(horticultural), te (traditional export), c (cereal). [b] Crop locations are: KAK (Kakamega), KIS (Kisii), NKU (Nakuru), NYE (Nyeri), SIA (Siaya).

Source: Calculated from data in Pearson and Monke, 1995.

supply of factors to the individual crops (although not to agriculture as a whole), and since the shadow exchange rate was carefully estimated, the *SCB* ranking is to be preferred.

Using *DRC*s, the large scale system appears to be more efficient (*DRC* = 0.54) than either of the smallholder systems (*DRC* = 0.60 on high potential land, and *DRC* = 0.68 on low potential land). But the *SCB* measure shows the large- and small-scale production systems in high potential areas to have almost identical efficiency levels (*SCB* = 0.67), while production in low potential areas is less efficient (*SCB* = 0.73). In this study the shadow exchange rate was carefully estimated, so the *SCB* is preferable. And since identical data are used for all measures, the greater accuracy of the *SCB* is due entirely to its functional form.

Among individual cropping activities, the *DRC* makes three ranking errors among the sixteen activities shown; the most important of these may be that the *DRC* wrongly ranks large scale commercial soyabeans above groundnuts from smallholders in low potential areas. These two crops are close substitutes in the edible oils industry, so the difference in ranking could affect such policy decisions as the location of processing facilities or the investment in crop research.

Data for Kenya come from a study of agricultural systems in five districts reported in Pearson and Monke (1995). All farms are located in areas of high agricultural potential. Thirty-six cropping systems were drawn from three broad classes of crops: cereals, traditional export crops, and horticultural crops. The traditional exports were introduced in the colonial period, while the horticultural products are now being promoted as new cash cropping alternatives.

The horticultural crops are the most dependent on purchased intermediate inputs (41 percent of total costs, as opposed to 24 percent for cereals and 16 percent for traditional exports). Although some of these crops can be produced only in specific locations (for example, pyrethrum, which is profitable only at high altitudes), as in Zimbabwe there is generally an elastic supply of land and labour for expanding production of each crop. And again, the best available estimate of the shadow exchange rate has been used, so the *SCB* is the preferred measure.

Table 2 compares the *DRC* and *SCB* measures calculated from the Pearson–Monke data. Clearly, the *DRC* favours the input-intensive mechanized wheat and horticultural crops, relative to more labour-intensive maize and traditional export crops. The *DRC* approach incorrectly ranks two of the mechanized wheat systems highly (second and seventh), while the *SCB* correctly ranks them lower (nineteenth and twentyfourth). Horticultural crops using substantial intermediate inputs are also ranked too high using the *DRC*, while traditional export crops which require more labour are ranked too low. None of the traditional export crops are in the top twelve under the *DRC*, but the *SCB* puts three in the top dozen (coffee, cotton and pyrethrum) and also raises the ranking of the major maize systems.

Many of the horticultural crops are unambiguously superior to other production choices; the same four horticultural crops rank in the top five under each method of analysis. Nonetheless, the *DRC* indicator consistently exaggerates the social profitability of horticultural crops and understates the contribution of maize and traditional export crops. These biases create the false impression that cereals and traditional exports contribute little to economic growth. In contrast, the *SCB* recognizes the value of these crops, and gives policy makers a more accurate picture of their social profitability relative to the new horticultural crops.

CONCLUSIONS

The appropriate use of indicators for ranking alternative activities is a long-standing theme of the project appraisal literature (for example, Gittinger 1982, pp.329–352). But policy analysts use them in slightly different circumstances, and ranking issues under these conditions have not been properly resolved in the literature. This paper has shown that in typical agricultural settings rankings based on domestic resource cost (*DRC*) ratios are biased against activities using domestic resources intensively. The use of the *DRC* is justified when the shadow exchange rate cannot be estimated, but where the best available shadow exchange rate is used, a social cost–benefit (*SCB*) ratio provides more accurate rankings of the social profitability of alternative activities. Evidence from Zimbabwe and Kenya shows the importance of using the more accurate indicator in policy analysis, particularly when comparing activities that have very different input combinations.

NOTE

[1] A similar source of error in the *SCB* arises from the need to separate costs and benefits: classifying costs as negative benefits could alter the ratio. For example, on-farm consumption of farm products could be put in any one of three budget categories: (a) a cost of production (hence added to the numerator), (b) a reduction in output (hence subtracted from the denominator), or (c) simply one of many sources of demand (which would not enter the measure at all). But this type of error affects the *DRC* as well, and is not a source of difference between the two measures.

REFERENCES

Alpine, R.W.L. and Pickett, J., 1993, *Agriculture, Liberalisation and Economic Growth in Ghana and Côte d'Ivoire, 1960–1990*, OECD Development Centre, Paris.

Appleyard, D., 1987, *Comparative Advantage of Agricultural Production Systems and its Policy Implications in Pakistan*, Economic and Social Development Paper 68, FAO, Rome.

Bruno, M., 1967, 'The Optimal Selection of Export-Promoting and Import-Substituting Projects', in *Planning the External Sector: Techniques, Problems and Policies*, Report on the First Inter-Regional Seminar on Development Planning, Ankara, Turkey, 6–17 September 1965, ST/TAO/SER.c/91, United Nations, New York, pp.88–135.

Dreze, J. and Stern, N., 1987, 'The Theory of Cost-Benefit Analysis', in Auerbach, A.J. and Feldstein, M. (eds.), *Handbook of Public Economics, Vol. II*, North Holland, Amsterdam.

Gittinger, P., 1982, *Economic Analysis of Agricultural Projects, Second Edition*, John Hopkins University Press, Baltimore.

Gonzales, L.A., Kasryno, F., Perez, N.D. and Rosegrant, M.W., 1993, *Economic Incentives and Comparative Advantage in Indonesian Food Crop Production*, International Food Policy Research Institute (IFPRI), Research Report No. 93, Washington, D.C.

Krueger, A.O., 1966, 'Some Economic Costs of Exchange Control: The Turkish Case', *Journal of Political Economics*, No. 74, pp.466–80.

Masters, W.A., 1994, *Government and Agriculture in Zimbabwe*, Praeger, Westport, Connecticut.

Monke, E.A. and Pearson, S.R., 1989, *The Policy Analysis Matrix for Agricultural Development*, Cornell University Press, Ithaca, New York.

Morris, M.L., 1988, *Comparative Advantage and Policy Incentives for Wheat in Zimbabwe*, CIMMYT Economics Working Paper 88/02, Mexico City.

Nelson, G.C. and Panggabean, M., 1991, 'The Costs of Indonesian Sugar Policy: A Policy Analysis Matrix Approach', *American Journal of Agricultural Econonomics*, Vol. 73, No. 3, pp.703–712.

Pearson, S.R. and Monke, E.A., 1995, *Agricultural Growth in Kenya: Applications of the Policy Analysis Matrix*, Cornell University Press, Ithaca, New York.

Srinivasan, T.N. and Bhagwati, J. N., 1978, 'Shadow Prices for Project Selection in the Presence of Distortions: Effective Rates of Protection and Domestic Resource Costs', *Journal of Political Economics*, Vol. 86, pp.97–116.

Tower, E., 1984, *Effective Protection, Domestic Resource Costs, and Shadow Prices*, World Bank Staff Working Paper No. 664, Washington, D.C.

Tsakok, I., 1990, *Agricultural Price Policy: A Practitioner's Guide to Partial Equilibrium Analysis*, Cornell University Press, Ithaca, New York.

Warr, P., 1983, 'The Domestic Resource Cost as an Investment Criterion', *Oxford Economic Papers*, Vol. 35, pp.302–306.

Williams, T.O., 1992, 'Comparative Advantage of Crop-Livestock Production Systems in Southwestern Nigeria and the Technical Research Implications', in Moock, J. and Rhoades, R. (eds.), *Diversity, Farmer Knowledge, and Sustainability*, Cornell University Press, Ithaca, New York.

World Bank, 1984, *Malawi Agricultural Diversification*, Report No. 4898-MAI, Washington, D.C.

World Bank, 1984, *Zambias Policy Options and Strategies for Agricultural Growth*, Report No. 4764-ZA, Washington, D.C.

DISCUSSION OPENING — Brent Swallow *(International Livestock Centre for Africa, Nairobi)*

In their paper, Masters and Winter-Nelson show that domestic resource cost is a biased measure of the economic efficiency of alternative activities. Instead of *DRC*, analysts should use a broader measure such as benefit-cost ratio. I agree with most of their analysis and conclusions. In fact, I think that the have been relatively generous to many of the studies that have used *DRC* as a major measure of economic efficiency.

I relied heavily on Price Gittinger's (1982) 'Economic Analysis of Agricultural Projects' while preparing my comments. Gittinger discusses the advantages and disadvantages of several measures of project worth: net present worth, internal rate of return, benefit–cost ratio, net benefit-investment ratio and domestic resource cost. I looked particularly for what gittinger said about the usefulness of these measures for ranking alternative projects. Net present worth is an absolute, rather than a relative, measure of project performance. Benefit–cost ratio discriminates against projects with relatively high gross returns and operating costs, even though they may have a greater wealth-generating capacity than other projects with higher benefit–cost ratios.

Internal rate of return (IRR) can be used to rank projects by the criterion of contribution to national income relative to the amount of resources used. But the criterion that Gittinger recommends most highly for ranking projects is the net benefit–investment ratio (N/K). N/K is calculated as the present worth of the net benefits divided by the present worth of the investment. The N/K ratio can be used to select projects on the basis of returns to investments made during the initial phase of the project.

A limitation of both IR and N/K is that they cannot be calculated for projects that don't have at least one year with negative net returns.

A criterion that has a very special use is domestic resource cost (*DRC*). Masters and Winter-Nelson discuss the justification for the use of *DRC* and show how it is calculated. They criticize its use when one has a good estimate of the shadow value of foreign exchange. They show that the domestic resource cost indicator is biased against activities using domestic resources intensively. This is quite obvious: the measure does not consider the costs of tradeable inputs, ceteris paribus, the higher the proportion of tradeable to non-tradeable inputs, the better the project looks according to the *DRC* criterion.

I would submit that another obvious problem with the *DRC* is that it completely discounts activities that generate non-tradeable benefits. Activities producing sorghum and millet can therefore not be ranked by the *DRC* criterion. I think that Masters and Winter-Nelson committed a bit of an error when they calculated *DRC*s for pearl millet, sorghum and finger millet in their analysis of the Zimbabwe and Kenya data. A few days ago, Chris Gerrard presented a paper at this conference in which he argued that even maize should be regarded as a non-tradeable in southern Africa because of the large disparities between import-parity and export parity prices.

So the next questions are, how prevalent is the use of this biased measure of project worth? An answer to that question can be found by a scan of the Proceedings of the Eastern and Southern African Session at this conference. Three of the papers used *DRC* to compare projects and policies. None of the three used the net benefit–investment criteria, nor the internal rate of return, nor the benefit–cost ratio. In most of the studies it is unclear, but perhaps the analysts weren't able to calculate internal rate of return or net benefit–investment ratio because all of the projects were very short term so that farmers incurred all costs and received all benefits during the same year.

So why didn't those analysts use the benefit–cost ratio? None of them mentioned any problems in calculating the shadow value of foreign exchange and none of them discussed any special policies related to import substitution or export promotion. All of them used the Policy Analysis Matrix as their analytical framework. My only guess, therefore, is that analysts applied the PAM in a mechanistic way and didn't consider the strengths and weaknesses of the different decision criteria that it generates.

Therefore, I wish to thank Masters and Winter-Nelson for the useful contribution. I hope that it causes economists to go back to consider some of the basics of welfare theory and benefit–cost analysis when they analyze their data and report and discuss their results.

S.K. EHUI AND M.A. JABBAR*

A Framework for Evaluating the Sustainability and Economic Viability of Crop–Livestock Systems in Sub-Saharan Africa

Abstract: Improved crop–livestock production systems and technologies are currently being developed in sub-Saharan Africa in response to the growing demand for food and the degradation of the natural resource base. These technologies must not only enhance food production, but they also need to maintain ecological stability and preserve the natural resource base, that is, they must be sustainable. However, the notion of sustainability has been of limited operational use to policy-makers and researchers attempting to evaluate new technologies and/or determine the effects of various policies and technologies. This paper discusses a methodology for measuring the sustainability and economic viability of crop–livestock systems. The approach is based on the concept of intertemporal and interspatial total factor productivity, paying particular attention to the valuation of natural resource stock and flows. The method is applied to a data set available at the International Livestock Centre for Africa. Intertemporal and interspatial total factor productivity indexes are computed for three farming systems in southwestern Nigeria. Results show that the sustainability and economic viability measures are sensitive to changes in the stock and flow of soil nutrients as well as material inputs and outputs. The advantage of this approach is that intertemporal and interspatial total factor productivity measures are computed using only price and quantity data, thus eliminating the need for econometric estimation.

INTRODUCTION

Livestock are an important component of farming systems in sub-Saharan Africa. They are raised mainly for meat, milk and skin, and provide a flexible financial reserve for farmers in years of crop failure. They also play a critical role in the agricultural intensification process by providing draught power and manure for fertilizer and fuel (Winrock, 1992; and Fitzhugh *et al.*, 1992). With increasing human population and economic changes, cultivated areas in many sub-Saharan African countries have expanded onto marginal lands and fallow periods are being shortened. As a result large areas of land are degrading and crop and animal yields are falling (IBRD, 1989; and Ehui and Hertel, 1992). It has been shown that where both crops and livestock are raised, technology is low, inputs scarce, and markets poorly developed, population pressures lead to the evolution of crop–livestock systems as the most efficient and sustainable means of increasing production from a fixed land base (McIntire *et al.*, 1992). Thus small holders will benefit from livestock if they can be successfully integrated with the cropping systems.

Improved crop–livestock production systems and technologies are currently being developed in response to the growing demand for food and the degradation of the natural resource base (ILCA, 1992). These technologies must not only enhance food production but also maintain ecological stability and preserve the natural resource base, that is, they must be sustainable. However the notion of sustainability has been of limited operational use to policy-makers and researchers attempting to evaluate new technologies and/or determine the effects of various policies and technologies. This paper discusses a

* International Livestock Centre for Africa, Addis Ababa, Ethiopia.

methodology for measuring the agricultural sustainability and economic viability of crop–livestock systems. The approach is based on the concept of intertemporal and interspatial total factor productivity (TFP), paying particular attention to valuation natural resource stock and flows (Ehui and Spencer, 1993).

The next section presents the model. Intertemporal and interspatial TFP indexes which are used to measure the sustainability and economic viability of production systems are derived. The third section presents data sources and construction. The empirical results are reported in the fourth section and the paper closes with some concluding comments.

DERIVATION OF INTERTEMPORAL AND INTERSPATIAL TFP INDEXES

The conventional approach to growth accounting uses TFP indexes to measure the residual growth in outputs not accounted for by the growth in factor inputs. The rate of growth of TFP is conventionally defined as the rate of growth of aggregate output minus the rate of growth of aggregate inputs (Capalbo and Antle, 1988).

Agriculture, however, is a sector which utilizes common pools of natural resources (e.g., air, water, soil nutrients etc.). The stock of these resources affects the production environment, but is in many cases beyond the control of the farmers. For example, soil nutrients are removed by crops, erosion or leaching beyond the crop root zone, or other processes such as volatilization of nitrogen. Agricultural production can also contribute to the stock of some of the nutrients, particularly of nitrogen by leguminous plants and animal manure.

When the stock of nutrients is reduced through nutrient losses, the farmer faces an implicit cost in terms of productivity loss. Conversely when the stock of resource is increased during the production process (e.g., via nitrogen fixation or manuring) the farmer derives an implicit benefit from the system. If these implicit costs and benefits are not accounted for when TFP is measured, results will be misleading.

The model used here builds on that developed recently by Ehui and Spencer (1993). They show that a system can be said to be sustainable if the associated intertemporal TFP index, which incorporates and values changes in the resource stock and flow, does not decrease. They also show that a system can be said to be economically more viable than another one if the interspatial TFP index associated with the former (which incorporates and values spatial differences in the resource stock and flow), is higher than the interspatial TFP index associated with the latter. While intertemporal TFP is about the productive capacity of a system over time (thus sustainability) interspatial TFP is a static concept which refers to the efficiency with which with which resources are employed in the production process at a given period. In both cases the measures include the unpriced contribution from natural resources and their unpriced production flows.

Figure 1 illustrates the difference between intertemporal and interspatial TFP for two hypothetical systems. System 1 is sustainable since its intertemporal TFP increases from a to d over the same period. On the other hand, System 2 is economically more viable (or efficient) than System 1 in year 2 (c is greater than a), but it is economically less viable in year n (d > b).

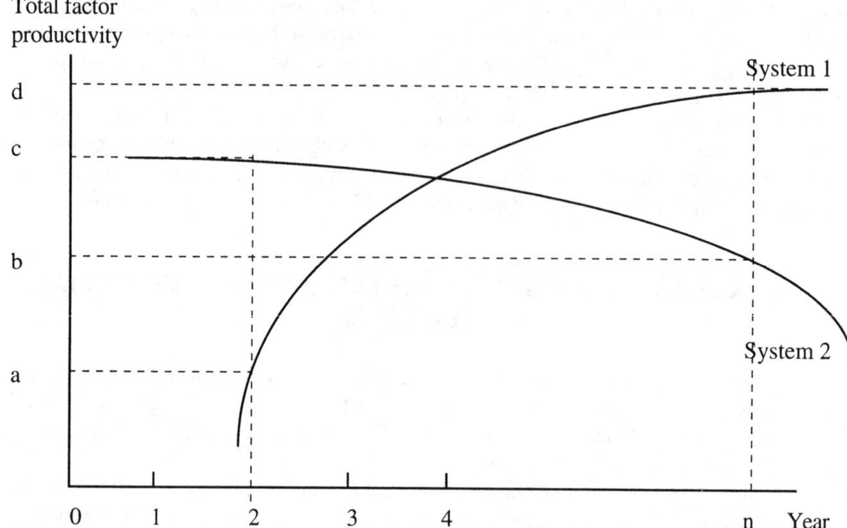

Figure 1 *Total Factor Productivity Changes for Two Hypothetical Agricultural Systems Over Time*

To derive the generalized model for TFP measurement, Ehui and Spencer (1993), solve a maximization problem. When changes in resource stock levels are positive, the problem is stated as:

$$\text{(1)} \quad \underset{[Y_t, Z_t]}{\text{Max}\,\pi_t} = P_{yt}Y_t + P_{zt}Z_t - G(Y_t, Z_t, W_t, B_t, t)$$

where π_t is a measure of aggregate profit in period t, including all benefits and costs of resource exploitation; Y_t is an index of crop outputs; Z_t is an externality denoting the net resource flow in period t, (when changes in resource abundance levels are positive, we have a positive externality and the resulting net resource flow); Z_t is treated as an output, thus contributing positively to the aggregate profit. P_{yt} and P_{zt} are the product and resource flow prices; B_t is a technology shift variable representing the level of resource abundance in period t. Equation (1) represents the case of 'open access' in which B_t is not a choice variable. The resource stock is beyond the control of farmers who thus ignore its opportunity cost. $G(\cdot)$ is the variable cost function for the optimal combination of variable inputs, where $\partial G(\cdot)/\partial B < 0$ and $\partial G(\cdot)/\partial Z > 0$. W_t is a vector of variable input prices; t, is the time trend representing the state of technical knowledge.

When the production process is depleting the resource at a rate faster than that required for sustainability, net changes in resource abundance levels are negative. Thus, we have a negative externality and Z_t is treated as a cost, contributing negatively to the aggregate profit. This requires modification of the objective function, Equation (1,) by replacing the (+) sign before $P_{zt}Z_t$ with a (–) sign, and in this case, $\partial G(\cdot)/\partial Z < 0$.

Using the first-order conditions of Equation (1), development of the continuous time Divisia index by the method of the growth accounting approach gives:

$$(2)\quad -\partial LnC/\partial t = [(P_y Y)/C]\dot{Y} + [(P_z Z)/C]\dot{Z} - \Sigma_j[(W_j X_j)/C]\dot{X}_j - \dot{B}$$

where, $C = \Sigma_j W_j X_j + P_y Y + P_z Z =$ total revenue, assuming constant returns to scale. Dots on variables imply the logarithm derivation of the associated variable with time.

When changes in the resource stock are negative, the productivity index becomes:

$$(3)\quad -\partial LnC/\partial t = [(P_y Y)/C]\dot{Y} - [(P_z Z)/C]\dot{Z} - \Sigma_j[(W_j X_j)/C]\dot{X}_j - \dot{B}$$

where $C = \Sigma_j W_j X_j + P_z Z = P_y Y$, assuming constant returns to scale.

Equations (2) and (3) indicate that TFP is measured as the residual after the growth rate of output $\{[P_y Y/C]\dot{Y}\}$ has been allocated among changes in inputs $\{\Sigma_j[(W_j X_j)/C]\dot{X}_j\}$ and resource abundance $\{\dot{B}\}$ and flows $[(P_z Z)/C]\dot{Z}$. The basic difference between Equations (2) and (3) is that in the former case the change in resource stock is assumed positive and the resulting flow is treated as a benefit. In the latter case, the change in resource stock is assumed to be negative and the resulting flow is treated as a cost.

It is clear from Equations (2) and (3) that total factor productivity measures are biased unless account is taken of variations in the resource stock abundance levels and resource flows. Note that although it is not a choice variable, B_t is part of the solution because it appears in the variable cost function, G.

A discrete-time approximation to the continuous time Divisia indexes of Equations (2) and (3) is given by the Tornqvist approximation (Diewert, 1976; and Ehui and Spencer, 1993). Allowing for resource abundance and flows, this approximation gives measures of the intertemporal and interspatial TFP indexes. As in Equations (2) and (3) we distinguish between two cases:

Case 1: Case of Net Positive Changes in Resource Stock

– intertemporal TFP

$$(4)\quad \tau_{st} = \tfrac{1}{2}\Sigma_j[R_{js} + R_{jt}].[LnY_{js} - LnY_{jt}] + \tfrac{1}{2}[R_{zs} + R_{zt}].[LnZ_s - LnZ_t] - \tfrac{1}{2}\Sigma_k[S_{ks} + S_{kt}].[LnX_{ks} - LnX_{kt}] - [LnB_s - LnB_t]$$

– interspatial TFP

$$(5)\quad \rho_{io} = \tfrac{1}{2}\Sigma_j[R_{ji} + R_{jo}].[LnY_{ji} - LnY_{jo}] + \tfrac{1}{2}[R_{zi} + R_{zo}].[LnZ_i - LnZ_o] - \tfrac{1}{2}\Sigma_k[S_{ki} + S_{ko}].[LnX_{ki} - LnX_{ko}] - [LnB_i - LnB_o]$$

Case 2: Case of Net Negative Changes in Resource Stock

– intertemporal TFP

(6)
$$\tau'_{st} = \Sigma_j [LnY_{js} - LnY_{jt}] - \tfrac{1}{2}[S_{zs} + S_{zt}].[LnZ_s - LnZ_t]$$
$$-\tfrac{1}{2}\Sigma_k [S_{ks} + S_{kt}].[LnX_{ks} - LnX_{kt}] - [LnB_s - LnB_t]$$

– interspatial TFP

(7)
$$\rho'_{io} = \Sigma_j [LnY_{ji} - LnY_{jo}] - \tfrac{1}{2}[S_{zi} + S_{zo}].[LnZ_i - LnZ_o]$$
$$-\tfrac{1}{2}\Sigma_k [S_{ki} + S_{ko}].[LnX_{ki} - LnX_{ko}] - [LnB_i - LnB_o]$$

In Equations (4)–(7) s and t represent two distinct time periods and i and o represent two distinct farming systems or two distinct geographical areas; B is the composite index of soil nutrient abundance; Z denotes the resource flow; $R_j = (P_j Y_j)/(\Sigma_j P_j Y_j)$ is the revenue share for output Y_j; $S = (W_k X_k)/(\Sigma_k W_k X_k)$ is the cost share for variable input k, and S_z and R_z are the cost and revenue shares of resource flow Z. The basic difference between τ_{st} and ρ_{io} and τ'_{π} and ρ'_{io} is that in Equations (4) and (5) the net increase in resource stock is treated as benefit while in Equations (6) and (7) it is treated as cost. It is clear from Equations (4)–(7) that the productivity differences across different farming systems and time periods can be broken into four components including: (a) an output effect (the first term in Equations (4)–(7), (b) a resource flow effect (the second term in Equations (4)–(7) effect, (c) an input effect (the third term in Equations (4)–(7) and (d) a resource stock effect (the last term in Equations (4)–(7)).

DATA SOURCES

The framework discussed above is demonstrated using a set of data generated during a nine-year study by the International Livestock Centre for Africa (ILCA) at one of its West African research sites in Ibadan (Southwestern Nigeria). The experiment comprised of three systems: (a) the traditional method of cultivation (System A), commonly known as bush fallow system; (b) the continuous alley farming systems (System B); and (c) alley farming with fallow (System C).

In the traditional system farmers fell and burn the fallow vegetation, cultivate the cleared land (typically one to three years) and then abandon the site (from four to twenty years) to forest or bush cover (Sanchez, 1976). This traditional agricultural production system, which is known to be stable and biologically efficient, operates effectively only where there is sufficient land to allow a long fallow period to restore soil productivity (Kang *et al.*, 1989). The fallow land also serves as a source of feed for the animals. In recent times, population growth and various economic changes have caused the fallow period to be shortened or eliminated. This is resulting in increased degradation of farm land, lower supply of quality feed, declining crop and animal yields, and reduced production of food from both crop and animal origins.

Alley farming is an agroforestry system in which crops are grown in alleys formed by hedgerows of trees and shrubs, preferably fast-growing leguminous species. The hedgerows are cut back at the time of planting of food crops and are periodically pruned during cropping to prevent shading and to reduce competition with the associated food crops. They may also be established along the slope to minimize erosion. A portion of the hedgerows' foliage is used as animal feed. Use of the woody legumes provides rich mulch and green manure to maintain soil fertility, enhance crop production, and provide protein-rich fodder for livestock. In the case of this experiment, small ruminants were part of the system and fed with part of the hedgerow foliage. One major advantage of alley farming over the traditional bush fallow system is that cropping, animal feeding and fallow phases can take place concurrently on the same land unit, allowing the farmer to crop the land and feed his/her animals for an extended period. However where it is technically feasible, it is possible to combine alley farming with some short cycle fallow periods as in System C.

Since the cropping systems have multiple crop outputs (maize and cowpea) an implicit output index is calculated by dividing the total value of all output by a price index. The latter is obtained by weighting the maize and cowpea prices by the revenue share of each crop.

Three major inputs are distinguished: planting materials, labour and fertilizer. While labour and fertilizer input quantities are used as observed, the planting material indexes are bilateral Tornqvist chain indexes for each type of planting materials. Planting materials for each crop are aggregated into a single index weighted by the cost share of each planting material.

The Divisia index for the soil nutrient stock is calculated by share-weighting the total quantities of main soil nutrients (nitrogen, phosphorous and potassium) available in the top soil (0–10cm). The opportunity cost of each soil nutrient is approximated by its replacement cost, that is, market price for chemical fertilizer. Resource (nutrient) flows are derived as the difference between nutrient abundance levels for a given production system between 1983 and 1984, and between 1983 and 1990. We chose these two periods to assess short-run and long-run effects.

EMPIRICAL RESULTS

Intertemporal and interspatial total factor productivity indexes for the three production systems under different scenarios were calculated and are reported in Tables 1 and 2, respectively. The basic analysis is conducted under two scenarios: (a) with and without resource stock and flows and (b) with and without a livestock component. Scenario (b) was evaluated in order to assess the impact of the livestock component on the TFP measures.

From column (5) in Table 1, over the period from 1983 to 1990, total factor productivity increased for the continuous alley farming systems (System B) and declined for both the traditional system (System A) and alley farming with fallow (System C). The continuous alley farming system produces 1.28 times as much output in 1990 as in 1983 using the 1983 input bundle. The continuous alley farming system can be said to be sustainable over the seven-year interval because, after properly accounting for temporal differences in input quality and quantity and resource flows and stocks, it produced more than in the reference year (1983). The traditional bush fallow system and the alley farming systems with fallow produced only 0.78 and 0.60 as much output in 1990 as in 1983 using the 1983 input bundle. Thus these two systems can be said to be non-sustainable. During the period 1983–84, the three systems had total factor productivity measures greater than one, indicating that they were sustainable over the relatively short one-year period (Table 1, column 3). Note from Table 1 that totally accounting for changes in resource stock levels and flows alters the productivity measures. For example, during 1983–90 when resource stock and flows are not accounted for, results indicate that the continuous alley farming system and the traditional bush fallow system produced 1.46 and 0.92 (Table 1, column 2) as much output as in 1983 using the 1983 input bundle. However, because over time there was a decline in nutrient stock levels in both systems, the gain in productivity levels was actually lower (1.28 and 0.28, respectively. see Table 1, column 5).

In Table 2, the economic viability of the three systems during 1983, 1984 and 1990 is compared. The traditional bush fallow system is used as the reference base system. In 1983, 1984, and 1990, after accounting for changes in resource abundance and flows, both the alley farming systems (continuous and with fallow) are shown to be relatively more productive than the traditional bush fallow system (Table 2, columns (4), (6), and (8)). The estimated interspatial TFP measures are largely greater than one, indicating that the two alley farming systems produced comparatively more output than the traditional bush fallow system using the latter system's input bundle. Comparison of columns (1)–(3) with columns (4), (6) and (8) indicate that, when resource stock and flows are accounted for, the productivity measures yield different results. The extent of these differences, of course, depends on how significant the changes are in resource stock and flows. In this case, changes in resource stock levels and flows have not been significant enough to alter substantially the productivity measures.

Table 1 *Intertemporal Total Factor Productivity (Sustainability) Indexes for Three Crop–Livestock Systems in Southwestern Nigeria, 1983–84 and 1983–1990*

	Not accounting for resource stock and flows		Accounting for resource stock flows			
	1983–84	1983–1990	1983–1984		1983–90	
			Live-stock	No live-stock	Live-stock	No live-stock
System	(1)	(2)	(3)	(4)	(5)	(6)
Traditional bush fallow (A)	1.24	0.92	1.17*	1.34*	0.78**	0.69**
Continuous alley farming (B)	1.31	1.46	1.08*	1.59*	1.28**	0.64**
Alley farming with fallow (C)	1.17	0.60	1.00*	1.47*	0.60*	0.56*

Note: Numbers with one asterisk indicate the case of a net positive resource flow and those with two asterisks indicate the case of a net negative resource flow.

In order to assess the relative importance of the livestock component in the TFP measures, the analysis was conducted with and without a livestock component. In all cases except for the measurement of the intertemporal TFP during 1983–84, all the productivity measures declined significantly, indicating that livestock do play a significant role in the total productivity of the farm. Therefore when farmers raise animals on the farm (as all of them do) and the productivity measures consider only the crop aspect, results will be biased. A system may said to be non-sustainable when in fact it is as in the case of the continuous alley farming during the period from 1983 to 1990. When the animal component is ignored, the intertemporal TFP measure is only 0.64. When the livestock component is taken into account, the same productivity measure doubles to 1.28 (Table 1, columns (5) and (6)). The same is true for interspatial TFP measures. For example during 1990, when the livestock component is omitted from the analysis, we conclude erroneously that continuous alley farming is economically less viable than the traditional bush fallow system (see Table 2, columns (8) and (9)).

Table 2 *Interspatial Total Factor Productivity (Economic Viability) Indexes for 3 Crop–livestock Systems, in Southwestern Nigeria, during 1983, 1984, 1989 and 1990*

Systems	Not acounting for resource stock and flows			Accounting for resource stock and flows					
	1983	1984	1990	1983		1984		1990	
				Live-stock	No live-stock	Live-stock	No live-stock	Live-stock	No live-stock
	(1)	(2)	(3)	(4)	(5)	(7)	(8)	(9)	(10)
Traditional bush fallow (A)	1	1	1	1	1	1	1	1	1
Continuous alley farming (B)	1.9	1.63	1.36	1.87*	1.045*	1.41*	0.94*	1.26*	0.95*
Alley farming with fallow (C)	2.11	2.14	1.45	2.06*	1.045*	1.93*	1.15*	1.18*	1.03*

Note: See Table 1.

CONCLUSIONS

Intertemporal and interspatial total factor productivities adjusted for resource flows and stock provide an excellent framework for evaluating the sustainability and economic viability of production systems. In this paper conventional TFPs are modified to develop a generalized TFP framework in which the contribution of crop and livestock outputs and the unpriced contribution of nutrient stock and flows are taken into account separately and properly. This paper shows that where resource flows and stocks are not negligible, the measures of TFP indexes provide markedly different results from conventional TFP approaches. Disentangling the productivity residual from changes in resource stock and flows honed the productivity residual to finer precision. While the analytical framework presented within this paper is appealing, its successful application depends greatly on data availability. In this paper only changes in major soil nutrients are taken into consideration. The model needs to take into consideration other indications of natural resource degradation, including vegetation and soil physical, chemical and microbiological properties.

REFERENCES

Capalbo, S.M. and Antle, J.M. (eds.), 1988, *Agricultural Productivity Measurement and Explanation*, Resources for the Future Inc., Washington, D.C.

Diewert, W.E., 1976, 'Exact and Superlative Index Numbers', *Journal of Econometrics*, Vol. 4, No. 2, pp.115–145.

Ehui, S.K. and Hertel, T.W., 1989, 'Deforestation and Agricultural Productivity in the Côte d'Ivoire', *American Journal of Agricultural Economics*, Vol. 71, No. 3, pp.703–711.

Ehui, S.K. and Spencer, D.S.C., 1993, 'Measuring the Sustainability and Economic Viability of Tropical Farming Systems: A Model From Sub-Saharan Africa', *Agricultural Economics*, Vol. 9, No. 4, pp.279–296.

Fitzhugh, H.A., Ehui, S.K. and Lahlou–Kassi, 1992, 'Research Strategies for Development of Animal Agriculture', *World Animal Review*, Vol. 72, No. 3, pp.9–19.

IBRD (International Bank for Reconstruction and Development), 1989, *Sub-Saharan Africa: from Crisis to Sustainable Growth, a Long-term Perspective Study*, World Bank, Washington, D.C.

ILCA (International Livestock Centre for Africa), 1993, *ILCA 1992: Annual Report and Programme Highlights*, ILCA, Addis Ababa, Ethiopia.

Kang, B.T., van der Kruijs, A.C.B.M. and Cooper, D.C., 1989, 'Alley Cropping for Food Production in the Humid and Subhumid Tropics', in Kang, B.T. and Reynolds. L. (eds.), *Alley Farming in the Humid and subhumid Tropics,* proceedings of an International Workshop held at Ibadan, Nigeria, 10–14 March 1986, International Development Research Centre, Ottawa, Canada.

McIntire, J., Bourzat, D. and Pingali, P., 1992, *Crop–Livestock Interaction in Sub-Saharan Africa*, The World Bank, Washington, D.C.

Sanchez, P.A., 1976, *Properties and Management of Soil in the Tropics*, Wiley, New York.

Winrock, 1992, *Assessment of Animal Agriculture in Sub-Saharan Africa*, Winrock International Institute for Agricultural Development, Morrilton, Arkansas.

JOHN H. SANDERS, SUNDER RAMASWAMY AND BARRY I. SHAPIRO*

Technology Development For Semi-Arid Sub-Saharan Africa: Theory, Performance and Constraints

Abstract: The paper proposes a theory of technology development for semi-arid regions. It then evaluates the theory by reviewing the characteristics of technologies successfully introduced into the regions and, with modeling, identifying some constraints to further technology introduction of the type proposed. Some specific policy recommendations to accelerate technology introduction are recommended.

INTRODUCTION

Declining food production per capita over the last three decades, especially in the Sahel, but also in other parts of sub-Saharan Africa, leads many to be pessimistic about future agricultural performance in this region. High population growth turns even moderate agricultural production growth rates into declining per capita trends (Sanders and Ramaswamy, 1995, Ch. 2). The per capita declines have been especially serious in the semi-arid regions where rainfall is low and irregular, and soils are often fragile with low fertility. Historically, these regions have been contributors to the labour pool of the most prosperous higher rainfall regions through out-migration. However, there have been some successes in agricultural performance especially with maize and sorghum in this semi-arid region. A closer look at these successes is useful to formulate approaches to technology development and leads to some optimism about the future of agricultural development in semi-arid sub-Saharan Africa.

This paper formulates a theory of technology development for the semi-arid sub-Saharan region of Africa. Next it evaluates this theory. First, the adequacy of the theory in explaining observed technology successes in semi-arid West Africa is reviewed. Secondly, potential technologies of the type recommended are modeled, and the predictions from these models are compared with the observed shifts in technology. The last two sections of the paper make some policy recommendations and conclusions.

A THEORY OF INTENSIVE AGRICULTURAL TECHNOLOGY DEVELOPMENT

In the semi-arid regions of sub-Saharan Africa, the principal constraint to crop-output increases is almost given by definition. Semi-arid regions have inadequate soil water for most crop production through most of the year. Nevertheless, in the last two decades there has been little investment in irrigation in this region, mainly due to prohibitive costs (Matlon, 1987, p.66). Both construction and rehabilitation of existing schemes were estimated to cost between $5000 and $20 000 per ha in the 1980s (Matlon, 1990, p.19).

* We benefitted from critical comments and suggestions of David Samonds, Jock Anderson, Steve Mason, Keijiro Otsuka and Doug Graham.

The effects of low and irregular rainfall on crop yields are frequently aggravated by soil crusting, which leads to reduced water infiltration. In these crusting soils, water-retention techniques such as dikes and ridging become critical to reduce runoff and to use the available rainfall. Fortunately, there are numerous techniques for water conservation or retention, and these are potentially very important (Carr, 1989, pp.46–48; Reij *et al.*, 1988; Sanders *et al.*, 1990).

Making water available when nutrient levels in the soil are very low often results in only a small yield response. Even at slightly higher nutrient levels, cereals will quickly deplete the available nutrients. Conversely, applying fertilizers (organic or inorganic) without an assured water supply is economically risky because the response to fertilizer depends upon the availability of water at the critical stages of plant development.

Combined technologies to increase soil water and crop nutrient levels have been shown to raise sorghum yields by 50–100 percent and to be highly profitable (Sanders *et al.*, 1990, pp.11–15; Nagy *et al.*, 1988). These combined technologies are land substituting and increase the demand for labour. To what extent would these technologies be economically appropriate and profitable and fit into farmers' production systems in the semi-arid environment of West Africa?

The semi-arid regions of West Africa have had increasing population pressure on the land, causing a breakdown of the traditional fallow periods of 10 to 15 years. Shorter fallow periods, without replacing soil nutrients with purchased inputs, cause crop yields to decrease over time. Farmers must then increase their cultivated area to maintain production levels, thereby pushing crop production into more marginal areas and then decreasing communal grazing areas. As cattle are sold or entrusted to migrating herders, availability of manure as fertilizer declines.

Soil nutrient depletion leading to lower yields becomes a widespread problem with increased population pressure (Southgate *et al.*, 1990). As cultivated areas are extended, wind and water erosion, and soil crusting often occur as farmers intensively cultivate the previously marginal crop or grazing areas and follow the traditional cultural practices of utilizing or burning crop residues. With declining organic matter and soil nutrient levels, farmers must increase their labour inputs to maintain the same level of production (see Sanders *et al.*, 1990, p.3).

The induced innovation theory considers technological change to be responsive to the economic signals from relative factor and product prices. In this case, the reduction in availability and quality of land and reduced productivity of labour induces researchers and governments to produce and promote, and farmers to adopt, new technologies which substitute increased use of labour and/or inputs for degraded land. Critics of such more intensive water retention technologies have emphasized the large increases in labour requirements (Matlon, 1990, p.27). This labour use change is substantial. However, the soil degradation and the consequent fall in the marginal productivity of labour already required an increased amount of labour to produce the same level of output with less land. Thus, it is the degradation and the decreased value of farm family labour with few non-farm alternatives that result in the increase in labour use. The technological change is a response to this demand for a technology that substitutes for land.

In the previous section, the principal constraints to output increases in semi-arid Sub-Saharan African agriculture are hypothesized to be water and soil nutrients. Are the new technologies being successfully introduced in semi-arid West Africa consistent with the above theory?

RECENT INTRODUCTION OF INTENSIVE TECHNOLOGIES: A PRELIMINARY EVALUATION OF THE THEORY

The Sahelian region exhibiting the most rapid technological change, the Sudano-Guinean zone, has the highest rainfall. Technically, this zone is in the transition to semi-humid rather than semi-arid, so fertilization can be practised with less concern for first improving water retention. Here, the introduction of new cotton cultivars has been combined with increasing levels of chemical fertilizer application (Table 1). Moderately high levels of inorganic fertilizer were utilized on both cotton and maize. Sorghum often benefits from being in the rotation. Introduction of new cotton and maize cultivars along with use of better production practices then complemented the yield effects of increased fertilizer application, enabling substantial increases in cotton and maize yields. New technology development and diffusion have been very successful in this region.

Dykes to slow runoff have been rapidly introduced in the last five years in the Sudanian and the Sahelo-Sudanian regions in Burkina Faso and Niger. In northern Burkina Faso alone, these dykes are found on 60 000 ha (World Bank, 1989, p.98; Sanders *et al.*, 1990)[1]. Dykes are predominantly found in the most severely degraded regions and are constructed in the off-season when opportunity costs of family labour are generally lower than during the crop season. This is consistent with the theory presented earlier. In the most degraded regions, the available opportunities for labour are much fewer compared to areas with higher population pressure and more adequate resources. Hence, sufficient labour becomes available for these extremely labour intensive technologies only with soil degradation and low opportunity costs. In the Sudanian zone of Mali, animal traction with oxen is predominant in contrast with the almost exclusive use of donkeys in the Sudanian zone of Burkina Faso. In Mali the use of ridging on the contour with animal traction is undertaken during the crop season when cultivating for weeds and has been shown to have almost as large a yield effect as tied ridges. As with the dykes the collection and spreading of the manure requires large labour inputs (Sanders, 1995, Ch. 4).

Another important innovation in both the Sudanian and the Sahelo-Sudanian zones has been development of shorter season cultivars (sorghum, millet, and cowpeas). There has been diffusion of new cultivars between farmers and from the experiment stations (Vierich and Stoop, 1990; Matlon, 1990, pp. 25, 26; Coulibaly, 1987). Since the start of the drought of 1968–73, rainfall has been one standard deviation below the long-term normal in semi-arid West Africa (Glantz, 1987, p.39). Hence, the payoff from early or short-season varieties has increased, since earliness allows drought escape. Moreover, improved farmer cultivars have been selected under low soil fertility conditions. Therefore, the early cultivars are a partial response to both constraints of water availability and soil nutrient levels. This introduction of new cultivars alone gives only small income increases in average years of good rainfall but raises yields in adverse rainfall seasons. This is only a temporary solution as all cultivars need fertilizers or they will mine the soil nutrients. In the sandy dune soils of the Sahelo-Sudanian zone of Niger, chemical phosphorous fertilization is being rapidly introduced in several regions (Mokwunye and Hammond, 1992). Here, crusting is less common, so fertilizer use alone is less risky than in the Sudanian zone (Shapiro *et al.*, 1993).

Due to high capital, maintenance, and recovery costs of irrigation, only small-scale and supplementary irrigation has tended to be promoted in Africa over the last two decades. Nevertheless, in some regions, old irrigation projects have been important for farmers. In

Niger, irrigation projects frequently serve as an income base for dryland farmers. In one zone, each farmer was given 0.4 ha of irrigated area; the farmers also produced crops on 4 to 5 ha of dryland. On the irrigated area, farmers produced rice with improved cultivars and high levels of chemical fertilizer. Clearly, these technologies resolved both constraints (Shapiro, *et al.*, 1993).

Table 1 *Rainfall by Region and Technologies Successfully Introduced in the Three Principal Agro-Ecological Regions for Crop Production of the Semi-Arid Tropics in West Africa*

Zones	Expected Rainfall at 90% Probability (mm)	Technologies	Responses to Principal Constraints	
			Water Availability	Soil Fertility
Sudano-Guinean	800–1100	New cotton and maize cultivars with chemical fertilizer and improved agronomic practices. Rapid increase in use of organic fertilizers	Sufficient rainfall in most years in this zone	Fertilizer used in the combined-technology package
Sudanian	600–800	Contour dykes and organic fertilizer. Early cereal and cowpea cultivars. In Mali, ridging and increases in organic fertilizers	Holds the runoff water. Earliness gives drought escape	Organic fertilizer. Selected for low soil-fertility conditions
Sahelo-Sudanian	350–600	Supplementary irrigation.[a] Early cereal and cowpea cultivars and P fertilizer. Contour dykes and organic fertilizers	Full water control. Drought escape with earliness. Holds the runoff	Rice heavily fertilized. In several regions, chemical fertilizers are being introduced. Organic fertilizers

Note: [a] Only small areas of supplementary irrigation (<1 ha) provided by the government of Niger to farmers; these are a type of income stabilization for dryland farmers.

Source: Sandra, Ramasaramy and Shapiro, 1995, Chapter 3.

In summary, sub-Saharan Africa is usually considered a land-surplus region, with seasonal labour availability as the main constraint to increased output. However, in semi-arid West Africa, the general failure to adopt animal traction, except where intensive, yield increasing technologies were introduced, may indicate the need for re-evaluation of this conventional analysis. The major thesis here is that the principal constraints to increasing agricultural output in much of sub-Saharan African agriculture are water availability and soil nutrient level. In semi-arid regions, improving soil nutrient level generally requires increased water availability at critical times of crop production, as well as higher nutrient levels. Water retention or conservation devices tend to be extremely labour intensive. Hence, they have been adopted first in those regions with land degradation and high population pressures where labour has the fewest alternatives. In regions with lower population densities and better resources, other technologies to increase water retention are expected to be adopted as the available crop area for expansion decreases and the value of agricultural products increases.

POTENTIAL TECHNOLOGIES AND CONSTRAINTS IN THE SUDANIAN REGION

There are many other high-yielding water-retention/soil-fertility techniques besides the dykes/organic-fertilizer combination, including the combination of tied ridges and inorganic fertilizer. Tied ridging is a water retention device constructed by creating perpendicular ridges, leaving a depression in the middle where water collects rather than running off[2]. As the available land is reduced with higher population pressure, model results predict an increasing area shift into the more intensive new technologies of tied ridges and fertilization. These combined technologies would be adopted by farmers, according to the model, and they provide moderate income increases even where there is severe degradation. Higher population pressures leading to decreasing land availability will induce more rapid shifts to the new technologies proposed (Ramaswamy and Sanders, 1992, p.368).

Another critical factor affecting technology introduction is the profitability of agriculture. As output and input prices are changed with improved transport and new policies, model results indicate that farmers shift to more intensive production practices, extending the area in tied ridges and increasing fertilization (Ramaswamy and Sanders, 1992, p.371). In the past, many African parastatal marketing agencies were not as concerned with the profitability of agriculture as with keeping food prices low and taxing agriculture to pay for public investments and services in urban areas (Bates, 1981, pp.30–44; World Bank, 1986, pp.61–73). Increased profitability of agriculture does result in the more rapid adoption of more intensive or sophisticated technologies.

The model results are confirmed by numerous field observations in the Sudanian region. First, as reported earlier, the dirt and stone dykes, combined with organic fertilizers, are being rapidly introduced on the Central Plateau of Burkina Faso, as is ridging on the contour with animal traction cultivators in Mali. Moreover, field studies in Burkina Faso during the 1980s indicated farmer adoption of several other intensive techniques, including the growth of a cash market for manure in Fulani regions, some utilization of inorganic fertilizer on sorghum, and increased out of season fruit and vegetable production with supplementary irrigation using organic fertilizer and watering by hand (Vierich and Stoop, 1990). Moreover, in the early 1990s, farmers introducing new maize cultivars with fertilizer were also reported as using tied ridges on the Central Plateau (Berry, Personal Communication, 1993). The areas in tied ridges have been expanding slowly, as this is an extremely labour intensive practice that has to be performed at one of the two peak labour demand periods. Expanding the areas in these intensive technologies in the Sudanian zone of Burkina Faso may require not only increased water availability and higher soil fertility but also an animal traction ridger to overcome the seasonal labour constraint.

The model results for potential technology introduction are consistent with our theory of technology development. The difficulty of simultaneously introducing three new inputs (a water retention technique, fertilizer, and a new animal traction implement) may explain previous failures in technology introduction (Byerlee and Hesse de Polanco, 1986). Now, with increasing pressure on the land, and African governments being encouraged by funding agencies to create a more profitable environment for agriculture, several of these intensive or yield increasing technologies are being adopted. This process needs to be adapted to different soils, labour availabilities, and economic environments (Sanders *et al.*, 1990; Shapiro *et al.*, 1993).

ACCELERATING THE INTRODUCTION OF INORGANIC FERTILIZER

In the agro-ecological zones discussed in the last two sections, a key technology component was inorganic fertilizer. Numerous alternatives to inorganic fertilizer have been researched. Most would substitute locally produced materials, by-products, or sophisticated production techniques such as inoculation. Many are claimed to be lower cost or lower risk. Unfortunately, in evaluating these alternatives in field trials in the Sahel, inorganic fertilizer was still the only viable alternative for increasing yields (Nagy *et al.*, 1988; for a brief policy article reviewing those alternatives to inorganic fertilization see Deuson and Sanders, 1990, p.197). There is a notable exception. Structural reform programs eliminated the subsidies on chemical inputs in the late 1980s in many countries. Moreover, the 50 percent devaluation of the currency (CFA) of the French Economic Community in January 1994 further reduced the relative prices of organic to inorganic fertilizers. Where farmers have animal stocks or can build them up, as in southern Mali, there have been increases in the manure production technology (covered compost heaps, cutting of millet and sorghum straw for the corrals), thus improving the quality and increasing the quantity of organic fertilizers from animals, household wastes, and crop residues. Again, these are extremely labour intensive processes. The supply is limited by the size of the animal herds and the transformation technologies available, so there are limits to the substitution potential between organic and inorganic fertilizers (Sanders, 1994, Ch. 4).

Substitutes for inorganic fertilizer in semi-arid regions have been evaluated by researchers for at least a decade. Further research to find low cost complementary activities to inorganic fertilizer and thereby reduce the costs to farmers should not affect the present development strategy. Inorganic fertilizer is a known technology backed by a substantial body of knowledge. It needs to be combined with increased water availability in the Sudanian region. Even higher returns are possible with the further addition of improved cereal cultivars for the Sudanian and Sahelo-Sudanian zones[3].

In the past, one principal constraint to fertilizer use was physical shortages. Government policy makers have typically put a low priority on fertilizer in their rationing of foreign exchange for imports. With the low priority given to fertilizer imports by governments, farmers often had to depend upon concessional imports from donors and upon irregular distribution systems. As sub-Saharan African countries adjust their overvalued exchange rates and remove import rationing by licensing and quotas, it will be easier for private or public distribution agencies to import fertilizer[4]. Achieving timely, low cost delivery of fertilizer to farmers needs to be an important public concern. With the generally poor state of transport infrastructure in most of sub-Saharan Africa, substantial public investments are required to assure the availability of fertilizers at the appropriate times and to facilitate the marketing of increased cereal yields.

CONCLUSIONS

Semi-arid sub-Saharan Africa has often been identified as a land-surplus region with seasonal labour as the limiting constraint. This paper challenges this view and argues that in the semi-arid regions, the dual problems of low soil fertility and lack of water availability at critical times of crop development are the factors leading to poor yields. Once the soil fertility and water management conditions are improved, there will be a much larger impact from the introduction of a new cultivar. The failure to identify these principal constraints has had important implications for both research and development policies.

Governments need to put a higher priority on fertilizer imports especially if they have not yet completely eliminated the overvaluation of their currencies. For some time, researchers and others have been claiming that a local input use, such as rock phosphate, a grain/legume rotation, crop residues, or the development of a low soil-fertility-tolerant cultivar would enable African governments to save foreign-exchange and the African farmers to avoid input purchases. Soil fertility improvement is a critical requirement for crop yield increases in this region and the gains from inorganic fertilizer use are well documented. Future research can reduce the long-run requirements for inorganic fertilizers by finding more efficient utilization methods. Nevertheless, African farmers need to take advantage now of the yield increases possible with this input. More public and private investments supporting the fertilizer and seed industries are also expected to accelerate the development of those agricultural systems.

NOTES

1 These dykes are constructed on the contour at fairly wide intervals of 10 to 30 metres, depending on the slope. The dykes accumulate soil from higher up on the toposequence for one or two metres behind them. This soil accumulation is often accompanied by the application of organic fertilizer (Wright, 1985, p.56). Higher value crops are planted here. These combined techniques respond to both of the key constraints; water availability and soil nutrient level.

2 A similar very labour intensive technique of digging small holes in the field ('zia') and planting around them has also been adopted in the degraded Sudanian regions of Burkina where farmers have utilized the rock and stone dykes. Again the labour input is undertaken outside the crop season.

3 Developing new cultivars for moderate input levels should be a higher return activity than attempting to develop genetic tolerances to drought and low soil fertility at low or zero input levels under harsh conditions. Increasing farm level yields and incomes without higher levels of input use may be impossible. The riskiness of fertilization alone is considerably reduced with increased water availability.

[4] There is a short run problem of the increasing price of inorganic fertilizer resulting from the elimination of fertilizer subsidies and from devaluation. However, devaluation also increases the price of imported food products relative to domestically produced food crops. This will increase the demand for domestic food crops increasing their prices. The relevant fertilizer price is then the cost of fertilizer relative to the domestically produced food price.

REFERENCES

Bates, R.H., 1981, *Markets and States in Tropical Africa: The Political Basis of Agricultural Policies*, University of California Press, Berkeley, California.

Byerlee, D. and Hesse de Polanco, E., 1986, 'Farmers' Stepwise Adoption of Technological Packages: Evidence From the Mexican Altiplano', *American Journal of Agricultural Economics*, Vol. 68, No. 3, pp.519–28.

Carr, S.J., 1989, *Technology for Small-Scale Farmers in Sub-Saharan Africa: Experience With Food Crop Production in Five Major Ecological Zones*, World Bank Technical Paper No. 109, Washington, D.C.

Coulibaly, O.N., 1987, 'Factors Affecting Adoption of Agricultural Technologies by Small Farmers in Sub-Saharan Africa: The Case of New Varieties of Cowpeas Around the Agricultural Research Station of Cinzana, Mali', Unpublished Master's thesis, Deptartment of Agricultural Economics, Michigan State University, pp.124.

Deuson, R.R. and Sanders, J.H., 1990, 'Cereal Technology Development in the Sahel' (Viewpoint), *Land Use Policy*, Vol. 7, No. 3, pp.195–197.

Glantz, M.H., 1987, 'Drought and Economic Development in Sub-Saharan Africa', in Glantz, M.H. (ed.), *Drought and Hunger in Africa: Denying Famine a Future*, Press Syndicate of the University of Cambridge, Cambridge, England, pp.37–58.

Matlon, P.J., 1987, 'The West African Semi-Arid Tropics', in Mellor, J.W. Delgado, C.L. and Blackie, M.J. (eds.), *Accelerating Food Production in Sub-Saharan Africa*, Johns Hopkins University Press, Baltimore, Maryland, pp.150–177.

Matlon, P.J., 1990, 'Improving Productivity in Sorghum and Pearl Millet in Semi-Arid Africa', *Food Research Institute Studies*, Vol. 22, No. 1, pp.1–44.

Mokwuyne, A. Uzo and Hammond, L.L., 1992, 'Myths and Science of Fertilizer Use in the Tropics', in Lal, R. and Sanchez, P.A. (eds.), *Myths and Science of Soils in the Tropics*, SSSA Special Publication No. 29, Soil Science of America, Inc., and American Society of Agronomy, Inc., Madison, Wisconsin, pp.121–34.

Nagy, J.G., Sanders, J.H. and Ohm, H.W., 1988, 'Cereal Technology Interventions for the West African Semi-Arid Tropics', *Agricultural Economics*, Vol. 2, pp.197–208.

Ramaswamy, S. and Sanders, J.H., 1992, 'Population Pressure, Land Degradation, and Sustainable Agricultural Technologies in the Sahel', *Agricultural Systems*, Vol. 40, No. 4, pp.361–378.

Reij, C., P. Mulder and L. Begeman, 1988, *Water Harvesting for Plant Production*, World Bank Technical Paper No. 9, Washington, D.C.

Sanders, J.H., 1995, 'Success Stories: New Crop and Input Technologies in the Sudano-Guinean Zone of Burkina Faso and Mali', Chapter 4 in Sanders, J.H., Ramaswamy, S. and Shapiro, B.I., *The Economics of Agricultural Technology in Semi-Arid Sub-Saharan Africa*, Johns Hopkins University Press, Baltimore, Maryland.

Sanders, J.H. and Ramaswamy, S., 1995, 'Economic and Agricultural Stagnation in Sub-Saharan Africa', Chapter 2 in Sanders, J.H., Ramaswamy, S. and Shapiro, B.I. *The Economics of Agricultural Technology in Semi-Arid Sub-Saharan Africa*, Johns Hopkins University Press, Baltimore, Maryland.

Sanders, J.H. and Shapiro, B.I., 1995, 'A Theory of Agricultural Technology Development for the Savanna Regions of Sub-Saharan Africa', Chapter 3 in Sanders, J.H., Ramaswamy, S. and Shapiro, B.I., *The Economics of Agricultural Technology in Semi-Arid Sub-Saharan Africa*, Johns Hopkins University Press, Baltimore, Maryland.

Sanders, J.H., Nagy, J.G. and Ramaswamy, S., 1990, 'Developing New Agricultural Technologies for the Sahelian Countries: The Burkina Faso Case', *Economic Development and Cultural Change*, Vol. 39, No. 1, pp.1–22.

Shapiro, B.I., Sanders, J.H., Reddy, K.C. and Baker, T.G., 1993, 'Evaluating and Adapting New Technologies in a High-Risk Agricultural System — Niger', *Agricultural Systems*, Vol. 42, pp.153–71.

Southgate, D., Sanders, J.H. and Ehui, S., 1990, 'Resource Degradation in Africa and Latin America: Population Pressure, Policies, and Property Arrangements', *American Journal of Agricultural Economics*, Vol. 72, No. 5, pp.1259–63.

Vierich, H.I.D. and Stoop, W.A., 1990, 'Changes in West African Savannah Agriculture in Response to Growing Population and Continuing Low Rainfall', *Agriculture, Ecosystems, and Environment*, Vol. 31, pp.115–32.

World Bank, 1986, *World Development Report 1986*, Washington, D.C.

World Bank, 1989, *Sub-Saharan Africa: From Crisis to Sustainable Growth*, Washington, D.C.

Wright, P., 1985. 'Water and Soil Conservation by Farmers', in Ohm, H.W. and Nagy, J.G. (eds.), *Appropriate Technologies for Farmers in Semi-Arid West Africa*, Purdue University, Department of International Programs, West Lafayette, Indiana.

DISCUSSION OPENING — Douglas Graham *(The Ohio State University, USA)*

My comments will focus on three areas; the strong recommendation for more focussed use of fertilizers, the suggestion that an induced innovation model is operating here and the question as to whether the study areas fall into the high potential or low potential area discussed earlier in the conferences for Africa by Otsuka and Delgado.

In my judgement the authors make a good case for qualifying the land surplus labour scarcity hypothesis with one that emphasizes the constraints of low soil fertility and lack of available water. They also argue that the failure to identify these constraints correctly has led to inappropriate research and development policies. I wish they would be more explicit and elaborate further on what these inappropriate policies were and how their current recommendations could correct this bias.

The authors also argue that governments should place a higher priority on fertilizer imports. I had always thought that, in the 1970s and early 1980s, governments in Africa had in fact given high priority to fertilizer imports and use through usually high subsidies to encourage fertilizer use. Of course, in the wake of structural adjustment policies, these subsidies are being removed and with higher real exchange rates emerging from these macro reforms, it is becoming expensive to use fertilizers across many crop lines in Africa.

In light of this it is not clear how the authors expect to overcome this high cost hurdle in recommending that governments support increased use of fertilizers in combination with their new water retention technology.

An additional issue is the authors' relative pessimism for the substitution of chemical fertilizers by organic manures and other local indigenous inputs or practices. In light of what I perceive to be a 'high cost' fertilizer solution, I am not sure how warranted this pessimism is for this region. Finally, there is mention at the end of the need for more public and private investment in fertilizer and seed industries. How do the authors see the logical division of labour here? Are private traders currently substituting for previous parastatal fertilizer distribution in these areas? If not, why not? What does this imply for the appropriate roles for each to achieve a cost effective fertilizer distribution network?

Secondly, what is the Induced Innovation path of technological change in the semi-arid region of SSA? The authors really do not address or explain this in the paper perhaps because of space limitations. Nevertheless, the paper does proprose a theory of technological development for semi-arid regions. Perhaps they could elaborate on this further. For example, in the classic induced innovation reasoning farmers suffering from an input constraint limiting their profits and growth, work through their farmer organizations to procure relevant government authorities and public research establishments to solve their problem by directing research to break, or at least reduce, the costs of this constraint. In the Hayami–Ruttan world this decentralized, bottom up path of including technological change in frequently cited with examples from Japan, the USA and European countries.

I don't see this political economy model of induced innovations in agricultural technology working out the same way in semi-arid west Africa. Farmers do not have the organizational 'clout' to pressure political authorities, and national research systems usually are weak or do not exist. No doubt regional or international centres or scientists come in to play a role here. This suggests a top down, not a bottom-up path of induced changed in agricultural technology. In this framework it is not clear what the relative roles of farmers, national governments, national and international research centres are and how they play out their respective roles to shape the path and direction of technical change in agriculture in this more rudimentary political and socio-economic setting. One thing is clear. It is not very likely to follow the decentalized institutional path of action and reaction that Hayami and Ruttan laid out for developed countries. At first glance it would appear that farmers would play less of a role and international research organizations more of a rule in shaping the priorities and policy initiatives.This this may be a necessary and logical fall back strategy given the level of socio-economic development in semi-arid African countries. It would be helpful if the authors would share their thoughts with us on this issue.

Finally, it would be instructive to get the authors' view on where they see the semi-arid regions of their study fitting into the high potential — low potential dichotomy laid out by Otsuka and Delgado in this conference. If it is a high potential area for yields, then the investment called for in this paper would make sense given the alleged high pay-off from these invested resources. On the other hand, if it is a low yield area, their recommendations could be questioned (if one accepts the Otsuka–Delgado position).

EDUARDO SEGARRA[*]

Depletion of a Ground Water Source: The Role of Irrigation Technology Adoption

Abstract: Under irrigated conditions agricultural producers are expected to adjust their crop patterns, irrigation systems, and production practices as ground water tables decline and irrigation costs increase. This study provides insight into the efficient path of irrigation technology adoption and the implications associated with this process. It is shown that: (a) the efficient crop pattern is related to the ground water supply condition; (b) declines in the proportion of high water requirement crops produced are rapid with high pumping lift and thin saturated thickness; and (c) declines in saturated thickness appear to have a greater impact on crop pattern and irrigated acreage than do increases in pumping lift. Furthermore, it is shown that the adoption rate of advanced irrigation systems is expected to be higher the more abundant is the ground water source.

INTRODUCTION

Irrigation has played an important role in the development and growth of agriculture in the USA. Irrigated farms contribute proportionally more to crop production than do dryland farms. For instance, in 1982, irrigated farms comprised only 12 percent of all farms, yet they produced nearly one-third of the total value of agricultural products (Moore, Crosswhite and Hostetler, 1987). Irrigation is particularly important to the agricultural economy in the semi-arid area of the High Plains: a large land resource area within the Great Plains region of the USA. This region is one of the most heavily irrigated areas in the USA, comprising some 20 percent of the national irrigated acreage. In the High Plains region, irrigation is essential in agricultural production because rainfall is either unreliable or insufficient. The main water source of irrigation in the High Plains region is the Ogallala aquifer, one of the most extensive and important interstate aquifers in the USA.

In the High Plains region, rapid expansion of irrigation practices using ground water began after World War II. In 1982, about 17 million acres of cropland were under irrigation and the total annual water withdrawal was 21 million acre feet (Moore *et al.*, 1987). Because recharge is insignificant compared to withdrawals, the continued overdraft has resulted in declines of ground water tables from 50 feet to 200 feet in some areas (High Plains Associates, 1982). The per unit energy cost of ground water pumping per foot of lift has increased dramatically since the early 1970s. Sloggett (1985) documented increases in energy costs of 182 percent for electricity to 700 percent for natural gas between 1974 and 1983. The increased pumping lift and decreased well yields, coupled with rising energy costs, have resulted in significant increases in the production cost of irrigated crops.

Given a ground water stock, the rate at which the ground water supply diminishes is determined by the amount of withdrawal, the technology of exploitation, and the input–output price relations. Due to the continued overdraft of ground water in the Texas High Plains region, in which about 30 percent of pre-development storage, on the average, has

* Texas Tech University, USA.

been depleted, this region has become the most critical ground water depletion area in the Ogallala formation (Gutentag *et al.*, 1984).

The objective of this study is to derive dynamically optimal rates of ground water use in agriculture which maximize the net present value of returns to the agricultural producer's ground water stock, land, capital, management, risk and overheads under alternative scenarios. Lubbock County was used as a representative area within the Texas High Plains. In particular, this study includes the determination of dynamically efficient crop patterns, irrigation technologies, and ground water use through time.

METHODS AND PROCEDURES

A dynamic framework whose components included a bio-simulation model of crop growth and a firm-level dynamic programming (DP) model were used to derive optimal decision rules of ground water use over time under alternative scenarios. The bio-simulation crop growth model used was the Erosion/Productivity Impact Calculator (EPIC) developed by Williams, Jones and Dyke (1984). This model was used to simulate data on crop yield–water responses under alternative combinations of cropping practices and irrigation technologies. The crop yield–water data simulated were used to estimate yield–water production functions using regression analysis and were used in the dynamic optimization models (Feng, 1992). The major underlying assumption of the DP models was that irrigators consider the total returns derived from irrigation over a long planning horizon. A 50-year planning horizon was used. These models are capable of determining optimal ground water use, cropping pattern, cropping practice, irrigation technology, and marginal user costs while adjusting ground water availability and extraction cost.

The crops considered in this study were cotton, grain sorghum and corn. These three crops encompass 91 percent of the total irrigated area and 47 percent of the non-irrigated area in Lubbock County. Numerous tillage practices and irrigation technologies exist, but the ones included in the optimization models were those which are widely used or show some acceptance in the study's region. Tillage practices considered in this study included conventional and conservation tillage. Conventional tillage was applied to all crop enterprises, while conservation tillage was only applied to cotton production. The conservation tillage method considered was a terminated wheat and cotton (TWH–CO) rotation. Six irrigation technologies were considered in this study. These included conventional furrow (CF), improved furrow (IF), sprinkler-high pressure (SH), sprinkler-drop (SD), low energy precision application (LEPA), and dryland farming. The optimization models in this study were formulated on a per acre basis with percentages being used to represent the proportion of a crop under a given tillage practice and irrigation technology.

The operating cost data used for the crops were the average projected costs for the 1981–1990 period, taken from the *Texas Crop Enterprise Budgets — Texas South Plains District* (Texas Agricultural Extension Services). These budgets included the basic operating costs for dryland and irrigated production, which include fertilizer, seed, herbicide, insecticide, machinery, harvesting costs, and irrigation well costs. The commodity prices used were the ten-year average prices received by farmers for the 1981–90 period as reported in the *Texas Agricultural Statistics* (Texas Department of Agriculture).

The per unit cost of pumping water is a function of pumping lift and well yield. Well yield decreases as the saturated thickness of the aquifer decreases. Therefore, the per unit cost of pumping water is a function of pumping lift and saturated thickness. Also, to evaluate the effect of pumping ground water on the water stock recursive equations, which consider the intertemporal adjustment of water availability, are necessary. All the assumptions and relationships used in deriving the hydrologic equations which describe the dynamics of the per unit cost of pumping water and the aquifer are described in Feng (1992).

Three additional constraints were used in the optimization models. The first constraint was a constraint on operating capital. Operating capital was assumed to be available from two sources. The first source was a fixed value of $250 per acre in each period of operation. The second source was the portion of the previous year's income which exceeds the average per acre return to land, management, and overhead estimated at $40 (Texas Agricultural Extension Service). The second constraint was land availability. The third constraint was a pumping capacity constraint at each time period.

SPECIFICATION OF THE DYNAMIC OPTIMIZATION MODEL

The objective function used in the models was that of maximizing the net present value of returns to land, management, ground water stock, risk, and investment in irrigation systems. Net returns are calculated as gross returns minus total costs. The total costs consist of variable costs and fixed costs. The variable costs are the costs directly associated with the level of the control variables, these are the costs of pumping ground water, investment and maintenance costs associated with the cropping practices, and investment and maintenance costs of the various irrigation systems. Given this information, a net return function in time t can be constructed as:

$$(1)\quad NR_t = \Sigma_i \Sigma_j \Sigma_k \Theta_{ijkt} \left\{ P_i Y_{ijkt} \left[WA_{ijkt} \left(WP_{ijkt} \right) \right] - C_{ijk} \left(WP_{ijkt}, X_t, ST_t \right) \right\}$$

where i represents the crops grown; j represents the cropping practices used; k represents the irrigation technologies used; Θ_{ijkt} is the percentage of crop i produced with cropping practice j and irrigated by irrigation technology k in time t; P_i is the price of crop i; WA_{ijkt} and WP_{ijkt} are per acre irrigation water available to the crop and ground water pumped, respectively, for crop i using jth cropping practice and kth irrigation technology at time t; $Y_{ijkt}[.]$ is the per acre yield production function of crop i using the jth cropping practice and the kth irrigation technology at time t; C_{ijk} is the total cost per acre associated with the production of the ith crop using the jth cropping practice and the kth irrigation technology; X_t is the pumping lift at time t; and ST_t is the saturated thickness of the ground water stock at time t.

The objective function to be optimized for the 50-year planning horizon is:

$$(2)\quad \text{Max } NPRV = \Sigma_{t=1}^{50} NR_t (1+r)^{-t}$$

where $NPRV$ is the net present value of returns, and r is the discount rate. The control variables in this optimization problem are WP_{ijkt} and Θ_{ijkt}. Substituting Equation (1) into Equation (2) and adding all the relevant constraints, the empirical dynamic programming model is:

$$(3)\quad \text{Max } NPRV = \Sigma_i \Sigma_j \Sigma_k \Sigma_t \Theta_{ijkt} \left\{ P_i Y_{ijkt} \left[WA_{ijkt} \left(WP_{ijkt} \right) \right] - C_{ijk} \left(WP_{ijkt}, X_t, ST_t \right) \right\} (1+r)^{-t}$$

subject to:

$$(4)\quad ST_{t+1} = ST_t - \left[(1-a) \left(\Sigma_i \Sigma_j \Sigma_k \Theta_{ijkt} * WP_{ijkt} \right) - R \right] K / As$$

$$(5)\quad X_{t+1} = X_t + \left[(1-a) \left(\Sigma_i \Sigma_j \Sigma_k \Theta_{ijkt} * WP_{ijkt} \right) - R \right] K / As$$

$$(6)\quad \Sigma_i \Sigma_j \Sigma_k WP_{ijkt} \leq 28.28 * (ST_t / 210)^2 \text{ for all } t$$

$$(7)\quad \Sigma_i \Sigma_j \Sigma_k \Theta_{ijkt} \leq 1 \text{ for all } t$$

$$(8)\quad \Sigma_i \Sigma_j \Sigma_k C_{ijkt} \leq 250 + \left(NR_{t-1} - 40 \right) \text{ for all } t$$

$$(9)\quad \Sigma_i \Sigma_j \Sigma_k C_{ijkt} = FC_{ijk} + HC_{ijkt} + PC_t + PEC_{ijkt}$$

$$(10)\quad PEC_{ijkt} = IC_{ijk} 1 / \left[125 - 1.5 \left(ST_t - S_o \right) \right]$$

$$(11)\quad PC_t = 0.0014539 * \left(X_t + (3.31 * PSI) * P \right) / (PE)$$

$$(12)\quad X_{t=1} = X_1$$

$$(13)\quad ST_{t=1} = ST_1$$

$$(14)\quad \Theta_{ijkt} \geq 0, WP_{ijkt} \geq 0$$

The two Equations of motion, Equations (4) and (5), update the state variables, saturated thickness (ST_t) and pumping lift (X_t). Equations (6), (7), and (8) are the water pumping capacity, land availability, and capital constraints, respectively. Equation (9) is the cost function, where FC_{ijkt} is the fixed cost component (basic operation costs), HC_{ijkt} is the harvest cost, IC_{ijk} is the irrigation system and crop practice investment costs, PC_t and PEC_{ijkt} are the pumping cost without the impact of saturated thickness and pumping cost induced by the change in saturated thickness. Equations (10) and (11) are the definitions of PEC_{ijkt} and PC_t. Equations (12) and (13) are the initial conditions of the aquifer, and (14) ensures that the values of the decision variables are non-negative.

The dynamically efficient solution to this problem is the one which maximizes the net present value of returns by selecting the rates of ground water pumped for each crop and the combination of crops, cropping practices and irrigation technologies used at each point in time, subject to the constraints. This model was also solved under the assumption of no adoption of new irrigation technologies. This was done by adding two more constraints to the model in equation (3) to (14). These constraints were:

(15) $\Sigma_i \Sigma_j \Theta_{ijkt} \leq D_k \;\; K = 1,2,...,Z$ for $t = 1,2...,50$; and

(16) $\Sigma_i \Sigma_k \Theta_{ijkt} \leq H_j \;\; j = 1,2,...,n$ for $t = 1,2...,50$

where D_k is the observed percentage of acres of irrigated cropland using the kth irrigation technology; and H_j is the observed percentage of acres of irrigated cropland using the jth cropping practice. Both D_k and H_j do not change over time. The difference between the allocation with and without these constraints represents the impact due to irrigation technology adoption.

RESULTS

The results of the DP models include the optimal crop pattern, irrigation technology adoption, and quantity of ground water pumped under the alternative scenarios which include four different ground water supply conditions, and with and without technological change. These scenarios are defined in Table 1. The 'Basic model' is the DP model under the ground water supply condition of 150 feet pumping lift and 130 feet saturated thickness, using average prices, and with irrigation technology adoption with a 2 percent discount rate. The other four scenarios of the model are similar to the Basic model except for the changes indicated in Table 1.

Table 1 *Definitions of the Model Scenarios*

Scenarios	Pumping lift (feet)	Saturated thickness (feet)	Irrigation technology (feet)
Basic	150	130	flexible
BasicP1	130	130	flexible
BasicP2	197	130	flexible
BasicS	150	50	flexible
BasicFT	150	130	fixed

Dynamic Optimal Crop Patterns

The solution of the Basic model is presented in Figure 1. The starting values (the values at time period 1) of the proportion of land by crop represent the current real crop pattern in Lubbock County. As shown in Figure 1, the current crop pattern is far from optimal under the specified ground water supply, capital constraint and price conditions. This is because the crop pattern quickly changes to a different crop combination once water use is optimized. Irrigated cotton increases from 40 percent to 74 percent, dryland cotton decreases from 36 percent to zero, irrigated sorghum drops from 6 percent to zero, and dryland sorghum increases from 13 percent to 23 percent, and irrigated corn decreases from 4.5 percent to zero over the first 40 time periods. The optimal crop pattern, as established in the solution, is kept approximately constant over 35 production periods. After the 35th time period, irrigated cotton declines and dryland cotton increases.

established in the solution, is kept approximately constant over 35 production periods. After the 35th time period, irrigated cotton declines and dryland cotton increases.

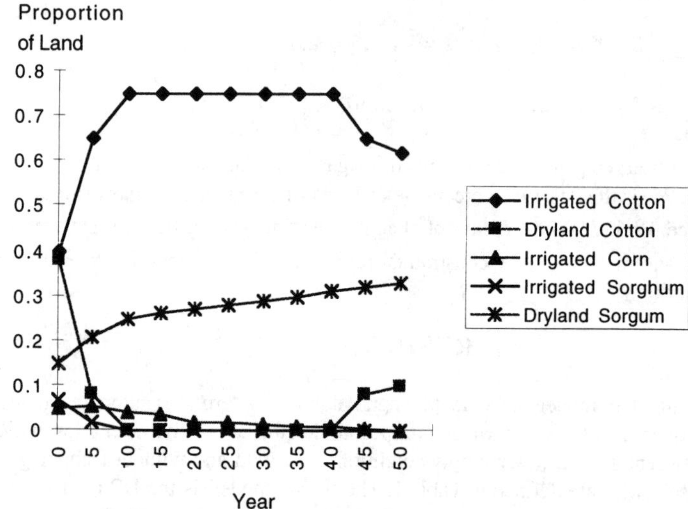

Figure 1 *Optimal Crop Pattern, Basic Model*

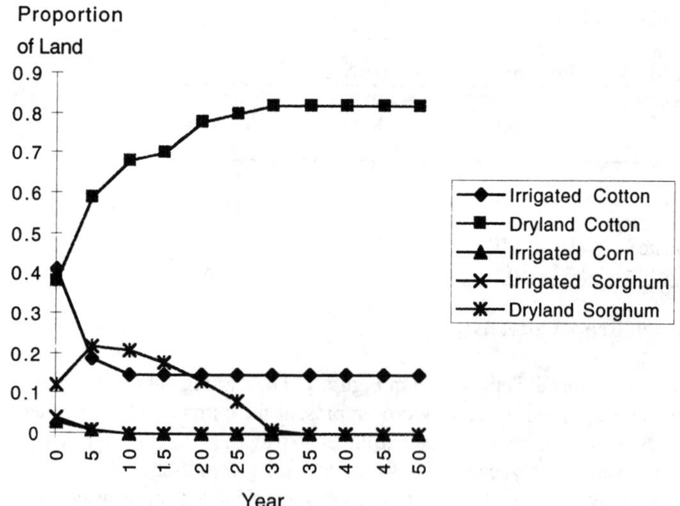

Figure 2 *Optimal Crop Pattern, BasicS Model*

This result suggests that the ground water resource is not utilized efficiently, given the Basic model assumptions. To obtain higher present value of returns from the ground water stock, irrigated production should be further developed. Also, ground water scarcity is not likely to be the factor limiting irrigated production in the next 40 years. This result shows that irrigated cotton is superior to irrigated sorghum and corn. Therefore most of the water is allocated to cotton, less to corn, and none to sorghum. The dynamic efficient crop pattern under the specified condition is approximately three-quarters of irrigated cotton and one-quarter of dryland sorghum.

The solution of the BasicP1 and BasicP2 models in which pumping lift is varied indicated similarities in the optimal crop pattern to that of the Basic model. These models' results showed a trend indicating that the greater the pumping lift, the smaller the irrigated crop percentage. The increased pumping cost due to greater pumping lift may affect irrigated acreage in two ways: (a) increased variable cost of irrigation results in greater production cost, which causes operational capital to become constrained, thus, less cropland can be irrigated; or (b) the increased pumping cost causes irrigated crop production to be less profitable, thus, less money is available for following periods operation and investment on irrigation systems which in turn causes less technological adoption and less percentage of irrigated acreage.

The results of the BasicS model which represents the scenario with poor ground water storage indicated a significantly different crop pattern to those of the previous models, Figure 2. That is, the proportion of irrigated acreage drops, and dryland cotton increases sharply. Thus, these results indicate that the optimal crop pattern is closely related to ground water pumping lift and saturated thickness. The reduction in the percentage of high water requirement crops, such as corn, would be faster in areas with higher pumping lift than in the areas with lower pumping lift, and the total irrigated percentage of cropland is reduced as the pumping lift increases. Declines in saturated thickness appeared to have a greater impact on irrigated production than did increases in pumping lift. Also, the reduction on well yields, due to declines in saturated thickness, result in a reduction in the number of acres that a irrigation system can cover, which in turn causes a great increase in per acre irrigation cost.

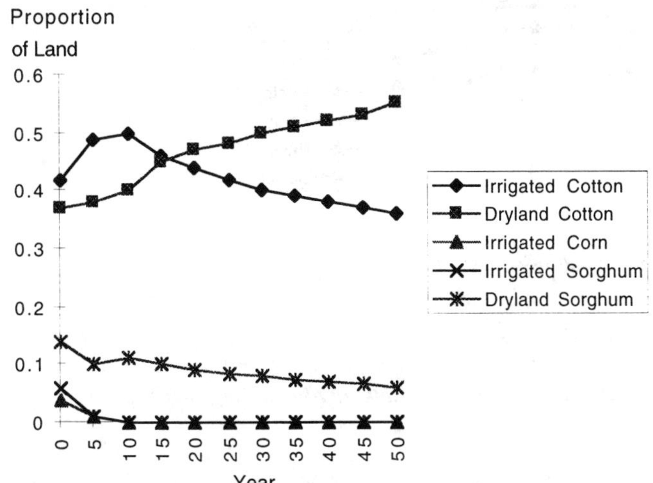

Figure 3 *Optimal Crop Pattern, BasicFT Model*

The results of the BasicFT model indicated that the current crop pattern in Lubbock County is close to the optimal, Figure 3. The differences in the cropping pattern between this model and the Basic model are due to the impact of the irrigation technology adoption assumption. The adoption of irrigation technologies with higher water application efficiency causes an increase in irrigated acreage and the production of crops with high water requirement (as shown in the Basic model). Therefore, the adoption of more efficient irrigation systems does not imply a long-term reduction in ground water use. If the increase in irrigated acreage were large enough to offset the decrease in per acre ground water usage, the net result of irrigation technology adoption would be to increase total water use and, thus, induce a faster depletion of the ground water stock.

Optimal Adoption of Irrigation Technology

The optimal paths of irrigation technology adoption are presented in this section. Among all the irrigation systems and tillage practices included, only three irrigation technologies and one tillage practice, the IF system, the low energy precision application (LEPA) system, dryland farming, and conventional tillage, appeared in the solutions of the DP models under all the scenarios. The LEPA system appeared to be the most efficient irrigation system for all the solutions of the models under all the scenarios. The general trend in the optimal irrigation system adoption under all the scenarios was that LEPA comprised more than 60 percent of cropland for most of the models, the IF system covered less than 5 percent of the cropland for most of the models, and dryland farming covered the remainder.

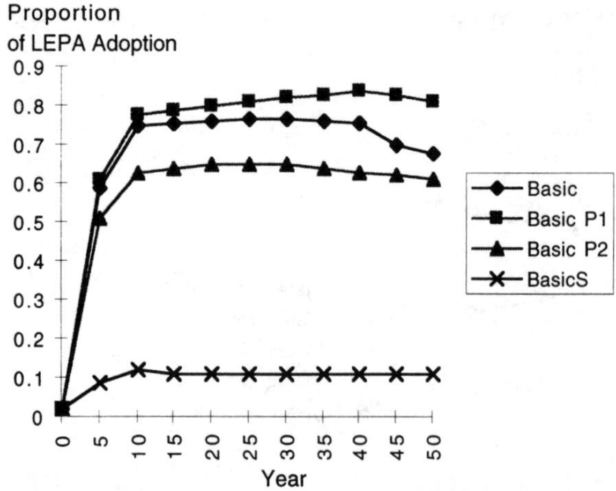

Figure 4 *Optimal LEPA System Adoption Rates at Alternative Water Supply Conditions*

The results of optimal LEPA system adoption for different ground water supply conditions, that is, the solutions for the models of Basic, BasicP1, BasicP2, and BasicS are presented in Figure 4. As shown in Figure 4, under the given cost and capital constraint current usage of LEPA in Lubbock County, 3.6 percent of total irrigated production, is far from optimal. To achieve higher returns to water, land, management, risk, and overhead, more LEPA should be adopted. Notice, however, that the optimal level of adoption of LEPA varies with the ground water supply condition. The optimal path of LEPA system adoption shows that the more abundant is the ground water storage, the higher the LEPA system adoption and the higher the proportion of irrigated production. The results also show that the proportion of irrigated acreage becomes closer to the proportion of LEPA system usage over time. This indicates that if operational capital is not binding, the LEPA system should be used in all irrigated acreage. With respect to the discount rate impact on irrigation technology adoption, it was found that LEPA system adoption is the same under the 2, 5, and 8 percent discount levels during the first 10 production periods. After the 10th production period, LEPA system adoption is lower under the 5 and 8 percent discount rates, than under the 2 percent discount rate, and there is not much difference in the adoption of the LEPA system under the 5 and the 8 percent discount rates.

Optimal Net Present Value of Returns

The per acre net present values of returns of the model under the five scenarios were: Basic, \$2713.70; BasicP1, \$3230.40; BasicP2, \$2250.40; BasicS, \$819.10; and BasicFT \$1775.80. As can be noticed, the net present value of returns is sensitive to the ground water supply condition. The highest net present value of returns among the different groundwater supply scenarios was \$3230.40 for the BasicP1 model. The lowest net present value was \$819.10 for the BasicS model. The reduction in the net present value of returns, as the scarcity on ground water increases, is contributed by both the increased ground water pumping cost, and the constraint imposed on irrigation technology adoption and irrigated acreage by the scarcity of ground water.

CONCLUSIONS AND POLICY IMPLICATIONS

Texas High Plains producers are expected to adjust their crop pattern, irrigation systems, and production practices as the ground water level declines and irrigation cost increases. This study provides insight into the efficient path of this adjustment process and implications associated with this process. It was found that the efficient crop pattern is related to the ground water supply condition. The declines in the proportion of high water requirement crops, such as corn, is fast with high pumping lift and thin saturated thickness. The declines in saturated thickness appear to have greater impact on crop pattern and irrigated acreage than do the increases in pumping lift. Thus, most of the ground water is allocated to irrigated cotton and less to non-irrigated corn and sorghum under all scenarios.

Irrigated acreage is not likely to decline within 20 to 30 years in the study region, if the adoption of irrigation technology follows the optimal path, except in areas underlying with thin saturated thickness (approaching 50 feet). The observed declines in irrigated acres in the Texas High Plains are mainly due to the utilization of low efficient irrigation systems, which combined with low crop prices result in low profitability. Declining ground water levels and depletion of the Ogallala aquifer are not the primary causes of the recent declines in irrigated acres, because these would increase if more efficient irrigation technology was used. Given that the total ground water withdrawals and total irrigated acres increase with the adoption of more efficient irrigation technologies, irrigation technology adoption could lead to substantial increases in the net present value of returns, but will not lead to ground water conservation. Public policies aimed at reducing total ground water withdrawals may not achieve their goal through increasing irrigation efficiency, since increases in profitability of irrigation bring about increases in irrigated acreage, and the increase in irrigated acreage will offset the reduction in per acre water use due to increased efficiency.

REFERENCES

Feng, Y., 1992, 'Optimal Intertemporal Allocation of Ground Water for Irrigation in the Texas High Plains', Unpublished dissertation, Department of Agricultural Economics, Texas Tech University, Lubbock, Texas, USA.

Gutentag, E. D., Heimes, F. J., Krothe, N. C., Lukey, R.R. and Weeks, J.B., 1984, *Geohydrology of the High Plains Aquifer in Parts of Colorado, Kansas, Nebraska, New Mexico, Oklahoma, South Dakota, Texas, and Wyoming*, US Geological Survey Professional paper 1400-B, Government Printing Office, Washington, D.C., USA.

High Plains Associates, 1982, *Six-State High Plain — Ogallala Aquifer Regional Resources Study*, Report to the US Department of Commerce and High Plains Study Council, Austin, Texas.

Moore, M. R., Crosswhite, W. M. and Hostetler, J. E., 1987, *Agricultural Water Use in the United States, 1950–1985*, US Geological Survey water-supply paper 2350, Government Printing Office, Washington, D.C., USA, pp.3–108.

Sloggett, J. E., 1985, *Energy and U.S. Agriculture-Irrigation Pumping, 1974–1983:* US Department of Agriculture, Economic Research Service, Agricultural Economic Report No. 545, Washington, D.C., USA.

Texas Agricultural Extension Service, 1981–1990, Texas Crop Enterprise Budgets — Texas South Plains District, Bulletin B–241.

Texas Department of Agriculture, 1981–1990, *Texas Agricultural Statistics*.

Williams, J. R., Jones, C. A. and Dyke, P.T., 1984, 'A Modelling Approach to Determining the Relationship Between Erosion and Soil Productivity', *Transactions of the American Society of Agricultural Engineers*, Vol. 27, No.1, pp.129–4.

DISCUSSION OPENING — Chamhuri Siwar *(University Kegangsaan, Malaysia)*

This highly technical paper is about adjustments in irrigation technology adoption that would maximize the net present value of returns under alternative scenarios given the ground water stock, land, capital, management and risk. Adjustments in optional crop patterns are made under four different ground water supply conditions, with and without technological change.

The result shows that producers respond to changing ground water level and increasing irrigation costs by adjusting their cropping pattern, irrigation systems and production practices.

The writer contends that the ground water supply conditions affect the efficient crop patterns but seems to contradict that contention with another statement that 'declining ground water levels...are not the primary causes of recent decline in irrigated acres'.

It seems that producers' response to prices (costs) may be the more dominant factor. Increasing pumping costs greatly affect irrigated acreage by eating into the profitability of investments on irrigation systems. The producer's objective to maximize net return alters his technology adoption and hence his cropping pattern, preferring the low energy precision application (LEPA) system under all scenarios. The net present value of returns is foremost affected by the increased ground water pumping cost, it seems, and is constrained by scarcity of ground water which affects irrigation technology adoption.

Two questions may be asked regarding the policy implications of the study. First, how would irrigation technology adoption adjust if ground water level reached its critical stage, where it may be no longer economical to pump water? What may be the impact on cropping patterns? Second, how will the social benefit–cost of ground water conservation compare with the social benefit–cost of increasing irrigated acreage?

MONIKA HARTMANN*

The Impact of EC Nitrogen Taxes on Agricultural Competitiveness and Welfare: Simulations with the World Trade Model TEPSIM

Abstract: In this paper the attempt is made to estimate the trade and welfare effects of nitrogen taxes in the European Community. The world trade simulation model TEPSIM was developed for this purpose. TEPSIM differs from conventional agricultural trade models in that it is not limited to agricultural output markets but explicitly considers 12 agricultural inputs. Thus, the model is not only suitable for the simulation of environmental policies in agriculture but also gives valuable insights into the intensification and specialization effects of current agricultural policy reforms. The results of the study reveal that the implementation of nitrogen taxes in the EC would lead to a loss in comparative advantage for agriculture in Europe. At the same time this policy would induce conventional welfare gains in the EC if the tax level did not exceed 44 percent. However, at that tax level the relative change in mineral nitrogen demand would be very low (13.5 percent). Higher nitrogen taxes, on the other hand, would induce net welfare losses in the Community. While these losses would increase exponentially with the tax rate, the decline in nitrogen use is not even linear. Thus, the implementation of extreme taxes would have high economic costs without inducing profound improvements in the ecological area.

INTRODUCTION

There is a growing concern in the European Community (EC) and in many other industrialized countries about the ecological consequences of current production and consumption structures. In the past the blame for environmental deterioration was laid primarily at the door of the industrial sector. However, as more is learned about the environmental impact of modern farming practices, agricultural producers also find themselves sitting in the dock. Farmers are accused of polluting ground and surface water with minerals, such as nitrogen and phosphorus and pesticides. Soil erosion and salinization are increasing problems, especially in Southern Europe. Air pollution due to intensive animal husbandry, manure spreading and crop spraying is a growing nuisance. Farming practices are also blamed for the accelerating rate at which species are disappearing. An important reason that farming places this increasing stress on the environment arises from the intensification and specialization of agricultural production, particularly to the increasing use of chemical inputs such as nitrogen and pesticides. This new awareness has led to the demand for environmental regulations, such as input taxes. Coinciding with these claims is a concern over the potential effects of these policies on agricultural production, farm income and agricultural trade. Producers in the EC fear that they might lose their competitiveness in world agricultural markets, especially in the case of unilateral EC implementation of environmental regulations.

While there is a vast literature on the economic effects of an agricultural trade liberalization, there are only a few empirical studies analyzing the trade and welfare effects of taxes on agricultural inputs[1].

* J.W. Goethe-University, Germany.

Given this background the paper attempts to step into this breach. The Multi-Output Multi-Input World Simulation Model TEPSIM has been developed for this purpose. In the paper attention is confined to the analysis of taxes on nitrogen, as one of the environmentally most damaging chemical inputs. To examine the sensitivity of the production, trade and welfare effects to the level of nitrogen tax, four different simulations are compared.

MODEL DESCRIPTION

To determine the trade and welfare effects of taxes on agricultural inputs, a partial analytical framework is not sufficient. Rather, an approach is needed which is able to capture the various horizontal and vertical interdependencies between agricultural outputs and farm inputs. The policy simulation model TEPSIM (Trade and Environmental Policy Simulation Model) was created to analyze the national and international impact of EC nitrogen taxes.

Economic Structure of TEPSIM

The Trade and Environmental Policy Simulation Model is a three region world trade model, covering; the European Community (EC-12), the United States of America (US) and the Rest of the World (RW)[2]. The basic structure of TEPSIM is borrowed from the SWOPSIM (Static World Policy Simulation) modeling framework developed by Roningen and others (Roningen, Sullivan and Dixit, 1991) at the USDA. Like all SWOPSIM variants, TEPSIM is of comparative static nature. These models can be solved to determine changes from the base year due to endogenous shocks such as changes in demand, supply or policy. Given the non-spatial character of the model, transport costs and product heterogeneity are neglected in the analysis. TEPSIM is based on constant elasticity functional forms for agricultural output supplies and consumer demand. The elasticities are not estimated endogenously in the model, but were taken from the literature.

TEPSIM belongs to the group of synthetic models. To ensure that the model is economically plausible, the elasticities in the EC and US model were chosen to be consistent with profit maximizing behaviour of producers and utility maximizing behaviour of consumers (elasticities are discussed further below). Given data limitations, a similar procedure was not possible for the 'Rest of the World' sector of the model. An important distinction between TEPSIM and traditional agricultural trade models arises from the Multi-Input Multi-Output nature of TEPSIM. Traditional trade models are Multi-Output equilibrium models. One limitation of these models is that they consider the effects on agricultural product markets, exclusively. Prices and quantities of farm inputs are assumed constant in this framework. To analyze the effects of taxes on nitrogen or other chemical inputs on production, trade and welfare, an extension of the model is necessary. For that reason TEPSIM covers 2 agricultural input markets in the EC and US, as well as 15 farm products[3]. These are: nitrogen fertilizer; other mineral fertilizers; pesticides; the feeds, wheat, corn and other coarse grains; soyabeans and other oilseeds; hired labour, arable land, pasture land and other inputs[4].

Data

Most prices and quantities for agricultural products were taken from the 1989 database of the USDA (Sullivan, Roningen, Leetmaa and Gray, 1992). However, modifications to the consumer prices seemed necessary. Valuing all products considered in TEPSIM at the database prices would account for only about 50 percent of food expenditure in the EC and the US. Those commodities actually account for about 75 percent of food expenditure (Hertel, Peterson and Stout, 1993). Thus, the marketing margins in the EC and US model were adjusted, using the calculations of Dunham (1991) (see also Hertel, Peterson and Stout, 1993).

To complete the output matrix, additional data were required for the aggregate 'Other agricultural products'. These were calculated from value data for the year 1989, assuming a producer price of 100 (Kommission der Europäischen Gemeinschaften 1992; United States Department of Agriculture, 1991; Putman and Allshouse, 1992; Bundesministerium für Ernährung Landwirtschaft und Forsten, 1991). Given the lack of information with respect to the trade activity for the aggregate Other agricultural products, no trade activity was considered on this product market in the reference scenario[5]. Information about the demand for and the prices of the newly integrated inputs was collected from different sources (Kommission der Europäischen Gemeinschaften, 1992; United States Department of Agriculture, 1991 and 1992; Barse, 1990; Food and Agriculture Organisation of the United Nations (FAO), 1991a and 1990b; Price, Seely and Tucker, 1991).

ELASTICITIES

Of utmost importance in creating a policy simulation model is the construction of a consistent and economically plausible elasticity matrix for product supply/input demand as well as for product demand. In TEPSIM the information in the USDA database was used as a starting point (Sullivan, Roningen, Leetmaa and Gray, 1992). However, considerable modifications and extensions to the EC and US sectors of the model were necessary, since the USDA database does not include any input markets. Thus, additional information was collected from various other published and unpublished sources. While a wide range of values for the own price elasticities of nitrogen demand are presented in the literature (Burrel, 1989 and the references therein), few estimates of elasticities for other inputs have been published. Information about the relationship between the input demand and producer prices for agricultural products is scarce as is that for consumer prices for other agricultural inputs. Additionally, the estimates in the literature often refer to a different country and/or product aggregation (for example, Anker and Schmitz, 1987; Boyle and O'Neill, 1990; Glass and McKillop, 1989; Michalek, 1988; Dubberke and Schmitz, 1993; Denbaly and Vroomen, 1991; Antle, 1984; Fernandez-Cornejo, 1993; Rendleman, 1993; Ball, 1989).

Given the limited applicability of the data in the literature to the present model it is important to secure the consistency of the chosen elasticities with profit maximizing behaviour of producers and utility maximizing behaviour of consumers. For that reason symmetry and homogeneity conditions were imposed on the product supply/input demand elasticity matrix as well as on the product demand elasticity matrix (Gardiner, Roningen and Liu, 1989; Haley, 1988). In TEPSIM separability of the utility function with respect to food and other consumer goods is assumed[6].

In the model, the supply of chemical inputs, hired labour and the aggregate other inputs is assumed to be perfectly elastic[7]. This implies that input supply equals input demand at constant prices. The own price elasticity of land supply is set equal to 0.2. Changes in the demand for land are thus reflected in its rental value.

Of considerable importance in world trade models is the determination of the world market price transmission elasticities for all countries/regions considered in the model. Given the price fixing policy in the European Community, the price transmission elasticity was set equal to 0 for all products but soyabeans and other oilseeds. Because of the deficiency payment system on these markets, consumer prices of these products will change with world market price changes. For the aggregate of other agricultural outputs a world price transmission elasticity of 0.7 was assumed. This parameter was set equal to 0.5 for all products in the Rest of the World model while in the US model product specific price transmission elasticities were used. The respective values were taken from the literature (Sullivan, 1990) and range from 0.2 for milk and sugar to 1 for grain, oilseeds and ruminant meat.

SIMULATIONS

Reference Scenario and Policy Options

The reference situation is characterized by the agricultural policies existing in 1989 in the three regions considered. Besides price intervention, the model takes into account quantity measures such as the quota policy on the EC milk market. Various policy options have been simulated with the Multi-Output Multi-Input model. In this paper the emphasis is on analyzing the effects of taxes on mineral nitrogen fertilizer in the European Community. Since it seems desirable to examine the sensitivity of the effects to the level of taxation, four different policy options are simulated which explore the impact of a 25 percent, 50 percent, 100 percent and 200 percent tax on nitrogen. In all scenarios the existing agricultural policies in the European Community are assumed constant. No policy changes are considered in third countries.

Quantity and Price Effects

The aim is imposing a nitrogen tax is to reduce the demand for this input and thus to lower the intensity of agricultural production. As expected, the relative change in nitrogen use depends heavily on the level of taxation (see Table 1). However, it is interesting to observe that a doubling of the tax leads to a less than proportional reduction in nitrogen use (see Table 1). Besides limiting nitrogen consumption, the taxation of this fertilizer induces a considerable decrease in the use of other chemical inputs, while the demand for feed, hired labour, land and other inputs is not very sensitive to this policy. Table 1 also summarizes the relative output supply changes in the European Community of the different simulations. Taxation of nitrogen use leads to a decline in crop and ruminant meat production, while the supply of pigmeat and poultry meat shows a slight increase. Apparently, the excrement from animal production becomes a valuable manure that is a substitute for mineral fertilizer[8]. From an environmental point of view this effect is not desirable.

Due to the EC milk quota policy, taxation of nitrogen fertilizer consumption has no supply effects on this market, since the shadow price for milk lies far below the EC market price. It would need an unrealistically high tax level to shift the marginal cost curve on the EC milk market sufficiently upward for the quota equivalent price to reach the market price. In this case milk supply would start to decrease and the quota would no longer be binding.

Table 1 *Impact of an EC Nitrogen Tax on Product Supply and Input Demand in Agriculture*

Commodity, commodity group or input	Level of nitrogen tax 25%	40%	100%	200%
Beef	–0.03	–0.06	–0.10	–0.16
Pork	0.08	0.15	0.26	0.41
Mutton and lamb	–0.02	–0.04	–0.07	–0.11
Poultry meat	0.03	0.05	0.08	0.13
Eggs	–0.01	–0.01	–0.02	–0.03
Milk and milk products	0.00	0.00	0.00	0.00
Wheat	–1.15	–2.09	–3.54	–5.55
Corn	–1.12	–2.02	–3.43	–5.37
Other coarse grains	–1.16	–2.10	–3.56	–5.58
Rice	–1.24	–2.24	–3.80	–5.96
Soybeans	–1.02	–1.85	–3.13	–4.92
Other oilseeds	–1.24	–2.24	–3.80	–5.96
Cotton	–1.15	–2.08	–3.54	–5.54
Sugar	–1.15	–2.08	–3.53	–5.53
Other agricultural products	–0.62	–1.13	–1.92	–3.04
Mineral nitrogen fertilizer	–8.49	–14.89	–24.11	–35.43
Other mineral fertilizers	–5.66	–10.05	–16.57	–24.98
Pesticides	–1.99	–3.60	–6.07	–9.47
Wheat for feed	0.00	0.00	0.00	0.01
Corn for feed	0.00	–0.01	–0.01	–0.01
Other feed grains	0.01	0.01	0.02	0.03
Soybeans	–0.09	–0.17	–0.29	–0.46
Other oilseeds	–0.31	–0.57	–0.95	–1.50
Hired labour	–0.59	–1.06	–1.81	–2.85
Arable land	0.26	0.48	0.82	1.30
Pasture land	0.09	0.17	0.29	0.46
Other agricultural inputs	–0.09	–0.17	–0.29	–0.46

Source: Own calculation utilizing the TEPSIM model described in the text.

With the decrease in crop and ruminant meat supply, net exports are discouraged on these markets in all scenarios (see Table 2). The relative change in net exports is far more pronounced than the relative supply change. For instance, while the supply of other coarse grains decreases by only 5.6 percent with a 200 percent nitrogen tax, net exports of this

Table 2 *EC Net Exports of Agricultural Products due to a Taxation of Nitrogen Use in Agriculture*

Commodity or commodity group	Reference scenario	Level of nitrogen tax 25%	40%	100%	200%
			(in '000 tons)		
Beef	574	572	569	566	562
Pork	791	802	812	826	847
Mutton and lamb	–199	–199	–199	–200	–200
Poultry meat	354	356	357	359	362
Eggs	69	68	68	68	67
Milk and milk products	10 578	10 578	10 578	10 578	10 578
Wheat	19 274	18 325	17 558	16 363	14 711
Corn	–2450	–2750	–2993	–3372	–3896
Other coarse grains	6145	5413	4822	3900	3625
Rice	–268	–285	–299	–321	–351
Soybeans	–13 045	–13 054	–13 061	–13 073	13 088
Other oilseeds	–2383	–2472	–2543	–2665	2809
Cotton	–965	969	–972	–977	–983
Sugar	2605	2427	2282	2058	1746
Other agricultural products	0	– 5084	–9224	–15 729	–24 844

Source: Own calculation utilizing the TEPSIM model described in the text.

Table 3 *World Market Price Changes Due to a Taxation of Nitrogen Use in EC Agriculture*

Commodity or commodity group	Level of nitrogen tax 25%	40%	100%	200%
Beef	0.25	0.45	0.76	1.20
Pork	0.26	0.46	0.78	1.23
Mutton and lamb	0.19	0.34	0.58	0.91
Poultry meat	0.48	0.86	1.47	2.30
Eggs	0.26	0.48	0.81	1.27
Milk and milk products	0.49	0.89	1.51	2.37
Wheat	1.57	2.85	4.87	7.71
Corn	1.15	2.09	3.57	5.64
Other coarse grains	1.75	3.18	5.43	8.59
Rice	0.35	0.63	1.06	1.68
Soybeans	0.45	0.82	1.39	2.18
Other oilseeds	0.54	0.98	1.68	2.64
Cotton	0.30	0.55	0.94	1.47
Sugar	1.09	1.98	3.36	5.29
Other agricultural products	2.65	4.84	–8.34	13.38

Source: Own calculation utilizing the TEPSIM model described in the text.

product decline by 57 percent. The relative importance of the EC as an exporter declines and its role as a net importer increases, revealing the loss in international competitiveness, especially on the grain markets. A different development can be observed on the markets for pig and poultry meat. On these markets EC exports increase slightly.

The impact of an EC nitrogen tax is not limited to internal effects. Given the important role the EC plays on world agricultural markets, this policy also induces world market price changes and thus has an impact on third countries. Table 3 reveals that world market prices increase on all product markets considered. The prices for wheat, corn and other coarse grain show by far the largest change from 1989 base prices. The introduction of a nitrogen tax induces an increase in supply and a decrease in demand on almost all agricultural product markets in the USA and the Rest of the World. In addition the rise in world market prices for all commodities leads to a considerable increase in the demand for nitrogen and other chemical inputs in the USA. Use of arable and pasture land increases only slightly due to the low supply elasticity of this input.

Welfare Effects

Table 4 *Welfare Change Due to a Taxation of Nitrogen Use in EC Agriculture $Billion*

Countries/ regions scenarios	Change in producer welfare	Change in land owner revenue	Equivalent Variation	Change in government revenue	Change in net welfare
European Community					
25% N-tax	–293	279	–1874	1937	50
50% N-tax	–700	511	–3422	3585	–27
100% N-tax	–1702	882	–5894	6338	–375
200% N-tax	–4014	1419	–9441	10 651	–1385
United States					
25% N-tax	1739	334	–1740	–3	331
50% N-tax	3182	606	–3172	–5	612
100% N-tax	5501	1035	–5452	–8	1077
200% N-tax	8857	1638	–8707	–12	1777
Rest of the world					
25% N-tax	1553	0	–1668	–68	–182
50% N-tax	2818	0	–3024	–122	–329
100% N-tax	4803	0	–5152	–208	–557
200% N-tax	7580	0	–8124	–327	–871
World					
25% N-tax	2999	613	–5282	1867	198
50% N-tax	5299	1117	–9618	3458	256
100% N-tax	8602	1918	–16 498	6123	144
200% N-tax	12 423	3057	–26 272	10 313	–479

Source: Own calculation using the TEPSIM model described in the text.

For all 4 policy runs the conventional welfare effects for the 3 regions considered are calculated. Only the change in real income is considered in the welfare measure. Possible benefits of environmental improvement (for example, reduction in pollution of ground and surface water with nitrogen, phosphorous and pesticides) resulting from the introduction of a nitrogen tax are not considered in this analysis. The method used for the measurement of the conventional welfare change is the sequential approach based on the Hicksian compensated curves (Hartmann, 1991; Just, Hueth and Schmitz, 1982).

The distributional and efficiency effects of the implementation of nitrogen taxes in the EC are summarized in Table 4. The results reveal that EC producers and consumers have to bear welfare losses in all policy scenarios while, on the other hand, land owners are beneficiaries of such a policy change. Government revenue will increase in two ways. First, due to the introduction of the nitrogen tax, government gains an additional revenue source. Second, this policy leads to a reduction in supply of most agricultural products in the EC (see Table 1) and to world market price increases (see Table 3), thus leading to a decline in product subsidies and export subsidies.

The net welfare effects will be positive only if the EC introduces a moderate tax on nitrogen fertilizer. Table 4 reveals, that a 25 percent tax increases conventional welfare in the EC by $50 million. This is due to the fact that the 'environmental policy' is implemented on already distorted markets. The input tax thus partly compensates for the price distortions on the product markets. The welfare gain reaches its peak at a nitrogen tax of 20 percent. If the tax level exceeds, 44 percent, the welfare effects become negative. Examination of Table 4 also shows that a linear increase in the level of the tax leads to an exponential rise in conventional welfare loss. The distributional and efficiency effects in third countries are also reported in Table 4. In common with land owners in the EC, those in third countries experience a welfare gain and consumers have to bear welfare losses in all policy scenarios considered. Producers in the USA and the Rest of the World will be beneficiaries from the implementation of a nitrogen tax in the EC while government revenues have to bear an additional burden in both countries/regions. In all simulations the net welfare change is positive for the USA but negative for the Rest of the World, reflecting the different net trade position of the two regions. The net welfare effects for the world as a whole depend on the level of the nitrogen tax. The world experiences real income gains in the case of a low 25 percent tax. Interesting enough these gains would increase if the tax level increases. World welfare is reduced by a 200 percent tax.

NOTES

1 See, for example, Liapis (1990 and 1992), Lueck, Haley and Liais (1993), Hartmann and Matthews (1993), Hartmann (1993), Haley (1993) and Gunasekera, Rodriguez and Andrews (1992). In most of these nitrogen fertilizer is the only agricultural input considered. Thus, the interdependencies between nitrogen and other agricultural inputs are neglected in these papers. This is not the case for the studies of LIAPIS (1990 and 1992). The author considers 5 input sectors in his model. One limitation of the analysis is, however, the high degree of aggregation. The simulation of taxes on fertilizer or pesticide is not possible with this framework.

2 In the EC-12, Germany is included in the borders before 3 October 1990.

3 The agricultural products considered in the analysis are: beef and veal; pork, mutton and lamb; poultry meat; poultry eggs; milk and milk products; wheat; corn; other coarse grains (barley, sorghum, mixed grains, oats, rye, and millet); soyabeans; other oilseeds (copra, cottonseed, flaxseed, palm kernels, peanuts, rapseed, safflower, and sesame seed); cotton; sugar and other agricultural products.

4 In contrast to the procedure in other SWOPSIM variants, the demand for wheat, corn, other coarse grain, soybean and other oilseeds is defined by two seperate equations; one equation for the final demand for human consumption and one equation for feed demand.

5 The consumer expenditures on the aggregate 'other agricultural products' are equal to all food

expenditure in the EC and the USA minus the expenditure for the products considered in the model.

[6] Interdependencies in input supply are not considered in the model.

[7] See also the discussion of this issue in Hartmann and Wiegand (1993).

REFERENCES

Anker, P. and Schmitz, P.M., 1987, 'Environmental Effects of Price Policies in Agriculture', Paper presented at the 5th Congress of the European Association of Agricultural Economists, Balatonszéplak, Hungary.

Antle, J.M., 1984, 'The Structure of U.S. Agricultural Technology', *American Journal of Agricultural Economics*, Vol. 66, No. 4, pp. 414–21.

Ball, V.E., 1989, *Estimating Supply Response of Multiproduct Farms*, Technical Bulletin No. 1750, Economic Research Service, United States Department of Agriculture, Washington, D.C.

Barse, J.R., 1990, *Seven Farm Input Industries*, Agricultural Economic Report No. 635, Economic Research Service, United States Department of Agriculture, Washington, D.C.

Boyle, G.E. and O'Neill, D., 1990, 'The Generation of Output Supply and Input Demand Elasticities for a Johansen-type model of the Irish Agricultural Sector', *European Review of Agricultural Economics*, Vol. 17, No. 4, pp.387–405.

Bundesministerium für Ernährung, Landwirtschaft und Forsten (BMELF, Ed.), 1991, *Statistisches Jahrbuch über Ernährung, Landwirtschaft und Forsten der Bundesrepublik Deutschland 1991*, Münster-Hiltrup.

Burrel, A., 1989, 'The Demand for Fertilizer in the United Kingdom', *Journal of Agricultural Economics*, Vol. 40, No.1, pp.1–20.

Denalby, M. and Vroomen, H., 1991, 'Elasticities of Fertilizer Demands for Corn in the Short and the Long Run. A Cointegrated and Error-Correcting System', Agricultural and Rural Economy Devision, Staff Report AGES No. 9137, Economic Research Service, United States Department of Agriculture, Washington, D.C.

Dubberke, H. and Schmitz, P.M., 1993, 'Ökonometrische Schätzung von Eigenpreis- und Kreuzpreiselastizitäten im Produkt- und Faktorbereich der deutschen Landwirtschaft auf der Basis einer Translog-Gewinnfunktion', in Schmitz, P.M. and Hartmann, M. (eds.), *Landwirtschaft und Chemie - Simulationsstudie zu den Auswirkungen einer Reduzierung des Einsatzes von Mineraldünger und Pflanzenschutzmitteln aus ökonomischer Sicht*, Kiel.

Dunham, D., 1991, *Food Cost Review 1990*, Agricultural Economic Report No. 651, Economic Research Service, United States Department of Agriculture, Washington, D.C.

Fernanadez-Cornejo, J., 1993, *Demand and Substitution of Agricultural Inputs in the Central Corn Belt States*, Technical Bulletin No. 1816. Economic Research Service, United States Department of Agriculture, Washington, D.C.

Food and Agriculture Organization of the United Nations (FAO), 1991a, *FAO Production Yearbook 1990*, Rome.

Food and Agriculture Organization of the United Nations (FAO), 1991b, *FAO Fertilizer Yearbook 1990*, Rome.

Gardiner, W.H., Roningen, V.O. and Liu, K., 1989, 'Elasticities in the Trade Liberalization Database', Staff Report No. AGES 89–20, United States Department of Agriculture, Washington, D.C.

Glass, J.C. and McKillop, D.G., 1989, 'A Multi-Product Multi-Input Cost Function Analysis of Northern Ireland Agriculture, 1955–1985', *Journal of Agricultural Economics*, Vol. 40, No. 1, pp.57–70.

Gunasekera, H.D.B.H., Rodriguez, G.R. and Andrews, N.P., 1992, 'Taxing Fertiliser Use in EC Farm Production. Implications for Agricultural Trade', Paper presented at the Agricultural Workshop 1992, Agricultural Policy, Trade and Development Task Force, Pacific Economic Cooperation Conference, East-West Center, Honolulu, May.

Haley, S., 1993, 'Environmental and Agricultural Policy Linkages in the European Community: The Nitrate Problem and CAP Reform', International Agricultural Trade Research Consortium, Working Paper No. 93–3, Washington, D.C.

Haley, S.L., 1988, 'Joint Products in the SWOPSIM Modeling Framework', Staff Report No. AGES 881024, Economic Research Service, United States Department of Agriculture, Washington, D.C.

Hartmann, M., 1991 'Wohlfahrtsmessung auf interdependenten und verzerrten Märkten: Die Europäische Agrarpolitik aus Sicht der Entwicklungsländer', Dissertation, Giessen.

Hartmann, M., 1993, 'The Effects of EC Environmental Policies on Agricultural Trade and Economic Welfare', *Journal of Economic Integration*, Special Issue on Agricultural Trade and Economic Integration in Europe and in North America, Vol. 8.

Hartmann, M. and Matthews, A., 1993, 'EC and International Implications of Chemical Restriction in Agriculture', in Soares, F.B. (ed.), *EC Agricultural Policy by the End of the Century*, Kiel.

Hartmann, M. and Wiegand, S., 1993, 'Auswirkungen einer Reduzierung des Einsatzes von Mineraldüngern und Pflanzenschutzmitteln in der Landwirtschaft. Ergebnisse einer schriftlichen Expertenbefragung', in Schmitz, P.M. and Hartmann, M. (eds.), *Landwirtschaft und Chemie - Simulationsstudie zu den Auswirkungen einer Reduzierung des Einsatzes von Mineraldünger und Pflanzenschutzmitteln aus ökonomischer Sicht*, Kiel.

Hertel, T.W., Peterson, E.B. and Stout, J.V., 1993, 'Adding Value to Existing Models of International Agricultural Trade', Unpublished Manuscript.

Just, R.E., Hueth, D.L. and Schmitz, A., 1982, *Applied Welfare Economics and Public Policy*, Englewood Cliffs.

Kommission der Europäischen G (ed.), Die Lage der Landwirtschaft in der Gemeinschaft, Bericht 1991, Brüssel und Luxemburg 1992.

Leuck, D., Haley, S. and Liapis, P., 1993, 'The Relationship between Selected Agricultural and Environmental Policies in the European Community', Paper presented at the International Conference on New Dimensions in North American-European Agricultural Trade Relations, Calabria, Italy, 20–23 June.

Liapis, P., 1990, *Incorporating Inputs in the Static World Policy Simulation Model (SWOPSIM)*, Technical Bulletin 1790, Economic Research Service, United States Department of Agriculture, Washington, D.C.

Liapis, P., 1992, 'Assessing the Results of Trade Liberalization: An Alternative Perspective', Paper presented at the Southern Agricultural Economics Association Annual Meetings, Lexington, Kentucky, 2–5 February.

Michalek, J., 1988, *Technological Progress in West German Agriculture - A Quantitative Approach*, Kiel.

Price, J.M., Seeley, R. and Tucker, C.K., 1991, *The Food and Agricultural Policy Simulator: Estimation of Farm Production Expenses*, Technical Bulletin No. 1803, Economic Research Service, United States Department of Agriculture, Washington, D.C.

Putman, J.J. and Allshouse, J.E., 1992, *Food Consumption, Prices, and Expenditures*, Statistical Bulletin No. 840, Economic Research Service, United States Department of Agriculture, Washington, D.C.

Rendleman, C.M., 1993, *Estimation of Aggregate U.S. Demands for Fertilizer, Pesticides, and Other Inputs*, Technical Bulletin No. 1813, Economic Research Service, United States Department of Agriculture, Washington, D.C.

Sullivan, J., 1990, *Price Transmission Elasticities in the Trade Liberalization (TLIB) Database*, Staff Report No. AGES 9034, Economic Research Service, United States Department of Agriculture, Washington, D.C.

Sullivan, J., Roningen, V., Leetmaa, S. and Gray, D., 1992, *A 1989 Global Database for the Static World Policy Simulation (SWOPSIM) Modeling Framework*, Staff Report No. AGES 9215, Economic Research Service, Washington, D.C.

United States Department of Agriculture, 1991, *Agricultural Statistics 1991*, Washington, D.C.

United States Department of Agriculture, 1992, *Agricultural Resources: Agricultural Land Values and Markets*, Situation and Outlook Report AR–26, Economic Research Service, United States Department of Agriculture, Washington, D.C.

DISCUSSION OPENING — Consuelo Varela-Ortega *(Polytechnica University, Madrid, Spain)*

This paper presents a method of estimating the trade and welfare effects of levying/applying different levels of nitrogen taxes in the EU agriculture. A trade simulation model is used (TEPSIM) in which the usual scope of agricultural trade models has been enlarged by introducing not only agricultural outputs but also agricultural inputs. (Multi-input, multi-output trade equilibrium model). This permits one to simulate different scenarios of input use (prices and/or quantities) valuable for policy analysis.

The model is a non-spatial aggregated three-regional static model (EU, US and the rest of the world) in which product and intra-regional heterogeneities are not considered. Elasticities are exogenous and the agricultural policy frameworks for the three regions is the one existing in base year 1989.

A sensitivity analysis is then carried out by simulating the impact of four different levels of taxation to mineral nitrogen fertilizer in the EU: 25 percent; 50 percent, 100 percent and 200 percent. The EU agricultural policy is assumed constant in all four scenarios. The welfare effects are measured as changes in real income using the approach based on Hicksian compensated demand curves.

My comments to this paper (aimed to stimulate the discussion from the floor) can be summarized in the form of 5 remarks.

With respect to policy analysis as referred to in the paper, I would say that this research focusses more on sensitivity analysis rather than on policy simulations. The EU policy has been held constant when envisaging a clear change in agricultural policy represented by the CAP reform. Thus no comparisons between pre- and post-CAP reform have been made. Also, for policy analysis the introduction of some dynamics into the model will surely enhance its simulation capacity.

With respect to the ecological benefits commented on in the paper (after all, the goal of reducing nitrogen use is environmental in nature), the estimates of environmental benefits cannot be conclusive due because this is an aggregated model without a spatial dimension. The effects on the environment of the reduction in mineral nitrogen fertilizer use are highly spatially specific. So we cannot conclude that any given reduction in nitrogen fertilizer use in the EU will necessarily lead to environmental benefits.

So, I think that it will be enhancing to integrate this analysis into a more comprehensive one that will integrate both the economic and environmental effects of such a measure of reducing nitrogen fertilizer use through taxing nitrates assumption. This will necessarily have to be spatially specific and thus have a lower level of aggregation.

With respect to the levels of taxation simulated (ranging from 25 percent to 200 percent), the upper bound appears to be too high and may cause problems with the consistency of elasticity measures, which in turn can lead to non-concluding results over that range of price variation.

The analysis of the land market, I think, needs further specification. When looking at the results, the ZUC column on Table 4 'Change in Land Owner Revenue' is confusing. If it refers to a change in the value of land for the land owner, the positive sign is realistic. The land value increase results from an increase in the demand for land as a response to the intensification process that results from a lower input use. However, the land supply elasticity is referred to in the text (0.2 percent) but no reference has been found to the demand response. Thus figures of land owner revenues have to be further explained.

Also, an increase in land prices for land owners will result in an increase in the value of their assets of land equity but cannot be considered a rental value (to add up). If this column refers to land rents (see page 6) the reduction of the producers' incomes will lead to a decrease in the demand for renting land and will induce a reduction in land rents received by land owners hiring out their plots. So, this column should have a negative sign and the positive sign shown will not be realistic.

As a general comment, I would conclude that based on the results of this research, a unilateral EU environmental policy of taxing nitrogen fertilizer use leads to net welfare losses for the EU as well as for the NGW, whereas it induces clear welfare gains in the USA. Thus, for an environmental policy (nitrate pollution reduction) to be well balanced and not a source of welfare disequilibria, it will have to be designed following a unilateral agreement scheme.

HENGLUN SUN AND JACK HOUSTON*

Economic Analysis of Best Management Practices in a Pilot Cost-Sharing Water Quality Program

Abstract: Simulated crop growth and nonpoint pollution yields under stochastic weather conditions generated farmers' expected net returns and the environmental effects of implementing 'Best Management Practices' (BMPs) under risky and uncertain conditions. Results from varying nitrogen fertilizer and irrigation management levels over a growing season show that, for production-optimal levels of nitrogen fertilization and irrigation without regard to pollution, nitrogen leaching is more serious, but soil loss and nitrogen runoff are lower, than for other scenarios tested. Voluntary implementation of BMPs to reduce levels of inputs and decrease water quality impacts would require substantial cost-sharing incentives. Farmers favour a cost-sharing program, with 87 percent willing to participate when government's cost-share is at the 80 percent level. When tight budgets restrict implementation of stricter pollution targets, a 20 percent cost-sharing would induce 27 percent of the farmers surveyed to voluntarily select BMPs.

INTRODUCTION TO THE GUM CREEK WATERSHED WATER QUALITY PROGRAM

Water quality pollution generated by agricultural production practices is regarded among the major environmental problems of the 1990s. The Gum Creek Watershed (GCW) in South Georgia was selected as one of 16 water quality demonstration projects in the US in which to examine potentially polluting agricultural practices. The Gum Creek Water Quality Project aims to reduce potential nonpoint source pollution by inducing farmers to voluntarily adopt 'best management practices' (BMPs) within a federal cost-sharing pilot program. This study compares activity levels through Multiple Objective Programming (MOP) analysis to search for economically optimal BMPs.

Gum Creek Watershed comprises approximately 53 000 acres in the coastal plain of Georgia. Average annual rainfall is 45 inches, generally well-distributed over the growing season. The topological relief in the area is gentle, with broad valley floors and 2 percent to 5 percent slopes dominating uplands. Tifton-Dothan-Raines and Tifton-Alapaha-Dothan are the dominant soil associations, while the dominant surface texture is loamy sand. Intensive agricultural production typifies land use in the watershed, with a diversity of crops produced. Several subwatersheds commonly plant more than 50 percent of their surface area to crops that have high fertilizer and/or pesticide requirements. Peanuts, the major crop in the watershed, comprises 5013 acres; other crops include soybeans, cotton, pecans, pasture, melons, and corn. In 1991, 25 percent of cropland in the watershed was irrigated using diverse systems. Soils with high or intermediate pesticide and nutrient leaching pollution potential cover most upland of the watershed (CGES, 1992).

* University of Georgia, Georgia, USA.

ANALYTICAL FRAMEWORK

Integrated Crop Management and Irrigation Water Management exemplify the two major BMPs analyzed in the economic evaluation of this project. Using results of individual farmer surveys in the GCW, we model a representative farm in the watershed to provide the framework for economic analysis of cost-sharing incentives to alter levels of fertilizer application and irrigation management. All related data — including topography, soil, weather, crop production and management practices, market prices and costs — were collected from project surveys and the Cooperative Extension Service (CES). The integrating approach for this analysis links (a) peanut and corn crop simulation models to predict crop yields under alternate (input) management practices, (b) selected water pollution and soil erosion simulation models to predict pollution levels, and (c) multiobjective programming analyses to assess irrigation and nitrogen management measures under risk and uncertainty for a representative profit-maximizing farm.

PNUTGRO version 1.02 (Boote *et al.*, 1989), a process-oriented peanut crop growth model, simulates and predicts peanut crop development, water and nitrogen balance, and the final peanut yield. CERES-Maize version 2.10 (Ritchie *et al.*, 1992) simulates the growth and yield of corn, produced in rotation with peanuts. GLEAMS (Groundwater Loading Effects of Agricultural Management Systems) version 2.0 (Knisel *et al.*, 1992), is selected to physically simulate agricultural management systems relating the movement of agricultural chemicals within and through the plant root zone and produce the chemical pollution and soil erosion output levels. A 100-acre peanut farm is simulated for the northwest sector of the watershed, using representative weather data (i.e., rainfall, temperature, and solar radiation data) from Tifton (Hook, 1991), the nearest weather station. Tifton loamy sand on average 3 percent of slope represents the soil type (Hook 1991, Knisel *et al.* 1991; and Thomas *et al.* 1989). The peanut crop typically rotates with grain corn annually. Only corn requires appreciable nitrogen fertilizer, because peanuts are leguminous. Other chemical applications, including phosphate and potash fertilizers, and varied use of pesticides are optimized by the simulators. Nitrogen is assumed to be applied twice in a cropping season — one-third of the total amount at sowing date and two-thirds 30 days later. Irrigation levels in the simulator are controlled by detection of the threshold soil water at a 0.50 metre depth, based on the calculations of the day-by-day soil water balance. GLEAMS uses the same weather, soil, crop planting, and management data, with irrigation water data imported from crop growth models and merged to the precipitation data files of GLEAMS day-by-day, to generate the pollution output parameters.

Ten-year (1982-91) peanut and corn yields of Crisp County validate the models, as in Hook (1991), with initial soil conditions appropriately adjusted to modify the simulated yields until simulated ten-year yields closely match the observed yields (i.e., paired comparisons of means of both simulated and actual yields tested equal at a statistically significant level of 5 percent using the t-test). Base models use no irrigation and a rate of 72 pounds of nitrogen fertilizer (CES). Validated base crop models are then extended to generate annual crop yields with the past 17-year weather data. Following Chavas *et al.* (1983), futures prices of corn are collected for the December contract when observed just prior to March 15 at the Chicago Board of Trade. Prices of peanuts, which do not have a futures market, cite peanut program quota prices as expected seasonal prices. All price levels are adjusted to real 1992 prices by the Producer Price Index. Costs for irrigation and chemical usage are based on CES (1993), with nitrogen fertilizer and irrigation costs computed to changing application levels and unit prices. The expected net return is defined as total expected revenue minus total costs (variable plus annualized fixed costs) of the enterprize under each management scenario.

To test the sensitivity of farmers' returns and pollution levels, differing amounts of nitrogen application are selected. One expects ENR to rise as nitrogen fertilizer application rates increase. However, while soil losses change very little among the management practices, nitrogen runoff losses grow quite measurably and nitrogen also much more likely percolates into ground water with increasing fertilizer usage and no irrigation (Table 1). Thus, maximizing farmers' expected annual net returns is not a sufficient criterion for a BMP. If all pollution levels that resulted from a management practice with the highest expected net return are below the environmental pollution target criteria, the management practice can be defined as BMP. However, if some pollution level generated from the management practice exceeds the environmental target, the management practice should be changed. A new alternative that meets the environmental criteria and has the least reduction from the highest return would be selected BMP. The reduction in expected net returns is then the opportunity cost, or loss in net returns, of implementing the BMP. The representative farm would attain, on average, a \$122 annual baseline ENR per acre at a rate of 72 lb. of nitrogen fertilizer usage while generating over 55 lb. of nitrogen leaching (Table 1).

Table 1 *Net Returns and Pollution Yields (per acre-year) for Low N Application Alternatives*

	Nitrogen fertilizer (lb)					
Key variables	24	36	48	60	72	84
Expected net return (\$)	67.3	84.6	100.3	113.0	122.3	130.4
Soil losses (t)	5.56	5.56	5.56	5.56	5.56	5.56
N losses by runoff (lb)	1.88	1.90	1.91	1.92	1.93	1.94
N losses by leaching (lb)	48.33	49.78	51.57	53.40	55.05	56.96

Farmers' Optimal Cost-Sharing Program

The optimal cost-sharing program can be considered by both farmers and government as a question of costs and benefits. The government decision is supported by their estimation of the potential environmental effect by a specific percentage of farmers implementing the BMP and by budget availability. However, farmers' attitudes toward the cost-sharing program are quite diverse, owing to their current management practices, their risk attitudes toward environmental problems, and their perceptions of a new program. Suppose current management practice generates annual net return A for a farmer and a new BMP would reduce the net return to B. Under a cost-sharing program, assuming each farmer has a p probability of adopting the new BMP and taking a k share subsidy from government (i.e., cost of the program $= A - B$) for doing so, the expected annual net return (ENR) for the farmer would sum the expectations of the net returns from two cases-maintaining current practice versus an altered practice (the BMP). That is,

$$(1)\quad ENR = E(A) + E(B) = (1-p)A + p[B + k(A-B)]$$

By algebraic manipulation, the expected net return is transformed:

$$(2)\quad ENR = A - p(1-k)(A-B)$$

A and *B* can be estimated and are considered constant in the cost-sharing decision procedure for a specific BMP. An optimal cost-sharing percentage can, from the farmer's perspective, be decided by the highest *ENR*, which would be determined by the term *p(1–k)*. Call that term the share parameter. The higher the value of the share parameter, the lower the *ENR* would appear, and the cost-sharing percentage would be less favored by farmers.

Table 2 *The Share Parameters for Cost-Sharing Program Alternatives*

Cost–sharing percent by Government *(k)*	Mean probability of adoption by farmers *(p)*	Share parameter *(p(1–k))*
80%	87%	0.174
60%	70%	0.280
40%	45%	0.270
20%	27%	0.216

Individual farmer surveys in the Gum Creek Project area provide the farmers' attitudes towards several alternatives of government cost-sharing levels and indicate the program could be helpful in approaching an optimal cost-sharing program. The questionnaire was designed to collect information about farmers' management practices, their attitudes toward environmental pollution and toward a cost-sharing program, as well as their socio-economic background. An estimated 61 farmers operate 70 farms in the Gum Creek Watershed. Participants' gross farm incomes in 1990 averaged just over $100 000 per farmer, and, on average, they applied 98 pounds of nitrogen per acre (or 110 kg/ha) of corn annually. The probability of their willingness to adopt a government cost-sharing BMP program decreases as government's percentage share declines. Using the mean of the probability of participation to represent farmers in the watershed, the parameters *p(1–k)* are shown in Table 2. Since the mean *p(1–k)* at 80 percent government share, with a mean at 0.174, is the lowest, the 80 percent cost-share level would be the option most favored by the farmers. The 20 percent level of government share, with a mean *p(1–k)* of 0.216, appears the second most-favorable option. However, the government must consider the potential effect of a higher percentage of farmers staying out of the program and retaining current management practices — higher expected pollution levels.

Multiple Criteria Optimization

The Gum Creek Water Quality Pilot Project poses a multiple-criteria decision-making problem in that it aims to control water pollution while not overly detracting from the maximization of farmers' profits. Multiple-criteria programming techniques, tackling the problem of simultaneous optimization of several objective functions subject to a set of constraints, can be used to find optimal solutions to such problems. That is, a feasible solution must be found such that there is no other feasible solution that can achieve the same or better performance for any one of the objectives without decreasing at least one of the other objectives. Therefore, multiple criteria optimization is equivalent to the concept of economic efficiency, and increasing numbers apply MOP for agricultural planning (Romero and Rechman, 1989; Berbel, Gallego, and Sagues, 1991; Maino, Berdegue, and Rivas, 1993) and resource management (Rosato and Stellin, 1993; Zekri and Albisu, 1993).

Multiple objective linear programming (MOLP) uses a vector-maximum algorithm, which computes an efficient point or points that 'maximize' the criterion vector and satisfy all constraints such that the resultant vector values are not dominated by any other points (Steuer, 1986). However, the 'maximization' of a vector of objectives generates a set of efficient solutions instead of one optimal solution. The entire set of efficient solutions is presented to a rational decision-maker, and he/she then selects the BMP alternative perceived most attractive. The decision maker, by reviewing the list of nondominated criterion vectors associated with the efficient extreme points, can identify his/her efficient extreme point of greatest utility (Steuer, 1986).

Three-fourths of the farmers in Gum Creek Watershed operate without irrigation. In order to examine N application alternatives, eight N levels centered around 72 lb. are simulated without irrigation. Farmers' net returns, nitrogen losses by runoff and leaching will increase with greater N fertilizer levels within this range (Table 1). Since cost-sharing is to be voluntarily adopted, farmers' attitudes toward adoption of the program will determine their net returns and pollution levels, as well as government expenditures. Let p be the farmer's probability of adopting the program in which government shares k percent of the cost of the management activity alternatives under the program. The cost of the program is the reduction in the farmers' net returns from adopting the new alternative, ΔR; i.e., the net return from current management, R_0, less that from new management, R_1. S_0, S_1, F_0, F_1, L_0, and L_1 refer to the soil losses, nitrogen to runoff, and nitrogen leaching from both current and new management practices, respectively. The expectations of farmers' net returns (*ENR*), soil losses (*ESL*), nitrogen losses by runoff (*ENF*) and nitrogen losses by leaching (*ENL*) will be summations of both probabilities. For example, a farmer's probability of adopting current management is $(1-p)$ with net return R_0 and that of new management is p with net return R_1 plus government cost-sharing ($\Delta R\ k$). The summation of both possibilities, $(1-p)R_0 + p(R_1 + \Delta Rk)$, would then be the farmer's *ENR*. The expected pollution levels would sum up outcomes of each alternative multiplied by its probability. The government's expected lump-sum costs (EGC) will also depend on the farmer's attitude toward adopting the program. These expectation functions follow:

(3) $ENR = (1-p)R_0 + p(R_1 + \Delta Rk)$

(4) $ESL = (1-p)S_0 + pS_1$

(5) $ENF = (1 - p)F_0 + pF_1$

(6) $ENL = (1 - p)L_0 + pL_1$

(7) $EGC = \Delta Rpk$

Table 3 *Regression Results of the Expectations on N Application and Government Cost-Share*

Dependent Vars. / Explanatory Vars.	Expected net returns	Expected N runoff	Expected N leaching	Expected government cost-sharing
Constant	93.83 (87.4)**	1.89 (1223)**	49.4 (203)**	15.8 (14.5)**
N fertilizer (lb/a)	0.324 (19.1)**	0.000524 (21.5)**	0.0825 (21.5)**	–0.344 (–20.0)**
Cost share rate (%)	11.9 (9.26)**	–0.00385 (–2.08)*	–0.606 (–2.08)*	16.3 (12.5)**
Adjusted R^2	0.44	0.45	0.45	0.49

Notes: *t*-values are in parentheses. ** and * indicate significance at 1 percent and 5 percent levels, respectively.

Five different management practices, simulated with 72 lb. N or below, provide expected output for new management options which cause the same or less N pollution. From the 29 farmers responding to four cost-sharing attitude questions in the Gum Creek Farmer Survey, 116 random observations of p are used to generate 580 randomized samples of expectations with respect to five N application alternatives. The expectations samples are then estimated by amount of N fertilizer applied and government cost share (k) using Ordinary Least Squares (Table 3) from varying usages of N fertilizer and government cost-sharing percentages (Equations 3 through 7). All the estimated coefficients have the expected signs and are statistically significant. The estimated functions define the dependency of *ENR, ENF, ENL,* and *EGC* on N fertilizer and government cost-sharing. MOLP uses the estimated functions as objectives and constraint, respectively, to search for an optimal N and government cost-sharing strategy.

Because current N control targets are not well defined, the *ENF* and *ENL* can be set as objective functions to be minimized, instead of constraints, in the MOLP. Thus, the MOLP problem uses the estimated relationships of *ENR, ENF, ENL,* and *EGC*, based on N fertilizer and cost-sharing percentage, to find efficient points for maximizing *ENR* and jointly minimizing *ENF* and ENL, subject to the constraints of government outlays. Substituting the estimated regression coefficients into the objective functions and setting the government budget constraint at $5.00 per acre, as the project planned, the MOLP solver provides three efficient extreme points (Table 4), when N fertilizer application ranges from 40.9 lbs. to 72 lbs per acre. Of the three efficient extreme points, option 3, which uses 72 lb. of N, has the highest ENR and N losses. All farmers would adopt option 3, if current pollution levels would not be a problem. Option 1, which uses 40.9 lb. of N, has the lowest *ENR* and N losses, and it is the most efficient option for reducing N losses to runoff and leaching with government cost-sharing at $5.00 per acre. However, farmers suffer higher losses of *ENR*. Compared to options 1 and 3, option 2 is a compromize point reflecting values other than efficiency. Farmers apply 69.2 lb. of N fertilizer, government shares $5 of the cost, and farmers attain higher *ENR* than option 1, while N losses would be less than the option 3.

Table 4 *Efficient Extreme Points of MOLP by ADBASE*

Variables	Option number		
	1	2	3
N fertilizer (lb/a)	40.9	69.2	72.0
Cost share rate (%)	20	80	80
Expected net return ($/a)	109.45	125.78	<u>126.67</u>
Expected N runoff (lb/a)	<u>1.92</u> (99.0%)	1.92 (99.5%)	1.93 (100.0%)
Expected N leaching (lb/a)	<u>52.66</u> (96.3%)	54.64 (99.9%)	54.87 (100.3%)
Expected government cost share ($/a)	5.00	5.00	4.05

Sensitivity Analysis of Government Budget Constraints

Decision-makers must weigh which efficient option would be the BMP when maximum allowable N losses to runoff and leaching are not clearly defined. MOLP can be used to search for optimal management options under varying government cost constraints. Table 5 compares the optimal solutions for minimizing N losses if the government budget were to be restricted to $2.50, $5.00, $7.50, and $10.00 per acre, respectively. The farmers' *ENRs* actually decline as the government's shared costs increase, because farmers' costs proportionately increase. As farmers and government pay more, the N losses to runoff and leaching from the crop growth processes both turn down and environmental benefits are gained. When government increases its lump-sum shared cost from $2.50 to $5.00 per acre, the optimal solution would reduce nitrogen runoff only from 1.917 to 1.913 lb/acre (or 0.2 percent) and N leaching from 53.26 to 52.66 lb/acre (or 1.0 percent). Farmers' expected net returns are reduced by $2.37 (from $111.80 to $109.43) per acre, after including the government payments. Pollution-minimum solutions cost more for both government and individual farmers. It is estimated that for every $2.50 government payment in the cost-sharing program, expected N losses to runoff are reduced by 0.2

percent, and expected N leaching is reduced by 1.5 percent. At the same time, the individual farmer pays (loses) about $2.35 from his prior expected net returns.

Table 5 *Optimal Solutions With Four Budget Constraint Alternatives*

Variables	Budget constraint ($/acre)				
	0	2.50	5.00	7.50	10.00
N fertilizer (lb/a)	72.0	48.1	40.9	33.6	26.3
Cost share rate (%)	55.1	20	20	20	20
Expected net returns ($)	123.71 (100%)	111.80 (90.4%)	109.43 (88.5%)	107.10 (86.6%)	104.74 (84.7%)
Expected N runoff (lb/a)	1.929 (100%)	1.917 (99.4%)	1.913 (99.2%)	1.909 (99.0%)	1.906 (98.8%)
Expected N leaching (lb/a)	54.71 (100%)	53.26 (97.3%)	52.66 (96.3%)	52.06 (95.2%)	51.46 (94.1%)
Expected government costs ($/a)	0	2.50	5.00	7.50	10.00

Note: The figures in the parentheses compare the ENR and pollution parameters to the outcome of a no-subsidy solution.

SUMMARY AND IMPLICATIONS

We simulated crop growth and nonpoint pollution yields under stochastic weather conditions to generate farmers' expected net returns and the environmental effects of implementing various BMPs under risky and uncertain conditions. A cost-sharing program can reduce the N leaching by subsidizing farmers for reducing their nitrogen fertilizer levels by considering benefits and costs of both farmers and other water users (the general public). Comparison of the simulated pollution levels with EPA target levels can be used to optimize the BMPs and find appropriate cost-sharing program incentives. The government decision supports their estimate of the potential beneficial environmental effects that can be attained by a specific percentage of farmers implementing the program subject to budget availability. However, farmers' attitudes to the cost-sharing program can be quite diverse, due to their current individual management practices and to their risk attitudes to environmental problems and a new government program. Survey response analysis shows that farmers favor a program with government's share at 80 percent of cost. A 20 percent government cost-sharing could induce higher expected net returns than those of 60 percent or 40 percent cost-sharing level, although fewer farmers would participate.

The conclusions derived from this research could be very site-specific, because the management alternatives are simulated through specific soil and weather conditions. However, the methodology used in this research could be extended to other geographic areas, as well as other management alternatives for searching the best management practices.

REFERENCES

Berbel, J., Gallego, J. and Sagues, H., 1991, 'Marketing Goals vs. Business Profitability: An Interactive Multiple Criteria Decision -Making Approach', *Agribusiness*, Vol. 7, No. 6, pp.536–49.

Boote, K.J., Jones, J.W., Hoogenboom, G., Wilkerson, G.G. and Jagtap, S.S., 1989, *Peanut Crop Growth Simulation Model: User's Guide (V 1.02)*, Florida Agricultural Experiment Station, Journal No. 8420, May.

Chavas, J.P., Pope, R.D. and Kao, R.S., 1983, 'An Analysis of the Role of Futures Prices, Cash Prices and Government Programs in Acreage Response', *Western Journal of Agricultural Economics*, Vol. 8, No. 1, pp.27–33.

GCES (Georgia Cooperative Extension Service), 1992, *Crop Enterprise Cost Analysis: South Georgia 1993*, AAE/AES /UGA, Athens, Georgia, October.

GCES (Georgia Cooperative Extension Service), 1992, *1992 USDA Demonstration Project Annual Report: Gum Creek Water Quality Project*, CES/UGA.

Hook, J.E., 1991, *Water Withdrawals for Irrigation in Drought Years*, ERC 03-91, The Coastal Plain Experiment Station, The University of Georgia, Tifton, Georgia.

Knisel, W.G., Davis, F.M. and Leonard, R.A., 1992, *GLEAMS Version 2.0: User Manual*, Southeast Watershed Research Laboratory/ARS/ USDA, Tifton, Georgia.

Knisel, W.G., Leonard, R.A., Davis, F.M. and Sheridan, J.M., 1991, 'Water Balance Components in the Georgia Coastal Plain: A GLEAMS Model Validation and Simulation', *Journal of Soil and Water Conservation*, Vol. 46, No. 6, pp.450–6.

Ritchie, J., Singh, U., Godwin, D. and Hunt, L., 1992, *A User's Guide to CERES Maize-V2.10*, 2nd edition, International Fertilizer Development Center, Muscle Shoals, Alaska.

Romero, C. and Rehman, T., 1989, *Multiple Criteria Analysis for Agricultural Decisions*, Series title: Developments in Agricultural Economics, Elsevier, Amsterdam.

Rosato, P. and Stellin, G., 1993, 'A Multi-criteria Approach to Territorial Management: The Case of the Carole and Bibione Langoon Nature Park', *Agricultural Systems*, Vol. 41, No. 3, pp.399–417.

Steuer, R.E., 1986, *Multiple Criteria Optimization: Theory, Computation, and Application*, John Wiley & Sons, Inc., New York.

Steuer, R.E., 1992, *Manual for the ADBASE: Multiple Objective Linear Programming Package*, Department of Management Science & Information Technology, The University of Georgia, Athens, Georgia.

Thomas, D.L., Smith, M.C., Leonard, R.A. and deSilva, F.J.K., 1990, 'Simulated Effects of Rapeseed Production Alternatives on Pollution Potential in the Georgia Coastal Plain', *Journal of Soil and Water Conservation*, Vol. 45, No. 1.

DISCUSSION OPENING — Slim Zekri *(University of Tunis)*

The paper tackles a serious environmental problem related to intensive agriculture. Farmers seek to maintain their revenue while the community looks for a reduction of the environmental burden which results from nitrate pollution. The multi-objective methodology is well suited to this type of issue where a conflict exists between the farmers and the community interests. Additionally, the authors are innovative in the sense that they consider four techniques: simulation models; multi-objective programming, willingness to participate in a cost sharing programme and econometric modelling. Nevertheless, it seems that the econometrically estimated Expected Net Return function lacks sense. In fact, a single farmer can either adopt a new Best Management Practice, use the current management practice or a combination of both. Thus the Expected Net Return cannot be the sum of the expectations of the net returns for both of the management practices. As presented, the Expected Net Return function could perhaps represent the community utility function of Gum Creek Watershed. But in such a case it does not represent the farmer's utility. With respect to the empirical data, I think that the case has been extremely simplified since only two crops are considered while a diversity of crops are grown on the farm. In the same way, peanuts and corn were thought to be non-irrigated. Irrigation is a major factor contributing to nitrogen leachate. Risk due to heavy rainfall events has not been taken into account. With respect to results, the figures in column 3 of table 4 differ from those presented in column 6 of Table 1. It would be useful to explain such differences.

POSTER ABSTRACTS

Trade, Policy and Competitiveness

Shankar Narayanan, Agriculture Canada, and **Fu Lai Tung** — *Comparison of capital labour ratios in Canadian and United States agriculture and implications on competitiveness.*

Transition in capital labour ratios of primary agriculture in Canada and USA over 1961–1990 indicates gradual substitution of capital for labour in general and a situation of relative overcapitalization in Canadian agriculture compared to the USA. Some of the key implied consequences for the competitiveness of Canada of higher capital costs include higher taxpayer funded farm income support, reduced effectiveness of farm finance programs (debt review), and weakening of the competitive position for Canadian agriculture products in the world markets in relation to the USA, due to reduced productivity.

John Parker, USDA — *Trends in the agricultural trade of North Africa and Southern Africa compared.*

North Africa's agricultural imports trended upward in the 1980s, and flattened out in the early 1990s because of lower prices, while its agricultural exports declined, especially cotton. Agricultural imports by Southern Africa fluctuated and peaked in 1992, while agricultural exports were steady.

Mary Mafuyai and **Richard Robbins**, North Carolina Agricultural and Technical State University, **Blake A. Brown**, North Carolina State University, and **Enefïok P. Ekanem**,Tennessee State University — *Impact of tobacco policy legislations on the United States and world economy.*

Tobacco is one of the most valuable crops in the USA. Farm level sales of tobacco were about $2.96 billion in 1992. Major tobacco exporters include USA, Brazil, Argentina and Zimbabwe. This research will evaluate legislation impacts on selected countries and world markets. An econometric model will be used in analysing the data.

R.W.M. Johnson, Ministry of Agriculture, New Zealand — *GATT and the regulation of technical barriers to trade.*

Major technical barriers to agricultural trade are sanitary and phytosanitary measures and environmental protection measures. Both could be justified in some circumstances and both are potentially covered by the provisions of Article XX of the GATT. Sanitary measures have been accepted as justified measures for a number of years for health reasons but it is only recently that environmental measures have been specifically discussed in the GATT context. The threats to trade can be resolved by reference to existing GATT provisions for exemptions and the possible development of new GATT rules for conflict resolution.

Mahmoud El-Jafari, Islamic University of Gaza City, Gaza Strip — *The international competitiveness of Palestinian agriculture.*

The purpose of this study is to identify and measure the impacts of factors which are expected to influence the competitiveness of Palestinian agriculture by using the market share approach with an econometric model. Over the past three decades, Palestinian agriculture has been subjected to increased international and regional competition. The impact of this competition is in part evidenced by trend decline in the West Bank and Gaza Strip agricultural exports on the one hand, and the increases in agricultural imports on the other. The empirical results indicate that the performance of domestic market and import shares could be improved through increasing the productivities of the major production factors, land, labour and capital. On the other hand, the competitiveness indicators of Palestinian agricultural exports have been found to be sensitive to changes in the export process prevailing in Jordan and Israel and to the changes in the relative real exchange rates of these countries. Also, the estimated coefficients of model have signified that Palestinian agricultural exports have deteriorated because of the non-tariff trade barriers (NTBs) imposed by Jordan and Israel. One could conclude that future farm export competitiveness will be closely linked to improvement agricultural factor productivities and marketing efficiency and eliminating NTBs imposed by Jordan and Israel.

Steve McCorriston, University of Exeter, UK and **Ian Sheldon**, The Ohio State University, USA — *Trade reform with market intermediaries.*

Most studies of agricultural and trade policy reform ignore the existence of market intermediaries. Yet casual observation suggests that such intermediaries play an important role in the agricultural and food system. Dealing with these intermediaries in applied work is complicated by the fact that a limited number of these intermediaries typically dominate specific markets such that the assumption of perfect competition — commonly assumed in applied policy analysis — no longer applies. This paper outlines a model for dealing with such features and is used to evaluate welfare changes following reform of the EC banana regime in 1992.

Jukka Kola, University of Helsinki, Finland — *A small country perspective on agricultural policy and trade disputes of large countries.*

Small EFTA countries depend heavily on international trade. Yet, their agricultural sectors are very protected due to the stabilized political economy of food security. In GATT, small countries can respond to large exporters' requirements of free trade and common markets by increasing agricultural efficiency, but also by emphasizing issues of new competitiveness based on environmental factors and full inclusion of externalities in production costs. Thus, the income redistribution effects illustrated by the surplus transformation framework may be more equally distributed, both between countries and within countries. In the search for local and global ecological and economic sustainability there is an important role for small countries.

Dennis R. Henderson and **Charles R. Hand**, Economic Research Service, USDA — *International commerce in food: market strategies of multinational firms.*

The annual value of international commerce in food is estimated to exceed $1.5 trillion. Much of this is carried out by multinational food firms, engaging a variety of strategies for accessing foreign markets. Of these, trade in dissimilar products plays a relatively minor role. More important by several orders of magnitude are shipments originating from foreign operations. Other important strategies include international product licensing, joint ventures and intra-industry trade. These strategies are motivated by profit opportunities associated with firm- or product-specific advantages. Both in-bound and out-bound international commerce are positively associated with a country's level of economic development. The economic impacts of such commerce are pro-competitive in both host and originating markets, measured in terms of increased product availability and lower prices.

A. Joaquín, University Politécnica, Madrid — *Money supply, exchange rates and relative prices.*

The dynamic response of money and both nominal and real exchange rates and relative agricultural and industrial prices is analysed in Austria, Germany and Spain, using VAR. The long-run neutrality hypothesis is rejected in general but the evidence is weak. Monetary and international factors also vary in importance, depending on the openness of instability of the economy. The main conclusion is that models using nominal or real exchange rates lead to almost exactly the same results.

Roland Hermann, University of Giessen, Germany — *How agricultural and exchange rate policies affect the level and instability of producer prices in developing countries: a cross-country approach for major commodities.*

This paper contains an explanation of how the average level of producer prices in developing countries was influenced by agricultural and macroeconomic policies, how the influence on the price level changed over time and how producer price instability was altered by the policies under consideration. The analysis focuses on two important food crops, wheat and rice, and one major export crop, coffee, over the period 1969–85.

It is found that exchange rate policies are an important source of total net protection in agriculture in developing countries, as they affect the average level of producer prices as well as its trend and instability strongly. However, in many cases agricultural policy is more important than macroeconomics policy with regard to total net protection. The latter finding is different from the results of the World Bank study by Krueger/Schiff/Valdes.

When exchange rate distortions are taken into account, many countries discriminate against agricultural producers. Apart from this, the export crop coffee is clearly taxed compared with the food crops wheat and rice. This result is mainly due to the differential treatment of food and export crops in agricultural policy. That policy sets more favourable food crop prices compared with the prices of export crops has been shown in earlier studies. The bias against export crops is also valid with regard to the weaker stabilization of producer prices and the deterioration of the policy-induced incentives over time.

Nicholas Samuel and Elton Li, The University of Adelaide, Australia — *Heterogenity in processed food and beverage markets in China: implications for competitive marketing.*

This study provides empirical support for the theoretical expectation that the Chinese market for processed food and beverages is made up of heterogeneous market segments. Analyses of primary survey data from four Chinese cities reveal significant inter-city difference in price levels and demand relationships, the latter in terms of price and income elasticities. This suggests dissimilar market growth prospects among the cities examined. The empirical evidence supports the need for businesses to consider geographical market segmentation analysis as a basis for target market selection and strategy formulation for marketing processed food in China.

Edith S. Obschatko, Interamerican Institute for Agricultural Cooperation (IICA) Argentina — *Competitiveness of the Argentine agro-industry.*

The competitiveness or 'agro-industrial complex' (primary and processed agricultural products) for Argentina is studied by means of several indicators; evolution of exports, Revealed Comparative Advantage coefficient and the Competitive Analysis of Nation (CAN) Model. Argentina's exports have increased during the eighties, with specalization in products in the OECD market in which the country has comparative advantage. Nevertheless, the agro-industrial complex as a whole has lost competitiveness in this market. Recent changes in macroeconomic policies — deregulation, price stabilization, privatization of public utilities — create conditions to increase competitiveness, but protectionism in developed countries poses a severe restriction. The private sector is undergoing organizational and technological changes to adapt to new conditions, such as a higher rate of adoption of available technologies, concentration of primary production in larger units, reduction in the number of small producers, diversification of production with non traditional crops, increased vertical and horizontal integration, associative arrangements, product differentiation and special arrangements related with the MERCOSUR.

Antonio Yunez-Naude, Centro de Estudios Ecónómicos, Mexico — *Agricultural price reforms; results of general equilibrium models applied to Mexico.*

The deep process of liberalization conducted recently by the Mexican government, together with its negotiations to reach a free trade agreement with Canada and the USA, have motivated the construction of several independent General Equilibrium Models (GEMs) to quantify the impacts of these changes on the Mexican economy and its agricultural sector. Although they have differences, it is argued that the main findings obtained from such applied models can be used to presentthe repercussions of policy reforms on Mexico's countryside, on solid grounds. Since the results of all of these GEMs point to the unfavourable consequences for Mexican rural poor and for its grain and oilseed subsectors that price reforms would bring about, their authors suggest that policies of transition towards the attainment of a more deregulated situation are required.

Carl Mabbs-Zeno, **Mesfin Bezuneh**, **John Chirwa** and **Barry Krissoff**, US Agency for International Development, Washington, D.C. — *Potential gains from reducing agricultural trade barriers.*

This paper examines the effect of the tariff differential extended by members of the Preferential Trade Agreement in Eastern and Southern Africa (PTA) to other members. It presents a static simulation model of trade by PTA members. The experiments summarized here highlight the limitations for the PTA of using tariff preferences to encourage agricultural production. Existing tariffs have little effect on international markets and the tariff preferences have almost no effect.

A.W. Mukhebi, **T. Munyombwe**, **C. Ncube**, **R.Kruska**, International Laboratory for Research on Animal Diseases, Kenya, **U. Ushewokunze-Obatolu**, Veterinary Research Laboratory, Zimbabwe and **B.D. Perry Mukhebi**, International Laboratory for Research on Animal Diseases, Kenya — *Livestock diseases and food security in the preferential trade area with a focus on Zimbabwe.*

This paper discusses livestock diseases as a major constraint to livestock production and food security in the Preferential Trade Area (PTA) region. It highlights economic costs of two major diseases in the region, namely theileriosis transmitted by ticks and trypanosomiasis transmitted by tsetse flies. It provides a more detailed analysis of the economic cost of theileriosis in Zimbabwe and the economics of its control by a new method based on immunization using the infection and treatment method.

Jamal B. Othman, **Jack E. Houston**, University of Georgia, USA and **Christopher S. McIntosh** — *Competition in US edible vegetable oil markets — persistence of structural changes.*

This study utilizes a time varying parameters model to examine evidence of transitory and permanent structural changes in the edible vegetable oils market in the USA and the resulting competitive effects of a promotional campaign focusing negative publicity on imported 'fatty tropical oils'. The relative magnitudes of the permanent and temporary components of changes in domestic demand elasticities for soybean, palm, coconut, and cottonseed oils are examined for periods prior to and following commencement of the 'tropical oils' campaign. Low estimated values of structural change persistence suggest that the negative impacts on palm and coconut oils were largely transitory until 1989, when food labelling legislation passed.

M. Ben Kaabia and **J.M. GilUnidad**, Servicio de Investigación Agraria, Spain — *The effect of macroeconomic variables on competitiveness of Spanish agricultural exports.*

This paper investigates empirical relationships among the interest rate, the real exchange rate, agricultural export prices and agricultural export sales in Spain using a restrictive vector autorregression model. Positive exchange rate shocks have less influence than prices on agricultural exports due to the compensatory mechanisms of the Common Agricultural Policy. Agricultural exports, on the other hand, have little influence on the macroeconomic variables.

Joseph Salvacruz and **Michael Reed**, University of Kentucky, USA — *Product cycle trade in the processed food industry.*

A study was conducted to describe the characteristics of traditional Product Cycle (PC) indicators of processed foods within the context of a three country model; developed, developing, and less developed economies – represented by the USA, South Korea, and the Philippines, respectively. The PC indicators studied were processed food exports, capital intensity of food exports, industry size, and productivity. Results revealed PC indicator trends consistent with the predictions of the PC theory in the maturity stage. Chow test results confirmed significant differences in PC indicator trends between the USA and South Korea, but not between South Korea and the Philippines. This study suggested that the USA possesses a technological advantage over the lesser developed countries. The role of other variables which may determine PC trends should be examined more closely. These variables are foreign investment flows, investment incentives, technological progress, and political factors.

Farms, Markets and Efficiency

Claude Freud and **Ellen Hanak Freud**, Centre de Coopération Internationale en Récherche Agronomique pour le Développement (CIRAD), France — *Is there a future for African robusta coffees?*

The competitiveness of robusta coffee producers is analysed using comparisons of the cost structure during and prior to the collapse in world prices in the late 1980s. The scope for African producers, whose intermediation costs are highest, to regain their footing via devaluation and via intensification of production is assessed.

Natalia Aldaz, University of Lleida, and **Joaquín A. Millan**, Polytechnic University of Madrid — *Agricultural efficiency of the Spanish autonomous communities.*

An empirical analysis using both parametric and nonparametric production frontiers is carried out for the agricultures of the Spanish Autonomous Communities. There are great differences in the estimated efficiencies and rankings between models. The main result is a trend toward convergence in productivity between regions.

W.J. Florkowski, **A.H. Elnagheeb**, **J.E. Houston** and **C.L. Huang**, The University of Georgia, USA — *Measuring risk perception of existing and new food production technologies.*

In this study, survey data were used to develop a model to measure the relationship between a set of socio-economic characteristics of consumers and their risk perception of feed additives and growth hormones used in livestock production. Perceptions were measured indirectly by constructs based on responses to multiple questions. Factor analysis was used to identify the perception measures. Next, two econometric approaches were applied to estimate the relationships between the explanatory variables and risk perceptions. Estimation results gave both the direct and total effects of each explanatory variable on the three constructs, risk perception due to the use of bio-engineering in food production or its specific example — the porcine somatotropin (pST) — the pig growth hormone, and support of pST use in pig production.

Franco Rosa, University of Udine, Italy — *Change in the EC food industry.*

The paper will focus on changes in the food industry in EC countries for the period 1980–90. The data, collected from Eurostat statistics referred to the 18sectors of the food industry with 20 or more persons engaged. This allowed calculation of the indexes signalling the change in productivity and investments of a selected group of EC countries for the period considered. Conclusions are for a consistent improvement of the food industry performance with structural convergence signalling the diffusion of technical innovation in the EC.

Wen S. Chern and **Guijing Wang**, The Ohio State University, USA — *Food consumption patterns and agricultural policy in China.*

This study estimates a linear approximate almost ideal demand system (LA/RAIDS) for 2 specifications by treating grains and oils as rationed or unrationed goods. The models are estimated using data from 28 cities and provinces (based on household surveys) over 1985–88. The results show that the rationsing model provides more plausible estimated demand elasticities than the nonrationing model. Furthermore, Chinese urban household demands for non-staple foods are shown to be elastic with respect to price and expenditure. These elastic demands will make future prediction of food demand in China more difficult.

Ian Jarratt and **Harold Brown**, Queensland Department of Primary Industries, Australia — *Commodity marketing board modernization: the Queensland experience.*

This paper describes and explains the recent very rapid reduction in the number of commodity marketing boards (CMBs) in Queensland as requested by their producers. The major influencing factors included: changed macroeconomic policies; changes to national marketing arrangements, reduced producer support for compulsory delivery, and producer demands for more flexible marketing systems. The key role of the Queensland Government in; encouraging reviews of the CMBs, providing innovative and flexible legislative changes, and providing information and other assistance, is emphasized. Research on the economic effects of the changes is suggested.

F. Sotle, Universita di Ancona, Italy — *Public transfers to Italian agriculture.*

The scope of the poster is to sketch the origin and destination of agricultural public transfers in Italy. The study focuses upon EU, MAF and Region expenditures for agriculture, together with the differentials, in terms of fiscal and social security benefits, between farmers and other sectors' workers. An estimate of the total amount of public money transferred to the agricultural sector is provided. Finally, in the light of recent CAP reforms and GATT agreement, we also attempt a preliminary analysis of recent changes in the distribution of costs and benefits of agricultural policy.

A. Gracia and **L.M. Albisu**, Unidad de Economia y Sociologie Agrarias, Servicio de Investigacion Agraria, Zaragoza, Spain — *A cross-section analysis of socio-demographic factors affecting food expenditure in Spain.*

This study examines the influence of socio-demographic factors on Spanish food consumption. Engel curves for food expenditures have been estimated. Data from the National Expenditure Survey conducted by the National Statistics Institute, in 1990–91 have been used. The large number of available observations have been aggregated into cohorts of representative households with common characteristics. Cohort averages have been taken to estimate a Working Leser model. The dependent variable has been the budget share for seven food products: (1) meat, (2) bread and cereals, (3) fish, (4) dairy, eggs and cheese, (5) fats and oils, (6) fruits, vegetables, pulses and potatoes and (7) other foodstuff. Per capita food expenditure has been introduced as a proxy for purchasing power because of the weak separability assumption. A set of socio-demographic variables (household size and composition, town size, seasonality and sex) have been incorporated into the model by the translation method. Estimations show that meat and fish are luxury products and cereals and dairy products, eggs and cheese are necessities. Sociodemographic variables revealed important determinants of food demand. Some economies of scale can be observed in meat, fish, bread and cereals and dairy products, eggs and cheese.

Jose Maria Sumpsi, Universidad Politecnica De Madrid, Spain; **Francisco Amador**, Universidad de Cordoba, Spain and Carlos Romera, Unviersidad Politecnical de Madrid, Spain — *On farmers objectives: the case of family farms in Andalusia Spain.*

In this paper a multi-criteria methodology aimed at researching the objectives actually followed by a farmer or by a homogeneous group of farmers is analyzed and used to predict the behaviour of family farms in 'Vega de Cordoba' (Spain). The proposed methodology has an algorithmic structure and is articulated within a goal programming formulation. The results obtained seem to corroborate previous findings in the literature which conjecture that the actual behaviour of farmers cannot be explained by the optimization of a single objective but by a compromise between multiple objectives. Some of the policy implications found are highlighted in the discussion.

Brent M. Swallow, International Livestock Centre for Africa, Nairobi, Kenya — *Economic analysis of techniques for controlling African animal trypanosomiasis.*

African animal trypanosomiasis can be controlled by a number of techniques: drugs can be given to protect or cure animals; trypanotolerant breeds of livestock can be raised; traps, targets or pour-ons can be used to suppress the tsetse flies that transmit the disease. Besides considering their total benefits and costs, research and policy regarding disease control need to also consider the excludability, security, multiplicity and externality attributes of the benefits and costs. In one area of south Ethiopia where targets were used, we focused our research on the local public good and insecurity attributes of the benefits. We used contingent valuation to assess people's willingness to contribute time and/or money. In a nearby area we used market and non-market surveys to assess the multiplicity and mixed public-private nature of the benefits derived by a pour-on.

Hamath A. Sy, **Merle D. Faminow**, **Gary V. Johnson** and **Gary Crow**, University of Manitoba, Canada — *Estimating the value of cattle characteristics using an ordered probit.*

Economists interested in the value of product characteristics have generally used hedonic analysis. However, in cases where market prices are not available a survey-based methodology called conjoint analysis can be used to value product characteristics. In this study, this technique is applied to beef cattle to appraise the value of genetic characteristics commonly used in beef improvement programmes. The conjoint analysis was conducted using an ordered probit model. Data from a beef producer survey in Manitoba, Canada were analysed to determine the relative values of reproduction traits (e.g., milking ability, calving ease) and final traits (e.g., carcass yield, feed efficiency).

Mayada Baydas, Ohio State University, USA — *Capital structure determinants among non-farm enterprises: the case study of developing financial markets in The Gambia.*

The focus of this study is the capital structure of non-farm manufacturing enterprizes in low income countries. The study examined the importance of different sources of financing, internal and external, in the capital structure of the firm and factors explaining entrepreneurial behaviour in using different financial contracts. The capital structure was modelled by considering a one-period world within a deterministic approach. A set of testable hypotheses derived from this model was applied to a sample of 153 micro, small and medium scale manufacturing enterprises in The Gambia. The findings of this study support the hypotheses that the characteristics of the enterprise, attributes of the entrepreneur, rates of return, interest rates, transaction costs of alternative sources of financing and the respective share of these securities simultaneously determine the capital structure of the enterprise.

C. Marian, University of Craiova, Romania — *Current analysis of agricultural produce markets in Romania.*

The author deals with problems in the distribution network for agricultural produce in Romania. Farmers and economic dealers involved in these networks face problems caused by aspects of the present social and economic conditions. In particular, there are frequent contradictions in economic signals and imbalances in agricultural yields. It is of particular importance that the transition should be as quick and profitable as possible and lead to high proficiency rates for farmers, processing and economic units. Consumers should also benefit from these changes. Details of expenditures are given for the agricultural distribution network in the district of Dolj.

Abebe Teferi, Ethiopian Tourism Commission — *Grain marketing structures and integration in Ethiopia.*

In the Ethiopian traditional society, market prices were determined traditionally and they had traditional trade connections. But in the past one and half decades the grain marketing system and the marketing was disrupted. Before the 1974 Revolution and before strong government intervention in the grain market, the grain market was positively integrated.

Prices were formed on the basis of market focus. Grains moved where the prices were highest. After the overthrow of the Marxist government, the disrupted market structures came back to normal. The formation of prices is based on market forces.

Ching-Kai Hsiao, National Chung Hsing University, Taiwan — *Analysis of demand for aquacultural water in Taiwan.*

The purpose in this paper is to construct a model of the demand for water by aquaculture, and to identify the technological relationship between output and inputs by estimating a production function for cultural fishery. The parameters of the models were estimated with data collected from a field survey of water use by different types of aquaculture in selected districts of Taiwan during 1991 and conducted the survey on the summer of 1992.

Jyrki Niemi, Agricultural Economics Research Institute, Finland — *Interrelated demands for factors of milk production in Finland.*

A multi-input translog cost function is applied to investigate the structure of Finnish milk production. The method allows a quantitative assessment of partial elasticities of substitution between inputs and the own- and cross price elasticities of input demand. The results suggest that the method used provides a reasonable framework for empirical analysis.

Amin Ismail Aboud, National Research Centre, Egypt — *Economic efficiency of human labour and nitrogenous fertilizers use in Egyptian new and old lands.*

Dramatic dispersion for levels of both labour and chemical fertilizer use was revealed, approaching 90 percent in new lands. Only 7 percent of producers there were close to efficient use based on equating the value of marginal product with the input's price. The corresponding estimate for old lands reached a maximum of 28 percent, inferring more serious need for efficient agricultural extension in new lands where experience is still young. Much lower applications revealed for larger farms and crop areas may be due to obligatory reliance upon hired labour and production requisites black markets.

Andrea Fantini, Institute of Agricultural Economics University Bari, Italy — *AGRISIM: farm simulation teaching model.*

A dynamic simulation model has been constructed to represent a livestock farm in the Marche region of Italy. Changes in the managerial environment are emphasized. These include increasing price instability following CAP reform and also the increasing importance of environmental constraints. The model is programmed using widely available spreadsheet software. Herd development and fixed equipment investment are modelled so that the user can see the effect of alternative strategies under different policy regimes. The program can be used as a business management simulator in order to instruct students in the management of farms or to train extension advizers when policy changes take place. Experience to date indicates that, after using the model, trainees can often construct their own versions of the models for application to the specific conditions of individual clients.

David Coleman, University of Manchester, UK — *Problems of measuring price distortion and price transmission: framework for analysis.*

In the contemporary condition where IMF and IBRD lending policies to less-developed countries involve imposing conditions for agricultural price and trade policy reform, and where the reform requirements are based on measures of price distortion and protection, this poster examines aspects of the robustness of these measures. It presents a framework for deriving measures of price distortion and price transmission. Using this, it considers the links between both types of results which can be expected. It also considers general aspects of the relationship of African and international prices, and argues that many studies use or assume, measures of price distortion and transmission which are flawed.

David D. Mainland, Economics Department, SAC Auchincruive, Ayr — *An approach to increasing dairy farm economic efficiency with reference to Scotland.*

If economic efficiency is to be achieved then it is necessary that farmers know and understand the concepts of marginality employed in economics. Current managerial techniques generally work in averages which is not at all helpful in achieving satisfactory economic outcomes. Instead a decision support system (DSS) is better suited to the task. Such a model is described and a derivative is used to analyse dairy herd production in Scotland since 1975 to compare actual feeding rates of concentrate feed against the economic optimum. Actual feeding rates were very much higher than the optimum until the introduction of quota brought more economic reality into dairy farm management. The model is further used so as to examine typical Scottish dairy farming problems in terms of marginality analysis.

K.L. Sharma, The University of the South Pacific, Western Samoa — *Acreage and yield responses in sugarcane production in the Fiji islands.*

This paper attempts to estimate the Nerlovian acreage and the neoclassical yield responses in sugarcane production to changes in price and non-price variables in the Fiji Islands during the period 1960–92. The results indicate that sugarcane farmers do respond positively to price changes. A favourable price regime is required to increase sugarcane production. Further, both the short-run acreage elasticity and the yield elasticity need to be considered to avoid underestimating the total supply elasticity.

R. Canero, University of Almeria, Spain and **J. Calatrava**, Department of Agricultural Economics, Granada, Spain — *Influence of the functional form and the estimation methods in frontier function efficiency analysis: the case of plastic covered horticulture in south-eastern Spain.*

Numerous studies have been carried out on productive efficiency in agriculture using production frontiers, particularly since 1980. However, the great majority of these limited themselves to using only one functional form and one or two frontier kinds. The aim in the present study is to analyse the effect that the choice of functional form and frontier kind has on the measurement of efficiency. Data obtained from horticultural businesses in south-eastern Spain have been used. Finally, conclusions regarding the above-mentioned effect are drawn.

Research, Technology and Innovation

Manuel Rapùn Gárate and **Belén Iráizoz Apezteguín**, Universidad Publica de Navarra Campus de Arrosadia , España — *Technical efficiency on the cereal sector and other by-products for the human consumption in Navarra.*

In this document we intend to carry out an estimation of the technical efficiency (TE) on the cereal subsector and other by-products for the human consumption, an outstanding feature in the regional economy because it accounts for the 14 percent of the employment of the agrofood industry in Navarra. Farrel's methodology has been applied in this case.

Hrabrin Bachev, Institute of Agricultural Economics in Sofia, Bulgaria and **Snehana Bacheva**, University of National and World Economy in Sofia, Bulgaria — *Agricultural research during transitional period.*

The paper examines the problems of organization and management of agricultural research in the transitional economies of Eastern Europe. The crisis created by the centralized bureaucratic management system of agricultural research in Bulgaria is analysed. The process of research management has been described from a formal structural aspect. The different models of agricultural research management have been analysed. A model for organization and management of agricultural research during the transitional economic period has been developed. The most effective governance structures for development of transactions in innovative cycle during transitional period have been designed. The new system should be based on the establishment of the National Council of Agrarian Research, responsible for setting the priorities of agrarian research and development, and the National Centre for Agricultural Research, carrying the organization and management of the State agricultural research system, research and a System of Agricultural Extension. Reorganization should involve formation of institutions with considerable autonomy, preventing revival of the monopoly in research management. Different and more flexible ways of financing agricultural research and mechanisms for developing private sector research (privatization and pseudo-privatization) have been proposed for the period of reorganization.

Heinrich Hockmann, University of Gottingen, Germany — *Price distortions and welfare effects of agricultural research activities.*

When government intervention leads to a distortion of market prices, the production enhancing effects of research and development induce positive (increase in producer rents) as well as negative (increase in dead weight losses) welfare effects. Partial equilibrium theory is used to derive a simple rule for estimating whether welfare gains or losses will occur. The sign of the welfare change depends on the elasticity of domestic supply, the demand elasticity in the world market, and the amount of price distortion. Technical change and the export share influence the amount of the overall welfare effect, but not its sign. The rule is applied to the development of hybrid rye in Germany. Since the demand in the world market is assumed to be elastic, this innovation has induced a positive net welfare effect.

Peter Karunga, University of Witwatersrand, South Africa, **Joseph Salvacruz** and **Michael Reed**, University of Kentucky, USA — *Technological progress and competitiveness in the food processing industry.*

A market share measure of international competitiveness in the world food market was determined for the USA and a group of less developed Southeast Asian countries (ASEAN LDCs) in 1970–89. The total factor productivity index in processed food was also computed and served as proxy measue for productivity competitiveness or technological progress. Research and development expenditures and market power were found to be driving technological progress in the USA, while poor market power was the only significant determinant of technological progress among the ASEAN LDCs. Results of regressing international marketing competitiveness against endogenous technology revealed a significant positive relationship between these two competitiveness measures.

Pareena G. Lawrence, University of Minnesota, USA and **John H. Sanders**, Purdue University, USA — *The impact of agricultural and household technologies on farm and female incomes in Burkina Faso.*

This paper investigates the impact of agricultural and household technologies on the income of the farm household and women for the Solenzo region in Burkina Faso. The Women in Development literature asserts that agricultural technologies can have an adverse effect on the income of women. This assertion, if true, creates a serious gender equity problem. Using the household decision-making theory and a programming model, this study shows that the impact of agricultural technologies depends upon the type of decision-making practised by the household. In contrast, household technologies increase the incomes of women independent of the type of household decision-making. Empirical evidence from various field studies suggests bargaining as the most prevalent form of household behaviour. According to model results, with bargaining, agricultural technologies benefit women, but women benefit most when both technologies are simultaneously introduced. The study also briefly examines the household investment decision in household technologies.

Shiva S. Makki and **Luther G. Tweeten**, Ohio State University, USA and **Cameron S. Thraen** — *Evaluating payoffs to research investments in agriculture: a co-integration approach.*

This paper examines the returns to USA agricultural research investments for the years 1930 through 1990 using the cointegration technique. Most previous research is based on time series regression analysis to evaluate the returns to research investments without correcting the data non-stationarity. According to Granger and Newbold, regressions estimated from nonstationary series frequently are seriously biased towards accepting spurious relationships. The cointegration approach corrects for data non-stationarity and provides a better estimate of the long run dynamic relationship among the time series variables. Results in this study indicate that agricultural productivity, public and private research investments, farmers' education, terms of trade, and commodity programs are cointegrated. The estimated internal rates of return are 27 percent for public research and 6 percent for private research in 1990 dollars. These estimates are from the most comprehensive and timely data assembled to date and indicate that returns to public agricultural research compare favourably to real returns on alternative long-run.

Mywish K. Maredia and **Carl K. Eicher**, Michigan State University, USA and **Derek Byerlee**, The World Bank, Washington, D.C. — *Strategies for increasing the efficiency of national wheat research programs in developing countries.*

Because of severe budget constraints, many National Agricultural Research Systems (NARSs) in developing countries have been forced to make hard scientific and financial decisions on the number, size and type of research programs. A cost–benefit model is used to determine the profitability of 71 wheat improvement programs in 35 developing countries. Many of these programs were found to be operating at uneconomic levels. NARSs can increase their research efficiency by consolidating wheat research programs, improving their capacity to import wheat technology, increasing collaborative regional research programs and relying more heavily on importing wheat from CIMMYT/NARS international collaborative breeding effort.

Paul W. Heisey, CIMMYT, Mexico — *What is a green revolution?*

Research reported here takes the following working definition of a 'Green Revolution'. Higher yielding, more input-responsive crop varieties based on a recognizable genetic innovation such as use of dwarfing genes in wheat, use of dwarfing genes or hybridization in rice, or hybridization in maize, are developed. Diffusion among farmers is observable. Yield-increasing technical change of this kind is thought to be more likely in land scarce countries. This research reviews historical data on periods of rapid yield increase for selected developing and developed countries and asks whether they are related to diffusion of high yielding varieties and increased input use. In general they are, but yield increases in countries that are not obviously land scarce, yield increases not easily ascribed to varietal improvement of the type defined, and varietal contributions to productivity that do not translate directly to rapid yield gains, are all cases requiring further study.

Duncan Boughton and **John M. Staatz**, Michigan State University, USA — *Using the commodity subsector approach to design agricultural research: the case of maize in Mali.*

This paper applies a subsector perspective to analyzing the design of agricultural production and processing technologies. The framework stresses how conditons at one level of a subsector influence constraints and opportunities for technical and institutional innovations at other levels. The paper also stresses the need to combine insights from the subsector and farming systems perspective when developing an agricultural research agenda. These points are illustrated by drawing on results from a recent maize subsector study in Mali.

Terrence S. Veeman and **Krishna B. Hamal**, University of Alberta, Canada — *Total factor productivity growth in the nepalese crop sector: an empirical analysis.*

Improved Crop Output and productivity is vitally important to Nepal, yet too little is known about agricultural productivity. In this paper, total factor productivity (TFP) growth is estimated and assessed in the Nepalese crop sector from 1961–62 to 1987–88. Two estimation procedures for TFP are used and compared; geometric aggregation, using factor shares and flexible weight aggregation, based on Tornqvist-Theil index numbers. Productivity in the crops sector in Nepal is estimated to have declined moderately over the period as a whole, at some 0.2 to 0.5 percent per year. However, crop productivity performance in the more recent sub-period of the 1980s has considerably strengthened with TFP growing at approximately one percent per annum. Since area is constrained, future crop output increases in Nepal will have to come largely from yield increases based upon improvements in technology and price policy.

Ronny Sibanda, MATAPOS Research Station, Bulawayo, Zimbabwe and **Benedict White**, University of Newcastle Upon Tyne, UK — *An economic evaluation of research and development expenditure on communal area livestock systems in Zimbabwe.*

The research aims to assess the uptake of new cattle breeds by small farmers in the communal areas of Southern Zimbabwe. Two sources of data are employed, the first is a survey of small farms, the second is data on breed potential trials carried out at Matopos Research Station. The representative farm models based on the survey data indicate only 21 percent of the farms in the survey would adopt the new breeds and these were the medium to large size farms. The resource base on most farms in the region was insufficient to support the requirements of breeds which had higher nutritional requirements than the unimproved breeds. The new breeds were also less well adapted to the multi-purpose role of cattle in the communal areas which includes draft power and milk production as well as meat production.

Policy and Infrastructure for and Performance of Smallholder Farms

Benon Gazinski, Agricultural University, Poland — *Between efficiency and equity: Indian agricultural policy seen from a Polish perspective.*

The objective in this paper is to give an overview of dilemmas of Indian agricultural policy from Independence to the 1990s. Four stages of agricultural policies were identified: land reforms and the Community Development Programme — late 1940s to early 1960s; intensive development and the 'Green Revolution' — early 1960s to mid 1970s; the Integrated Rural Development Programma and related programmes — mid 1970s to late 1980s, and emerging new economic policy and market reforms — 1990s. It is shown that the economic system of India as framed by Nehru in the 1950s remained virtually unchanged until the end of the 1980s. Many elements of the Nehru vision typical of the Soviet-type socialist economy are cited. These include: the principle of central planning; priority to industry, excessive centralization, emphasis on the public sector etc. The objective of rural policy — to obtain growth with justice and to eradicate poverty — has remained unattainable and the inefficiency of the system has increased, leading to the shift toward the market economy reforms.

Nicholas T. Christodoulou, Development Bank of Southern Africa and **Joan C. Van Rooyen**, Republic of South Africa — *Shaping the impact of small farmer support programs (FSPs) in South Africa.*

Black smallholder farmers in South Africa emerged as a separate group operating without the benefit of Government assistance enjoyed by white commercial farmers. The FSP was formally introduced in South Africa by the Development Bank of Southern Africa (DBSA) in 1987 as one of the major agricultural development strategies to support black farmers who have been historically denied access to basic support services. This paper examines the events leading to the conceptualization and introduction of the FSP and subsequent implementation problems experienced. It also analyses changes in the orientation of the FSP approach and the DBSA management systems and funding arrangements which helped to reshape and improve the impact of the FSP to address existing and future development challenges in South Africa.

Barry I. Shapiro, ILCA, Ethiopia, and **John H. Sanders**, Purdue University, USA — *Intensification of improved integration of livestock with crops in the savannas of sub-Saharan Africa?*

Intensification occurs where high man-land ratios and access to urban markets exist. Opportunities for livestock intensification in mixed systems include animal traction, fattening of small ruminants, intensified milk production with crossbreeds or improved breeds, and strategic fattening to meet demand peaks. Like improved crops, forages to overcome the critical feed constraint require increased soil fertility through purchased inputs in the savannas. Potential for improved integration of mixed systems is thus limited.

Specialized systems occur where livestock profitability is higher than for crops, either near urban markets or where crops cannot thrive. Specialized, intensified peri-urban dairy and finishing operations present important, but limited development opportunities. In drier areas, on-going currency devaluation results in increased, but still highly variable livestock income. Future research will be needed to cut livestock losses and stabilize prices, and provide better market opportunities and information. Migration due to low income potential in marginal smallholder mixed systems will ultimately lead to improved larger scale livestock operations.

Saa Dittoh, University for Development Studies, Ghana — *No magic in markets: evidence from the agricultural sector of Nigeria.*

Exchange rate deregulation and other structural adjustment policies were instituted in the Nigerian economy to stem distortions in the economy, increase productivity (especially in the agricultural sector) and improve the standards of living of the people. However, analyses and arguments in this paper show that the policies had little positive effect on the production and export of cocoa, palm kernel and rubber, as well as the production of food and other agricultural products. Market forces actually had the effect of pauperizing farmers and being an 'invisible exploiter'. The paper argues for a more holistic approach to the analysis of the agricultural sectors of developing economies. Macroeconomic analyses should be strongly supported by microeconomic, sociological and other analyses if effective development policies are to be arrived at.

Jozsef Popp, Hungary — *Hungarian experience with adjustment and transition in the agrifood sector and the development of market economies.*

The Hungarian agriculture and food industry has a dominant role in domestic food supply, exports and rural development. Difficult decisions have been made about very complex issues such as: collective farm reforms; privatization, compensation and market regulation. Most of the market institutions have been established. There has been successful change of ownership, with private property becoming predominant, although there have been delays in the compensation process. The transformation of co-operatives to strengthen the diverse co-operative sector continues. Investment has increased from rock bottom. Improved market conditions are necessary for a progress in investment. Financial 'obligations' accumulated in the food sector are substantial, with credit in the sector influenced by preferential interest rates and state guarantees.

K.N. Ninan, Institute for Social and Economic Change, Bangalore, India — *Agricultural growth, institutional intervention and rural poverty trends in India: their linkages in the context of structural adjustment and liberalization.*

Against the background of Structural Adjustment Programma (SAP) and Liberalization, the paper analyses the trends and factors behind rural poverty in India from 1957–58 to 1986–87. It notes that, contrary to earlier findings, not only are there distinct time trends in the incidence of rural poverty in India and for most states, but also while these trends were positive and significant in period I (1957–58 to 1968–69), they were negative and significant in period II (1969–70 to 1986–87). Also, the rate of decline in the incidence of rural poverty in the latter period was much higher than that in the preceding period for both all-India and across states, using alternate measures of poverty. It then probes into the role of agricultural growth, inflation, access to subsidized food through the public distribution system, population pressure on environmental resources, rural consumption levels and inequality and infrastructure development on rural poverty using time series and cross-section data. Its findings suggest that policies to accelerate agricultural growth, infrastructure development and provide better access to subsidized food, along with measures to control inflation and population growth as also promoting environmental conservation promise to be most effective in reducing rural poverty in India. It then assesses the implications of SAP and other policy reforms in India and suggests that if the poor are to be protected and agricultural growth accelerated and sustained public investment will need to be stepped up, which however, conflicts with SAP's objective to reduce public expenditures.

Pramod K. Mishra, University of Sussex, UK — *Crop insurance and crop credit: impact of India's comprehensive crop insurance scheme on co-operative credit in Gujarat 1985–91.*

Discussions in the analytical literature hold out only a limited role for crop insurance in improving the flow of agricultural credit. On the basis of empirical data from Gujarat, this paper examines the impact of India's Comprehensive Crop Insurance Scheme (CCIS) on production credit to farmers, especially small farmers. The findings show that there is a significant increase in the flow of credit to insured farmers after the introduction of the CCIS. There is an increase in the number of borrowers, and also in credit per borrower, as well as per hectare. The share of small farmers in total loans increased from 19 percent to 27 percent. There is significant increase in the repayment of loans in absolute terms — repayment per farmer and repayment per hectare, but it is not clear if the propensity to repay improved. The expansion of credit is due to a collateral effect.

Donald W. Larson, **Douglas H. Graham**, Ohio State University, USA and **Fernandez Zaque** — *Why users prefer informal financial market services: the case of Mozambique.*

Informal financial matters (IFMs) are controversial, widely discussed, growing rapidly and poorly understood in Mozambique as well as in many other developing countries. The controversy results from views held by many people that IFMs are monopolistic, exploitative, illegal, usurious and unproductive marginal enterprizes. Government intervention leading to repression of the formal financial institutions contributes to the growing importance of IFMs in Mozambique and other countries. Because IFMs demonstrate considerable flexibility in their operations, many users prefer their financial services. Their diversity and flexibility has allowed IFMs to serve far more clients than are served by formal financial markets and institutions in spite of the hostility often expressed by formal sector agents and by policy makers and government officials charged with financial sector regulation. Even if the formal financial system were operating efficiently in a free market environment IFMs would exist. Thus attempts to eliminate IFMs by government regulators would appear to be neither possible nor desirable.

Mark Wenner, **John Holtzman** and **Gary Ender**, ABT Associates Inc, USA — *Agribusiness promotion in developing countries: policy regimes and institutional support.*

This paper reviews the economic and institutional policies needed to launch and sustain an agribusiness export promotion campaign. It is directed to policy makers in small open economies, as well as donor officials who work in such countries who accept an outward oriented growth strategy as appropriate. It examines first and second-best economic policy instruments and discusses the most appropriate roles for public and private sector actors in supporting agribusiness development. The main policy objectives are (1) a flexible and realistic exchange rate; (2) a liberal trade regime; (3) competitive primary input markets; (4) competitive financial markets; (5) non-discriminatory tax system; and (6) a transparent and rational regulatory system. Institutionally, the goal is to foster a set of units that collaborate in a consistent manner and deliver timely, useful services thus contributing to an enabling environment.

Antoon G. Vergroesen, Deutsche Gesellschaft fuer Technische Zusammenarbeit (GTZ) in co-operation with the Ministry of Lands and Housing German Assisted Settlement Project, Kenya — *Integrated rural development in settlement schemes in the Coast Province in Kenya; guidelines and criteria for community participation and project selection towards a sustainable settlement policy.*

The main focus in the paper is on the the lessons learned from a 10 year settlement experience in the Coast Province of Kenya. The guidelines show the need for: integrated physical planning for all departments; a clear definition of community borders; the timely demarcation of plots; the promotion of cluster settlement, the need to avoid balloting of plots but the emphasis on block-wise land development on a communal basis and; the proper selection of community development projects for integration of new farmers in settlement schemes. The set up of village development committees allows settlers and local residents to take responsibility for community life and projects in settlement schemes. Successful implementation of community development projects requires proper ex-ante project evaluation according to at least three described criteria. Only technicallly sound, economically feasible and socially acceptable projects chosen by the settlers and implemented through community participation will result in the sustainable development of settlement schemes.

Yony Sampaio and **Ana Lucia Petry**, University Federal de Pernambuco, Brazil — *The economics of scarcity: food consumption effects of the Cruzado Plan in Brazil.*

The macroeconomic policy called Cruzado Plan involved a price and wage freeze that ended up leading to scarcity and black markets. The income and scarcity effects on consumption of some important food commodities are studied, along with the total effect on caloric and protein consumption. It is concluded that consumption by low income families increased and that by higher income families decreased.

D. Sheikh, Small Ruminant Programme, Nairobi and **C. Valdivia**, University of Missouri, USA — *Gender roles in the production of dual purpose goats.*

This study addresses differences in adoptive behaviour among male and female farm operators with respect to the Dual Purpose Goat technological (DPGT) package. The study also addresses access and control of resources and tries to find out whether this can explain the differential adoptive behaviour.

Mohamed A. Elfeil and **John Davis**, Queen's University, UK — *The economic constraints on producing field crops in the Northern Province of Sudan: an econometric approach.*

This research set out to determine the main economic constraints in the production of field crops in the Northern Province of Sudan. Results indicated the most important constraints as being the low level of application of inputs, especially, irrigation and chemical fertilizer and the unavailability of credit.

Ali Nguisa, **Slim Zekri** and **Moncef Ben Said**, University of Tunis — *Evolution and performance of family farming: a case study in Northern Tunisia.*

The paper analyses the evolution over the last 15 years of a homogeneous group of family farmers located in a region close to the Tunisian capital. The methodology used is based on cluster analysis and multiobjective programming. The results obtained showed that the farmers invested only in stables. On average they increased the housing capacity by 75 percent. They still depend on hired machinery, and reduced their dependence on loans. The compromise solution showed, on the other hand, that these farmers should better use the stable housing capacity and specialize in dairy cows. The gross margin will improve by 76 percent and the number of crops should be reduced considerably.

T.S. Jayne, Michigan State University, USA, **Tobias Takavarasha**, **E.A. Attwood**, Ministry of Lands, Agriculture and Water Development, Zimbabwe, **Bernard Kupfuma**, Michigan State University and **Mandivamba Rukuni**, Uiversity of Zimbabwe — *Postscript to Zimbabwe's maize success story: policy lessons for easterna and southern Africa.*

Since independence, Zimbabwe has received wide international acclaim for the rapid growth in smallholder maize production. However, there has been a largely unnoticed structural decline in production since 1985, associated with a contraction of public sector support programs that had contributed to the dramatic rise in smallholder production during the early 1980s but involved large treasury outlays. However, the adverse effects of this production decline on urban food security appear to have been considerably mitigated by recent maize marketing reforms that have reduced distribution and milling costs of staple maize meal available to consumers. The experience of Zimbabwe raises important policy issues for potential economic transition in South Africa: (1) how to restructure (rather than abandon under budget pressure) key public sector programs and policies to raise agricultural productivity and meet the needs of a vastly expanded agricultural client base in a sustainable way; (2) how to capture potential gains from market liberalization without exposing producers, consumers and government to the economic, nutritional and political costs of price instability; and (3) how to allow the preferences of lower-income consumers to be better articulated through the food marketing system to promote food security.

Mulugetta Mekuria, University of the North, Republic of South Africa and **Eric W. Crawford**, Michigan State University, USA — *Economic analysis of constraints and opportunities to increase smallholder wheat production in Ethiopia.*

In Ethiopia, wheat is an important crop and half of the wheat consumed is imported. Yields are lower than in other African countries. Probit analysis identified critical variables influencing farmers' decisions to use different fertilizer rates. Partial budget and marginal returns analysis confirmed the profitability of recommended production packages.

Naomi Ngwira and **Scott Swinton**, Michigan State University, USA — *Managing maize production risk using horticultural crops: a new approach to solving household food insecurity in Malawi.*

The potential of non-rainfed cultivation to improve food security is investigated using safety first Target MOTAD to model farmers' risk avoidance behaviour. Results indicate that stable, high yields of non-rainfed crops can enhance adoption of fertilizer and hybrid maize varieties leading to higher mean maize harvests and income.

Memoona R. Khan and **James F. Oekmke**, Michigan State University — *Commercial and institutional infrastructure at the village level in Punjab.*

Village access to 13 key indicators of physical transport, commercial, institutional, administrative and social infrastructural services are measured. Cluster analysis indicated that most sample villages enjoy reasonably good access to infrastructural services. Off-farm labour allocation differed significantly across villages with more and less accessible infrastructure.

Sureah Babu, IFPRI, Malawi, **Arne Hallam**, Iowa State University, USA, and **B. Rajasekaran** — *Agroforestry and household food security interactions: implications for multi-disciplinary research policy.*

A general framework is developed in this paper to study the interactions between agroforestry and household food security. The contribution of various components of agroforestry to the dynamics of household food security of smallholder farmers is discussed in a growth theoretical framework. Recognising the slow adoption of an agroforestry system by resource-poor farmers, conditions for switching between systems of monocropping and agroforestry are derived using model results. Policy implications for multi-disciplinary research are derived.

T.O. Williams, International Livestock Centre for Africa, Niger, **Fernandez-Rivera** and **J.M. Powell**, Sahelian Centre, Niamey, Niger — *A risk programming model of crop-live-stock production alternatives in the Sahelt.*

Integrated crop and livestock production is growing in importance in semi-arid West Africa as previously independent pastoral and crop production systems are becoming less relevant. Realistic economic assessments of the complex interactions between crop and livestock production are needed in order to determine the complementarities and trade-offs inherent in the production system and how best to exploit these to improve the welfare of producers. This paper uses a MOTAD programming model to evaluate (a) the impact of integrating crop and livestock production on farm income, and (b) the implications of farmers' risk aversion for long-term farm profitability. The results indicate that farmers can make significant economic gains by integrating crop and livestock production, but inadequate working capital and farmers' risk aversion are major constraints to maximizing income from crop-livestock production activities. Opportunities exist for raising farm income if the liquidity position of the farmer at the beginning of the growing season can be improved. In an average rainfall year, an increase in cash availability would enable the farmer to purchase fertilizer, hire labour and buy replacement breeding animals — all of which would serve to increase farm incomes and rural welfare in the long run.

G. Schiefer, University of Bonn, Germany and **C.H. Gotsch**, Stanford University, USA — *Computer supported policy advisory systems for developing countries: background, potential and development framework.*

The (market) policy decision situation in developing countries and the emerging market economies in Eastern Europe makes these countries especially dependent on the availability of appropriate policy information and decision support systems. New developments in information requirements analysis, information systems research, and information technology have demonstrated their potential for executive decision support in corporate environments of industrial countries. The paper reviews these developments and relates them to the specific conditions in policy institutions in development environments. It is argued (and supported by early empirical evidence) that these developments, if appropriately applied and administered, could initiate a major thrift towards the emergence of computer-based policy support systems with substantial potential for executive policy support in developing countries. The paper is summarized in a 10-step development framework which is being used in on-going system development efforts and could serve as a guide to similar activities elsewhere.

Agriculture and Sustainable Development

Hosein Shapouri and **James Duffield**, USDA — *Biomass energy outlook for developing countries.*

Energy use in developing countries is expected to increase more rapidly in the future. Traditionally, these countries have relied on imported oil for their increased energy needs. However, with current economic conditions and expected higher oil prices it may be beneficial to invest in alternative domestic sources of energy. Biomass energy is the primary feedstock for energy in developing countries. Agricultural and forestry residues, animal dung, by-products from agribusiness industries, such as sugar cane, pulp and paper, and municipal solid waste, are readily available energy sources in developing countries. There are many simple technologies that could be introduced to increase the efficiencies of biomass energy use in rural areas, and some advanced technologies for industries. These technologies have the potential of saving energy, diminishing adverse environmental effects, improving living standards and reducing energy dependency.

Javier Calatrava, Department of Agricultural Economics, Granada, Spain — *Contingent analysis of the scenic value of sugar cane in the subtropical coast of Granada (Spain). Some factors related to willingness to pay (WTP).*

Natural resources valuation is currently receiving increasing attention from agricultural economists. An application of the contingent value method (CVM) to estimation of the scenic value of sugar cane on the subtropical coast of Granada (Spain) is presented here.

Bruno Barbierpost-doc, Washington D.C. and **Michel Benoit-Cattin**, CIRAD, France — *Modelling agricultural sustainability at the village level in West Africa.*

Linear programming is used in a recursive way to discuss the medium and long term perspectives of agricultural systems in cotton zones of western Africa. Interactions between population growth, land fertility management, needs for food and energy, cattle, trees, crops, and evolution of prices are included in the model and discussed according to different scenarios.

K.J. Thomson and **D. Psaltopoulos**, University of Aberdeen, Scotland, UK — *Forestry and rural development in agriculturally over-extended areas: the cases of Scotland and Ireland.*

The objective of this paper is to provide estimates of the impact of forestry, as a land-use alternative to agriculture, on rural development in areas of Scotland and Ireland characterized by depopulation, remoteness from main population centres, and adverse soil and climatic conditions. It describes work conducted at and from Aberdeen as part of tripartite 1991–94 CEC CAMAR[i] study of Afforestation in Rural Development in

Scotland, Northern Ireland and the Republic of Ireland. In particular, two aspects of this work are focussed upon: (i) the interrelationships between the forestry sector and other components of the rural economy investigated through surveys of forestry sub-sectors and input–output analysis, and (ii) analysis of alternative afforestation scenarios over the next several decades. The study as a whole is intended to throw light on the implications of afforestation for economy-wide output, job creation and income levels.

A. Alverez, **A.C. Herruzo**, University of Cordoba, Spain and **S. Zekri**, University of Tunis — *Intertemporal profits from soil conservation practices in Mediterranean dry farming.*

An approach to compare conventional (non-soil conserving) practices with conservation practices in Mediterranean dry farming is presented. This approach involves the application of an economic damage function to determine the present value of the net income stream lost from maintaining conventional tillage practices instead of adopting reduced tillage techniques (direct drilling systems). The GAMES model is used to estimate soil erosion rates under both conservation and non-conservation practices. A soil productivity index is then used to quantify the relation between soil erosion and soil productivity. Finally, production costs and yields under both tillage systems are estimated to calculate the erosion damage function. The results of the analysis indicate the profitability of conservation tillage for the growing conditions of the area.

Gamini Herath, La Trobe University, Australia — *The algal bloom probem in Australian waterways: some control issues.*

Algal blooms have created considerable concern in Australia in recent years. Australia experienced the worst algal bloom in the Darling-Barwon River System in 1990. The Government has appointed a Task Force to study the algal bloom problem and to develop appropriate control measures. Simultaneously control measures are being taken in several fronts. The lion's share of attention seems to have gone to technological solutions such as upgrading sewage plants. There is considerable potential for institutional measures such as community education, informal group formation etc. to enhance the effectiveness of government control measures. The effort in these areas appears to be inadequate and if this is not overcome the effectiveness of technological solutions may be lowered. Control of detergent phosphorus appears to be an area needing attention and there is potential to reduce phosphorous considerably if this aspect is carefully worked out.

Habibullah Khan, National University of Singapore — *Strategies for sustainable development in a city-state economy: the case of Singapore.*

The paper provides a theoretical framework for analysing sustainable growth and development in city-state economies, which are, by definition, small in size and deficient in land and natural resources. For illustration, the case of Singapore is highlighted. Growth and environmental objectives were fulfilled in an integrated fashion, as suggested by the theory, through an efficient physical planning system in Singapore. The government played an important role in implementing sustainable growth strategies but the interventionist measures did not hinder the process of market mechanism, as argued in the paper.

Guillermo Flichman, Institut Agronomique Méditerranéen de Montpellier, France, **Consuelo Varela-Ortega** and **Aberto Garrido**, Universidad Politécnía de Madrid, Spain — *Agricultural policy, choice of technologies and environmental impacts under uncertainty and market imperfections: a regional comparison in southern Europe.*

This paper analysis the effects of the reform of the Common Agricultural Policy (CAP) on the choice of technologies, crop pattern and environmental damage. We consider 2 regions of southern Europe, South West France and Andalucía in Spain. The methodology used is based on the integration of an agronomic model (AM) with a mathematical programming model (MPM). The AM allows us to generate a wide specification of techniques, both actual and potential, overcoming the lack of information on potential techniques that may be feasible as a response to drastic changes in the price structure. The MPM is recursive and takes into account risk and uncertainty. The results are presented for a period of 5 years for 2 different scenarios, one that assumes a continuation of the previous policy and the other that considers implementation of the CAP reform.

Danilo Tomic and **Zorica Vasiljevic**, Institute of Agricultural Economics, Belgrade, Yugoslavia, and **Miladin Sevarlic**, University of Belgrade,Yugoslavia — *The land degradation processes, causes and consequences: the case of Yugoslavia.*

In this paper the authors analyse land potentials in some selected countries which are important food producers and consumers. First, this analysis refers to cultivable areas per resident as well as per economically active agricultural producer (farmer). It includes some countries characterized by cultivable area as a factor 'in abundance', others with cultivable area as a 'limiting' factor, and some with satisfactory available land potential. Imbalance between decrease incultivable and arable areas on one side, and growth of population number on the other are pointed out. The paper includes analysis of degradation of soil caused by: a) water and wind erosion; b) chemicals and fertilizer application; c) irrigation; d) utilization of heavy mechanization. Particular attention is been paid to the causes and consequences of soil compaction. It is pointed out that there is a need for more rational land utilization, first of all by increased utilization of organic substances and manure, decreased utilization of chemicals, as well as by subsoiling, having respect to the crop rotation etc. Particular attention is paid to the mentioned problems in Yugoslav agriculture.

Philip Szmedra, Economic Research Service, USDA — *Pesticides in sub-Sahara Africa.*

The use of agricultural pesticides in the SSA region has increased with the growth in area devoted to cash crops for export. Prevailing agricultural development philosophies by donor groups influenced the SSA nations in establishing subsidy structures which promoted the use of chemical pesticides. Institutional structures to regulate the distribution and use of these materials are either absent or lack sufficient financial and technical resources. Though many nations have accepted the concept of IPM as an important aspect of agricultural policy, adoption of alternative pest control methods has been sporadic. This paper details the pesticide use situation in the region including data for the 1992 harvest year for Cote D'Ivoire, Kenya and Zimbabwe. Use trends in important pesticide market crops such as cotton, coffee, cocoa, and tobacco are described. Regulatory environments are evaluated with implications for future use of chemical and non-chemical pest control methods.

Policy Reform and Transition in Rural Economies

G.C.G. Fraser, University of Fort Hare, and **Alice G.G. Antrobus**, Rhodes University — *The availability of commercial farm land for redistribution via the market in the Eastern Cape province of South Africa.*

The intention of the South African Government to establish a significant number of black farmers as commercial producers could be achieved in part through the purchase of land on the open market. The paper attempts to establish the extent to which this would be possible by examining the transfers of rural immovable property in the Eastern Cape province over a period of time. A greater proportion of smaller properties change hands each year than larger properties. Many of these are in the vicinity of the metropolitan areas (Port Elizabeth and East London) and not all can be considered as viable units for full-time farming. While smaller properties are more expensive per unit area, more extensive farm are generally situated in areas unsuited to subdivision into small scale units. It is concluded that the amount of land becoming available each year without intervention on the part of the State would be insufficient to establish a significant number of black commercial farmers in the Eastern Cape. Opportunities for livestock intensification in mixed systems include animal traction, fattening of small ruminants, intensified milk production with crossbreeds or improved breeds, and strategic fattening to meet demand peaks. Like improved crops, forages to overcome the critical feed constraint require increased soil fertility through purchased inputs in the savannas. The potential for improved integration of mixed systems is thus limited. Specialized systems occur where profitability is higher for livestock than for crops, either near urban markets or where crops cannot thrive. Specialized, intensified peri-urban dairy and finishing operations present important, but limited development opportunities. In drier areas, on-going currency devaluation results in increased, but still highly variable livestock income. Future research will be needed to cut livestock losses and stabilize prices, and provide better market opportunities and information. Migration due to low income potential in marginal smallholder mixed systems will ultimately lead to improved larger scale livestock operations.

Katalin Daubner, Budapest University of Economic Sciences, Hungary, and **Donald B. Erickson**, Kansas State University, USA — *New policies and forms of co-operation for Hungarian agricultural transition.*

Economic forces strongly favour privatization. Production efficiency provided by private farms is clearly evident. Presently agriculture has a surplus of resources that will have to be corrected over time based on accurate costs and returns. The length of time required to make the transition to a free market economy will depend on politicians' and farmers' willingness to change. Marketing regulations have been established to handle production flows and price fluctuations resulting from the transition to a free market. Support from the Ministry of Agriculture and the Product Councils will establish regulated agricultural markets that are specific to each product. Marketing surplus products will be toward Western Europe but tariffs and restrictive quotas entering the European Common Community will prevent major expansions. The transition to a free market economy in

Hungary should be faster with fewer disruptions than in most of the other centrally planned economies.

Xavier Bejarano, **David R. Lee** and **Duty Greene**, Panamerican Agricultural School, Honduras, Cornell University, USA and Agricultural Policy Institure, Ecuador — *Exchange rate reform and agricultural export response in Ecuador.*

Real exchange rate devaluation has been a centerpiece of macroeconomic reforms in many developing countries in the 1980s and 1990s. This paper analyzes the effects of variations in the real exchange rate, export prices, and other factors on the performance of three major agricultural export markets (coffee, cocoa, bananas) in Ecuador for the period 1978–89, over which significant macroeconomic changes occurred. Exchange rate and price transmission models and export supply models are estimated to analyze the structure of price determination and export responsiveness. The empirical results demonstrate that: (1) the real exchange rate is a primary determinant and world prices are a secondary determinant of export responsiveness; (2) measures of market segmentatio;n and integration can be used to assess the domestic market effects of variations in the real exchange rate, world prices, and border prices and (3) unique structural characteristics of individual export markets influence price and exchange rate pass-through at different levels.

Peter Calkins, **Frederic Martin** and **Sylvain Lariviere**, Laval University, Canada — *Identifying and involving the poor in structural adjustment and transition auto- and exo-perceptions from rural Burkina Faso.*

Subjective (auto) perceptions of well-being, solicited from rural residents through focus-groups and voting exercises, included not just material goods like food, but public goods like health and ethical values like family harmony. Spearman-rank correlations among young, old; male, female; and favoured, disfavoured villagers demonstrated that all ranked children's welfare, cattle, health, clothing, better harvests and enhanced women's contributions above money. Guttman scales were also developed to rank households' well-being by objectively observable (exo) perceptions. Extension and relief workers can use ploughs, primary school registers, and bicycles to distinguish rapidly and accurately among comfortable, vulnerable, poor and destitute households, even in villages that have never been visited before. Regression analysis further determined that government could reduce poverty by promoting a larger workforce per household, more off-season employment, investment in new technology and intensification of the cropping index. Special attention should be given to female-headed households and those belonging to certain religious communities.

M.R.G. Daroch and **D.F. van der Riet**, University of Natal, Republic of South Africa — *Impact on land values of deregulation in the South African sugar industry.*

Much uncertainty surrounds the direction of future land values in the South African sugar industry following proposals to abolish sucrose production quotas and set a new tariff on raw sugar imports. Results of an econometric model of sugar quota land values show that expected real net realization revenue per hectare and real interest rates drive real quota land values. Acceptance of the new tariff, and successful lobbying by growers for a bigger share of sugar sales proceeds, will prevent farm income and hence sugar land value from falling to the extent expected if quota abolition alone occurred. Using representative North Coast area data, a net 10 percent fall in real sugar farm income per hectare sugar land value per hectare by an estimated 5.5 percent, ceteris paribus. Given the prospect of sugar quota land owners incurring asset value losses, it is entirely predictable that the Industry proposes to phase in only partial deregulation and growers will lobby for compensation to reduce this economic shock.

Natalija Kazlauskiene, Lithuania Institute of Agrarian Economy and **William H. Meyers**, Iowa, USA — *Macroeconomic adjustment and the economic transition in agriculture: the case of Lithuania.*

Experience in transition economies have shown that the simultaneity of macroeconomic and sectoral reforms is important to the success of both. In Lithuania, macroeconomic, agrarian and other sectoral reforms were implemented concurrently. Real wages and income have declined sharply. Inflation has been reduced to low single digit levels, the real exchange rate has appreciated substantially and stabilized, and the real value of foreign trade and trade dependence on the East has fallen substantially. Restructuring and privatization of state and collective farms has been progressing rapidly, and the privatization of other enterprizes in the food and agricultural chain has been going at a slower pace. Input prices and retail prices have increased in real terms while real farm prices have declined. The food and agricultural sector has contracted and in a market economy will likely remain far less dependent on imported inputs and on export markets for products.

John Omiti, **Simeon Ehui**, **Kevin Parton** and **Sagary Nokoe**, International Livestock Centre for Africa, Ethiopia (for all but Kevin Parton who is with the University of New England, Australia) — *Changing farm resource use systems from socialist to partially liberalized agrarian structure in the Ethiopian highlands.*

The military (1974–91) government nationalized and redistributed all agricultural land amongst peasants following the Land Reform Proclamation in 1975 in Ethiopia. Land redistribution was meant to achieve equal land size per household and improve agricultural performance. Sale of land and hiring of agricultural labour were prohibited. Following the ousting of the military regime in 1991, there has been a reduction of imperfections in rural factor markets. Selling/hiring, renting andexchanging of agricultural land, farm labour and animal traction are increasing. These changes will influence agricultural production in many ways if government policies with respect to rural factor markets and infrastructural development are encouraged and implemented. Policy reform regarding land tenure would be of utmost importance in guiding agricultural productivity.

Korotoumou Oattara, **Carlos E. Cuevas**, and **Douglas H. Graham**, Ohio State University, USA — *Financial innovation and donor intervention in Africa: village savings and credit associations in The Gambia.*

This paper documents the unusual performance of the Village Savings and Credit Association (VISACAs) in The Gambia. Important organizational and operational technologies are highlighted in successfully supplying a range of financial services to their members. The important issue of the appropriate type of donor intervention is also explored.

Johan van Rooyen, **Johan van Zyl**, University of Pretoria, Republic of South Africa, **Thedi Matsetela** and **Masipula Mbongwa**, Development Bank of Southern Africa — *A framework for agricultural land redistribution in South Africa.*

A complex set of factors will influence agricultural land reform in South Africa. These include the nature of agriculture, political and social considerations, institutional arrangements, macroeconomic policy and spatial dimensions. This complexity requires a multi-pronged approach to land reform. A framework for land redistribution is discussed where various redistribution models are linked to dimensions of the 'South African land issue' and the present status of land. Models range from private land acquisition through market purchases to expropriation by the state. Land use models for land reform are also discussed. Land status ranges from tribal land to private land. Land subject to forced removals and disputed claims is also considered in the framework.

Prafulla Chandra Sarkar and **Annil Bhuimali**, University of North Bengal — *The required reforms of agricultural cooperative credit societies of West Bengal.*

The study shows that an agricultural co-operative credit society with unlimited liability is infinitely superior to the one with limited liability. Yet Acts on co-operative societies in West Bengal have prevented the growth in West Bengal of agricultural co-operative societies with unlimited liability. Revision of legislation is, therefore, urgent. The merit of the Raiffeisen model of agricultural co-operative credit society (or an agricultural co-operative society with unlimited liability) is two-fold. Firstly, since the members' liability is not limited to their amounts of shares, the savers who open accounts with or deposits money for a longer term at the society feel that their savings are insured without the existence of an external deposit insurance corporation. Secondly, since the inefficient management of funds might cause sudden depletion of their personal assets, the members are obliged to be ever vigilant to make sure that their society does not commit errors. A measurement of the institutional power of this type of agricultural co-operative credit societies is relevant.

Anikó Souphanthong, Hungarian Development Foundation — *The agricultural restructuring programme of the Hungarian Development Foundation.*

Agriculture in Hungary is undergoing major and complex change. Important factors arisen over the past years include: the return of ownership of agricultural land and assets to individuals, which is pressuring state farms and co-operatives to split up into smaller operating units; the loss of the former guaranteed COMECON markets for agricultural produce; lack of capital, limited availability of loan finance and interest rates that are too high for the sector, and the removal of many subsidies. Recognising these factors, the Hungarian Development Foundation has developed a Restructuring programma to support the transformation of agro- businesses. The goal of the Restructuring Programma overall is to enable enterprise managers to take more effective control of their businesses and plan and implement a range of measures to improve performance and profitability. The programma started in June 1993 has been delivered flexibly to meet the needs of the participating enterprizes and adapted to specific enterprize requirements as needed. Based on our experiences to date in addition to the objectives set as a result, we see other positive outcomes of the programma. These include: establishing of contact between the organizations; ensuring that the process of decentralization follows business sense, keeping in mind future operational ability, providing small entrepreneurs with guidelines to become contributors to supporters of larger companies and promotion of regional level agrarian strategies.